Understanding Reading Problems

Assessment and Instruction

Fifth Edition

Jean Wallace Gillet

Orange County (VA) Schools

Charles Temple

College of William and Mary

with

Alan N. Crawford

California State University/Los Angeles

Samuel R. Mathews II

University of West Florida

Josephine Peyton Young

University of Georgia

LONGMAN

An imprint of Addison Wesley Longman, Inc.

New York • Reading, Massachusetts • Menlo Park, California • Harlow, England
Don Mills, Ontario • Sydney • Mexico City • Madrid • Amsterdam

Sr. Acquisitions Editor: Virginia L. Blanford
Full Service Production Manager: Joseph Vella
Project Coordination and Text Design: York Production Services
Electronic Page Makeup: York Production Services
Cover Design Manager: Nancy Danahy
Cover Designer: Keithly and Associates
Cover Illustration/Photo: © Photo Disc
Senior Print Buyer: Hugh Crawford
Printer and Binder: Maple-Vail Book Manufacturing Group
Cover Printer: Coral Graphic Services, Inc.

Library of Congress Cataloging-in-Publication Data

Gillet, Jean Wallace.
    Understanding reading problems : assessment and instruction / Jean
  Wallace Gillet, Charles Temple, with Alan Crawford, Samuel R.
  Matthews II, Josephine Peyton Young. — 5th ed.
     p.   cm.
  Includes bibliographical references and index.
  ISBN 0-321-01333-6
    1. Reading—Ability testing.   2. Reading—Remedial teaching.
  I. Temple, Charles A., 1974–   . II. Title.
  LB1050.46.G55   1999
  372.48—dc21   99-29907
                                            CIP

Please visit our website at http://www.awlonline.com

ISBN 0-321-01333-6

45678910—MA—02

Contents

Preface

Helping all students to become effective, strategic readers who read and write enthusiastically and purposefully is one of the greatest challenges facing teachers today. Teachers need to know how to

- use a wide variety of teaching methods, materials, and strategies to help children learn to read,
- monitor and document students' progress, strengths, and needs,
- diagnose difficulties in reading and related areas,
- apply corrective instruction when appropriate, and
- prevent literacy problems from arising in the future.

To do so, teachers need well-informed diagnostic judgment and the tools and strategies to monitor students' development effectively. Such strategies and tools must be flexible and practical, tapping the kinds of everyday reading and writing that students use in and out of the classroom.

Teachers must also undertake corrective instruction within the context of regular ongoing instruction, without setting problem readers apart from others. Such diagnostic and instructional strategies are the heart of this book.

When the first edition of this book appeared in 1982, we wrote in that preface that the field of reading education was undergoing exciting changes. In each successive edition, we have reiterated this thought, because it remained true. The first few editions saw the growing use of informal diagnostic techniques gradually supplant the use of formal, standardized diagnostic tests, as well as a growing responsibility for classroom teachers to undertake their own diagnostic assessment. Basal reading systems and skills management systems, once the linchpin of reading instruction, were challenged by literature-based approaches and collaborative learning.

Today, new emphases on authentic assessment that accurately represents what students can do challenge our thinking about measurement and evaluation. Simultaneously, many states are struggling to define ways to increase student achievement and ensure accountability to the public. Today's teachers are expected to use continuous developmental assessment devices; to use portfolios of student work to demonstrate and evaluate student achievement; to teach reading using authentic literature and a wide variety of teaching methods; to integrate reading and writing across all curricular areas; and to help all students, regardless of their level of literacy, to become effective, strategic readers.

This book provides the kind of clear, detailed, realistic help teachers need to fulfill these expectations.

The concepts and principles that guided the development of the first four editions, and which made this book a leader in its field, have been strengthened and expanded in the fifth edition. We have

- updated and expanded our treatment of important trends in research and practice, including emergent literacy, portfolio assessment, strategic reading, literature-based instruction, learning English as a second language, and developmentally appropriate assessment and instruction;
- described the primary purposes for assessment and the important differences between assessments for internal and external audiences;
- expanded and elaborated upon our extensive coverage of instructional approaches and methods, including new material on emergent literacy, beginning and developmental literacy, the development of reading strategies, word recognition, developing predictive thinking, teaching adolescent poor readers, increasing students' time spent reading, and content-area reading strategies; and
- added all-new material on teaching students whose first language is other than English and on authentic assessment, with an emphasis on lifelong literacy.

Convincing case studies of real readers and examples of real students, work are used throughout the book to illustrate points and help users develop diagnostic-corrective judgment.

The fifth edition examines both traditional and contemporary means of assessing reading strengths and needs, as well as developmental and corrective instruction; our goal has been to combine the best tried-and-true methods with the best new strategies for diagnosing and teaching. Emphasis is placed on preventing reading problems by providing necessary experiences for children to develop and progress as readers, as well as on correction and remediation.

The first five chapters comprise Part One, dealing with assessment topics and issues. Chapter 1 describes what teachers need to know about the reading process and its assessment, including the internal and external audiences for assessment data, an overview of reading developmental stages, and an introduction to principles that underlie authentic assessment.

Chapter 2 describes various types of ongoing assessments teachers often use, including running records, systematic observation of students, reading strategies, the use of cloze procedures, and monitoring growth in spelling and composition.

Chapter 3 details widely used methods for the periodic, in-depth assessment of reading progress, including how to select, administer, score and interpret informal reading inventories and related devices.

Chapter 4 describes in detail the purposes of classroom portfolios and how to begin and manage a portfolio assessment program. Included are strategies for enlisting the support of administrators and parents, conferring with parents and fostering students' self-evaluation.

Chapter 5 deals with formal assessments, including fundamental measurement concepts, characteristics of tests, norm-referenced and criterion-referenced tests, and minimum competency tests.

The remaining six chapters deal primarily with instructional topics and issues.

Chapter 6 details the stages of emergent and beginning reading, including assessing and teaching print concepts and phonemic awareness, fostering reading comprehension, and early intervention programs.

Chapter 7 deals with teaching developing readers who are beyond the beginning reading stage. Developing word recognition strategies, including sight recognition and word analysis strategies, reading fluency, and reading and listening comprehension are major themes. The critical issue of how much time students spend actually reading is discussed, with implications for teachers and parents.

Chapter 8 deals with teaching older students and adolescents who are reluctant or disabled readers. The special challenges of dealing with older beginning readers are detailed, with authentic case studies and a wealth of instructional recommendations.

Chapter 9 details how students progress to mature reading and writing, in which students are no longer learning to read but are now using reading to learn. The reading-to-learn operations of *anticipation, investigation,* and *reflection* are described with numerous teaching strategies. Predictable patterns of nonfiction text organization and effective vocabulary teaching are presented.

Chapter 10, an entirely new chapter in the fifth edition, describes strategies for teaching reading and writing to students whose first language is not English. Principles and processes of second language learning and bilingualism are detailed, along with ways to adapt phonics, decoding and spelling instruction for students who may struggle with some English phonemes, and scaffolding to improve comprehension of written English.

Chapter 11 deals with philosophical, legal, and instructional issues related to the teaching of students with special learning needs. Relevant legislation, issues of inclusion, and ways of identifying and assessing special-needs students are outlined. Intellectual factors and tests of intelligence and learning aptitude, physical factors related to vision and hearing, language development and disorders, and the special challenges of learning disabilities and dyslexia are discussed.

As in the previous four editions, we are indebted to a growing list of friends, colleagues, and strangers for their influence, advice, and encouragement. Our friend and colleague Alan Crawford wrote Chapter 10 and gave us invaluable insight and support. Samuel R. Mathews II and Josephine Peyton Young provided generous contributions to the fourth edition which are still felt in this edition. Jackson-Via Elementary School's Karyl Reynolds, media specialist, and Tracy Snead, first-grade teacher, contributed their special expertise in the development of bibliographies and literature searches, as well as their friendship and support. Our colleagues in the Reading and Writing for Critical Thinking Project—Jeannie

Steele, Kurt Meredith, Scott Walter, Donna Ogle, and Alan Crawford—along with 70 volunteer teacher educators and hundreds of international colleagues—have deeply affected our thinking on reading-to-learn issues.

We are grateful for the careful reading and insightful criticism of our fifth edition manuscript reviewers: Mariam Jean Dreher, University of Maryland; Lee A. Dubert, Boise State University; Ann Harris, Austin Peay State University; Ellen Jampole, SUNY-Cortland; Barbara Laster, Towson University; David C. Little, Samford University; Patrick McCabe, Nova Southeastern University; Richard Osterberg, California State University, Fresno; Barbara Pugh, California State University, Bakersfield; Mark Sadoski, Texas A&M University; and Rebecca Swearingen, Southwest Missouri State University. We also gratefully acknowledge the many helpful suggestions we have received since the first edition appeared from the reviewers and users of previous editions.

We also extend our heartfelt thanks to our editor, Virginia Blanford, and her staff at Addison Wesley Longman; our editor on previous editions, Christopher Jennison; and to Susan Free and the production staff at York Production Services.

Finally, we are grateful to our students and colleagues at Hobart and William Smith Colleges, Mary Baldwin College, and the Charlottesville, Virginia, Public Schools. Many, many people helped make this book what it is; we acknowledge their many influences with gratitude and offer our work to you with pride.

Jean Wallace Gillet
Charles Temple

PART ONE

ASSESSMENT

CHAPTER 1

Reading and Its Assessment

As educators, we want to believe that most people share our fundamental beliefs about literacy, which are:

- that reading is **functional;** that is, useful and necessary every day to work at most jobs, raise children, keep ourselves safe, and exercise our citizenship.
- that reading is **integral to development;** that is, necessary to grow intellectually, to acquire new information and skills, to experience vicariously things and events that could not be experienced in reality, and to develop a sense of personal competence in a literate world.
- that reading is **social;** that is, a fundamental part of the culture of schooling, a basic expectation of the outcome of schooling, and a part of daily family life. It is also social in that literacy is, in effect, handed down in families from adults to children and in that literacy provides common bonds and experiences among people who otherwise might have little else in common.
- that reading is **enjoyable;** that is, a source of pleasure, fun, recreation, relaxation, escape, and even adult–child bonding.

Although we would like to believe that almost everyone shares at least some of these attitudes about literacy, our daily lives show us a different reality. Reality intrudes whenever our lives touch those of preliterate elementary children whose self-esteem has been stunted by academic failure; of disaffected young people who gave up on school before it could give up on them; of wage earners whose literacy skills are so primitive that they have no hope of ever getting a better-paying, more-skilled job; or of displaced workers whose marginal literacy might have been sufficient for many years of manual work but who find themselves without even the basic skills necessary to become reemployed.

To millions of North Americans, reading is neither functional, developmental, social, nor enjoyable. Instead, it is an onerous chore, a secret source of embarrassment, an obstacle to getting or keeping a fulfilling job. It is to be avoided whenever possible.

Teaching children to read is still the schools' most important academic task. Identifying students who, for a variety of reasons, were considered at risk of school failure and providing effective corrective instruction used to be the most important parts of that task. Today, schools have an equally urgent priority: to cultivate in students a love of books and a habit of reading so that they will read.

These two priorities reflect fundamental themes that run throughout this book. The first theme is that *while children can experience many kinds of difficulty in learning to read, there are only a few basic causes of reading failure that occur in case after case.* We need to be able to effectively and accurately identify children who have these difficulties and provide immediate instructional intervention.

The second theme is that *not reading also causes reading failure,* which leads to failure in all subject areas, as well as causing incalculable damage to children's sense of competence. Reading is one of those things that you must do a lot of to get very good at it.

These two themes suggest a third: that ***it is necessary for teachers to understand how children learn to read to help them through their problems.*** These issues form the basis for this chapter and those that follow it.

When we seriously consider how children learn to read, the issues are not as obvious as some experts have suggested. (Some so-called reading experts offer simplistic explanations of reading and reading difficulties as a rationale for selling commercial products such as kits, programs, videos and audiotapes, flashcards, workbooks, and other money-making schemes. Ask yourself: If it were really this easy for every person to read successfully, why would reading problems still exist?)

Reading requires the subtle interplay and coordination of many skills and processes, among which are sensory information, language fluency, thinking and problem-solving skills, and issues of interest, motivation, and tolerance for error. In spite of the hundreds of books and thousands of research studies that reading has inspired over the years, exactly how reading occurs and why some people read so effectively while others do so with great difficulty are still misunderstood.

But we should not take this to mean that the process of learning to read cannot be understood or explained, or that helping struggling readers requires luck and magic as much as anything else. On the contrary, in the past decade, dramatic breakthroughs in our understanding of the way children learn to read have occurred, and we are able to help children far more effectively now than ever before.

WHAT TEACHERS NEED TO KNOW ABOUT READING ASSESSMENT

In the olden days, which might have been only twenty or so years ago in some places, teachers needed to know the essentials of the subjects they were to teach and a smattering of "methods," or generic ways to present material and motivate students. Knowledge of subject matter was the most important criterion of teacher effectiveness; how children learn, and so how best to teach them, was not considered particularly important, and classroom management skills were largely presumed. In the main, teachers received little, if any, formal training in identification of students with special needs, instructional assessment, corrective or remedial teaching procedures, individualizing instruction, issues of motivation and behavior management, and so forth.

Students who experienced difficulty of one sort or another were typically referred to some sort of educational specialist (if the school division employed one), who was responsible for testing students and communicating scores and other results to teachers. Because those specialists rarely were teachers themselves, they often communicated to teachers in ways that were less than helpful in effecting instructional change. In any event, the responsibility for assessment and interpretation of it was typically somebody else's, not the teacher's.

Today, most teachers are expected to know how to conduct and interpret many kinds of assessment devices in the classroom; to communicate results and their implications to administrators, colleagues, and parents accurately and clearly; and to implement instructional change on the basis of their findings.

Teachers are routinely required to document student progress in a variety of ways that include not only teacher-made classroom tests, but also periodic student work samples and commercially available assessment devices. Teachers now bear the responsibility of doing much of their own assessment.

Assessment for Internal Audiences

There are two fundamental reasons for teachers' assessments, whether they use a weekly spelling test, a pop quiz on yesterday's assigned reading, a commercial diagnostic reading inventory, a districtwide skills checklist, or a language arts system placement test. One reason is to gather information about students that will be of direct, immediate usefulness to the teacher herself or himself to organize, plan, and evaluate the effectiveness of instruction. These are referred to as **assessments for internal audiences,** because they are used internally, at the school and classroom level.

The audience for internal assessments is the classroom teacher, who needs them to plan where to begin teaching, what to review, when to introduce new material, and how students can be grouped for effective learning and socialization. A second internal audience is often the other half of the teaching-learning team, the student. Assessment results are often shared with students to show them their progress and help them to recognize their achievements and where they still need to continue working. Perhaps the most widely recognized vehicle for communicating with students via periodic assessments is the classroom portfolio, which you will read about in Chapter 4.

Baseline Assessments

The kinds of assessments that are used for internal audiences depend on several factors, among which are the grade being taught and the age and/or developmental level of the students.

For example, a kindergarten teacher likely needs to know where each entering kindergartner is in oral language development and recognition of letters, numbers, and colors; whether the child yet has basic concepts of "numberness" such as one-to-one correspondence; whether the child can write his or her first name; and so forth. These assessments, as well as selected others that are of immediate usefulness, are undertaken as early in the year as possible, perhaps upon school registration or in the days immediately before the start of school, certainly within the first couple of weeks in school.

They are typically done individually by the teacher, instructional assistant, and other school personnel such as the school nurse or language teacher who are trained in administration of these measures. They are carried out in as relaxed, reassuring a manner as possible, and the children usually don't even know they are being assessed. You will read more about preliteracy assessment in Chapter 6.

Primary-grade teachers need some of the same information as their kindergarten counterparts, as well as some very different information. They need to know, first, which children are entering the primary grades, especially first grade, without having successfully completed or achieved all the benchmarks of kindergarten.

Primary teachers will assess letter recognition, sight word recognition, and ability to "track" or match words read orally with their printed counterparts in a memorized utterance such as "Mary had a little lamb" or "Brown bear, brown bear, what do you see?" They will assess each child's ability to retell a familiar story or fairy tale in a cohesive manner and to listen to and understand an engaging new story, evidenced by their predictions and answers to questions about it.

They will assess phonemic segmentation, decoding and encoding skills, use of letters to represent sounds in spelling and writing, and children's use of strategies to figure out unfamiliar words in texts. Like the kindergarten teacher, primary-grade teachers will use these data and observations to form flexible instructional groups, to choose stories and texts to read to and with children, and to introduce new operations at a level of comfortable challenge.

The same is true for teachers at every grade level and subject. If every teacher's goal is to meet children "where they are" and take them to further developmental levels, then teachers' need to assess where they are at the outset is obvious. Without baseline data, the teacher will not know what students already know and can do, what they need to progress to the next developmental level, or how to teach to their interests.

Ongoing and Periodic Assessments

In the same way, teachers need to assess students' progress at periodic intervals after instruction has been undertaken to judge the effectiveness of the instruction. Teacher-made tests and quizzes are most often used to demonstrate students' mastery of factual information, ability to apply knowledge in new situations, and problem-solving skills. But chapter or unit tests are not enough to show progress or development in many developmental areas such as language fluency, vocabulary growth, and growing complexity of spelling knowledge, nor do they document progress in areas such as developing literary tastes and preferences, improving attitudes about reading and general literacy, or growth in independent work skills, persistence, project completion, and so forth.

So periodic updating of the baseline records is an important component of the assessment program for every teacher. How long the periods are, or how often students are reassessed, depends on the grade and subject being taught. In general, most teachers reassess monthly, quarterly, or biannually. Typical ongoing assessments include:

- reassessing knowledge, mastery, and so forth at intervals after instruction,
- reassessing developmental processes at intervals after growth and experience,
- selecting and keeping dated samples of student work,
- keeping records of systematic teacher observations,
- keeping classroom portfolios (see Chapter 4).

To reiterate, assessment for internal audiences is undertaken to gather immediately useful data on students so that teachers can form instructional groups, plan and implement instruction, and document students' growth, development, progress, and/or subject mastery.

Assessment for External Audiences

The other major reason teachers and schools use assessment is to provide data to people and organizations *beyond the classroom and building level.* That is why these are referred to as **assessments for external audiences.** Those people and organizations include the families of students in the school division and the community at large, which may be represented by a city or town council, a district planning commission, and so forth. Beyond the building level, we find the divisional superintendent and the school board or other similar school governing body; beyond the community level, we find the state-level department of education and/or state superintendent of schools; special programs personnel (such as the federally funded Title I program, for example) at the division, state, regional, and/or federal levels; and so forth.

The kinds of data that are most useful to external audiences are nearly the opposite of what is useful to the teacher or student. External audiences want to compare programs, school divisions within a state, or even states themselves rather than comparing students or comparing what a single student can do at quarterly intervals.

Although documented teacher observations and student portfolios are information-rich within the classroom, they are not suitable for comparing one large group to another. Tests yielding numerical scores that can be transformed into percentages and percentiles, stanines and graphs, pie charts, and rank-ordered lists are more useful. Tests and other assessments must be given to everyone in a particular group (with the exception of students whose special educational circumstances exempt them), such as all nonexempt students in the fourth grade across the state. State-mandated achievement tests, college admissions tests, minimal competency tests, and the like provide numerical and statistical data that are used to measure the effectiveness of established programs, instructional initiatives, and ongoing classroom instruction within school divisions, among school divisions, and among states.

Legislative and Governing Bodies

Assessments for external audiences are not given at the discretion of the teacher or even the building. For effective comparison, such measures must be given in a very standard way, at the same approximate times, and on the same dates.

Common sense dictates why. Let's say that teachers at Alpha Elementary give the state-mandated fifth-grade achievement test six weeks later than any other school in their division; they give their students all the time they need rather than only the required number of minutes; and they read test items aloud to their classes instead of requiring students to read the items themselves. Alpha

Elementary's scores are likely to be higher than those of their counterparts because Alpha's students enjoyed advantages that their peers in other schools did not: more instruction, more time, and having items read to them.

Strict adherence to both the spirit and the letter of the rules and dates for administration is necessary if scores are to be considered comparable. Compliance is routinely checked by state and local school officials, and dreadful penalties await those who seek to pad their scores with nonstandard administrations. Typically, a week-long "testing window" is mandated so that all students are tested after the same, or very nearly the same, number of instructional days in the year. Access to test forms before the scheduled test day is restricted to the building principal and designees to avoid the possibility of "teaching the test" or compromising its contents.

With evidence of compliance in administration, the legislative and governing bodies at the local, regional, state, and federal levels take the data they receive and draw conclusions about the effectiveness of instruction at various levels. Funding is usually involved in, and sometimes at the heart of, these conclusions; in some places, high-achieving or most-improved schools or programs earn fiscal rewards, while other programs face either status quo funding or reductions. But this isn't always the case; district superintendents from poor localities are vociferous in demanding a fiscally level playing field for all students in the state, while those from affluent divisions with a greater tax base energetically defend the "dollars for scores" initiatives.

Parents and the Local Community

The other major external audience is the parents of our students and the community in which the schools exist. In most localities, public schools are furnished and maintained, and personnel are hired and paid, by the taxpayers of the local community. These taxpayers include not only the parents of children in those schools, but also people whose interest in schools might be less immediate: people who have no children, older folks whose children are grown, people whose children go to private schools or are home-schooled, businesses, and property owners other than homeowners with children. All of these diverse groups have the right to expect that the schools will function effectively, playing their part in preparing students for adulthood.

The local community expects that schools will be accountable for what is done with their tax dollars and with their children. Accountability consists of school leaders communicating the achievements, needs, and visions of its students and staff to the community in ways that build confidence, invite involvement, and promote pride in that community's students and schools.

Assessment results should not be the only means of assessing school effectiveness. For example, achievement test scores might remain the same or even dip slightly over, say, a five-year period; looking only at those data, one might conclude that achievement was either stagnating or actually dropping. However, if the high school dropout rate was halved in the same five-year period, minority enrollment in foreign languages and higher-level math/science courses increased significantly, and parent involvement in the elementary schools tripled, then most community members would agree that good things were indeed going on in the community's schools.

The use of test scores alone to rank-order schools or whole communities, a common practice in local newspapers; the use of test scores by real estate agents to steer prospective clients toward or away from whole neighborhoods or towns; and the highly publicized mass firing, demotion, or transfer of administrators at "failing" schools (often by school superintendents whose crusades are focused more on personal advancement than on the local schools) can only be seen as divisive, self-serving, and ultimately destructive.

THE READING PROCESS AND READING PROBLEMS

The rest of this book is about assessing reading difficulties and helping readers to overcome them, as well as helping teachers to prevent them. We start here, though, by creating an overview of how children learn to read and what normally happens to them as they progress from prebeginner status to mature readers. Naturally, readers face different possibilities and problems at different stages, and this introduction will help us later by showing us what to expect as we go about assessing and correcting the reading problems students might develop at different points in their lives.

The reading stages that follow are not written on stone tablets; they are, for us, a convenient way to organize our thinking about reading and our discussions about children. The stages into which we divide the process of learning to read are as follows:

- ■ *Emergent Literacy.* Children in the stage of emergent literacy are discovering basic concepts about print and learning to associate pleasure with reading, books, and being read to. Usually, these children are found in preschool, kindergarten, and first grade.
- ■ *Beginning Reading.* Children in the beginning reading stage know enough, at least on a tacit or nonverbal level, about reading and print to begin to learn individual words, or acquire a *sight vocabulary,* from their encounters with them. These children are often first-graders, but both younger and older students may be beginning readers.
- ■ *Building Fluency.* Children who are building fluency, typically in grades two and three, can recognize many words automatically and are reading passages that are several sentences long without too much stumbling over words. They are comprehending what they read, for the most part, so their reading has become fairly rapid and accurate and their oral reading is fairly expressive. Children at this stage are no longer beginners, but they are not yet fluent independent readers for the most part. At this stage, the amount of reading that children do and their degree of success with it have a tremendous impact on their progress to the next stage.

- *Reading to Learn and for Pleasure.* Children in this stage, usually from grade three on up, may be reading chapter books for pleasure and homework assignments for learning. By this stage, good readers are pulling dramatically farther ahead of struggling readers in their ease of reading, the amount of time they spend reading outside of school, and the amount of reading they do.
- *Mature Reading.* Mature readers are those who read and compare many sources of information on a topic. They can read "against the grain" of a text and use the reading experience as a way of generating original ideas of their own. They can also recognize and appreciate an author's style and technique. Although many readers do these things in the lower grades, this kind of adultlike reading is more common in about middle school and above; high school or college students who don't have these advanced reading skills have an increasingly difficult time.

Of course, individual students will go through stages of reading at different rates, but if they vary too much from the norm, difficulties can occur. As you can see from these descriptions, in each stage, students develop new reading abilities, and new challenges are placed on those abilities by the curriculum.

If students' reading development gets too far out of step with the demands of the curriculum, they might find themselves in real trouble. In first grade, for example, children struggle to recognize words, while in fourth grade, reading is normally fluent, automatic, and often purposeful: Fourth-graders are required to write book reports and read for homework. Some children in fourth grade still struggle to recognize words, and in that way, their reading is like the reading of first-graders. Their situation is very different, however, because these troubled readers have fewer chances to practice reading using material written on their grade level than first-graders do (Allington, 1983). That is, these readers will have an impoverished opportunity to get better at reading. Moreover, if they cannot easily read for information, they might find themselves competing with classmates who have a richer knowledge base. This is a recipe for failure.

Let us now take a closer look at these stages, beginning with the earliest one: emergent literacy.

Emergent Literacy

The stage that once was called *reading readiness* or *prereading* is now known as *emergent literacy* (Teale and Sulzby, 1986). Emergent literacy refers to a process that represents the child's growing discoveries about print: that writing corresponds to spoken words; that the print, not the pictures, tells the story; that print is composed of a certain set of letters arranged just so on a page; and that those letters stand for spoken words in a certain way.

These concepts are so naturally learned by many children, usually by those who are read to often at home, that in the past, teachers usually launched right into beginning reading instruction without taking into account the prereading concepts that children might already have. Now, thanks to a dynamic body of research in emergent literacy, we understand the critical set of concepts that children must have to benefit from reading instruction. We know how to identify children who still need to develop emergent literacy concepts and experiences, and we have strategies to help them learn. We can even give families and community volunteers ways to help all children get off to a good start in literacy acquisition. These are important breakthroughs.

Now we will highlight the key developments of the stage of emergent literacy. Much of this discussion will focus on writing as well as on reading, because children's discoveries of how print works come from not only recognizing print (reading) but also from producing it (writing).

Concepts about Print

In the following excerpt from *What Did I Write?* (1975), Marie Clay, a pioneer in the study of emergent literacy, gives a compelling example of what we mean by *concepts about print*. (In this excerpt, Clay's term "new entrant group," refers to New Zealand children who have just attained the age of 5 and have begun school in a class for "infants," our version of kindergartners.)

> Suppose a teacher has placed an attractive picture on the wall and has asked her children for a story, which she will record under it. They offer the text "Mother is cooking," which the teacher alters slightly to introduce some features she wishes to teach. She writes:
>
>
>
> Mother said,
> "I am baking."
>
>
>
> If she says, "Now look at our *story,*" 30 percent of a new entrant group will attend to the *picture.* If she says, "Look at the words and find some you know," between 50 and 90 percent will be looking for *letters.* If she says, "Can you see *Mother?*" most will agree that they can, but some see her in the picture, some can locate *M* and others will locate the word *Mother.*
>
> Perhaps the children read in unison "Mother is . . ." and the teacher tries to sort this out. Pointing to *said,* she asks, "Does this say *is?*" Half agree that it does because it has *s* in it. "What letter does it start with?" Now the teacher is really in trouble. She assumes that the children *know* that a word is built out of letters, but 50 percent of the children still confuse the verbal labels *word* and *letter* after six months of instruction. She also assumes that the children know that the left-hand letter following a space is the "start" of a word. Often they do not. (Clay, 1975, pp. 3–4)

In this vignette, Clay has pointed out that even with beginners, we often assume that children have concepts and labels for concepts that they might very well lack. Some of these concepts turn out to be more difficult for some young children to acquire than others. These concepts about print include knowing that:

- a book has a front and a back and a cover;
- we read the words in a book, not the pictures;
- print goes from left to right and from top to bottom;
- language is made out of words;
- words are made out of sounds;
- sounds can be matched with letters;
- there is a limited set of those letters;

- the letters have names; and
- other parts of print have names, too, such as *sentence, word, letter, beginning,* and *end.*

The terms that we use for these fundamental emergent literacy concepts and operations include *concept of word, phonological awareness, alphabet recognition, emergent storybook reading,* and *early writing/invented spelling.*

Concept of Word   A longstanding procedure to introduce children to reading is to teach them to memorize a catchy phrase or rhyme and then show them the phrase or rhyme written down. It seems natural that a child who has memorized the words of a poem should find it easy to read the printed version, pointing at the words as she or he goes. In fact, it might not be so easy.

To do this supposedly simple speech-to-print matching (Morris, 1981) requires the understanding that language comes in units of words and that those units correspond exactly to the clusters of letters on the page with spaces at either end. Only in late kindergarten or early first grade do many children develop this *concept of word* (Morris, 1981), and many children still don't have it even in early first grade.

It is easy to see why the concept of word should be important in learning to read. Darrell Morris has demonstrated that children who can point to words as they say them are more likely to learn words from seeing them in print. Other researchers (Ehri and Sweet, 1991; Reutzel et al., 1989) agree.

What other abilities support the concept of word? Morris (1989) found that children were more likely to *voice-point* accurately (that is, to point to a written word in a line of text that has been memorized at the same time that they say the spoken word) if they were able to recognize some beginning letters and associate them with sounds. That is, a child who knows the letter T and associates the sound /t/ with T will have an easier time pointing to word units in "Twinkle, twinkle, little star."

On the other hand, Ehri and Sweet (1991) found that children who were aware that words were composed of individual sounds (see the following section) were better able to voice-point. For now, we can say that children's instruction in emergent literacy should develop all of these concepts: knowledge of letters and awareness of their sounds, manipulation of sound units in spoken words, and voice-pointing to develop a concept of word.

Phonological Awareness   After children have the concept of word, they must be able to break a word down into its component sounds, or *phonemes.* For example, they must perceive that the spoken word *cape* contains the sequence of sounds /k/,/ā/, and /p/. Why is this important? The short answer is that it's the way our alphabetic writing system works. Written words, for all their apparent irregularity, use letters to spell the individual sounds of spoken words. Children who are not able to sense the individual sound units of spoken words won't be able to sound out that word when they try to read it.

But that's only part of the answer. Some researchers, such as Isabel Liberman et al. (1977) and Linnea Ehri (1978), believe that even when we have learned to recognize a word as a whole, the sort of memory process that we use stores the word part by part, or phoneme by phoneme, with an awareness of the graphic representation or spelling of those phonemes. So the more adept we are at breaking words into sounds, the more efficient we'll be at remembering those words for later recognition.

As we just saw, another aspect of phonological awareness should be an *awareness of letter-to-sound correspondences,* that is, knowing what sounds are usually represented by what letters. We are not saying that children in the emergent literacy stage need to know all of the letter-sound relationships. At first, we care only that they realize that such relationships exist. They are likely to see this first in the case of familiar words they see often in meaningful contexts: their names, brand names, words on street signs, and so forth.

Alphabet Recognition   It is certainly not necessary for children to know all of the letters of the alphabet to read, but research suggests that it helps if they know most of them (Walsh, et al., 1986). For one thing, we know that the practice of *invented* or *temporary spelling,* discussed in the next section, helps children develop phonological awareness and later word recognition (Clarke, 1988). Children need to be able to name and form letters to invent spellings.

A thorough assessment of children's emergent literacy will include an inventory of the letters that they can recognize and write. A sound instructional program will teach them the alphabet, along with more natural literacy activities such as listening to stories, reading picture books, writing, and retelling and acting out stories.

Emergent Storybook Reading   We have described the aspects of emergent literacy as if they developed separately. In fact, these aspects develop naturally in the context of reading events: Children are read storybooks and soon try to read storybooks themselves.

Elizabeth Sulzby (1985) observed hundreds of preschool children of different ages reading storybooks and discerned clear patterns of evolution in the strategies that younger to older children use in such activities. These strategies, in turn, reflect children's growing awareness of decontextualized language, of the reality of words, of the speech-to-print match, and of some other learnings as well. Figure 1.1 summarizes these strategies.

The youngest subjects (some as young as age 2 or 3) "read" by pointing to the pictures and naming them. They treat the pictures rather than the print as the primary conveyors of meaning in texts; also, for them, reading consists of commenting on each picture as a separate exhibit. They do not attempt to weave a story across several pictures. Their commentary, also, is directed at the person who is reading with them. Reading at this stage is deeply embedded in conversation.

Children then begin to form stories from texts; this occurs before they pay attention to the print. The first stories are still highly conversational: "And do you know what she did then?" Children might begin to tell a little story about each picture separately, without reference to preceding or subsequent pictures.

Later reading attempts are conducted in voices that sound like people reading, though the children still orient themselves in the story by the pictures, not

BROAD CATEGORIES	BRIEF EXPLANATION OF CATEGORIES
1. Attending to Pictures, Not Forming Stories	The child is "reading" by looking at the storybook's pictures. The child's speech is just about the picture in view: the child is not "weaving a story" across the pages.
2. Attending to Pictures, Forming *Oral* Stories	The child is "reading" by looking at the storybook's pictures. The child's speech weaves a story across the pages but the wording and the intonation are like that of someone telling a story, either like a conversation about the pictures or like a fully recited story, in which the listener can see the pictures (and often *must* see them to understand the child's story).
3. Attending to Pictures, Reading and Storytelling	The child is "reading" by looking at the storybook's pictures. The child's speech fluctuates between sounding like Mixeda story-teller, with oral intonation, and sounding like a reader, with reading intonation. To fit this category, the majority of the reading attempt must show fluctuations between storytelling and reading.
4. Attending to Pictures Forming *Written* Stories	The child is "reading" by looking at the storybook's pictures. The child's speech sounds as if the child is reading, both in the wording and intonation. The listener does not need to look at the pictures (or rarely does) in order to understand the story. If the listener closes her or his eyes, most of the time she or he would think the child is reading from print.
5. Attending to Print	There are four subcategories of attending to print. Only the *final* one is what is typically called "real reading." In the others the child is exploring the print by such strategies as refusing to read based on print-related reasons, or using only some of the aspects of print.

FIGURE 1.1 Simplified Version of Sulzby's Classification Scheme for Children's Emergent Reading of Favorite Storybooks: Category Summaries

Source: From "Children's Emergent Reading of Favorite Storybooks: A Developmental Study." Elizabeth Sulzby, *Reading Research Quarterly* 20, 1985. Reprinted with permission of Elizabeth Sulzby and the International Reading Association.

the print. But the idea is dawning that a book tells a certain story, just so: in these words and no others. This reflects an awareness of decontextualized language, but it also prepares the children to start looking seriously at the print to see what part of the story it tells.

One of the first signs that children are looking to the print as a source of the spoken words might come as a refusal to read: They know that they should be able to read the print, and they know that they can't. Thus, a child who would have cheerfully trotted out a story the month before might now hesitate or refuse.

But hearing a favorite story over and over and seeing someone point to the words (or at least to the line of print) as they read eventually enable children to match spoken words with written ones. This leads to their learning the vivid words and the

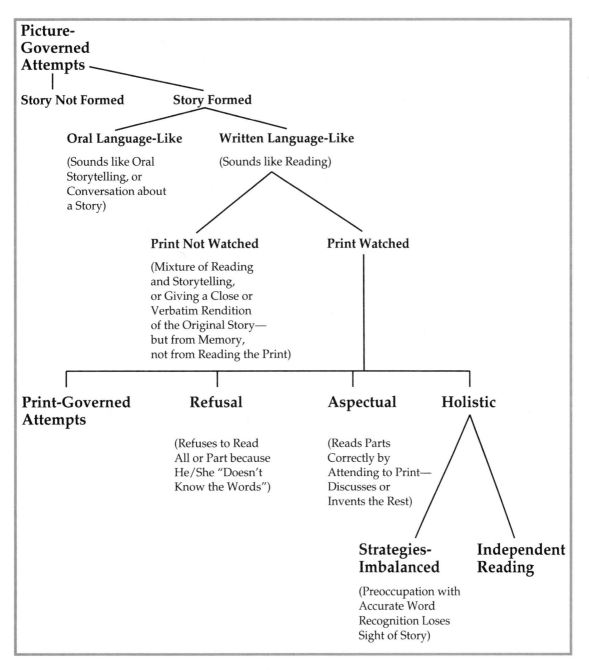

Picture-Governed Attempts

Story Not Formed   Story Formed

Oral Language-Like   Written Language-Like

(Sounds like Oral
Storytelling, or
Conversation about
a Story)

(Sounds like Reading)

Print Not Watched   Print Watched

(Mixture of Reading
and Storytelling,
or Giving a Close or
Verbatim Rendition
of the Original Story—
but from Memory,
not from Reading the Print)

Print-Governed Attempts   **Refusal**   **Aspectual**   **Holistic**

(Refuses to Read
All or Part because
He/She "Doesn't
Know the Words")

(Reads Parts
Correctly by
Attending to Print—
Discusses or
Invents the Rest)

Strategies-Imbalanced   **Independent Reading**

(Preoccupation with
Accurate Word
Recognition Loses
Sight of Story)

FIGURE 1.1 *(continued)*

ones that are often repeated. At some point, a reading might consist of finding these known words, even at the expense of losing the thread of the story, before children actually succeed in reading the story by tracking along with the written words.

Young children's attempts to read a favorite story show us aspects of their understanding of the functions of print and the nature of language in print. As a practical matter, storybook reading can provide a useful context for observing these concepts in action. Giving children good books on their level, and then encouraging them to read these books in their own fashion, turns out to be a natural way to encourage the emergence of children's literacy, whether at home, in preschool, or in school.

Early Writing and Invented/Temporary Spelling   Discovery plays a crucial role in children's learning about literacy. English has an alphabetic writing system, in which words are represented by a set of relationships between letters and phonemes. Children have to discover these relationships to learn to read and write.

Ferreiro and Teberosky (1982) investigated children's understanding of these issues by asking them to draw pictures and write captions under the pictures. When they questioned the children about the marks the children produced as they were "writing," the researchers identified stages that the development of writing goes through.

The first stage we might call *concrete writing*. A child draws a cat and labels it, using a few large letterlike characters. He draws a kitten and labels it, using similar characters, only smaller. He draws a family of kittens and labels them, using repetitions of the small characters used to label "kitten." It appears that the child believes that there should be a concrete relationship between the thing he is labeling and the marks that he uses. Names for similar objects (*cat* and *kitten*) should be similar. Names for big or numerous things should have big, numerous characters, and names for small and few things should have few, small characters. This *concrete strategy* bypasses any attempt to represent the spoken word for the object and represents features of the object itself.

A more mature child draws an alligator and writes the following:

The child draws a butterfly and writes the following:

As you can see, the child is now trying to represent the names of the things. He or she is using marks to count out the syllables in the words *alligator* and *butterfly*. But there is no further relationship between the marks and the sounds of those syllables. In this *syllabic strategy*, marks are used as counters only.

A sightly more mature child draws a foot and writes the following:

He draws a bird and writes the following:

As the beginning (left-hand) letter of each string shows, the child is now trying to represent a sound that he hears in the name of the thing with a particular letter. No longer are letters mere counters; the child is thinking about writing as a way of finding correspondences between the sound-constituents of words and the letters of the alphabet. This *alphabetic strategy,* as we have already said, is essentially the one our writing system is based upon.

As Marie Clay's work (1975) has shown us, when children make marks on a page and call them writing, we can begin to tell what defining concepts they have in mind when they think of print. Often, young writers create print by repeating the same move over and over. Clay called this idea the *recurring principle.*

When children learn to make a few discrete marks, they often use the same marks over and over to generate a large amount of writing. Clay called this insight the *generative principle:* A small number of characters can be reproduced in varying orders to make a large amount of writing. The generative principle is, of course, the basis for alphabetic writing: Twenty-six letters can be combined and recombined to fill all the books in the Library of Congress.

Once children know a few letters, they often begin to play with them, to draw them in different ways. Sometimes they happily produce letters that they didn't already know. Sometimes they just seem to be testing the limits of the different ways they can make letters without changing them into something else. Marie Clay used the term *flexibility principle* to refer to the insights that come from exploring print by varying the forms of letters.

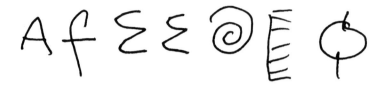

Psychologists of perception (such as Gibson and Levin, 1975) have shown that perceptual learning proceeds from whole to part and from gross distinctions to finer ones. We learn to tell birds from bugs, then robins from wrens and gypsy moths from monarch butterflies. Clay found basically the same thing in children's writing. Children discover graphic principles related to the writing system as a whole before they master many individual letters. That being the case, then, if we give children opportunities in preschool and kindergarten to produce scribbles and other pretend writing, we'll be making it easier for them to focus on individual letters when the time comes. In other words, scribbling and pretend writing are useful early practices for learning to form and recognize letters.

Once children know the names of some of the letters of the alphabet and can begin to segment phonemes in spoken words, it is natural that they should discover the *alphabetic principle* and begin to use letters to spell words by their individual sounds. So many children of age 5 or 6 do this, even before they have learned to read in the conventional sense, that the phenomenon is now well known.

Thanks to the research of Charles Read (1986), Edmund Henderson (1992), and others, the stage-bound set of discoveries by which many people learn to spell have been mapped out in detail. The stages are described in Box 1.1. For now, we should note that when children produce spellings such as those in Figure 1.2 (on page 23), they show that they are

- segmenting the phonemes in words and
- actively exploring the relationships between writing and reading, between letters and sounds.

When we look at one child's spelling over a period of months, we see that even without being taught, the words take on more and more features of standard spelling and that by reading and writing, the child is discovering the spelling structures of the writing system. Capitalizing on this discovery process, many teachers offer authentic daily opportunities to write, representing ideas and words however they can, with drawings, scribbles, and invented spellings.

STAGES OF INVENTED/ TEMPORARY SPELLING

We used to think that people learned to spell by memorizing thousands of individual spellings. Now we know that learners look for patterns in spelling that relate letters to sounds. As when they learn to talk, children learning to spell put forward their own ideas of how the patterns work, and often make some bizarre-looking spellings in the process. Also like learning to talk is the fact that children seem to go through a rough set of stages in spelling development. These stages, which represent characteristic strategies for inventing their own spellings for words, are outlined below. You will note that these stages cover the range from preschool through high school.

Characteristics of Prephonemic Spelling
Phillip, Kindergartner

CHARACTERISTICS OF PREPHONEMIC SPELLING

Prephonemic spelling:

- Is made up of letters and letterlike forms, such as numerals and incorrectly formed or made-up letters.
- Is unreadable; letters and forms are used randomly, not to represent sounds.
- Is usually arranged in horizontal lines.
- May be made up of unbroken lines of letters or arranged in wordlike configurations with spaces between.
- Shows that the child is aware that words are made up of letters and that print is arranged horizontally.
- Is typical of older preschoolers, kindergartners, and many first-graders.

CHARACTERISTICS OF EARLY PHONEMIC SPELLING

Early phonemic spelling:

- Is made up entirely of letters, usually in short strings of one to four letters; single letters are often used to represent whole words.
- Represents the discovery of the alphabetic principle. Letters are used to represent some of the sounds in words.

(continued)

BOX 1.1 *(continued)*

I love my mother. Me and my mother. Me and my dog.

- Commonly features the use of consonants to represent initial sounds; sometimes, final sounds and/or other important, clearly discernible sounds are represented too, but the spellings are very incomplete.
- Shows the child's discovery that letters in print represent sounds in spoken words and indicates the beginning of the ability to segment phonemes.
- Is typical of very beginning readers, some kindergartners, most early first-graders, and some older children who are just beginning to read.

CHARACTERISTICS OF LETTER-NAME SPELLING

Letter-name spelling:

- Shows children's firm awareness that letters represent sounds, so the letters they use stand for sounds with no silent letters included.
- Is still incomplete: Some sounds clearly evident in words are systematically omitted, such as m's and n's before consonants, vowels in unstressed syllables, and many short vowels until late in this stage; however, more sound features are represented than in earlier spelling stages.
- Uses the *names* of letters to represent sounds in words as well as the *sounds* of letters.
- Is often characterized by long vowels used appropriately but unmarked (as with a silent *e*); short vowels predictably substituted by using vowel-letter names or omitted altogether; verb tenses and plural endings spelled as they sound: T, D, and ID; S, Z, and IZ; use of JR, GR, and CHR for sounds adults spell with *tr-* and *dr-*.
- Is typical of beginning readers, who can read a little but are not yet fluent. Most first-graders and many second-graders fall into this group.

(continued)

BOX 1.1 *(continued)*

My TEETH

Last nit I pold oht my lustuth and
I put it ondr my pelr. And wan I wok
up I Fid a two dilr bel. The End.

Characteristics of Letter-Name Spelling

Billy's Spelling: Letter-Name

CHARACTERISTICS OF TRANSITIONAL SPELLING

Transitional spelling:

- Is nearly complete; all phonemes are represented, long and short vowel sounds are generally spelled correctly or typically: HED (head).
- Shows an awareness of marking systems such as silent letters and consonant doubling but uses markers inappropriately: RUNING (running), MAKKING (making), DUCKE (duck).
- Is largely readable by others.
- May show several different attempts at the same word, sometimes abandoning a correct for an incorrect spelling.
- Show an awareness of inflectional endings, but words are often spelled phonemically: PICKT (picked), WANTID (wanted).
- Is typical of young pupils beyond the beginning reading stage and older ones who are still unfluent readers.

CHARACTERISTICS OF DERIVATIONAL SPELLING

Derivational spelling:

- Shows mastery of most of the phonemic and rule-governed spelling patterns, such as vowel marking and consonant doubling, that trip up transitional spellers.
- Shows lack of awareness of relational patterns among words derived from the same source.
- Is typical of older students and adults who have not read widely, written copiously, and studied word derivations directly.

(continued)

BOX 1.1 *(continued)*

Make a vest.
If you want to make a rest, you hare
to get some meatium-size
buttens and then some neadles
a in threds and then some
light Mateerial for the back
Make sure it is white matea
and Make sure that the ves
is brown or tan then start
Soing. Make sure it has
no arms eather. Make sure it
has three buttens then you hare
a rest to wear.
You will Know how to make a vest

Josiah

Characteristics of
Transitional Spelling
Source: Josiah,
First Grade,
Transitional Speller

definate   sergen   natchrel   reverse
version   nature   surgery
saler   sail   definition

Characteristics of Derivational Spelling

Reading and Writing at This Stage

Children at this stage can successfully read simple, predictable texts with few
words and many supportive pictures. These books have proliferated in recent
years. Major publishers of attractive predictable books include The Wright

Group, Rigby Publishing, Scholastic, and Addison-Wesley. Emergent readers love to zoom through familiar books, counting and sorting the books they know. Individual copies tend to be small paperbacks with few pages, easy for little hands to manipulate. There should be a good balance of fiction and nonfiction material from which children can choose. Alphabet books, counting books, and concept books that illustrate colors, animal families, machines, and so forth are good.

Children's writing and attempts to spell in the emergent stage may include everything from *scribbles* with various graphic features showing up, to early *phonemic spelling*. The examples in Box 1.1 illustrate some of these features.

Problems in the Emergent Stage

Emergent literacy is fascinating for adults to observe, and many of the things young children say and do with writing, spelling, reading, and books are delightful and amusing. But for children, moving toward literacy is serious business. Children who successfully explore concepts about print during this period lay down a foundation that helps them to profit from reading and writing instruction later on.

Children who do not acquire foundational concepts about print will very likely struggle with beginning reading and subsequently fall farther and farther behind their peers unless extraordinary steps are taken to help them. Connie Juel (1988) has shown that nearly 90 percent of the first-graders who were behind their peers in reading were still in the bottom group four years later; but by then, the distance between them and the average readers was immense. This occurred in spite of a whole arsenal of special intervention services that were available to assist them.

For this reason, in recent years, intensive early intervention programs such as Reading Recovery (Clay, 1985; Pinnell, 1989), Success for All (Slavin et al., 1991), and First Steps (Morris, 1993a) have been developed. These programs have been quite successful in preventing early reading failure (Johnston, 1991). However, they also raise troubling questions for educators and communities: Should priorities for special reading instruction be concentrated on children in the first few grades, where they might do the most good, or should they be used to support children at all levels of schooling? The dynamics of emergent literacy that we described in this section are certain to gain more attention in coming years as we strive to make all our children literate. Teaching strategies for helping children

FIGURE 1.2 Invented Spelling by Annabrook, a Five-Year-Old, Not Yet Reading
Translation: "I am going to Virginia and I have a headache."

through the stage of emergent literacy are the subject of Chapter 6, "Emergent and Beginning Literacy."

Beginning Reading

Children reach the beginning reading stage when they learn to recognize words appearing in different contexts. For example, a child who recognizes *McDonald's* only when it appears on the restaurant sign but not when it appears on a road sign or newspaper ad is recognizing the word as a meaningful symbol but not as a word. When the same child suddenly realizes that *McDonald's* is the same word, thus readable to him or her, on signs, hamburger wrappers, newspaper coupons, and Mom's "To Do" list, then the child has acquired it as a *sight word,* a word that is immediately recognizable without analysis.

This stage marks the beginning of true reading, but it comes only after much prior learning. As we saw in the discussion of emergent literacy, before children can begin to acquire a *sight vocabulary,* or a corpus of words that they recognize immediately at sight, they must

- be able to pay attention to spoken language and its parts,
- understand something about the way reading is done, and
- know a good deal about the nature of print.

An additional challenge in the period of beginning reading is to learn to recognize words and attend to their meaning at the same time. If all we do is teach children to recognize words, we will give them a distorted idea of what reading is, for reading is much more than identifying the words on a page. On the other hand, we can't get around the fact that children must learn to recognize words with increasing accuracy and automaticity if they are to progress in reading. In this section, we will consider *word recognition, comprehension,* and *reading fluency.*

For years, experts have debated whether it is better to encourage children to recognize words as wholes or to teach them to use *phonics,* the process of sounding out words by associating speech sounds with letters. But this should not be an either-or proposition. Good readers use both immediate recognition of whole words and a variety of decoding or word analysis operations, so the best approach is to acknowledge what children are doing at different points in their development as they try to recognize words and to give them a variety of strategies that they can use flexibly and purposefully.

Beginning readers usually have fairly small sight vocabularies, and if the texts that they read are not highly supportive and predictable, they will have to try to figure out a good number of the words that they encounter in print. For that reason, in the following discussion, we will talk about word recognition or word analysis strategies first and the role of sight words second.

Recognizing and Analyzing Words

Recent studies suggest that children look at words differently as they gain experience in beginning reading. Marsh et al. (1981) found that children go through a series of stages in figuring out words:

■ ***Glance and Guess.*** Children who are reading very familiar text, such as a memorized favorite book or rhyme, will glance at a word and identify it according to what makes sense. This identification is a form of guessing, based on context, perhaps according to the shape of the word or other visual features. The word that they guess is always drawn from words that they have in their spoken vocabulary.

■ ***Sophisticated Guessing.*** With more experience, children begin to focus on an initial or final letter in a word and use its letter-sound correspondence to reduce the number of possible alternatives. If the sentence says, "We went to the fire *station,*" they might say "We went to the fire *store.*" The word that they guess is still supplied from words that they know. If they didn't know the word, they wouldn't be able to sound it out.

■ ***Simple Phoneme-Grapheme Correspondences.*** As children get better at sounding out, their reading of unknown words might become somewhat bizarre, such as "We went to the fire *statone.*" By now, they might be so heavily involved in sounding out words that they forget about the meaning. Note that the letter-sound correspondences that children use at this stage are based on small units and the sounding goes almost letter by letter.

■ ***Recognition by Analogy.*** At a more advanced level, children recognize words not just by their individual letter-sound correspondences, but by larger patterns. If one knows *night,* then one can correctly reads the new word, *might,* because one recognizes the known pattern *-ight* in the new word. Word parts like this are commonly known as *phonogram patterns;* words that share the same pattern but change the beginning are often called *word families.* More technical terms are *onset* and *rime* (Trieman, 1979), which name the beginning element of a word and the phonogram pattern that follows it. For example, C or /k/ is the onset in *cat,* and AT or /æ t/ is the rime. Either way we describe these patterns, children who become familiar with them are more sophisticated at recognizing words and spelling, too (Temple et al., 1993).

■ ***Later Word Recognition.*** At a still more advanced stage, readers recognize unknown words by identifying known parts in them. One example of this strategy is seen in reading compound words, for example, recognizing *playground* by recognizing *play* and *ground.* On a still more advanced level, words are deciphered by the *morphemes* or meaningful word units they contain; for example, as the unfamiliar word *equidistant* is broken into *equi-,* a word that is related to the known word *equal,* and *distant,* a known word. This later phase of word recognition lasts from the middle elementary grades into adulthood.

Paying attention to the growth of children's word recognition strategies can help us to give them the help they need. For example, children at the glance-and-guess stage should be given plenty of supported practice reading simple and familiar text, according to ways that we will describe in the next chapter. When they have about fifty or more words at sight (Stauffer, 1975), we can begin calling their attention to the beginnings of words and show them that words beginning with the same letter often begin with the same sound. We'll encourage them to write using temporary or invented spellings, too; when they want to write words they can't spell, we'll encourage them to say the word slowly and write whatever letters they can produce to represent the sounds, or as many of the sounds as they can.

When children have reached the point of sophisticated guessing, we'll give them more practice identifying beginning sounds to consolidate their strength, and we'll also begin to call attention to sounds at the ends of words and in the middle. Their somewhat more complex invented spellings will give them more opportunities to think about the relationship between sounds and letters. (Look again at Box 1.1 for a review of how invented spellings become progressively more complex as children grow in literacy.)

When they reach the point of sounding out by means of simple phoneme-grapheme (i.e., sound-letter) correspondences, we'll encourage the children to find those individual sound-to-letter matches, but also we'll begin to call their attention to phonogram patterns in words, especially by studying rhyming words, word families, and other ways of categorizing similar words, called *word sorting* (see Chapter 6). Once children expect to find familiar phonogram patterns in words, we can continue to discuss these patterns with them, again using rhymes and word sorts.

Although we are discussing word recognition as though it proceeded in an orderly sequence of stages and related teaching strategies, such a sequence is only approximate and should never replace providing children at all developmental levels with an environment that is rich in real literature, songs, poetry, storytelling, informative nonfiction, and so forth. Even children who are at the earliest stages of word recognition can surprise us by discovering, well before we expect them to, that similar letter sequences make similar sounds. When this discovery is made, it appears to be a profound one; we have seen children's faces light up in amazement when they discover that two words rhyme or that because they can read *not*, they can also read and spell *hot*. The sheer power that children feel over words when they make these discoveries never fails to delight them—and us as well.

In teaching beginning readers, we sometimes emphasize word recognition operations at the expense of comprehension and enjoyment. Even when beginning readers are preoccupied with studying and practicing word recognition skills, we need to emphasize that reading is supposed to make sense. As children become more engrossed in puzzling out words, they might lose sight of this larger purpose of reading. We should frequently remind readers to ask themselves what makes sense as they try to read unfamiliar words, especially as they practice using decoding strategies. When children use word parts and decoding to produce words that look and sound like the word in the text but make no sense, we have not helped them much. Effective reading is not just good decoding or reading aloud accurately but with little understanding. Expecting meaning, trying to decode, and considering what makes sense: These are the means by which children learn to recognize words.

Normally, as children advance into second grade and beyond, their word analysis strategies grow more sophisticated. They will take more complex word patterns and meanings into account as they analyze words. At the same time, they will continue to acquire sight words, and teachers will often refer to a child's growing sight vocabulary. The combination of a larger sight vocabulary and more effective word analysis strategies allows these developing readers to read increasingly difficult texts fluently and with good comprehension.

Acquiring Sight Words   Eventually, to read efficiently, readers must recognize most of the words in running text quickly and accurately. Trying to get meaning from text while having to analyze and figure out one word after another results in frustration, confusion, loss of comprehension, and fatigue. It is much easier to read for meaning if you can recognize words quickly and accurately and have to decode only a few of the words. If you are not sure, see how long it takes you to read this out loud:

> *Owwer entint heeriz tughshoa yugh whuttah dissuhgrieuhbull choware iddizz tuh sowndowt evirie wurrd ennalign uvtegst, wunnbighwunn.*

Did it take you longer than reading the following?

> Our intent here is to show you how disagreeable a chore it is to sound out every word in a line of text, one by one.

Even so, you decoded more quickly than the average poor reader, because you could quickly translate *tughshoa* into *to show*. Even though we tried to make our example somewhat difficult for you, it is very hard to overcome all the thousands of pieces of information you already have in your head as a fluent, mature reader. But perhaps you had just a taste of what poor readers experience as they claw their way along a line of text, with few whole words that they can recognize.

But if efficient reading means recognizing words as wholes, why shouldn't we just teach whole words and skip decoding altogether? The answer is that, as we stated earlier, learning to break words into sounds and to match sounds with letters actually gives us a more efficient memory for recognizing words. People with sophisticated decoding knowledge, or *orthographic awareness,* are not only proficient at figuring out words in the first place, but also proficient at remembering them.

Also, we cannot expect to be able to teach children to recognize at sight every word that they will ever encounter in print. So we have to help readers acquire effective word analysis strategies as well as sight words. But because reading text with lots of words that have to be figured out, as in the example above, is fatiguing and discouraging, we should make sure that what students read is made up mostly of words that they can read at sight.

Readers should not have to struggle with, or stop to figure out, more than about one word in twenty, as a rule. Unfortunately, the farther below grade level students are reading, the less likely it is that they will be placed in text of an appropriate level of difficulty, in which readers can already recognize most of the words (Allington, 1983). (You will learn more about assessing the difficulty of text and the importance of placing students in texts that have enough known words to be comfortable in Chapters 2 and 3 and about matching texts to readers' abilities in Chapters 6 and 7.)

Sometimes, there is confusion between *sight words,* which are any words that a reader can recognize immediately, and *basic sight words,* a term that is often used for the two hundred or three hundred high-utility, or frequently occurring, words that are often directly taught as wholes. The role of these high-utility words in reading is an important one.

A very few words account for a large percentage of all running text. Look at the words on this page; many of the same words appear again and again, such as *a, the, and, is, of, be, not, for, it, will, you, that,* and *like.* You would find these same words, and a few other very common ones, repeated over and over in almost any text you examined, whether it was another college textbook, a popular novel, a children's book, a set of directions, a letter from a friend, or a newspaper article. In fact, just ten words account for 20 percent of all words in many popular children's books, and only 188 words account for 70 percent of the running text in the same books (Durr, 1973).

The usefulness of a small body of common words is not a new idea. A century ago, children were given lists of common words to memorize, and fifty years ago, the Dolch Basic Sight Vocabulary flashcards could be found in nearly every first-grade classroom in the United States. As recently as thirty or so years ago, many basal readers and supplementary materials featured highly controlled vocabularies, meaning that entire stories were constructed from the same small number of words, supplemented of course by pictures that supplied much of the meaning. (Who could forget the adventures of Dick, Jane, and Sally, immortalized in texts such as "Oh, oh, oh. Look, look, look. See the funny thing," or so-called "linguistic reader" texts such as "Pat has a flat pan. Dan has a fat hat."?)

Teaching children to recognize the most basic words is useful in theory, but there is a catch. Many of the most frequently occurring words are conjunctions, articles, pronouns, and prepositions; they don't refer to anything directly, but rather serve a grammatical function in sentences. (How would you describe the meaning of *of*? Can you say what *in* means without using the word *in*? It's much easier to say what *the* signals to us when we see it before a noun than to tell what *the* means.) The most common words are vague in meaning and rather hard to remember outside the meaningful context of a sentence. If you can remember your teachers using flashcards, you might remember struggling to remember the difference between similar-looking words such as *these* and *those, when* and *where,* or *of* and *off.*

Even worse, one can recognize all of the basic sight words and still not know what is going on in a passage. Consider, for example, the following sentences, from which we have deleted all of the words except for those that are most common and often considered "first-grade words":

_____ _____ and his _____ _____ _____ in the _____. They _____ in green. They _____ the _____ for _____ with their _____ and _____.

Hmmm, ready to answer some comprehension questions about that passage now?

Here is the same passage with the basic sight words taken out and the other words put back in:

Robin Hood _____ _____ merry men lived _____ _____ forest. _____ dressed _____ _____. _____ shot _____ deer _____ food _____ _____ bows _____ arrows.
(Manning-Sanders, 1977, p. 1)

It is much easier to get at least the gist of what is going on if you can read the more difficult, colorful, memorable words than if you can read only the basic sight words. As we see, it is fairly easy to guess the high-frequency words if we know the low-frequency words; but knowing the high-frequency words, the basic sight words, without the other words is of little help in understanding the passage.

Children are apt to learn low-frequency words with fewer exposures than they will basic sight words, simply because the former are more vivid. Today, many teachers do not bother with teaching children basic sight words *in isolation;*

instead, they teach students to recognize these very useful words as they occur in the context of sentences and paragraphs. Instruction in word recognition is generally better in a meaningful context.

Comprehending Text

Comprehension, or understanding what we read, is the whole point of reading. However, the process of comprehension is not understood by all teachers and, for this reason, has not always been taught effectively.

Comprehension involves *prior knowledge, knowledge of text structure,* and an *active search for information.* Let us describe each of these and put them together into an understanding of reading comprehension.

Comprehension and Prior Knowledge
The simplest definition of comprehension is *understanding new information in light of what we already know.* We understand new things and events we encounter by matching them with our store of mental frameworks that are called *schemes* or *schemata* (Piaget, 1959/1964).

The same process is at work when we try to make sense of what we read. We use the words on the page to trigger our existing knowledge of whatever the words refer to, and in doing so, we often supply as much information as the words on the page do. Here is an illustration of what we mean:

Read this passage:

> Johnny was nearly in tears. It was Susan's birthday, and he'd forgotten to tell his mother, so Johnny had gone to the party empty-handed. He stood behind a cluster of other children who were greeting Susan at the door. Through the open door, he could see the cake on the table, and brightly colored balloons and streamers taped to the wall and hanging from the ceiling.
>
> The other children went inside. Susan turned and saw him.
>
> "Hi, Johnny," she said. "I'm glad you could come."
>
> "Hi, Susan." With his hands behind his back he stepped forward, feeling his face blush bright red.

Without looking back at the story:

1. Retell the story events in chronological order.
2. Summarize the story in one sentence.
3. Why was Johnny "nearly in tears"?
4. Why was he empty-handed?
5. Describe the cake.

If you are like most readers, you began making some decisions about this story fairly early on. You probably decided without conscious thought that Johnny's problem is his lack of a present for Susan.

The point of the exercise, as you might have guessed, is to demonstrate how much of the meaning of the passage you supplied for yourself. Nowhere in the text is a present explicitly mentioned, nor is the cake described, or Johnny's age referred to. Yet readers have no trouble filling in this missing information and generally agree in their judgments. Indeed, they find it so natural that most are unaware that they are doing it.

Current theories of how we comprehend text (e.g., Anderson and Pearson, 1984; Bartlett, 1932; Minsky, 1975; Rosenblatt, 1978) stress the reader's active role in constructing meaning. According to one version called *schema theory,* readers have mental frameworks that organize their knowledge of the world. Schemata are abstract; that is, they are inexact enough to be called in to fit a range of new situations. They are also incomplete; they have slots in them that are available to be filled by the details in the text that is being considered (we say "text," but this theory of comprehension can apply, of course, to events in the world as well). When we fit details from the text into the slots in our schema, we actively create the meaning that is partially supplied by the text.

In the case of the birthday party example, the text provided words about the characters and their actions, but you supplied your own understanding of the situation: the birthday party. You provided even more, however; to consider Johnny and Susan as characters, you demonstrated a set of expectations about narratives: that they involve characters in causally motivated sequences of actions. Thus, from the very beginning we want to know why Johnny is upset (and we can easily guess from the details we are given), and we want to know what will happen next.

Readers are thought to have both kinds of schemata: schemata that organize *world knowledge* and schemata for *text structure.*

World Knowledge   *World knowledge* is all the things readers know that enable them to fill in the gaps when they are reading or listening to someone talk or read.

We can make three points about world knowledge. First, while fourth-graders might know a lot about birthday parties, they might know little or nothing about Europe or the way we elect the President of the United States. If they encounter text about a country in Europe or a presidential election, they might not be able to fill in the gaps or organize the new information sufficiently. They will not understand the text. Thus, the amount of background knowledge that students have will affect their reading comprehension, a fact that had led E.D. Hirsch, Jr., to suggest that schools might attack reading problems by increasing the information content of the curriculum (Hirsch, 1987).

Text Structure   Becoming a good reader also requires that one be familiar with the *structure of the text* and be able to use that structure to guide the student's search for meaning. The text structure that we're talking about can be as basic as sentence structure. Consider the following sentence:

> *Shirley reached into her pocket and found a b* _____.

A reader who is guided by awareness of sentence structure would supply *button, buck, bean,* or some other noun or noun phrase beginning with B to fill the slot. The reader would realize that a noun must follow as the object of the verb *found* and the lead word for the noun phrase denoted by the article *a,* though the reader might not be able to explain it in these terms. Even without considering what would make sense, readers with text structure awareness can reduce the possibilities for the last word by many thousands. Add to that the sense-making structures that effective readers have, and those thousands of possibilities are reduced even further, since many nouns beginning with B would not make sense in this sentence; Shirley could hardly find a *buffalo,* a *birdcage* or a *Bernese mountain dog* in her pocket. Of all the English words beginning with B, only a relative few would work in this sentence.

Story Structure   There are larger structures than the structure of a sentence, which even beginning readers use to help them understand what they read. The most familiar structure is probably that which we call a *story.* Consider this example:

The Dog and His Shadow

Once there was a big brown dog named Sam. One day Sam found a piece of meat and was carrying it home in his mouth to eat. Now on his way home, he had to cross a plank lying across a brook. As he crossed the brook, he looked down and saw his own shadow reflected in the water beneath.

He thought it was another dog with another piece of meat and he made up his mind to have that piece also. So he made a snap at the shadow, but as he opened his mouth, the piece of meat fell out. The meat dropped into the water and sank out of sight. Sam never saw the meat again. (McConaughty, 1980, p. 158)

Short as it is, the story of Sam nonetheless has all of the structural elements that we expect in a simple story, and it has them in the right order.

It begins with a *setting,* in which a character is introduced in some context of time and place, which may be directly stated or inferred:

Once there was a big brown dog named Sam. One day Sam found a piece of meat and was carrying it home in his mouth to eat. Now on his way home, he had to cross a plank lying across a brook.

Next in the story comes an *initiating event,* which is either some occurrence or some idea that strikes someone and sets events in motion in the story or that causes some important response in the main character:

As he crossed the brook, he looked down and saw his shadow reflected in the water beneath.

As a result of the initiating event, the main character has an *internal response;* that is, the character thinks, judges, decides, or otherwise responds in some way to the initiative event:

He thought it was another dog with another piece of meat . . .

He then sets a *goal:*

. . . and he made up his mind to have that piece also.

(Sometimes the response and the goal occur at the same time, as the character's response is to set a goal.)

To achieve the goal, the main character makes an *attempt,* some overt action to reach the goal:

So he made a snap at the shadow . . .

and this attempt has an *outcome:*

. . . but as he opened his mouth, the piece of meat fell out.

(In typical stories which are not as short as this one, more than one attempt might occur; each attempt has its outcome, either stated directly or inferred, and successive attempts are unsuccessful until the final one.)

Following the attempt(s) and outcome(s), there is a *consequence;* that is, some new action or situation results from the character's success or failure to achieve the goal:

> *The meat dropped into the water and sank out of sight. Sam never saw the meat again.*

The last story structure is the only one that may be considered optional. There may be a *reaction,* that is, an idea, an emotion, or some further action that indicates the main character's feelings about achieving or not achieving the goal or a response that relates the events of the story to some larger set of concerns. "The Dog and His Shadow" did not include a reaction, but if it had, it might have taken the form of a moral or lesson statement, such as the following:

> *Sam was indeed a sadder but wiser dog!* or,
>   *A steak in the mouth is worth two in the brook!*

Taken together, the elements of stories and the order in which they are presented are sometimes called a *story grammar* because they describe story elements and their allowable orders in ways that remind us of sentence grammars, which do the same thing for the elements of a sentence. A schematic rendering of the structure or grammar of stories like "The Dog and His Shadow" is found in Figure 1.3. The grammar that we just saw might be made more elaborate by making provision for *episodes* in it.

As we mentioned above, episodes exist when a story is made up of more than one series of attempts and outcomes, as when the main character tries first one method to achieve the goal but fails, tries another method but also fails, then tries another method and finally succeeds.

Such is not the pattern of "The Dog and His Shadow," but it is the pattern of a great many other stories. When we consider the addition of episodes and the interaction of more than one principal character, each having a goal, then even so-called simple stories such as *The Three Little Pigs* can be shown to have a fairly complicated structure.

Story = Setting + Initiating Event →

Goal → { Attempt → Outcome / Attempt → Outcome / Etc. } → Consequence (→ Reaction)

Key: = means "is made up of"
→ means "causes or leads to"
{ } mean "choose one or more of the enclosed elements"
( ) mean "you may choose or omit the enclosed element"

FIGURE 1.3 A Diagram of the Structure of "The Dog and His Shadow"

Many children begin school with a tacit inner awareness of these structures; that is, they already have in their minds a very complicated yet orderly idea of what stories should be like, although they would find it very hard to tell you what these structures are because their story awareness is at a tacit, or nonverbal, level. But they recognize a story and can distinguish stories from other kinds of texts such as expository nonfiction and poems. Thus, when they hear a reader or storyteller mention a time and place early in the story, they register these elements as constituting a setting (although of course they don't use the term *setting*). When a person or personified animal is mentioned, they consider it the main character, and so on.

There is more to stories than story grammar, just as there is more to language than sentence grammar. Without an appreciation of structure, however, readers cannot tell how all the elements fit together, and they will miss the significance of much that goes on in stories.

Other Text Structures   By the time they leave the primary grades, children have begun to encounter material other than stories. Some texts will describe things; others will explain how certain things work or how to carry out a procedure. Later texts will give opinions and try to persuade the students to adopt certain attitudes and beliefs, while the students' own writings will still largely take the form of expressions of their personal feelings and responses. Each of these purposes of writing tends to have its own structure, and each structure has a name. For example, material that describes is called *descriptive writing*. Writing that explains or gives directions is called *expository writing*. Writing that persuades is variously called *argumentative* or *persuasive writing*. All of these forms fall under the general heading of *nonfiction*.

Far less research has been focused on these other text structures than on fiction, but it is clear that:

- knowing nonfiction text structures helps readers to comprehend nonfiction text (Meyer, 1977);
- students who don't have a sense of these structures have more difficulty comprehending nonfiction text than those who do (Marshall and Glock, 1978–1979);
- many older students lack an adequate sense of nonfiction text structures and hence do not know how to read nonfiction text effectively (Marshall and Glock, 1978–1979);
- many students who can read adequately in fictional text begin to founder at about fourth or fifth grade when nonfictional text is relied upon more heavily as a medium for learning other content (Richards, 1978).

Problems in reading nonfiction text are most acute in the content areas of science, social studies, health, and math, in which students are expected to read nonfiction text and acquire new information from it. We will devote a large portion of Chapters 7 and 8 to these issues, so our present discussion will be brief.

The Active Search for Information

Let's return to our example of Johnny and the birthday party. Some readers won't understand that passage. Yes, they've been to birthday parties, and yes, they've heard stories before; but it won't occur to them to make the inferences that are required to weave the information given in the passage into what they already know about stories in general, birthday parties, and how a guest without a present might feel (Anderson and Pearson, 1984).

Such readers read passively, as if they were sitting in the middle of a stream letting the water flow over them. We've seen them in our classes; they are the readers who seem to acquire nothing from their reading, in spite of having gone through the motions of reading the text. In fact, going through the motions is exactly what they were doing. We might have attempted to engage them in pre-reading discussion designed to activate their prior knowledge, and watched them run their eyes over the words. But when we ask them to retell, summarize, state the main idea or moral, put story events in order, or in fact do much of anything with what they've read, they come up empty.

In addition to having background knowledge and knowledge of text structures, these readers need to work on the thinking processes of comprehension; that is, practicing the *active search for information*. As we have seen in our previous examples, meaning is not contained only in the words on the page, but also in the mind of the reader, and must be actively constructed by the reader. Because many students might not have developed the habit of pursuing meaning actively, teachers need to model this practice for them and encourage them to seek meaning actively each time they read. This, of course, requires that they be reading texts that are meaningful, not the contrived "Pat has a pan" types of "easy-reading" materials, which have little or no meaning to construct.

In summary, *reading comprehension is the search for meaning, actively using our knowledge of the world and of texts to understand each new thing we read.* This one sentence identifies three elements of reading for comprehension:

- we need knowledge of the world to understand new things;
- we need to be familiar with the variety of text structures we're likely to encounter; and
- we need to seek meaning, and not wait passively for it to rise up from the page.

Reading and Writing at This Stage

In the stage of beginning reading, children still do not have an *independent reading level* (see Chapter 3); that is, there are very few books that they can pick up and read successfully without support. They will continue to thrive in highly predictable text, supported by pictures, especially if the book has been read to them first. Predictable books with a repeating sentence structure or refrain and highly supportive illustrations, like Bill Martin, Jr.'s *Brown Bear, Brown Bear, What Do You See?* and hundreds of others, are good bets as long as someone reads them through a few times first so that the children get the pattern.

A great many simple books and predictable books are now available as *Big Books*. As the name suggests, these are "super-sized" versions of picture books, often about 18 inches by 24 inches in size. Their size makes them perfect for shared reading with a group; everyone can clearly see each individual word and space between, every punctuation mark, and every detail of the illustrations. (No more struggling to hold and read a library book with the print facing away from you while listeners whine, "I can't SEE it!") Big books provide an excellent way for teachers to introduce a book to the whole class before children attempt to read smaller versions on their own. (Don't be surprised, though, if the children prefer reading the big version and want to read it to each other, exactly as you just did!) Dictated experience stories, class poems and class songs, nursery rhymes, and similar predictable or easily memorized texts are also very useful. (You will read more about big books, dictated experience stories, and so forth in Chapter 6.)

Children's writing in the beginning reading stage will take the form of *letter-name spelling* (see Box 1.1). During this period, you will see children using more letters to represent more of the sounds they hear in words. Toward the end of this period, as children begin building fluency, you will see more standard spellings for vowel sounds and consonant digraphs showing up in children's spelling. The spellings are still sound by sound, however, rather than pattern by pattern. That is, children who can spell *went* correctly might still spell *bent* "BET" because they don't yet think of the phonogram *-ent* as a pattern that can show up in other words. When they do make this discovery, when they are well along in beginning reading, they will suddenly find that they can read and write many more words. Reading and writing take a huge leap forward as children discover that knowing one word often gives them the key to figuring out many similar words.

Problems in the Beginning Reading Stage

The problems that children experience in the beginning reading stage usually center on word decoding, sight vocabulary, and comprehension. One noted researcher argues that these problems are causally related. Keith Stanovich (1986) used the term *Matthew effects* (inspired by the Biblical assertion that the rich get richer and the poor get poorer) to describe a process in which students who have initial difficulties see those difficulties compounded, while children who get off to a good start pile success upon success. More specifically, children who lack adequate phonological awareness, which, as we saw, should have been the outcome of the emergent literacy stage, will have difficulty decoding words. They will be slow to build sight vocabularies; and without adequate sight vocabularies, their comprehension will be limited. They will use up so much of their available attention deciphering the words that they won't have enough left to concentrate on meaning.

If Stanovich's claims are correct, and a growing consensus of current research suggests that they are (see Juel, 1991, for a review), then helping children to comprehend what they are reading will not be a substitute for helping them learn to read words accurately and efficiently. To be good readers, they have to be good at recognizing words. There seems to be no way around that. A great many children with reading problems at the beginning reading stage need help in learning to decode words and developing a sight vocabulary.

Beginning reading methods such as Reading Recovery (Clay, 1985, 1993; Pinnell, 1989; Pinnell et al., 1994), language experience (Stauffer, 1975), and variations of these approaches focus primarily on having children read predictable texts so they can activate their use of context and sense-making strategies, reread familiar material numerous times to reinforce sight recognition of high-utility words, and transfer of skills from decoding to spelling. You will read more about these and other beginning reading methods in Chapter 6.

Good readers are not just good at recognizing and figuring out words. They are also active meaning-seekers who read for pleasure and information. To make sure readers develop balance in their skills, we need to make sure that they have sufficient prior information about reading topics, see relationships between pieces of information, are familiar with structures of texts, and know how to actively seek meaning from texts.

Building Fluency

In a sense, *beginning reading* is like learning to balance on a bicycle and to ride for short stretches without falling over. *Building fluency,* then, is like pedaling successfully for longer and longer stretches, though the bicycle is still not your main means of getting around and the process is not yet thoroughly automatic. However, the more you do it, the more automatic it becomes; the more automatic it is, the more enjoyable and fun it is. Eventually, you will have ridden so much, and so successfully and enjoyably, that the old expression *It's just like riding a bicycle* will mean doing something that is unforgettably automatic.

In learning to read, children go through a period in which they are learning to orchestrate word recognition and comprehension and do both automatically and quickly. This is the stage of *building fluency.* This stage follows on the heels of beginning reading, and for the typical reader, it often occurs between the end of first grade and the end of third.

Children's reading rates climb dramatically during this time, from an average of 60 words per minute at the end of first grade to about 110 words per minute towards the end of second grade to 150–200 words per minute by middle school. Figure 1.4 shows the progression of typical reading rates from first grade through college (Carver, 1992).

If reading proceeds very slowly, as is the case with unfluent readers, comprehension suffers; but with a faster reading rate, comprehension improves. As word recognition becomes automatic, readers can concentrate more on the meaning of what they've read. Also, the faster the reading, the more likely the reader is to process the text in increasingly larger, more meaningful units: words, then phrases, then clauses, then sentences, then concepts.

The main learning task of this fluency-building stage, then, is to practice, practice, practice reading. The amount of time a child spends reading for meaning becomes a critical factor in his or her progress. Skilled teachers have moved away from round-robin oral reading, in which children in a group read one after another, because they don't get enough practice reading in such arrangements. Allington (1983) showed that in such traditional formats, most children spend only a few minutes actually reading every day. Since the goal is fluency and fluency grows with practice, we need to provide children with many more opportunities to read. We will discuss strategies for fostering oral reading practice in Chapter 7.

As Figure 1.4 shows, the sharpest increase in children's rates of reading occurs during the period from the end of first grade through the end of second grade. However, most students' reading rates continue to climb at an average of

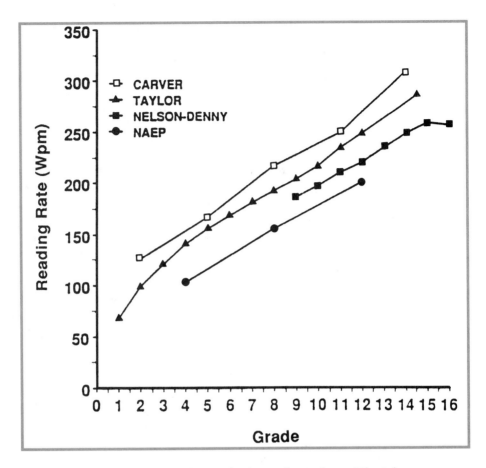

FIGURE 1.4 Reading Rate, in Standard Length Words per Minute*

*Words per minute from grades 1 to 16, according to data reported in four different sources.

Source: Ron P. Carver. *Reading Rate: A Review of Research and Theory.* New York: Academic Press, 1992, Figure 1.

20 words per minute per year, every year thereafter through high school and college. This increase should remind us that building reading fluency continues as a goal of instruction throughout the school years.

Reading and Writing at This Stage

Children at last have a fledging *independent reading level* (see Chapter 3). That is, there are some simple books that they can pick up and read independently.

Children in the fluency-building stage of development have moved beyond the highly predictable books that beginners enjoy; most children at this stage are very sensitive to what they think of as "baby books." These postbeginners enjoy what are often called *easy readers.* Examples of these books are Arnold Lobel's Frog and Toad stories (*Days with Frog and Toad, Frog and Toad Are Friends,* and so forth), James Marshall's Fox books (*Fox on Wheels, Fox in Love, Fox at*

School, and so forth), Cynthia Rylant's Henry and Mudge books, Else Holmelund Minarik's Little Bear books, and many of Dr. Seuss's books.

Easy readers often consist of either a single story or three or four short, catchy episodes per title, in books of about 40–60 pages each. They feature relatively short words that are often repeated, with one to three sentences on each page accompanied by supportive pictures. The Bank Street *Ready-to-Read* series, Scholastic's *Hello Reader!* series, Random House *Step into Reading* books, and Harper Trophy's *I Can Read* books are typical. Since they are widely available in inexpensive paperback versions, every first-, second-, and third-grade classroom should have a good supply of these books. Any school librarian will be able to advise on their selection.

Children in the fluency-building stage can also enjoy picture-story books, especially if the books have been read to them once or twice already. Books such as Mercer Mayer's *Just Me and My Dad* or Norman Bridwell's *Clifford the Big Red Dog* contain vocabulary that is challenging to some children, so the children should be familiar with them before trying to read them on their own.

Children at this stage are typically prolific writers. Their reading and their spelling instruction give them a larger writing vocabulary of words they can spell readily as well as a set of sound-to-letter correspondences that they can quickly use to spell unknown words. Writing is still an adventure, unmixed by the realization that their style or their spelling might not be as developed as that of the professional writers whose works they read.

Specifically, their spelling may show trends from the *transitional stage of spelling* (see Box 1.1). They learn a great deal about features such as story plots, dialogue, and characterization from the literature that surrounds them in the classroom as well as at home. For example, children at the fluency stage will often incorporate familiar story characters into their own writings, creating an original adventure for a character with whom they and their readers are already familiar, and may incorporate features of familiar books such as plots and problems into their own stories. They have little or no concept of plagiarism, fortunately; for writers at this stage, imitation really *is* the sincerest form of flattery.

Problems in the Fluency-Building Stage

If children haven't learned to recognize many words automatically by early second grade, they will not fully experience the spurt in reading rate and fluency that we associate with this period. The gap between these lagging readers and their classmates will be growing. Unfortunately, they often begin to feel like failures, and that attitude itself may compound the problem. We must keep working to build these children's abilities to recognize words, and we'll want to provide lots of easy books so that they can practice reading. We can't neglect reading *to* them, either. They need to keep up their intake of written language for the information, vocabulary, and text structure that it yields. Otherwise, their future hurdles will loom even higher.

Reading to Learn and for Pleasure

The stage of *reading to learn and for pleasure* may begin in late second grade or early third grade and last from then on, though most students will diversify their reading with what we call *mature reading* by the time they reach middle school or even sooner. To return to our bicycle-riding analogy, children in this stage are reading to get somewhere. The operations of bike riding have become mostly automatic now, and their full attention can be focused on reading for meaning. Reading has truly become the vehicle for learning. After students have built fluency in their reading, they enter a long period in which their reading ability is put to use, when we hope that they *will* read a great deal, because they find reading both an enjoyable pastime and a source of information that they wouldn't get otherwise.

The Benefits of Reading

At this point, reading becomes its own best teacher. Students who have the habit of reading are consuming dozens of books, thousands of pages, and hundreds of thousands of words a year. This reading practice equips them with an expanded vocabulary, familiarity with varied sentence structures, a broad knowledge of the forms of written language, and acquaintance with most of the topics they are likely to come across in print. Until recently, few would have considered any of these to be components of reading ability, but now we realize that these achievements, all of them gained through practice in reading, probably make as much difference to a person's ability to read as any of the traditional skills of reading do.

Much of this difference has stayed beyond our direct control. Traditionally, children have done very little reading at school, only a few minutes per day (Allington, 1983). Although many children do read outside of school, there are truly staggering differences in the amount of extracurricular reading any classroom full of children will do. These astonishing differences contribute to what we referred to earlier as Stanovich's "Matthew effect" in which the better readers continue to get better and better, while the poorer readers lag farther and farther behind.

Figure 1.5 shows Stanovich's (1986) interpretation of data collected by Wilson, Fielding, and Anderson on sixth-graders' out-of-school reading. The Percentile column on the left represents sixth-graders' reading achievement, from highest (98th percentile) to lowest (2nd percentile); the average sixth-grade reader may be considered to be at the 50th percentile. Reading across, we can see the average number of minutes per day students at each reading achievement level spend independently reading books, reading informational text, and reading of any kind and the average number of words students at each achievement level read per year.

What do these figures tell us? That "the rich," in Stanovich's literary terms, really do get "richer" by reading some thirty to ninety times as much as "the poor"— in this sense the poorest readers, who most would agree need to be reading more than anyone else! Assuming a typical, heterogenous class of sixth-graders, *in one school year, the top three readers will read more words than the lowest three readers will read in 46 years!* In addition, *it would take the lowest reader in the sixth grade 591 years to read as many words as the top reader!*

Good readers are gaining a wealth of information about the world and a wealth of vocabulary. This knowledge and this vocabulary are what readers comprehend with: As the schema theory of comprehension predicts, we need to know a little bit about the topic before we can learn something new about it.

MINUTES OF READING PER DAY				WORDS READ PER YEAR	
PERCENTILE	BOOKS	TEXT	ALL READING	BOOKS	TEXT
98	65.0	67.3	90.7	4,358,000	4,733,000
90	21.1	33.4	40.4	1,823,000	2,357,000
80	14.2	24.6	31.1	1,146,000	1,697,000
70	9.6	16.9	21.7	622,000	1,168,000
60	6.5	13.1	18.1	432,000	722,000
50	4.6	9.2	12.9	282,000	601,000
40	3.2	6.2	8.6	200,000	421,000
30	1.3	4.3	5.8	106,000	251,000
20	0.7	2.4	3.1	21,000	134,000
10	0.1	1.0	1.6	8,000	51,000
2	0.0	0.0	0.2	0	8,000

FIGURE 1.5   Variation in Amount of Independent Reading

Source: Keith E. Stanovich. "Matthew Effects in Reading." *Reading Research Quarterly* 21 (1986): 360–406.

Readers who read a lot are going to know a little bit about a lot more topics and will be better readers because of it (Hirsch, 1987).

What about those readers at the other end of the scale? Children who read less will generally show overall inefficiency in reading, that is, slow, inaccurate reading with generally poor recall and comprehension of what they read. In the classroom, they will often be seen fidgeting instead of giving sustained attention to reading tasks. They will show up without having read their assignments. Their oral reading will be halting and uncertain.

Not so long ago, assessments of such students' reading behavior might have indicated that they needed to develop this or that comprehension ability and to work on word recognition. Now we recognize that such judgments, while true, miss the larger point. To focus on the skill deficits of a person who doesn't read is like doing an expensive diagnosis of a car that is never driven. The car will surely have problems, and they must surely be fixed before it can be driven, but the problems will only return if the car is still not used. In the case of people who don't read, instruction in reading skills might well be called for, and reading diagnosis will help us decide when and what sort, but *the real issue will be to get them to read.*

Let us point out one more scary fact: *The students who read too little are the majority of our children.* Look again at Figure 1.5. The amount of book reading done outside of school by the average readers (50th percentile) was *only 4.6 minutes a day* in this sixth-grade sample. *The lowest readers didn't read at all.* As Paul Wilson (1992) concluded after collecting and studying these data,

> [W]e must face the fact that when we visit the typical elementary classroom, we find ourselves, at present, among nonreaders . . . . Knowing this, our first goal for school reading programs must be to cultivate literacy, to cultivate that headlong rush toward meaning that leads to large volumes of motivated voluntary reading. (p. 168)

Reading instruction must help children learn to love reading by making sure that children have books available to them at school and at home that are interesting to them and are written on a level they can read easily as well as incentives for them to read.

We will revisit the issues of time spent reading and how reading makes people smart in Chapter 7, "Assessing and Teaching Developing Readers."

Reading for Information

After second grade, students are expected to use their reading to learn content. Learning from reading raises a new set of problems. How are questions posed in texts? How are they answered? How are arguments set up in texts? How are they resolved? For those who up to now have thought of reading as pronouncing words aloud or following a story line, these new tasks are real challenges. How will children learn to meet them?

Clearly, many children will not learn how to learn from text without guided practice. That is, teachers need to *show them how to do it.* The best approaches for teaching children to learn from reading is for teachers, as skilled readers, to figure out exactly what *we* do as we learn from a text and demonstrate these operations to our students. In other words, we use *think-alouds* (Palincsar, 1986) to make our own thought processes explicit as we read and question our way through a text, as in this example:

> *Teacher:* The next section of this chapter is called "Desert Neighbors." Hmmm. The picture here doesn't show any houses around, so my guess is that it's not talking about what people are neighbors in the desert. Maybe the "desert neighbors" are animals that live near each other in the desert. Does that sound right? If so, I wonder which ones it'll mention? Anybody have any ideas?

We also encourage children to think aloud as they read, to help them pursue meaning and also to demonstrate how they are processing the information in the text. This type of instruction fits the instructional model of *cognitive apprenticeships* (Palincsar, 1986), in which teachers teach reading and writing as if these activities were to be taught through demonstrations by a master practitioner, followed by the learners' guided practice.

Explicit instruction may be used to teach students to learn from reading. Question-Answer Relationships, or QAR (Raphael, 1984), and KWL (What I Know, Want to Know, and Learn) activity (Ogle, 1986) are ways to teach students how to learn from reading. So are the various study guides for reading that are often referred to as "graphic organizers" in the reading in content areas texts. These approaches will be discussed in detail in Chapters 7 and 9.

Nonetheless, knowing how to learn from text is not enough to make a reader successful. Readers also need a wealth of background knowledge and a classroom in which knowledge is acquired, used, and explored.

Responding to Reading

When we speak of comprehension in reading, should we make a distinction between what readers do with fiction and what they do with nonfiction? The literary critic Louise Rosenblatt (1978) suggests that we should. There is a difference, she points out, between reading in which we gain information, such as reading a history text or a bus schedule, and reading for more indirect enlightenment and vicarious pleasure, such as reading a novel. She calls the first kind *efferent reading;* the second kind, she calls *aesthetic reading.*

In the moments when we are reading aesthetically, Rosenblatt believes, we are summoning up our own experiences and fantasies in response to the words in a book. The meaning of the text resides in just this event: It is a real-time experience of orchestrated thinking and reverie, jointly created by the text and our minds.

Rosenblatt's position is referred to as *reader-response criticism,* and it raises interesting questions about the ways in which we should understand and teach reading comprehension. If a good part of the meaning of a text comes from the reader, not just from the book, then teaching reading for meaning means thinking about texts and bringing associations from personal experiences to the reading. It means that we should consider readers to be authorities on their own understanding. It means that we cannot ever fully measure reading comprehension. It also means that the potential for human misunderstanding is very great, because the meaning of anything resides ultimately in what every individual makes of it. In fact, sharing books and discussing our responses to them turn out to be one of the best ways we have of building a community of understanding, or an *interpretive community,* as David Bleich (1975) has called it. Building community in this sense is the central task of the schools.

Teachers who take reader-response theory seriously arrange regular opportunities for students to read books, to say what the books make them think of, to write response journals about them, and to compare their responses with others.

Reading and Writing at This Stage

There is a bonanza of books for children in the stage of *reading for pleasure and to learn.* There are thousands of new titles, fiction and nonfiction, and if your school library hasn't acquired *lots* of new books in recent years, your students might be missing out on a whole category of books that teach and expand their curiosity. Especially suited to this age group are *chapter books,* in which a single story is sustained for 50–100 pages, with the support of occasional illustrations.

The high ratio of text to picture might make it difficult for some children to get into a book. So Wilson (1992) prompts teachers to help children learn strategies for choosing books that they will enjoy. Having children recommend books to each other is one good way. So is the strategy of featuring different children's authors every few weeks: reading aloud from their books, inviting students to do reports and make posters from their work, and even writing them letters. (The school media specialist should be able to assist with biographical information, publishing company addresses, and so forth.) It helps to feature authors who have written a string of books that are suitable for the same age group, such as Beverly Cleary, Betsy Byars, Roald Dahl, E. Nesbit, Cynthia Rylant, Katherine Paterson, Virginia Hamilton, Gary Paulsen, or Avi, for example. If students have enjoyed one of these authors' books, they will know where to get others that they will like.

As for writing, children in the reading for pleasure and to learn stage should be writing fluently for a variety of authentic purposes. Thoughtful language arts curricula have opportunities for children to use the following:

- *expressive writing,* as in journal entries, letters to pen pals, rough notes written to themselves to explore a topic before giving it more formal treatment;
- *poetic writing,* not just poetry, but also stories for their own and others' enjoyment;
- *expository writing,* as in reports, directions for carrying out activities, and interviews with interesting people; and
- *persuasive writing,* as in arguments to persuade people for or against certain positions or actions.

Children might choose for themselves the topics for writing, but the teacher should sometimes set up challenges for writing so that children write for different purposes and in different forms. We should show children models of others' writings in each of the forms we're interested in. Here we mean "modeling" in both senses of the word: We should have examples around of things that are written in each form, and the teacher and other writers (including students themselves) should occasionally show *how* they write.

In terms of spelling development, students in this stage are spelling most words correctly. They might be struggling with the challenge of *consonant doubling* (that *bat + ing* is spelled "batting") and of the spelling of *grammatical markers* (that the past tense of *wish, flow,* and *want* are all spelled with *-ed*). By the fourth or fifth grade, they will find a need to pay attention to the *derivational origin* of a word to spell it: knowing that *graph* and all its related words are spelled with *ph,* for example.

Problems in the Reading for Pleasure/Reading to Learn Stage

Children who become adequate readers read a great deal, usually from about third grade on. It's certainly possible for people to get the habit of reading later than this, but we believe that a price will be paid in terms of what the person will have missed out on reading, especially the content reading that would have made that person's school studies more meaningful. The academic achievement of U.S. students surely would not rank behind that of every other highly industrialized nation if even *half* of our students had the habit of reading.

Students who have difficulty in reading are especially likely to avoid reading. Therefore, we must continue to work on their particular reading abilities and help them to find materials that they *can* read and will *want* to read. We all need to become more imaginative and aggressive in providing interesting classroom libraries, family literacy projects that put books in homes and encourage parents to get involved in literacy, and community projects that distribute books and offer incentives for people to read them. But we must not limit these initiatives to the "problem readers." As we have argued in this section, *most* students do not read enough. We need to encourage all students to read, help them learn to choose books that they will enjoy, and even provide time in school for students to read. If Wilson's data reflect the time most children spend reading books, then we can greatly increase the national average if we have children reading books for just twenty minutes a day in school!

Mature Reading

This last developmental reading stage is hard to quantify in terms of grade levels, for as the grades increase, the span of reading levels in any classroom widens geometrically. The best readers in an elementary school are probably mature readers while only in fourth or fifth grade, whereas the poorest readers in those grades are likely beginning readers. The same is true for middle schoolers and high school students; the best readers in middle or high school typically can read college texts and adult best-sellers comfortably. They are mature readers, regardless of their grade. Likewise, millions of adults are not and never will be mature readers, largely because they don't read enough to ever get very good at it.

Mature readers have arrived, through instruction and years of sustained practice, at the apex of reading development; they can read almost anything they choose to, comfortably and successfully. That is not to say that they won't ever struggle with reading; one could find college textbooks, toy assembly directions, or government documents to challenge the reading abilities of even the best adult readers. But most of what they want to read will be accessible. Because they don't struggle with it, mature readers generally read a great deal; they are the ones at the top end of Stanovich's scale, who read four or five million words a year.

Mature reading includes what is sometimes called *critical reading*, or mentally arguing with texts. It also includes what Mortimer Adler (1940) called *syntopical reading*, that is, reading several sources on a topic to get a rounded picture of it. It further includes *aesthetic reading*, reading for an appreciation of the craft of good writing. Let's look at each of these in turn.

Critical Reading

Some years ago, parent "watchdog" groups asked the U.S. government to place restrictions on the amount of violence and commercialism in children's television programming. The government backed away, in effect giving an old response: *caveat emptor* ("Let the buyer beware"). Since the "buyers" in this case were young children, the government's response raised the question "Should we teach our children to be critical of what they hear and read so that they can defend themselves against the manipulation of those who want their money or their loyalty for cynical purposes?" Many educators believe that we should; therefore, the term *critical reading* is heard more and more these days. Critical reading means arguing with books or authors, in particular analyzing books for hidden biases or subtle suggestions that one group is superior to another. Box 1.2 contains an example of critical reading, in which a group of seven- and eight-year-olds discuss gender bias in fairy tales.

Syntopical Reading

Mature reading also includes the practice of reading widely on a single topic, especially for the purpose of seeing how different authors handle the same topic.

AN EXAMPLE OF
CRITICAL READING

BOX 1.2

A mixed group of second- and third-graders are discussing the story *Beauty and the Beast*.

"Suppose," says the teacher, "Beauty had been a boy in this story, and the Beast had been a girl."

A howl goes up from the class.

Alice looks troubled. "But then Beauty, the boy, would be *younger* than Beast, the girl . . ."

"So? Why would that matter? Besides, they don't tell you how old they are," says Alexander.

"But then, I mean, it's not right for a girl to ask a boy to go to the prom or something . . ." Alice still looks troubled.

"I've heard—this is what my Mom says—there's not a law against it or anything, but it's not right for a girl to ask a boy to marry her. This is what my Mom says. I don't know if it's true," says Charlotte.

"So why should that matter?" says Julian. "But I have another problem. The boys in the story are always the worse ones. I mean, the boys in the fairy tales just run up to a girl they don't even know and say 'Will you marry me?'"

"I know," adds Sarah. "I wish they'd say, 'Why no! How can I marry you? I don't even know you. I don't know what your *attitude is!*'"

"Boys in the fairy tales want to marry somebody they don't know anything about. I mean, they might not even *change their underwear!*" says Charlotte.

Allison takes a different tack. "I'm going to be a person who's the exact opposite of Beauty. Pretend there's a fire in here. You go up to that person and he says, 'So? Why'd you ask me? You help 'em!' But Beauty . . . You wouldn't have to tell her anything. She'd just go!"

"What does that have to do with how boys are and how girls are?" asks the teacher.

"Well, I'm not saying boys are *always* selfish . . ." Allison doesn't want to go further.

"What bugs me is that in the fairy tales, the guys are always doing things outside, and the girls are just basking around in their beautiful dresses," says Joanne. Several children nod.

Source: Charles Temple. "Suppose *Beauty* Had Been Ugly? Reading Against the Grain of Gender Bias in Children's Literature." *Language Arts* (March 1993).

An example is an experience one of the authors had with a freshman college seminar. On the topic of Columbus's fifteenth-century explorations, the students read materials written by Spaniards, by Native Americans, by Latinos, and by Italian nationalist groups living in the United States, as well as by Columbus himself. Comparisons of these strikingly different readings told us a great deal about Columbus but also gave us a greater appreciation of the points of view of each of these different groups of people, each of which felt strongly about the Columbian legacy.

Syntopical reading is reading not just for information, but also for nuances of the meanings, for the *meanings of the meanings* in their social contexts.

Aesthetic Reading

Another dimension of mature reading is *aesthetic reading*, savoring the artistry (or examining the shortcomings) of well-crafted or slapdash prose. An illustration of aesthetic reading is found in David Bleich's (1975) approach to reader response. Bleich first asks his students to retell a work that they have all read, and he notes the variety in what students choose to include in their summaries. Then he asks students to name the most important parts of a work, and again he notes the effect of each reader's individual experiences and tastes in making such seemingly straightforward judgments, because there is invariably much variety in what readers choose. Next, he asks students to comment on the most important *devices* in the work; he hears the students commenting on such things as voice, characterization, description, plot, and irony long before he has introduced the technical terms for these things.

A kind of aesthetic reading that teachers and students sometimes do, often without realizing it as such, is to connect reading and writing. For example, some time after they have read and discussed *Maniac Magee* by Jerry Spinelli, a teacher asks a fifth-grade class to reread the first chapter and lays out this challenge: Find all the tricks you can that the author used to make the story of Maniac Magee seem like a legend. The students work in groups and come up with the jump-rope rhyme, the way the author introduced characters as if they were already famous, and the way the author mentioned several exaggerated versions of Maniac's background. After discussing those, the teacher then invites the students to use some of these devices in writing original legends of their own.

Now that we have described these three aspects of mature reading, it should be clear that these kinds of reading need not wait until high school or college. Indeed, the example of critical reading came from a second- and third-grade group. Children just as young are capable of making aesthetic responses to written works. Elementary-grade children can do syntopical readings as well. We only chose to call these activities *mature reading* because they strike us as the most mature kinds of reading we do, even though in many case, we begin doing them at an early age.

Reading and Writing at This Stage

The practices of mature reading, that is, critical reading, syntopical reading, and aesthetic reading, can be applied to any sort of text. Of course, as students grow in their reading maturity, they will seek out more challenging books. Our question is not so much *what* they read at this point but *how they think about* what they read.

In writing, demands will grow in school for students' writing to develop themes and arguments, to take positions clearly, and to provide details to support those positions. Students who have been encouraged to write often about what they really think and have had their ideas taken seriously should not have much difficulty meeting these later demands, but a great many students find these demands difficult or impossible to meet.

Problems in the Mature Reading Stage

Few students will be referred to a remedial reading teacher for failing to read or write in the ways that we have just described. We have included this discussion, though, because it is important for reading teachers to know where reading development is headed. The ultimate goal is not just that students understand what somebody else has written, but that they know where they stand on the author's claims or be able to find an interesting interpretation of the work and be able to state their positions clearly. Aspects of these goals, of course, might be included in our instruction at any level.

CHANGING TRENDS IN ASSESSMENT

In the preceding sections, we attempted to outline in broad strokes the generic kinds of assessments that classroom teachers find themselves responsible for today and the general stages of development that normal readers go through as they move from prereaders to mature readers. To close this chapter, we return to the topic of assessment once again to describe some general directions in which assessment is moving today and how teachers' needs are changing in the area of student assessment.

Authentic Assessment

This term refers to the kinds of tasks students are asked to perform, tasks that we use to make decisions about their progress and mastery of operations or subject matter. In this sense, *authentic* means *realistic* or *natural*. In the past, students have been assessed in ways that many found to be inauthentic; for example, reading comprehension was commonly tested by having students read a sentence or two, or a short paragraph, and select a word from several choices that best completed a sentence. But in real-life reading, we rarely, if ever, have to perform this task. Instead, our real-life comprehension of text is more often measured by what we can *do* with the information; for example, if we can read a series of steps and then correctly complete a procedure, our performance shows that we have comprehended the steps.

Likewise, typical inauthentic writing assessment sometimes included having students choose the sentence in a paragraph that was incorrectly stated or grammatically incorrect, whereas authentic writing assessment requires students to actually write a composition. Similarly, an inauthentic paragraph-writing task might be to put five sentences in the correct order in paragraph form, while an authentic task might be to actually write a well-structured paragraph on a topic of one's choosing. An inauthentic, but common, standardized spelling test procedure is to have students choose, again from several choices, the one correctly spelled word, or even the "best" misspelling; an authentic spelling assessment requires students to actually spell words from scratch, particularly in the context of writing.

Today, teachers are expected to be able to recognize inauthentic assessment procedures and develop authentic ways of assessing the processes and content we want students to master. They are also expected to be able to interpret assessment results to students and their parents and to explain why authentic assessment procedures are more informative than inauthentic ones.

Portfolio Assessment

As you will read in Chapter 4, portfolios are a widely used way of documenting student performance in authentic ways. A portfolio is a system for collecting, organizing, and displaying samples of student work. These can run the gamut from a simple work folder arrangement, containing samples of current work in a single area (say, writing or math) to a highly elaborate collection of written work, photographs, videos, realia, and other materials representing a student's finest achievements in a single area or across the curriculum. There are even portfolios that represent students' achievements outside of school, in sports, community work, scouting, and so forth.

In Chapter 4, you will learn what various kinds of portfolios students can develop; how to help students to select material for inclusion; how to guide students in developing self-evaluation skills and the ability to reflect on their own learning and progress; and how to share portfolios with parents, school administrators, and others who are interested in this method of documenting student performance and achievement.

SUMMARY

In this chapter, we described in general terms what comprises the two main areas of assessment: *assessment for internal audiences,* or what the teacher, parents, and students will find most helpful in evaluating student progress, and *assessment for external audiences,* by which agencies or groups beyond the school level, such as school boards, state legislatures, and federal programs, evaluate schools' effectiveness.

We also described, again in general terms, reading development as it progresses through five stages: *emergent literacy* (when children acquire foundational concepts about print), *beginning reading* (when children begin to recognize words and read with rudimentary comprehension), *building fluency* (when children learn to recognize so many words that their reading becomes more rapid and expressive), *reading for pleasure and to learn* (when children develop the habit of reading for pleasure, and also can reliably read for information), and *mature reading* (when students read critically, syntopically, and aesthetically). We expanded the description of each stage with brief accounts of the sorts of books students are reading at each stage and the kinds of writing and spelling they produce. Also included was a discussion of the problems associated with each stage.

Each of the next three chapters, Chapters 2 through 4, details a particular aspect of assessment for internal audiences: ongoing assessments based largely on systematic observation of reading and reading-related behaviors, periodic in-depth assessments that are diagnostic in nature and typically carried out by the classroom teacher, and assessment portfolios.

REFERENCES

Adler, Mortimer J. *How to Read a Book.* New York: Simon & Schuster, 1940.

Allington, Richard L. "The Reading Instruction Provided Readers of Differing Abilities." *Elementary School Journal* 83 (1983): 548–559.

Anderson, Richard C., and P. David Pearson. "A Schema Theoretic View of Basic Processes in Reading Comprehension." In *Handbook of Reading Research*, ed. P. David Pearson, Rebecca Barr, Michael L. Kamil, and Peter Mosenthal. White Plains, NY: Longman, 1984.

Bartlett, Frederick. *Remembering.* New York: Cambridge University Press, 1932.

Bleich, David. *Readings and Feelings.* Urbana, IL: National Council of Teachers of English, 1975.

Carver, Ronald P. *Reading Rate: A Review of Research and Theory.* New York: Academic Press, 1992.

Clarke, Linda K. "Invented versus Traditional Spelling in First Graders' Writings: Effects on Learning to Spell and Read." *Research in the Teaching of English* 22 (1988): 281–309.

Clay, Marie M. *What Did I Write?* Portsmouth, NH: Heinemann Educational Books, 1975.

Clay, Marie M. *The Early Detection of Reading Difficulties.* Portsmouth, NH: Heinemann Educational Books, 1985.

Clay, Marie M. *Reading Recovery: A Guidebook for Teachers in Training.* Portsmouth, NH: Heinemann Educational Books, 1993.

Durr, William. "Computer Study of High-Frequency Words in Popular Trade Juveniles." *The Reading Teacher,* 27 (1973): 37–43.

Ehri, Linnea. "Beginning Reading from a Psycholinguistic Perspective: Amalgamation of Word Identities." In *Development of the Reading Process*, IRA Monograph no. 3, ed. Frank B. Murray. Newark, DE: International Reading Association, 1978.

Ehri, Linnea, and Jennifer Sweet. "Fingerpoint-Reading of Memorized Text: What Enables Beginning Readers to Process Print?" *Reading Research Quarterly* 26 (1991): 442–462.

Ferreiro, Emilia, and Ana Teberosky. *Writing before Schooling.* Portsmouth, NH: Heinemann, 1982.

Gibson, Eleanor, and Harry Levin. *The Psychology of Reading.* Cambridge, MA: MIT Press, 1975.

Henderson, Edmund H. *Teaching Spelling,* 2d ed. Boston: Houghton Mifflin, 1992.

Hirsch, Edgar Donald, Jr. *Cultural Literacy.* Boston: Houghton Mifflin, 1987.

Johnston, Peter A. "Remediation." In *Handbook of Reading Research,* Vol. 2, ed. Rebecca Barr, Michael L. Kamil, Peter B. Mosenthal, and P. David Pearson. White Plains, NY: Longman, 1991.

Juel, Connie. "Learning to Read and Write: A Longitudinal Study of Fifty-Four Children from First through Fourth Grade." *Journal of Educational Psychology* 80 (1988): 437–447.

Juel, Connie. "Beginning Reading." In *Handbook of Reading Research,* Vol. 2, ed. Rebecca Barr, Michael L. Kamil, Peter B. Mosenthal, and P. David Pearson. White Plains, NY: Longman, 1991.

Liberman, Isabel, D. Shankweiler, A. Liberman, M. Fowler, and W. Fischer. "Phonemic Segmentation and Recoding in the Beginning Reader." In *Toward a Psychology of Reading*, ed. A.S. Reber and D. L. Scarborough. Hillsdale, NJ: Lawrence Erlbaum Associates, 1977, pp. 207–225.

Manning-Sanders, R. *Robin Hood and Little John.* London: Methuen, 1977.

Marsh, G., M. Friedman, V. Welch, and P. Desberg. "A Cognitive-Developmental Theory of Reading Acquisition." In *Reading Research: Advances in Theory and Practice*, Vol 3., ed. G. E. Mackinnon and T. G. Waller. New York: Plenum, 1981, pp. 199–221.

Marshall, Nancy, and Marvin Glock. "Comprehension of Connected Discourse." *Reading Research Quarterly* 14 (1978–1979): 10–56.

McConaughy, Stephanie. "Using Story Structure in the Classroom." *Language Arts* 57 (1980): 157–165.

Meyer, Bonnie F. "The Structure of Prose: Effects on Learning and Memory and Implications for Educational Practice." In *Schooling and the Acquisition of Knowledge*, ed. Richard Anderson and Rand Spiro. Hillsdale, NJ: Lawrence Erlbaum Associates, 1977.

Minsky, Marvin. "A Framework for Representing Knowledge." In *A Theory of Computer Vision,* ed. P. H. Winston. New York: McGraw-Hill, 1975.

Morris, R. Darrell. "Concept of Word: A Developmental Phenomenon in the Beginning Reading and Writing Processes." *Language Arts,* 58 (1981): 659–668.

Morris, R. Darrell. "The Relationship between Word Awareness and Phoneme Awareness in Learning to Read: A Longitudinal Study in Kindergarten." Boone, NC: Appalachian State University, 1989.

Morris, R. Darrell. "First Steps: An Early Reading Intervention Program." Boone, NC: Appalachian State University, 1993a.

Morris, R. Darrell. "The Relationship between Children's Concept of Word in Text and Phoneme Awareness in Learning to Read: A Longitudinal Study." *Research in the Teaching of English* 27, no. 2 (May 1993b): 133–154.

Ogle, Donna. M. "K-W-L: A Teaching Model That Develops Active Reading of Expository Text." *The Reading Teacher* 39 (1986): 564–570.

Palincsar, Annemarie S. "The Role of Dialogue in Providing Scaffolded Instruction." *Educational Psychologist* 21 (1986): 73–98.

Piaget, Jean. *The Early Growth of Logic in the Child.* Neuchatel: Delachaux & Niestle, 1959/London: Routledge & Kegan Paul, 1964.

Pinnell, Gay Su. "Reading Recovery: Helping At-Risk Children Learn to Read." *Elementary School Journal* 90 (1989): 161–182.

Pinnell, G., C. Lyons, D. DeFord, A. Bryk, & M. Seltzer. "Comparing Instructional Models for the Literacy Education of High-Risk First Graders." *Reading Research Quarterly* 29 (1994), 8–39.

Raphael, Taffy E. "Teaching Learners about Sources of Information for Answering Comprehension Questions." *Journal of Reading* 27 (1984): 303–311.

Read, Charles. *Children's Creative Spelling.* New York: Allen and Unwin, 1986.

Reutzel, D. Ray, L. K. Oda, and B. H. Moore. "Developing Print Awareness: The Effect of Three Instructional Approaches on Kindergartners' Print Awareness, Reading Readiness, and Word Reading." *Journal of Reading Behavior* 21 (1989): 197–217.

Richards, Jill. *Classroom Language: What Sorts?* London: Allen & Unwin, 1978.

Rosenblatt, Louise. *The Reader, the Text, and the Poem.* Carbondale, IL: Southern Illinois University Press, 1978.

Slavin, Robert E., Nancy A. Madden, Nancy L. Karweit, Lawrence J. Dolan, and Barbara A. Wasik. "Success for All: Ending Reading Failure from the Beginning." *Language Arts* 68, no. 5 (September 1991): 404–409.

Stanovich, Keith E. "Matthew Effects in Reading: Some Consequences of Individual Differences in the Acquisition of Literacy." *Reading Research Quarterly* 21 (1986): 360–406.

Stauffer, Russell. G. *The Language-Experience Approach to the Teaching of Reading.* New York: Harper and Row, 1975.

Sulzby, Elizabeth Tucker. "Children's Emergent Reading of Favorite Storybooks: A Developmental Study." *Reading Research Quarterly* 20 (1985): 458–481.

Teale, William and Elizabeth Tucker Sulzby, ed. *Emergent Literacy.* Norwood, NJ: Ablex, 1986.

Temple, Charles, Ruth Nathan, Frances Temple, and Nancy Burris. *The Beginnings of Writing,* 3d ed. Boston: Allyn & Bacon, 1993.

Trieman, Rebecca. "Onsets and Rimes as Units of Spoken Syllables: Evidence from Children." *Journal of Experimental Child Psychology* 39 (1979): 161–181.

Walsh, D., G. G. Price, and M. G. Gillingham. "The Crucial but Fleeting Skill of Alphabet Knowledge." *Reading Research Quarterly* 23 (1986): 108–122.

Wilson, Paul. "Among Nonreaders: Voluntary Reading, Reading Achievement, and the Development of Reading Habits." In *Stories and Readers: New Perspectives on Literature in the Elementary Classroom,* ed. Charles Temple and Patrick Collins. Norwood, MA: Christopher-Gordon, 1992.

CHAPTER 2

Assessment for Internal Audiences: Ongoing Assessments

Carly Adams, a fourth-grade teacher, keeps an assessment folder for each student in her class. Each student's folder contains different kinds of assessment information collected over the course of the year. Carly is preparing for a parent-teacher conference with Ben's parents. During the conference, she will share with them the numerous ways in which Ben's growth and progress have been assessed this year and will answer their questions about assessment results and implications.

A review of Ben's various assessments will help Carly to be fully informed for the conference. Also, it allows us a chance to peer over her shoulder, so to speak, and consider the kinds of assessments that are typically used with students, both formal and informal, periodic and ongoing. (The latter variety is discussed in detail in this chapter; periodic, in-depth internal assessments are discussed in Chapter 3, and portfolio assessment is discussed in Chapter 4. Assessments for external audiences, such as standardized group achievement tests, are discussed in Chapter 5.)

First, Carly scans a sheet that contains all of Ben's most recent standardized achievement test scores. She studies it carefully, for she knows that Ben's parents will probably have many questions about the results and how they are to be interpreted. On the reading section of the test, Ben's scores fell in the 30th percentile, with subtest scores ranging from the 16th to the 41st percentile. Carly looks at this sheet first, but not because it is the most important; in fact, she considers these standardized test scores to be among the *least* informative to her in teaching Ben. However, she familiarizes herself with them because she knows that standardized test data have great importance to her principal, as well as to Ben's parents.

These results indicate that Ben is functioning well below average in reading in comparison to others of his age and grade in the norm group and in the local group being tested at the same time; in fact, they show that Ben performed as well as or better than only about 30 percent of other fourth-graders taking the test, while about 70 percent performed better than Ben. His performance was also significantly below the *mean*, or average, score at about the 50th percentile.

Carly can use these data to explain to Ben's parents where he stands in comparison to others on this particular test, but they do little to help her teach him. For example, they do not help her to know what areas of strength Ben has, what specific difficulties he had, or the degree of Ben's motivation, interest, or prior information. Also, they might paint an unnecessarily bleak picture of Ben's reading ability to his parents while revealing little of his strengths and nothing about his progress during the time he has been in Carly's classroom.

Carly next turns to a sheaf of forms she has completed on Ben at many points across the previous months. These include:

- *running records*, or annotated copies of material Ben has read aloud, with miscues and other reading behaviors noted;
- *informal reading inventories* given at the beginning of the year and again a few weeks ago, showing Ben's oral and silent reading rates, oral reading accuracy, types of miscues that occurred, and comprehension after oral and silent reading of passages at successive grade levels;

- *observation records,* or notes Carly took while observing Ben working in a variety of learning situations;
- *cloze procedures,* or reading passages with certain words deleted and replaced by blanks, to be filled in by the reader;
- *spelling records* showing patterns and high-utility words that Ben has mastered and the date they were successfully tested;
- *a list of books read* this year; and
- *a writing progress inventory,* showing Ben's progress in using various forms and voices in writing.

Carly Adams's choice of assessments demonstrates her philosophy of reading and instruction. Because she collects a number of different measures and samples of reading and reading-related behaviors, we can infer that she believes that reading is not a single operation, nor is reading the same each time it occurs, regardless of the material being read or the reader's purpose for reading it. Carly uses *multiple indicators of student performance* to build a "corroborative framework" (Vacca et al., 1991, p. 427) that strengthens decision making; that is, information from one source builds on, or is contrasted by, information from other data sources. The result is a multidimensional picture of the student's reading performance in a variety of situations and with a variety of kinds of materials—in other words, an authentic, dynamic portrait of a reader.

Similarly, we can infer that Carly holds an *interactive view* of the reading process; that is, she believes that reading is a complex process involving the coordination of a variety of skills, processes, and operations that occur simultaneously and in concert with one another. This is in direct contrast to the now largely outmoded, but still widely held, *summative view:* that reading is the result of mastery of a set of skills that can be learned and practiced in isolation from each other but sum up to effective reading when each has been mastered.

We sometimes illustrate this view of reading to our students by comparing it to learning to swim. One could be taught each discrete operation in swimming separately from the others and practice each operation in isolation. For example, one could learn the arm movements that are necessary to do the front crawl and practice them, first standing on the side of the pool, then lying prone on a bench, and finally while standing in shallow water. One could then be taught and practice turning the head to the side and breathing in, then turning the head down and blowing out, again first on the side of the pool, then standing or crouching in water, and so forth. But *at no point* would one be swimming. Even more important, one could master each and every separate skill, demonstrate mastery of each on the side of the pool and then while standing or crouching in the water, and then *fail to swim* when trying to put the skills together in one operation.

As any swimmer knows, swimming is more than the sum of its separate skills, and so it is with reading. Carly Adams knows that reading is not just the sum of all its parts, but the result of the *interaction* of all the necessary operations, in concert with each other, combined with what the reader knows and brings to the reading, his or her motivation and purposes for the reading, and the complexity of the text being read, in authentic (not testlike) reading situations. So when preparing an assessment picture of a reader, she prefers to use a variety of behavior samples in as many real reading acts as possible, combined with her informed observations of the reader in authentic learning situations, to strengthen and support the instructional decisions she makes. And she makes sure that the data she collects are gathered at regular, frequent intervals so that an accurate record of the reader's progress is developed.

As Carly Adams prepares for her conference with Ben's parents, she organizes these forms and the information they contain into a packet that will help Ben's parents to see and understand his progress and growth this year, as well as his continuing difficulty with many kinds of reading. Carly does not wish to sugar-coat Ben's difficulty, for she is concerned about what future grades hold for Ben if his reading does not improve drastically. However, she knows that standardized test scores do little to help parents, teachers, or students themselves to develop an accurate picture of the whole reader. Although Ben's achievement test scores are discouraging, he has made significant progress in several areas this year, which Carly has documented. Understanding this will help Ben and his parents, and Ben's teacher next year, to see that Ben has strengths as well as needs, potential for improvement, and the capability to succeed when motivation is present and instruction is appropriately challenging. Without the ongoing assessments that Carly herself provided, the picture of Ben's achievement would be one-sided and, in this case, unnecessarily grim.

In the following sections, we will discuss some kinds of informal, ongoing assessments that many teachers find helpful in compiling a complete picture of a student's literacy achievement.

RUNNING RECORDS

One of the most common ongoing assessments teachers conduct are *running records* of students' oral reading. As described by Marie Clay (1985), running records are transcripts of texts, or text portions, at a comfortable level of difficulty (referred to as the *instructional level*), with the reader's miscues, correction attempts, comments made during the reading, and other reading behaviors marked by using a standardized system of marks. Running records may be made periodically to show the reader's mastery of successively difficult texts, types of miscues made, strategies used in figuring out unfamiliar words, and comprehension.

Running records were first used in conjunction with the individual tutorial program called Reading Recovery, an early intervention program designed by Marie Clay and described in detail in her book *The Early Detection of Reading Difficulties* (1985). Clay devised running records as a way of keeping careful track, on a daily basis, of a reader's use of key *strategies* and growth toward higher levels of difficulty of text. A Reading Recovery teacher takes a running record of the reader's second reading of a new book, done the day after the child has read the new book independently for the first time. Since a new book is introduced daily in a Reading Recovery lesson, a running record is taken daily as an ongoing measure of the child's progress.

Running Records to Document Progress

In the years since Reading Recovery was first introduced in the United States, running records have become widely used outside the format of the Reading Recovery lesson. Many teachers find running records helpful in documenting a reader's progress at systematic intervals because they take place during authentic reading tasks and can be done during ongoing instruction without interrupting the flow of a lesson. Also, several modifications of Reading Recovery have been developed, including a group adaptation sometimes called a *Readers' Circle*.

In a Readers' Circle lesson, the teacher takes a running record of one student reading yesterday's new book while the others listen; in this way, each child in the group is assessed about once a week. Other teachers find it most useful to take a running record every few weeks; for older students, this generally provides sufficient information about reading progress without becoming burdensome for the teacher. In our own classrooms, we take running records daily during Reading Recovery and Reader's Circle lessons; weekly for remedial students in small groups who are reading short, easy materials; and monthly or less often for developmental readers who are reading longer texts such as chapter books and novels. Whatever the interval, we keep dated copies of each reader's running records in his or her assessment file, since they provide concrete, easy-to-understand documentation of the reader's growing facility with text.

Figure 2.1 shows an example of a running record.

Running Records and Text Difficulty

Another important use of running records is to determine whether readers are self-selecting materials that are too easy, too difficult, or, like Baby Bear's chair, "just right." A growing trend in classrooms using a reading workshop approach is to have students self-select much of their reading material. Although this practice has undeniable appeal in helping children to read more and develop literary tastes and preferences, it can also mean that much of what students read is not challenging enough to spur their development as readers.

Why students would self-select easy material is not hard to understand. Material that is easy is usually very enjoyable, if only because the reader doesn't have to work very hard at it. Look at your own and other adults' self-selected pleasure reading materials. If you are like most adults, you would rather read popular fiction such as mysteries, thrillers, romances, and best-sellers or popular nonfiction such as celebrity biographies, self-help books, and how-to books than the "good-for-you" novels that your English teachers assigned you. Most of us would choose the latest crime novel over *War and Peace*, a Danielle Steele over an Emily Bronte, or the biography of a contemporary sports star over the biography of a long-dead President.

Children are no different. Leave it entirely up to them, and they'll generally choose the easy, the familiar, and the popular over material that might make

2   "I'm sorry," said the dog. "I don't know how to get

home."

1   "Are you lost?" asked a kind elephant.

"Yes, we are," said the goldfish.

"Then I will take you home," said the elephant.

"This is very kind of you," said the dog.

1   "It is fun to go places and see things," said the

elephant. "But it is good to go home, too."

"Yes, it is," said the dog.

Before long the dog and her goldfish were home.

"That was so much fun," said the goldfish.

"Where will we go now?"

1   "Now we will sit at home by the fire," said the

dog. "That is what I want to do."

"Anything to keep you happy," said the goldfish.

"You are very kind," said the dog.

Scoring for Oral Reading:

# of Errors	0	1	2	3	4	5	6	7+
%	100	99	98	97	97	96	95	

| Independent | Instructional | Frustration
Go to next lower level |

FIGURE 2.1 A Running Record

them think, wonder, or struggle the least bit. But it is the materials that are a stretch for us, in terms of our reading, that help us to become better readers, thinkers, and communicators. Issues related to text difficulty will be discussed further in the section "Monitoring Types and Difficulty of Texts Read" in this chapter and again in Chapter 3.

Teachers can use running records to check periodically whether what students are choosing is very easy for them. If students are reading material orally for the first time (i.e., "reading it cold") at close to 100% accuracy with few oral reading errors, or *miscues*, then the material represents their *independent, or "easy," reading level*. Some self-selected material at the independent level is good for you, but a steady diet of it will not help you to grow as a reader.

If students are reading at around 90–97 percent accuracy, making a few miscues that don't cause much meaning interruption and many of which are spontaneously corrected, then the material represents their *instructional, or "comfortable," reading level*. This is ideal for growth in reading—easy enough to be read without too much of a struggle but not so easy that it can be done with the mind on automatic pilot.

Of course, if students are reading at much below 90 percent accuracy and their miscues generally don't make sense, or if they are making many uncorrected miscues or unsuccessful correction attempts, then we infer that the material is at the *frustration, or "too difficult," reading level*. Reading much at this level is generally unpleasant and discouraging; little is learned from the reading, but negative attitudes about reading might quickly develop. You will read more about these functional reading levels in Chapter 3.

OBSERVATIONS OF READING BEHAVIORS AND STRATEGIES

Observing students and recording objective statements about what each individual is attempting, achieving, and struggling with can be invaluable in helping you to plan instruction and communicate with students, parents, and administrators.

Observing Readers

The classroom teacher is in the best possible position to observe and record students' daily interactions with text. These observations can be very helpful in communicating with parents, completing report cards and progress reports, talking with students about their progress, and meeting their instructional needs.

The lists that follow show many of the behaviors that we observe and record in our work with students. You might wish to add other behaviors you observe.

PHYSICAL BEHAVIORS
Points to words accurately during reading (for beginners)
Frequently loses place during silent or oral reading
Subvocalizes during silent reading

Reads quickly; appears not to look carefully at print; skips large portions of text; typically tries to finish before anyone else

Appears to be very absorbed in reading for pleasure; is not distracted by activity in environment during reading

Is easily interrupted or distracted by activity in the environment during reading

Does not read during sustained reading; leafs through the text, draws, puts head down, looks out the window, annoys others, etc.

Squints, turns head to the side, closes one eye, holds text closer or farther away from eyes than normal; vision appears uncomfortable during reading

COGNITIVE BEHAVIORS

Predicts easily about material to be read, or rarely offers a prediction

Recalls directly stated information easily or with difficulty

Demonstrates understanding of cause-and-effect relationships or little understanding

Produces inferences, conclusions, applications easily, with difficulty, or rarely

Offers personal opinions and/or experiences related to the reading

Uses background knowledge or prior information to understand text

Responds critically to aspects of plot, characters, author's style, illustrations

Draws comparisons between this material and other texts

Expresses enjoyment of an activity or text or pride in success

SOCIAL INTERACTIONS RELATED TO READING

Participates enthusiastically in group discussions/projects, participates hesitantly, or is typically nonparticipatory

Exchanges information and opinions with others or rejects others' contributions

Works cooperatively with a partner or small group or has difficulty cooperating with others

Often monopolizes group discussions

Appears to enjoy cooperative work (projects, buddy reading, etc.)

Waits for a peer to signal a need for help before giving assistance

Gives helpful clues or strategy suggestions to others when needed

READING STRATEGIES OBSERVED

Uses one or more strategies spontaneously before seeking assistance or rarely attempts a strategy before seeking help

Uses only one strategy exclusively (this is usually decoding or sounding out or, less often, contextual guessing)

Tries another strategy when the first attempt isn't successful

Uses context or sense-making and decoding together

Gets his or her mouth ready to say the beginning sound

Reruns or rereads to get a "running start" past a difficult part or to self-check

Indicates when what was read doesn't sound right or doesn't make sense with words or gestures ("What?" "Huh?" "Wait a minute," a puzzled look, etc.)

Cross-checks by checking picture and text, rereading, or using more than one strategy

Often attempts self-correction, whether successful or not

Assists others by giving clues and/or suggesting helpful strategies

Effectively uses text aids such as headings, bold print, charts, maps, tables, and summaries

Recording Observations

There are several ways in which you can keep track of your observations of students' reading behaviors and strategies while ensuring that you observe each student systematically. One way to do this is to make copies of an observation record sheet marked with a square for each student like the one in Figure 2.2. The squares should be large enough to accommodate a self-sticking note paper; many teachers use the 1 ½ × 2 inch size. Each square is labeled with a student's name. Observations are noted on the sticky notes, which are then attached to that student's square. As additional observations are made, the notes are stacked one atop the other. Many observations can be kept on one sheet, and there is no need to transfer your comments to another sheet. A drawback of this system is that sticky notes can fall off.

Another way to record observations is to write them directly on a sheet marked with labeled squares, as above. Sheets may be kept on a clipboard at hand, for convenience. A calendar page can be used, with a student's name in each weekday square; the month is already printed on it, and dates are jotted in each student's square as they occur, as shown in Figure 2.3. Or you can make a number of blank sheets with the squares ruled. Notes are made directly on the sheet, with the date marked. This system eliminates having to recopy notes from one place onto the sheet, but space for numerous comments is limited.

A third system involves making notes on index cards that may be carried in a pocket or on a clipboard (see Figure 2.4). This system might be most convenient for teachers who move about a great deal and who might find keeping a clipboard or sticky notes inconvenient. Index cards allow room for numerous or extended comments, but the notes may have to be transferred to another sheet for permanence, a process that many teachers find unnecessarily time consuming.

A fourth system involves keeping a separate observation sheet for each student (see Figure 2.5). This system is more convenient for keeping track of a small number of students, for example, members of a small remedial group. Sheets may be kept in students' daily work folders, in a ring binder, or on a clipboard.

Blair	Brianna	Vincent	Luke
	Jan. 12 – Made two self-corrections during reading		
Raquel	Lauren	Carla	Richard
Antoine	Kevin	Carlos	Marisa
		Jan. 14 – Volunteered to read first today!	
Scott	Terri	Sherita	Denzel
Jan 9 – Helped Huang check spelling during writing.			
Anthony	Jamahl	Huang	Paula
			Jan 10 – Used a dictionary for first time, self-initiated.

FIGURE 2.2   Observation Record Sheet with Sticky Notes

This system is cumbersome for large groups but allows plenty of room for each observation and eliminates recopying.

Whatever system you choose to record your observations, you must be careful of several issues.

1. *Use Objective Language.* Note what was said or done in factual terms, rather than your interpretation of the behavior. For example, "Richard repeatedly pulled the book away from his reading partner" is a factual report of what was done; "Richard has trouble sharing a book with a partner" is less specific and more judgmental. "Joanne looks out the window for most of the sustained reading period" is factual; "Joanne wastes her reading time" is judgmental. In general,

SEPTEMBER

Sunday	Monday	Tuesday	Wednesday	Thursday	Friday	Saturday
1 Last Quarter	2 Blair LABOR DAY	3 Brianna 9/8 Self-corr. during reading	4 Vincent	5 Luke	6 Raquel	7
8 New Moon GRANDPARENT'S DAY	9 Lauren ROSH HASHANAH	10 Carla	11 Richard	12 Antoine	13 Kevin 9-13 Beginning to space bet. words	14
15 First Quarter	16 Carlos	17 Marisa 9-17 Volunteered to read for first time CITIZENSHIP DAY	18 Scott YOM KIPPUR	19 Terri	20 Sherita	21
22	23 Denzel Full Moon FIRST DAY OF AUTUMN	24 Anthony 9-19 Has much difficulty pointing to each word	25 Jamahl	26 Huang	27 Paula	28
29	30				AUGUST S M T W T F S 1 2 3 4 5 6 7 8 9 10 11 12 13 14 15 16 17 18 19 20 21 22 23 24 25 26 27 28 29 30 31	OCTOBER S M T W T F S 1 2 3 4 5 6 7 8 9 10 11 12 13 14 15 16 17 18 19 20 21 22 23 24 25 26 27 28 29 30 31

FIGURE 2.3 Observations on Calendar Page

use terms such as "_____ did" or "_____ said" rather than "_____ is." Be especially wary of sweeping generalizations such as "_____ hates to read," "_____ works well in groups," or "_____ is uncooperative." And avoid using categorical terms such as "always" and "never," as they are rarely literally true.

The more precise you can be in describing what was observed, the more helpful your observations will be to you, the reader, and/or the reader's parents. We once saw this comment on a kindergartner's report card: "_____ can really act ugly sometimes." We all know intuitively what "acting ugly sometimes" might mean, but your idea of "ugly" behavior might be very different from mine and different from the child's parent as well. Such an imprecise comment doesn't help the child or parent to see *what* the behavior is or *how often* or *in what circumstances* the behavior occurs. Document behavior specifically, rather than judgmentally.

2. ***Observe Every Student.*** You might sometimes observe certain students more often than others, especially if they are having particular difficulty or showing a growth spurt, but in general, you should make sure you observe every child before starting another round of observations. The record-keeping systems shown in Figures 2.2 and 2.3, in which all notes are kept on one sheet with

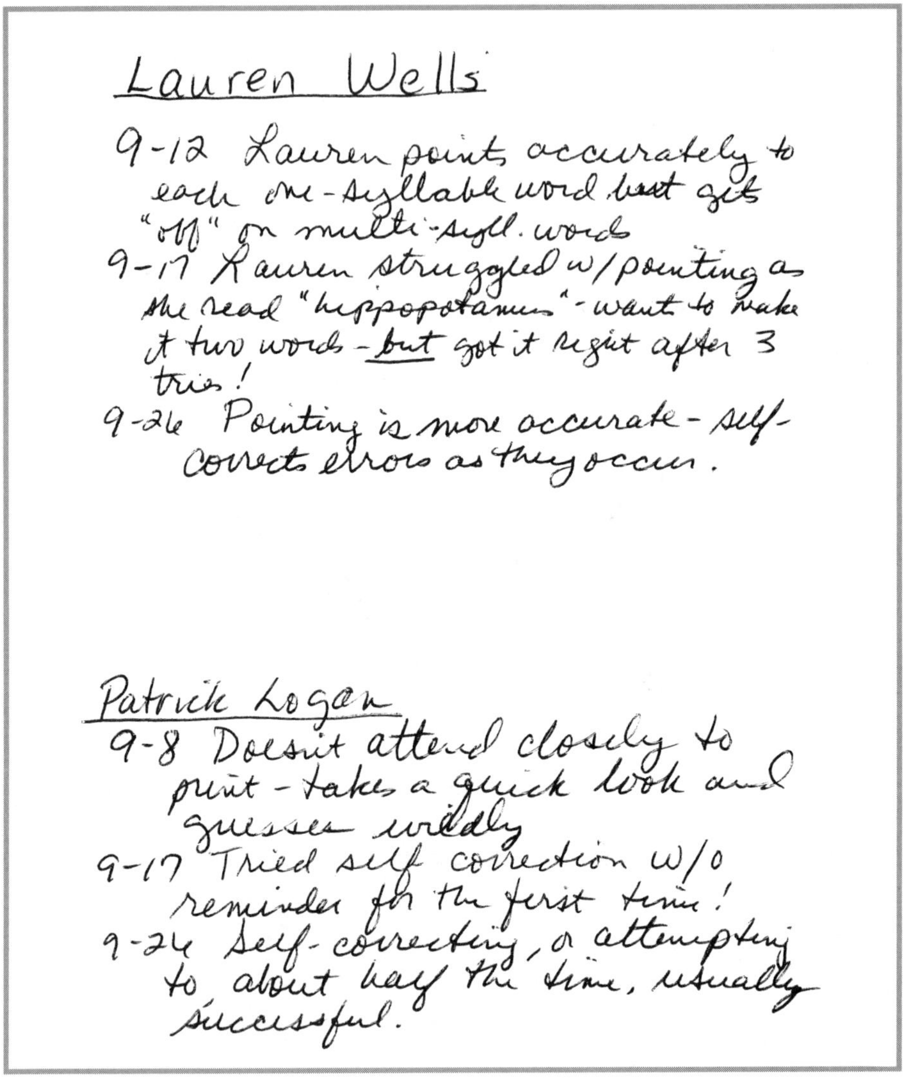

Lauren Wells

9-12 Lauren points accurately to each one-syllable word but gets "off" on multi-syll. words
9-17 Lauren struggled w/pointing as she read "hippopotamus" - want to make it two words - but got it right after 3 tries!
9-26 Pointing is more accurate - self-corrects errors as they occur.

Patrick Logan

9-8 Doesn't attend closely to print - takes a quick look and guesses wildly
9-17 Tried self correction w/o reminder for the first time!
9-24 Self-correcting, or attempting to about half the time, usually successful.

FIGURE 2.4 Observation Index Cards

labeled squares, help you to keep track of which students you have observed recently. An empty square indicates that you need to observe that individual.

If we don't pay attention to this, it can be easy to unwittingly observe one or a few students many more times than others. There are many reasons for this, some better than others. Frequently observed students tend to be having great difficulty or creating discipline or management problems for the teacher or can just be more engaging or likeable than others. Whatever the reason, it is unfair to observe some students many times and others few times, if at all. Every student is equally deserving of attention, no matter how difficult or likeable, successful or unsuccessful.

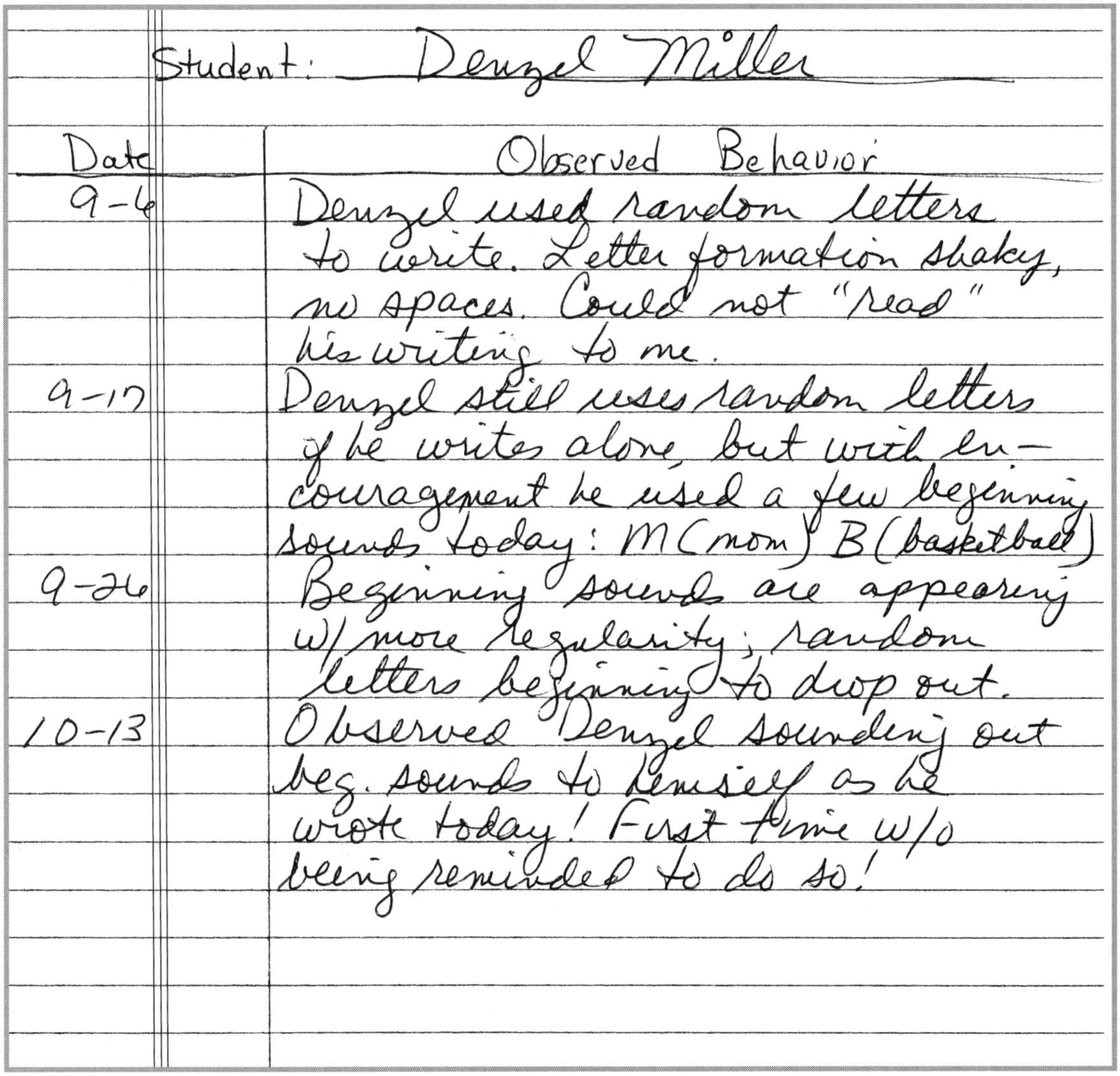

Student: Denzel Miller

Date	Observed Behavior
9-6	Denzel used random letters to write. Letter formation shaky, no spaces. Could not "read" his writing to me.
9-17	Denzel still uses random letters if he writes alone, but with encouragement he used a few beginning sounds today: M (mom) B (basketball)
9-26	Beginning sounds are appearing w/ more regularity; random letters beginning to drop out.
10-13	Observed Denzel sounding out beg. sounds to himself as he wrote today! First time w/o being reminded to do so!

FIGURE 2.5 Individual Student Observation Sheet

3. ***Build Systematic Observation Time into the Schedule.*** Set aside time on a regular basis for student observations. Whether you take a few minutes daily or a longer block of time once a week or every other week, be sure to block off such time in your schedule. If you don't, you might find that observation gets pushed aside by the daily demands of teaching and responding to students.

If you keep in mind that observing students is as important a part of your evaluation responsibilities as, say, giving tests or grading homework, you'll find it easier to make time for it. If you look at your last observation notes and find that it's been longer than a few weeks since you kept any observation records, you'll know that you need to carve out some time on a more regular basis. By doing so, you can often head off more serious problems and prevent them from becoming habitual.

MONITORING TYPES AND DIFFICULTY OF TEXTS READ

Another important record to keep is what texts students are reading, what types or genres are preferred, and how difficult the texts are. These are most important in programs in which students are self-selecting at least a portion of what they read, as they should be. But required or teacher-selected material should also be documented.

One way to do this is to keep a running list in each child's work folder or portfolio or in a binder that shows the materials being read, their genres, and some indication of their difficulty, either in terms of grade-level readability or in comparison to what the child can comfortably read. Another way is for students to keep such a list individually and share it with you in periodic conferences. Older students can easily keep their own records; they might record the title and author, the type of material (joke book, short story collection, historical or contemporary fiction, biography, science, etc.), and their self-assessment of its difficulty for them (easy to read, pretty hard book, over 100 pages long, etc.). For longer works that take more than a day or so to finish, the starting and ending dates may be recorded. Examples of such records are shown in Chapter 4, "Assessment for Internal Audiences: Portfolio Assessment."

Such lists show you at a glance how much and what kind of reading the child is doing. If a student appears to be reading one kind of material exclusively, you can consider encouraging him or her to try another author, topic, or genre. If only very easy books are attempted, you might introduce the student to a little more challenging material; conversely, for the one who always chooses too-difficult, discouraging texts, guidance in selecting more manageable books might be needed. The child who takes several months to read a single novel might benefit from introduction to shorter works or collections.

These records can also be very effective in demonstrating to parents just what their children are capable of and interested in. This can help them to provide appropriate materials for reading at home. And most students enjoy getting a panoramic look at what they are reading and often get great satisfaction in watching their lists grow and change. Such information can help students to become more reflective and self-evaluative.

There are several ways to informally determine the difficulty level of different materials. One tried and true method is to use the publisher's estimate of the text's readability, often shown on the back or front cover. Readability estimates are determined by using arithmetic readability formulas and are expressed as decimal numbers showing the estimated grade level of difficulty in years and months. A reading level, sometimes called the RL, of 4.0, for example, is read as fourth grade, no months, or the beginning of fourth grade; a reading level of 4.5 is read as the fourth grade plus five months, or about mid-fourth grade. Above sixth grade, readability levels might simply be expressed as MS, or middle school; HS, or high school; or YA, or young adult (usually middle to older teens). Conversely, materials for beginning readers might be marked P, or primer, or Beginning Reader, or the like.

Teachers can also use readability formulas to determine for themselves the approximate or estimated readability level of a book. Difficulty, in this sense, is considered to be a function of word and sentence length rather than of the information that is conveyed. The assumption behind readability formulas is that easy-to-read texts have short words and many short sentences, while harder-to-read texts have many longer words and fewer, longer sentences. Many school media specialists have simple computer programs that compute the readability level of texts using several comparable formulas when three 100-word samples are typed in. It is also possible, although cumbersome, to compute these levels by hand using readability formula charts. Two widely-used formulas follow:

THE FRY READABILITY FORMULA

1. Select three 100-word passages from near the beginning, the middle, and the end of the text. Count proper nouns, dates (1776), numerals (5,380), number words (5th), acronyms (NATO), and symbols (+, &) as single words. Mark the text after the 100th word.
2. Count the **number of sentences** in each 100-word passage, estimating to the nearest tenth of a sentence in the case of an incomplete sentence at the end of a passage. Average these three numbers by adding them and dividing by 3.
3. Count the total **number of syllables** in each 100-word passage. Do so by reading the words *aloud*; there is a vowel sound in each syllable of a word. Do not be misled by size; *idle* is short but has two syllables, but *through* is long and has only one. For dates, acronyms, symbols, and the like, count each *character* as a syllable; 1918 has four, GNP has three, and = has two. Average the number of syllables by adding and dividing by 3 as above.
4. Plot on the graph in Figure 2.6 the location of the average number of syllables and the average number of sentences. Most will occur near the curved line on the graph. The perpendicular lines show the approximate grade-level areas. If the syllable and sentence averages fall outside or at the extremes of a grade-level band, check your arithmetic for error and, if necessary, recalculate using three new samples.

THE RAYGOR READABILITY FORMULA

1. Select three 100-word passages as for the Fry formula, selecting passages from near the beginning, middle, and end of the work.
2. Count the **number of sentences** in each sample, estimating to the nearest tenth of a sentence for an incomplete sentence at the end of a passage. Average the number of sentences by adding and dividing by 3.
3. Count the **number of words with more than six letters** in each passage. Average the number of "long words" by adding them and dividing

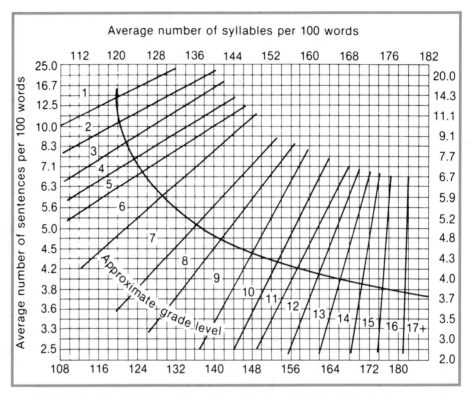

FIGURE 2.6   Fry's Graph for Estimating Readability—Extended

Source: Edward Fry. "Fry's Readability Graph: Clarifications, Validity, and Extension to Level 17." *Journal of Reading* 21, no. 3 (Dec. 1977):242–252.

by 3. If one sample of 100 words yields very different numbers than the other two, select another passage. For example, if two passages have about twenty-five or thirty "long words" and one has only four, add one more sample, count the long words, and average over four samples.

4. Find the point on the graph in Figure 2.7 where the average number of sentences and long words intersect. The number of the band running across the chart tells you the grade level of the text. If the intersection falls in the areas marked "Invalid," do not try to interpret this finding. First check your arithmetic; then do the procedure again with different passages. If the same results occur, the text does not conform to typical norms of grade level difficulty.

CLOZE PROCEDURES

A cloze procedure is another way of determining the approximate difficulty level of a text. However, the result is not a grade-level estimate, as you get using a

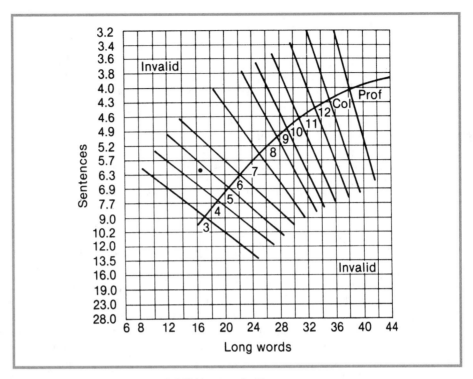

FIGURE 2.7 Raygor Readability Formula Chart

Source: From R. Scott Baldwin and Rhonda K. Kaufman. "A Concurrent Validity Study of the Raygor Readability Estimate." *Journal of Reading* (Nov. 1979):148–153.

readability formula, but rather an estimate of whether an individual, group, or class is likely to find the material too easy, comfortable, or too hard.

Figure 2.8 shows a portion of a cloze procedure. After the first sentence, you will find blanks in the text. Can you figure out what might make sense in each blank? (Only one word has been deleted each time.)

In a cloze procedure (Taylor, 1953), students read material from which words have been systematically deleted; that is, every *nth* word has been left out. Frequently, every *fifth* word after the first complete sentence is replaced with a blank, as in our example. Our aim is to see how accurately students can predict or infer the words that should fill the blanks, thus creating *closure,* or wholeness, in the passage.

A completely accurate prediction of every deleted word is almost impossible unless the material is extremely simple in content and vocabulary, but it is not necessary to fill in each deletion with total accuracy. If an adequate proportion of words to blanks is supplied, readers can usually use their sense of what is going on in the passage to supply words that will complete the author's text. Can you give a good guess for each of the deleted words in Figure 2.8? You probably could fill in more than half of the blanks accurately but not every one. For some of the deletions, only one or two words could possibly fit; for others, there are more alternatives. The ninth blank, for example, occurs in the phrase, "had come from the

"When Emily Johnson came home one evening to her furnished room and found three of her best handkerchiefs missing from the dresser drawer, she was sure who had taken them and what to do. She had lived in _____ furnished room for about _____ weeks and for the _____ two weeks she had _____ missing small things occasionally. _____ had been several handkerchiefs _____, and an initial pin _____ Emily rarely wore and _____ had come from the _____ -and-ten. And once _____ had missed a small _____ of perfume and one _____ a set of china _____. Emily had known for _____ time who was taking _____ things, but it was _____ tonight that she had _____ what to do."

FIGURE 2.8   Portion of a Cloze Procedure

Source: Shirley Jackson. "Trial by Combat." in *The Lottery.* New York: Farrar, Straus, 1949, p. 35.

_____-and-ten." You probably recognized almost immediately the expression "five-and-ten" and would have trouble thinking of a better alternative. On the other hand, what about "a set of china _____"? You could probably think of several good alternatives for that blank: *plates, figurines,* or *animals.* In spite of some uncertainty, the whole passage is not too frustrating or difficult to complete.

The cloze procedure indicates the extent to which readers are able to follow the sense of a reading passage. In fact, studies have shown that the percentages of correct words readers are able to supply in a cloze passage constitute as reliable a measure of general comprehension as much more elaborate devices (Bormuth, 1966; Jones and Pikulski, 1974; Rankin and Culhane, 1969).

There are two common purposes for using a cloze procedure:

1. to determine whether a particular piece of written text represents an individual's independent, instructional, or frustration reading level (placement purposes) and
2. to assess the quality of an individual reader's use of context as a strategy for understanding what is read (diagnostic purposes).

Using a Cloze for Placement

A cloze placement test is a fast and accurate device for determining whether an individual, group, or whole class can comfortably read a given book or other material. In classes in which everyone must read the same required textbooks, cloze results can help the teacher form groups for differential instruction. Where students are reading trade books and novels, cloze results are invaluable for determining whether selections are easy, too hard, or just right.

When constructing a cloze passage, omit systematically every fifth word, that is, 20 percent of the words. Leaving 80 percent intact gives sufficient context for the reader to supply the remaining words. Deleting every fifth word in order ensures that words of all grammatical classes and levels of difficulty are sampled, not just all nouns or all long words, for example.

Here are the steps for constructing a cloze passage for placement purposes (Estes and Vaughn, 1985):

1. Select a passage the students have not read before, about 300 words long.
2. Leave the first sentence intact to get the readers started. Then begin counting words, replacing every fifth word with a blank 15 spaces long. If any word to be deleted is a proper noun, leave it in and delete the next word. (Proper nouns are harder to predict from context than other words.) Continue counting until you have 50 blanks.
3. Finish the sentence in which the last deletion occurs. Type one more sentence intact.

Administering and scoring a cloze are simple:

1. On the blackboard, show the students how to complete the passage. Give example sentences and discuss how to use context clues. Let students work together on short passages for practice. This step is important because even good readers will do poorly if they are unfamiliar with the demands of the task.
2. Direct the students to use only one word for each blank and to try to use the precise word the author would have used.
3. Explain that no one will get each word correct and that about 50 percent correct is a good score. If the students don't know this in advance, anxiety can affect their performance.
4. Give ample time for completing the passage without rushing. The students should not use their books because we want to see whether they can read and understand the material without aid.

In scoring, accept only the *exact replacement*. Studies (Bormuth, 1966; Miller and Coleman, 1967; Ruddell, 1964) have shown this to be the most valid scoring system for placement purposes. When you use this activity instructionally to teach the use of context clues or work on vocabulary, you might choose to accept synonyms or make other changes. The rank order of scores changes little, if at all, if synonyms are accepted, but interpreting the results can be difficult. Also, you can drive yourself crazy deciding what is "close enough."

Determine the percentage of correct responses, adding 2 percent for each correct word. (Don't count incorrect *spellings* as errors on the cloze.) You can judge more accurately by averaging each student's scores on two or more passages from the same text.

A score of 60 percent correct or higher indicates that the material is easy for these students and that the material can be used for *independent* reading. A score between 40 and 60 percent indicates that these students can comfortably read the material and that it is suitable for direct instruction because it represents their *instructional* reading level. A score below 40 percent correct indicates that the material is too difficult and that it represents the reader's *frustration* level (Bormuth, 1968a, 1968b; Rankin and Culhane, 1969).

The cloze procedure can be very useful in classes in which a single text or set of materials is required, as is typical of many secondary-level classes and some upper-elementary content area classes. It enables the teacher to determine quickly and accurately which students will find that particular material too difficult (Jones and Pikulski, 1974). It is an effective procedure for gathering information about students' reading ability in the first days of school, before their teachers get to know them, especially when a teacher has more than one class. If the same text or material is used year after year, the initial cloze can be used again and again or shared by several teachers who use the same textbooks or trade books.

Using the Cloze Diagnostically

The cloze procedure can be used diagnostically to find out what students know, to help them focus on context clues, and to read critically.

For diagnostic purposes, it is not necessary to delete words systematically. Instead, *key words* can be deleted, words that convey much of the information. When used *after* a reading assignment, the cloze can show a good deal about the concepts and vocabulary that students have gained from the assignment. Used *before* the assignment, the cloze can show their need for vocabulary and concept development prior to the reading.

A reader's tacit grasp of syntactic structures can be explored by deleting words of a particular grammatical class, such as verbs, prepositions, or adjectives. If used on a regular basis, the cloze can help students to focus on grammatical forms, learn concepts of parts of speech, become aware of context clues, and infer the meaning of new words. Simplified cloze activities can be made up from students' dictated experience stories and their own written productions. This approach will help reinforce recognition of sight words and can be especially helpful for youngsters who are having trouble recognizing those troublesome structure words (*the, is, there, at,* and so forth). The *oral cloze,* in which selected word are left out and suggestions solicited while the teacher reads aloud to students, can be very useful in encouraging critical listening and comprehension (Blachowicz, 1977).

Cloze activities are particularly worthwhile for students who have relatively good word recognition but poor comprehension. Because they help students to focus on the meaning and sense of the material, these activities can be invaluable in helping the word caller to improve reading and listening comprehension (Bortnick and Lopardo, 1973, 1976).

MONITORING SPELLING PROGRESS AND PROBLEMS

Another kind of ongoing assessment is a record of students' growth in spelling. Learning to read words requires the operation of *recognition;* learning to spell them requires the more difficult but related operation of *production.* Thus, children's ability to read words usually outstrips their ability to spell them; this generally holds true for adults as well. (It's likely that you can easily read any number of words that you might have difficulty spelling correctly. However, it's almost inconceivable that you could spell a word you couldn't read.)

For beginning readers, spelling attempts can be windows that reveal the child's growing phonemic segmentation ability. In fact, phonemic segmentation is often assessed by having children try to write unfamiliar words or whole sentences and looking at how many phonemes they are able to represent accurately or acceptably. Marie Clay has long used a dictation test as part of her Diagnostic Survey for Reading Recovery (Clay, 1985), in which children are asked to write as much of a standard sentence as they can; there are five different sentences, each consisting of thirty-seven phonemes. Children who can represent at least half of the sounds in one of these sentences are considered to be well on their way to developing phonemic segmentation ability. Figure 2.9 shows a first-grader's performance on a sentence dictation task in September and in April.

Developmental Spelling Stages

Twenty or more years of spelling research have shown that young children apply systematic strategies to relate speech sounds to letters and words and that these strategies develop in a predictable stagewise sequence. As children grow and gain more experience with print, their *invented spellings* approximate correct spellings more and more closely. This developmental sequence appears to take from three to six years to complete (e.g., Bissex, 1980; Clay, 1979; Henderson & Beers, 1980; Read, 1971, 1975). These developmental stages are briefly described below.

Prephonemic Spelling

Children have enough experience with print to know that it is made up of letters and that it conveys a message, but they do not yet understand that letters represent speech sounds. At this stage, letters are used randomly, representing a message that only the writer can "read." For example, a four-year-old wrote "FLLMLMFMLMFL" to stand for "This is a flock of butterflies." Later she read it as, "These butterflies are very pretty." Numerals and other characters are sometimes included. Prephonemic spelling is usually arranged linearly but without spacing.

Semiphonemic, or Early Phonemic, Spelling

As children are taught the alphabet, they begin to recognize that letters have a sound associated with them. They begin to try out this concept by representing one or more sounds, usually the initial and sometimes the final sound, with letters that have that sound. Whole words might be represented with a single letter, or a few random letters might be added. For example, a first-grader wrote "ILMMR" for "I love my mother." Spaces between the units intended for words might appear late in this stage.

FIGURE 2.9 Sentence Dictation Test

Phonemic Spelling

As children move into beginning reading, they learn more and more about the ways in which letters represent sounds in written words, and they use this information both to decode in reading and encode, or spell, in writing. First, inventions become more wordlike, with more consonant sounds represented, as in "LFNT" for "elephant." Then vowels begin to appear; first the long vowels, since they "say their names," as in "EGL" for "eagle" or "BOLN" for "bowling." Late in this stage, short vowels appear; they are usually incorrect because children try to use the *name* of the letter to approximate its sound, which works with long vowels and most consonants but rarely works with short vowels. Typical late phonemic, or *letter-name* spellings, are "HIT" for "hot" and "BAT" for "bent."

Transitional Spelling

This very extended stage encompasses many strategies of growing sophistication and generally lasts from roughly second to fourth or fifth grade with typical spellers. As a result of their growing reading ability and systematic decoding and spelling instruction throughout these years, children gradually abandon the primarily phonemic, or sound-based, spelling on which they previously relied and begin to develop strategies for spelling whole syllables and word parts, "silent" letters, and entire words, as well as developing a visual memory for hundreds of words. They now learn words by patterns, as most spelling programs advocate, and can generate many words based on learning common patterns such as CVC/get, CVCe/cake, CVVC/hear, and so forth. Learning word families and rules for dividing words into syllables and consonant doubling allows them to spell many words correctly and to produce very readable spelling errors. Transitional-stage errors often result from overusing or misusing spelling rules, such as using both a vowel digraph and a silent e in a long vowel word, or putting an extra vowel in an unstressed syllable. Examples of transitional errors are WEAKE/weak, APPAL/apple, OWNLEY/only, and PEPPEL/people.

Derivational Spelling

As students learn more and more about our spelling system and move farther from the phonemic strategy, they are faced with reading and writing more difficult, complex words. Negotiating this final developmental stage requires that spellers develop a "spelling conscience," a sense of "what looks right" in spellings and consequently an awareness of when an error has been made. It also requires that they develop a sense of how words are related by meaning and by their historical, or *etymological*, roots, so that spelling patterns can be preserved across these *derived forms*. For example, derivational spellers may confuse -*tion* and -*sion*, as in CONSTITUSION/constitution, but they are unlikely to spell this affix as it sounds, as a transitional speller would with "CONSTITUSHUN." Common derivational errors are confusing -*ily* and -*aly*, -*tion* and -*sion*, and the like and failing to preserve the *derivational constancy* of related words such as sign/signal and decide/decision, which may include changes in pronunciation while maintaining the spelling pattern.

Documenting Spelling Progress

With the stages of spelling development in mind, it is useful for teachers to monitor and document their students' spelling development across time. One way to accomplish this is to have students deliberately attempt to spell a group of unfamiliar words at points across the year and contrast their attempts on the same words at intervals of several months. Another way is to collect misspellings of the same words from their writing at intervals, contrasting the attempts as above.

The first method involves giving a sort of spelling test, but with words that the students have not been taught. This provides information about how they handle different common spelling features such as vowel patterns, blends and digraphs, prefixes and suffixes, and consonant doubling. Using a *features list* in this way allows you to collect information on how students manipulate various spelling features. However, since the words should be unfamiliar, students might feel uncomfortable taking a "spelling test," or something that looks and feels like a spelling test, on words that they haven't learned to spell. They will need plenty of explanation that you don't expect them to spell many, if any, of the words correctly but that you are looking at how they spell particular parts of each word, and they will need reassurance throughout the assessment.

We have had good results using a single answer sheet with vertical rows of numbered blanks; before the assessment, each student's sheet is folded so that only one row of blanks is visible, and the folded sheets are paper-clipped closed for security. We give the same words in the same order each time, so after two or more assessments, we have successive attempts at each word arrayed across each set of blanks. As shown in Figure 2.10, dating each list at the top allows us to see at a glance how each student is progressing in handling the various spelling features. This sheet also clearly shows parents how their children's spelling is advancing as the year progresses and which features might be continuing to be troublesome. Finally, near the end of the year, students delight in looking at their spelling attempts on each word and seeing the concrete evidence of their growth.

Developmental Spelling Inventory

Students' spelling can also be analyzed by using a spelling inventory. The spelling inventories that we have developed are collections of words we expect children will not be able to spell correctly. We hope that they will misspell each word on the list so that we can analyze those errors. In this case, correct spellings are not helpful. So we reassure students that they have probably not yet learned to spell these words, that we do not expect they will be able to spell very many correctly, and that we are most interested in the ways they try to spell a word they are not sure of. (Students who are familiar with traditional spelling tests need this reassurance as they discover that they do not "know" these words.)

Tables 2.1 and 2.2 contain suggested lists; the first is for students in grades K and through 2, and the second is for pupils in third grade and above. Lists can be

Name **Raquel**

Grade **2** HR Teacher **Smith**

9-6
date

1. **fh**
2. **Bd**
3. **jut**
4. _____
5. _____
6. _____
7. _____
8. _____
9. _____
10. _____
11. _____
12. _____
13. _____
14. _____
15. _____
16. _____
17. _____
18. _____
19. _____
20. _____

1-23
date

1. **fesh**
2. **bnd**
3. **jumpt**

Fold here

6-3
date

1. **fish**
2. **band**
3. **jumpted**

fold here

FIGURE 2.10 Multiuse Spelling Sheet

administered to whole classes or smaller groups, with younger children attempting the words in several sittings. All students should be told beforehand that these are *new* words that they have not studied before, that not knowing some (or even all the words) is expected, and that it is their *attempts* you are interested in. Papers are not scored; instead, you should analyze each pupil's attempts for strategies that represent an overall developmental level.

Classifying the Errors

Do not analyze correct spellings. If a child gets more than half of the beginners' list correct, administer the advanced list. Use these guidelines for assigning each misspelling to a category, whether it occurs in a writing sample or on the spelling lists:

TABLE 2.1 Developmental Spelling Inventory I: Primary Grades K–2

Part I: One Session*

Fish	I caught a fish.
Bend	You can bend your arm.
Jumped	I jumped over a log.
Yell	We can yell all we want outside.
Learned	I learned to count in school.
Shove	Don't shove your neighbor in the lunch line.
Witch	Hansel and Gretel met a witch.
Piece	I want a piece of cake.

Part II: Another Session

Late	I stayed up late.
Bench	We sat down on a bench.
Drive	I'm too young to drive a car.
Wet	Your hair is all wet.
Chirped	The cricket chirped in the yard last night.
Neck	She wore a gold chain around her neck.
Trained	I trained my dog to shake hands.
Tick	There was a tick on my dog.

*May be given at one sitting if the children don't tire too quickly.

Note: Repeat each word two to three times, but don't exaggerate its pronunciation.

1. ***Prephonemic.*** Consider a spelling prephonemic if there is no evidence that any of the letters in the spelling stand for any of the phonemes in the test word. Assign each prephonemic spelling a 1.

Examples: DLD for *once*, RZF for *witch*

2. ***Semiphonemic.*** Consider a spelling semiphonemic if salient phonemes in the test word are omitted (but not *n* or *m* before consonants, or vowels before *m*, *n*, *l*, or *r*, in unstressed syllables; these are omissions associated with the following letter-name stage of spelling). Assign each semiphonemic spelling a 2.

Examples: ND for *wind*, JD for *jumped*, HD for *shed*

TABLE 2.2 Developmental Spelling Inventory II: Grade 3 and Above

Setter	My dog is an Irish setter.
Shove	Don't shove your neighbor in the lunch line.
Grocery	I'm going to the grocery store.
Button	A button popped off his jacket.
Sailor	My cousin is a sailor.
Prison	If you break the law, you may go to prison.
Nature	We went for a hike on the nature trail.
Peeked	The spy peeked out from his hiding place.
Special	Birthdays are special days.
Preacher	The preacher talked for an hour.
Slowed	The truck slowed down for the curve.
Sail	The boat had a torn sail.
Feature	We went to see a double feature.
Batter	The first batter struck out.

3. **Phonemic.** Consider a spelling phonemic if most of the phonemes in the test word are represented on the basis of a similarity between the phonemes and the sound of the letter name. Silent letters are omitted, as are *n* and *m* before consonants and vowels in unstressed syllables ending in *n, m, l,* or *r.* Short vowels are often spelled by the closest long vowel-letter name; *i* for *ŏ, e* for *ĭ.* Long vowels will be spelled without markers. Assign each phonemic spelling a 3.

Examples: HEK for *chick,* LRND for *learned,* PECT for *picked*

4. **Transitional.** Consider a spelling transitional if short vowels and digraphs (*ch, sh, th*) are spelled correctly and if the letters *y, w, c* ("soft sounds"), and *g* ("soft sound") have their conventional spellings. Silent letters can be present but incorrectly used. Consonant blends such as *tr* and *dr* can be spelled CHR and JR, respectively. The /sh/ or /ch/ sounds in *nature, grocery,* and *special* can be spelled CH, S, and SH, respectively. Past tense endings will be spelled incorrectly, just as they sound. Consonant doubling may be omitted in two-syllable words. Assign each transitional spelling a 4.

Examples: LURND for *learned,* GROSHRY for *grocery,* CHRAEND for *trained,* BUTUN for *button*

5. **Derivational.** Consider spellings derivational if the /ch/ or /sh/ sounds in *grocery, special, preacher,* or *feature* are spelled with *ti, si, ci, sy,* or *ty* but not with *ch* or *sh.* Consider spellings derivational if the stems in *sail* and *sailor* are spelled the same way. *Prison* might be spelled PRISION. Assigned each derivational spelling a 5.

Examples: SAILER for *sailor,* NATIUR for *nature,* SPETIAL for *special*

After some practice with these guidelines, you will have little difficulty in assigning each misspelling to a category. If you get completely stuck on a word, discount it and concentrate on the others.

For each child, determine which category has the most examples. If there are large accumulations of errors in other categories, these too can be revealing. Spelling development tends to be unidirectional. It moves from prephonemic to semiphonemic to phonemic, and so on, not the other way around. Thus, if students have 50 percent of their errors in the transitional category and 30 percent in the phonemic category, it is an indication that they are acquiring transitional spelling strategies with vestiges of the earlier phonemic strategies remaining. If they have 60 percent in the transitional and 30 percent in the derivational stage, this suggests that they are moving beyond transitional spelling and into derivational spelling (Temple and Gillet, 1996).

Another way of comparing children's spelling inventions across time is to cull errors from their writing at periodic intervals, recording them on a sheet like the one in Figure 2.10 and dating the entries. This method involves more work for the teacher, since it requires that you select and read samples of each student's writing done at intervals and find the same or very similar words that are misspelled each time. The only advantage that this method offers is that the words you analyze are all words students actually tried to use in their writing. However, if the misspellings occurred in early drafts of a piece, it might well be that the student did not try particularly hard to spell the words correctly, knowing that spelling errors could be cleaned up later in the writing cycle. So, even though the words come from authentic writing, the writer might not have given each one his or her best effort. For these reasons, we prefer to use periodic features testing with our students.

MONITORING GROWTH IN WRITING

As is the case with spelling, many teachers find it useful to monitor and document students' progress in composition and the use of writing strategies across the year. This can be accomplished in several ways. One way is to collect dated writing samples for comparison across time; another is to compile a checklist of writing features and strategies that students might reasonably be expected to gain facility with across time. Of course, these will necessarily be different depending on the age and grade of the students.

Writing Samples

Collecting dated writing samples is easy, and you can either set aside time for everyone to write a piece to be collected or select and photocopy a piece from each student's writing folder or portfolio at intervals. When you set aside time for everyone to write an assessment sample, you can either assign a general topic or form of writing or allow students to choose. Letting them choose their own topics makes the writing somewhat more authentic, but asking everyone to write on the same broad topic (e.g., a lost animal, a description of an object or picture, or a holiday celebration) or to produce the same type of writing (e.g., a letter to a friend, a story from the imagination, or a descriptive paragraph) makes comparison easier. You can also have students use the same topic or genre each time the samples are collected; this makes comparing the individual's pieces across time easy. If students are self-selecting topics most of the time, an occasional structured writing assignment is unlikely to hurt them.

However, some teachers resist the notion of assigning writing topics or styles even for purposes of assessment, and some don't even like to ask students to write "on demand," especially in the primary grades. In this case, reviewing each student's writing folder or portfolio at intervals and selecting pieces to collect and compare seems the only course. Older students might share in this selection process. The samples collected are more likely to represent authentic writing in which the writer has some ownership, but the temptation might be great to select samples that are particularly strong, especially close to the end of the year, and so the samples might not represent what the writer typically produces. Keep in mind that the purpose of this selection is not to showcase the student's best writing, but to show growth across a number of fronts from one part of the year to another.

When we collect dated samples across a school year, we typically write an evaluative comment either on the copy of the sample or on a comment sheet that is attached to the samples. We usually note how the student appears to be managing tasks such as selecting a topic; forming sentences and paragraphs; using the writing cycle to first develop and elaborate on ideas, then check for mechanical problems; and aspects of writing mechanics such as capitalization, punctuation,

	October	February	May
Composing Easily thinks of topic Can talk about topic before writing Maintains focus Expresses complete thoughts Produces at least 3 related sentences/ thought units			
Style Has a personal "voice" Uses vivid vocabulary Uses descriptive words Organization appropriate to topic and genre			
Usage Inflects plurals Inflects verbs Uses pronouns Subject-verb agreement Complete sentences, not fragments or run-ons			
Mechanics Beginning capitals Proper noun capitals, including I End punctuation Indented paragraphs Spelling checked			

FIGURE 2.11 Writing Benchmarks for Primary Grades

and spelling. We also note things that we observed during the writing, if possible, such as great difficulty finding a topic, ease and fluency of the writing, the writer's degree of independence during the writing or efforts to get help from others, ability to reread the piece, and what, if anything, the writer had to say about the topic or the piece. You will find examples of these observations in Chapter 4, "Assessment for Internal Audiences: Portfolio Assessment."

Writing Checklists

A checklist of writing skills and strategies can also be used to show how and when students have achieved certain benchmarks of writing across the school year. This can be used instead of dated samples or in conjunction with them. The latter, of course, provides the most comprehensive documentation of the student's writing progress.

Figures 2.11 and 2.12 are examples of writing progress checklists that can be adapted for a range of grades. The benchmarks can be considered typical of students' writing at different ages, but you might have different expectations for

	October	February	May
Composing Establishes topic easily Topic sentence Supporting sentences Concluding sentence Minimum one complete paragraph Maintains focus			

Style
Has a personal "voice"
Maintains voice throughout
Vivid vocabulary
Uses descriptive adjectives/
  adverbs
Organization appropriate
  to topic and genre
Varied sentence length and style			

Usage
Inflects plurals correctly
Inflects verbs correctly
Pronoun-referent agreement
Subject-verb agreement
Complete sentences
Some evidence of subordinate
  clauses in sentences
Vocabulary appropriate for topic,
  audience, and genre			

Mechanics Capitalization correct End punctuation correct Commas correct w/in sentences Quotation marks in dialogue Indented paragraphs High-utility words spelled correctly Spelling appropriate for age/grade			

F I G U R E 2.12 Writing Benchmarks for Elementary Grades

your students that can be incorporated into your own checklists. These lists are for primary and elementary grades; middle school teachers could easily adapt the elementary standards for middle school grades.

SUMMARY

This chapter describes a variety of assessments that a teacher might make on an ongoing basis throughout the year. These assessments and observations can add to other, more in-depth or formal measures to compile a complete picture of a student's literacy development and achievement.

Running records are transcripts of text that a student reads aloud, with the reader's miscues, correction attempts, comments, and other reading behaviors marked. Running records may be collected periodically to show the reader's progress in mastering progressively more difficult text, word recognition and word analysis strategies, and comprehension. They are also used to show how well a reader is handling self-selected materials and whether such materials are challenging enough to promote reading growth.

Observations of reading behaviors and strategies can be informative in planning instruction and in communicating about students' progress with students themselves, their parents, and other teachers. Physical and cognitive behaviors, social interactions during reading and reading strategies that may be observed during reading are listed in the chapter. Several methods of recording observations are illustrated, including using a sheet of labeled squares, a calendar page, index cards, and individual student observation sheets. Maintaining objectivity, using objective language to describe behaviors, systematic planning for observations, and being sure to observe each student regularly are discussed.

Types and difficulty of texts can be recorded on individual reading lists. *Readability formulas* are one way to estimate the difficulty of texts, yielding a grade-equivalent reading level. However, these formulas are based on the notion that text difficulty is a function of sentence and word length, rather than a function of the information conveyed or the reader's interaction with it. *Cloze procedures,* or portions of text with words systematically deleted, can also be used to determine whether a particular text represents a reader's or group's independent, instructional or frustration reading level, rather than yielding a grade-equivalent reading level.

Spelling progress and development can be documented by using a *dictated sentence task*, a *developmental spelling inventory,* or periodic samples of *misspellings from writing*. A sentence dictation task may be used with young children or emergent and beginning readers to show their ability to segment phonemes in spoken utterances. A developmental spelling inventory may be used for beginning and developmental readers/writers, to show their mastery of the successive developmental stages of spelling acquisition. Culling spelling errors from student writing is useful to document writers' use of spelling strategies in words they choose to use in their writing.

Growth in writing can be documented by collecting *writing samples* for comparison over time and by using *writing checklists*, which show how and when each student has achieved certain *benchmarks* of writing development.

REFERENCES

Bissex, Glenda. *GNYS AT WRK: A Child Learns to Write and Read.* Cambridge, MA: Harvard University Press, 1980.

Blachowicz, Camille. "Cloze Activities for Primary Readers." *The Reading Teacher* 31, no. 3 (December 1977): 300–302.

Bormuth, John R. "Readability: A New Approach." *Reading Research Quarterly* 1, no. 3 (1966): 79–132.

Bormuth, John R. "The Cloze Readability Procedure." *Elementary English* 55 (April 1968a): 429–436.

Bormuth, John R. "Cloze Test Reliability: Criterion Reference Scores." *Journal of Educational Measurement* 5 (Fall 1968b): 189–196.

Bortnick, Robert, and Genevieve S. Lopardo. "An Instructional Application of the Cloze Procedure." *Journal of Reading* 16, no. 4 (Jan. 1973): 296–300.

Bortnick, Robert, and Genevieve S. Lopardo. "The Cloze Procedure: A Multi-Purpose Classroom Tool." *Reading Improvement* 13, no. 2 (Summer 1976): 113–117.

Clay, Marie M. *Reading: The Patterning of Complex Behavior,* 2d ed. Auckland, NZ/ Portsmouth, NH: Heinemann Educational Books, 1979.

Clay, Marie M. *The Early Detection of Reading Difficulties.* Portsmouth, NH: Heinemann Educational Books, 1985.

Estes, Thomas H., and Joseph L. Vaughan. *Reading and Learning in the Content Classroom,* 2d ed. Boston: Allyn & Bacon, 1985.

Henderson, Edmund H., and James W. Beers, Eds. *Developmental and Cognitive Aspects of Learning to Spell: A Reflection of Word Knowledge.* Newark, DE: International Reading Association, 1980.

Jones, Margaret, and Edna Pikulski. "Cloze for the Classroom." *The Reading Teacher* 17, no. 6 (March 1974): 432–438.

Miller, G. R., and E. G. Coleman. "A Set of 36 Prose Passages Calibrated for Complexity." *Journal of Verbal Learning and Verbal Behavior* 6 (1967): 851–854.

Rankin, Earl F., and Joseph W. Culhane. "Comparable Cloze and Multiple Choice Comprehension Test Scores." *Journal of Reading* 13, no. 3 (Dec. 1969): 193–198.

Read, Charles. "Preschool Children's Knowledge of English Phonology." *Harvard Educational Review* 41 (1971): 1–34.

Read, Charles. *Children's Categorization of Speech Sounds in English.* Urbana, IL: National Council of Teachers of English, 1975.

Ruddell, Robert. "A Study of Cloze Comprehension Technique in Relation to Structurally Controlled Reading Material." *Proceedings of the International Reading Association* 9 (1964): 298–303.

Taylor, Wilson. "Cloze Procedure: A New Tool for Measuring Readability." *Journalism Quarterly* 30, (Fall 1953): 415–433.

Temple, Charles, and Jean Wallace Gillet. *Language and Literacy.* New York: HarperCollins, 1996.

Vacca, Jo Anne, Richard T. Vacca, and Mary K. Gove. *Reading and Learning to Read,* 2d ed. New York: HarperCollins, 1991.

Assessment for Internal Audiences: Periodic In-Depth Assessments

In this chapter, we continue our discussion of assessment that is designed to aid instruction, or internal assessment. Here, we will examine the kinds of periodic, in-depth assessments that teachers typically undertake in their classrooms, often at the beginning of the year and near the end to show growth or at various times during the year to diagnose areas of difficulty.

As we discussed previously, so-called *internal assessment*, which is designed to inform students, teachers, parents and building-level administrators and drive instruction, differs in important ways from so-called *external assessment*, which is typically undertaken for accountability purposes for audiences outside the school, often for school division administrators, school boards, and state boards of education. Figure 3.1 contrasts the purposes, criteria, and pragmatics of these two assessment models (from Calfee & Hiebert, 1991, p. 283).

In this chapter, we discuss informal reading inventories; functional reading levels and their meaning in everyday teaching; and informal tests of oral reading miscues, decoding, reading strategies and interests.

FIGURE 3.1 Comparison of Assessment Instruments Designed for Different Purposes

Source: Robert Calfee and Elfrieda Hiebert. "Classroom Assessment of Reading." *Handbook of Reading Research, Vol. 2.* White Plains, NY: Longman Publishers, 1991, p. 283.

ASSESSMENT DESIGNED FOR INSTRUCTION	ASSESSMENT DESIGNED FOR EXTERNAL ACCOUNTABILITY
Purpose and Source	
Teacher-designed for classroom decisions	Designed by experts for policy makers
Combines several sources of information	Stand-alone, single index
Strong link to curriculum and instruction	Independent of curriculum and instruction
Criteria	
Valid for guiding instruction	Predictive validity
Profile reliability—strengths and weaknesses	Total test reliability
Sensitive to dynamic changes in performance	Stable over time and situations
Performance is often all-or-none	Normally distributed scores
Pragmatics	
Judgmental, quick turnaround, flexible	Objective, cost and time efficient, standardized
Performance-based, "real" task	Multiple-choice, recognition
Administer whenever needed	Once-a-year, sometimes twice

LEVELS OF READING ABILITY

Parents, teachers, and students alike are concerned about reading levels, which are often linked to issues of retention, promotion, and graduation. Usually, the statements and questions that we hear about reading levels assume that a reader has one single reading level, but this is an oversimplification. Most readers who have progressed beyond beginning reading have three reading levels. Each level is appropriate for reading different kinds of texts and for different purposes.

The Independent Level

At the independent level of difficulty, students can read text *easily,* without help. Comprehension is generally excellent, and silent reading at this level of difficulty is rapid because almost all the words are recognized and understood at sight. Students rarely have to stop reading to analyze an unfamiliar word. Oral reading is generally fluent, and occasional miscues, or divergences from the written text, rarely interfere with comprehension. Independent-level reading is easy and typically enjoyable for the reader.

The Instructional Level

At the instructional level, the material is not really easy but is still *comfortable.* Students are comfortably challenged and will benefit most from instruction. Comprehension is good, but help may be needed to understand some concepts or vocabulary. Silent reading is fairly rapid, though somewhat slower than at the independent level; however, it is rapid enough to allow for good comprehension. Some word analysis is usually necessary, but most words are recognized on sight; when an unfamiliar word must be decoded, the reader can usually do this successfully within a few seconds. Oral reading is fairly smooth and accurate, and oral divergences from the written text usually make sense in the context and do not cause a loss of meaning. Occasional miscues that interrupt the flow of meaning do occur, but they are rare enough that the reader (and the listener, if the reading is oral) maintain adequate to good comprehension.

The Frustration Level

At the frustration level, the material is *too difficult* to be read successfully. In materials that represent a reader's frustration level, comprehension is poor, with major ideas missed, forgotten, or misunderstood. Both oral and silent reading are usually slow and labored, with frequent stops to analyze unknown words. Too often, attempts to figure out unfamiliar words are unsuccessful. Oral reading miscues are frequent, often causing the reader to lose the sense of what was read. Because of this difficulty, it is frustrating for students to attempt to read such material for sustained periods of time, and their efforts often fail. This level is to be avoided in instruction.

Figure 3.2 shows the characteristics of each level and some typical kinds of reading a student might do at each level.

	CHARACTERISTICS	TYPICAL READING
Independent Level: Easy	Excellent comprehension Excellent accuracy in word recognition Few words need analysis Rapid, smooth rate Very few errors of any kind	All pleasure reading All self-selected reading for information Homework, tests, seatwork, learning centers, and all other assigned work to be done alone
Instructional Level: Comfortable	Good comprehension Good accuracy in word recognition Fairly rapid rate Some word analysis needed	School textbooks and basal reader Guided classroom reading assignments Study guides and other work done with guidance Forms and applications
Frustration Level: Too hard	Poor comprehension Slow, stumbling rate Much word analysis necessary	No assigned material Reading for diagnostic purposes Self-selected material where student's interest is very high in spite of difficulty

FIGURE 3.2 Functional Reading Levels

The instructional level, at which the student is comfortable yet challenged and will benefit most from instruction, is the level that we usually mean when we refer to a student's reading level. The other two levels, however, are also very important.

At the independent level, we want students to read for pleasure, information, and enrichment. Anything that is to be read and understood independently, such as tests, homework, and independent assignments at centers, should ideally be at students' independent levels. Harder material will make it difficult for them to complete this reading without help.

We want students reading at the instructional level in materials for direct instruction such as trade books, basals, subject area textbooks, study guides, workbooks, skills activities, and worksheets that are read in class where the teacher can provide help and guidance. But to do so, we must determine what material represents the frustration level. This means that we have to have students attempt to read difficult material. Unless we explore the limits of the student's reading ability, we will not know how far he or she can go. The teacher has to see what strategies a student can use when pushed and what strategies continue to serve well. After the frustration level has been determined, a reader should never be assigned to read material that difficult. (However, students sometimes choose to read frustration level materials, as we will discuss in the next section.)

The Listening Level

Although it is not an actual reading level, there is one more level that is important because it relates to a student's reading abilities: the listening level. This is the highest grade level of text material that a student can understand when he or she listens to it being read aloud. The listening level provides an estimate of the student's present potential for reading improvement.

Most readers who have not yet reached their full potential as readers, who are still developing their reading skills, can listen to and understand text read aloud to them that they cannot yet read for themselves. This is most obvious with beginning readers, who can understand many books and kinds of text by listening to them but might not yet be able to read anything independently. As students are exposed to text by being read to and their ability to read grows, the gap between what they can understand by listening and what they can read independently begins to close. By the time they become fluent, mature readers, there might be no difference at all; that is, they can understand material as well by reading it as by listening to it. But for students who have not yet completed their development as readers, the listening level is usually higher than the instructional reading level. The listening level gives us an indication of how much their reading may be expected to advance at this point in time. We will return to consideration of the listening level later in this chapter, when we interpret informal reading inventory (IRI) findings.

The Usefulness of Grade-Equivalent Reading Levels

In the past, when almost everyone used basal readers or similar language arts materials of graded difficulty for reading instruction, the usefulness of grade-equivalent reading levels was obvious. If Tommy's instructional level was late first grade, or level 5 in his basal reader, then teachers knew that Tommy would be most appropriately placed in the level 5 book or in materials of similar, but not greater, difficulty. If Tommy had completed all the stories in his level 5 book but could not read the level 6 book comfortably, he could be placed in a "supplemental basal" or some other alternative materials until his instructional level advanced. (Many schools kept copies of either another, similar basal series or the previous edition of their current basal for this purpose.) The most common use of a student's instructional level was to place him or her in an appropriate basal reader.

Today, fewer teachers use basal readers for reading instruction, although it has been estimated that "from 80% to 90% of the children in U.S. schools learn to read in the context of basal reading programs" (Hoffman et al., 1998, p. 171). Many teachers use basals occasionally, in conjunction with other nonbasal materials, picking and choosing particular stories, articles, or poems to supplement a thematic unit or an author study. Others use trade books and novels entirely, more often at the middle and upper elementary grades. Do teachers still need to know about students' reading levels?

There is still usefulness in the concept of reading levels, even for teachers who haven't touched a basal reader in years, because the concept of grade-equivalent reading levels is not limited only to basals. Many teachers still form reading groups of children with similar reading abilities, although today, children are much less likely to stay in the same group all year than they were in the past. All the same, many teachers use reading levels to decide, for example, which students will read which of that grade level's required novels for the year or in what order they will tackle them.

Trade books are still subjected to readability studies, and approximate reading levels are usually indicated somewhere on the back cover. Textbooks and classroom materials in subject areas such as social studies, science, and health still have grade levels assigned to them. Parents still want to know whether their children can read as well as others in the same grade. When students receive special help in reading, their present reading levels are among the first information required to document their progress.

It is certainly true that children who are functioning at a particular instructional reading level differ widely in the materials that they can and do successfully read. The importance of a reader's interest in particular materials or topics cannot be overemphasized. We all know of many examples of students successfully and enjoyably reading materials thought to be too hard for them just because they are fascinated by the topic.

But while Jennifer might choose Beverly Cleary novels because all her friends love them, and so plow through one after another, we cannot count on her motivation to expand to other novels of the same level of difficulty. Likewise, Wayne might read anything he can get his hands on about hunting, his particular passion, but be stumped by material of similar difficulty on other topics. In the classic *Hooked on Books*, Daniel Fader (1976) described a marginally literate incarcerated teenager who doggedly struggled all the way through *The Scarlet Letter* because he had heard it was about what he called "a whore."

Students might self-select very difficult materials because of interest in the topic or author but might not be able to deal with assigned materials that are just as difficult. We should not discourage them from self-selecting hard books, but we need to know what they can read effectively for the many assigned materials that we use. In most classrooms, much of what children read is still teacher-selected. Reading and reading instruction are not limited to the language arts block but extend throughout the school day and across many topics and genres.

INFORMAL READING INVENTORIES

An *informal reading inventory* (IRI) consists of text passages corresponding in difficulty to literature and textbook materials at grade levels from primer through secondary school and sets of questions for each passage that are intended to test readers' comprehension and recall after reading. Passages are arranged in order of difficulty from easiest (primer and primary grades) to hardest (usually ninth grade or beyond). There are usually at least three different but relatively equivalent passages at each grade level. IRIs usually also contain a word recognition inventory, lists of individual words arranged in levels like those of the reading passages. In addition, many commercial IRIs have supplementary tests such as phonics inventories, cloze tests, and spelling inventories.

Figures 3.3 and 3.4 show a student page and corresponding examiner's pages from a commercial IRI.

Many basal reading and language arts series provide an IRI to be used for placement within that series and for diagnostic use. There are also a number of commercial IRIs, most of them essentially similar; a list of those follows at the end of the next section.

Language arts series IRIs have passages that are selected from that series. Commercial IRIs have passages that are either selected from different sources or specially written for the test. Usually, passages are 50–250 words long, and they can be read comfortably in a few minutes. An IRI consists of a student's copy of the reading passages and an examiner's copy of the instrument. The examiner's copy contains the reading passages and the corresponding comprehension questions with their correct answers. The example in Figure 3.4 also includes a score sheet for unaided retellings.

So that an examiner can assess oral and silent reading separately, a good IRI should have two or more different passages at each grade level. The passages should be from different stories but comparable in difficulty. To be most useful in testing children of various abilities and ages, the grade levels that are represented should range from preprimer or primer through at least sixth-grade text, preferably through ninth- or even twelfth-grade material.

Like all assessment devices, IRIs have both advantages and disadvantages. They offer the teacher a complete set of word lists, passages, and questions already compiled and ready to reproduce and use. They feature multiple forms at each grade level, which allow the teacher to assess oral and silent reading or to retest later with new material. They are inexpensive and widely available.

They do have shortcomings, however. IRIs that accompany a basal reading series are made up of passages from that series, so students who are being tested might have previously read one or more of the stories from which the passages came. Therefore, their comprehension scores on those passages might be falsely inflated. Administrators sometimes "reserve" those passages, meaning that teachers are told to skip those stories in the basals, but students might have read them on their own or in another school or district.

Commercial IRIs have passages that are specially written to conform to readability levels or passages selected from sources other than basal readers, but the quality of such passages varies widely. If the test passages are very short, this will severely limit the number of ideas available to the reader and the number of questions that can be asked.

Particularly at the lower levels, some IRI passages are written in short, stilted sentences that don't sound much like real language. Some carry on the same story from passage to passage, making it difficult to omit the lower levels or move from a higher to a lower level during administration. Some are taken from the middle of a story, but no introduction is provided to help the reader understand what con-

Cats: Lions and Tigers in Your House

House cats, lions, and tigers are part of the same family. When animals are part of the same family, they are alike in many ways. House cats are like lions and tigers in many ways, too. When kittens are first born, they drink milk from their mothers. Lions and tigers drink milk from their mothers, too. When kittens are born, they have claws, just like big cats. Claws are used by lions, tigers, and kittens to help them keep away enemies. As kittens get bigger, they learn to hunt from their mother. House cats hunt in the same way that lions and tigers do. They hide and lie very still. When the animal they are hunting comes close, they jump on it and grab it by the back of the neck. Cats kill other animals by shaking them and breaking their necks.

Lions, tigers, and house cats show when they are afraid in the same ways, too. Their fur puffs up, making them look bigger. They hiss and spit, too. Those are their ways of saying, "I'm afraid, don't come closer."

A cat's tongue has many uses. Because it is rough with little bumps on it, it can be used as a spoon. A cat drinks milk by lapping it. Because of the bumps the milk stays on the tongue until the cat can swallow it. If you feel the top of a cat's tongue, it is rough. This makes the tongue good for brushing the cat's hair. Lions and tigers clean themselves with their tongues just like house cats do.

FIGURE 3.3   Commercial IRI Pupil Page

Source: Lauren, Leslie, and JoAnne Caldwell. *Qualitative Reading Inventory II.* New York: HarperCollins, 1995, p. 167.

Level: Three

Expository

Concept Questions:

What is the cat family?

_____

_____

_____ (3-2-1-0)

How do cats protect themselves?

_____

_____

_____ (3-2-1-0)

What does a cat's tongue look like?

_____

_____

_____ (3-2-1-0)

What are cat sounds?

_____

_____

_____ (3-2-1-0)

Score: _____ /12 = _____ %

_____ FAM _____ UNFAM

Prediction:

_____

_____

_____

Cats: Lions and Tigers in Your House

House cats, lions, and tigers are part of the same family. When animals are part of the same family, they are alike in many ways. House cats are like lions and tigers in many ways, too. When kittens are first born, they drink milk from their mothers. Lions and tigers drink milk from their mothers, too. When kittens are born, they have claws just like big cats. Claws are used by lions, tigers, and kittens to help them keep away enemies. As kittens get bigger, they learn to hunt from their mother. House cats hunt in the same way that lions and tigers do. They hide and lie very still. When the animal they are hunting comes close, they jump on it and grab it by the back of the neck. Cats kill other animals by shaking them and breaking their necks.

Lions, tigers, and house cats show when they are afraid in the same ways, too. Their fur puffs up, making them look bigger. They hiss and spit, too. Those are their ways of saying, "I'm afraid, don't come closer."

A cat's tongue has many uses. Because it is rough with little bumps on it, it can be used as a spoon. A cat drinks milk by lapping it. Because of the bumps the milk stays on the tongue until the cat can swallow it. If you feel the top of a cat's tongue, it is

FIGURE 3.4 Commercial IRI Examiner's Pages

Source: Lauren, Leslie, and JoAnne Caldwell. *Qualitative Reading Inventory II.* New York: HarperCollins, 1995, pp. 180–182.

tent preceded the passage. Some have fairly interesting passages but use factual recall questions almost exclusively while ignoring other aspects of comprehension.

When considering which IRI to use, use judgment and care in evaluating these instruments. The following section will help you to consider the most important aspects of commercial IRIs.

Level: Three

rough. This makes the <u>tongue</u> good for brushing the cat's hair. Lions and tigers clean themselves with their <u>tongues</u> just like house cats do. (261 words)

Number of Total Miscues
(Total Accuracy): _____

Number of Meaning Change Miscues
(Total Acceptability): _____

Total Accuracy		Total Acceptability	
0–6 miscues	_____ Independent	_____ 0–6 miscues	
7–27 miscues	_____ Instructional	_____ 7–14 miscues	
28+ miscues	_____ Frustration	_____ 15+ miscues	

Rate: 261 x 60/_____ seconds = _____ WPM

Retelling Scoring Sheet for Cats: Lions and Tigers in Your House

Main Idea

____ Cats,
____ lions,
____ and tigers
____ are part of the same family.
____ They are alike
____ in many ways.

Details

____ When kittens are first born,
____ they drink milk
____ from their mothers.
____ Lions
____ and tigers
____ drink milk
____ from their mothers.
____ Kittens have claws.

____ Lions,
____ tigers,
____ and kittens use claws
____ to keep away enemies.
____ Cats hunt
____ in the same way
____ that lions
____ and tigers do.
____ They jump on the animal
____ and grab it
____ by the neck.
____ Cats kill animals
____ by breaking their necks.
____ When lions,
____ tigers,
____ and cats are afraid,
____ their fur puffs up.
____ They hiss
____ and spit.
____ Because a cat's tongue is rough
____ with bumps,
____ it can be used
____ as a spoon.
____ A cat drinks milk
____ by lapping it.
____ Because of the bumps,
____ the milk stays
____ on the tongue
____ until the cat can swallow it.
____ Lions
____ and tigers clean themselves
____ with their tongues
____ just like cats.

Other ideas recalled, including inferences

_____

FIGURE 3.4 *(continued)*

Selecting a Commercial or Language Arts Series IRI

Commercial IRIs include the following:

Bader, Lois A. *Bader Reading and Language Inventory*, 3d ed. Upper Saddle River, NJ: Prentice Hall, 1997.

Burns, Paul C., and Betty D. Roe. *Informal Reading Inventory*, 4th ed. Boston, MA: Houghton Mifflin, 1992.

Ekwall, Hayward E., and James L. Shanker. *Ekwall-Shanker Reading Inventory,* 3d ed. Boston: Allyn & Bacon, 1993.

Level: Three

Questions for
Cats: Lions and Tigers in Your House

1. What is this passage mostly about?
   Implicit: that cats, lions, and tigers are alike in many ways

2. How are lions, tigers, and cats alike?
   Explicit: any one of the ways presented in the story: milk from their mothers as babies; they have claws; the way they hunt; the way they show fear; the uses of their tongues

3. What is another way that lions, tigers, and cats are alike?
   Explicit: any other of the above responses

4. What is still another way that lions, tigers, and cats are alike?
   Explicit: any other of the above responses

5. What do you think a cat would do if you cornered it?
   Implicit: it would hiss, spit, or puff up

6. Why is it important for cats to have claws when they're born?
   Implicit: for protection from their enemies

7. Why is the top of a cat's tongue rough?
   Implicit: because of the bumps on it; or so it can drink

8. Why doesn't milk fall off a cat's tongue?
   Explicit: because of the bumps which make cups on the tongue

---

Number Correct Explicit: _____

Number Correct Implicit: _____

Total: _____

_____ Independent: 8 correct

_____ Instructional: 6–7 correct

_____ Frustration: 0–5 correct

FIGURE 3.4 *(continued)*

Flynt, E. Sutton, and Robert B. Cooter. *Flynt-Cooter Reading Inventory for the Classroom,* 3d ed. Upper Saddle River, NJ: Prentice Hall, 1997.

Johns, Jerry L. *Secondary and College Reading Inventory.* Dubuque, IA: Kendall/Hunt, 1988.

Johns, Jerry L. *Basic Reading Inventory,* 5th ed. Dubuque, IA: Kendall/Hunt, 1997.

Leslie, Lauren, and Joanne Caldwell. *Qualitative Reading Inventory II.* New York: Addison Wesley Longman, 1995.

Manzo, Anthony V., Ula C. Manzo, and Michael C. McKenna. *Informal Reading-Thinking Inventory.* New York: Harcourt Brace College Publishers, 1994.

Silvaroli, Nicholas J. *Classroom Reading Inventory*, 8th ed. Dubuque, IA: Brown and Benchmark, 1996.

Stieglitz, Ezra L. *Stieglitz Informal Reading Inventory*, 2d ed. Boston: Allyn & Bacon, 1997.

Woods, Mary Lynn, and Alden J. Moe. *Analytical Reading Inventory*, 5th ed. Columbus, OH: Merrill, 1995.

To choose the best IRI for your use, you must examine and compare several, then select the one you believe has the most strengths and will serve your diagnostic needs best.

We believe that the following aspects are of critical importance in choosing an IRI:

1. literary quality of reading passages;
2. clarity and relevance of questions;
3. balance of question types, including a range of comprehension skills and both explicit and implicit questions;
4. convenient format;
5. complete instructions, including examples;
6. balanced use of both narrative and expository texts, ideally featuring use of both types at each level; and
7. some means of assessing readers' prior knowledge of topics before passages are read for assessment.

Literary Quality of Passages

The heart of an IRI is the reading passages. When you consider an IRI, read the passages. Are they generally interesting, with topics that many children will likely know something about and be interested in? We cannot expect good comprehension of dull text.

Does the language sound natural? When there is dialogue, do the speakers sound like real people? Are descriptive passages colorful and memorable? At the upper levels and in nonfiction passages, is the language clear and straightforward? Are sequences and cause-and-effect relationships presented clearly? Are the words and ideas in the passages appropriate for the grade levels and ages for which they are intended? In the primary levels, is some story or sequence of events present? If there are illustrations, are they necessary to an understanding of the passages? Keep in mind that all information should be presented in the text, not in the illustrations.

You might not expect brilliant prose in an IRI, but do look for one that has consistently interesting, clearly written, straightforward passages with natural-sounding dialogue, colorful descriptions, and topics that a wide range of students can recognize and understand. Look for passages that are complete in themselves; that is, they should not sound like paragraphs taken from the middle of a story with preceding material omitted. This is an important consideration in IRIs that accompany basal readers, since the reading passages have been taken from basal stories, and they may be only part of a longer story.

Quality of Questions

Most often, the questions that we ask are the primary means we have of assessing comprehension. (Retelling, or spontaneously recalling what was read, is another useful means that will be described later.) If the IRI questions that we use are confusing, picky, or limited in the thinking skills they require, we will not get an accurate picture of the reader's comprehension. To get good answers, we must ask good questions.

Good questions should be clear and simple, should follow the organization of the passage, should tap the most important information conveyed, should call on a variety of comprehension skills, and should be answerable only after reading, not by general knowledge, prior experience, or illustrations.

Poor IRI questions can be answered *before* the reader reads the passage, so they do not assess reading comprehension but rather general knowledge. For example, in a fifth-grade passage about trash disposal, one question is, "Name one product that can be recycled." Many children can answer this question from general knowledge or personal experience without reading the passage. A better question would be "Name something that can be recycled *that was mentioned in this passage.*" In one primer-level passage, a commercial IRI asks, "What is a sidewalk?" Most children could answer this without reading the passage.

Good questions should require extended responses (not one-word answers), should call on both convergent and divergent thinking, and should not be answerable by yes or no without explanation or elaboration. They should not be repetitious.

As in the "sidewalk" example above, vocabulary questions are often very poorly worded. They should feature passage-based contexts for the words; for example, "In the sentence *Jim put the package on the bar*, what did *bar* mean?" is a better question than "What does *bar* mean in this story?" or, worse, "What is a *bar?*"

Vocabulary questions should require readers to use context to figure out the meaning of a word or phrase; this means that the most common meaning of a word might not make the best question. The meaning of the word or phrase *must* be indicated by the surrounding context.

IRI comprehension questions should not call for the reader's personal opinion or experience or for answers that cannot be evaluated objectively. The following are examples of such questions:

"Would you like to have a dog like Sandy?"

"What is something you are afraid of?"

"What do you think might happen in the next part of the story?"

There is nothing wrong with questions like these *in instruction,* but they are not appropriate testing questions. How would you score each of the questions above? Could anyone get one of them "wrong"? If not, then the question does not require comprehension of the reading passage to answer. Asking for children's opinions, personal experiences, and predictions is good pedagogy, but it does not necessarily make for good assessment of reading comprehension.

Format and Instructions

For you to assess oral and silent reading comprehension separately, the IRI that you use should have *at least* three different passages of equivalent length and difficulty for each level. Most commercial IRIs have three to six equivalent forms, allowing you to use alternate passages for retesting or for assessing listening comprehension. The instrument's format should make it easy for you to locate and to use the appropriate passages and questions during the testing.

Are the different forms and grade levels clearly labeled and easy to locate? Are pupil pages coded in some way so that the grade level of the passage is not apparent to the student? Is a record or summary sheet provided to help you summarize your observations, findings, and conclusions?

Are the directions for administering the IRI clear and concise? Are there directions for interpreting findings? Are there examples of students' responses for you to study and practice interpreting?

If your basal reading series includes an IRI, you should examine it critically before you use it, just as you would if you were choosing a commercial IRI. Basal series IRIs have an advantage in that they closely match the kind of text students read every day *if* what students read mostly is basal material. This is because the IRI passages are usually taken directly from the reading books. However, if the students who are being tested have previously read the material, their comprehension might be falsely inflated. And if students are reading mostly trade books, what they actually read might be considerably harder or easier than the IRI passages for that grade. The ideal basal IRI would feature test passages that are very similar to the text material in difficulty, quality of writing, and topical interest but not taken directly from the basal readers.

Types of Text in Informal Reading Inventories

Some commercial IRIs are made up entirely or primarily of fiction passages. However, students must read both fiction and nonfiction, or narrative and expository, texts effectively. A good IRI will have a balance of both narrative and expository material at each level. This allows us to systematically assess a student's reading of both these types of texts.

It is not sufficient for an IRI to include both types of text but have only fiction selections at some levels while including nonfiction at other levels. (It is not unusual to see a preponderance of fiction passages at the primary levels and a preponderance of nonfiction at the upper levels.) A good IRI will have both fiction and nonfiction passages, equivalent in difficulty and length, at each level.

The Role of Prior Knowledge in Comprehension

Likewise, some means of assessing whether a reader has sufficient prior knowledge of a topic to read a passage with adequate comprehension is a very useful feature. As we know, what a reader already knows about a topic has a significant effect on what the reader might understand and remember from reading and on readers' ability to locate information in text (e.g., Symons & Pressley, 1993). Indeed,

> the crucial role of prior information in text comprehension has become conventional wisdom in the reading field. This conventional wisdom is supported by a considerable body of instructional research demonstrating the effectiveness of activating and building students' prior knowledge before reading a text. (Dole et al., 1996, p. 62)

In the classroom, helping students to recall and organize what they already know before reading is quite common and is considered good pedagogy, but it is rare in assessment. But when we are attempting to determine how well a reader comprehends what is read and are trying to do so in as authentic a way as we can, doesn't it make sense to at least attempt to determine what, if anything, a student already knows about a topic before reading material for assessment purposes? This is an example of how what we know about teaching and learning does not always extend into our assessment methods. Few tests take readers' prior knowledge into account, but Leslie and Caldwell's *Qualitative Reading Inventory II* (1995) is an example of a commercial IRI that includes this feature for every passage.

Before reading, the examiner asks the reader to tell something about two or three key terms or concepts from the passage and notes on the examiner's page whether the student knows *a lot*, *some*, *a little*, or *nothing* about the term or concept. Points are given for the completeness of the answer:

- A precise answer gets 3 points. (Example: *Why do people work? To earn money so they can buy stuff.*)
- An example, specific attribute, or function gets 2 points. (Example: *Where do people work? At hospitals. What is a bear? It's furry and it eats blueberries.*)
- A general association or solely personal association gets 1 point. (Example: *What is a field trip? We went on a field trip in first grade.*)
- An unconnected or clearly incorrect response gets no points.

The passage topic is then rated as familiar or unfamiliar before it is read, and, if it is unfamiliar, a different passage is substituted.

For example, before reading *Cats: Lions and Tigers in Your Home* (Figure 3.4 on pages 91–93), the reader is asked to answer these prior knowledge questions:

- What is the cat family?
- How do cats protect themselves?
- What does a cat's tongue look like?
- What are cat sounds?

Responses are noted in the box labeled "Concept Questions" at the top of Figure 3.4. This quick assessment of prior knowledge before reading a passage requires time and effort, but in the long run, it prevents us from attempting to assess readers' comprehension of passages they know little or nothing about before they start.

The following sources might provide more information about informal reading inventories and evaluating commercial IRIs:

Arno, Kevin S. "Test Review: Burns/Roe Informal Reading Inventory." *Journal of Reading* 33, no. 6 (March 1990): 470–471.

Cheek, Earl H., Jr. "Selecting Appropriate Informal Reading Assessment Procedures." *Middle School Journal* 24, no. 1 (September 1992): 33–36.

Johns, Jerry L., & Anne Marie Magliari. "Informal Reading Inventories: Are the Betts Criteria the Best Criteria?" *Reading Improvement* 26, no. 2 (Summer 1989): 124–132.

Kinney, Martha A., and Ann L. Harry. "An Informal Inventory for Adolescents That Assesses the Reader, the Text and the Task." *Journal of Reading* 34, no. 8 (May 1991): 643–647.

Martin-Rehrmann, James. "Test Review: Analytic Reading Inventory (ARI), Fourth Edition." *Journal of Reading* 33, no. 7 (April 1990): 564–565.

Michel, Pamela A. "Test Review: Secondary and College Reading Inventory." *Journal of Reading* 33, no. 4 (January 1990): 308–310.

Pikulski, John J. "Informal Reading Inventories." *The Reading Teacher* 43, no. 7 (March 1990): 514–516.

Robinson, Richard. "An Interview with Dr. Jerry L. Johns (Leaders in Reading Research and Instruction Series)." *Reading Psychology* 11, no. 4 (1990): 335–346.

Siedow, Mary Dunn. "Informal Assessment of Older Readers' Abilities." *Forum for Reading* 22, no. 2 (Spring–Summer 1991): 12–18.

Smith, Lawrence L., and C. Rosanne Joyner. "Comparing Recreational Reading Levels with Reading Levels from an Informal Reading Inventory." *Reading Horizons* 30, no. 4 (Summer 1990): 293–299.

Tindal, Gerald, & Douglas Marston. "Technical Adequacy of Alternative Reading Measures as Performance Assessments." *Exceptionality* 6, no. 4 (1996): 201–230.

Valencia, Shiela W. "Authentic Classroom Assessment of Early Reading: Alternatives to Standardized Tests." *Preventing School Failure* 41, no. 2 (Winter 1997): 63–70.

Wepner, Shelley B. "On the Cutting Edge with Computerized Assessment." *Journal of Reading* 35, no. 1 (September 1991): 62–65.

ADMINISTERING AN INFORMAL READING INVENTORY

Giving an IRI takes roughly 30–50 minutes, but how long it takes depends on how well the student reads, how many passages are read, and how many parts of the IRI are used. It does *not* all have to be done at one sitting. If you are giving an IRI in class during regular instruction time, break up the testing into a number of short sittings, with the student reading one or two passages at a time and finishing the IRI over a period of several days. This allows you to give an individual test without taking too much time away from other students or activities. You will need a student copy of the passages, an examiner's copy for recording each student's responses, pencils, and a stopwatch for timing the reading.

Where to Start

One of the first questions inexperienced IRI users ask is "Where should I begin testing?" It would certainly be uneconomical to begin at the lowest level and proceed upward until the frustration level was reached. Where to begin depends in part on your purpose for giving the IRI. If you are testing to see whether material at a particular level of difficulty would be comfortable reading, begin there. If the student is successful, you may proceed to higher levels or stop. If the student is unsuccessful, you should drop down to an easier level.

Some experts advocate giving the word recognition test, graded lists of words in isolation, as a way of determining where to start. Administration procedures for the word lists are included in the section of the chapter entitled "Assessing Recognition of Words in Isolation." In essence, the word lists are given first, and the examiner begins giving the reading passages at the level at which the reader began to miss more than 90% of the words on the list.

In our experience, a drawback to this procedure is that many students can recognize words with good accuracy but cannot comprehend text material at the same level of difficulty. So we would end up starting the IRI considerably above the reader's real instructional level. For that reason, we usually don't give the word recognition inventory until after we have assessed oral reading, reading comprehension, and listening comprehension.

For this discussion, we'll assume that you intend to administer the word lists later. Let's say that a new child has just been enrolled in your third-grade class. Records from his previous school can take some time to arrive; even with them, you wish to form your own best judgment of his instructional level so that he can be appropriately placed immediately. So your first, most general question might be, "Is he instructional at grade level?" You begin the IRI with a third-grade passage. His oral reading is fairly fluent and largely correct, with some miscues that mostly make sense. He answers seven of nine comprehension questions correctly. He also reads another third-grade passage silently within a reasonable length of time and again answers most of the questions accurately. You decide that third-grade material is comfortable for him, a good instructional level. Your first diagnostic question has been answered. You can, for the time being, stop giving the IRI and place him on a temporary basis in a group that is reading at grade level, whether that be in a basal, trade books, or whatever.

However, you still don't know several things: Is his instructional level significantly above grade level? What is his approximate listening level? Later, perhaps in the next week or so, you will want to continue IRI testing with this student, determining his *independent level* by administering passages below his instructional level, his *frustration level,* by continuing to give successively harder passages until the frustration level is reached, and his *listening level,* by reading successively harder passages to him until he can no longer answer questions about what he has listened to. (These procedures are detailed in the sections to follow.)

Your purpose for testing a child might not be to determine whether or not he or she is instructional at grade level, but more generally to determine just what his or her instructional level is. In this case, begin one or two grade levels below the student's present grade. For primary graders, begin at primer or first grade. If the student is not reading easily and experiencing immediate success at that level, drop back to lower levels. If the first passage seems easy, go on to higher levels.

Let's return for the moment to our example of the new student in your class. Let's say that your first diagnostic question is not, "Is he instructional at third grade?" but rather, "What is this child's instructional level?" You can start with third-grade passages, or you can begin lower. Let's say that you begin with a second-grade passage. His oral reading is rapid, expressive, and accurate, and his comprehension is excellent; he answers all questions correctly and even supplies details that are not called for in the answers. Second grade seems like his independent level, doesn't it? You'll proceed upward then; you could skip the second-grade silent passage for the moment and go on to third grade or even skip third and go to fourth if you thought his reading was that strong.

But let's change the scenario a bit: When he reads the second-grade passage, he struggles with it, reading fairly slowly with numerous miscues, many of which don't make any sense. In this case, of course, you will want to move *down*, to first-grade passages and lower if necessary, until you determine a level that is comfortable and successful for him. With an IRI, you can move in either direction, or even skip a level and come back to it later if necessary, with ease.

Where to Stop

The next big question inexperienced IRI users generally ask is, "When should I stop testing?" Some commercial IRIs, such as the *Qualitative Reading Inventory II*, feature a scoring key after each passage that allows you to determine whether the passage was at the reader's independent, instructional, or frustration level without having to figure any percentages.

For example, look at Figure 3.4 on pp. 91–93 again. After the oral reading passage, you'll see a box that tells you how many miscues may be made for the passage to fall within each reading level; in this case, up to six miscues represent an independent level, from seven to twenty-seven miscues represent the instructional level, and more than twenty-eight miscues represent the frustration level. (We'll explain the difference between *total accuracy* and *total acceptability* in a section to follow; for now, *total accuracy* means the total number of miscues, regardless of whether or not they made sense.)

After the comprehension questions for this passage, you'll see another box into which you enter the number of comprehension questions the reader answered correctly, regardless of their type. In this example, answering all eight questions correctly indicates the independent level, six or seven correct answers indicate the instructional level, and five or fewer correct answers indicate the frustration level.

If the IRI that you're using does not contain such a feature, you will have to quickly figure the percentage of accuracy for the comprehension questions on the spot. When the reader's comprehension score reaches about 50%, the frustration level has been reached. (We'll discuss scoring procedures in more detail in a section to follow.)

When the reader's responses indicate that the grade level just read was clearly at his or her frustration level, you should stop the reading portion of the testing. If there is any ambiguity, any doubt in your mind that the reader really cannot go any farther, then another level may be given then or in another sitting. When the reader's frustration level has been reached, the listening comprehension portion of the assessment begins. This procedure will be detailed in the section "Assessing Listening Comprehension" later in this chapter.

Step-by-Step Administration

In this section, we'll go back over the general procedures that we described above and fill in the details.

1. Begin the IRI at a level at which you think the student will be able to read easily. (If you overestimated, you can drop back to lower levels.) Or you might give the word recognition inventory (WRI) first to find out where to begin the IRI. This practice is discussed in the section "Analyzing Word Recognition in Isolation" later in this chapter.

2. For each passage, assess the student's prior knowledge of the topic by asking the prereading concept questions or by asking the student to tell you something about the topic or explain two or three key terms or concepts. If the student knows little or nothing about the topic of the passage, use a different passage at the same difficulty level.

3. At each level tested, give the oral reading passage first. Show the student where to begin reading and where to stop and say, "Please read this passage out loud to me. When you are finished, close the book and I will ask you some questions about what you have read."

4. Follow the reading on your copy and carefully mark down the responses that diverge from the text. These divergent responses, or *miscues,* happen naturally when we read aloud. The miscues will be analyzed later to provide detailed information about the reader's use of phonic and structural analysis, syntax, and word meanings during oral reading. The marks that are used for oral reading miscues are listed and discussed in the section "Marking Oral Reading Miscues" later in this chapter.

5. When the oral reading is completed and the passage is covered or removed, ask the comprehension questions. Jot down key words or phrases from the student's answers. Don't hesitate to probe for more information or ask a student to explain or justify an answer. (If you change the wording of a question, or the order of questions asked, note it on the examiner's page.)

6. Give the silent reading passage for that level. Show the student where to begin and stop reading silently. Remove or cover the passage when the reader is finished. Then ask the comprehension questions for that passage as before.

7. If the student answered 50 percent or more of the comprehension questions correctly or is within the instructional-level criteria for the test you're using, proceed to the next level. In general, it's best to test both oral and silent reading at each level, but not always. If comprehension scores following oral reading are low but comprehension after silent reading is still above 50 percent, discontinue the oral reading but continue silent reading at higher levels until these scores also drop below 50 percent and remain there. If the student shows poor silent comprehension but oral comprehension scores are still above 50 percent, discontinue the silent reading but continue oral reading. Discontinue the reading portion of the IRI when both oral and silent reading comprehension have fallen to the frustration level. If you're not sure, administer one more level.

Reinspection and Comprehension

Most often, readers' comprehension of IRI passages is assessed by asking comprehension questions and by expecting *unaided recall,* that is, answering without looking back to the passage. Most IRI directions tell you to cover or remove the passage after reading so that student can't look back at it. Several problems are inherent in this approach:

- When *reinspection* (looking back to the passage) is not allowed, both recall and comprehension are being tested. Readers might comprehend but fail to recall information, resulting in our underestimating their comprehension (Baker and Stein, 1981).

■ Readers might fail to include information in a response because, to the reader, it appeared obvious, redundant, or secondary to other information. Reinspection tends to encourage more complete answers.

■ Recall without reinspection is more a test-taking skill than an everyday reading strategy. In classroom reading, students usually discuss material and answer questions with the material before them rather than with books closed. In real, everyday reading, we are typically able to look back at, or reread portions of, material we did not understand. (Think about everyday reading tasks such as reading a computer manual, a complicated recipe, or a Tom Clancy novel. How would these tasks be different if we had to understand and remember everything in only one reading and were not allowed to go back?)

When we do not allow readers to reinspect an IRI passage when they answer questions, we place an unreasonably heavy burden on the process of recall and short-term memory (Rubenstein et al., 1988). Yet most IRI directions clearly state that students should not reinspect except when they are specifically asked to do so in a question assessing their locational skills (e.g., *Find and read me the sentence that tells you the goldfish was happy.*)

Therefore, we must face the question of whether we are testing reading comprehension, which surely involves memory but involves other factors as well, or whether we are instead testing the reader's short-term memory. One of our reasons for using an informal reading inventory was to assess students' reading in as natural a way as possible. But disallowing reinspection appears to run counter to what people really do when they read.

Reinspection can significantly affect students' ability to answer comprehension questions on IRIs. This particularly seems to affect poorer readers and to help all readers effectively deal with inferential questions (Cardarelli, 1988; Kender and Rubenstein, 1977; Rubenstein et al., 1988). We agree with these and other writers who have urged that standard IRI procedures be changed to allow students to reinspect passages if they need to when answering inferential and higher-level comprehension questions.

The issue of whether or not to allow reinspection is an important one, and you can incorporate reinspection fairly easily into standard IRI administration. To do so, you should direct the reader to look back to the passage and locate some specific information after the retelling and questioning.

Some commercial IRIs include so-called reinspection items in the comprehension questions, but many do not. In this case, it is a simple procedure to direct the reader to "Look back and find the place where it says that . . ." or the like, noting whether the reader is able to scan for the desired information or must begin reading all over again and whether or not the information can be located. One reinspection item per reading passage is probably enough. If the IRI that you're using doesn't have such items, you might want to add one to each passage, adjusting the scoring criteria accordingly.

Retelling and Comprehension

Another issue involves the use of questions alone, rather than allowing students to *retell*, or recall in their own words, what they remember from passages. By the very act of asking questions, we shape students' comprehension; questions provide clues to what we believe is important for readers to remember and include in their answers. Because of this, an effective way to learn more about students' comprehension is to ask them to retell what they have read and either record what each student tells you or use a checklist of all of the information in a passage, allowing the student to use his or her own words in recalling these items. Retelling should be done *before* comprehension questions are asked.

Some commercial IRIs have incorporated retellings into their comprehension assessment. As we mentioned previously, Figure 3.4 shows an examiner's page from one that does. You will see that both a checklist for retelling and a set of questions are included for each passage. Students are first asked to retell the passage without prompting or probes, before questions are asked.

Synonyms and paraphrases are acceptable; readers are not expected to recall verbatim, and few do. The examiner decides whether the retelling matches the information in the passage. Information that is recalled may be checked off on the list, or items may be numbered in the order in which the reader recalled them. The latter method helps the examiner to determine whether the reader recalled information in roughly the same order as it occurred in the passage or whether the retelling was not sequentially ordered. Information that is included in a retelling but was not in the passage may be noted as well.

Retellings are not scored quantitatively, but rather are judged globally and subjectively based on the sheer number of ideas recalled. Retellings may be informally evaluated for completeness, accuracy, and inclusion of the most important information or ideas in the passage. These judgments contribute to our diagnosis and implications for instruction, although they are not included in determining overall reading levels.

If you wish to assess readers' unaided recall by using retellings, an IRI that features a retelling checklist for each passage will make the job easier. However, if you prefer to use an IRI that does not have this feature, there are several ways to incorporate retelling.

- The easiest procedure is to listen to the reader retell the passage without prompting, then make an evaluative note right then about the completeness of the retelling. Examples of such comments might be, *"Recalled most passage details in correct order," "Retelling fairly complete but haphazard, in jumbled order,"* or *"Very sketchy retelling, included only beginning and ending."* This gives you the least information; you don't have a record of what was recalled or in what order, and your subjective judgment of a complete or sketchy recall might differ considerably from someone else's.
- More effort is required to jot down key bits of information as the reader recalls them. This will give you a record of the recall, but you can quickly get bogged down, and you'll interfere with the reader's recall if you ask him or her to slow down!

■ The most complete way is the most time-consuming, at least at the out-set—that is, to construct a recall checklist for each passage, like the one shown in Figure 3.4. It can be typed, duplicated, and stapled into each examiner's copy of the IRI. This tedious job is ideally undertaken by a team of users, dividing the labor. The best thing about this method is that it has to be done only once.

Marking Oral Reading Miscues

While the student is reading aloud, you will mark all of the oral divergences from the text, or *miscues*, on your copy of the passage. Miscues are important reading behaviors and are considered in two ways: They are *counted* to determine the reader's degree of oral reading accuracy and *analyzed* to determine what word attack strategies the reader used during the oral reading.

Miscues include

■ *substitutions* of real or nonsense words,
■ *insertions* of extra words,
■ *omissions* of whole words or phrases,
■ *corrections* made by the reader either at the time the miscue occurred or later during the reading,
■ *words provided* by the examiner, and
■ *reversals* of word order.

Very long *pauses* and *repetitions* of words or phrases may also be marked but are not counted as errors.

Box 3.1 contains a simple coding system that will allow you to record all miscues accurately. Most commercial and reading series IRIs have a suggested system for marking miscues; these are usually very similar. There might be small differences. For example, some systems show self-corrections marked with a check; some with the letters SC and a line showing which part of the word, phrase, or sentence was corrected; and some with a C in a circle. All these marks mean the same thing. Small differences are unimportant, but it is important to be able to read what another examiner has marked. It's best if everyone uses the same system, but if everyone using IRIs in your school or team doesn't use the same marks, be sure that you are familiar with the variations.

Figure 3.5 shows a sample passage with miscues marked.

Assessing Listening Comprehension

When the student can answer correctly only about half of the questions for a passage, functional reading has broken down. One very important aspect remains to be tested, however: the student's listening comprehension. As we discussed earlier in this chapter, the listening level, the highest level of text a reader can comprehend when listening to another read aloud, provides a rough estimate of one's potential for reading improvement. It helps us to form reasonable expectations for growth in reading.

A SYSTEM FOR MARKETING ORAL READING MISCUES

BOX 3.1

1. *Substitution of a word or phrase:* the student's word written over a word in text

   The doll fell from the shelf. *(dog written over doll)*

2. *Insertion of a word not in text:* a word written in over a caret or small arrow

   The doll fell from the shelf. *(down written over caret)*

3. *Omission of a word or phrase:* the omitted elemented circled

   The (big) dog ran away.

4. *A word given by the examiner:* parentheses placed around that word

   The climbers were assisted by (Sherpa) tribesmen.

5. *Miscue spontaneously corrected by the reader:* check mark next to original coding

   The big dog ran away. *(doll ✔ written over dog)*

   or © next to original coding

   The big dog ran away. *(doll © written over dog)*

   or sc with line showing corrected element

   The big dog ran away. *(doll sc written over dog)*

6. *Reversal of order of words:* proofreader's symbol of inversion used

   "Let's go," shouted Sally.

7. *Repetition of word or phrase:* wavy line under repeated element

   The climbers were assisted . . .

8. *Pauses longer than normal:* slashes for pauses, one per second

   The // controversial theory . . .

When reading comprehension scores indicate that the reader has become frustrated (scores of 50 percent or less), read one of the next level passages aloud to the student and then ask the comprehension questions. Before you read, say something like, "You've worked hard and the last story was difficult. This time I want you to listen carefully while I read the story. Afterward I'll ask you questions as I did before." Read normally, not too slowly or with exaggerated expression. If the student gets more than half of the questions correct, read a passage from the next level in the same way. Proceed until you reach a level at which the student gets 50 percent or fewer of the questions correct, then stop.

Assessing Recognition of Words in Isolation

A component of an informal reading inventory that is used to assess recognition of words in isolation (i.e., in lists, not in context) is the *word recognition inven-*

Level: Two

Expository

Concept Questions:

What do flowers need to grow?

_____

_____

_____ (3-2-1-0)

What does "forest animals in the winter" mean to you?

_____

_____

_____ (3-2-1-0)

What does "changing seasons" mean to you?

_____

_____

_____ (3-2-1-0)

Score: _____ /9 = _____ %

_____ FAM _____ UNFAM

Prediction:

_____

_____

_____

Seasons

There are four seasons in a year. They are spring, summer, fall, and winter. Each season lasts about three months. Spring is the season when new life <u>begins</u>. The <u>weather</u> becomes warmer. Warm <u>weather</u>, rain, and <u>light</u> make plants grow. Some plants which looked dead during the winter grow again. Tulips are plants which come up every spring.

Summer <u>begins</u> on June 20th for people who live in the United States. June 20th is the longest day of the year for us. We have more sunlight that day than on any other day. <u>Insects</u> come out in summer. One bug that comes out in summer likes to bite. The bite hurts and it itches. Do you know what that bug is? It's the deer fly.

Summer <u>ends</u> and fall <u>begins</u> during September. In fall we <u>begin</u> to get less <u>light</u> from the sun. In the North, leaves <u>begin</u> to die. When they die they turn brown. Then they fall off. Nuts fall from trees. They are saved by squirrels to eat in the winter.

Winter <u>begins</u> just a few days before Christmas. December 21st is the shortest day of the year for us. We have less <u>light</u> that day than on any other day. In winter many animals have to live on <u>food</u> that they stored during the fall. There are no green plants for the animals to eat. Winter <u>ends</u> when spring <u>begins</u> on March 20th. The seasons keep changing. Plant life <u>begins</u> and <u>ends</u> each year. (249 words)

FIGURE 3.5 Sample IRI Passage with Miscues Marked

Source: Lauren, Leslie, and JoAnne Caldwell. *Qualitative Reading Inventory II.* New York: HarperCollins, 1995, p. 160.

tory (WRI). This instrument consists of graded lists of individual words, usually primer-level through grade six, typically included in commercial IRIs.

The word recognition inventory is used to assess sight recognition and some aspects of phonic and structural analysis. Since the words appear in isolation, the WRI is not used to assess how students recognize words in context or to assess comprehension in any way.

As was mentioned previously, a secondary purpose of the WRI is to help determine where to begin administering the reading passages of the IRI. When it is used for this purpose, the WRI is given first, before the IRI, and the examiner begins having the student read story passages at the grade level where he or she first began to miss some words. When not used for this purpose but only to provide information about the student's word recognition, the WRI can be administered after the rest of the IRI.

The WRI consists of graded word lists for the student to read and a corresponding set of examiner's pages for the teacher to mark and score as the instrument is administered. The student's copy contains only the individual words, arranged in lists. On the examiner's copy, each word is followed by two blanks for filling in what the reader said when errors occurred.

Figure 3.6 shows two levels of word lists from a commercial IRI.

Typically, each word in succession is shown to the student for a very brief exposure of less than one second; the word is uncovered for a second, longer look if it is not identified immediately. There are several similar ways to reveal each word for only a brief exposure. One is to use a file card to cover each word, drawing the card down the list to briefly reveal each word as the student reads down the list; another is to use two file cards, moving one to briefly uncover the word, then covering it again with the other card; a third is to use a card with a small rectangular window cut in it and slide the card down the list so that each successive word appears briefly in the window. Most teachers find that with a bit of practice, one or another of these methods is most comfortable for them. The means that are used to show the words are less important than whether each word is revealed briefly yet completely and that the administration is smooth and fluent. This might take a little practice.

Words that the reader recognizes immediately and accurately are checked off on the examiner's copy; words that are incorrectly identified or sounded out are noted in the blanks following each word. Some commercial IRIs have only one column of blanks, but most have two; those that have two blanks after each word are providing spaces for the examiner to note whether the word was recognized automatically or had to be decoded by the reader. Percentages of accuracy are derived for each list of words by counting the errors made.

The point is really academic, since we are not interested in setting a functional reading level from reading word lists but rather in analyzing the student's word recognition strategies and assessing how well the student recognizes words automatically. Scores for each list may be entered on the IRI record sheet.

To summarize, the steps in administering an IRI are shown in Box 3.2.

SCORING AN INFORMAL READING INVENTORY

Scoring procedures for an IRI are fairly simple. Word recognition in isolation, oral reading accuracy, and comprehension are scored by percentages, which help the teacher to determine the student's independent, instructional, and frustration levels.

Because IRIs are often used to determine a student's independent and instructional levels, the criteria for setting these levels are very important. IRIs have been widely used since the 1940s, when Betts (1941, 1957) and others popularized their use, and the criteria for setting levels were derived largely from clinical experience. For many years, the minimum instructional-level criteria

Examiner Word Lists

First			Second		
	Identified Automatically	*Identified*		*Identified Automatically*	*Identified*
1. bear	_____	_____	1. morning	_____	_____
2. father	_____	_____	2. toy	_____	_____
3. find	_____	_____	3. room	_____	_____
4. rabbit	_____	_____	4. old	_____	_____
5. friend	_____	_____	5. trade	_____	_____
6. song	_____	_____	6. promise	_____	_____
7. thought	_____	_____	7. pieces	_____	_____
8. there	_____	_____	8. hatch	_____	_____
9. run	_____	_____	9. push	_____	_____
10. then	_____	_____	10. though	_____	_____
11. move	_____	_____	11. begins	_____	_____
12. group	_____	_____	12. food	_____	_____
13. eat	_____	_____	13. light	_____	_____
14. air	_____	_____	14. ends	_____	_____
15. bread	_____	_____	15. clue	_____	_____
16. have	_____	_____	16. breathe	_____	_____
17. wind	_____	_____	17. insects	_____	_____
18. get	_____	_____	18. weather	_____	_____
19. put	_____	_____	19. noticed	_____	_____
20. looked	_____	_____	20. money	_____	_____

Total Correct Automatic	____ /20 = ____ %		Total Correct Automatic	____ /20 = ____ %	
Total Correct Identified	____ /20 = ____ %		Total Correct Identified	____ /20 = ____ %	
Total Number Correct	____ /20 = ____ %		Total Number Correct	____ /20 = ____ %	

LEVELS		
Independent	Instructional	Frustration
18–20	14–17	below 14
90–100%	70–85%	below 70%

FIGURE 3.6   Word Recognition Inventory, Examiner's Page

Source: Lauren, Leslie, and JoAnne Caldwell. *Qualitative Reading Inventory II.* New York: HarperCollins, 1995, p. 95.

attributed to Betts, 95 percent oral reading accuracy and 75 percent comprehension, were widely accepted.

Today, some authorities still use the Betts criteria, although 70 percent comprehension is most often used. However, the oral reading accuracy criteria

STEPS IN ADMINISTERING AN INFORMAL READING INVENTORY

BOX 3.2

1. Begin the assessment one or two grade levels below the student's present grade or basal level or at a level that you think will be easy for the student. Remember, you can move back as well as forward in the IRI if the reading is still too difficult. Assess the reader's prior knowledge of each topic before reading.
2. Administer the first oral reading passage. Code the miscues during the oral reading. You may tape-record the oral reading for greater accuracy if it does not distract or annoy the reader. Record the retelling. Ask the comprehension questions and record the gist of the answers.
3. Administer the silent reading passage at the same level. Ask the comprehension questions and record the gist of the answers.
4. If the student was not reading comfortably and successfully at this level, move back to a lower level and administer the oral and silent reading passages as before. Then continue to move forward in the IRI, skipping the level that you already administered when you come to it.
5. If the student was reading comfortably at the level on which you began testing, continue to move forward in the IRI, giving oral and silent passages as above, until the comprehension scores drop to 50 percent or less.
6. When you have located the frustration level, read one of the next-level passages aloud to the student and ask the comprehension questions as before. Continue assessing listening with one passage per level until the listening comprehension score drops below 50 percent. Then stop the IRI.

have been challenged as too stringent, and 90 percent is widely accepted as the lower end of the instructional range for oral reading accuracy (Johns & Magliari, 1989; Powell, 1970). These are the same percentages that Reading Recovery teachers use when they take running records each day to determine whether a Reading Recovery student is reading instructional-level material (Clay, 1985).

Oral Reading Accuracy

For each oral passage of the IRI that is used, score the oral reading accuracy by counting the number of uncorrected miscues, which are shown in Box 3.1.

The issue of whether to count miscues that the reader corrected is an important one. Many people, including ourselves, do not count self-corrected miscues. Self-correction shows that the reader is monitoring whether the passage makes sense, a critically important reading strategy. Some people count all miscues, however, whether corrected or not, and some commercial IRIs instruct users to do so. Likewise, some people count repetitions and even pauses as scorable miscues; we do not, because these are not *divergences* from the written text. In informal assessment, there are some issues on which practitioners do not agree.

You should discuss these issues with experienced IRI users and with your colleagues and use your best judgment as a teacher.

While you are learning to give and score an IRI, it is helpful to tape-record the oral reading so that you can replay it and be sure that you caught all the miscues. It might also help you to make a check or tally mark at the end of each line of print, one for each uncorrected miscue in that line. It makes counting up easier.

To obtain a reader's total accuracy score, you need to know not only how many miscues occurred, but also how many words are in the whole passage. In other words, what percentage of the total words does each individual word contribute?

Most commercial IRIs do all the arithmetic for you, providing a box or chart showing how many miscues represent the independent, instructional, and frustration levels for that passage. As we mentioned in the previous section on administration, if you look back at Figure 3.4, you will see a box at the end of the passage indicating how many miscues may be made for the passage to fall within each reading level; in this case, up to six miscues represent an independent level, from seven to twenty-seven miscues represent the instructional level, and more than twenty-eight miscues represent the frustration level. (These scores do not reflect whether the miscues made sense within the passage or not; that issue is discussed in the section to follow, entitled "Qualitative Analysis of Oral Reading Miscues." This discussion refers only to the total accuracy of the oral reading.)

If you are using an IRI that provides you only the total number of words in the passage, you will have to calculate the oral reading accuracy score. This requires only simple arithmetic.

Let's use the marked oral reading passage in Figure 3.5, *Seasons*, as an example. This passage contains 249 words. The reader made thirteen uncorrected miscues.

To calculate oral reading accuracy:

1. Determine the number of words that were read correctly by subtracting the number of miscues from the number of words in the passage.
2. Divide the number of words in the passage into the number of words correct.
3. Multiply the resulting decimal number by 100 to get the total accuracy score. Round off to the nearest whole number.

1) 249   2) $249 \overline{) 236}$ gives .947   3) .947 x 100 = 94.7%, or 95%
    -13
    ───
    236

By making 13 uncorrected miscues in a passage of 249 words, the reader read with 95 percent accuracy.

As you score each oral reading passage, write the percentage of accuracy on the examiner's copy of the passage. The oral reading accuracy scores will contribute to your determination of the student's independent, instructional, and frustration levels.

The most widely accepted criteria for oral reading accuracy are as follows:

Independent level: 97 percent or higher

Instructional level: 90–96 percent
Frustration level: below 90 percent

If these criteria seem high, remember that sentence context provides a powerful word recognition aid. In sentences, words are constrained by their grammatical usage and meaning. An unknown word in a sentence does not appear there arbitrarily, as it might in a list, but because it fits grammatically and semantically. The number of alternatives for any individual word is therefore small, and this makes it easier to recognize words in context than in isolation. A student who misses more than about one in ten running words is likely not understanding what is being read.

Reading and Listening Comprehension

Score the silent and oral reading comprehension questions separately for each passage and determine the percentage of questions answered correctly. Do the same for any passages that you used for listening comprehension. These passages are all scored in the same way.

If the IRI that you are using does not have a box for checking off the number of correct answers and the corresponding level, you will have to determine the percent of correct answers, as you would if you were grading a test or quiz. To determine how much each question counts, divide the number of questions into 100. The answer represent the percentage that each question counts. Multiply the number of correct answers by this number to get the comprehension score for each passage.

Jot the score for each passage on the examiner's copy of that passage. Repeat the same procedure for all passages that are read to the student. The comprehension scores will contribute to your determination of the reader's independent, instructional, frustration, and listening levels.

The most widely accepted criteria for reading and listening comprehension scores are as follows:

Independent level: 90 percent or higher
Instructional level: 70–90 percent
Frustration level: below 70 percent

(In our discussion of administering IRIs, you were told to continue testing until a score of 50 percent or lower was attained. By doing so, you can be sure that the frustration level has been reached.)

Scoring the Word Recognition Inventory

The WRI is easy to give and score. When a word is correctly identified during the brief exposure, it is checked off in the column labeled *Automatic* (or whatever the designation is on your IRI for the brief exposure of each word) on the examiner's sheet; if an error is made, the error is written on the blank instead of a check. Then the word is uncovered for a longer exposure, and the student's second attempts are written in the column labeled *Decoded* (or whatever the designation is on your IRI for the longer, or untimed, exposure of the word). If the reader corrects the error after looking at the word again, a check may be placed in that blank.

Each column is scored separately for each level. Some commercial IRIs, like the one shown in Figure 3.6, show you how to derive an independent, instructional, or frustration level from these scores. If not, you will derive a percentage score for each column, as though you were grading a quiz.

The widely accepted criteria for word recognition in isolation are as follows:

Independent level: 90–100 percent accuracy

Instructional level: 70–85 percent

Frustration level: below 70 percent

These levels are most useful when the WRI is used to show where to begin the reading passages. We are not interested in setting a functional reading level from reading word lists alone, but we do use this information in analyzing the student's word recognition strategies and assessing how well the student recognizes words automatically.

Keeping Track of Scores

After you have derived scores for word recognition in isolation, oral reading accuracy, oral and silent reading comprehension, and listening comprehension, enter the scores on a record sheet, which can be stapled to the front of the examiner's copy of the student's IRI. Having all the pertinent scores and observational notes that you made during the testing on one sheet aids in interpreting the student's performance. (Interpreting IRI results is discussed in the next section.)

A model score record sheet is shown in Figure 3.7. On this sheet are spaces for recording all scores from the IRI, notes and observations, information about the student such as age and grade, and scores from the word recognition inventory.

The necessary scores for determining the functional reading and listening levels from an IRI are summarized in Table 3.1. If the IRI that you prefer to use specifies somewhat different score criteria, use those given in the IRI instructions.

INTERPRETING AN INFORMAL READING INVENTORY

As with all assessment procedures, IRI scores are not an end in themselves. They should be interpreted and then applied in instructional planning. To do so, the student's functional reading levels must be determined, and patterns of strength and need must be noted and addressed.

Establishing Reading and Listening Levels

The scores that are derived from the oral reading and comprehension measures are used to determine overall levels. Scores for *both* oral reading and comprehension areas should meet the criteria for the instructional level to be sure that the reader will be comfortable at that level. The necessary scores are shown in Box 3.3.

Examples 1 and 2 (Figures 3.8 and 3.9) show oral reading and comprehension scores for a second-grader and a sixth-grader. Let's look at each example and determine what the scores tell us about each one's reading levels.

Student _____ Age _____ Grade _____
Date tested _____ Tested by _____

Level	WORD RECOGNITION INVENTORY		ORAL READING	COMPREHENSION		
	Automatic	Decoded	Total Accuracy / Total Acceptability	Oral Reading	Silent Reading	Listening
P						
1st						
2nd						
3rd						
4th						
5th						
6th						
7th						
8th						
9th						

READING LEVELS

Independent _____

Instructional _____

Frustration _____

Listening _____

Retelling: _____

_____

_____

Strengths: _____

_____

_____

Needs: _____

_____

Prior Knowledge: _____

_____

Recommendations: _____
_____
_____
_____
_____
_____

FIGURE 3.7   Informal Reading Inventory Record Sheet

TABLE 3.1 **Criterion Scores for Establishing Reading and Listening Levels with an IRI**

	Oral Reading	Comprehension
Independent Level	97%	90%
Instructional Level	90%	70%
Frustration Level	Below 90%	Below 70%
Listening Level	—	70%

The child in Example 1 is reading comfortably at the primer (P) level with accurate word recognition and excellent comprehension. All scores are at the independent level.

At the first-grade (1) level, her oral reading accuracy is still good, although she made more miscues, and comprehension is good in both oral and silent reading. An oral reading accuracy score of 94 percent and comprehension scores of 75 percent and 80 percent are within the instructional level. First-grade material represents a good instructional level for this youngster. In second-grade material, both word recognition and comprehension break down. Second-grade material represents her frustration level.

The listening comprehension score of 80 percent at third grade shows that she can listen to and understand material at a third-grade level of difficulty, while the listening score of 60 percent at fourth grade shows that this level of material is currently too hard for her to understand adequately even when she hears it. The 80 percent score at third grade also represents this youngster's *potential* reading level; that is, she has the vocabulary and verbal concepts to understand material appropriate for third-graders, when she hears it. This is a positive sign; she has demonstrable potential for improving her reading. However, she currently is able to read only first-grade material, about two levels below her potential at this time.

In Example 2, the student's scores at second grade in oral reading and both oral and silent comprehension are within the independent level. (Since independent-level scores were obtained at second grade, first grade and primer levels were not assessed.) His scores at both third and fourth grades fall within the instructional range, so we can

FIGURE 3.8 **Example 1: Scores for a Second Grader (in Percentages)**

		COMPREHENSION		
GRADE	ORAL READING	ORAL	SILENT	LISTENING
P	97	100	100	—
1	94	75	80	—
2	88	60	50	—
3	—	—	—	80
4	—	—	—	60

		COMPREHENSION		
GRADE	ORAL READING	ORAL	SILENT	LISTENING
2	99	100	90	—
3	94	85	80	—
4	91	70	70	—
5	86	50	55	—
6	—	—	—	90

FIGURE 3.9 Example 2: Scores for a Fifth Grader (in Percentages)

say that fourth-grade material represents his highest instructional level; his instructional reading level actually encompasses both third- and fourth-grade material.

With all fifth-grade scores falling into the frustration range, we conclude that fifth-grade material is too difficult for this youngster to read, but the 90 percent listening comprehension score at sixth grade shows that he can understand material at his present grade level when he hears it. This youngster's listening comprehension score shows that he has the potential to read at grade level, although he is currently reading at a fourth-grade level.

The process of deriving percentages of correct responses and using these scores to determine reading levels is called *quantitative analysis.* It shows how many correct and incorrect responses the reader has made. This analysis is useful, but it is incomplete because it lacks the essential element of in-depth analysis of the student's responses. (However, in reality, this is as far as most classroom diagnosis goes.)

To determine what the reader knows and where help is needed, we must determine the strategies underlying the correct and incorrect responses. We have to look for patterns of strengths and weaknesses. From this perspective, it is not as important *how many* correct responses the student made as *which* responses were right and *why.* This assessment is termed *qualitative analysis,* because it focuses on the quality of responses and the strategies that the reader demonstrated.

Quantitative analysis will aid us in determining the levels of difficulty of text the reader can deal with successfully. Qualitative analysis aids us in determining what the student has mastered and what skills and processes are lacking. Both kinds of analyses are needed to develop a prescriptive program for a reader.

Qualitative Analysis of Oral Reading Miscues

The context in which a word occurs is a powerful aid to word recognition, but context is provided only by connected text. When we make a transcript of the oral reading of IRI passages, we can analyze word recognition within the real act of reading. Therefore, accurate marking and analysis of miscues are important.

Even very fluent readers make occasional miscues, especially when they have not read the material before. Some miscues change the meaning of the sentence or passage very little; others change the author's meaning significantly and can interfere with the reader's comprehension.

By examining and evaluating a reader's miscues, we can add greatly to our understanding of what the reader is doing during the reading. We can see more than just whether the reading is highly accurate or not. We can see, through the miscues themselves, whether the reader is using context and sense-making strategies to try to actively construct the author's meaning. Students who generally make acceptable, or qualitatively "good," miscues need a different kind of word-attack instruction to help them read more accurately than those whose miscues generally don't make sense.

Comparing Miscue Quality

For example, let's say two readers read the following three sentences aloud:

The day was warm and sunny. Tom and Mandy packed a lunch. They brought ham sandwiches, chips, and pickles.

One student reads:

The day was **hot** and sunny. Tom and Mandy packed **their** lunch. They brought ham sandwiches, chips, and **peaches**.

The other student reads:

The day was warm and **sandy**. Tom and Mandy **picked** a lunch. They brought ham sandwiches, chips, and **pirckles**.

Each reader made three uncorrected miscues. Their overall accuracy scores for this paragraph would be the same, but the first reader's miscues more nearly preserved the meaning of the paragraph, while the second reader's miscues made less sense and probably interfered more with her comprehension.

Hot and *warm*, when discussing weather, are closer in meaning than *sunny* and *sandy*. It makes better sense, and is more like the meaning of the text sentence, to say that the day was *hot and sunny* than *warm and sandy*. Likewise, "packed *their* lunch" is closer to the original meaning of the sentence than "*picked* a lunch," although it isn't grammatically correct. *Peaches* aren't much like *pickles*, but they are at least both foods that might be found in a picnic lunch; *pirckles* is a nonsense word, even though it looks and sounds more like *pickles* than *peaches* does. Although both readers made three miscues, the first reader's miscues were qualitatively better, in the sense of preserving the intended meaning, than the second reader's.

Scoring Miscue Acceptability

When considering the quality of miscues, we reread the passage as the reader read it, with all the miscues just as we marked them, and decide whether each miscue significantly changes the meaning of the passage or sentence in which it occurs. We do not look only at the individual word, but at the miscue within the phrase, sentence, or passage context. Miscues that do significantly alter the meaning may be marked by circling them, marking them with a highlighting marker, or marking them *MC* for *meaning change*. If we were marking the paragraphs read in the foregoing examples, we would mark only *peaches* as a

> *hot* *their*
> **First reader:** The day was warm and sunny. Tom and Mandy packed a lunch.
> They brought ham sandwiches, chips and (peaches) pickles. MC
>
> MC MC
> (sandy) (picked)
> **Second reader:** The day was warm and sunny. Tom and Mandy packed a lunch.
> (Pirckles) MC
> They brought ham sandwiches, chips and pickles. MC

meaning-changing miscue by the first reader and all three of the second reader's miscues as meaning changes, as shown below:

Then we can rescore the oral reading passage to arrive at a percentage of accuracy that includes only the *significant*, or *meaning-changing*, miscues. Some commercial IRIs, such as Leslie and Caldwell's *Qualitative Reading Inventory II*, which we use in this chapter as an example, direct users to do this with each oral passage. Look back at Figure 3.5; as was mentioned previously, you will see in the box following the passage that miscues are counted to arrive at two different scores: *Total Accuracy*, derived by counting all uncorrected miscues, and *Total Acceptability*, derived by counting only meaning-changing miscues. For this passage to be at the reader's instructional level, a reader could make as many as twenty-one miscues, but no more than eleven of them could be meaning-changing miscues. If a reader made more than twelve meaning-changing miscues, the passage would represent a frustration level of difficulty.

Just What Makes a Miscue Acceptable?

At this point, inexperienced users often begin to wonder how much a miscue must change meaning to be considered significant. It can be argued that any change in the author's words, no matter how small, changes the author's meaning, and this might indeed be true. But we are not concerned here with tiny or subtle meaning changes. Instead of asking ourselves, "Does this miscue change the meaning?" we ask, "Does this miscue change the meaning *significantly*? Is this a *big* meaning change?"

Whether the meaning is changed a lot, a little or hardly at all depends on the miscue *and its surrounding context.* That's why miscues must be considered in their context, not taken out of context, placed in a list, and evaluated, as some IRI instructions say. We try not to split hairs, in terms of meaning, but to be aware of big changes in meaning. We keep in mind that a word, phrase, or sentence can make good sense even when it is grammatically incorrect, so we avoid making hard-and-fast rules such as "changes in parts of speech always result in meaning change."

With experience, we've found that there's little ambiguity about most miscues; it's clear either that little or no meaning was lost or that the miscue changed the meaning a great deal, and the ones we have to puzzle over are rare. With these, we usually ask someone else what they think; we read them what the sentence was supposed to say and what the reader said and ask whether they think it was a significant miscue or not. Then we try not to "sweat the small stuff" and get on with it.

By taking the extra time and effort to examine and evaluate the miscues that occur during oral reading, we can add greatly to our understanding of what the reader is doing during the reading. We can see more than just whether or not the reading was highly accurate. We can see, through the miscues themselves, whether the reader is using context and sense-making strategies to try to actively construct meaning. Students whose miscues generally make sense in context need a different kind of word-attack instruction to help them read more accurately than do those whose miscues generally don't make sense.

Dialect or Miscue?

An important issue in analyzing a reader's miscues is the role of nonstandard English dialects in oral reading accuracy. As we have seen, simply counting all the miscues and deriving an accuracy score do not take into account whether the reader's errors make sense. Likewise, this process does not take into account whether the reader might be translating standard English text into his or her own familiar, albeit nonstandard, oral dialect.

For example, let's say the sentence reads, **Rose said, "This is my mother."** The reader, a dialect speaker, reads, **Rose say, "This my mother."** In quantitative terms, the reader has made two uncorrected miscues: the omission of *is* and the substitution of *say* for *said*. Qualitatively, the oral reading does not correspond exactly to the written words, but it does represent an accurate translation into a widely used nonstandard dialect, with no loss of meaning. In most dialect usages, it is grammar, not meaning, that differs from the written text.

It is important not to confuse dialect miscues with true word recognition errors, because doing so results in underestimating the word recognition abilities of many dialect speakers. Likewise, it is not helpful to assume that all miscues produced by dialect speakers will be acceptable, and not provide the help they might need to develop greater accuracy and automaticity in word recognition. By listening closely to the informal speech of your dialect-speaking students, you will gain enough familiarity with its conventions to distinguish true dialect miscues, which are generally acceptable, from those that interfere with comprehension.

When you are marking a dialect speaker's oral reading, it's best to mark what the reader says, then rescore the passage for acceptability as above. If they are dialect usages, most of the miscues will be insignificant.

What about Names?

Names are especially tricky for readers. Often, students stumble over names in a passage even when they read harder words correctly. We generally don't count names as miscues more than once in a passage, provided that the reader calls the character by the same wrong name each time. That is, if "Phillip" is read as "Phil" or even as "Pillip" throughout a passage, we count it only the first time. If "Phillip" were read as "Phil" a few times, then changed to "Flip," we would count each change *once*.

Some people count name miscues as a separate error each time; this seems excessively strict. Others count it if the name seems to change the gender (calling Phillip "Phyllis," for example). Check the instructions for administering your IRI and follow what the authors recommend if it makes sense to you.

A useful device for analyzing a reader's miscues in great detail, or for teaching yourself everything there is to know about miscue analysis, is the venerable *reading miscue inventory (RMI)* by Yetta Goodman, Dorothy Watson, and Carolyn Burke (1987). This device provides a highly detailed analysis of twenty-five consecutive miscues. Each is analyzed according to the degree of correction or dialect involvement, graphic and phonological features, syntactic function and grammatical acceptability, and the degree to which the original meaning was preserved by the miscue.

Although it is time consuming to administer and score, the RMI makes evaluation of the quality of miscues more objective and less subject to examiner opinion than informal miscue analysis, takes account of the oral reading and comprehension of a whole story or complete passage rather than only a text portion as in an IRI, and can include analysis of the reader's comprehension of the passage as well as accuracy of the reading. It can be used independent of an IRI or as a miscue analysis training device.

Analyzing Reading Comprehension

By looking at oral and silent reading comprehension scores across several grade levels, we can determine whether the reader's comprehension during either oral or silent reading is particularly weak or strong and whether this pattern is consistent with what others of the same age do. We can also spot a pattern by looking at responses to the different types of comprehension questions within a grade level and across levels that tell us whether the student has particular strengths or weaknesses in recalling main ideas or details, forming inferences, and other comprehension skills required by the questions.

If readers consistently show better comprehension performance after reading orally and lower comprehension scores after reading silently, we can conclude that they have to hear themselves say the words aloud to understand them. Such readers translate, or *recode*, print into speech and derive meaning from the spoken words. This is fairly typical of beginning readers, especially those whose initial reading instruction has been primarily oral.

When asked to read silently, they sometimes lose their places because when they read aloud, their voices help to "anchor" them in the print. It is not surprising when they read aloud and show consistently better oral than silent comprehension, since oral reading is still so widely used in primary classrooms. However, if we see a student older than about age 8 or 9 reading this way, we might be concerned. Beyond the primary grades, emphasis shifts to rapid, silent reading for meaning. An older student who has to read audibly might have trouble keeping up with the volume of material that is required in upper grades.

For readers beyond the beginning stage, silent reading tends to be faster than oral reading. Oral reading speed is limited by how rapidly we can speak clearly; about 200 words per minute is very rapid speech, and even very fluent oral readers do not read aloud that fast. However, fluent silent reading may vary between 200 and 400 words per minute, depending on the difficulty of the material, the reader's purpose in doing the reading, and whether or not the material is familiar. Fluent mature reading of challenging material proceeds at about 250 words per minute (Perfetti, 1985), while fluent mature reading of easy interesting material that is read for pleasure may be considerably faster. Thus, the reading demands of the upper grades require that students shift from the primary oral reading of beginning reading toward fluent silent reading with comprehension.

Somewhere between the second and the fourth grade, most readers begin to shift toward more silent reading and characteristically show better comprehension after silent than after oral reading. This is developmentally appropriate; it certainly does not indicate that these older students show an oral reading weakness or that they should begin a lot of remedial oral reading. On the contrary, oral reading should be deemphasized and silent reading emphasized in the upper grades.

Comprehension Skill Patterns

Some readers have consistent difficulty with one or another kind of comprehension question. One might, for example, usually not have difficulty with questions requiring direct recall of explicitly stated information but have much more difficulty with inferential questions, main ideas, or vocabulary items. If we go back to the comprehension questions following the IRI passages and consider what kind of question each one was, we can discern whether there was a particular type of question that gave a student consistent difficulty. Figure 3.10 shows the major types of questions that usually appear in IRIs.

FIGURE 3.10 Sample Comprehension Questions

Literal Comprehension (Answers to questions explicitly stated in passage)

TOPIC:	What event was this story about?
	What might make a good title for this passage?
MAIN IDEA:	What was the most important thing the author said about dogs?
	How would you describe in one sentence the information about dogs given here?
IMPORTANT DETAIL:	What kind of animal was Nitwit?
	What did Bob do as soon as he got home?
SEQUENCE:	What happened after Jill heard the window break?
	Where did the children go first?
CHARACTERIZATION:	What did Ms. Willis do that showed she was angry?
	How did Bruce act when he saw Jamie again?
REINSPECTION:	Find the sentence that describes Ben's new bike and read it to me.
	Find the place in the story where the children began to argue, and read it out loud.

Interpretation and Judgment (Answers to questions not explicitly stated in passage)

INFERENCE:	Why do you think Jim spoke roughly to the dog?
	What makes you believe Cathy might enjoy flying?
VOCABULARY:	What did Rita mean when she said "I'm simply green"?
	What is a "chopper" in this story?
PREDICTION:	What might happen if the delivery boy loses the package?
	If Shana runs away, where might she go?

By systematically looking from one grade level to another, we can see what, if any, pattern emerges. Was there a type of question that repeatedly gave the student difficulty at different levels or one that the student consistently answered correctly? Looking for individual patterns in comprehension responses allows us to design appropriate comprehension activities for students according to their individual needs.

However, we must be quite certain that the questions really tap the comprehension skills that they purport to. IRI questions are notoriously hard to classify. Even experienced teachers attempting to classify comprehension questions by type often classified questions quite differently from the authors of a particular IRI (Schell & Hanna, 1981).

Unquestioning acceptance of IRI question classifications, and indeed unquestioning acceptance of all IRI questions as good questions because they appear in a commercial IRI, is unwise. Comprehension patterns can often be discerned, however, and helpful teaching strategies devised from these judgments, *if* teachers continually use critical judgment when they use IRI questions (Peterson, Greenlaw, & Tierney, 1978).

Don't take either the quality of questions or the way the author classified them on faith. Read the passages and each of the questions, and consider carefully whether you think the questions are appropriately labeled by type. Then, if you discern a consistent pattern in a student's response to particular question types, consider your judgment as a working hypothesis about the student's needs.

Begin instruction based on your hypothesis that a student needs practice in particular areas, but continue to evaluate on the basis of how the student responds to that instruction. Further teaching may reveal that what looked like a comprehension skill weakness on the IRI did not persist or that what looked like an area of strength did not continue to be a strength for the reader beyond the IRI, in real text. Only further teaching will reveal whether your judgments were accurate.

Patterns in Listening Comprehension

If students achieve 70 percent or better on the comprehension questions after listening to a passage read aloud by the examiner, we assume that they can understand similar concepts and vocabulary when they hear it, although they cannot read that level of material for themselves. We refer to the highest grade level at which the student had 70 percent or better as the student's *listening level*. This level is important because it helps us to determine what we can expect this student to achieve and thus makes it possible to set reasonable instructional goals.

As we discussed earlier in this chapter, most students who are not fluent, mature readers can listen to someone else reading aloud and understand material that they cannot yet read successfully. Most of them, especially the younger ones, are still learning and developing as readers while they have been competent listeners and language users for a lot longer. Therefore, their listening levels are somewhat above their instructional reading levels, which is predictable, for it shows that they are not yet able to read as well as they can think.

Some youngsters will have instructional reading and listening comprehension levels that are the same. Material that is too difficult for them to read is also too difficult for them to understand on an auditory basis. This is fine. What it shows is that they are reading just as well as they can and that at the present time, there is not much room for improvement. These pupils are reading right at their potential, using all their ability to read as well as they do. They need support and further instruction, but if they are poor readers, they will probably make steady but not spectacular gains in reading. The listening comprehension level represents a sort of overall goal in reading improvement.

The listening comprehension level is dynamic, not fixed or static. As children grow older and have more experiences, they can understand more and more difficult material because they have gained knowledge and experiences to which new information and experiences can be related. The average 7-year-old can listen to and understand stories that are appropriate for second- or third-graders and understand them, but ninth-grade material would be too difficult conceptually. By the time the child is 12 or 13, however, ninth-grade materials might well be comprehensible because vocabulary, store of concepts, and experiences have grown in those five years. The listening level represents an estimate of *present* functioning. Establishing a student's listening level once and using it as an ongoing standard, however, is no more appropriate than expecting last year's instructional level to be the same next year.

Here are three examples, all second-graders:

JENNY:

Jenny's listening comprehension level is late second grade. Since she is in second grade, we infer that her verbal intelligence is roughly average for her age and that she has the necessary concepts and vocabulary to learn to read second-grade material successfully, although at the present time, she has a first-grade instructional level. Although her instructional level is low, she can improve her reading with appropriate instruction and support.

MATT:

Matt has a listening comprehension level of sixth grade. He has the concepts and vocabulary to listen to and understand very advanced material, and he is obviously very bright. In spite of his potential, he is achieving at grade level and has an instructional level of late second grade. Therefore, his achievement is average for his grade, although he has the potential for higher achievement. The finding that Matt is not performing at his full potential is not necessarily negative. If he is comfortable, motivated, and interested, there is no need for concern. If he appears to be apathetic, bored, or frustrated, then he certainly needs greater intellectual challenge.

SANDY:

Sandy has an instructional level of first grade, and his listening level is also first grade. Although Sandy's achievement is below grade level, it is in line with his present potential. Sandy might be a slow learner or of below-average verbal intelligence; he might have learned to read later than others or may have a limited background of experience with print. At any rate, his performance and potential appear to be in line at the present. Sandy needs much support and instruction, and as he becomes a more proficient reader, his listening level will increase. This in turn will make greater reading improvement possible.

Analyzing Word Recognition in Isolation

As we discussed in earlier sections, the word recognition inventory, consisting of graded lists of words, is used to assess students' automatic recognition of words at each level, as well as some aspects of word analysis and decoding. Since words appear in isolation rather than in context, the student's use of context and word meaning as a cue to recognition is not assessed with this device, but rather by oral reading of IRI passages. The WRI is administered by showing each word for a very brief exposure, using either a file card or a card with a window cut in it, to briefly reveal each word in this list. Words that are not recognized immediately or that are misidentified are shown for a longer, untimed exposure.

The size of the student's immediate sight word recognition is inferred from performance on the Automatic, or timed exposure, portion of the instrument. A large and stable sight vocabulary forms the basis of fluent, effective reading. A reader who has a good sight vocabulary of common, frequently occurring words will usually score around 90 percent or better on automatic recognition of words, at least at the lower grade levels. At any grade level, scores much below 70 percent indicate that the student probably does not recognize enough of the words at that level to read fluently and effectively at that level of difficulty.

The responses in the Decoded, or untimed exposure, columns give us information about the phonic and word analysis strategies that a student can use when he or she does not recognize a word immediately. Students who typically correct an initial error when decoding the word show us that though sight recognition is weak, decoding skills are solid. Students who make unsuccessful attempts to decode unrecognized words but who typically preserve the initial consonant or blend sounds in their attempts show us that they have a grasp of initial sounds but might be weak in decoding medial or final sounds. By looking for patterns in both correct and incorrect responses, we can begin to determine what word attack skills need to be reviewed or taught.

SUPPLEMENTING INFORMAL ASSESSMENTS

A number of other assessment procedures and devices may be used periodically to supplement informal measures and explore particular areas of students' reading in detail. These include procedures that help us to obtain information about how readers attempt to construct meaning from text and tests of word recognition and decoding.

Helping Students to Become Strategic Readers

We know that effective readers are actively involved in the process of comprehending what they read. They use strategies such as previewing the text, creating predictions about the content, self-questioning, summarizing at various points in the story, and continually monitoring their own understanding as they read (Dole et al., 1996; Schmitt, 1990). Effective readers do not simply take in meanings found in text; they actively construct meaning for themselves by interacting with the text, reviewing what is already known, and integrating new information with prior information (Flood and Lapp, 1990; Symons and Pressley, 1993).

Metacomprehension Strategies

When readers activate what they already know and integrate new information in ways that make sense to them, when they select and use appropriate strategies to help them understand and remember what they read, they are becoming *strategic* readers. When readers fail to use prior information or lack sufficient prior information to make sense of new information, when they overrely on word-attack skills at the expense of context, or when they fail to monitor their understanding, they are not making progress toward becoming strategic readers. They might need a program of instruction that teaches them how and when to use effective strategies as they read.

Schmitt (1990) developed a 25-item multiple-choice questionnaire, called the Metacomprehension Strategy Index (MSI), that teachers can use to evaluate children's awareness of reading strategies in middle elementary grades and beyond. The MSI measures awareness of predicting and verifying, previewing, purpose setting, self-questioning, drawing from background knowledge, and applying "fix-up" strategies (Schmitt, 1990, p. 455). The questionnaire can be administered orally by the teacher or read silently by students. It can be given individually or in groups. Students respond to items by indicating what would be good strategies to use before, during, and after reading. Here is an example item (Schmitt, 1990, p. 459):

Before I begin reading, it's a good idea to:

 a. Think of what I already know about the things I see in the pictures.
 b. See how many pages are in the story.
 c. Choose the best part of the story to read again.
 d. Read the story aloud to someone.

After scoring students' MSIs, the teacher can determine which strategies students are aware of and which strategies students need to learn and practice using. Since the MSI is a self-report instrument, it might be that students *say* that they use particular strategies but in reality fail to use them; teacher observation is necessary to determine whether they really use what they say. The MSI appears to provide useful information about students' strategic awareness when combined with other diagnostic information.

Think-Alouds

Thinking aloud during reading can help students' comprehension (Loxterman et al., 1994). Readers' verbal self-reports about their thinking processes during reading, called *think-alouds,* can be used to obtain information about how readers construct meaning from text (Wade, 1990).

During a think-aloud, a reader reads short portions of a passage, one or a few sentences at a time. After each portion is read, the reader is asked to tell what the passage is about, what is happening in the passage, or what clues the reader is using to understand the passage. Nondirective probes such as "Tell me more about that" or "Why do you think so?" are used to extend the reader's responses.

The procedure may be tape-recorded and the record analyzed to determine whether the reader generates tentative hypotheses about the topic, uses information from the text to support hypotheses, relates information in the text to prior knowledge, integrates new with old information, and deals with conflicts between new and old information. Behaviors that may reveal the use of strategies such as rereading, as well as indications of anxiety, uncertainty, and the like, are noted by the examiner.

Box 3.3 shows the procedure for administering and interpreting a think-aloud.

BOX 3.3 — PROCEDURE FOR ADMINISTERING AND INTERPRETING A COMPREHENSION THINK-ALOUD

I. **Preparing the text**

Choose a short passage (expository or narrative) written to meet the following criteria:

A. The text should be from 80 to 200 words in length, depending on the reader's age and reading ability.

B. The text should be new to the reader, but on a topic that is familiar to him or her. (Determine whether the reader has relevant background knowledge by means of an interview or questionnaire administered at a session prior to this assessment.)

C. The text should be at the reader's instructional level, which can be determined by use of an informal reading inventory. Passages at this level are most likely to be somewhat challenging while not overwhelming readers with word identification problems.

D. The topic sentence should appear last, and the passage should be untitled. Altering the text in this way will elicit information about the reader's strategies for making sense of the passage and inferring the topic.

E. The text should be divided into segments of one to four sentences each.

II. **Administering the think-aloud procedure**

A. Tell the reader that he or she will be reading a story in short segments of one or more sentences.

B. Tell the reader that after reading each section, he or she will be asked to tell what the story is about.

(continued)

BOX 3.3 *(continued)*

    C. Have the student read a segment aloud. After each segment is read, ask the reader to tell what is happening, followed by nondirective probe questions as necessary. The questions should encourage the reader to generate hypotheses (what do you think this is about?) and to describe what he or she based the hypotheses on (what clues in the story helped you?).

    D. Continue the procedure until the entire passage is read. Then ask the reader to retell the entire passage in his or her own words. (The reader may reread the story first.)

    E. The examiner might also ask the reader to find the most important sentence(s) in the passage.

    F. The session should be tape-recorded and transcribed. The examiner should also record observations of the child's behaviors.

III. **Analyzing results**

Ask the following questions when analyzing the transcript:

    A. Does the reader generate hypotheses?

    B. Does he/she support hypotheses with information from the passage?

    C. What information from the text does the reader use?

    D. Does he/she relate material in the text to background knowledge or previous experience?

    E. Does the reader integrate new information with the schema he/she has already activated?

    F. What does the reader do if there is information that conflicts with the schema he/she has generated?

    G. At what point does the reader recognize what the story is about?

    H. How does the reader deal with unfamiliar words?

    I. What kinds of integration strategies does the reader use (e.g., visualization)?

    J. How confident is the reader of his/her hypotheses?

    K. What other observations can be made about the reader's behavior, strategies, etc.?

Source: Suzanne E. Wade, "Using Think Alouds to Assess Comprehension." *The Reading Teacher* 43, no. 7 (March 1990): 445.

Word Recognition and Phonics Tests

Most often, children's decoding ability is assessed by asking them to decode nonsense words that are similar to real words, such as *dap, rike, faught, blunch,* and so forth. The validity of such measures might be questionable, since such assessments are most probably the only time children are ever asked to attempt to read nonwords. In fact, teachers are cautioned against using nonsense words in teaching, since we are trying to help children to make sense of the act of reading and apply sense-making strategies when they encounter unfamiliar words.

Many children are confused by such a task and attempt to read nonsense words as real words, believing that their teachers would never ask them to read something that makes no sense. Cunningham (1990) suggested an alternative to nonsense word decoding assessments called "The Names Test," a list of first and last names of fictitious children. Each of the names is "fully decodable given commonly taught vowel rules and/or analogy approaches to decoding" (1990, p. 125).

A student is asked to pretend to be a teacher reading a class list of students' names as if he or she were taking attendance, a task that is familiar to most students. A name is counted correct if all syllables are pronounced correctly, regardless of where the student places the stress or accent (for example, YO-lan-da or Yo-LAN-da). Errors are noted phonetically and analyzed to reveal what phonic patterns the student needs to review or learn.

The Names Test and administration procedures are shown in Figures 3.11 and 3.12.

A number of commercial tests that are intended to test mastery of phonics skills and decoding are available. Usually, they consist of letters and letter groups to identify and sound out, real words and pseudo-words (nonsense words such as *mif, grake,* or *faught*) to sound out using common phonic generalizations, and letters-plus-word-stems (such as *p – in* or *s – ate*) to combine, or blend, into pronounceable words.

Some commercial IRIs such as Silvaroli's Classroom Reading Inventory, the Ekwall-Shanker Reading Inventory and the Bader Reading and Language Inventory include separate phonics inventories. A few standardized achievement tests, such as the Woodcock Reading Mastery Test-Revised, the Peabody Individual Achievement Test-Revised, and the Gray Oral Reading Test, 3rd edition include phonics and word blending subtests.

FIGURE 3.11   The Names Test

Source: Cunningham, Pat. "The Names Test: A Quick Assessment of Decoding Ability." *The Reading Teacher* 44, no. 2 (Oct. 1990): 127.

THE NAMES TEST

Jay Conway	Wendy Swain
Tim Cornell	Glen Spencer
Chuck Hoke	Fred Sherwood
Yolanda Clark	Flo Thornton
Kimberly Blake	Dee Skidmore
Roberta Slade	Grace Brewster
Homer Preston	Ned Westmoreland
Gus Quincy	Ron Smitherman
Cindy Sampson	Troy Whitlock
Chester Wright	Vance Middleton
Ginger Yale	Zane Anderson
Patrick Tweed	Bernard Pendergraph
Stanley Shaw	

Preparing the Instrument

1. Type or print legibly the 25 names on a sheet of paper or card stock. Make sure the print size is appropriate for the age or grade level of the students being tested.
2. For students who might perceive reading an entire list of names as being too formidable, type or print the names on index cards, so they can be read individually.
3. Prepare a protocol (scoring) sheet. Do this by typing the list of names in a column and following each name with a blank line to be used for recording a student's responses.

Administering the Names Test

1. Administer the Names Test individually. Select a quiet, distraction-free location.
2. Explain to the student that she or he is to pretend to be a teacher who must read a list of names of students in the class. Direct the student to read the names as if taking attendance.
3. Have the student read the entire list. Inform the student that you will not be able to help with difficult names, and encourage him or her to "make a guess if you are not sure." This way you will have sufficient responses for analysis.
4. Write a check on the protocol sheet for each name read correctly. Write phonetic spellings for names that are mispronounced.

Scoring and Interpreting the Names Test

1. Count a word correct if all syllables are pronounced correctly regardless of where the student places the accent. For example, either Yó/lan/da or Yo/lan´/da would be acceptable.
2. For words where the vowel pronunciation depends on which syllable the consonant is placed with, count them correct for either pronunciation. For example, either Ho/mer or Hom/er would be acceptable.
3. Count the number of names read correctly, and analyze those mispronounced, looking for patterns indicative of decoding strengths and weaknesses.

FIGURE 3.12 Procedures for Administering and Scoring the Names Test

Source: Cunningham, Pat. "The Names Test: A Quick Assessment of Decoding Ability." *The Reading Teacher* 44, no. 2 (Oct. 1990): 127.

Tests like these may be useful for screening purposes, since they are fairly quick to administer and do not require analyzing the student's WRI responses. However, it is just this analysis that helps teachers to develop the diagnostic skills and judgment that they need to fully explore students' abilities. Commercial word-attack tests are adequate for screening purposes but should not be depended on to replace careful study of what a child can do.

SUMMARY

This chapter discusses the assessment of student performance based on informed teacher judgment. *Internal assessments*, designed for instruction, include teacher-made tests and procedures, observations, interviews, informal diagnostic procedures and so forth. *External assessments*, designed for accountability, include norm- and criterion-referenced tests.

Informal diagnostic procedures make possible *qualitative* analysis of reading behaviors as well as use of *quantitative* scores. They are useful in determining a reader's *independent, instructional,* and *frustration* reading levels and reading strength and needs.

An *informal reading inventory (IRI)* is individually administered for these purposes. IRIs consist of story passages for oral and silent reading at consecutive grade levels from primer through high school and corresponding comprehension questions. During oral reading, *miscues,* or divergences from the text, are recorded, counted to determine a reader's oral reading fluency, and analyzed to reveal word recognition strategies and use of context. Responses to comprehension questions are used to determine reading levels and reveal comprehension skills and strategies. *Retellings* may be used in addition to questions. When the frustration reading level is reached, subsequent passages may be read aloud to the reader to determine his or her *listening comprehension* level, an indicator of potential for reading improvement.

An informal *word recognition inventory (WRI)* consisting of graded lists of individual words may be used to assess sight vocabulary and decoding skills out of context. Sight recognition is assessed by flashing individual words for a very brief moment, and phonic and structural analysis skills are assessed by reexamining missed words in an untimed exposure.

Think-alouds, or students' verbal self-reports of their thinking during reading, may be used to assess students' use of strategies and attempts to construct meaning from text. *Supplementary phonics tests* may be used to further study the reader's decoding skills.

REFERENCES

Baker, Linda, and Nancy Stein. "The Development of Prose Comprehension Skills." In *Children's Prose Comprehension: Research and Practice,* ed. Carol M. Santa and Bernard L. Hayes. Newark, DE: International Reading Association, 1981.

Betts, Emmett A. "Reading Problems at the Intermediate Grade Level." *Elementary School Journal* 40 (June 1941): 737–746.

Betts, Emmett A. *Foundations of Reading Instruction.* New York: American Book, 1957.

Calfee, Robert, and Elfrieda Hiebert. "Classroom Assessment of Reading." In *Handbook of Reading Research,* Vol. 2, ed. Rebecca Barr, Michael L. Kamil, Peter Mosenthal, and P. David Pearson. White Plains, NY: Longman, 1991.

Cardarelli, Aldo F. "The Influence of Reinspection on Students' IRI Results." *The Reading Teacher* 41, no. 7 (March 1988): 664–667.

Clay, Marie. *The Early Detection of Reading Difficulties*, 3d ed. Portsmouth, NH: Heinemann Educational Books, 1985.

Cunningham, Pat. "The Names Test: A Quick Assessment of Decoding Ability." *The Reading Teacher* 44, no. 2 (Oct. 1990): 124–129.

Dole, Janice A., Kathleen J. Brown, and Woodrow Trathen. "The Effects of Strategy Instruction on the Comprehension Performance of At-Risk Students." *Reading Research Quarterly* 31, no. 1 (Jan.–March 1996): 62–88.

Fader, Daniel. *The New Hooked on Books.* New York: Berkley, 1976.

Flood, James, and Diane Lapp. "Reading Comprehension Instruction for At-Risk Students: Research-Based Practices That Can Make a Difference," *Journal of Reading* 33, no. 7 (April 1990): 490–496.

Goodman, Yetta M., Dorothy J. Watson, and Carolyn L. Burke. *Reading Miscue Inventory: Alternative Procedures.* New York: Richard C. Owen, 1987.

Hoffman, James V., Sarah J. McCarthey, Bonnie Elliott, Debra L. Bayles, Debra P. Price, Angela Ferree, and Judy A. Abbott. "The Literature-Based Basals in First Grade Classrooms: Savior, Satan, or Same-Old, Same-Old?" *Reading Research Quarterly* 33, no. 2 (April–June 1998): 168–197.

Johns, Jerry L., and Anne Marie Magliari. "Informal Reading Inventories: Are the Betts Criteria the Best Criteria?" *Reading Improvement* 26, no. 2 (Summer 1989): 124–132.

Kender, Joseph P. and Herbert Rubenstein. "Recall versus Reinspection in IRI Comprehension Tests." *The Reading Teacher* 30, no. 8 (April 1977): 776–779.

Leslie, Lauren, and JoAnne Caldwell. *Qualitative Reading Inventory II.* New York: HarperCollins, 1995.

Loxterman, Jane A., Isabel L. Beck, and Margaret G. McKeown. "The Effects of Thinking Aloud during Reading on Students' Comprehension of More or Less Coherent Text." *Reading Research Quarterly* 29, no. 4 (October–December 1994): 352–367.

Perfetti, Charles A. *Reading Ability.* New York: Oxford University Press, 1985.

Peterson, Joe, M., Jean Greenlaw, and Robert J. Tierney. "Assessing Instructional Placement with the IRI: The Effectiveness of Comprehension Questions." *Journal of Educational Research* 71, no. 5 (May–June 1978): 247–250.

Powell, William R. "Reappraising the Criteria for Interpreting Informal Reading Inventories." In *Reading Diagnosis and Evaluation,* ed. D. L. DeBoer. Newark, DE: International Reading Association, 1970.

Rubenstein, Herbert, Joseph P. Kender, and F. Charles Mace. "Do Tests Penalize Readers for Short-Term Memory?" *Journal of Reading* 32, no. 1 (Oct. 1988): 4–10.

Schell, Leo M., and Gerald S. Hanna. "Can Informal Reading Inventories Reveal Strengths and Weaknesses in Comprehension Subskills?" *The Reading Teacher* 35, no. 3 (Dec. 1981): 263–268.

Schmitt, Maribeth Cassidy. "A Questionnaire to Measure Children's Awareness of Strategic Reading Processes." *The Reading Teacher* 43, no. 7 (March 1990): 454–461.

Symons, Sonya, and Michael Pressley. "Prior Knowledge Affects Text Search Success and Extraction of Information and Recall." *Reading Research Quarterly* 28, no. 3 (July–Sept. 1993): 250–261.

Wade, Suzanne E. "Using Think Alouds to Assess Comprehension." *The Reading Teacher* 43, no. 7 (March 1990): 442–453.

CHAPTER 4

Assessment for Internal Audiences: Portfolio Assessment

PERSPECTIVES ON AUTHENTIC ASSESSMENT AND EVALUATION

As you have read in previous chapters, assessment is undergoing fundamental changes. Perhaps never before have educators, parents, and students so closely examined and challenged long-held beliefs and practices regarding the assessment and evaluation of student learning.

For many years, annually conducted standardized achievement tests have been used to quantify the progress of students and measure the effectiveness of our schools. For almost as long, concerns have existed about the nature and accuracy of how students' achievement and progress are measured. In broad terms, these concerns include the following:

- Standardized achievement test content might not match local emphases or desired outcomes for students.
- Demographics of standardized test norm groups might not closely match local population demographics.
- Standardized achievement tests might measure only operations or processes that are easy to quantify.
- Students' own purposes, interests, and learning styles are divorced from assessment.
- Student progress is difficult to interpret when test results are largely quantitative.
- Teachers, students, and parents have no part in what is tested or how testing is accomplished, other than to try to interpret the results.

What do these concerns mean in real, human terms? The following real-life examples illustrate why such concerns exist.

- Susan's parents attend a parent-teacher conference to discuss Susan's standardized achievement test results. These results indicate that Susan's reading is almost two years below test norms for her grade level. While Susan's teacher tells them about the many ways in which Susan has grown and made progress this year, her parents are preoccupied with the thought that their child is failing in reading.
- As the state-mandated testing period approaches, teachers begin teaching test-taking skills such as accurately marking machine-scored response sheets, strategies for answering multiple-choice questions, and how long to puzzle over an item before proceeding to another one. Large blocks of subject matter instructional time are given over to teaching test-taking skills.
- Local newspapers print test results as if they were sports scores. Neighboring school divisions are compared, "winners" are headlined, and superintendents are asked for official statements that might somehow explain their students' perceived progress or lack thereof. School boards hold hastily called, closed-door meetings while reporters wait in hallways as if for a jury verdict.
- Individual schools within a division are rank-ordered by scores; principals of those schools at the bottom of the list cringe and begin updating their

resumes. Real estate agents photocopy the lists and begin directing clients toward the neighborhoods with "good" schools.

■ As teachers meet in the lounge and hallways, their comments reflect their concern and feelings of helplessness as they watch their students take the tests:

"Maria put her head down on the desk and started to cry. I didn't become a teacher to make kids cry!"

"After all the work we did on not giving up, continuing to look for the easy items, Matthew tried the first three problems, then gave up! I tried to get him to keep trying, but he just looked at me like I'd lied to him."

"Quentin didn't even try; he just colored the ovals in a geometric design! And he can do so MUCH!"

"I really hate this. All this class time given over to learning to take the tests, and for what? When there's so much they *need* to learn?"

Educators and parents ask whether there are other ways of assessing and evaluating students' progress and development that might be more authentic than traditional achievement tests. Teachers want ways to show what students can do and are doing, rather than what they are not doing; to show how students are progressing developmentally, rather than in relation to grade level norms; and to match assessment to local instructional goals and emphases. They also want to help students become reflective and self-evaluative, moving toward independence as learners. Parents want ways to understand what their children are learning, how they are growing toward mastery of subject matter and processes, and how their interests and abilities are changing over time. They want to know how their own children are growing, rather than only how they compare to others. And they, too, want their children to become more committed to their own learning, more reflective about their work, and more able to evaluate what they have done and what they are capable of.

What drives these needs is a search for *authenticity* in instruction and assessment. Authentic instruction consists of learning tasks that are real, not artificial; it produces real learning that can be used in everyday life, not learning which is circumscribed by the classroom or divorced from real life. Authentic assessment consists of analyzing how students demonstrate that learning by performing meaningful, real-life tasks for real purposes (Kieffer & Morrison, 1994; Rief & Barbieri, 1995).

WHY KEEP PORTFOLIOS?

Portfolios provide just such a means of fulfilling these needs. A portfolio is a collection of materials that demonstrate how each student is progressing across time in learning content, mastering operations, broadening and/or refining tastes and interests, and progressing in development toward more mature or complex stages.

Portfolios are established when students and teachers systematically collect representative samples of work over time and reflect on what such samples show about the students' achievement, goals, and capabilities. Portfolios can be used with any grade level, across the curriculum, to fulfill a variety of purposes: to showcase achievement, to document progress over time, to demonstrate effort in a variety of areas, and to foster students' decision making, self-evaluation, and reflection (Clemmons et al., 1993; Jasmine, 1992).

Showcasing Achievement

One purpose of portfolios is to showcase one's best work. Students might choose work that represents to them the pinnacle of their achievement in one or more curricular areas. The emphasis here is on products, rather than processes. Another way in which students can think about their "best work" is to consider what work they feel particularly proud of. This might not always be work that received the highest grades but might represent results they are especially pleased with. For example, a student might select his or her best spelling papers, perfect math tests, or best pieces of writing.

Documenting Progress

Another purpose of portfolios is to show progress in a particular subject area, skill, or process across time. For this purpose, work samples that show increasing complexity, mastery, or difficulty are chosen. For example, a student might select first drafts of original stories at monthly intervals, dated spelling tests showing mastery of increasingly difficult patterns, or math worksheets moving from simple to complex computations. Such examples are particularly useful for communicating with students and parents about how students are progressing developmentally.

Demonstrating Effort

Another useful purpose is to demonstrate areas or processes in which the student might not excel but is putting forth considerable effort. For example, reluctant writers might feel discouraged about the amount of writing they can produce but might be surprised to see that over time and with effort, their written pieces are growing considerably longer and more readable. Likewise, a writer might choose to include a composition that represents a great deal of work, even though the final product was not outstanding. Or a student who rarely persists long enough to finish a project might be encouraged to select work that demonstrates persistence and completion.

Fostering Students' Self-Evaluation and Reflection

For many teachers, especially those who teach middle schoolers and older students, the most important function of portfolios is to help students develop reflection and self-evaluation; that is, the objectivity to step back from their own work, reflect on its quality and importance to them, and evaluate their own strengths and abilities. When students do this, they move toward becoming independent learners, able to rely on their own judgments rather than being bound by what teachers or peers think of their work. This has particular value for adolescents, who might be negatively affected by their peers' judgments of their work and abilities. Self-evaluation helps students to retain their self-respect when others don't value their work and to value their own instincts and judgments. Self-evaluation is necessary if students are to feel ownership of and responsibility for their work (Hansen, 1994, 1999; Jervis, 1996).

BEGINNING A PORTFOLIO PROGRAM

Most teachers already have some system of keeping track of students' work, whether it be a work folder in which students keep current work to collect and send home, a drop file in which all graded student work is kept for displays and parent conferences, or even a bulletin board of excellent work. So beginning to use portfolios is not as difficult as it might seem.

The first thing you will need to decide is how comprehensive your portfolios should be. That is, what subject areas or skills do you want to document in this way? If you have never used portfolios before, it might be best to keep things very simple at first. You might decide to choose one particular area, such as reading, writing, or math and include only materials related to that area at first. These are, after all, fundamental subjects in which students and parents are very interested. Whether you choose to include one subject area, several, or all areas, don't try to do too much at once. If students are new to the portfolio process, it is easier to start simply and add complexity later than to have to cut back or streamline later. The section entitled "What Goes into a Portfolio?" later in this chapter, will show you what kinds of materials can be included in portfolios.

At the beginning, you will need to prepare some basic materials for storage and communicate what you are doing to students and their families. You will also want to inform your administrator that you are trying a new way of documenting student progress, one that will supplement your classroom grades, standardized test scores and other numerical data on student progress.

First, each student needs a sturdy folder. Many teachers use either sturdy cardboard folders with pockets or expanding file folders that can accomodate a lot of "stuff." Regular open-sided file folders can't hold very much, and papers begin to spill out. Also, they are not good for holding nonpaper materials, such as artwork, audiotapes of oral reading, and so forth. Students can decorate or otherwise make their folders unique.

Then find an accessible place for portfolio storage. Plastic "milk crate" storage boxes, plastic storage tubs, or even a cut-down cardboard box can house the folders, as long as it is easily accessible to students. (File drawers are unsafe; when opened, file cabinets can tip over if students lean on the drawer while looking for their folders.)

In classrooms where teachers have job charts or rotating duties, a new job may be added: portfolio helper, who makes sure the portfolios are neatly stored in alphabetical order at the end of the day. For students who might not have mastered alphabetical order, each student can be assigned a number and folders can be arranged in order. Checking folder order daily reinforces alphabetical and numerical ordering, and each student will get this practice when his or her turn comes.

Next, prepare a letter to parents explaining in simple terms that students will be collecting much of their work in a special folder to document what they are doing and how they are progressing. Explain that students will be asked to share the responsibility for choosing what work goes into their portfolios and that such choices require students to consider what might be their best work, their most challenging work, work of which they are most proud, and so forth. Invite parents to view the collected work at conferences, at open houses, and during visits to the classroom.

Finally, explain to students what they will be doing. If possible, have another teacher who already uses portfolios come to your room, perhaps with a few of his or her students, to show what portfolios look like and why students keep them. Or borrow a few portfolios from another classroom—with students' permission, of course—to demonstrate. Explain that many professionals, such as artists, photographers, actors, and models, compile portfolios that visually represent the depth and breadth of their experience and achievements and that the students' portfolios will likewise show their talents and progress. Pass out the empty portfolios for personalization, show how they are to be stored, and perhaps ask students to find one or more current pieces of work to be included.

Teach your students that all work must be dated. Many teachers use rubber stamps for this purpose. Office-type date stamps work well and look very official. Some teachers use different stamps to indicate the stage of some written work: "1st Draft," "Revised," "To Be Edited," and "Completed" are useful categories, with space for the student to write in the date. Dating all work helps students to see their progress across time, as well as how long a particular project took.

Primary Grades

Primary graders' portfolios will necessarily be simpler than those of older students. A simple drop file, into which students drop all of their current work in the chosen subject, works well. At regular intervals, say, once each week, time should be set aside for students to look at everything in their folders, choose particular pieces on the basis of some general criteria, and remove other pieces. The pieces that are removed can be sent home immediately.

For example, a first-grade teacher using portfolios for the first time set aside time on Friday afternoon for portfolio review. Students were to look at everything in their folders and set aside several work samples:

- their best writing done that week,
- something they had worked very hard on, or
- something they were very proud of.

Other work was put into large, sturdy envelopes to take home that afternoon. Parents were to review the work, sign the empty envelope, and return it to school on Monday. Work that was selected to include in portfolios was briefly shared and either discussed with the whole class, a small group, or a friend or discussed with the teacher in a brief portfolio conference (Vizyak, 1994–1995). Here is an example of part of a quick whole-group sharing:

TEACHER: As we go around the circle, hold up one piece you chose and tell us why you chose it. Yolanda, will you begin?

YOLANDA: I chose this story about my dog because I think it's a good story and because I drew a picture of my dog on the back.

BRUCE: I chose my word study test because I got all the words right.

Portfolio conferences are an important part of helping students to become reflective and self-evaluative. (You will read more about them in the section entitled "Portfolio Conferences.") Some teachers cringe at the thought of yet another teacher-student conference, wondering where the time will come from. It is important to keep in mind that a brief conference need take no more than a few minutes and that such a conference might occur no more often than once every several weeks.

Two second-grade teachers who have used portfolios for several years conduct these "miniconferences" during the time when students are looking over their work and reflecting on what to include, but they do their record keeping somewhat differently. Each teacher calls students individually to a small table to show one selection and tell briefly why it was selected. The teachers note the date of the discussion in their grade books. One jots a sentence or two about the selected work and what the student had to say about it on a portfolio conference form that is kept in each portfolio (see Figure 4.1); the other writes notes on file cards paper-clipped to the work. A glance at their grade books shows with whom they still need to meet.

In early primary grades, most of children's self-evaluations will be oral, and teachers' records of portfolio conferences are important ways of documenting children's decision making and reflection. As they learn to write, children can begin to complete some of their own reflective records. Teachers in one first-grade unit have students complete a simple response form once a week beginning in January; the form is a half sheet of paper with space at the top for the student's name, the date, and the question, "Why did you choose this for your portfolio?" Students complete the form on their own, paper-clip or staple it to the selected work, and read it to the teacher or assistant when finished. The adult may write what the student has read if it is difficult for others to read.

In second and third grades, students should begin to respond in writing to their own work periodically. A variety of questions, or reflection starters, can be used so that the process does not become rote. Some useful questions are the following:

- How does this work show what you are learning?
- What makes this work your best?
- Why are you proud of this work?
- How does this story (report, project, etc.) compare with other stories (reports, projects, etc.) you've done this year?
- How has your writing (reading, math, etc.) changed this year?
- Why did you choose this sample?

Student-Teacher Portfolio Conference

Student ___Carrie M.___ Date ___11-12___

Student Comments/Evaluation:

"... my best story so far."
(what makes it good?)
   it's long
   I've been working a long time
      on it
   I just like it

Student Goals:

   finish it
   publish it

Teacher Comments/Evaluation:

Carrie spoke w/ great enthusiasm
about this piece; shows real pride.
Her comments show awareness of
her effort. Goals vague – doesn't
yet have clear idea of what's next.

Student signature _____
Teacher signature _____

FIGURE 4.1 **Student-Teacher Portfolio Conference Form**

Figure 4.2 shows some third-grade responses. You will read more about student self-evaluations in the section entitled "Evaluating Portfolios" later in this chapter.

Middle and Upper Grades

Older students can take more responsibility for selecting work to be included, keeping some of their own records, and responding thoughtfully to their own work and effort. They can also arrive at more sophisticated judgments about how their work is changing and how they are progressing (Graves & Sunstein, 1992).

Student Self-Evaluation Card

Name Steve   Date

Think About: Why did I choose this piece?

My Self-Evaluation: This is my best poem. I used good words and made word pictures. I read it to my friends.

Student Self-Evaluation Card

Name Irma   Date

Think About: How does this report compare to your first one?

My Self-Evaluation: I put in lots more information. I used more books and I used two encyclopedias. My spelling was better too.

FIGURE 4.2 Student Self-Evaluations

If students are inexperienced at keeping portfolios, they will need a hands-on demonstration of what portfolios are, just as younger students do. Again, bringing in samples can be very helpful. At one middle school, the art teachers visit each language arts class to show their own and others' professional art portfolios. They explain how artists use portfolios to visually demonstrate their talents and invite students to draw comparisons between an artist's portfolio and a student's language arts portfolio. Students from other classes with portfolio experience can also visit classes to share their portfolios and their part in the evaluation process.

If portfolios are to follow students from one grade to the next, a selection of the previous year's portfolios can be studied. On the other hand, if portfolios are routinely returned to students at the end of the year, other teachers might have a few that they kept as samples from students who moved out of district or for other reasons.

Teachers who are new to the portfolio process might make a note to keep one or two portfolios for this purpose, perhaps photocopying the contents at year's end so that the students can keep theirs. Another way is to build a sample portfolio by photocopying exemplary pieces from a variety of students' work. (Protect students' privacy by securing permission from them and by removing names from photocopied work.)

Gaining the Support of Administrators and Parents

Letting people know what you are doing is important to the success of a portfolio effort. Be sure to discuss what you are going to do with your supervisor and/or building administrator *before* you inform either parents or students. Administrators typically don't like surprises; they *especially* don't like having parents call with questions that they can't answer because they don't know what you are doing! The concept of keeping portfolios is probably not new to your administrators, since they are a familiar part of so many classrooms today. But your administration might not know in detail how such records are kept, the extent to which students are or should be involved in the evaluation process, or how parents might receive the idea. So be prepared to sell your administrators on your plan.

First, arm yourself with enthusiasm and confidence. Assume that your administrators will approve any plan that will help students to become more responsible and more reflective about their own progress and abilities and that will help parents to better understand the school's curriculum and their students' progress. Emphasize these as your primary purposes. Approach administrators as partners, not as potential roadblocks.

Next, be prepared with concrete details of how the process works. Describe what curricular areas will be included and why you chose them. Outline how portfolios will be organized and stored, how work will be selected for inclusion, and how students will be involved in the evaluation process. It might be useful to share a few of the forms or other record-keeping aids that will be used. Be careful not to get bogged down with too many nuts-and-bolts details, but be ready to answer questions about specific operations.

Then describe your plan to involve parents in the portfolio process. Building good public relations is a part of an administrator's job, and increasing parent involvement is always a priority. Tell how you will use students' portfolios in parent-teacher conferences, at Open House or Back-to-School Night, and by sending portfolio samples or copies of samples home periodically. If portfolios are to be used in grading students, be ready to describe how portfolio contents will tangibly support and demonstrate how grades were earned. Emphasize that portfolios help parents to understand the school's expectations and how their students are developing across time.

By now, your administrator is probably already sold on your plan. If he or she is still uncertain, assure him or her that you plan to start small, to continually reevaluate the effectiveness of your plan, and to seek input from colleagues, parents, and students as you progress. Invite your administrator to visit your room as you introduce the plan to students, preview communications you will send home, and meet with you again before Open House or parent-teacher conferences. If desired, arrange to meet periodically for updates, and plan for selected students to share their portfolios individually with the administrator.

With your administration behind you, you are ready to inform parents of your plan. Some parents might question the validity of any new type of assessment, and some might resist what they perceive as nontraditional assessment. Many parents are used to letter grades based on test scores and graded assignments and to thinking about how their children compare to others. Portfolios help them to think about how their children are progressing on a developmental continuum. Parents also want to be assured that your principal supports you and that their children will be prepared for other teachers and other means of assessment.

The best way to enlist parents is to keep them fully informed and involved. Parents need to understand why portfolios are being used and what they might be expected to do. When they see their children's work progressing, compare their latest work with earlier work rather than with other students' work, and watch their children participate in self-evaluation, they are more likely to support the use of portfolios.

As we mentioned earlier in this chapter, you should send home a letter to let parents know what portfolios are, why students will be keeping them, how work will be evaluated, and how families can have input. The letter should be warm and positive in tone and free of jargon. Figures 4.3 and 4.4 show examples of parent letters that are informative and concise.

Any event that brings parents into the school is an opportunity for them to review their child's portfolio, ask questions, and make comments about progress and effort. These typically include Open House, Back-to-School Night, and parent-teacher conferences. But there are other opportunities, too; class parties and holiday celebrations, plays and concerts, awards assemblies, and PTA/PTO meetings are a few. Parents should be reminded often that they are welcome in your classroom, that their children *want* them to come and look over their portfolios, and that their ideas and input are important and valued. A Portfolio Party is a special event; Figure 4.5 shows a sample invitation. If many parents cannot attend during the school day, consider an evening event, perhaps in conjunction with another event such as a PTO meeting, Book Fair, Science Fair, or performance (Jasmine, 1992).

Don't expect all parents to be able or willing to come to school. There are many reasons why some parents are never seen at school, including (but not limited to) conflicting or unpredictable work schedules, transportation and child

Dear Parent or Guardian,

Welcome to the new school year! Our classroom will be an exciting place to grow and learn this year.

This year students will keep portfolios of their work in several subjects. It will be easy for students, other teachers, and you to see how your student is progressing. Students and I will work together to choose work to be included, and to evaluate the work.

I will explain more about student portfolios, and show you some examples, at Back-To-School Night. If you would like to know more before then, please call me at school or stop by our classroom. We would love to show you our work!

Sincerely,

FIGURE 4.3 Sample Parent Letter, Primary Grade

care difficulties, prior unfortunate experiences at conferences, custody conflicts, and negative or ambivalent feelings about their own schooling. But we must assume that all parents want their children to be educated and successful and want to help their children. It might seem clear to teachers that coming to school for conferences and meetings is important, but it might not seem so to all parents.

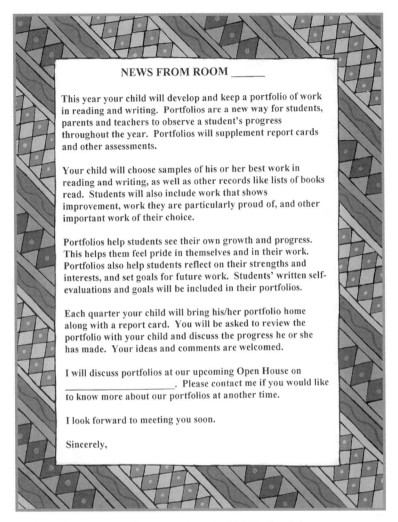

NEWS FROM ROOM _____

This year your child will develop and keep a portfolio of work in reading and writing. Portfolios are a new way for students, parents and teachers to observe a student's progress throughout the year. Portfolios will supplement report cards and other assessments.

Your child will choose samples of his or her best work in reading and writing, as well as other records like lists of books read. Students will also include work that shows improvement, work they are particularly proud of, and other important work of their choice.

Portfolios help students see their own growth and progress. This helps them feel pride in themselves and in their work. Portfolios also help students reflect on their strengths and interests, and set goals for future work. Students' written self-evaluations and goals will be included in their portfolios.

Each quarter your child will bring his/her portfolio home along with a report card. You will be asked to review the portfolio with your child and discuss the progress he or she has made. Your ideas and comments are welcomed.

I will discuss portfolios at our upcoming Open House on _____. Please contact me if you would like to know more about our portfolios at another time.

I look forward to meeting you soon.

Sincerely,

FIGURE 4.4 Sample Parent Letter, Middle Grades

We must reach out to parents who don't come to school as well as those who do. One way to do this is to send home samples or copies of work from the portfolio, or the whole portfolio if you are confident that it will be returned promptly, along with a parent response form that parents can fill out with the student and return for inclusion in the portfolio. You will learn more about parent evaluations, including a sample form that may be used for parent comments, in the section entitled "Evaluating Portfolios" later in this chapter.

If possible, phone parents to tell them when their child is bringing portfolio samples home. If you make a home visit, you might take the child's portfolio along to share with parents. When you can, involve the child by explaining the portfolio to the parent, selecting some old and new work to compare, or showing something particularly significant. The student's enthusiasm will be contagious.

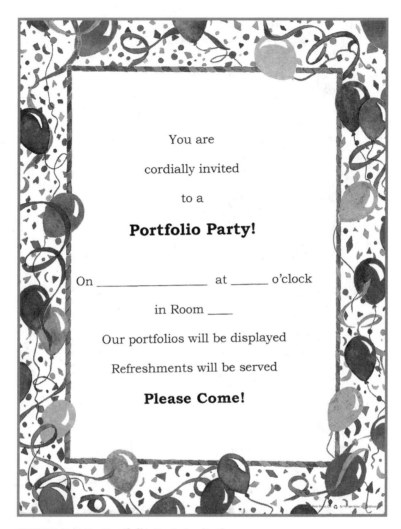

You are

cordially invited

to a

Portfolio Party!

On _____ at _____ o'clock

in Room ____

Our portfolios will be displayed

Refreshments will be served

Please Come!

FIGURE 4.5   Portfolio Party Invitation

Keeping Portfolios

Before you can determine what will go into students' portfolios, you must decide the purpose for keeping them.

The content of a portfolio depends on:

- the **intended audience** and
- the **purpose** for developing a portfolio.

A simple **collection portfolio** contains a wide variety of all kinds of work because its purpose is to form a pool of materials from which certain pieces or samples may be drawn for other purposes, such as to create another kind of portfolio, demonstrate growth across a variety of fronts, or familiarize students with the fundamentals of portfolio collection. Its audience is the teacher and the student. This kind of portfolio is sometimes referred to as a *work folder* or *drop file* and is widely used in many classrooms, even when teachers don't think they are using portfolios.

A **showcase** or **display portfolio** contains examples of the student's best work, chosen specifically to show growth and achievement in a particular area or areas. It might be restricted to one subject area in which the student excels, such as math, art, or writing. Its purpose is to display the depth and breadth of the student's talents. The audience is the student, teacher, parents, and others whom the student wants to impress, such as college admissions officers, competition judges, or leaders of selective programs. Showcase portfolios are fairly common in high schools and in programs for gifted and talented students.

The **progress** or **assessment portfolio** is the kind that most teachers think of when they think of student portfolios. This portfolio contains examples of the student's best work and work that shows marked growth, as does the showcase. However, it also contains selected work in progress, work that represents significant effort even if the product is not extraordinary, and copies of relevant assessment devices. These might include chapter and unit tests, standardized achievement tests, interest and attitude inventories, developmental checklists, lists of achievement benchmarks, lists of books read, running records of oral reading, videotapes and/or audiotapes, students' goal statements and written self-evaluations, teachers' evaluations and anecdotal records, notes on student-teacher portfolio conferences, and parent comment sheets. The purpose of an assessment or progress portfolio is to demonstrate progress, achievement, and effort. Its audience is the student, teacher, and parents.

Selecting Curricular Areas to Be Sampled

With your purpose in mind, your next task is to decide what areas of the curriculum you want to document with portfolios.

Your teaching assignment, of course, will play a large part in this decision, as will your school's major instructional goals. For teachers whose primary teaching assignment is in one area, such as language arts, math, or science, this is one less decision to make. Those who teach multiple subjects throughout the day, like the typical elementary classroom teacher, should decide in what subject area they wish to begin. If you decide to use student portfolios for more than one subject area, for example for language arts and math, students should sort their work into piles and keep a separate folder within a folder for each area. Alternatively, they can keep separate portfolios for each selected subject. But trying to keep up with more than one portfolio can be cumbersome.

Whether you decide to use portfolios to document just one subject area, such as language arts, math, or social studies, or keep more inclusive portfolios representing most or all of what students do throughout their day, remember to **start small.** Until you are experienced at portfolio assessment, it is much easier to begin with one area and add others as you and your students become familiar with the process.

In elementary grades, the areas that most regular classroom teachers document with portfolios are reading and writing. In part, this is because these subjects seem made to order for the process of using work samples to document progress.

Conversely, it is difficult to quantify growth in these areas that are so developmental in nature, and test scores, grades, and numbers often fail to capture the real nature of children's growth; witness teachers' and parents' annual struggle to make sense of standardized reading achievement test scores. Periodic work samples, however, show vividly what students are doing and how they are developing.

In this section, we will primarily discuss the components of reading and writing portfolios. Information can easily be adapted for portfolios in other subject areas. Because these literacy fundamentals are necessarily a part of all school subjects, the components that you select will also reflect students' growth and achievement in science, social studies, health, and, to some extent, math. Including work from these subject areas helps to build a more complete picture of each student's development.

What Goes into a Portfolio?

Here is a list of possible inclusions in a reading-writing portfolio. Some items listed might not be available or are not used in your classroom or school; some items you consider important might not be listed. Adapt it to fit your purposes and students. Box 4.1 summarizes these elements.

POSSIBLE INCLUSIONS IN READING-WRITING PORTFOLIOS

BOX 4.1

Baseline or entry writing samples, running records, reading inventories, other assessments
Interest inventories
Lists of books read
Book reports or reviews
Book summaries
Reading response journal entries
Running records of oral reading
Literature logs
Character studies
Personal journal entries
Original creative writing: stories, poetry, plays, etc.
Successive drafts of work showing the writing process
Subject area reports and projects
Photographs, audiotapes, and/or videotapes of student work
Teacher-student conference records
Student self-evaluations and goal statements
Parent review and comment forms
Records of extracurricular achievements

- *Baseline or Beginning Samples.* These are the students' earliest samples of work in any area, for example, reading journal entries, running records, audiotapes of oral reading, and first writings. These are collected to establish a baseline with which to compare later work.

- *Reading Journal Entries.* Reading journals, also known as *reading response logs* and *literature logs*, are notebooks that students use to record their responses to what they are currently reading. Simple summaries should give way to more thoughtful responses such as character studies, opinions about the characters' actions, and so forth. Reading journal entries can be collected quarterly, monthly, or at other intervals to show growth in critical thinking and types of literature selected.

- *Learning Log Entries.* Like reading journals, learning logs are often used to have students respond in writing to topics in subject areas such as science, math, and social studies. For example, students might write their thoughts or opinions about subject area topics such as pollution, rain forest preservation, or the dangers of smoking; describe the steps to be followed in solving a math problem; or summarize the new information that they learned from a reading assignment, discussion, or demonstration. Periodic sampling from the learning log helps to develop a picture of the student's growth in thinking, writing clarity, and subject area knowledge.

- *Writing Samples.* A common component of elementary portfolios is the sampling of students' writing at periodic intervals. Earlier writings can be contrasted with later efforts to show growth in any or all of the writing areas: use of prewriting strategies, development of early and later drafts, use of strategies to clarify and extend content, mastery of mechanics such as sentence formation, standard English usage and grammar, spelling, punctuation, and so forth. In addition to selecting pieces from different times of the year, students should be guided to select pieces that were written for different purposes and audiences: original stories, retellings of familiar stories, nonfiction or expository writing, persuasive pieces, letters, poetry, and so forth. At least twice a year, they should choose pieces that illustrate the steps in the writing process, from prewriting through successive revised drafts to editing, polishing, and sharing of the completed piece. In doing so, students and parents can observe the process of composing as well as the final product, the various ways writing is used in everyday life, and their growth in many areas (Barnes, Morgan, & Weinhold, 1998).

- *Records of Oral Reading.* Many teachers use **running records** (see Chapter 3) to document students' growth in oral reading accuracy, fluency, and use of reading strategies as they progress to more challenging reading levels. Teachers use a system of conventional marks to record everything a reader says and does while reading a portion of text. Running records are used to determine the accuracy and fluency of a student's oral reading and his or her use of decoding, syntax, and context strategies to identify unfamiliar words when reading material of a comfortable level of difficulty. **Audiotapes** of the student reading aloud at timely intervals may also be included, as they graphically demonstrate to the student and parents how the student's oral reading fluency and accuracy are progressing. The student might use the same tape for a number of readings; before each reading, the student records the date of the reading and might keep a simple chart listing the date of the reading, the title and author of the selection, and the beginning and ending numbers on the tape counter. (This allows you to quickly find and listen to a particular reading without having to listen to the whole tape.)

- **Lists of Books Read**. Each student should keep a list of books read in and out of school, noting the title, author, number of pages read, type or genre of literature, and beginning and ending dates. At intervals of several weeks, such as quarterly or at the end of a grading period, students can evaluate their reading habits in a number of ways. For example, they can graph the number of books read each month or the number of fiction and nonfiction books read each quarter. They can evaluate whether they are developing balance in their reading habits by selecting various genres or authors or limiting their reading to a particular series, author, or genre and set appropriate goals for the next period. They can also evaluate the amount of time they spend reading. Lists of books read help students, parents, and teachers to see what and how much students are reading and whether they are developing wide reading habits.

- **Text Samples with Written Responses.** Periodically, students can choose a current or recently completed book and photocopy a page or two to illustrate the types and difficulty of text they are reading. This makes a good accompaniment to the list of books read, which might not convey much to parents if the books are unfamiliar to them. To accompany text samples, students could include a written rationale for their choices, a response to an open-ended question about the text, a summary or critique of the book up to that point, or other written commentary.

- **Audiotapes of Oral Presentations**. Audiotapes are useful for capturing students' story retellings, oral reports, and book talks as well as oral readings. They are an excellent way of documenting students' growth in oral language use, fluency, vocabulary development, and sentence structure.

- **Videotapes.** Videotapes are invaluable in offering students a chance to observe and evaluate their reading, speaking, and listening skills and ability to work with others. They also offer parents and other observers a unique opportunity to see students in classroom situations that they would otherwise miss as well as providing a way to include three-dimensional projects in portfolios that otherwise could not be included. Videotapes can be used to record drama activities such as improvisations, reader's theater, skits and plays, presentation of projects and research, book talks and read-aloud activities, poetry readings, dramatic choral readings, debates, panel discussions, and so forth. Videotaping should be used as a part of the self-evaluation process. Participants should view the tape as soon after recording as possible and identify their strengths and possibilities for improvement. Peers may be invited to give helpful suggestions. If you plan to use videotaping for documentation, it is helpful for each student to have one blank videocassette to use for the year. Blank videotapes are often donated by parents, the PTO, or local civic groups or businesses, and the school's media specialist can copy relevant segments onto the tape belonging to each student involved in the activity.

- **Photographs.** Although they are less compelling than videotapes, photographs are simpler and less expensive to use while still offering a way of capturing students' projects, plays, and other strictly visual work. Photographs can be useful in documenting learning activities such as plays, skits, artwork, science projects, animal care, and constructions. If you use photographs, be sure to capture every class member in a variety of situations.

- **Assessment Devices.** These may include results of standardized tests, classroom tests, informal reading inventories, interest inventories, anecdotal records, skills or benchmark checklists, and so forth. These document student achievement and progress that may be mandated by the school or district and are more informative to teachers and parents than to students. Some teachers prefer to keep assessment devices in private folders that are separate from students' daily work, shared with parents at conferences, and transferred with portfolios to the next grade at the end of the year.

- **Conference and Student Self-Evaluation Records.** These include forms that are used to document when the student and teacher met to discuss the portfolio and students' written reflections on their progress and achievements. These inclusions document students' ability to reflect on their strengths, make decisions, set goals, and work toward achieving them. A sample of a conference form is shown in Figure 4.1 (p.138).

- **The Self-Esteem Folder.** Some teachers and students choose to include material such as awards, certificates, newspaper clippings and photos, memorabilia from extracurricular activities such as clubs and student government, and performance programs that represent special school achievements. Items relating to a student's achievements outside of school in clubs, sports, music, drama, art, and so forth can also be included as tangible reminders of achievements that enhance pride and self-esteem. Allowing students to celebrate their lives in and out of school in as many ways as possible may help them to connect school and the real world.

Helping Students to Select Work for Inclusion

In the previous section, we described what kinds of materials might be included in a language arts or reading-writing portfolio. How are decisions made about what to include?

A basic tenet to keep in mind is that a portfolio is a cooperative effort shared by teacher, student, and parents. Batzle (1992) wrote,

> The working portfolio is one in which the teacher and child assess and evaluate together. The student chooses samples that show his/her growth, parents contribute comments, and the teacher adds samples and other records. All perspectives (student, teacher and parent) are included to present a realistic picture. (p. 24)

In this way, the portfolio represents a panoramic picture of the whole student, showing both process and product.

Students' choice items typically include

- writing samples,
- reading responses,
- portfolio reflections and goals,
- published books,
- list of books read,
- photos, audiotapes, and videotapes,
- text samples and responses,
- "best work" samples,
- self-esteem items,
- samples of work in progress, showing stages of development of the work, and
- other items the student wants to include.

Teachers' choice items typically include

- running records,
- tests and other assessment devices,
- conference records,
- anecdotal records,
- progress checklists,
- interest inventories,
- work samples agreed on by teacher and student,
- parent comments, and
- other items the teacher wants to include.

Teachers should avoid dominating the selection process. Allow free access to the portfolios, and respect students' selection choices and reasons. When teachers dominate, students' sense of ownership erodes, and much of the portfolio's potential is lost. Students are most invested in their work and progress when they have authentic input into the process.

An overall plan for reviewing portfolios, selecting work, and reflecting on it should be developed. Work may be reviewed and selected monthly, quarterly, or at the end of each report card period, depending on the grade level, subject area, type of work being done, and other defining characteristics of the class. For example, young students might benefit from more frequent reviews; important work that takes a long time to complete, such as research reports, projects, and ambitious writing efforts, needs fairly long intervals between reviews; and students with low self-esteem might need frequent reviews to feel successful.

Let's say, for example, that you decide to have your third-grade class select work in reading and writing on a monthly basis. You have reviewed the list of possible inclusions found in the previous section, and posted a list of the things students will be selecting to include. (You will include items from the teacher's choice list above as they occur.) You have secured administrative support for your program; sent a letter home informing parents; introduced your class to the concept and purpose of portfolios; had students personalize folders; and taught them how portfolios are to be stored, ordered, and retrieved.

The first entries in portfolios will be the *baseline samples* referred to in the previous section. In each area, have students collect their first pieces of work, for example, their initial writing samples, reading journal entries, reading response log entries, and first oral readings on tape. (If students use composition books for reading response logs and learning logs, as most do, they will include dated photocopies of their first entries.) In the first weeks, you will add each student's first running records, informal reading inventory, interest inventory, skills checklist, and so forth.

One way to organize the baseline samples is to have each student tuck his/hers into a construction paper pocket or "minifolder" (a 12 inch × 18 inch sheet of construction paper, folded in half and stapled on the sides) with the date or month on the front. This keeps all the baseline samples together. Another way is to separate the samples into areas (e.g., reading, writing, and assessments), place them in separate minifolders, and add later related samples to them.

Now, at monthly intervals, you will build in periods in your planning for students to review their current work, select samples for that month to add to their portfolios, and compare earlier and later work. Using the same organizational scheme, students might collect all of that month's samples in a minifolder of a different color, dating the front, or they might add later samples to the separate minifolders they are keeping for each subject area. However they are organized, keep reminding students to date everything and to refrain from just tossing stuff into their portfolios with the intention of organizing it some other time. Portfolios can quickly become chaotic! Allow time for your "organizationally challenged" students to sort and arrange their portfolios frequently.

Along with the selection of work, students will engage in self-evaluation, goal setting, and portfolio conferences with the teacher. Evaluation and conferring with students and parents are discussed in the next sections.

EVALUATING PORTFOLIOS

Portfolios are more than just a way to document progress. They are also an effective way of helping students to become reflective and self-evaluative. After your baseline samples have been selected, begin teaching students how to self-evaluate and set goals for themselves. After they master these processes, they will use them each time they select new material to be included in their portfolios. Students of all ages, even the youngest, can learn to evaluate their own work and set goals for themselves.

Teaching Self-Evaluation

Teach students to self-evaluate the same way you would teach any new operation: by defining what students are to do, modeling the operation for them to observe while you talk through what you are demonstrating, having them practice the operation in small groups and discuss what they did, and then practice the operation individually. This is the basic scaffold for teaching self-evaluation in any subject area.

Let's say, for example, that you decide to begin this process by having students practice self-evaluating their writing. Compositions lend themselves particularly well to subjective evaluation. In this case, you would define the criteria for evaluating a composition by listing with students the things that make writing effective; these would include the writing skills and content that are appropriate for your grade and your students' developmental levels. With the whole group, using a sample that you made up or one from a previous year, "walk through" comparing the piece with the listed criteria and noting its strengths. The whole-group modeling may be repeated with other samples until students are comfortable with it (Hansen, 1989, 1994). (*IMPORTANT:* Initially, self-evaluation will focus on strengths only; later, needs for improvement can be added to the process, but *only* after students are habituated to looking for strengths and making positive comments.)

After one or more whole-group walk-throughs, and in another lesson, present small groups with a piece that is similar to the one you used for your demonstration. Have each group use the criteria chart to write an evaluation stating the strengths of the sample. (Young students can share their findings orally.) Repeat as necessary, changing the composition of each group so that students work with a variety of peers. When they are able to do this easily in small groups, they can work individually on a sample you provide. Or they can apply what they have learned in an individual evaluation of a current composition of their own. For their first time doing this individually, baseline samples are fine.

Students can also learn to self-evaluate their selections of other kinds of work. After they have learned how to self-evaluate their writing samples, they can practice the same process using selections from their reading response journals and learning logs, selections of content area work, and so forth. You might need to reteach the process for each different kind of portfolio selection, or your students might need only to review the procedure described above and develop criteria charts for good work in each area.

For example, criteria for effective literature responses might include writing the date, title, author, and copyright date; describing a character and the reasons for certain actions; explaining a conflict and its resolution; discussing the author's writing style or use of dialogue, narration, and so forth; and using correct writing mechanics. Criteria for effective learning log entries might include writing the date and subject area, writing the question or issue being responded to, using correct sentence structure and mechanics, and including drawings or diagrams to illustrate the entry. Criteria for effective research might include selecting a topic of interest to the researcher, using various sources of information, taking notes, creating an outline, organizing information, and producing an edited final draft.

Criteria charts should be developed with students and displayed for them to refer to when they are evaluating their portfolio selections. As time passes, the charts can be updated, and additional criteria can be added. As students become more proficient at self-evaluation, they will begin to internalize the criteria for good work and will have less need for charts and prompts.

Teaching Goal Setting

After students have practiced self-evaluation and are comfortable finding their own strengths, they are ready to begin setting goals by finding areas for improvement. Self-evaluation helps students to see the positives and feel pride in their work. Goal setting helps them to strive toward greater challenge, growth, and mastery. The criteria charts for effective work are used again, this time to find things that students need to continue practicing.

You might need to explain what goals are in this context and that goals should be realistic and specific. You might list some hypothetical needs, followed by examples of goal statements that are either vague or unrealistic.

Let's say that you use the example of a student who doesn't read very much. A goal for him might be to read more. *"I will read more,"* however, is too vague, while *"I will read 100 pages every day"* is unrealistic. Students can brainstorm better goals for this example: *"I will read for 20 minutes every night," "I will read five books this month,"* or *"I will finish reading (title) by (date)."*

You can then return to the criteria chart developed for a particular area, review how a selection may be evaluated for its strengths, and then extend the lesson by having students brainstorm how it could be improved. As a class or in small groups, have students write specific, reasonable goals as if the piece were their own. Repeat this process until students are able to confidently find strengths, then areas of need, and write one or more "good" goals for sample selections.

Then have students write goals for the improvement of their own individual selections. It might be helpful to have volunteers share their initial goals and invite peer feedback so that students practice writing goals that they really can work toward. Some examples of specific, realistic goals are *"I want to make my stories more interesting by using more colorful words," "I will use an outline to help me organize my next report,"* and *"My goal is to make sure I have a punctuation mark at the end of each sentence."* Remind students that working toward one or two goals at a time is plenty; trying to master too many things at once can be discouraging, even overwhelming. Reviewing goals and how students are working toward them is discussed in the next section, "Portfolio Conferences."

Teacher Evaluations

Teachers' evaluations of students' strengths and needs are a fundamental part of the portfolio process. First, these evaluations provide important information about students' abilities and progress, which might be more balanced and objective than students' and parents' viewpoints. Second, you provide validation for students' efforts, helping them to see their achievement and growth and guiding them to explore new areas and interests. Third, your evaluations provide an important means of evaluating and modifying your instructional program; awareness of students' strengths and needs gives direction to instructional change. There are several ways in which you can use the portfolio process to document students' achievement, progress, and needs (Graves & Sunstein, 1992; Jervis, 1996).

One way is through **portfolio conferences.** We briefly referred to the conference in the section entitled "Beginning a Portfolio Program." Because the student-teacher portfolio conference is such an important part of the process, we describe in detail how to conduct these sessions in the section to follow, "Portfolio Conferences." To avoid unnecessary redundancy, we will say here that the input that you provide in these conferences and the records that you keep of their content provide crucial documentation of students' progress and effort, their growth in goal setting and decision making, and your attention to individual instruction.

A second important source of teacher evaluations is **anecdotal records**. This term refers to notes that teachers make while they are observing students in various classroom situations. Yetta Goodman (1978) referred to teachers' informed observations of students' learning processes as **kid watching**. Kid watching includes two perspectives: *involved observations*, which take place while the teacher is actively working with students, and *objective observations*, which take place while students function independently. Anecdotal records are notes kept during kid watching or shortly thereafter while the observation is fresh in the teacher's mind. They should report, rather than judge or interpret; they are intended to document what student do and say, thus forming an objective record of students' day-to-day operations.

Batzle (1992) suggests several ways to keep anecdotal records systematically: using a grid on a clipboard with a square for each student and carrying the clipboard around the room, keeping an index card for each student and making dated entries on each card, using a calendar page with a student's name on each square and recording observations on self-sticking notes, and writing dated notes in a notebook with a divider for each student. The last method, she notes, might be easiest and most effective, since it does not involve later transferring temporary notes into portfolios and forms a diary of observations on each child.

Many teachers try several ways of keeping anecdotal records before they find a method that works best for them. Whatever the method, it is important to make sure that every child is observed periodically and that notes reflect observed behavior in specific ways. For example, *"Jose helped Ronnie find a word in the dictionary"* tells what Jose did; *"Jose was helpful to Ronnie"* and *"Jose has good dictionary skills"* are neither specific nor objective comments and would be less informative to the teacher, student, or parents.

A third way of incorporating teacher evaluations into portfolios involves traditional **grading**. In a sense, report card grades and portfolios are like oil and vinegar; they share fundamental characteristics but don't mix very well. In salad dressing, oil and vinegar contribute different but compatible flavors to the salad; in student evaluation, traditional grades and portfolio documentation contribute different but compatible information to the portrait of students' progress.

Grades purport to show where students are in comparison to others. When they are compared to their peers, we might think of this as "grading on a curve," or determining where the individual stands in comparison to a distribution with the performance of the lowest and highest students as the boundaries. When students are compared to a set of preestablished criteria, as on a criterion-referenced test or a teacher-made test for which the teacher knows what a "typical" class might do, they are being compared to a hypothetical peer group or to a set of expectations designed to fit a hypothetical group of peers. Either way, students are compared to each other. Portfolios, in contrast, allow comparison of students to themselves, in the sense that earlier work or effort is compared to later work or effort by the same student (Tchudi, 1997). Both kinds of comparisons are valid; both communicate to students, parents, and other teachers, and both contribute to each other.

Many teachers believe that work that is selected to be included in a portfolio should not be graded, since the portfolio is intended in large part to be a celebration of the student's unique abilities, achievements, and progress. Instead of assigning a letter grade, such work might be evaluated in narrative form, with comments attached to the work. Since the portfolio is designed to hold only a sampling of a student's work, this should pose no problem; other, similar work can be graded and sent home to parents.

Comments attached to portfolio work samples may vary in length but should be concise and positive, noting specifically what the student did well and, as necessary, indicating areas for possible further practice. Such evaluations should be done *after* students have self-evaluated the sample, to avoid influencing what students think of their own work. The student "owns" the portfolio, so comments should be addressed to the student by name and should be written on cards or notes attached to the work, not directly on the work itself.

In the beginning, you might find that writing a comment for each selected sample is time consuming; however, as you get into the process, you will find that it takes less time to write more meaningful, less general comments. For one thing, not every work sample needs to be accompanied by a teacher comment. Often, students' self-evaluations, plus comments you make about the sample in a conference with the student, are sufficient. Also, a few minutes are not too long for you to spend commenting on work that might have taken the student days, even weeks, to complete. As a general rule, the longer it took the student to complete the work, the more time its evaluation deserves. Samples that were quickly completed, such as a worksheet, spelling quiz, or "math minute," can be evaluated quite quickly; for example, "Look how many more problems you completed this time, Liz!" or "Alex, this sample shows me how hard you've worked on spelling vowel sounds" would be sufficient for short assignments. Figure 4.6 shows some sample narrative comments that are more substantive.

Parent Evaluations

Parents' input into their children's portfolios is tremendously valuable for several reasons. First, their comments show that they are aware of at least some of the things their child does in the classroom.

Second, their comments show whether or not they understand some of the fundamentals of today's instruction, such as the importance of home reading, children's use of invented spelling and the stages of the writing cycle. Parents' comments can show you where you need to make an explanatory phone call, invite parents in to observe or talk informally, send samples home more often, plan a parent education event, or make other efforts to better inform parents.

Third, parents' comments can give you valuable insight into variables in the children's lives outside of school that might bear on their interests, difficulties,

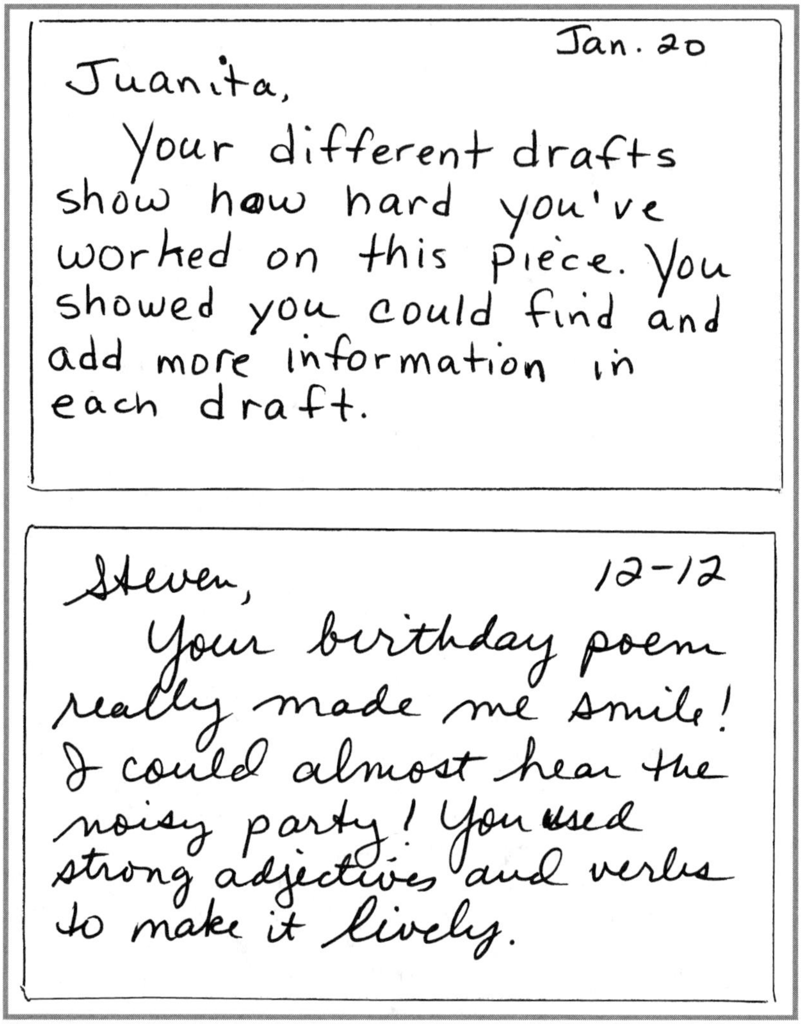

Jan. 20

Juanita,

   Your different drafts show how hard you've worked on this piece. You showed you could find and add more information in each draft.

Steven,   12-12

   Your birthday poem really made me smile! I could almost hear the noisy party! You used strong adjectives and verbs to make it lively.

FIGURE 4.6 Sample Teacher Evaluation Comments

areas of strength, behavior, motivation, and the like. Being aware of home influences in the child's life helps you to teach the whole child.

Fourth, parents' comments can be tremendously validating and encouraging to the student. As students get older, it might become harder for parents to understand what their children are doing in school and harder for children to explain. This can contribute to a growing gulf between home and school as parents are left to wonder just what their children are doing in school and how or why their children are doing particular work or studying particular topics. Encouraging parents to share in the portfolio process is an important way of bridging the home-school gulf.

Parents welcome opportunities to observe their children's progress and development. Portfolios offer the perfect opportunity to inform and involve them. Parents can get a much clearer understanding of their children's strengths and weaknesses from seeing sequential work samples than from test scores or grades. Parents also appreciate that teachers see their children as unique individuals, too. And parents become active participants in their children's education, even if they cannot participate in traditional parent activities such as classroom volunteering or parent-teacher organizations.

One way in which parents can contribute to the evaluation process is by completing a **parent response form** to be returned to school with the portfolio or selected samples after review at home. Figure 4.7 shows two samples of this kind of form. They should be kept short and simple but allow room for parents to write their comments.

Parents should be invited to review their children's portfolios regularly, whether during a scheduled conference, open house, classroom event, or drop-in visit to the classroom. Questions and concerns can be addressed in conferences or on the phone. You will read more about portfolio conferences with parents in the next section.

PORTFOLIO CONFERENCES

Students' evaluation and goal setting culminate in portfolio conferences. When the teacher and student confer, they become collaborators in the evaluation process. When students confer with peers about portfolio selections, they give and receive encouragement on their efforts and achievements and may discover strengths that they were unaware they had. And when students and teachers confer with parents, they can help parents to gain a comprehensive view of the student's work and abilities and a better understanding of their child's development.

Conferring with Students

Formal teacher-student conferences often occur in the latter part of the quarter or report card period. However, informal conferences can be held much more often at your discretion. Conferences vary in length depending on the student's age, the portfolio contents, and other factors; however, ten minutes or so for most elementary students is a fair estimate. Conferences with middle and high school students may take longer, unless the conference is limited to discussing one sample or goal. Some teachers post lists showing which students will have their conferences that day and hold conferences while students are working independently or in small groups. Others "grab" students as they can.

Students should review their portfolios before the conference so that they are ready to discuss their progress, strengths, and goals. Nothing is gained by trying to discuss the portfolio of a student who doesn't remember what his current

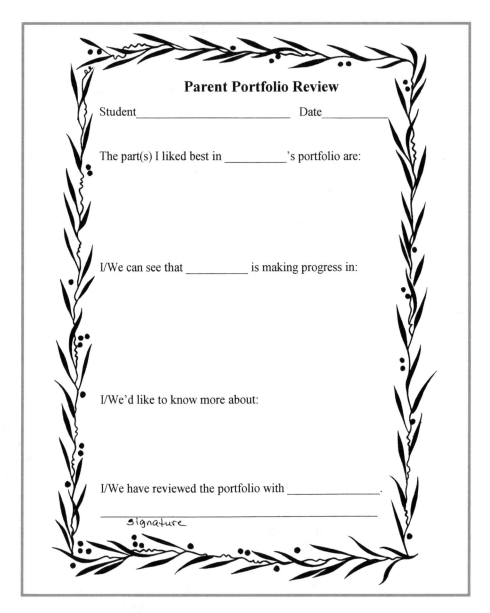

Parent Portfolio Review

Student_____ Date_____

The part(s) I liked best in _____'s portfolio are:

I/We can see that _____ is making progress in:

I/We'd like to know more about:

I/We have reviewed the portfolio with _____.

_____
signature

FIGURE 4.7 Sample Parent Response Forms

goal is, which piece is his best, or where he has made progress! Having students review their portfolios purposefully, with specific areas to look for, helps them to become more reflective; it also makes conferences more effective and efficient (Hansen, 1992).

Student-teacher conferences typically have three main parts:

Parent Response Form

Student_____ Date_____

Student comments: I chose this work because ...

It shows my progress because....

Parent comments: I/We think that this work shows...

Parent questions:

Parent(s) signature_____

FIGURE 4.7 *(continued)*

1. The *teacher compliments* the student on some aspect of the portfolio, such as organization, selection of samples, and thoughtful self-evaluations. The conference should begin on a positive note.
2. The *student recognizes areas of growth* shown by selected samples and discusses his or her reading and writing progress with the teacher. This might include discussion of how previous goals have been met or worked toward.
3. The *student sets goals* for the next quarter or interval, with the teacher's help if necessary.

You can see why students need time to review their portfolios before conferences and to know what they should look for. If you need to draw a student out during a conference, you can use questions like these:

- How does your portfolio show what you are learning?
- How can you tell from your work that you are growing as a reader (writer, etc.)?
- What can you do well in writing?
- What might your portfolio tell about you to person who didn't know you?
- What kinds of things do you like to read (write) about?
- What does this piece tell about you as a reader (writer)?
- How have you worked toward the goal(s) you set for yourself last quarter?

These open-ended questions are intended to get the student thinking and talking about the work. The student should talk more about the work than the teacher does. Avoid dominating the conference or making the student feel as though he or she is being cross-examined.

Students should review their previous goals and reflect on how they are progressing toward meeting them. This will help them to set goals for the next quarter or marking period. Some students might need help in setting realistic or attainable goals. Some whose goals were ambitious or long-range might continue working toward them. Not every student will have attained the previous goals or set new ones, but it is important for every student to reflect on his or her progress toward attaining them in the portfolio conference. It might be helpful for students to write what their most recent goal was and how they have attained it.

Portfolio conference records should reflect the dates of student-teacher conferences, areas discussed, goal setting, and other relevant comments. Figure 4.8 shows a sample portfolio conference form that is added to after each scheduled conference. A different kind of conference form, completed separately after each conference, is shown in Figure 4.8.)

Peer Conferences

Older students with portfolio experience can also benefit from conferring with peers about their portfolios. Peer conferences are less for evaluation purposes than for sharing selected work, explaining choices and goals, and getting helpful feedback from others. Like other examples of cooperative learning, peer

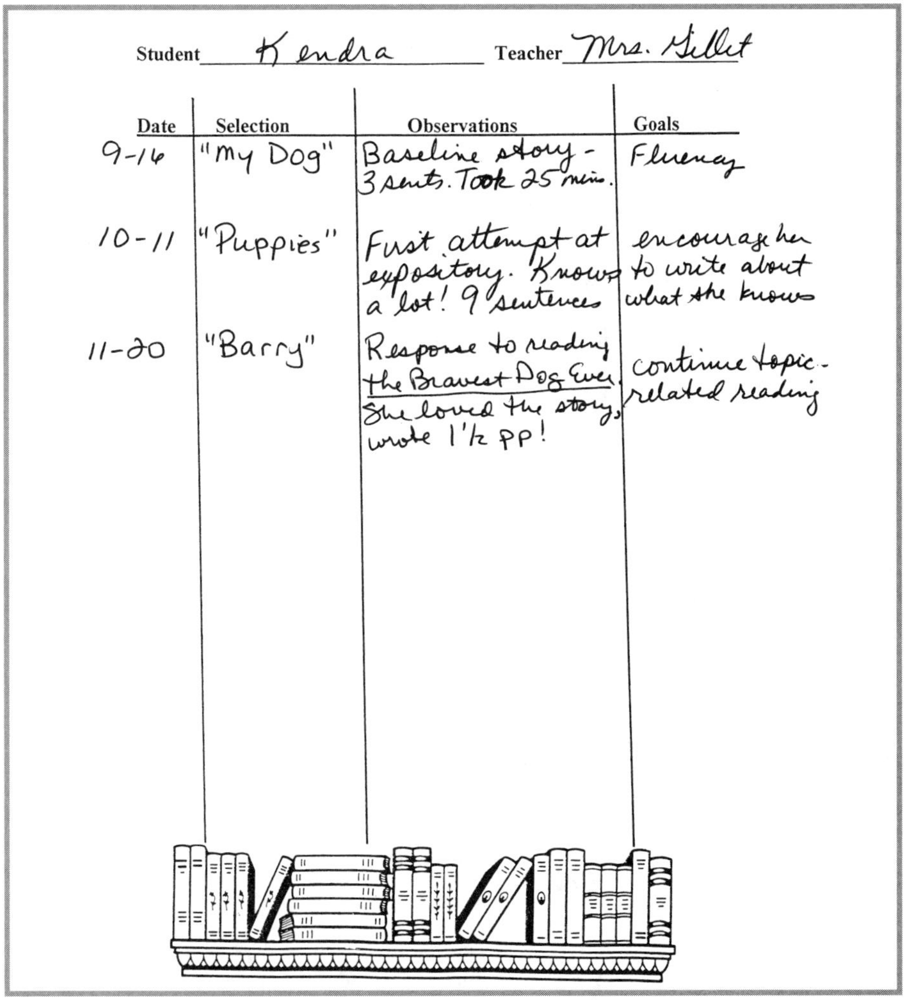

Date	Selection	Observations	Goals
9-16	"My Dog"	Baseline story - 3 sents. Took 25 min.	Fluency
10-11	"Puppies"	First attempt at expository. Knows a lot! 9 sentences	encourage her to write about what she knows
11-20	"Barry"	Response to reading the Bravest Dog Ever. She loved the story, wrote 1½ pp!	continue topic-related reading

Student: Kendra   Teacher: Mrs. Gillet

FIGURE 4.8 Portfolio Conference Form

conferences can be beneficial for both parties; the owner of the portfolio gets to show off some of his or her best work and accomplishments, and the partner gets to see what others are including in their portfolios and offer encouragement. Positive feedback from peers can be very validating, especially for adolescents.

Students need to be taught, however, how to conduct these conferences so that they are positive and helpful. Just as you would directly teach how to conduct any other activity, demonstrate with one student how to listen attentively, make positive comments about specific aspects of the work, and ask thoughtful

Portfolio Partner Review

Name_____ Date of review_____

I reviewed _____'s work sample.

I think this sample shows that _____ can...

I think _____ did these things well in this sample:

I think _____ learned....

And I learned.....

Signature_____

FIGURE 4.9 Portfolio Partner Review Form

questions. Then let students practice conferring with a partner and evaluate what they did in groups before you begin having students schedule peer conferences. Students could create a list of Peer Conference Do's and Don'ts to which they could refer as they work together. Figure 4.9 shows a sample partner review form.

Conferring with Parents

Portfolios can be invaluable in helping you to explain to parents what their children are working on, where their academic strengths lie, what skills and processes they need to develop, and how they are progressing. Portfolios give parents a "bird's-eye view" of their children's work that report cards, test scores, and other evaluative information cannot provide.

When you confer with parents, begin by highlighting the student's strengths and using portfolio samples to show how far the student has progressed to date.

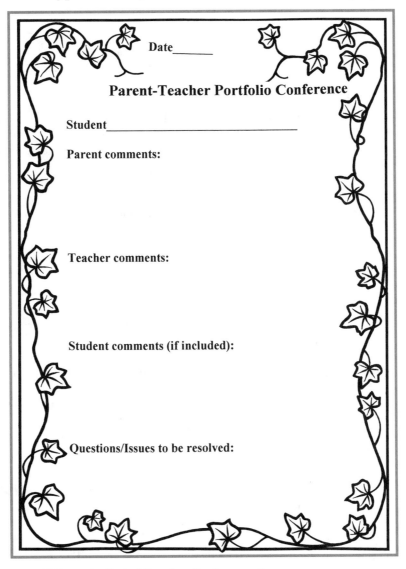

Date_____

Parent-Teacher Portfolio Conference

Student_____

Parent comments:

Teacher comments:

Student comments (if included):

Questions/Issues to be resolved:

FIGURE 4.10   Parent-Teacher Conference Form

It is much easier for parents to understand and accept statements of their child's needs *after* they have heard you acknowledge the child's strengths. Portfolio samples can be used to show areas that students need to practice and to reinforce or illustrate test scores, report card grades, and so forth. Goal statements and conference records document students' active role in learning.

Parents' comments and concerns should be noted on the teacher's copy of the parent-teacher conference form that you use to document such conferences. If your school does not already have such a form, you can adapt the one shown in Figure 4.10.

SUMMARY

Authentic assessment refers to assessment of students' demonstrated learning by performing meaningful, real-life tasks for real purposes. *Portfolios* provide a means of collecting materials that demonstrate how a student is progressing in learning content, mastering operations, and/or showing developmental progress or growth. Portfolios are typically used to *showcase achievement, document progress, demonstrate effort,* and *foster self-evaluation and reflection.*

Beginning a portfolio program requires teachers to determine the subject areas or skills in which such documentation is desired; prepare basic materials for storage; and communicate purposes and procedures to students, parents, and administrators. Primary-grade students often use a simple drop file system, periodically choosing work to keep and taking the rest home. Older students can select work for inclusion on the basis of a variety of criteria, and engage in self-evaluation as well as teacher-student and peer *portfolio conferences.* A variety of kinds of materials are suggested for inclusion in reading-writing portfolios.

Teaching students self-evaluation is important in the portfolio assessment process. Students confer with teachers, peers, and parents to share their observations about their own progress, strengths, and goals for further learning. A variety of *sample forms* are included to document these conferences and their outcomes.

REFERENCES

Barnes, Donna, Katherine Morgan, and Karen Weinhold, eds. *Writing Process Revisited: Sharing Our Stories.* Urbana, IL: National Council of Teachers of English, 1998.

Batzel, Janine. *Portfolio Assessment and Evaluation: Developing and Using Portfolios in the Classroom.* Cypress, CA: Creative Teaching Press, 1992.

Clemmons, Joan, Lois Laase, DonnaLynne Cooper, Nancy Areglado, and Mary Dill. *Portfolios in the Classroom: A Teacher's Sourcebook.* New York: Scholastic Professional Books, 1993.

Goodman, Yetta. "Kid Watching: An Alternative to Testing." *National Elementary Principals* 57, no. 4 (June 1978): 41–45.

Graves, Donald, and Bonnie Sunstein, eds. *Portfolio Portraits.* Portsmouth, NH: Heinemann Educational Books, 1992.

Hansen, Jane. "Anna Evaluates Herself." In *Risk Takers, Risk Makers, Risk Breakers,* eds. JoBeth Allen and Jane Mason. Portsmouth, NH: Heinemann Educational Books, 1989.

—. "Literacy Portfolios: Helping Students Know Themselves." *Educational Leadership* 49, no. 8 (August 1992): 66–68.

—. "Literacy Portfolios: Windows on Potential." In *Authentic Reading Assessment: Practices and Possibilities,* eds. Sheila Valencia, Elfrieda Hiebert, and Peter Afflerbach. Newark, DE: International Reading Assoiation, 1994.

—. *Doing What Counts: Learners Become Better Evaluators.* Portsmouth, NH: Heinemann Educational Books, 1999.

Jasmine, Julia. *Portolio Assessment for Your Whole Language Classroom.* Huntington Beach, CA: Teacher Created Materials, Inc., 1992.

Jervis, Kathy. *Eyes on the Child: Three Portfolio Stories.* New York: Teachers College Press, 1996.

Kieffer, Ron, and Linda Morrison. "Changing Portfolio Process: One Journey Toward Authentic Assessment. *Language Arts* 71, no. 6 (October 1994): 411–418.

Rief, Linda, and Maureen Barbieri, eds. *All That Matters: What Is It We Value in School and Beyond?* Portsmouth, NH: Heinemann Educational Books, 1995.

Tchudi, Stephen, ed. *Alternatives to Grading Student Writing.* Urbana, IL: National Council of Teachers of English, 1997.

Vizyak, Lindy. "Student Portfolios: Building Self-Reflection in a First-Grade Classroom." *The Reading Teacher* 48, no. 4 (December 1994/January 1995): 362–364.

REPRODUCIBLE FORMS

Student-Teacher Portfolio Conference

Student_____ Date_____

Student Comments/Evaluation:

Student Goals:

Teacher Comments/Evaluation:

Student signature_____
Teacher signature_____

Student-Teacher Portfolio Conference

Student_____ Date_____

Student Comments/Evaluation:

Student Goals:

Teacher Comments/Evaluation:

Student Signature_____

Teacher Signature_____

Student Self-Evaluation Card

Name_____Date_____

Think About:_____
_____

My Self-Evaluation:_____
_____
_____
_____
_____
_____
_____

Student Self-Evaluation Card

Name_____Date_____

Think About:_____
_____

My Self-Evaluation:_____
_____
_____
_____
_____
_____
_____

Student Self-Evaluation Card

Name_____Date_____

Think About:_____

_____

My Self-Evaluation:_____

_____

_____

_____

_____

_____

Student Self-Evaluation Card

Name_____Date_____

Think About:_____

_____

My Self-Evaluation:_____

_____

_____

_____

_____

_____

Dear Parent or Guardian,

Welcome to the new school year! Our classroom will be an exciting place to grow and learn this year.

This year students will keep portfolios of their work in several subjects. It will be easy for students, other teachers, and you to see how your student is progressing. Students and I will work together to choose work to be included, and to evaluate the work.

I will explain more about student portfolios, and show you some examples, at Back-To-School Night. If you would like to know more before then, please call me at school or stop by our classroom. We would love to show you our work!

Sincerely,

NEWS FROM ROOM _____

This year your child will develop and keep a portfolio of work in reading and writing. Portfolios are a new way for students, parents and teachers to observe a student's progress throughout the year. Portfolios will supplement report cards and other assessments.

Your child will choose samples of his or her best work in reading and writing, as well as other records like lists of books read. Students will also include work that shows improvement, work they are particularly proud of, and other important work of their choice.

Portfolios help students see their own growth and progress. This helps them feel pride in themselves and in their work. Portfolios also help students reflect on their strengths and interests, and set goals for future work. Students' written self-evaluations and goals will be included in their portfolios.

Each quarter your child will bring his/her portfolio home along with a report card. You will be asked to review the portfolio with your child and discuss the progress he or she has made. Your ideas and comments are welcomed.

I will discuss portfolios at our upcoming Open House on _____. Please contact me if you would like to know more about our portfolios at another time.

I look forward to meeting you soon.

Sincerely,

Parent Portfolio Review

Student_____   Date_____

The part(s) I liked best in _____'s portfolio are:

I/We can see that _____ is making progress in:

I/We'd like to know more about:

I/We have reviewed the portfolio with _____.

_____

Parent Response Form

Student_____ Date_____

Student comments: I chose this work because ...

It shows my progress because....

Parent comments: I/We think that this work shows...

Parent questions:

Parent(s) signature_____

Parent Response Form

Student_____ Date_____

Student comments: I chose this work because ...

It shows my progress because....

Parent comments: I/We think that this work shows...

Parent questions:

Parent(s) signature_____

Portfolio Conference Form

Student_____ Teacher_____

Date	Selection	Observations	Goals

Portfolio Partner Review

Name_____ Date of review_____

I reviewed _____'s work sample.

I think this sample shows that _____ can...

I think _____ did these things well in this sample:

I think _____ learned....

And I learned.....

Signature_____

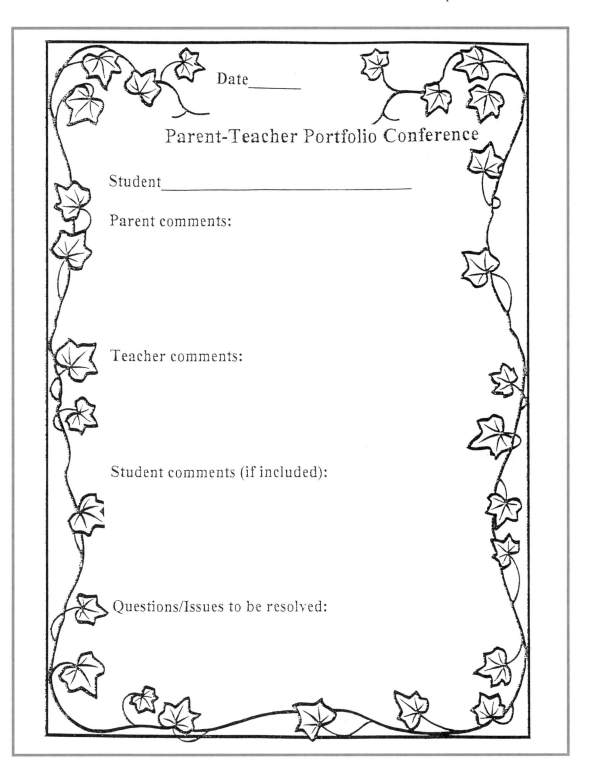

Date_____

Parent-Teacher Portfolio Conference

Student_____

Parent comments:

Teacher comments:

Student comments (if included):

Questions/Issues to be resolved:

Parent-Teacher Portfolio Conference

Student_____ Date_____

Parent comments:

Teacher comments:

Student comments (if included):

Questions/Issues to be resolved:

CHAPTER **5**

Assessment for External Audiences: Formal Measures

This chapter is devoted to formal measures of reading. Two principal types of formal measures are norm-referenced standardized tests and criterion-referenced tests. Most students encounter these formal measures in the form of group achievement tests administered during the elementary and secondary grades and in college admissions tests such as the Scholastic Aptitude Test and the Graduate Record Examination. The results of formal assessments of reading are often used to assess school, district, or state reading programs; to identify individual strengths and weaknesses within a curriculum; and to compare achievement patterns of schools, districts, and states.

This chapter will provide you with information that will help in determining the appropriateness of formal assessments for particular uses and interpreting their results. Our goal is to help you to make accurate responses to parents' questions and determine whether a particular test should be used to assess individual students' scores. To use and interpret test scores, teachers must be knowledgeable about characteristics of tests in general and any peculiarities of specific tests. Without this knowledge, interpretations can be difficult at best and inaccurate at worst.

UNDERSTANDING FORMAL TESTS

For decades, formal tests were used to quantify student achievement and to assess instructional effectiveness. They are still used for these purposes, but in recent years, criticism of the validity and authenticity of such tests has increased. Today, most schools and school divisions are required to administer and interpret formal measures and to supplement them with a variety of informal and observational assessments. What are the major criticisms of formal tests, particularly reading tests?

First, and perhaps most important to reading educators, is that formal reading tests do not reflect what we know about the process of reading. We know that reading is a complex, constructive process in which meaning results from interaction among the reader, the text, and the context in which the reading occurs. The prior experiences, background knowledge, interests, motivation, and knowledge of the reading process are *reader factors*. The amount and nature of the information conveyed, organizational structures, vocabulary, grammatical complexity, writing style, and even size and clarity of type are *text factors*. The setting in which the reading takes place, the purpose for the reading, the locus of purpose setting (i.e., whether the purpose is set by the text, the reader, or another person), the frequency of interruptions during reading, and so forth are *context factors*. These factors combine to enable the reader to actively construct meaning from reading.

But formal reading tests most often treat reading as a series of isolated, discrete skills. Test results show how readers perform on one separate skill after another, and these scores are generally added together to yield a global or overall reading score. This practice is a holdover from the outdated summative view that effective reading requires mastery of a list of discrete skills, each of which can be taught, practiced and mastered in isolation. This model of reading has largely been abandoned in favor of the interactive, constructive model.

Second, formal reading tests typically do not assess reading in authentic ways. In real life, comprehension is often demonstrated by doing something with the information that is gained. But in test reading, comprehension is usually demonstrated by answering questions about it, often in a multiple-choice format. In real life, readers often read fairly lengthy selections, including whole stories, chapters, and whole books. In test reading, selections are usually much shorter; they may be as short as a single sentence and are rarely longer than a single page.

In real life, reading is rarely timed, and the reader determines how quickly or slowly to read the material. In test reading, most selections are timed, and readers who don't finish the section are penalized. Most educators agree that formal tests create artificial contexts for effective reading.

Third, formal reading tests often do not match the goals of instruction. Most are geared toward retention of a quantity of factual information, which may be thought of as *product.* Yet most instructional programs emphasize *process* as much as product. Especially in the elementary grades, we are as interested in teaching students the process of learning as we are in teaching information and are as concerned with the learning process as with the products of such learning. But formal tests do not take process into account; indeed, they can create the appearance of a lack of success because of this.

For example, imagine a class of low-achieving, reluctant readers and writers. Their teacher hopes that their test scores will increase this year; but she is even more hopeful that the students will modify their negative attitudes about reading, spend more time reading and enjoy it more, and use writing more effectively for communication and self-awareness. As the year progresses, she documents dramatic increases in the amount of reading and writing her students are doing and the amount of time they spend reading and writing. Their reading habits and comments about reading reflect an increase in positive feelings about reading and about themselves as successful students. However, end-of-year standardized achievement tests show only a very modest increase in average reading level. If just these scores were available, it might appear that the class had made little progress in reading improvement. In this case, the formal measures that the school division required were not compatible with the goals of instruction.

Finally, and related to the foregoing point, formal tests most often measure skills and operations that are easily quantified and tested. Often, students are required to recognize, rather than produce, correct information. For example, they might be asked to choose the best title for a paragraph from several alternatives, rather than to create a good title for it. Or they might be asked to choose the correct spelling from several incorrect versions of the same word, rather than to spell the word correctly.

Recognition is easier than production; it is easier to do, to score, and to measure. But it is generally not what we want students to learn. We teach spelling so that students can produce correctly spelled words, not so that they can merely recognize misspellings. We teach them to recognize main ideas so that they can use the information gained by reading, not so that they can choose the main idea from a list. The operations that result in increased test scores might not result in real, useful learning.

In spite of these criticisms of formal tests, their widespread use continues. Why?

Communities expect their schools to do an effective job of teaching young people the information and skills they need to live productive lives and be good citizens. When students reach high school, or leave it, lacking basic skills in reading, writing, science, and mathematics, communities are rightfully concerned. They seek to make their schools accountable in a variety of ways. Most of these ways hinge on achieving test scores that show what students have mastered.

Formal tests don't test all of the things we want students to know or do, but they do show mastery over certain kinds of information and operations. They yield numerical results that are fairly easy to interpret and compare. They are much more economical of time and effort than many informal measures. And because they have standardized administration procedures that everyone must follow to the letter, they ensure that all students will have the same instructions, examples, time limits, and so forth. This makes it easier to compare scores from one locality to another.

Finally, many people feel more comfortable with numerical scores than with other types of test results that depend more upon examiner or teacher judgments. The idea that "numbers don't lie" dies hard. Numerical scores somehow seem less subjective than other results. So many communities and legislative bodies have continued to require formal test results to ensure educational accountability.

With these issues in mind, it is imperative that teachers understand the characteristics, purposes, and features of formal tests.

CHARACTERISTICS OF TESTS

When we select a tool to do a job, we typically know the nature of the job, the level of skill we possess, and the tools we have available. The same is true for selecting a formal measure of reading. When that selection is made, we, or those who do the selection, should know what we want to do with the results, the level of skill or support we have in administering and interpreting the test, and the options that are available for selecting a test. Most districts have selected one test or a small group of tests that will be purchased and administered to its students.

In the sections that follow, we will briefly describe some fundamental concepts of testing and measurement that apply to all standardized tests, not just reading tests. These basic concepts are necessary to an understanding of such reading tests.

The quality of the tool that is selected to do a certain job is directly related to the quality of the outcome of the job. For formal tests, two qualities are critical to the performance of a test: *reliability* and *validity*. Both are necessary for a good test, but of the two, validity is the more important.

Reliability

Reliability is a measure of how stable test scores are. It refers to the results obtained from a test, not to the test itself. There are several aspects of reliability to be considered. One is *stability*, or the consistency of test scores across time, from one administration to another with the same group of subjects. Another is *internal consistency*, or the consistency of items within a test. A third is *equivalence*, or consistency across different forms of the same test.

Stability

If a group of students took Test 1 several times, each individual's score would be somewhat different each time. If the scores are consistent, or reliable, the students' rank order would remain very similar from one testing to another. Therefore, the student with the highest score the first time would have the highest, or nearly the highest, score the second time; the student with the lowest score would retain very low standing, and the order of students between highest and lowest would remain nearly unchanged. If stability is lacking, a score that is attained once is unrelated to the score that is attained another time. Obviously, such scores would have little meaning or usefulness because they would be heavily affected by random chance.

Stability is estimated by using the *test-retest method*. The same test is given twice to the same group of subjects, and the rank order of their scores on each one is compared. If the interval between administrations is fairly short, students will remember a number of items and will be familiar with the format. This method will tend to raise everyone's scores, but the rank order of the scores will remain much the same. The rank order of the scores, not the numerical value of the scores themselves, is what is important here. If the interval between administrations is very long, maturation and the acquiring of new information will affect performance.

Internal Consistency

This term refers to the degree to which items within a test are related. Internal consistency is determined by comparing a student's performance on an entire test to her or his performance on two halves of the same test administered separately. However, since the more difficult items often come toward the end, it would not be a good practice to split a test at the middle. Instead, alternate items should be selected: one half with all the odd-numbered items, the other half with all the even-numbered items. If the scores on each half are closely related, a measure of good internal consistency has been provided. If performance on the two halves is not closely related, the total test score will not be reliable, and its value is questionable.

Sometimes internal consistency is estimated by the *split-halves method* in which students take the two halves of a test as separate tests. The scores on each half are correlated, and an arithmetic formula is applied to relate the correlation to the entire test. Other ways of estimating internal consistency involve giving the whole test once and applying one of several arithmetic formulas to the total score. The computations are beyond the scope of this discussion, but you will find detailed information in almost any text on tests and measurement methods.

Equivalence

When alternate forms of a test are being used, equivalence is important. Many standardized reading tests feature alternative forms that are used for pretesting and posttesting, but they must be highly equivalent if the scores are to have any usefulness.

The *equivalent forms method* is used to estimate this aspect of reliability. It requires the construction of two different tests, each one an equally good sampling of the content being tested. Each form must also be equivalent in difficulty and length. The two forms are administered to the same students in close succession, and the scores on the two forms are correlated. This method usually yields the most conservative estimate of reliability.

Every standardized reading test that you consider for use should have reported reliability estimates and should indicate what methods were used to determine such estimates. Reliability can be expressed in numerical terms by a *reliability coefficient*. This coefficient, a decimal number between 0 and 1, shows how consistent the scores were after using the test-retest, split-halves, or equivalent forms assessments. The closer to 1.0 the reliability coefficient is, the more reliable the scores are.

Overall reliability can be profoundly affected, for good or bad, by the consistency of individual subtests. Survey reading tests, generally used for screening large numbers of students, usually have few subtests, and the expressed reliability coefficients refer to the test as a whole. Quite a few reading achievement tests and most standardized reading diagnostic tests, however, have many separate subtests, and the reliability of subtest scores can vary widely. These tests should have reported subtest reliabilities as well as a coefficient for the entire test, and scores on subtests of questionable reliability must be discounted. If a test that is under consideration has more than one or two subtests of low reliability, another test should be considered.

A final point about judging reliability concerns the *standard error of measurement*. This term does not mean that there are mistakes in the test; it refers to the fact that no score is absolutely precise. The standard error of measurement is a number that indicates how much an individual's score might have varied depending on random chance factors. The standard error shows numerically how accurate any score is likely to be. A small standard error indicates high reliability, and we can be fairly confident that the student's test score and the true score closely approximate each other.

Validity

Reliability is necessary, but not sufficient, for a test to be a good one. A test can yield consistent scores but still not truly measure what it was intended to measure. This quality of actually measuring what was supposed to be measured is referred to as *test validity*. There are several types of validity that are often referred to in test reviews and manuals, and teachers should understand how validity is developed in test evaluation.

Although reliability is a quantitative concept, validity involves qualitative judgments as well.

Content Validity

In assessing content validity, we ask whether the test is an adequate sample of the content area or process being tested. Content validity is particularly important in achievement tests, which are designed to show subject mastery.

A spelling achievement test for elementary students that included only very difficult, infrequently used words from college textbooks would lack content validity because it would not represent what elementary children study in spelling. A reading test that was made up primarily of answering multiple choice questions about reading passages only a few sentences long probably would not be considered a good test of reading ability by many teachers today.

Content validity is established when test makers study school curricula and tests and submit their tests to the scrutiny of subject area experts. Some authorities claim that many reading achievement tests lack content validity because they measure only a narrow range of real reading behaviors, artificially partition the reading process into a host of separate skills, and ask trivial questions about meaningless passages.

The content validity of current reading tests is an issue of major importance. In recent years, our understanding of literacy and effective reading has changed, and the content of tests and methodology of testing has not kept up. If test content does not closely match what we understand reading is and what we teach our students about reading, then the tests' content validity is questionable. Lipson and Wixon (1991) claim that "the degree of mismatch between theory, instruction and assessment has become quite alarming" (p. 223). The situation has not improved since that statement was written.

Criterion-Related Validity

One way of establishing a test's validity is to relate it to other validated measures of the same ability or knowledge. The predetermined *criterion* may be other test scores, grades or subject area performance, or other observable behaviors. A test has criterion-related validity if it calls for responses that relate closely to actual performance. Concurrent validity and predictive validity are both criterion-related.

When a new test is found to be highly correlated to an existing test of established validity, it is said to have *concurrent validity*. Test makers frequently report coefficients of concurrent validity. But just because two tests are closely related does not necessarily mean that either one is valid, only that they measure the same attribute.

When a score is closely related to later performance on some criterion, the test is said to have *predictive validity*. This aspect is critically important in aptitude tests, since they purport to determine whether someone has the potential to become skilled in a particular field at a later time. If students who do well on a test of mechanical aptitude later excel in school courses such as woodshop and drafting and then go on to college engineering and technical schools or seek careers as engineers, architects, and machinists, that test is a good predictor of mechanical aptitude. The Scholastic Aptitude Test (SAT), used to predict the potential of high school students for college studies, is believed to be high in predictive validity because SAT scores and subsequent college grade-point averages are closely related.

Construct Validity

Traits or qualities that are not directly observable or measurable, but are widely inferred from behaviors, are called constructs. Traits such as attitudes, intelligence, or aptitudes are not directly measurable and must be inferred from observable behaviors. Thus, intelligence, musical or mechanical aptitude, judgment, problem solving, attitudes, and interests are constructs.

If a test has good construct validity, it allows the students to demonstrate behaviors that are directly related to the construct. In a test of attitudes toward reading, for example, students should be able to show how positively or negatively they would feel about getting a book for a gift, hearing a book discussed, going to the library or bookstore, or seeing someone vandalizing a book. Construct validity is important in all tests, but it is critical in psychological and personality tests and attitude inventories.

INTERPRETING TEST RESULTS

Once a reliable and valid test is selected and administered, the tests are scored and the results are reported to various interested groups (e.g., teachers, administrators, parents, governmental officials, news media). Test results are often presented in three ways:

- the distribution of test scores,
- measures of central tendency, and
- measures of dispersion.

Distributions of Test Scores

Descriptions of the *distribution* of test scores provide visual representations and other indicators of a group's performance on a given test. Two dimensions are typically used to describe the distribution of test scores. One is the score on the test itself, and the other is the number of students obtaining a particular score. Most of us are probably familiar with the *bell-shaped curve* or the *normal distribution* (see Figure 5.1). In this distribution, more students scored in the average range than in either the high range or the low range.

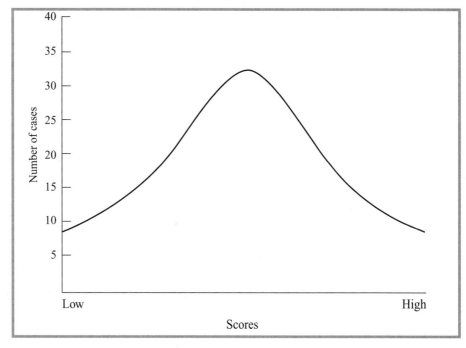

FIGURE 5.1 Normal Distribution

Not all distributions are normal. Instead of most of the scores clustering in the middle, a test might yield a distribution with many very high or very low scores. This is called a *skewed* or *asymmetrical distribution* (see Figure 5.2). The

FIGURE 5.2 Skewed or Asymmetrical Distributions

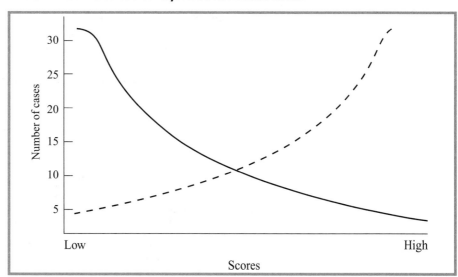

shape of the distribution of scores for a class, school, or district graphically represents the overall performance of a group or groups of students.

Compare the distribution of scores in Figure 5.1 to the two distributions in Figure 5.2. At least on the surface, the three sets of scores are distributed differently for different groups of students who completed the test. There are several possible explanations for this difference.

One is that for the asymmetrical distributions, the test might not have adequately measured the construct that was the object of instruction. The distribution that shows many high scores and few low scores was probably very easy for most of those taking the test, while the opposite is true for the distribution showing many low scores and few high scores.

In the latter case, the test might have been too hard for most of those who took it; in addition, variables such as disruptions during the testing, uncomfortable testing conditions, test bias, and so forth could have negatively influenced a large number of scores. Whatever the reasons, distributions that are highly skewed should be viewed with caution (Kubiszyn and Borich, 1990).

Measures of Central Tendency: Mean, Median, and Mode

Scores are most often thought of in relation to where they lie on some distribution. The most common measure of central tendency is the *mean,* or average. For example, many teachers use averages in assigning report card grades; a student who got math test scores of 67, 89, 73, 66, 92, and 80 had an average score of 78, which is represented by a grade of, say, C+. To get a mean score, add all the scores together and divide the sum by the number of scores added together.

Other measures of central tendency are the median and mode. The *median* is the point on a distribution at which there are equal numbers of scores above and below it. For example, if four students took a spelling test and got scores of 14, 15, 16, and 17, the median score would be 15.5, since there are two scores below 15.5 and two scores above it.

The *mode* represents the most frequently occurring score. In general, the closer together the mean, median, and mode of a set of scores are, the more symmetrical the distribution will be. If these measures of central tendency are widely dissimilar, the distribution will be asymmetrical.

When the media report on test scores or school achievement, they most often refer to "averages" or mean test scores of a school or school district derived from standardized tests or the Scholastic Aptitude Test. It is fairly common to see mean scores for a particular school grade compared to the scores of other schools in the same division, divisions compared to each other, and divisions compared to state averages.

For example, let's consider Alpha Public Schools, a district that contains four elementary schools. The average reading scores for, say, sixth-graders at West Elementary School may be compared to those for sixth-graders at North, South and East Elementary Schools, and the average for all sixth-graders in the Alpha district may be compared to those of the neighboring Beta, Delta, and Omega school districts. Averages for each district may be compared to the average scores of sixth-graders across the state.

Measures of Dispersion: Range and Standard Deviation

Measures of dispersion of a set of scores can be expressed in several ways. The *range* of scores on a test represents the breadth of performance by a group of students. It is obtained when the lowest score is subtracted from the highest score and 1 added to the result. A range of scores is only a gross indication of the dispersion of scores by a group of students. A more common measure of the dispersion of scores is the standard deviation (Ebel & Frisbie, 1991).

The *standard deviation* is an index of how scores are spread out around the mean, regardless of the shape of the distribution. For convenience, we will return to the normal distribution concept to illustrate the standard deviation.

In a normal distribution, we said that most of the scores would be grouped near the mean. But how many is "most"? How near is "near"? Statisticians have determined that 68 percent of the scores would be arrayed around or at the mean, with smaller percentages near the extremes, as in Figure 5.3.

If a student's score were one standard deviation (1SD) below the mean, we would know where the score lay on the distribution; we would know that the student did as well as or better than 16 percent of the norm group but that 84 percent did better. The range around the mean, from −1SD to +1SD, is considered the average range. A score of −1SD would be at the bottom of the average range.

The concepts of mean and standard deviation are fundamental to understanding how most scores such as those described below are reported.

Forms of Test Scores

When formal assessment instruments are administered, scored, and returned to the teacher for interpretation, the scores are often reported in several different forms. Although each of the forms of test scores is based on an individual student's performance, the final form of the score can vary depending upon the computations performed upon the raw score. The *raw score* shows simply how many items the student got right on the test or on each subtest. Interpreting a raw score directly may be misleading, so raw scores are converted to more easily comparable forms. The most frequently encountered forms of test scores are

FIGURE 5.3 Percentages of Scores within Standard Deviation (SD) Units

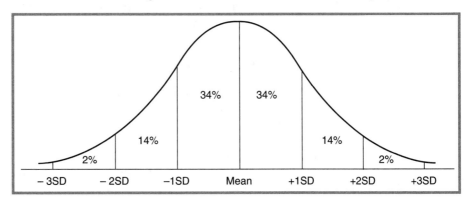

grade equivalents, percentiles, stanines, Normal Curve Equivalents (NCEs), *T*-scores, and *z*-scores.

Grade-Equivalent Scores

Grade-equivalent scores, often called simply *grade scores,* are frequently used in reporting reading test scores. They represent a level of achievement that is considered average for a particular grade and month of school within that grade. Grade scores are expressed in two-part numbers; the first number indicates the grade level, and the second number indicates the month within that grade. A grade score of 3.1, for example, stands for the first month (September) of third grade.

Grade scores seem easy to understand, and many parents place great faith in them. They hope to hear that their children have achieved grade scores that are in line with the children's present grade placement; it is easy to understand scores that seem to say that your child is reading just as he or she "should be" for his or her grade. But is this what grade scores do?

Grade scores imply that there is some objective, generally accepted standard of achievement for every month of each school grade. But in reality, no such agreement exists on what skills or competencies readers should have at any given point. Such expectations are too heavily influenced by local standards, curricular goals, scope and sequences of skills within commercial programs, and learner characteristics for any one standard of achievement to exist. Grade scores are often considered and interpreted to parents, however, as though there *were* such objective standards. Therefore, they are often overinterpreted.

Percentile Scores

Percentiles are more easily understood than grade scores. Percentiles range from 1 to 99; where a score lies within this range indicates relative performance compared with the norm group. A score at the 10th percentile means the student did as well as or better than 10 percent but worse than 89 percent of the students in the norm group. A score at the 98th percentile means that the student did as well as or better than 98 percent of the norm group and that only 1 percent attained higher scores.

Sometimes, parents misunderstand percentile scores, believing that they represent the number of items that the child answered correctly. Such a parent, whose child scored at the 50th percentile, would judge that the child had gotten only 50 percent of the items right, instead of correctly viewing the score as average.

Stanines, NCEs, T-scores, and z-scores

Other forms of scores take the distribution of scores of the norm group into account and provide comparable units across the range of scores. These are standardized scores, which include stanines, NCEs, *T*-scores, and *z*-scores (Thorndike et al., 1991).

Stanines are similar to percentiles. The term is derived from "standard nines," which means that the distribution of possible scores had been divided into nine parts. Stanine scores range from 1 to 9; a score of 5 is the mean, and scores from just below 4 to just above 6 are considered average, scores of 1 to 3 being below average and scores of 7 to 9 being above average.

Normal Curve Equivalents (NCEs) are derived from the average and standard deviation of a set of scores. They range from 1 to 99, with a mean of 50. NCEs have become more common, since they are widely used in the evaluation of federally funded reading and math programs such as Title I.

T-scores and *z-scores* are fairly common standard scores. Like NCEs and stanine scores, the *T*- and *z*-scores are based on the standard deviation. The *T*-scores range from 20 to 80, with a mean of 50. These values are computed from the standard deviations and indicate how close to the mean of the normal distribution a particular score lies. The *z*-score is based more directly on the standard deviation, with a mean of 0 and a standard deviation of 1. Scores ranging from −1.0 through 1.0 are considered average. The range for *z*-scores is based on the number of standard deviations in the distribution of scores. If Figure 5.3 represented the distribution of scores on a particular test, the *z*-score range would be from −3.0 to +3.0.

Decisions about how scores will be reported are often made at the school district level. Most reports include a grade equivalent and percentile, and an increasing number now include one of the standardized scores (stanine, NCE, *T*-score, or *z*-score). As a teacher, the selection of which information to use in conferences with parents will depend on which scores are available to you, your own knowledge of each form of test score, and the type of information you wish to convey. Grade-equivalent scores are easy for parents to understand but frequently misinterpreted; percentiles and stanines are probably more accurate and representative if they are properly explained.

Interpreting Standardized Scores to Parents

Figure 5.4 is a transcript of a parent-teacher conference in which the test results are discussed. The questions that the parent asked are like those encountered by many teachers. The goal of conferences like this one should be to share information for instructional decision making.

NORM-REFERENCED TESTS

Norm-referenced tests are developed by publishers, which administer them to large numbers of students to develop *norms*. The norms represent average performances of many students in various age, grade, and demographic groups and are used to compare the performance of individuals or special groups to the performance of those in the norm group.

Most test makers go to great lengths to include students from various geographic areas, urban and rural communities, racial and ethnic groups, and economic groups. Many tests feature several different sets of norms for local groups that might be unlike national averages—for example, urban schools, rural schools, high-achieving gifted populations, highly affluent areas, and the like.

FIGURE 5.4   Parent-Teacher Conference on Test Results

Parent: I'm worried about the reading scores on the test Dana took last month. They seem so low! What does this mean?

Reading Teacher: I share your concern about Dana's reading. Dana is having difficulty with reading, and these test results confirm my observations. Even though reading is a struggle for her, she is making progress in several areas. I'd like to describe a little about the test Dana took and what the scores mean.

Our district uses these tests to determine how our schools compare to other school districts and to provide a general indication of how individual students are doing when compared to others in the same grade.

The first section of Dana's score report includes *Normed Scores.* They reflect how Dana did when compared to other sixth-grade students. These first two scores, the *National Stanine* and the *Normal Curve Equivalent,* indicate that Dana performed below the average of other sixth-graders. The other two scores, the *Local Percentile* and the *National Percentile,* show within our district and across the nation how many students performed below Dana on the test. These percentile scores show that, on the total reading battery, Dana performed better than 12 percent of sixth-graders in this district and better than 22 percent of sixth-graders nationally.

Parent: Sounds like Dana is really having problems in reading and doing poorly overall. Does this score mean that she only got ten problems right on the vocabulary part of the test?

Reading Teacher: No, it doesn't show how many items Dana got right or wrong. The score of 10 on vocabulary is a Local Percentile score. It means that 10 percent of the sixth-graders in this school district scored below her, getting fewer right, on that part of the test. But 90 percent did better on this part of the test. The total reading score matches what I have seen in her classwork. She is in the bottom half of the class in reading. In addition to her classwork in language arts, I believe that the test is accurate because of her difficulty in other areas such as study skills, science, social studies, word analysis, and spelling.

Parent: I just don't understand how Dana did so poorly on the test. It looks as though she has passed or mastered more items than she has not mastered.

Reading Teacher: The skills scores indicate whether Dana mastered, passed, or has not mastered each skill. In this section, we must be very careful when we draw conclusions, because each skill is probably evaluated with only a few questions. Remember, the scores in the Normed-Score section are based on a comparison of Dana's performance with that of other sixth-graders. This means that more of Dana's peers scored above her than below her.

Parent: Well, what do we do now?

Reading Teacher: There are a number of directions we can go in at this point. A group conference with all of Dana's teachers would help to clarify how she's doing in all of her classes and what she needs to work on. I'd certainly recommend further assessment, using individual diagnostic tests that can pinpoint her strengths and weaknesses. Such tests would tell us a great deal more about what Dana can and cannot do than this standardized test. There are other kinds of intervention that we can organize to help Dana after we have gathered some more information.

Regardless of the type of test, the form of score, or the quality of the test, formal assessment of reading is only a single indication of a student's performance. Scores on norm-referenced standardized tests *must* be combined with other, more qualitative information to make the most valid instructional decisions.

Norm-referenced tests serve two general purposes. Many norm-referenced tests are designed to measure achievement or past learnings. These *achievement tests* vary in the scope of topics covered and the detail with which students' results are reported. Tests that assess specific knowledge and strategies associated with reading provide a range of difficulty which begins at a lower level. These tests, designed to show growth in these areas, are considered to be *diagnostic tests*.

Achievement Tests

Achievement tests are designed to measure the current level of learners' performance in a variety of areas. Many achievement tests are actually batteries of subtests representing different content or skill areas such as language arts, mathematics, science, and social studies. Tests that provide only a general performance score in each area are often called *survey tests*. Although survey tests can be helpful in pointing to areas in need of additional assessment, very little detailed information can be obtained.

Other achievement tests provide more detailed information within each subject area. These tests can often aid teachers, schools, and school districts in assessing the overall impact of their curricula.

Achievement tests are designed to show the depth of one's knowledge and mastery of subject area curricula. Because they are designed to assess mastery or achievement, they are usually administered *after* the appropriate instruction has been given. Tests that are used for diagnostic purposes are often given *before* a program of instruction, or early on, to reveal strengths and so that instruction can be modified appropriately. The content of diagnostic and survey tests is sometimes very similar to that of achievement tests, but the purpose and timing of the testing differ.

Standardized achievement tests are probably the most common type of formal tests used in schools. Many students take a standardized achievement test of some kind yearly, often a battery covering the major curricular areas. Because subtests are usually given in separate sittings, completion of a battery can take several days or a week. Achievement tests must be given under strictly standard conditions for results to be compared across groups, so sometimes a team of school personnel administers all the tests, and sometimes the regular daily schedule is suspended so that all students can be tested simultaneously. The tests are machine-scored by the publishers, and results are sent back to the school.

Almost all achievement tests are group tests. They should be used only to evaluate groups of students, not individuals. For this reason, they are of very limited diagnostic use. They are useful only for evaluating the progress of large groups such as whole schools or all the students from one grade.

Publishers make every attempt to make the content of their achievement tests represent typical school curricula. A math test, for example, will generally be made up of problems and calculations that are common to most school math programs for a particular grade. What is considered typical is decided by consulting subject area experts, by studying textbooks and materials that are in wide use, and by field-testing experimental test forms. Content validity, or how well a test represents the major aspects of the subject area, is of particular importance, but how closely the curriculum of an individual district, school, or classroom coincides with national trends is difficult to say. Achievement tests in any subject area should be carefully evaluated to determine how well their content matches the local programs and materials in use.

Most of the widely used achievement batteries measure reading, English language usage, science, math, and social studies. Most have forms for every grade from early elementary through high school, although some school districts do not begin using them until third or fourth grade. Some batteries have reading readiness tests for kindergarten and first grade.

Among the typical wide-ranging achievement batteries are the following:

The Metropolitan Achievement Test, Seventh Edition. For kindergarten through grade 12, this battery includes prereading, math, and language subtests for kindergarten; word recognition (first and second grades only), reading vocabulary, reading comprehension, language, science, math concepts and problem solving, math procedures, and social studies subtests and a separate diagnostic battery for grades 1 through 12; and a separate, norm-referenced writing test for grades 1 through 12.

The Comprehensive Test of Basic Skills, Fourth Edition. For kindergarten through grade 12, this battery includes readiness (K and 1 only), reading vocabulary, reading comprehension, spelling, language, math, social studies, science, and study skills subtests.

The Stanford Achievement Test, Ninth Edition. For kindergarten through grade 13, this battery includes reading, language, study skills, spelling, math, science, social sciences, and listening subtests.

There are a few reading achievement tests for individual administration. Two examples are the **Peabody Individual Achievement Test, Revised Edition (PIAT-R)** and the **Wide Range Achievement Test, Third Edition (WRAT–3).** These instruments are hybrids with characteristics of both group achievement tests and individual survey tests. Both tests are often given as diagnostic screening devices to students who are experiencing difficulty in either reading or math or to those with generally poor school achievement. Like other achievement tests, however, the results that they yield are solely quantitative, with little, if any, diagnostic value.

The PIAT-R contains reading recognition, reading comprehension, spelling, math, and general information subtests. Because it includes math as well as various reading skills and general information, the PIAT-R measures mastery of the largest part of typical elementary curricula.

The PIAT-R, for kindergarten through grade 12, has two sections. Reading Recognition includes sixteen multiple-choice questions requiring students to identify and match letters and words to the given stimulus. Students are also given eighty-four words in isolation to pronounce. The Reading Comprehension subtest requires silent reading of one or several sentences and then matching pictures to the text. Pictures are in a multiple-choice format, and written sentences cannot be referred to by the student. At the upper levels, the comprehension sentences are extremely complex, and words are highly unusual.

The WRAT-3, often used in screening students for special education programs, is designed for ages 5 through senior adulthood. The WRAT-3 has reading, spelling, and arithmetic subtests. Like the PIAT-R, it covers the areas that are most heavily concentrated on in elementary school.

The reading portion of the WRAT-3 is made up entirely of lists of single words. Pronunciation within ten seconds is the only criterion. It does not measure comprehension of either text or words, and no reading of connected text is included. Consequently, it does not measure real reading at all. If the test makers do not include comprehension in their view of reading, they should at least acknowledge what the test does *not* do. This test purports to provide accurate diagnoses of reading disabilities and placement of students in instructional groups, all without reading of words in sentences. These claims, and the content validity of the reading subtest, are suspect.

Advantages

First, like other group tests, group achievement measures offer schools a reliable, uncomplicated way to gather information on large numbers of students. Second, a maximum amount of data can be gathered in a minimum of time. If the batteries include a number of subjects, many curricular areas and processes can be assessed at one time.

Third, if properly administered and scored, they yield potentially informative data on the progress of groups of students, such as the total population of a given grade. When patterns of progress or lack of progress are discerned, curricular changes at the school and district levels can take place.

Fourth, these tests are usually extensively field-tested and standardized with great precision. Norming and validating achievement batteries is a big and complex business, and since millions of tests are taken yearly, test manufacturers try to make them as reliable and valid as they can.

Disadvantages

Standardized reading achievement tests are not designed to give diagnostic data, so they cannot be criticized for not doing so; but if used for their proper purposes, they can be effective measures of prior learning. However, some cautions should be kept in mind.

First, administration procedures must be followed to the letter. Students should take these tests in their regular classrooms rather than in huge groups in the cafeteria or gym, as sometimes happens.

Second, as with diagnostic reading tests, subtests are sometimes quite short, and their reliability coefficients might be low because of this and other factors.

Third, the time and cost that are involved sometimes contribute to gross over-interpretation of their scores. Retention of students because of scores on a single achievement battery or public humiliation of school groups and personnel because of score comparisons are clear abuses of test scores, yet such abuses do occur.

Fourth, achievement tests tend to call upon recall of factual material rather than higher-level thinking skills. Factual learning and recall are among the easiest processes to measure, but they do not represent all learning or achievement. We must not lose sight of the many additional aspects in reading and other subject areas, such as learning rate, interest, or creative thinking, which achievement tests do not typically measure.

Diagnostic Tests

Norm-referenced standardized achievement tests are designed to measure what a reader has already learned and are usually administered to groups of students on a yearly basis. Scores are reported by state, district, school, class, and student. *Diagnostic tests* are norm-referenced and standardized but are designed to be administered to students who are showing signs of reading difficulties. Most diagnostic tests are individually administered. Diagnostic tests differ from achievement tests in three major ways:

- They have a large number of subtest scores (sometimes called *part scores*) and a larger number of items.
- The items are devised to measure specific skills.
- Difficulty tends to be lower to provide adequate discrimination among students with reading problems.

Diagnostic tests, both the group and individual types, have numerous subtests and yield a profile of scores. Each subtest assesses a particular skill area. Developers of these tests maintain that analysis of a profile of subtest scores will reveal strengths and weaknesses in skill areas and that it is this analysis that makes them more diagnostic than survey tests.

Diagnostic tests for group administration frequently include subtests assessing some or most of the following skills: reading comprehension, vocabulary, visual and auditory discrimination, structural analysis, numerous aspects of phonic analysis, sound blending, skimming and scanning, syllabication, sight-word recognition, and spelling. Because of the number of separate subtests, they usually have to be administered in several sittings.

An example of a group diagnostic test is the **Stanford Diagnostic Reading Test, Third Edition.** The Stanford, testing grades 1 through 12, includes subtests assessing auditory discrimination, auditory vocabulary, word meanings, phonic and structural analysis, and literal and inferential reading comprehension. Levels for grade 4 and beyond include reading rate, and those for grade 8 and beyond include skimming/scanning/fast reading subtests. Scores are reported in grade scores, percentiles, and stanines. The Stanford test takes about two hours to administer.

There are many diagnostic reading tests for individual administration. They attempt a broad-based analysis of skills, with assessment of word recognition and decoding skills and comprehension of prose passages. An example is the **Diagnostic Reading Scales.**

Some standardized diagnostic tests focus more heavily on word recognition and word analysis skills. Among these are the **Diagnostic Screening Test—Reading, Third Edition,** the **Diagnostic Achievement Battery-2,** and the **Gates-McKillop-Horowitz Reading Diagnostic Test, Second Edition.** The latter is probably the best known of this type of test. Designed for students with reading problems in grades 1 through 6, the Gates-McKillop-Horowitz-2 assesses oral reading fluency of story passages without comprehension assessment, flashed and untimed recognition of whole words, recognition of nonsense words, dividing words into syllables, producing letter sounds, letter naming, sound blending, auditory discrimination, spelling, and informal writing. The test yields grade-equivalent scores and overall reading ratings of average, above average, and below average. No estimate of reading comprehension is available, and all scores depend on the student's oral reading level.

Some specialized diagnostic tests focus on oral reading ability only. The Slosson Oral Reading Test (SORT-R) is one of these. The student does not read connected text; the test is made up of lists of words in isolation. It purports to furnish an instructional reading level for the student on the basis of word pronunciation alone. Because this level is derived from reading words in lists, it is largely useless.

More typical of true oral reading tests are the **Gray Oral Reading Tests, Third Edition,** and the **Gilmore Oral Reading Test.** In these tests, comprehension results are less important to the overall scoring than oral reading accuracy and speed. The Gray Oral Reading Test is not intended as a comprehension test, but it does include comprehension questions following passages and yields a comprehension score as well as an Oral Reading Quotient that combines the oral fluency and comprehension scores. The Gilmore Oral Reading Test yields separate oral fluency and comprehension scores. Testing is discontinued when a ceiling number of word recognition errors occur, even if comprehension continues to be adequate.

A number of individual diagnostic tests resemble informal reading inventories, with silent and oral reading passages followed by comprehension questions. They differ from informal reading inventories in that they are norm-referenced. **The Durrell Analysis of Reading Difficulty, Third Edition,** and the **Diagnostic Reading Scales—Revised** are examples of these. As in a typical IRI, these tests assess sight vocabulary recognition, word analysis in isolation and in context, and silent and oral comprehension. They include graded word lists, graded story passages with comprehension questions, supplemental tests of phonics and decoding skills, and systems for determining reading levels by counting errors. Assessment of oral fluency includes counting the oral reading miscues, but no miscue analysis.

The Diagnostic Reading Scales-Revised assess comprehension with a preponderance of questions requiring short answers and literal recall; some questions are answered by yes or no. Rate of reading is measured but does not take into account that good readers vary their rate for different reading purposes. In this test, the instructional level is the student's *oral* reading level, and the independent level is the student's *silent* reading level. This test also includes supplementary phonics subtests that assess initial and final consonant sounds, blends and digraph sounds, initial consonant substitution, auditory recognition of consonant sounds, long and short vowel sounds and variant vowels, recognition of syllables and phonograms, sound blending, and auditory discrimination.

The Durrell Analysis of Reading Difficulty also assesses word recognition and word analysis, oral fluency, and silent and oral comprehension. It includes listening comprehension, identifying meanings of individual words, recognition of sounds of individual letters, blends, digraphs, phonograms and initial and final affixes, spelling, visual memory of words, and "prereading phonics abilities" including matching spoken with written sentences ("syntax matching"), identifying letter names in spoken names (such as *s* in *Esther*), and identifying and writing letters.

The Woodcock Reading Mastery Test—Revised is often used in special education. The Woodcock consists of six subtests: visual-auditory learning, letter identification, word identification, word attack, word comprehension, and passage comprehension. Designed for use in all grades from kindergarten through twelfth, it takes about 30–60 minutes to administer.

The letter identification subtest requires the student to identify letters shown in eight styles of type. The word identification subtest consists of 150 words in order of difficulty from preprimer (*the* and *and*) to twelfth grade (*facetious* and *picayune*). They are listed in isolation, and the student pronounces the words in an untimed presentation. The word attack subtest consists of fifty nonsense words to be decoded and pronounced. Items range in difficulty from *bim* to *wubfambif*. The word comprehension subtest contains seventy verbal analogies: *bird–fly, fish–_____*. The subject reads the analogy silently and says a word to complete the set. The passage comprehension subtest consists of modified cloze items; a word is omitted from a sentence, and the subject reads the item silently, then gives a word to complete it. Early items are single sentences with a picture clue; later items contain two or three sentences and have no picture.

The Woodcock yields percentiles, grade-equivalent scores, and age-equivalent scores for each subtest and a Total Reading score representing the combined subtest scores.

Advantages

First, as with group survey tests, the most obvious advantage is economy of time. With a *group diagnostic test* such as the Stanford, a large group can be tested in less than two hours. Second, some teachers find the information generated by such a test more specific than the results of a general survey test, with its relatively undifferentiated subtests and global scores. Third, group diagnostic tests, like their survey counterparts, are easy to administer without special preparation and are usually easy to score.

An advantage of using a standardized individual diagnostic test lies in the opportunity to closely observe one student's reading. A second advantage is the detailed analysis of discrete skills that some of these tests allow.

Disadvantages

The first disadvantage of using multiple subtests is that each usually represents a very limited sample of the behavior. Subtests are usually kept very short to save time, but subtest length critically affects reliability. Although there is no general rule of thumb, tests in which individual subtests have few responses should be suspect because they might sacrifice in-depth analysis of specific things for a quick glimpse of many things.

Second, tests can be seriously flawed by poor passages and poor questions. The passages are usually written to conform to readability formulas, which make them sound stilted. Often, they are bland, dull, and sometimes very short. A student's comprehension will be radically affected by interest in and prior knowledge of what is read. Dull passages that are written poorly do little to promote anyone's reading comprehension. The number of questions following a passage is another important variable. Ten questions of different types will make a fairly good sample, but ten questions all requiring literal recall will not, and asking only four or five questions is usually not enough to really test comprehension.

Third, tests that yield an overall reading level but do not assess comprehension are of dubious value. The heart of reading is comprehension, and a reading level that has not included comprehension, even indirectly, is not very useful.

Fourth, many of these tests, particularly those that focus on word analysis skills, excessively partition the process of reading into minute parts. Word analysis skills serve to facilitate word recognition, but they do not add up to effective reading. Improvement in word-attack skills does not guarantee that the student will be able to read effectively with comprehension.

So, as with all formal assessments of reading, the results of norm-referenced, standardized diagnostic tests should be interpreted only in light of other formal and informal assessments that reflect real reading tasks.

CRITERION-REFERENCED TESTS

While norm-referenced tests aid in comparing students' performance to that of others, criterion-referenced tests enable teachers to compare a student's performance to a predetermined goal or outcome. Criterion-referenced tests provide a way of determining whether a student has met instructional goals, or *criteria*.

Characteristics of Criterion-Referenced Tests

In individualized reading programs, each student works toward mastery of skills that he or she has not yet learned. Pretests are most often used to determine which skills need improvement. In theory, every student in a classroom might be working on mastering a different skill at any given time. In practice, few teachers could effectively manage such a program, and students are temporarily grouped with others who need work on the same skill or process. Even though the instruction usually takes place in groups, these programs are called *individualized* because each student works on those particular skills in which she or he is thought to be deficient.

This instructional model requires a measurement method that helps the teacher to determine not how students compare with one another, but rather how each student's performance compares with the goals of the program. Criterion-referenced tests compare a student's level of proficiency or mastery of some skill or set of skills to a standard of mastery, or *criterion* (Kubiszyn and Borich, 1990).

Goals and Objectives

Criterion-referenced testing is really the final stage in a three-part instructional model. First, the overall *instructional program goals* must be decided on and stated. These goals are usually broad statements of general educational outcomes. Examples of reading program goals might be as follows:

- ■ to read different kinds of text with adequate comprehension,
- ■ to appreciate different literary genres,
- ■ to recognize words fluently.

Program goals are often developed at the district or state level. Such goals do not specify either how such behaviors or attitudes will be conveyed or what specific levels of competency are required. However, they do serve to define the general directions in which instruction will move.

Program objectives follow from curricular goals. They are also general, but they are more specific than goals. They define more narrowly the desired outcomes of the instruction, such as the following:

- ■ Students will recognize and discriminate among basic speech sounds.
- ■ Students will demonstrate effective listening skills.
- ■ Students will identify characteristics that distinguish major literary genres.

Program objectives are usually developed at the school district level or at the local school level. They apply to specific educational programs, but they usually do not specify the level of proficiency desired or how such objectives will be implemented.

Instructional objectives are the specific statements of learner behavior or outcomes that are expected after a unit of instruction. (The instructional period might be a five-minute minilesson, a one-week lesson or a month-long unit; in each case, the unit of instruction is usually defined.) Instructional objectives define what specific content is taught, as in these examples:

- ■ After completion of the Level 1 reader, students will recognize at sight all the basal words listed at the end of the book.
- ■ After reading this story, students will formulate two inferences about the possible results of the main character's actions.

■ By the end of November of kindergarten, students will name the months of the year, in order, from memory.

Instructional objectives are often referred to as *behavioral objectives* because they describe the behaviors that learners are to demonstrate. Objectives that call for students to "appreciate" or "understand" are common, but they do not describe the behaviors to be shown. Because of this, instructional objectives often do not take into account attitudes or generally unmeasurable behaviors, instead focusing on discrete, measurable behaviors. It is this that many educators object to about such objectives.

Good instructional objectives identify the *behavior* to be demonstrated, which is the observable learning outcome. They state the *conditions* under which the student will demonstrate the outcome: *from memory, by Friday, orally, in writing, given a list of 20 misspelled words,* and the like. Sometimes, these conditions are referred to as "the givens"; they are contained in such objective statements as the following:

■ *Given* a list of 30 basal words from the Level 2 reader, the student will identify 25 words at sight.
■ *Given* 20 two-digit addition problems, the student will compute all answers correctly.

Good instructional objectives also state the *criterion level* of mastery desired: the number of items correct, a percentage of accuracy, the number of consecutive times performed, the prescribed time limit (where speed of performance is required), or the essential features to be included (as in a composition or essay response).

From instructional objectives come the items that are used on criterion-referenced tests. To achieve its purpose of determining how closely a student has achieved mastery of a skill or objective, each test item must define the criterion or skill being assessed. Criterion-referenced test items are often taken directly from instructional objectives, when such tests are developed locally. When the instructional objectives have been written so that they are sufficiently clear, precise, and measurable, developing such test items is easy. For example, with an instructional objective such as *"After completing the Level 1 reader, students will recognize all of the basal words at sight,"* a criterion-referenced test item such as *"From the list provided, read these words with 90 percent accuracy"* might follow.

As with any other kind of test, criterion-referenced test items must fairly and adequately sample the essential skills or knowledge that is being tested. Test items must match the learning outcomes and conditions specified in the instructional objectives; this ensures test validity (Kubiszyn and Borich, 1990).

If, for example, an instructional objective calls for students to discriminate between statements of fact and opinion in newspaper articles, then test items that require them to discriminate between statements of fact and opinion in a letter to the editor is a good match, but an item that requires them to state an opinion about the use of letters to the editor is not a good match.

Likewise, if an instructional objective requires students to use an illustration to identify twenty bones of the human body, then a test item giving them a picture of a skeleton with twenty bones to be labeled would be a good match, but a test item requiring them to name twenty bones from memory would not.

When instructional programs and tests are developed locally, the tests usually match the instructional goals quite closely. So, too, do commercial skills programs that feature their own criterion-referenced tests. When tests are purchased separately from programs or when test programs are purchased but instructional programs are developed locally, a mismatch might occur between what is taught and what, or how, that content is tested. In some situations, expensive commercial test programs lock teachers into a particular sequence of skills. This is a case of the tail wagging the dog, since tests should be tailored to meet instructional programs, not the reverse.

When judging the objectives for a commercial criterion-referenced test or test program, keep these questions in mind:

1. Do these objectives call for learning outcomes that are appropriate for this subject area? What are the most important outcomes to be desired from instruction? Are they included in this testing program?
2. Do these objectives represent a balance of thinking and learning skills? Is factual knowledge emphasized at the expense of higher-level thinking skills?
3. Are the desired outcomes realistically attainable by our students? What modifications should be made to fit the needs of our students and the realities of our teaching facilities?
4. Do these objectives fit the philosophy of our school(s) and teachers? If not, how can the objectives of the test be modified to better represent our overall goals and philosophy?

Advantages

One of the most important assets of criterion-referenced tests is their diagnostic potential. They can indicate with great clarity and precision what a student can or cannot yet do, and so appropriate instructional modifications can be made, which is the major goal of any diagnostic procedure. They have much greater diagnostic power than norm-referenced tests because they yield information that is related to specific goals rather than information relating the performance of students to one another.

Second, it is possible for parents and students to see how test scores are related to instructional methods and materials, whereas ordinarily, it is difficult for them to see any relationship. This advantage can help to eliminate a misunderstanding between home and school.

Third, criterion-referenced tests make it very clear to the public what goals the school has developed and how these goals are to be attained. There is therefore greater public confidence in the accountability of schools.

Fourth, they can be made to conform to local standards, teaching conditions, and practices and thus reflect the actual abilities and achievement of local students more accurately than standardized norm-referenced tests.

Fifth, they tend to minimize damaging competition among students, since a student's achievement is not measured in terms of someone else's achievement but rather in terms of a preset criterion. Both parents and students can then concentrate on the goals to be attained rather than on invidious comparisons among individuals or groups.

Sixth, they are particularly useful for evaluating the effectiveness of a program innovation or a completely new program.

Disadvantages

First, criterion-referenced tests might be top-heavy with the objectives that are easiest to measure, such as factual material. The higher-order learning processes, such as evaluation and application of knowledge to novel situations, are naturally harder to assess and may be underrepresented in the objectives.

Second, the necessity of being clear and precise might encourage partitioning of reading acts into many molecular units. Excessive partitioning leads to a proliferation of objectives, and reading as an integrated process can get lost. Criterion-referenced tests tend to encourage teachers to think of reading as a conglomerate of hundreds of discrete skills instead of a complex thinking and language process.

Third, since criteria of quality or accuracy are always arbitrary, they should be considered carefully. There is nothing magical about 80 percent, 90 percent, or 100 percent accuracy. If skills are truly hierarchical, like some math skills, then perfection might be necessary before the student goes on to more difficult skills. If there is no particular sequence of skills in one area or no generally agreed-upon progression, then all quality criteria are arbitrary, and one might be just as good as another. Teachers using any test with predetermined criteria for mastery should decide for themselves if the criteria seem unnecessarily rigid.

Fourth, we must remember that we don't want students to demonstrate mastery only on a one-time basis. We want them to retain what they have learned and be able to apply it to new situations. Important objectives should be tested more than once, and mastery should be shown in more than one way.

Fifth, many criterion-referenced tests assess specific skills with very few items per skill. This can reduce reliability. An option is to include a larger number of items for each skill; but the longer the test, the more difficult it is for students to complete.

Perhaps the biggest drawback in criterion-referenced tests is that objectives to be tested have a way of *becoming* the reading curriculum itself. Some educators maintain that programs that emphasize testing of discrete skills encourage teaching the skills in the same manner. It is difficult, if not impossible, to isolate skills in actual reading because meaningful reading requires the use of many skills and processes simultaneously, and partitioning overlooks this important factor.

MINIMUM COMPETENCY TESTING

In recent decades, the accountability movement has affected education in a number of ways. One major impact has been in the area of *minimum competency testing.* In an effort to provide accountability in schools, some groups attempted to determine minimum levels of competence that students should possess before promotion to the next grade or graduation from high school with a diploma. To assess these minimum competencies, *minimum competency testing* programs were established in many states (Thorndike et al., 1991). Today, most states have such programs in place.

Minimum competency tests may be considered a special kind of criterion-referenced tests, because success on these instruments depends upon students' achieving certain predetermined levels of mastery on the required competencies.

Minimum competency programs differ from state to state and from one school district to another. Most commonly, however, they feature the following components:

- statements of specific skills, often called *standards of learning, basic competencies,* or *learning objectives,* in reading, writing, and mathematics that schools are responsible for teaching all children and that all students are responsible for mastering;
- tests to determine whether students have mastered the required skills;
- requirements that students cannot be promoted to the next grade and/or cannot graduate unless the tests are passed; and
- requirements concerning extra courses, placement in special programs, remediation, and other interventions that are intended to correct deficiencies

Issues of Minimum Competency Programs

A number of complex issues are involved in this movement. In general, supporters believe minimum competency testing will

- help to identify and better serve the students with the greatest educational needs;
- motivate students toward greater achievement in school;
- motivate teachers to teach all students more effectively;
- make high school diplomas more meaningful (in states that have *diploma sanctions,* regulations requiring mastery on tests before a diploma may be awarded);
- place pressure on schools to provide more instruction in basic skills and to become more accountable for student achievement; and
- create an objective database regarding school achievement patterns.

Problems of Minimum Competency Programs

Since minimum competency testing programs first appeared, a number of concerns have been expressed by educators. These include the following:

1. Minimum competency testing might exclude more children from schools and stigmatize underachievers. When such programs result in denial of pro-

motion or graduation and even implicitly encourage dropping out of school, such programs might be percieved as punitive, even exclusionary.

2. Programs might focus on identifying students with basic skill deficiencies without aggressively pursuing effective remediation. Testing is certainly easier than remediating, and effective long-term remediation is both difficult and expensive.

3. Such programs and the rhetoric that is associated with them might oversimplify the basic competency issues, seeking or creating pat answers to exceedingly complex issues of adult literacy.

4. Such programs might be viewed as a quick fix to the problem of the community's loss of confidence in the schools or as an attempt to restore such confidence while actually having little effect on the complex underlying causes of illiteracy.

5. Students with special educational needs might be penalized or further shut out from equal educational opportunity by their failure to meet standard objectives or pass the typical group-administered, paper-and-pencil tests of basic skills. Many states are rigorously examining the implications of these programs for special-needs students.

6. The emphasis such programs place on minimum competencies might result in a narrowing of curricular goals, with greater emphasis on so-called basics and less emphasis on a broad range of school topics and educational experiences for all learners.

7. Although students who fail such tests are the ones who ultimately pay the penalty, teachers might be forced by community pressure to restrict the range of topics and methods to those most likely to be tested so that they can more clearly justify the use of student time and effort. This can result in students' passing the required tests but being poorly prepared in more global reading, writing, and thinking applications.

8. So much emphasis on minimums might create a climate in which *the minimum becomes the maximum.* Critics already charge that schools in general do not fully challenge average or talented pupils but seek only to ensure that everyone has a minimum level of achievement. The motivation and achievement of average and above-average students might suffer as a result.

9. When such programs are mandated by the state, local school districts might wonder who will absorb the cost. The state might finance the actual testing but not the remedial programs that must be a necessary part of the process if it is to serve the students' needs. Localities might balk at subsidizing the necessarily expensive remedial efforts if they feel that the state has usurped local autonomy.

10. Finally, the question of whether students' competence in applying school literacy skills to life experience can be accurately, fairly, and comprehensively tested by means available today must be addressed.

Although there are many problems and concerns with minimum competency testing, the courts have upheld states' rights to establish such testing programs (Thorndike et al., 1991). The pressure for accountability in schools continues, but many states are beginning to take a broader view of assessment that includes both formal and informal assessments.

SOURCES OF TEST INFORMATION

Information on a commercial test or battery can be obtained from a number of sources such as measurement yearbooks, test publishers' catalogs, and technical reports, bulletins, and journals.

Measurement Yearbooks and Indexes

These sources are compendia of information and reviews of all current published tests. They can be found in libraries, although many school divisions have a set of their own. Many are now available online as well.

Measurement Yearbooks

The most valuable source, and the first place to which many teachers turn with questions about tests, is the series of *Mental Measurement Yearbooks* (MMYs). The first MMY was published in 1938; for many years, these were edited by Oscar K. Buros, until his death. The ninth and subsequent MMYs were edited by others. The most current is the *Thirteenth Mental Measurement Yearbook*, published in 1998.

Each MMY lists tests that have appeared or been revised since publication of the previous volume. Age and grade levels, time needed for administration, subtests included, publishers, and costs are listed for each test. This information is helpful in initially screening a number of tests, and it makes ordering sample sets easy. Most important, these yearbooks contain extensive reviews of many tests written by qualified experts in the field, synopses of reviews appearing in journals and other sources, lists of pertinent books and monographs, and the names of people and journals that review tests.

Measurement Indexes

The MMYs are not cumulative; a test that was reviewed in a previous MMY might not appear in subsequent volumes. To aid in locating reviews and pertinent information without having to go through each MMY, Buros developed *Tests in Print I* (1961), *Tests in Print II* (1974), *Tests in Print III* (1983), and *Tests in Print IV* (1994). Another source of information is *Tests: A Comprehensive Reference for Assessments in Psychology, Education and Business,* Third Edition, edited by Richard C. Sweetland and Daniel J. Keyser (1993).

Test Publishers' Catalogs

Publishers of commercial tests usually provide informational catalogs and technical manuals without charge to educators. These can provide a wealth of very current information to add to what Buros's reference books provide. The catalogs usually provide descriptions of the tests, subtests included, time limitations, normative information, types of scores yielded, scoring services, costs, and related specific information. Because catalogs are sales devices, they tend to present the tests in the most positive light, so the publisher's claims should be compared with the critical reviews in the MMY and current journals.

The 13th MMY lists names and addresses of all test publishers as of 1998. The Educational Testing Service (ETS), Princeton, NJ 08541, publishes the *Test Collection Bulletin*, a quarterly publication listing the most current addresses and services of test publishers.

Technical manuals often accompany specimen sets of tests, which usually must be purchased from the publisher. They provide detailed information about the populations that were used in standardizing the tests, reliability and validity estimates for individual subtests and the entire test, and other statistical data that are very useful for evaluation purposes.

Bulletins

Free or inexpensive bulletins about tests, publishers, and measurement issues are available from a number of sources. ETS publishes the nominally priced *Tests and Measurement Kit,* which includes guides for developing teacher-made tests and selecting commercial ones. ETS also publishes *TM News* and *TM Reports,* bulletins that report on measurement trends and issues and summarizing papers presented at national meetings of the American Educational Research Association (AERA). *TM Reports* also includes bibliographies on a wide variety of testing topics, which are extremely helpful to those who are interested in extended readings. In addition to these bulletins, ETS issues *A Directory of Information on Tests,* which will help in locating other information sources.

The National Council on Measurement in Education (NCME) (1230 17th St. N.W., Washington, DC 20036) publishes quarterly reports (*Journal of Educational Measurement, Measurement in Education,* and *Measurement News*) on a wide variety of topics such as performance contracting, criterion-referenced testing, grading practices, reporting of test scores to parents, and interpreting of national norms.

The Psychological Corporation (555 Academic Court, San Antonio, TX 78204) publishes a number of free or inexpensive bulletins on topics such as aptitude testing, test score accuracy, interpretation of reliability coefficients, the costs of tests, and the development of local norms. The Psychological Corporation also provides free single copies of their *Test Service Notebooks,* including reports on such topics as secondary school testing and what parents must know about testing and test selection, as well as their *Focus on Evaluation* monographs, which cover topics such as mandated assessment and the political use of test results.

The American Psychological Association, Inc. (APA) (1200 17th St. N.W., Washington, DC 20036) publishes a bulletin entitled *Standards for Educational and Psychological Tests* to guide test developers and test users. It contains information on the proper development and reporting of tests, results and research findings, and the use and interpretation of tests.

Journals

Published several times yearly, professional journals often contain the most current information. Many journals routinely review new or revised tests in many areas as well as reporting research findings related to testing. In the area of measurement and evaluation are such journals as the *American Psychologist, Journal of Educational Measurement, American Educational Research Journal, Psychological Bulletin,* and *Applied Psychological Measurement.* Reading journals such as *Language Arts, The Reading Teacher, Journal of Reading,* and *Reading Research Quarterly* often include test reviews and critical articles.

SUMMARY

The basic test characteristics that teachers should be familiar with are *reliability* and *validity.* Reliability refers to the consistency of scores a test yields. Aspects of reliability are *stability,* or consistency across repeated administrations; *internal consistency,* or consistency among test items; and *equivalence,* or consistency across alternate test forms. Validity refers to how well a test measures what it was intended to measure. *Content validity* is the quality of adequately sampling the subject area or process being assessed. *Criterion-related validity* is made up of *concurrent validity,* or how closely a test is related to another test of established validity, and *predictive validity,* the degree to which test performance is related to some other established criterion, such as grades in college or job success. *Construct validity* refers to how well the test measures traits or constructs that are not directly observable but must be inferred from observable behavior. Intelligence is an example of a construct.

Commonly used descriptive statistics include *distributions, indices of central tendency and dispersion,* and forms of *standard scores.* A distribution is an array of scores from highest to lowest. Many standardized tests assume a *normal distribution,* a symmetrical array with most scores falling near the mean and progressively fewer scores at the extreme high and low ends. Asymmetrical distributions are referred to as *skewed.* Indices of central tendency in distributions include the *mean,* an arithmetic average, and the *median,* the point in a distribution at which there are equal numbers of higher and lower scores. Indices of dispersion in a distribution describe how far apart scores are from one another. They include the *range,* or the span from highest to lowest score, and the *standard deviation,* which shows how far from the mean each score is in standard or equal increments.

Standardized reading tests usually yield several forms of test scores. *Grade scores* are two-part numbers that indicate achievement such as we might expect at a given grade level and a number of months within that grade. These scores are meant to represent the performance of an average student in the grade and month indicated. *Percentiles* are standard scores that show what percentage of the norm population scored higher or lower than the individual tested. *Stanines* are scores in which the distribution has been divided into nine parts; a stanine score indicates which ninth a score fell in. *T-scores* and *z-scores* use the concepts of mean and standard deviation to show where a score lies in relation to the mean of a normal distribution.

Norm-referenced tests are developed by publishers, which administer them to large numbers of students to develop *norms,* or average performances across grades, ages, and demographic groups. Norms are used to compare the performance of local students and groups to these averages. *Achievement tests* are designed to measure what students have already learned in major curricular areas and to assess the effectiveness of instructional programs. *Diagnostic tests* are designed to reveal individuals' strengths and weaknesses in particular areas.

Criterion-referenced tests compare a student's performance to a preset goal or criterion rather than to the performance of other students. Such tests are thought to be effective in showing student mastery of particular skills. *Minimum competency tests* are a kind of criterion-referenced test.

Sources of test information include measurement yearbooks and indexes, test publishers' catalogs and bulletins, and professional journal reviews.

REFERENCES

Buros, Oscar K. *Tests in Print IV.* Highland Park, NJ: Gryphon Press, 1994. (Previous editions: 1983, 1974, 1961.)

Ebel, Robert L., and David A. Frisbie. *Essentials of Educational Measurement,* 5th ed. Englewood Cliffs NJ: Prentice Hall, 1991.

Kubiszyn, Tom, and Gary Borich. *Educational Testing and Measurement: Classroom Application and Practice,* 3d ed. Glenview, IL: Scott, Foresman, 1990.

Lipson, Marjorie Y., and Karen K. Wixon. *Assessment and Instruction of Reading Disability: An Interactive Approach.* New York: HarperCollins, 1991.

Sweetland, Richard C., and Daniel J. Keyser, eds. Tests: *A Comprehensive Reference for Assessment in Psychology, Education and Business,* 3d ed. Austin, TX: PRO-ED, 1993.

Thirteenth Mental Measurement Yearbook. Lincoln, NB: Buros Institute Mental Measurements of the University of Nebraska–Lincoln, 1998.

Thorndike, Robert M., George K. Cunningham, Robert L. Thorndike, and Elizabeth P. Hagen. *Measurement and Evaluation in Psychology and Education,* 5th ed. New York: Macmillan Publishing Company, 1991.

PART TWO

INSTRUCTION

CHAPTER **6**

Emergent and Beginning Literacy

Ｔhe first five chapters of this book gave an overview of the learning-to-read process, considered the ways in which reading assessment is used for internal and external audiences, and looked in detail at both "informal" approaches to assessment, exemplified by the Informal Reading Inventory, and at "authentic" approaches (exemplified by the use of portfolios). The next four chapters will look into the special challenges of assessing and teaching each age group of students. This chapter considers emergent and beginning readers. Chapter 7 will look at developing readers, and Chapter 8 will examine mature readers. Chapter 9 will be devoted to adolescent readers with reading problems. We turn now to early literacy.

DIFFERENT CONCEPTIONS OF EARLY LITERACY

Over the years, educators' thinking about the early stages of reading and writing has evolved through phases. Ideas current in earlier periods rarely vanish completely, so the approaches to early reading that one still observes in some classrooms, and assumptions that underlie public discussions of the topic, may well be a pastiche of old and new ideas. Moreover, there are heated debates among theorists writing currently about early reading—so contemporary ideas do not all come from a common viewpoint, either. We will review some of the former ideas about early reading, as well as some contemporary debates on the topic, before launching into the heart of this chapter.

The "Magic Moment" of Readiness to Read

From earlier in the 20th century comes one prominent influence on educators' thinking about early literacy. This is the once widely held idea that no effort should be made to help children learn to read until they reach the moment when they are "ready." Followers of the famous child developmentalist Arnold Gessell advanced the claim in the 1930s that children had to mature until the appropriate moment for reading instruction to begin (Gessell and Ilg, 1949). At that moment, reading instruction would easily bear fruit. Before that moment of "readiness," efforts at instruction would be frustrated.

In line with this way of thinking, one teacher we knew had her first graders reach their right arms over the tops of their heads and touch their left ears. Those who could do this were considered ready to learn to read; those who could not may have to wait several months longer. This teacher's thinking was more sophisticated than it may at first seem. Infants' heads are large in proportion to their arms. As children grow through their first six or seven years, their arms grow faster than their heads do; and a point will one day be reached when they will at last be able to reach their arms across their heads. What is dubious about this teacher's thinking, though, is that this physical maturation alone should be a sufficient indicator of readiness for reading.

Of course it is reasonable to claim that maturation has *something* to do with the appropriate timing of reading instruction: Few people would try to teach toddlers to read. Yet contemporary psychologists see a role for both maturation and stimulation—heredity and environment. The Gessellian view credits maturation alone, and if teachers are persuaded by it, they may withhold from children the early experiences in literacy that could help them learn to read and write.

Teaching Isolated Skills: The Behaviorist Approach

With the advent of behaviorist psychology at mid-century came the popularity of teaching reading as many discrete skills. The complex behavior of early reading was broken down, in some programs, into discriminating shapes (straight lines from curves, circles from squares, then C's from T's) and discriminating sounds (bells from dog barks). Then these skills (along with many others) were taught through isolated drill-and-practice, with the expectation that they would add up to form competent reading.

There were three problems with this view. First, in their purest formulation, behaviorist views put a large burden on a child to make sense of what all of the discrete parts added up to. By analogy, these approaches were like showing a person how to turn wheels and mash petals, and then expecting her to drive an automobile. Those children who did not already have a strong concept of what fluent readers did could be left as confused by such instruction as the would-be driver who had never watched someone drive a car.

Second, the discrete skills themselves were more often identified by a curriculum designer's logic rather than from direct observation of children. When many of the skills taught in behaviorally based readiness curricula were subjected to scrutiny, they turned out not to matter very much in reading (see, for instance, Vellutino, 1977).

Third, the behaviorist approaches underestimated children's innate powers of discovery, and their powers to direct their own learning. Without recognizing children's role in their own learning, these approaches failed to immerse children in print, to present for them models of good readers and writers, or to show them strategies they could use to read well. In short, by breaking reading tasks into small parts, they left children at the mercy of the curriculum developers' understanding of the reading act—which, as we have just said, was often inadequate.

"Learning to Read by Discovery"

From the late 1960s, our understanding of early reading received a boost from the newly emerging fields of cognitive psychology and psycholinguistics. Both of these fields credited the child's powers of discovery in learning to read. Cognitive developmental theories, such as that of the monumental Swiss psychologist Jean Piaget, stressed both the power of children's discovery in learning and also the stage-by-stage nature of that learning. Psycholinguists pointed out that the capacity to talk and understand language is our greatest intellectual achievement, yet it results not from direct instruction by adults but from children's discovery of patterns in the sounds, words, and sentences they hears adults use. Adults are not teachers but models, argued the pioneer psycholinguist Noam Chomsky (1968). It is true that other psycholinguists later credited adults with more importance in the language-learning process: Rather than mere models, adults became partners in the learning process (Bruner, 1985). But the children still had the initiative. Developmental views of reading such as Smith's (1971) and Goodman's (1976) derived from psycholinguistics. So did the discoveries of children's emergent writing (Clay, 1975) and invented spelling (Read, 1975).

The teaching implications of the cognitive and psycholinguistic revolutions (they were such a dramatic change from the behaviorist theories that they really do deserve to be called revolutionary) in learning theory led to the current emphasis on immersing children in books, modeling fluent reading and writing for children, encouraging children to read and write at emergent levels before and during the time they are formally taught, and appealing directly to children as deliberate partners in their learning. All of these approaches are still highly valued in promoting children's early literacy. However, there are two instructional implications of the developmental psycholinguistic view of reading that have been challenged in recent years.

One aspect of psycholinguistic-oriented instruction that has been questioned is the degree to which discovery processes can be relied upon in learning to be literate. To what extent do children also need instruction in letter identification, letter-to-sound correspondences, and the like? Should they memorize spelling words, or can they invent and write their way to correct spelling? Current research suggests that for most children, the answer lies somewhere between complete reliance on discovery on the one hand, and complete reliance on direct instruction, on the other hand.

An issue from cognitive psychology that has become controversial is the emphasis on *developmentally appropriate instruction.* Cognitive developmentalists such as Jean Piaget have demonstrated that at least some domains of learning proceed through stages, and that later concepts would not be easily acquired until children had "constructed" certain foundational concepts. Enthusiastic followers of cognitive developmental theory have argued on the basis of Piaget's theory that it must be inappropriate to teach children aspects of literacy before they are ready to discover them anyway. This idea can be misapplied, however: There are school districts in which kindergarten teachers have been told that it is "developmentally inappropriate" to teach children the alphabet until they produce several letters on their own, without prompting. Such an approach surely favors children who have had more exposure to literacy at home, while it allows children who need more direct support to languish. Children's discovery processes are important, certainly; but *not* to teach a kindergarten child the letters of the alphabet and other important concepts about literacy may be putting that child at a real disadvantage. Used in this way, so-called developmentally appropriate instruction becomes, in the words of Anne McGill-Franzen, "a trap for poor children" (1992, p. 57).

Early Literacy: A Research-Based View

The reader might be wondering, after this review of conflicting ideas in the field, "what *are* the important components in early literacy?" In a nutshell, research suggests that literacy begins early in childhood, well before school entry. Though maturity is a factor, there is no "magic moment" when children are ready to read. It helps to surround children with print and read to them a great deal, but direct instruction will still be needed to help many children learn to read.

Although many component skills of early reading do little good when taught in isolation, there *are* a small number of component skills whose presence or absence have proved to make a large difference in a child's eventual success in becoming a reader.

Recently, a panel of experts charged by the National Academy of Sciences reached these conclusions about early literacy:

> Reducing the number of children who enter school with inadequate literacy-related knowledge and skill is an important primary step toward preventing reading difficulties. . . . Children who are particularly likely to have difficulty with learning to read

in the primary grades are those who begin school with less prior knowledge and skill in relevant domains, most notably, *(1) general verbal abilities, (2) the ability to attend to the sounds of language as distinct from its meaning, (3) familiarity with the basic purposes and mechanisms of reading, and (4) letter knowledge* [Emphasis added]. (Snow et al., 1998, p. 5)

All of these priorities are addressed in this chapter.

THE TRANSITION FROM EMERGENT LITERACY TO BEGINNING READING

Traditionally, the phase of beginning reading was considered to have started when a child could read several words. But when we view the early stages of reading and writing with what we know about emergent literacy in mind, the boundary to beginning reading becomes continuous and overlapping, rather than distinct.

Consider two hypothetical children. One cannot yet read more than three or four words but knows that the print, not the pictures, is "what you say when you read." Although this child cannot yet write more than a few letters, he has learned to use scribbles as "place-holders" (Harste et al., 1984) for his thoughts. He follows stories knowledgeably, cheering when "Amazing Grace" succeeds in landing the role of Peter Pan in the book by Mary Hoffman (1991). He knows to expect a different listening experience from a poem by Shel Silverstein than a concept book by Richard Scarry. The other is a child who has been taught to read a dozen words, has memorized many of the letters, and even has learned to associate sounds with many of them. He happens to be lacking most of the insights and concepts the first child possesses, however, and therefore seems to have a limited ability to apply what he has learned about reading. The second child was traditionally considered a "beginning reader," while the first was not—yet the first child might be more likely to make good progress in learning to read than the second one.

Learning to read words is obviously important. The first child in the example still requires someone else to read to him, and his scribbles are not usually intelligible to others. Of course, he will have to learn to read in the conventional sense. The point is that a teacher will need to know about a young child's emergent concepts about literacy—whether or not that child can read words—and also that learning about print and literacy should be part of children's early education, even before first grade or even kindergarten.

UNDERSTANDING AND ASSESSING EMERGENT AND BEGINNING LITERACY

We turn now to several sections that describe procedures for assessing children's emergent and beginning literacy. Each of the procedures looks at a different aspect of emergent and beginning literacy:

- oral language fluency,
- storybook reading,

- print concepts,
- the concept of word,
- letter knowledge,
- phonemic awareness,
- knowledge of letter-to-sound correspondences or phonics,
- word recognition, and
- comprehension.

We begin by discussing the importance of each of these aspects to students' literacy and then set out specific procedures to assessing the development of those aspects. In the second half of the chapter, we will describe teaching and tutoring procedures that help students to develop these components, separately when it is appropriate, and also together. The chapter closes with a discussion of early intervention programs.

Oral Language Fluency

Up until about fourth grade, children's oral language is normally more advanced than the language they can read (Loban, 1963). Children first learn to recognize words in print that they are used to hearing in speech; and a teacher's goal for a student reading aloud is often that the child "make it sound like talk." But what if a student's English language fluency is limited? That can cause a lag on reading development. A careful instructional program will pay attention to developing students' oral language fluency as well as their development in literacy.

The Importance of Oral Language Fluency

Fluency in the language one is reading has been shown repeatedly to predict success in learning to read (Snow et al., 1998). Reading is an exercise in language use, and successful reading draws heavily on what children know about language. A reader needs to associate ideas with words, to use language elaborately to express fine shades of meaning that go beyond informal conversation, and to recognize the effects of grammatical structures on the meaning of word strings.

Assessing Oral Language Fluency

In this section, we describe two procedures that allow teachers to assess the oral language fluency of children in the context of activities that teach as well as test. The first is the *dictated experience account,* an activity to which we will return throughout this chapter because it offers other diagnostic insights beyond the assessment of oral language fluency. The second is *echo-reading,* a sentence imitation task based in the language of books. We will also describe two more assessment approaches, each with a more limited focus. Marie Clay and her associates' *Record of Oral Language and Biks and Gutches* (1983) deals with syntactical knowledge; Joan Tough's (1973) observational procedure identifies the functions to which children are able to address their utterances.

Dictated Experience Accounts

Dictated experience accounts are told aloud by a child and printed, exactly as spoken, by another person. One child can dictate a complete account, or a group can collaborate, with several children or each child contributing individual sentences.

Dictated experience accounts are a part of the language experience approach to beginning reading (Stauffer, 1980). Language experience is usually thought of as an instructional method, but dictations and rereadings have considerable value as diagnostic techniques for a small group or an individual child.

Materials A dictated experience account needs relatively few materials.

1. Individual account
   a. a stimulus (a hamster, arrowhead collection, picture book, or other concrete object or actual experience the child has just had)
   b. paper and pencil
2. Group story
   a. a stimulus (concrete object or event the group has just experienced together)
   b. an experience chart (a pad of large newsprint)
   c. a felt-tip pen or crayon

Procedure Whether with an individual or group, the dictated experience account starts with a concrete stimulus, which the children experience directly. The stimulus should be unique enough to (1) give the children an urge to talk about it and (2) enable them to remember it two or three days later when the dictation is reread.

After the students have enjoyed and discussed the experience, sit down with them and explain that together you are going to write an account of what has happened. You can begin by having the children talk about the stimulus and writing down some key words they use. Then ask each child to tell something about the experience and write down each one's contribution, including the child's name, like this:

The Strip Mine

John said, *"We went and saw a strip mine."*
Avery said, *"It was real deep"*
Sheila said, *"I was scared we would fall in."*
Bobby said, *"They dig up coal with big machines."*
Sue said, *"My Daddy works on a strip mine."*

Be careful to write down exactly what the children say, regardless of whether the sentences are complete or have errors in syntax, to preserve the integrity of their language. When it is all written down, read the whole account aloud two or three times, rapidly pointing to each word or line as it is read. Then ask the children to read the piece chorally with you. The idea is to have them memorize it so that the sentences become firmly anchored in their minds. When they have choral-read it twice or more and they seem confident, ask for volunteers to come forward and read a sentence, or the whole piece, if they can do so. As they recite the sentences, they should point to or underline individual words they know.

You can then make up a duplicating master of the group account and reproduce a copy for each child. These can be illustrated and reread many times; as additional single words are recognized, they should be underlined. Many children collect these accounts in booklets.

The dictated experience account can be done with one child, a small group of children, or a whole class. For diagnostic purposes, it is best used with an individual or small group.

The activity can be spread over a number of days: the dictation one day, the choral and individual reading on the second day, and the distribution of copies to the children for individual reading on the third day.

What to Look for in Dictated Experience Accounts   When a child dictates an experience account, the teacher can get an indication of the child's fluency as a language user. Some aspects to consider are the following:

- Does the child speak in sentences or in single words and word clusters?
- Does the child use descriptive names for objects and events or many ambiguous terms such as "it," "that," "this thing"?
- Does the child speak slowly and distinctly, repeating as necessary for the teacher to take the dictation, or blurt out or mumble sentences and then forget what was said?
- Does the child provide information that a reader who had not experienced the stimulus would need to reconstruct the event, or does the child assume that everyone has the same information about the event?

The more precise their terms, the more inclusive their sentences, and the more their speech takes into account the listener's informational needs, then the more we would say that the children are speaking in an elaborated code. This speech style is closest to the language of books. Children who speak in an elaborated code will learn to read that language more easily than children who speak in a less elaborated code. Perhaps the best summary of the expressive use of language is this: A dictated experience story is "talk written down" (Allen, 1976); nevertheless, the more children's talk sounds like book language, the better their oral language prepares them for learning to read.

Echo-Reading

Language fluency has two aspects that are particularly important. One is the expressive use of language, using elaborate sentences that make meanings adequately explicit. The expressive use of language can be examined informally by using the dictated story. The other aspect, the development of grammar or syntax, can be examined by using an *echo-reading* procedure.

In echo-reading, the teacher reads a sentence aloud, and the child repeats or *echoes* the teacher's words, verbatim if possible, while looking at the line of print.

The reading is not done independently but is accomplished in a highly supportive setting. What we are interested in is the precision with which the child can echo the teacher's words, not how well she or he can read the words.

Syntax is a system of ordering and inflecting words within sentences and ordering sentences within utterances. An intuitive understanding of syntax helps in constructing and understanding sentences with many components. Syntax is a complicated topic, but in the present context of reading diagnosis, we are concerned with only a minor aspect of it—namely, that syntactic development can limit the number of words a child can speak in a single sentence, which in turn can hinder the child's reading and discussion or written language, so it is a matter of concern in diagnosis.

Ordinarily, by the time children are about 5 years old, their utterances are complex and lengthy, and counting the number of words in their sentences has ceased to be a worthwhile enterprise, as it was when they began talking. Some children, however, are still limited in the number of words they can comfortably handle in one sentence when they reach the first or second grade. When this is the case, it is sometimes hard to spot, since the paucity of speech can be mistaken for shyness. If the teacher does have a child who is a reluctant speaker, using echo reading is a fairly straightforward means of deciding whether there is a lack of syntax.

The procedure for echo reading is as follows:

Materials   Select an eight-line passage from a book written at approximately a first-grade level. To record the echo-reading, make a copy of the lines. To keep records on several students, type the lines, triple spaced, and duplicate a copy for each student.

Procedure   Here are the steps to carrying out the echo-reading procedure.

1. Sit down with one student at a time in a place that is relatively free of distractions.
2. Explain that you will read the lines aloud and that as you do so, you want the student to repeat the words you just read, exactly as you read them.
3. Read a line clearly, stop, and have the student echo it.
4. Repeat for each of the eight lines.
5. As the student echoes, record his or her words on your copy. You might it find it convenient to tape-record these sessions and score the echo-reading later.

Code the echo-reading as follows:

1. Place a check mark over each word repeated correctly.
2. Circle words, word parts, or phrases that are omitted.
3. Write in words substituted for those in the line and draw a line through the words that were not repeated.
4. Write in words inserted in the line; use a caret (^) to indicate where the insertion was made.

Here are some examples:

✔✔ ✔ ✔ ✔ ✔ ✔

My new red wagon has (four shiny) red wheels. (correct and omission)

✔ friend ✔✔✔ ✔ ✔ ✔✔

My ~~brother~~ and I pull things in it. (correct, substitution, and insertion)

Why is the ability to repeat sentences important? It is a curious fact of language development that children cannot accurately repeat a sentence that is more syntactically advanced than one that they can produce spontaneously.

If you ask children to repeat a sentence that is more complicated than one they can produce themselves, they will normally simplify the sentence in the repeated version (Slobin and Welsh, 1971). Here, for example, are some sentence repetitions by young children between 2 and 4 years old.

1. *Adult:* Look at the doggy.
   Child: Doggy.
2. *Adult:* This boy is all wet.
   Child: Boy all wet.
3. *Adult:* The new bikes and roller skates are over there.
   Child: A new bikes are there and a skates are over there.

The link between children's ability to imitate sentences and the limits of their syntactic ability is fortuitous for language assessment. It enables us to get an idea of the limits of the complexity of their sentences by asking them to repeat sentences that we read to them. Thus, the method of echo-reading can indicate whether a child's syntax is sufficiently developed to encompass the sentence patterns encountered in reading books written on a given level. Experience tells us that if the language patterns of a book do not lie within the children's control, they will be at a disadvantage in reading that book. And occasionally, reading teachers encounter children whose syntax is not adequate for any but the simplest books.

What to Look for in Echo-Reading   One or two words deleted or substituted per sentence are not a cause for alarm, especially if the child substituted a familiar for a less familiar word such as *store* for *shop*. Similarly, if the child leaves off grammatical endings, plural markers on nouns, or tense markers on verbs, it is considered normal if he or she belongs to a dialect group that usually omits these endings. However, if the child regularly leaves out important words or rewords whole phrases, it is more serious. In the previous examples, the first two show important elements omitted.

If children have a great deal of trouble with a certain book, it is helpful to find out what they *can* successfully echo-read. It is easier to echo-read material that is written with predictable patterns of language, such as nursery rhymes, simple poems, and jingles. If the children are still having trouble even with this kind of material, you should observe whether or not they are taking advantage of the rhythm of the sentences. Do they repeat the sentences rhythmically? If not, make them tap their hands on the table along with you as they recite. Getting into the rhythm of the language will often help them to repeat longer sentence patterns.

The important thing here is to find out what the children *can* do once the limits of their syntactic development have been found—that is, the length and type of sentence in which their repetition falls below about 80 percent of the words, dialectical variances excluded. In these cases, their language in response to books will have to be drawn out before reading instruction can successfully proceed. Songs, poems, rhythm games and chants, and dictated experience accounts should all be used lavishly, as well as any simple books with a pattern or a rhyming or rhythmic element, as many books for young children have.

A Structured Sentence Imitation Task: The Record of Oral Language

While the level of difficulty of the echo-reading task can be set to any level of text by the selection of the sentences out of which it is constructed, a more standardized version of the same task assigns kindergartners and first-graders high, average, and low levels of syntactical development. This assessment tool, *The Record of Oral Language* by Marie Clay and associates, also has provisions for pinpointing the kinds of sentence constructions (the *basic sentence patterns*), as well as specific transformations of these patterns (including *passives, imperatives, interrogatives,* and several types of *imbeddings*).

The Record of Oral Language is a test based on the same principle as echo-reading. The groups of sentences to be repeated are carefully controlled for their form and their complexity, however, and they are arranged in three levels of difficulty. It comes bound in book form (the pages can be reproduced) with clear instructions for administering it and scoring the children's responses. Also provided is a detailed discussion of the syntactic structures being tested, the origins of the test, and the average scores of large groups of students for purposes of comparison. Because these students were all in New Zealand, however, it is inadvisable for U.S. teachers to use these data *verbatim* in judging the performance of their students. A safer approach will be to administer the test to one or more whole classes of students and determine the range of scores that emerge.

A sample page from *The Record of Oral Language* is found in Figure 6.1.

Storybook Reading

The benefits of reading storybooks alouds to children are well known—witness the popularity of Jim Trelease's read-aloud books (Trelease, 1989). Less well known is the diagnostic significance of the child's side of the read-aloud routine. As research has shown, however, a child's "pretend reading" of storybooks provides a valuable window into his or her growing conceptions on literacy.

The Importance of Storybook Reading

Children who show familiarity with and delight in storybooks not only show us that they have had many pleasurable encounters with books in their early lives; they also have a base of knowledge and expectation that will serve them well in the months and years ahead as they learn to read.

CLASS: _____ SCHOOL: _____ CHILD'S NAME: _____

DATE OF
BIRTH: _____ DATE: _____ AGE: _____ RECORDER: _____

THE LEVELS SENTENCES

Level 2 Part 1		Level 2 Part 2	
Type		Type	
A	*That big dog over there is going to be my brother's.* ☐	A	*That old truck in there used to be my father's.* ☐
B	*The boy by the pond was sailing his boat.* ☐	B	*The cat from next door was chasing a bird.* ☐
C	*The bird flew to the* top of the tree. ☐	C	*The dog ran through* the hole in the *fence.* ☐
D	*For his birthday Kiri gave him a truck.* ☐	D	*For the holidays Grandpa* bought us a ball. ☐
E	*Can you see what is climbing up the wall?* ☐	E	*The boy saw what the man* was doing *to the car.* ☐
F	*Here comes a big elephant with* children sitting on his back. ☐	F	*There is my baby riding* in his pushchair. ☐
G	*My brother turned the radio up very loud.* ☐	G	*The girl threw her book* right across the room. ☐

Total for Level 2 ☐

Enter 14 on the next page if all Level is credited.

FIGURE 6.1 Sample Page from *The Record of Oral Language*

Source: From Marie Clay, Malcolm Gill, Ted Glynn, Tony McNaughton, and Keith Salmon, *The Record of Oral Language and Biks and Gutches,* p. 20 (Auckland: Heinemann Publishers Ltd., 1983). Reprinted by permission.

Assessing Storybook Reading

Elizabeth Sulzby (1985) developed a research technique that can also be used to assess children's early reading knowledge. She chooses a book that she believes is appropriate for a child of a particular age and reads that book to the child at least twice, making sure that the child has become interested in the storybook. The reading of the book to the child may take place on several occasions over several days.

When it appears that the child is familiar with the book, she invites the child to "read" the book to her. She observes the child's pretend reading very carefully and then characterizes it according to one of the strategies found in Figure 6.2.

In practice, she might carry out this procedure more than once with a given child—after all, the activity of pretend reading itself is a worthwhile literary activity—

Biks and gutches

11 This is a bik and here is another bik.
There are two _____. (biks)
12 There is a gutch and here is another gutch.
There are two _____. (gutches)

Open the door

The children said to the lady. 'Open the door.
4 The lady is _____ the door. (opening)
5 But she is careful when she _____ it. (opens)
6 Yesterday she nearly knocked the little girl over
when she _____ the door. (opened)

FIGURE 6.2   Sample Questions to Test Syntactical Knowledge

Source: From Marie Clay, Malcolm Gill, Ted Glynn, Tony McNaughton, and Keith Salmon, *The Record of Oral Language and Biks and Gutches,* p. 20 (Auckland: Heinemann Publishers Ltd., 1982). Reprinted by permission.

to make sure she has found a strategy that the child seems to be using consistently. Sulzby's research suggests that children do use a particular strategy with some consistency, although they might revert to an easier strategy sometimes or experiment with a more difficult one on some occasions. On the whole, she found that children move in the direction from her earlier-named strategies to her later ones.

What does a child's use of these strategies tell us? If used repeatedly in assessment, Sulzby's categories eventually come to have meaning of themselves. In the meantime, as we noted in Chapter 2, the child's use of one or another strategy gives an indication of his or her understanding of the functions of print, of the decontextualized and highly structured language that print represents, and, finally, of the form—including the spelling-to-sound code—that print embodies.

Print Orientation Concepts

The Importance of Print Orientation Concepts

As we saw above, the National Research Council (Snow et al., 1998, p. 5) stressed the importance of acquainting young children with "the basic purposes and mechanisms of reading." New Zealand educator Marie Clay has shown a particular genius for seeing these basic purposes and mechanisms from a child's point of view. One whole set of challenges facing a young child is knowing his or her way around a book. Imagine a child in a reading circle who hears instructions such as these:

> "Open the book to the first page. Look at the first word. Go on to the next word. What letter does it begin with? Look at the end of the line: Don't you see that the author is asking a question? Now go on to the next page."

The teacher in this situation is assuming that the child knows how an English book is opened (it's different in Chinese); knows what a "page" is and where to find the "first" one; knows what a word is and that words in written English are arranged on a page from left to right and from top to bottom (not so in Chinese or Hebrew; and in ancient Greek, the words on the same page were alternately arranged from left to right and from right to left); knows what a letter is and that the "first letter" in a word refers to the one farthest to the left; understands marks of punctuation; and so on.

Assessing Print Orientation Concepts

It is unwise to assume that children who are just entering school understand the mechanisms of print. There are many children in kindergarten and first grade who do not; so Clay developed the *Concepts About Print Test* (1979) to assess these aspects of a child's orientation to books and to written language. This test is highly recommended for kindergarten and primary-grade teachers as well as for reading clinics. It comes with one of two reusable books and is available from Heinemann Educational Books, 361 Hanover Street, Portsmouth, New Hampshire 03801-3959.

The aspects of the *Concepts About Print Test* that are especially relevant to the present discussion of emergent literacy are:

- book orientation knowledge;
- principles involving the directional arrangement of print on the page;
- the knowledge that print, not the picture, contains the story;
- understanding of important reading terminology such as *word, letter, beginning of the sentence,* and *top of the page;* and
- understanding of simple punctuation marks.

The assessment of orientation concepts about written language can be carried out by using a simple illustrated children's book, one that the child being tested has not seen before. The *Concepts About Print Test* has two specially made books (*Sand* and *Stones*), but teachers can get much of the flavor of the procedure with a book of their own choosing. The following are some concepts that can be tested and the procedures to use with them.

1. ***Knowledge of the Layout of Books.*** Hand the child a book, with the spine facing the child, and say, "Show me the *front* of the book." Note whether the child correctly identifies the front.

2. ***Knowledge That Print, Not Pictures, Is What We Read.*** Open the book directly to a place where print is on one page and a picture is on the other (you should make sure beforehand that the book has such a pair of pages, and have it bookmarked for easy location). Then say, "Show me where I begin reading." Observe carefully to see whether the child points to the print or the picture. If the pointing gesture is vague, say, "Where, exactly?" If the child points to the print, note whether or not the child points to the upper left-hand corner of the page.

3. ***Directional Orientation of Print on the Page.*** Stay on the same set of pages, and after the child points at some spot on the printed page, say, "Show me with your finger where I go next." Then observe whether the child sweeps his or her finger across the printed line from left to right or moves it in some other direction.

Then ask, "Where do I go from there?" and observe whether the child correctly makes the return sweep to the left and drops down one line.

Note that a correct directional pattern is like this:

If the child indicates some other directional pattern, make a note of it.

4. ***Knowledge of the Concepts of Beginning and End.*** Turning now to a new page, say, "Point to the beginning of the story on this page" and then "Point to the end of the story on this page." Observe whether the child interprets both requests properly.

5. ***Knowledge of the Terms "Top" and "Bottom."*** Turning to another pair of pages that have print on one page and a picture on the other, point to the *middle* of the printed page and say, "Show me the bottom of the page" and then "Show me the top of the page." Then point to the *middle* of the picture and say, "Show me the top of the picture" and then "Show me the bottom of the picture." Note whether or not the child responds accurately to all four requests.

6. ***Knowledge of the Terms "Word" and "Letter."*** Now hand the child two blank index cards and say, "Put these cards on the page so that just *one word* shows between them" and then "Now move them so that *two words* show between them. Now move them again so that *one letter* shows between them" and then "Now move them so that *two letters* show between them." Make note of the child's response to all four requests.

7. ***Knowledge of Uppercase and Lowercase Letters.*** On the same page, point to a capital letter with your pencil and say, "Show me a little letter that is the same as this one." (Beforehand, make sure that there is a corresponding lowercase letter on the page.) Next point to a lowercase letter and say, "Now point to a capital letter that is the same as this one." (Again, make sure that there *is* one.) Repeat this procedure with other pairs of letters if the child's response seems uncertain.

8. ***Knowledge of Punctuation.*** Turn to a page that has a period, an exclamation point, a question mark, a comma, and a set of quotation marks. Pointing to each one in turn, ask, "What is this? What is it for?" Note whether or not the child answers correctly for each of the five punctuation marks.

To follow this assessment procedure efficiently, you will have to choose a book carefully and practice using the assessment questions enough times to become proficient. The procedure is easily carried out with Marie Clay's own test booklet, which is well worth the nominal cost.

The Concepts About Print Test was extensively reviewed by Yetta Goodman (1981), who has long been interested in what young children know about print and who has suggested several perceptive adaptations to the test. She recommended using a trade book that is relevant to the children's experience rather than using Clay's *Sand* or *Stones,* which accompany the test. Goodman believed that the particular children who are pictured and their particular activities might not be culturally relevant to all. She also urged that teachers read the entire book to the children before asking the orientation questions because she found that some of the children she worked with became impatient with the interruptions of the story for the questioning.

It is advisable to make up a record sheet that provides for the quick recording of information yielded by the assessment. Clay's own test is matched with a scoring system. We believe, however, that it is sufficient simply to make a list of those print orientation competencies the children do or do not have. Then, as you work with them in simple trade books and basals, with dictated stories, and by reading aloud to them, you can begin to draw their attention to the concepts they have not yet mastered: the direction of print, capital and lowercase letters, periods, and the like.

Letter Knowledge

The Importance of Letter Knowledge

Knowledge of letters of the alphabet has been shown to be an early predictor of later reading success (Walsh et al., 1988). Part of the reason for this, no doubt, is that those children who know more letters have had more exposure to print. But knowing letters is important in itself, for several reasons. First, even children who seemingly learn to recognize words as wholes, rather than analyzing them by their parts (see a discussion of this in the section entitled "Sight-Word Recognition" later in this chapter) need enough letter knowledge to identify at least a salient part of a word (Ehri, 1991). Second, and related to the previous point, children who *voice-point* (who focus visually on word units as they recite to themselves a known line of text) seem to rely on at least beginning letters to orient themselves to word units (Morris, 1993). Third, as children begin to sound out words, or begin to use what their fledgling knowledge of the relations between letters and sounds to read words, they will obviously need to be able to recognize several letters. Fourth, as children begin to invent spellings for words—itself an activity that helps children learn to segment words into phonemes, and also to explore the relationships between letters and sounds (Clarke, 1988)—they will need to know how to name and produce several alphabet letters. Indeed, before any direct instruction in reading is likely to be of much benefit to children, those children must be able to recognize and produce most of the letters of the alphabet (Morris, 1990).

Assessing Letter Knowledge

When testing students' alphabet knowledge, we ask them to recognize all of the letters of the alphabet in both uppercase and lowercase. We also ask them to write all of the letters once each, without specifying uppercase or lowercase. The letters are always presented in a scrambled sequence so that the children cannot use serial order as a cue to identifying a letter.

For a Letter Recognition Inventory, prepare the following letters as a separate display. Prepare another copy to use as a record sheet.

> **d f t g n b e h l v o y m a**
> **r c q z u p j s i x k w g**

> **D F T G N B E H L V O Y M A**
> **R C Q Z U P J S I X K W G**

As you proceed from left to right across the line, point to each letter and ask the child to identify it. Enter on the record sheet only a notation of what letters were misidentified or unnamed.

Many beginning readers will have difficulty recognizing Z, Q, V, and perhaps one or two letters that they encounter out of sequence. Difficulty with *b, d, p, q,* and *g* is also common because of directional confusion.

Children who confuse letters in isolation might still read them correctly in words, though they will be more uncertain than those who do not confuse them. Children who have difficulty identifying letters other than these will need more experience with print and letters as a top priority.

The Speech-to-Print Match

The Importance of the Speech-to-Print Match

As described in Chapter 1, the speech-to-print match or concept of word refers to one's ability to match spoken words with the same words as they appear in print. Children gain this ability only after they have acquired the following concepts about written language: (1) words are separable units, (2) printed words have spaces on either side that separate them from other words, and (3) words and syllables are not necessarily the same things. Therefore, dividing a line of writing up into its audible syllables, or "beats," will not necessarily be an accurate way to separate the line into words (Morris, 1981).

Assessing the Speech-to-Print Match

The speech-to-print match can be assessed by informal means, either in a special *voice-pointing* procedure or as a follow-up to a dictated experience story.

The Voice-Pointing Procedure This technique is best carried out by the teacher with one child at a time.

Materials You will need a short poem or a very memorable story, four lines long and preferably clearly supported by illustrations. Print or type the lines on paper or tagboard and triple space the lines. Reproduce a separate picture to support the learning of each line.

We have found that rhythmic children's stories work well with prereaders because they have just the right elements of rhythmic, repetitious language and strong picture clues to make the lines easy to memorize and repeat. It is necessary for the child to learn to recite the lines confidently before the procedure begins, so choose some easily memorized text. Be sure that at least two of the words within the four lines have more than one syllable.

An optional part of the test is to determine whether the child has learned new words from this task, since the voice-pointing assessment procedure very much resembles a rich teaching episode, in which the student encounters in print, with an attentive teacher present, the written form of words that have become meaningful. If you choose to assess the child's word recognition, you should prepare a set of eight word cards from the text.

In any case, choose two words from the beginnings of lines, two words from the ends of lines, and four words from the middles of lines. Two of the eight words that you choose should be longer than one syllable. Prepare two versions of the text, one with the text intact and the other with certain words underlines and a scoring sheet for each line, as shown:

The procedure is as follows:

1. (*Optional.*) Use the word cards to pretest recognition of the words.
2. Recite the lines, holding up the picture for each line, until the child has memorized them but has *not yet seen them* in print.
3. Read the lines aloud, pointing to each word as you read.
4. Have the child recite the lines and point to the words while doing so.
5. Read selected words aloud and ask the child to point them out.
6. (*Optional.*) Use the word cards to posttest recognition of those words; the child might now recognize some or all of them as a result of the activity.

The first and sixth steps, using the word cards, are intended to show, respectively, whether the child already knew any of the words before the exercise and whether any of those selected were learned during the exercise. You should take note of the number of words recognized, if any, during steps 1 and 6.

The second step, memorizing the lines, is not timed or scored. You should show the picture as you recite the lines, but it is important not to show the child the printed lines until after this stage is completed. Later on, you might want to see how easily he or she can form associations between spoken words and printed ones, so it is important not to teach these associations inadvertently at this stage. Make sure that the child knows the lines before going on, since children differ in how many repetitions they need to memorize the lines.

In step 3, you model the voice-pointing procedure. Read each line at a normal speed and point to each word as you read, but make sure that the child is watching your finger.

Old Sam, the baker man
Washed his face in a frying pan
Combed his hair with a wagon wheel
And died with a toothache in his heel.

[DRAW ONE PICTURE TO SUPPORT EACH LINE, AND INSERT AS A LARGE
FIGURE, DIVIDED INTO SQUARES(ONE PICTURE IN EACH SQUARE).]

	Line Pointing	Word Pointing	Word Pointing
Old Sam, the baker _man_	_____	_____	_____
Washed his _face_ in a _frying_ pan	_____	_____	_____
Combed _his_ hair with a _wagon_ wheel	_____	_____	_____
And _died_ with a toothache in his _heel_.	_____	_____	_____

(Note that the scoring sheet is designed to record the child's performance in voice pointing only.)

In step 4, now ask the child to say the words aloud in a line as she or he points to each word. As the words in each line are recited and pointed to, observe how accurately the child matches the spoken and printed words. Award the child one point for each line through which he or she correctly voice-points, by putting a "1" in the blank for "Line Pointing" beside that line.

In step 5, you put your finger beside the first line and say, "Point to the word, 'Old.' Now, point to the word 'man.'" Award the child one point for each word correctly pointed to, by putting a "1" in the blanks for "Word Pointing" beside that line. Repeat the procedure for the underlined words in the second, third, and fourth lines and score the child's voice-pointing for each line.

Step 6 is optional. If you wish to see whether the child has learned to recognize any of the words, you should now call out the eight words that you put on the word cards in scrambled order, one at a time, and ask the child to read them. Subtract the number of words the child identified in the pretest (step 1) to arrive at a word learning score.

At the conclusion of this activity, you should have:

- *(optional)* pretest and posttest scores of the child's recognition of words from the text in isolation;
- observations of the child's voice-pointing performance; and
- a score of the number of spoken words he or she could identify in the context of the printed lines.

What to Look for in the Voice-Pointing Procedure This procedure directly tests two important components of beginning reading:

- the concept of the word as a written unit in print and
- the ability to learn new words from a supported reading activity.

Using Voice-Pointing with a Dictated Experience Story Dictated experience stories provide excellent opportunities for teachers to test and develop a child's speech-to-print match. Later in this chapter, we introduce the dictated story "The Strip Mine," in which John dictates a sentence and the teacher reads the passage twice and then chorally reads it with the children. There is a good probability that John will remember his sentence, because he just said it: "John said, 'We went and saw a strip mine.'" He probably can recognize his own name, too. If the teacher asks him to read the sentence aloud, he will be able to do so, perhaps even with his eyes closed. If the teacher asks him to point to his name, *John,* he should be able to do it. If she asks him to point to each word in the sentence as he says it, he probably will do so even though he might be a little hesitant. Now the question is: Can he point to a single word such as *mine* or *saw?* If he can, he is showing signs of the speech-to-print match. He can recognize that bound configurations on the page correspond to spoken words in his head. This is how the sixth word, for example, in his spoken sentence comes to match the sixth word in his written sentence.

Phonemic Awareness

Phonemic awareness is the consciousness of the smaller units of sounds that make up speech. Being aware of speech sounds is not as easy as it might sound because we are far more used to paying attention to what language *means* than how it sounds.

There are several levels of phonemic awareness. Griffith and Olson (1992) suggest three:

1. rhyming and recognizing rhymes;
2. segmenting the beginning sound (onset) from the remainder of the syllable (rime), as in /b/ -*ack;* and
3. completely segmenting the phonemes in spoken words (/b/-/a/-/k/ and manipulating them to form new words, as in back-buck-duck-dull.

The latter two levels will especially concern us here, since sounds at the phoneme level have been shown repeatedly to present the most difficulty to children who are attempting to learn to read and write in alphabetic languages such as English (Ehri, 1991).

The Importance of Phonemic Awareness

To read in any writing system, a person should be able to make accurate mappings between the spoken units of language and the written units. A logographic writing system such as that of Chinese is made up of written characters, or zi, that correspond to the spoken language at the whole word level. In a mixed logographic and syllabic writing system, such as that of Japanese, some of the units of written language (the *kanji*) correspond to whole words, and some (the *katakana* and the *hiragana*) correspond to spoken syllables. In an alphabetic writing system, such as we use in English, the units of written language (the letters) correspond to the spoken language at the level of *phonemes*. Phonemes are small units of sound, smaller than syllables. They are the sounds to which the letters in C-A-T correspond. Every language has phonemes, of course, but only alphabetic languages base their writing systems on them. This is a mixed blessing.

On the positive side, an alphabetic writing system gives us remarkable economy. We would need half a million characters at the word level to write our immense vocabulary in English. We would need 5,000 characters at the syllable level to spell that same vocabulary. But by writing our words at the phonemic level, we can make do with twenty-six letters.[1] On the negative side, phonemes are difficult things to manipulate. Of the three sounds in CAT, for instance, only the middle sound—the vowel sound—is identifiable when spoken in isolation. The consonants cannot be understood when spoken alone. It has been shown that many adult illiterates cannot separate words into their phonemes (Morais, 1987), an ability that we often take for granted in our 6-year-olds. And it has been shown that teenage nonreaders could be taught to read syllabaries when they could not read words spelled alphabetically (Lesgold et al., 1985). Indeed, there is much evidence that difficulties in the awareness of phonemes lies at the heart of perhaps a majority of the cases of reading disability (Vellutino, 1979).

Phonemic awareness is different from phonemic perception. Most 5-year-old children will pick up the cat and not the bat when you ask them to, showing that they can perceive the difference between the phonemes /k/ and /b/. Most will hesitate and some will balk completely, though, if you ask them to tap their finger on the table to each of the three constituent sounds in CAT. The difference is one of responding to the meaning of language—which young children find relatively natural—and thinking about language, or *metalinguistic awareness*, which doesn't come so easily.

Why is phonemic awareness important? Obviously, when beginning readers want to sound out words, they must be aware of units of sound. Yet even beyond the beginning stage, phonemic awareness has been shown to be important. Ehri's hypothesis (Ehri, 1991) is that phonemic awareness somehow corresponds to the kind of memory storage we have for words. So a person who has strong phonemic awareness has a well-differentiated memory storage for words and will therefore in time be able to recognize many words instantaneously—clearly a prerequisite for fluent and effortless reading.

---

[1] It's not an exact match at that. English has forty-four distinct phonemes, and our twenty-six letters have to do double and triple duty to spell them all. At the same time, the alphabet contain some redundancies, such as the letter S, which sometimes sounds like S and sometimes like K.

In the rest of this section, we will demonstrate two ways of assessing children's phonemic awareness.

Assessing Phonemic Awareness by Means of Invented Spelling

One way to observe whether or not a first-grade child has phonemic awareness is to ask him or her to spell words that he or she does not already know. By asking the child to spell unknown words, we ask the child to rely upon his or her *invented spelling*, the inner capacity to forge connections between letters and sounds. Children have an amazing intuitive ability to invent spellings, and we can learn much about their word knowledge by looking at their invented productions.

A procedure for testing phonemic segmentation (after Morris, 1992), then, is to have the child spell the following list of words as you call them out. Then you can count the number of phonemes the child reasonably attempted to represent. (Guides to scoring each word are presented in parentheses.)

bite	(three phonemes: BIT = 3 points; BT = 2 points; BRRY, etc. = 1 point)
seat	(three phonemes: SET or CET = 3 points; ST, CT = 2 points)
dear	(three phonemes: DER = 3 points; DIR or DR = 2 points)
bones	(four phonemes: BONS or BONZ = 4 points; BOS or BOZ = 3 points)
mint	(four phonemes: MENT or MINT = 4 points; MET or MIT = 3 points; MT = 2 points)
rolled	(four phonemes: ROLD = 4 points; ROL or ROD = 3 points)
race	(three phonemes: RAS, RAC, or RAEC = 3 points; RC or RS = 2 points)
roar	(three phonemes: ROR or ROER = 3 points; RR = 2 points)
beast	(four phonemes: BEST = 4 points; BES or BST = 3 points; BS or BT = 2 points)
groan	(four phonemes: GRON = 4 points; GRN = 3 points; GN = 2 points)
TOTAL:	Thirty-five points.

Explain to the child that you are going to ask the child to spell some words you know the child doesn't know how to spell. The child will have to figure out the spellings as best she or he can. After you call out each word (at least twice, and as many more times as the student requests), ask the student to try to spell each sound in the word. If the student says he or she can't, ask the student to listen to the way the word begins. What sound does it start with? Ask the student to write down a letter for that sound and letters for any other sounds he or she can hear. If the student is not sure how to spell a sound, ask the student to write a little dash (—).

After reading all ten words (fewer if the test seems too arduous for a particular child), count the number of reasonable letters the child wrote for each word, and compare that to the number of phonemes in the word. A child who consistently writes three or four letters that show some reasonable connection to the sounds in the word appears to be able to segment phonemes. A child who writes nothing or strings together many letters indiscriminately is not yet able to segment phonemes, and a child who writes one or two reasonable letters per word is just beginning to segment phonemes. You might calculate a score for phonemic segmentation by scoring each word according to the table at the right of each word and then comparing the total number of points the child receives to the total possible.

A Spoken Test of Phonemic Segmentation

Invented spelling is a natural means both to assess and to practice phonemic segmentation, but it does have one drawback. To demonstrate that they can segment words into phonemes, children must also be able to match phonemes with letters, know what the letters look like, and know how to form them on paper. These latter abilities have nothing to do with segmenting phonemes. Hence, invented spelling both tests and exercises more than phonemic segmentation ability.

A procedure that does not depend upon spelling and writing is an oral test of phonemic segmentation developed by Hallie Kay Yopp (Yopp, 1988). This procedure is done with one child at a time, and it takes between five and ten minutes to administer. The test consists of a series of twenty-two one-syllable words. The child's task is to pronounce the words slowly to highlight the phonemes, after the tester shows the child how. Yopp's directions to the children work as follows:

> Today we're going to play a word game. I'm going to say a word, and I want you to break the word apart. You are going to tell me each sound of the word in order. For example, if I say old, you will say o-l-d. Let's try a few words together. (Yopp, 1988, p. 166)

She follows with three more demonstration words: *ride, go,* and *man.* She praises the child if the child is correct and corrects the child if he or she is wrong. After the trials, she reads twenty-two words to the child, and the child breaks the words apart one at a time as they are read. Again, the teacher gives praise or correction after each word. The words are as follows:

dog	*lay*	*keep*	*race*
fine	*zoo*	*no*	*three*
she	*job*	*wave*	*in*
grew	*ice*	*that*	*at*
red	*top*	*me*	*by*
sat	*do*		

Yopp gives the child a point for each word correctly segmented (there is no partial credit), so the scores can range from 0 to 22. When the test was given in the spring of the year to a group of ninety-four kindergartners in southern California—children with a median age of 5 years, 10 months—the children got an average of nearly twelve items correct.

Yopp gives data that suggest that her task predicts children's ability to learn to sound out words more reliably than nine other phonemic segmentation tasks against which she compared it. Unfortunately, she did not compare her task against invented spelling. Mann, Tobin, and Wilson (1988), however, did find that invented spelling, when measured as a test of phonemic segmentation in kindergarten, significantly predicted reading ability in first grade.

Phoneme-to-Grapheme Correspondences

Phonemic awareness, or phonemic segmentation—the topic of the previous section—is something that relates to spoken language directly (We can practice segmenting words into phonemes without ever referring to print.) Phoneme-to-grapheme correspondences, in contrast, have to do with our ability to match those speech sounds with letters of the alphabet. Phoneme-to-grapheme correspondences are the domain of what most people think of when they think of *phonics*.

The Importance of Phoneme-to-Grapheme Correspondences

Several major studies have concluded that having knowledge of phoneme-to-grapheme correspondences is essential if children are going to learn to read. These studies range from Jeanne Chall's 1960's comprehensive survey of research to the most recent report of the National Academy of Sciences (Snow et al., 1998). Although some children might learn what they need to know about phoneme-to-grapheme correspondences without explicit instruction, a great many children need such instruction. Since knowledge of phoneme-to-grapheme correspondences is so important, one researcher has concluded that

> "The only sure way to prevent a child from learning to read is to preclude all opportunity to make appropriate associations between written letters and the sounds they represent." (quoted in Graves, et al., 1998, p. 99)

Knowing phoneme-to-grapheme correspondences is important because it is a key means by which a reader may sound out unfamiliar words. It is true that other means exist. For example, if a child were puzzled by *refrigerator* in the written sentence, "My brother put the milk into the *refrigerator*," she might have several ways available to identify the word. If there were an illustration, she might use the picture cues. She could use the grammatical context to know that the unknown word had to be a noun, the object of the preposition "into." And she could use the meaning of the sentence, the semantic context, to narrow the possibilities to "something into which you put milk." Nonetheless, as a panel of reading experts recently concluded, phoneme-to-grapheme correspondences is the *most important* means of determining a word's identity. It is one means teachers should be sure every child has available.

The Nature of Learning Phoneme-to-Grapheme Correspondences

Learning phoneme-to-grapheme correspondences is not a static, once-and-for-all occurrence. As children begin to explore the relationships between letters and sounds, they notice different features at different points in their development. Their discoveries tend to follow a similar pattern (Marsh et al., 1981), which has been described as follows.

Beginning Letter Only   At a primitive level, children may notice the first (or another salient) letter in a word and ignore the other letters. For the young child, the word "beach" might appear something like this: **b####.**

Each Letter Represents a Sound   Later, the child's ability to work out letter-to-sound correspondences might enable him or her to "see" more letters in "beach." However, the child might process these letters as if each one by itself corresponded to a unit of sound: yielding a bizarre pronunciation, such "be-ah-cuh-huh."

"Onset" and "Rime"   Still later, the child will begin to realize that letters work in teams: that the word "beach" can be approached as a combination of *b + each*. The child may further realize that the *b* can be substituted by *r, t,* and *p* to make other words. This beginning element plus following letter string has been called *onset* and *rime* by Rebecca Trieman (1993).

Assessing Knowledge of Phoneme-to-Grapheme Correspondences

There are two reliable ways to assess students' knowledge of phoneme-to-grapheme correspondences. One is by means of **invented spelling.** The other is by means of **picture sorts,** which we describe here.

Picture-Sound Identification   Prepare a set of picture cards similar to those shown in Figure 6.3 depicting the following items or concepts:

apple	otter	gun	jar	pin	vest
ape	oats	hat	lamp	rat	wall
egg	bat	kangaroo	map	sun	zoo
eagle	dog	fan	net	tack	

Demonstrate the task. Show the child the picture of the hat. Say, "Look. Here's a picture of a hat. Can you say the word? 'Hat'). Good. Let's see: What is the first sound we hear in 'hat'? I know. It's 'huh.'" Can you hear the 'huh' sound in 'hat'? What letter spells the "huh" sound in 'hat'? I know: It's **H.**"

Now show the student another picture, and tell the student the name of the item or concept in the picture. Ask the student to repeat the word. Correct the student if she or he does not say the word correctly. Make sure the student says the word.

Ask the student to say the sound the word begins with. Now ask the student to tell you what letter spells that sound.

Repeat the procedure until you have shown the student all of the consonant cards and vowel cards.

Record on the record sheet (see Figure 6.4) the student's accuracy in matching letters with sounds. Make a note to help that student learn those phoneme-to-grapheme matches that he or she is unsure about.

Sight-Word Recognition

Repeated exposure to written words, including some ability to sound words out by their phoneme-to-grapheme correspondences, enables a reader to acquire *sight words,* words that can be recognized instantly.

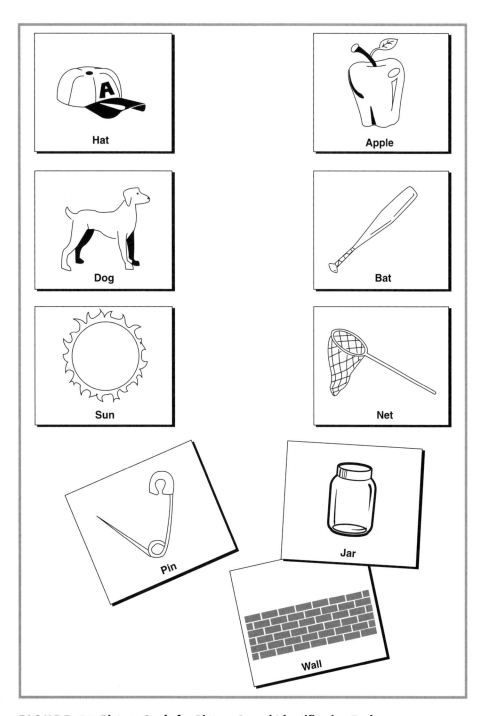

FIGURE 6.3 Picture Cards for Picture-Sound Identification Tasks

Phoneme	Correct?	Comments
/a/ (apple)		
/a/ (ape)		
/e/ (egg)		
/e/ (eagle)		
/o/ (otter)		
/o/ (oats)		
/b/ (bat)		
/d/ (dog)		
/g/ (gun)		
/h/ (hat)		
/k/ (kangaroo)		
/f/ (fan)		
/j/ (jar)		
/l/ (lamp)		
/m/ (map)		
/n/ (net)		
/p/ (pin)		
/r/ (rat)		
/s/ (sun)		
/t/ (tack)		
/v/ (vest)		
/w/ (wall)		
/z/ (zoo)		

FIGURE 6.4 Record Sheet for Picture-Sound Identification Tasks

The Importance of Sight-Word Recognition

At the stage of emergent literacy, children's ability to recognize some words is an indicator of their general exposure to print. We won't expect children to recognize very many words in later kindergarten or early first grade. Nonetheless, before children can read independently (that is, before they can make sense of text they have not dictated or heard read aloud), they must amass a number of sight words, words that they can recognize with little effort. Words that children recognize immediately are stepping stones that help them to get through text that contains unknown words. Without sight words, reading is reduced to word-by-word decoding, and although this resembles reading in some superficial ways, it is not reading in a meaningful sense.

It is therefore important to see whether children have begun to acquire some sight words. We cannot productively ask them to identify all the words they can recognize in print, however. We must instead construct a sample list of words that they are likely to encounter in beginning reading, test them on those, and estimate from their performance what proportion of typical words they are apt to recognize as sight words in other contexts.

Assessing Sight-Word Recognition

A useful sight word inventory has two kinds of words: *high-frequency words,* or those that often appear in print but do not necessarily follow common spelling patterns, and *decodable words,* words that follow some of the spelling patterns that children encounter in first grade.

HIGH-FREQUENCY WORDS

are

was

you

they

house

friend

school

what

out

love

some

DECODABLE WORDS

cat

hot

rob

it

up

mop

sad

cot

net

bug

The assessment is done with one child at a time. If you are right-handed, sit with child on your left. Put the tag board with the word list in front of the child and a duplicated copy of the list by your right hand. (If you are left-handed, the placement is reversed.) Using two index cards, frame one word at a time to the child, asking, "What is this word? . . . How about this one?" Put a check mark on your sheet next to every word that the child recognizes. You can put an X next to any word the child does not know at sight but is able to figure out. Continue until all the words have been exposed unless the student becomes frustrated or unhappy with this experience, which might happen if the child knows only a few sight words. Use your judgment, and stop if the child gets discouraged.

Comprehension

Comprehension, making meaning from text, is the ultimate purpose of reading. Every concept and strategy that we introduce in this chapter is pointed toward the goal of comprehension. We sometimes hear of instructional programs that seek to teach the "skills" of reading first and deal with comprehension later, or we hear it said that younger children are not yet ready to work on comprehension. Most reading experts agree, though, that comprehension should be the goal of all reading instruction at every level. Certainly, children should begin with their very first experiences with reading to expect to make sense of what they read.

Aspects of Comprehension

There appears to be a right way and a wrong way to approach comprehension. The wrong way was brought to light ninety years ago by the famous educational philosopher John Dewey (1910). On a visit to a sixth-grade class in Chicago, Dr. Dewey asked the students this question: "Boys and girls, suppose we could dig a hole right through this floor, say, 4,000 miles deep. What would it be like at the bottom of it?" The students stared at him blankly. The teacher, with a look of irritation, walked to the front of the room and said, "Why, Dr. Dewey. You didn't ask the question properly." Then to the students she said, "Class, what is the state of the center of the earth?" In one hypnotic voice, the children responded, **"A state of igneous fusion!"**

As Dewey noted, it is possible, dangerously possible, to get students to memorize information that makes no sense to them.

The better way to approach comprehension was described by the psychologist Jean Piaget. According to Piaget, at its simplest, comprehension is understanding new information in light of old information: using what we already knew to make sense of what we didn't know. When we are faced with a new topic, we begin by searching our prior knowledge about the topic and asking questions about it. We might even predict what we will find out. Then we inquire to answer our questions. We make inferences as we go and keep track of our own understanding. Then we look back on what we found out; we sum it up; we consider the implications of it; relate it to our lives, apply it, interpret it, debate it; and possibly modify our ideas about the topic in light of what we've learned.

Dewey's observation was repeated more recently by the contemporary psychologist Howard Gardner (1991). Gardner pointed out that children gain many of their most basic ideas about the world by means of discovery. They also obviously learn a great deal of formal knowledge through schooling. Unfortunately, "school knowledge" is too often learned passively, without discovery or examination. As a result, Gardner demonstrates, it is possible to enter advanced university science classes and find students who behave like young children when asked to solve problems that they have not been taught how to solve. What is needed is to cultivate approaches to teaching that engage students actively in understanding and learning. If such approaches are followed from the earliest years, the hope is that the problem of useless school knowledge can be largely avoided.

Graves et al. (1998) suggest that several key component abilities are involved in reading comprehension. They include summoning up our prior knowledge and asking ourselves what we know about the topic of the text what we want to know. These components also include *finding main ideas, drawing inferences,* and *imaging.* They include summarizing information and monitoring our comprehension.

Prior Knowledge   According to models of understanding such as that of Jean Piaget, students understand by interpreting new information in light of their prior knowledge. That means, first, that they should *have* prior knowledge about the topics they are likely to read about and, second, that they be ready to remind themselves of what they already know about the topic. The first takes wide reading and an information-rich curriculum, and the second takes energy and a habit of curiosity.

Asking Questions   Once students have summoned up their prior knowledge—or, in simpler terms, remembered what they already knew about a topic—they might then ask what they now want to know. Alternatively, if the text itself has planted some mystery or otherwise raised a question about its own contents, good comprehenders rise to the challenge and approach the text with questions in mind.

Finding Main Ideas   This is a necessary part of comprehension because more information is usually conveyed in a text than a reader can recall after reading. Since it is not possible to remember everything, students should remember what is most important—but they must first be able to identify what those important ideas are.

Making Inferences   Besides stating their points explicitly, authors frequently leave gaps in their works that must be either supplied from the readers' background knowledge or derived from hints the author had given or both (Raphael, 1982).

For a familiar example, consider Harry Allard and James Marshall's picture book, *Miss Nelson Is Missing* (1977). In this book, we readers are never told whence came Miss Viola Swamp, the no-nonsense substitute teacher. Nor are we told where she went. But at the end of the story, we're shown Miss Nelson reading in bed, next to a closet with an ugly black dress hanging in it—just like the one Viola Swamp wore. And there's a box on the shelf marked in upside-down letters that spell "WIG!" The inference that Viola Swamp was Miss Nelson in disguise is left for the young readers to make.

For a more elaborate example, consider a text about General Robert E. Lee. A text says that he was the commander of the Confederate forces in the Civil War and that he had difficulty communicating with some of his generals during their campaigns. It also says that General Hampton of South Carolina took some actions in the field that General Lee did not agree with.

The reader is given two pieces of explicit information and is called on to make two kinds of inferences to make full sense of this information.

One inference is that General Hampton might have taken the actions without General Lee's approval because timely approval was impossible to get. That inference was derived from the information that was given.

Another inference is that difficulties in communication were caused by slowly evolving technology. That inference is derived from the reader's background knowledge. The reader might know from background knowledge that the Civil War was fought from 1861 to 1865, before the invention of radio but during the early days of the telegraph. Telegraph signals traveled through metal lines strung above ground, and they were easily disrupted in wartime if they were available at all. Otherwise, the fastest communication would have used the physical conveyance of messages by means of railroad trains or horseback riders. Therefore, the difficulty in communication was to be expected.

Imaging or Visualizing   Another important (as well as enjoyable) ability is imaging or visualizing, being able to picture what is described in a text. Imaging means being able to bring to life in one's "mind's eye" what is described in the words on the page.

Summarizing   Summarizing means restating in a few words the essence of what was written in a passage. Brown and Day (1983) have described the process of summarizing in some detail. After reading a passage, students should:

- delete trivial or irrelevant information,
- delete repeated information,
- provide a superordinate term for members of a category,
- find and use generalizations the author has made,
- create your own generalizations when the author has not provided them (Graves et al., 1998).

Comprehension Monitoring   Knowing whether or not what you are reading makes sense and whether your questions are being answered is referred to as *comprehension monitoring*. Students who practice comprehension monitoring are able to stop and "repair" lapses in comprehension, as when a misread word skews the meaning of a passage.

Assessing Comprehension

It follows from the discussion immediately above that assessing students' comprehension should observe the aspects of comprehension that were described in the previous section. Specifically, a good assessment of comprehension should observe:

- the students' readiness to summon up their relevant *prior knowledge* when approaching a new text;

- their disposition to *ask questions and make predictions* and the relevance of those questions and predictions to the content and the genre of the text;
- whether or not the students make the more obvious *inferences* suggested by the text—and whether those inferences are derived from information in the text or from the student's prior knowledge;
- their ability to *visualize*—that is, to describe out loud or act out, scenes, and actions in the text;
- their ability to point to *main ideas* in the text; and
- their ability to *summarize* the information in the text.

These aspects of comprehension are assessed especially well using two strategies that have already been presented in this text: the *running record*, discussed in Chapter 2, and the *Informal Reading Inventory*, discussed in Chapter 5.

TEACHING FOR EMERGENT AND BEGINNING LITERACY

The techniques that are used to help each youngster's literacy emerge, whether in classroom or in clinic, should derive from two guiding principles: First, they should involve real reading and real writing in real contexts; second, they should respond to what the child knows and needs to know about reading and writing. In the following section, we suggest activities that are related to each of these assessment areas.

READING STORYBOOKS

As you will recall from our discussion of emergent storybook earlier in this chapter, by paging through and pretending to read favorite storybooks, in imitation of adults they have seen reading, children develop concepts about the form and function of written text and the kind of language that is used in print. Therefore, good instruction for emerging readers will include providing individual books on their level, with simple text, that they will enjoy. The teacher introduces the books by reading them to a child or group of children more than once and then giving them to the children and encouraging them to "read" the books to friends or parents. Opportunities for such storybook reading should be provided daily for children on all levels.

Reading Many Books, Repeatedly

Reading to children familiarizes them with books, acquaints them with characters and plots and other patterns of literature, and gradually helps them to learn the elaborated syntax and special vocabulary of written language. Best of all, it helps them come to enjoy books and feel at home with them. Reading six to eight books a day is not too many. Choose books that are simple and highly patterned at first—by either rhyming lines, repeated actions, or a strong plot.

It's fine to read the same book through more than once at a sitting. On subsequent days, reread some of the books that you read before. Repeated reading familiarizes the children with the pattern of the book. Some literary patterns are shared by many books, so if children get the pattern, they will appreciate a similar book that much more readily. This is especially true of books by the same author. Bill Martin's *Brown Bear, Brown Bear, What Do You See?* leads nicely into his *Polar Bear, Polar Bear, What Do You Hear?* Each of Cynthia Rylant's *Henry and Mudge* books prepares children for the next, as do Arnold Lobel's *Frog and Toad* series, Norman Bridwell's *Clifford* books, and James Marshall's *George and Martha* books. Folktales can do this, too, such as Ivan Bilibin's collection of *Russian Folktales*, many of which feature magical transformations of the hero and the exploits of the remarkable witch Baba Yaga or the many *Anansi* stories.

Repeatedly reading the same book serves another purpose, too: Once the children are familiar with a book, you can leave it out and invite them to "reread it" themselves or to other students. By regularly supporting and encouraging them in pretend reading, you are giving them close encounters with literature from which they will gradually learn about print.

Reading Expressively

Listen closely to a parent talking to a baby. The parent's voice makes exaggerated swoops, from high to low, from quiet to loud, from pauses to dramatic emphases. Parents' speech, sometimes called "Motherese," is thought to use these exaggerated moves to attract and hold the child's attention and even show the child the significant features of speech (Stern, 1982).

Reading a book to children is like that. As we read through a story, we deliberately exaggerate the changes in our voices: from especially bright and cheerful to doleful and sad, to slow and suspenseful, to rapid and excited. We make the rhythms of language march, and we savor delightful words. By reading that way, we are showing children the dramatic contours of stories, the ebb and flow of emotions, the force and conflicts of characters, the pull of the plot, the music and cadence of rich language. Children might not sense these things unless we make them very clear and put them out there to be appreciated.

If you are new to reading aloud to children, the odds are that you will have to work on your voice to make it as expressive as it should be. Box 6.1 offers suggestions for practicing reading aloud expressively.

LITTLE BOOKS

Christine McCormick and Jana Mason (1989) developed a simple but effective means of boosting young children's early experience with books. They created a series of "little books," each made from a single sheet of paper printed on both sides, cut in half horizontally, and folded (see Figure 6.5). One book, called, appropriately, *Stop,* said

TEN POINTERS FOR READING ALOUD

BOX 6.1

1. Read the book to yourself first to get familiar with it. You need to know whether this book is suitable for the children. If it is, you also need to think out how the characters' voices should sound, which parts have suspense, which parts are comical, and which parts are sad.
2. Arrange the children in front of you in a quiet area where they won't be distracted for the duration of the reading.
3. Preview the book for them. Show the cover and a few pictures from inside. Ask children to talk about what they see. Invite them to speculate on what might happen in the story.
4. As you read, go slowly and put animation and drama into your voice. Come up with slightly distinct voices for the characters—but don't overdo them.
5. Stop and show them the pictures. (In fact, you should practice reading books upside down so that you can show children the pictures as you read.) Allow time for the children to talk about what they notice.
6. Stop at the exciting parts and ask the children to predict what they think is going to happen.
7. After you've read on a ways, stop and ask them if it happened. Were we right about our predictions?
8. Read the book again, and invite the children to chime in on the repeated parts. Reread it another day, too. It's good for children to really get to know books.
9. Follow up. Ask them what they thought was the best (scariest, funniest, most exciting) part.
10. Leave the book out where they can look at it on their own after you've read it to them.

Stop, car.
Stop, truck.
Stop, bus.
Stop, stop, stop.
Stop for the cat.

One line was written on each page, and each page had an illustration. The books were given to the mothers of low-income kindergarten children, a high percentage of whom could be at risk of reading failure later on. Each mother was encouraged to read the book to her child at least once and then encourage that child to read the book on his or her own. Every six weeks or so during the year, McCormick and Mason mailed each family another little book with the same instructions. The

FIGURE 6.5 A "Little Book"

children thus received six books during the course of the year. When the children who had received the books were compared with a control group that had not, it was clear that the little books had helped them to learn letters and develop a concept of word. They boosted the children's potential for learning to recognize words. The benefits of the little books were large in proportion to the amount of effort they took to produce and share; thus, starting little book sharing programs seems like a very good idea for kindergarten and first-grade classes with children who are not likely to have many books of their own at home.

SERIES BOOKS

From New Zealand has come a host of short and colorful books that are written on carefully graduated levels of difficulty. Many of these books, published by companies such as the Wright Group, Rigby, and Richard C. Owen, have strongly patterned, yet meaningful texts. Because these books are often skillfully written and their vocabularies are not limited to words with the simplest letter-to-sound correspondences, the books can be surprisingly meaningful and enjoyable.

When reading through one of these books with a child, it helps if you follow these steps:

First, determine whether the level of the book is right. After previewing the book (that is, reading several pages aloud to the child and discussing the pictures), ask the child to read the book alone. If she or he misreads or needs help on fewer than one word out of nine, that book is at a suitable level for instructional work.

When you are reading a book proper, begin by previewing the book. Consider the title. Call the student's attention to the cover and discuss it. Ask for predictions of what will happen. If the child doesn't offer any, offer two alternate predictions yourself and ask, "Do you think X will happen or Y? Let's read and find out." Open the book and look at a more pictures.

Encourage the child to do as much reading as she or he can without your help.

Praise lavishly but honestly. Praise specifically. Say, "I like the way you read to the end of the line and then went back and corrected the word you read wrong the first time." This calls children's attention to strategies that good readers use.

In some books, children may begin to read by the pattern alone, plus the picture cues. Call the student's attention to individual words from time to time. Ask the student to point to the words while reading them.

If the child's energy and enthusiasm flags, you can use these support techniques: Do echo-reading (you read a line or a page, then the child reads), or do choral-reading (you both read the text together).

Stress meaning. Stop and discuss what is happening. Ask the student to make predictions (and make them yourself when the child won't).

Since you are likely to be doing some form of word study in the same lesson you are reading this book, remind the student of words she or he has studied that appear in the text.

Don't spend too much time sounding out. You are after fluency and success here; sounding will come later.

TEACHING PRINT ORIENTATION CONCEPTS

How do we help children to develop print orientation concepts? Don Holdaway (1979), a careful reader of his compatriot, Marie Clay, has tackled this question for us. He begins by noting that there are practical problems to be overcome in teaching groups of children about print. Books, after all, are usually just big enough to be read by one person. If a teacher tries to point out features of print to a group of children sitting around him or her, it's not likely that they will be able to see the spaces between words if the teacher uses a textbook to point them out. Besides, if the teacher sits so that he or she is facing them, the book will be oriented upside down to them unless the teacher holds it up so that it is upside down to him or her.

The solution, Holdaway proposed, is the "big book": a giant, three-foot-high version of the readers the children are using (see Figure 6.6). The teacher can place a big book on a chart stand, where it can be readily seen by a group of children. The teacher can have them read along as she or he points out features of print: where the text begins on a page, the left-to-right direction of reading, the return sweep, the spaces that demarcate words, and punctuation.

In New Zealand, these big books are usually made by the teacher or a parent volunteer. They might be chosen to accompany a reading series of which the children have copies; that way the children can look for the features on the page in front of them that the teacher points out in the big book. Big book versions are also made up from favorite trade books. When children already know and are excited about the story line, they can more easily pay attention to the way print portrays the text,

FIGURE 6.6   Teaching Print Orientation Concepts Using the Big Book

Source: Don Holdaway. *The Foundations of Literacy,* p. 65. Gosford, N.S.W.: Ashton Scholastic, 1979. (Reprinted by permission.)

which is the point of this sort of lesson. After some initial reluctance by U.S. publishers, big book versions of children's books are now available from many sources.

We will say more about Holdaway's approach later in this chapter, in the section on shared reading.

TEACHING THE ALPHABET

Many children enter kindergarten knowing most of their letters. Middle-class children are often able to point to and name all but *Q, Z, J,* and *Y*—unless, of course, their own names contain some of these letters—and write a dozen or more letters. Some children, however, enter kindergarten knowing very few letters and come to know letters in school only slowly and with difficulty (Ehri, 1989). Although it might be possible to recognize a few words by memorizing their overall appearance (focusing on the "eyes" in *look*, for example), knowing the letters is necessary for learning to read appreciable numbers of words and to write using invented spelling.

Marie Clay's work (1975) and the work of Harste et al. (1984) suggest that many children can invent their way to letter knowledge if they have models of print around them and are given early opportunities to write. However, by kindergarten, and certainly by first grade, those children who do not know most of their letters need more explicit teaching. Indeed, many studies show that children who know many letters in kindergarten are more likely to read by the end of first grade than are children who know few (Walsh et al., 1986).

How can we teach children the alphabet?

Alphabet Books

Alphabet books are arranged A to Z, usually with examples of both uppercase and lowercase letters and an illustrative picture that begins with the sound of the letter. Kate Greenaway's alphabet book, first published a century ago, is still in print, and more and more gorgeous and innovative alphabet books come out every year.

Older children in the school can make alphabet books for younger children. Or younger children can prepare alphabet books themselves, with guidance from the teacher. Either way, it is highly desirable for every preschool and kindergarten child to have his or her own personal alphabet book.

When children take alphabet books home, send along instructions to the parent to take the time to listen to the child read his or her alphabet book. Remind the parent to make this an enjoyable occasion—certainly not a drill session.

Letter-Matching Games

Once the children are beginning to know some letters, you can play letter-matching games with them along the lines of the concentration game. First, make up two sets of five different lowercase letters on cards. Turn these cards face down on the table, and turn up a pair. If they are the same, you have to name them, and then you can have them. Work through all of the lowercase letters in this way. Then do the same with the uppercase letters. After children become proficient at matching lowercase letters in this way, they are ready to play with uppercase and lowercase versions of the same letters.

Sound and Letters

As you will undoubtedly note from the foregoing discussion of concepts about print, the following procedure assumes that children are well along in their awareness of sounds in words and their notions of beginning and ends of words. For children who have reached these milestones, this procedure, from the work of the McCrackens (1987), is a worthwhile activity.

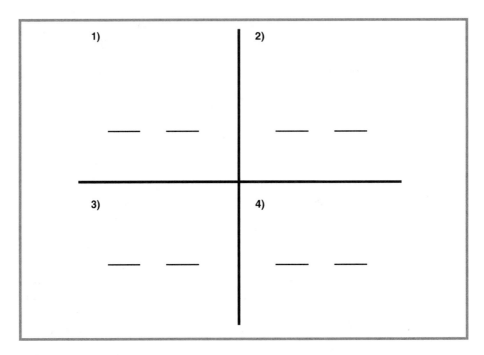

FIGURE 6.7 The McCrackens' Procedure for Teaching Letters

Working with first graders, they will introduce a letter, say, M:

1. They write M on the board.
2. They pronounce the letter slowly and ask the children to watch their mouths as they say it.
3. They ask the children to pronounce the letter slowly and pay attention to how it feels in their mouths.
4. They ask the children to write the letter on their individual chalk tablets, saying the letter aloud as they do so.
5. Later, they hand the children specially prepared tablets, as shown in Figure 6.7.

The teacher says the word "me" and asks the child to write the letter M in the appropriate slot in the square marked 1. Does the M come at the beginning of the word "me" or at the end? For square 2, the word is "may"; for square 3, the word is "am"; and for square 4, the word is "um."

TEACHING THE CONCEPT OF WORD

The concept of word, as we have seen, is the important ability to relate words in the mind with words on the page. Research by Morris (1981, 1995) has suggested that children need to develop this ability before they will advance very far in their word recognition ability, because they need a concept of word to be able to focus their attention properly on word units in print. Several of the tasks that we have already introduced in this chapter as assessment devices work quite well as instructional devices, too.

The Voice-Pointing Procedure

One way is to read text aloud—say, a big book, or a dictated chant on the chart—pointing to the print, one word at a time. Also, call attention to the word saying, "See? That word is 'fish.' See the F it begins with? That's the word 'fish.'"

When children have memorized a text, as in a little book, encourage them to point to the words as they read.

Cut-Apart Words

Have a child memorize a four- or five-word sentence or a line of poetry. Then, on a piece of tag board, write down the sentence as the child says the words. Read the words several times, pointing to them. Then cut the words apart, scramble them, and ask the child to rearrange them correctly.

If the child can rearrange them successfully, take away a word, and ask the child which word it was. If the child cannot rearrange the words successfully, make a copy of the line, leave it intact, and ask the child to rearrange the cut-apart words underneath by matching them to the words in the intact version.

Dictated Experience Accounts

Again we meet this technique in this chapter. The procedure that we outlined above for voice-pointing can be used very effectively with text that a child or group of children have dictated and that the teacher has written in large letters on chart paper.

Another effective use of a dictated account goes as follows. Write a small version of text and duplicate it so that each child has two copies. Instruct the children to cut the paper so that each sentence is on its own strip of paper. Then they should cut these sentence strips into individual words. The teacher should circulate among them to identify the words they are cutting apart and encourage the children to identify them. Once the words are cut apart, the children should match the cut-apart words with the same words on the other, intact sheet, laying each word above the intact word so that it does not cover it.

Once children can do this sort of activity fairly easily, they can arrange the cut-apart words into sentences without using the intact words as a guide.

EXERCISES TO DEVELOP PHONEMIC AWARENESS

For many children, the practice of writing freely and meaningfully using invented spelling provides all the exercise in developing phonemic awareness they will need.

Invented Spelling

Some kindergartners and first-graders might be reluctant to write with invented spelling. It is best to begin the year by encouraging the whole group to use invented spelling, in the following way. First, you should plan to have regular, at best daily, occasions for children to write and have meaningful and interesting topics for them to write about. In a pre-first-grade room, for example, the teacher read the children *Where the Wild Things Are* and *There's a Nightmare in My Closet*. After a discussion of monsters and nightmares, she passed out drawing paper and water colors and invited the children to paint their own monster. Next the children were instructed to write the names of their monsters on the pages. Finally, they were told to write what they do to defend or protect themselves from the monster.

Had the children not had plenty of experience by now writing with invented spelling, the teacher might have kept the children in the group and asked them to think of a monster's name. Once they agreed on one, she might say, "'Long Arm Monster.' How are were going to write that? Who can think of a letter to begin it with? Long: luh, luh, luh." As each child thinks of a plausible letter, she can write it on the board—even if the result is LIG RM MISTR (one version of "long arm monster" in invented spelling). Several group demonstrations of this sort might be necessary before children will begin to use invented spelling; but before long, the children will find it natural to sound out words to write them. If they ask for help, they will be more likely to ask for the spelling of a sound than for the whole word.

Other Exercises to Develop Phonemic Awareness

When children are not using invented spelling and an assessment of phonemic segmentation suggests that they are having difficulty with this ability, direct tutoring in phonemic segmentation can be tried. Such tutoring violates one of the principles we set out above—namely, that instruction should take place in the context of meaningful reading and writing activities to the greatest extent possible. We recommend doing this only with children who really need it and also making sure that the children are supported with other more natural reading activities at the same time, such as storybook reading and using dictated experience accounts.

One effective procedure, described by Marie Clay (1986), is discussed in Box 6.2.

A RUSSIAN DEVICE TO TEACH PHONEMIC SEGMENTATION

BOX 6.2

In the 1950s, the Russian psychologist Daniel Elkonin developed what are now the most widely used procedures for training children to segment phonemes. Elkonin was a student of the pioneer cognitive psychologist, Lev Vygotsky. Because he and his colleagues were among the first to determine that difficulties in hearing the sound constituents of words were more likely than distortions in visual perception to lie behind many children's reading problems, they were searching for ways to teach this ability.

(continued)

BOX 6.2 *(continued)*

At first, Elkonin worked at pronouncing words slowly and asking children to tap their fingers to count out the phonemes in the words. However, he soon realized that this task was too difficult for children. A colleague, P.J. Galperin, persuaded him that the training of a mental operation worked best if it proceeded by first making sure the children understood the task, then leading them to master the operation using concrete objects, then mastering the task using overt oral speech, then transferring the operation to the mental level, and then having them carry out the task on an entirely mental level.

Accordingly, Elkonin drew up picture cards of words. For each word indicated by a picture, he made a matrix card—a long rectangle divided by vertical lines into horizontal arrays of squares, one square per phoneme of the word.

He began the task by showing a child a picture card. Then, as he slowly pronounced the word, he pushed a small wooden token into a square for each phoneme of the word (at first the token was blank, since at this point he did not wish to complicate the task with letters).

After demonstrating the procedure several times, he then invited the child to look at a card, pronounce the word, and push one token onto a square for each phoneme heard. When the child could easily do this, Elkonin removed the matrix card and had the child simply move a token for each phoneme the child heard in the word, without the guidance of the card. Later, Elkonin removed the picture card, and finally, the tokens. At the end, the child was asked questions such as these: "How many sounds are in the word? In which position is such and such a sound when you count from the beginning? Which sound is first? Which is last? Which sound comes before (or after) such and such a word?" (Elkonin, 1973, p. 568)

Soviet teachers who tried Elkonin's task succeeded in twelve to fifteen short lessons to teach kindergarten children to segment phonemes. So successful was this procedure that it has been incorporated into the corrective teaching procedures promoted by Clay (1986) and Bryant and Bradley (1985).

Source: Daniel Elkonin. "Reading in the USSR." In *Comparative Reading,* ed. John Dowling. New York: Macmillan, 1973.

A more elaborate program to raise children's awareness of sounds in words was developed in Portugal by Ines Sim-Sim (Sim-Sim, 1994). Sim-Sim designed her plan to help teachers boost the early reading success of immigrant children from former Portuguese colonies in Africa, who had little home experience with books and who spoke a Creole version of Portuguese. Sim-Sim based her approach on street rhymes that the children already knew; in the presentation in Box 6.3, though, we have substituted English-language rhymes and words for Sim-Sim's Portuguese-language examples.

USING STREET RHYMES TO BUILD LINGUISTIC AWARENESS

BOX 6.3

The method used by Ines Sim-Sim begins with a street rhyme familiar to the children:

> **Miss Mary Mack**
> **Dressed in black,**
> **Silver buckles**
> **Up and down her back.**

It then follows these sequences of steps:

1. To make children aware of sounds, tell or sing the rhymes to the children until they know them by heart.
2. Repeat the rhyme without the word *black* and ask the children to supply the missing word.
3. Take the word *Mack* and ask the children which other words in the poem end the same way, in the same rhyme.
4. Ask children to think of other words that end in the same rhyme, *-ack,* and contrast them with words that do not rhyme, to give the children the concept of rhyme.

RAISING AWARENESS OF LANGUAGE SEGMENTS

1. *To raise children's awareness of the concept of a word:*
   a. Say the first line of a rhyme and ask the children to show (tap, count, sign) the number of words they hear in it.
   b. Ask the children to identify the first, middle, and last words in the line. Then ask them to repeat the line without pronouncing the first, middle, and last words.
   c. Ask them to substitute another word for the first, middle, or last word in the line.

2. *To raise children's awareness of the syllable:*
   a. Pronounce words to the children slowly, with the syllables segmented—*sil-ver, buc-kle.* Then ask them to rebuild them.
   b. Tell them a word (for example, *silver*), and ask them to segment it into pieces (*sil-ver*) by tapping, counting, and signing.
   c. Ask the children to name the first and last "piece" and then ask them to repeat the word without pronouncing the first or last "piece."

3. *To raise children's awareness of phonemes:*
   a. Say to the children words that begin with vowels or with fricatives (sounds such as /f/, /v/, and /s/), and ask them to pronounce the words slowly, emphasizing the first sounds. For example, if the words were *up* and *silver,* ask them to emphasize the [u] and the [s].

(continued)

BOX 6.3 *(continued)*

    b. Then say the word with the sounds separated—M . . . a . . . ck—and ask the children to put them together.

    c. Next ask the children to do the opposite: That is, say the word *Mack* and ask the children to pronounce the first sound [m], or the last one [k].

    d. Play a game in which children have to say beginning or ending sounds of words.

With all of these activities, when children can isolate vowels and fricatives, move on to lateral sounds, such as [r] and [l], and then to stop consonants, such as [t], [p], and [k].

Source: Ines Sim-Sim. "Reading Around the World: News from Portugal." *The Reading Teacher,* 1994.

EXERCISES TO TEACH WORD RECOGNITION AND LETTER-TO-SOUND CORRESPONDENCES

In this section, we treat teaching word recognition and letter-to-sound correspondences together. Several of the strategies that follow teach both at once: especially the word sorting activity, which begins this section.

Word Sorts

The practice of *word sorts* (Temple & Gillet, 1978; Morris, 1982; Bear et al., 1996) is a naturalistic, whole-to-part way to draw children's attention to the sound elements in words and the letter patterns that typically spell those elements. Word sorts can be used at nearly all levels of literacy development, but they are especially useful for emergent and beginning readers.

Word sorts provide students practice in identifying words, but they are meant to do more than that. They also help students to generalize patterns learned in one group of words to other words. That is, they develop *orthographic concepts* ("orthography" is another way of saying "spelling" or "letter-to-sound correspondences"). When word sorts are successful, students learn many important patterns about the ways words are put together, and these patterns help them to recognize new words.

Picture Sorts

Before children are ready to study letter-to-sound correspondences in written words, they can use a sorting strategy to develop awareness of sounds in words.

Given a collection of small cards with pictures of a pig, a pie, a duck, a penguin, a doll, a door, a pumpkin, a dog, and a paddle, children can be asked to sort together all of the pictures whose names begin like "pig" and to make a separate grouping of the pictures whose names begin like "duck." The picture cards, like all word sort cards, should be written on stiff paper of about calling card size. See Figure 6.8.

Picture sorts practice the categorization of sounds without relying upon reading ability. They also familiarize children with a learning strategy that can be used with written words (see below).

Beginning Consonant Sorts

Once children have become adept at picture sorts, and after they have learned to recognize many consonants and vowels, you can move on the beginning consonant sorts. Prepare two groups of five or six words that begin with the same con-

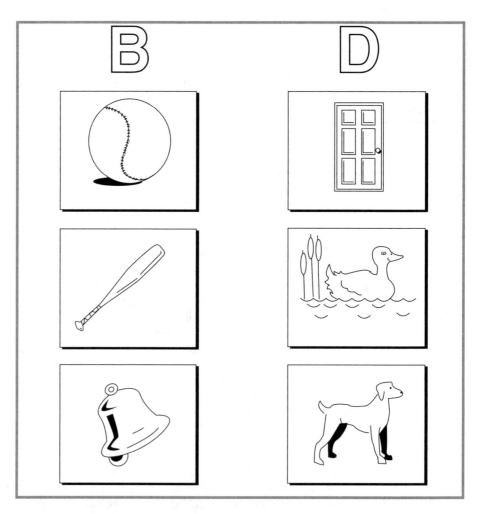

F I G U R E 6.8 Picture Sort Cards

sonant. Choose beginning consonant pairs that are visually distinct: *b and t*, but not *b and p.* To call maximum attention to the sound element, put down two picture cards of words that begin with the "b" sound (such as a bat) and the "t" sound (such as in "tip"). Then take the scrambled word cards, read one aloud, and ask the child where it goes: "Does this word begin like 'bat' or like 'tip'?" After you read three of the cards, ask the child to read and sort the rest of them, giving help where needed. Once children are adept with the *b and t* words, go on to sorting more words with different beginning consonants, still two at a time.

Phonogram Pattern Sorts

Once children can attend to beginning consonants, we can move on to one-syllable words with short vowel *phonogram patterns*. A *phonogram* is a spelling unit that consists of a vowel plus a following consonant or consonant group. For example *at, it, ut, atch, ight,* and *oat* are phonogram patterns. Another way of putting it is that the phonogram pattern is the part that rhymes in two rhyming words, as Rebecca Trieman (1993) has pointed out.

Begin with short vowel phonogram patterns, since these are far more regular and consistent that long vowel patterns. Prepare two groups of word cards with four or five words that contain different phonogram patterns, such as *at* words ("cat," "fat," "hat," "sat") and *ip* words ("lip," "sip," "rip," "tip"). Scramble these words, and then place one word from each group (the *guide word*) face up on the table. As the child picks up each new word in the pile, he or she places it in the appropriate column. See Figure 6.9.

Note that children might be able to match a word with the others in the column before they can read it. If so, you should have the child place the word in the appropriate column and then read from the guide word down the other words in the column. With encouragement, the child should now be able to read the new word. If so, the child made an important step: She or he is learning to read new words by attending to the beginning consonant plus the phonogram pattern.

Making and Breaking Words

As an enhancement of the word study component of the Reading Recovery program™ (see below for a discussion), Iverson and Tunmer (1993) developed a procedure for "making and breaking words." The procedure is carried out with a set of plastic letters and a magnetic board (available in most toy stores) and is conducted one-on-one.

The teacher asks the child to move the letters around to construct new words that have similar spellings and sound patterns. For instance, the teacher arranges letters to make the word *and.* The teacher announces that the letters spell "and" then asks the child what the word says. If the child seems uncertain, the teacher forms the word again, using different letters, says its name, and asks the child to name the word.

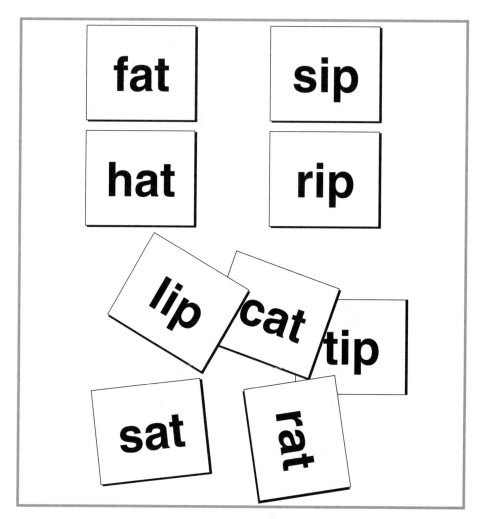

FIGURE 6.9 Word Cards for a Phonogram Pattern Sort

As a next step, the teacher scrambles the letters and asks the child to make "and." Again, if assembling scrambled letters proves difficult, the teacher spreads the letters apart, in the proper order, at the bottom of the magnetic board and asks the student to make the word "and" with them in the middle of the board. When the child has made the word, the teacher asks the child to name the word. If the child responds correctly, the teacher scrambles the letters and asks the child to make the word again and to name the word afterward. The teacher repeats the procedure until the child is readily able to assemble the letters and name "and."

As a next step, the teacher puts the letter *s* in front of *and* and announces what she or he has just done. The teacher takes a finger and moves the *s* away and then back and says, "Do you see? If I put *s* in front of *and*, it says *sand*. The teacher asks the child to read the word *sand,* and the child runs a finger under it. Now the teacher removes the *s* and points out that with the *s* removed, the word is now *and.* With the *s* pushed aside, the teacher asks the child to make *sand.* If the child correctly makes the word, the teacher asks the child to name the word she or he has made. Next the teacher instructs the child to make *and.* As a next step, the whole procedure is repeated, making *hand* and *band.* Now the teacher can make *sand,* then *band,* then *hand,* and *and,* asking the child to name each word as it is made. When the child can do so successfully, the teacher scrambles the letters *and* on the board, and puts the letters *s, b,* and *h* to one side. Now the teacher challenges the child to make *and.* If the child can do so, the child is now challenged to make *hand, sand,* and *band.* The child is asked to read each word after it is made.

Connecting Children's Literature with Phonics Instruction

An important way to connect phonics instruction with the words children read is to integrate it with children's literature. Before and while children are learning about words, letters, and sounds, they need to be surrounded with a rich language environment. The richer the language environment, the more children learn about language, both spoken and written.

Phyllis Trachtenburg has described a "whole-part-whole" sequence integrating phonics instruction with children's literature (1990, p. 649) in this way:

1. Whole: Read, comprehend, and enjoy a whole high-quality literature selection.
2. Part: Provide instruction in a high-utility phonic element by drawing from or extending the preceding literature selection.
3. Whole: Apply the new phonic skill when reading (and enjoying) another whole high-quality literature selection.

For example, the teacher reads aloud *Angus and the Cat.* Extension activities include dramatizing parts of the story or comparing the story to other dog-and-cat stories. The teacher then introduces the short-*a* sound and shows the students a printed portion of the story containing a number of short-*a* words, such as *cat, that, back,* and *glad.* The teacher rereads the story portion while emphasizing and underlining the target words. Students and teacher choral-read the excerpt several times, with emphasis on the target words. Students then work with a "word slotter," made of tagboard strips with a medial short *a* and movable strips with beginning and ending consonants. Students experiment with moving the initial and final letters to create new short-*a* words. (Students could use linking letters, letter cards, or plastic letters as well.) Students then use a "sentence slotter" to construct sentences with short-*a* words. (Students could use word cards for this activity as well.) Finally, a new story is presented that also features many short-*a* words, such as *The Cat in the Hat.* Choral and individual readings of the new book help to reinforce the use of the phonic pattern in new text. The following is a list of trade books that feature short and long vowel elements, as suggested by Trachtenburg (1990):

SHORT *a*

Flack, Marjorie. *Angus and the Cat.* Doubleday, 1931.

Griffith, Helen. *Alex and the Cat.* Greenwillow, 1982.

Kent, Jack. *The Fat Cat.* Scholastic, 1971.

Most, Bernard. *There's an Ant in Anthony.* William Morrow, 1980.

Nodset, Joan. *Who Took the Farmer's Hat?* Harper & Row, 1963.

Robins, Joan. *Addie Meets Max.* Harper & Row, 1985.

Schmidt, Karen. *The Gingerbread Man.* Scholastic, 1985.

Seuss, Dr. *The Cat in the Hat.* Random House, 1957.

LONG *a*

Aardema, Verna. *Bringing the Rain to Kapitl Plain.* Dial, 1981.

Bang, Molly. *The Paper Crane.* Greenwillow, 1985.

Blume, Judy. *The Pain and the Great One.* Bradbury, 1974.

Byars, Betsy. *The Lace Snail.* Viking, 1975.

Henkes, Kevin. *Sheila Rae, the Brave.* Greenwillow, 1987.

Hines, Anna G. *Taste the Raindrops.* Greenwillow, 1983.

SHORT AND LONG *a*

Aliki. *Jack and Jake.* Greenwillow, 1986.

Slobodkina, Esphyr. *Caps for Sale.* Addison-Wesley, 1940.

SHORT *e*

Ets, Marie Hall. *Elephant in a Well.* Viking, 1972.

Galdone, Paul. *The Little Red Hen.* Scholastic, 1973.

Ness, Evaline. *Yeck Eck.* E.P. Dutton, 1974.

Shecter, Ben. *Hester the Jester.* Harper & Row, 1977.

Thayer, Jane. *I Don't Believe in Elves.* William Morrow, 1975.

Wing, Henry Ritchet. *Ten Pennies for Candy.* Holt, Rinehart & Winston, 1963.

LONG *e*

Galdone, Paul. *Little Bo-Peep.* Clarion/Ticknor & Fields, 1986.

Keller, Holly. *Ten Sleepy Sheep.* Greenwillow, 1983.

Martin, Bill. *Brown Bear, Brown Bear, What Do You See?* Henry Holt, 1967.

Oppenheim, Joanne. *Have You Seen Trees?* Young Scott Books, 1967.

Soule, Jean C. *Never Tease a Weasel.* Parents' Magazine Press, 1964.

Thomas, Patricia. *"Stand Back," said the Elephant, "I'm Going to Sneeze!"* Lothrop, Lee & Shepard, 1971.

SHORT *i*

Browne, Anthony. *Willy the Wimp.* Alfred A. Knopf, 1984.

Ets, Marie Hall. *Gilberto and the Wind.* Viking, 1966.

Hutchins, Pat. *Titch.* Macmillan, 1971.

Keats, Ezra Jack. *Whistle for Willie.* Viking, 1964.

Lewis, Thomas P. *Call for Mr. Sniff.* Harper & Row, 1981.

Lobel, Arnold. *Small Pig.* Harper & Row, 1969.

McPhail, David. *Fix-It.* E.P. Dutton, 1984.

Patrick, Gloria. *This Is . . . .* Carolrhoda, 1970.

Robins, Joan. *My Brother, Will.* Greenwillow, 1986.

LONG *i*

Berenstain, Stan and Jan. *The Bike Lesson.* Random House, 1964.

Cameron, John. *If Mice Could Fly.* Atheneum, 1979.

Cole, Sheila. *When the Tide Is Low.* Lothrop, Lee & Shepard, 1985.

Gelman, Rita. *Why Can't I Fly?* Scholastic, 1976.

Hazen, Barbara S. *Tight Times.* Viking, 1979.

SHORT *o*

Benchley, Nathaniel. *Oscar Otter.* Harper & Row, 1966.

Dunrea, Olivier. *Mogwogs on the March!* Holiday House, 1985.

Emberley, Barbara. *Drummer Hoff.* Prentice-Hall, 1967.

McKissack, Patricia C. *Flossie & the Fox.* Dial, 1986.

Miller, Patricia, and Iran Seligman. *Big Frogs, Little Frogs.* Holt, Rinehart & Winston, 1963.

Rice, Eve. "The Frog and the Ox" from *Once in a Wood.* Greenwillow, 1979.

Seuss, Dr. *Fox in Socks.* Random House, 1965.

LONG *o*

Cole, Brock. *The Giant's Toe.* Farrar, Straus, & Giroux, 1986.

Gerstein, Mordicai. *Roll Over!* Crown, 1984.

Johnston, Tony. *The Adventures of Mole and Troll.* G.P. Putnam's Sons, 1972.

Johnston, Tony. *Night Noises and Other Mole and Troll Stories.* G.P. Putnam's Sons, 1977.

Shulevitz, Uri. *One Monday Morning.* Charles Scribner's Sons, 1967.

Tresselt, Alvin. *White Snow, Bright Snow.* Lothrop, Lee & Shepard, 1947.

SHORT *u*

Carroll, Ruth. *Where's the Bunny?* Henry Z. Walck, 1950.

Cooney, Nancy E. *Donald Says Thumbs Down.* G.P. Putnam's Sons, 1987.

Friskey, Margaret. *Seven Little Ducks.* Children's Press, 1940.

Lorenz, Lee. *Big Gus and Little Gus.* Prentice-Hall, 1982.

Marshall, James. *The Cut-Ups.* Viking Kestrel, 1984.

Udry, Janice May. *Thump and Plunk.* Harper & Row, 1981.

Yashima, Taro. *Umbrella.* Viking Penguin, 1958.

LONG *u*

Lobel, Anita. *The Troll Music.* Harper & Row, 1966.

Segal, Lore. *Tell Me a Trudy.* Farrar, Straus, & Giroux, 1977.

Slobodkin, Louis. *"Excuse Me—Certainly!"* Vanguard Press, 1959.

Enhanced Writing

At the end of one lesson, ask the child to think of a sentence he or she wants to write the next time. Then, have the child tell you the sentence several times. If necessary, shorten it for the child to five or six words.

Ask the child to write the sentence as best he or she can. Accept a reasonable letter for each sound, but don't accept nonsense. As he writes, have the child put his or her finger between individual words.

When the child has finished writing a word, fill in letters for sounds he or she can't hear. Don't worry about silent letters for now. We are concerned at this stage about beginning consonants, vowels in each syllable, and ending consonants.

Later, rewrite the sentence correctly, twice, and proceed to the cut-apart words exercise.

Early Writing Workshops

Early writing workshops teach the concept of word, phonemic awareness, and the beginnings of letter-to-sound correspondences. Kindergarten is not too early to begin writing workshops with children. What do we mean by "writing workshop" at this age? A writing workshop is a time when children are encouraged to create a story or some other sort of expression on a page, confer with their teacher and their classmates as they produce it, and share the result with the class.

Naturally, kindergarten children will draw their story first. But with nudging from the teacher and support from their classmates, we should see children begin to use letters or pseudo-letters to stand for some of their ideas, especially if the writing workshop is repeated daily or at least several days a week.

We're not aiming for perfection or even partial correctness now. We know that children learn to write by getting into the game. They pick up concepts about writing by putting marks on the page, thinking about how those marks might represent ideas, and then looking with growing curiosity at the ways in which others use marks to stand for language. Little by little, the children's strategies for using marks will grow more sophisticated and will progress through something like the stages described in Chapter 1.

Demonstrating Invented Spelling: A Group Writing Workshop

When many children know ten or more letters, are beginning to attend to sounds in words, and are ready to explore the ways letters and sounds work in words, it is time to show them how spelling works. The best way is to demonstrate the process of inventing spelling, and draw the whole class into the activity.

After the children have drawn pictures, the teacher asks for a volunteer to share her picture with the class. The child comes and sits in the "author's chair," in the front of the classroom, and tells about her picture. Then the teacher asks,

"If we wanted to write *one thing* about this picture what would it be?" The child says, "My dog is nice."

The teacher repeats the sentence several times and asks the other children to repeat it. The teacher wants the sentence firmly in everyone's mind for what comes next.

Now the teacher says, "Suppose we wanted to write 'My dog is nice.' What word do we want to write first?"

"My dog," someone says.

"Let's say 'My,'" says the teacher. "We want to write 'my.'" (The teacher is exaggerating the pronunciation.)

"What sound do we hear in 'my'? Watch my lips as I say it."

"Mmmmm," someone says.

"Mmmmmm," repeats the teacher. "Does anyone know what letter makes the sound 'Mmmmmm'?"

"M?"

"M!" says the teacher and writes the M on the board, describing the writing motions as she goes.

"Does anyone hear another sound in "My"? asks the teacher.

The children look at her blankly, so she goes on to the word "dog."

If someone *had* heard the vowel sound in "my" and later offered a letter for it, chances are that letter would have been I, not Y. The teacher would have accepted the I. She knows that children aren't learning individual spellings at this stage; they are just learning that letters represent sounds. On the other hand, she would not accept A or U or T. Those letters bear no logical relationship to the sound of I. Since this logic is what she's aiming for, to accept random letters in a demonstration like this would just confuse children.

The teacher might repeat these group demonstrations several times a week. At first, she is showing children that it is acceptable to try to invent spellings, and she is encouraging them to do it themselves. As the demonstrations proceed, she is showing children sound-to-letter relationships, modeling the logic of alphabetic writing.

Early Writing Workshop: Individual Children

The writing workshop is offered daily or at least several days a week. At first, the children will draw and will share their drawings with the class, telling the story as they do. The teacher or a parent volunteer might also ask the child to dictate a sentence about the picture, which the teacher can write across the bottom or on the back. The child can take the picture home and reread the sentence with a family member.

Once children know some letters, the teacher might open one or two sessions each week with a group dictation demonstration (see above) and then invite children to write about their own drawings.

If the group demonstration has done its job, children need only be encouraged to write one thing about their picture. If a child is reluctant, the teacher might approach the child, invite him or her to tell about the contents of his drawing, and then ask, "If you could write *one thing* about this story right down here (pointing to some white space at the bottom of the page) what would it be?" Then the teacher will encourage the child to put down letters for his or her words on the page. If the child knows some letters and seems able to think about sounds in words, the teacher can take the child through the steps of sounding out and recording some of the sounds in his or her words. This is sophisticated stuff for kindergarten, though. Many children will be making random marks and pseudo-writing, at least until the latter part of the kindergarten year.

Let us hasten to add that even with young children, writing workshop is about a lot more than spelling. The activity of thinking up messages, inscribing them in some form on paper, and sharing them later with interested classmates is the essence of authorship that is valuable in its own right.

TEACHING FOR COMPREHENSION

The most successful strategies for developing comprehension follow most of the steps just described. The Directed Listening-Thinking Activity (Stauffer, 1975), which we describe on pages 322–323, uses a text that is read aloud and begins with questions and predictions and includes pauses for the confirmation of predictions and the making of new ones. The Directed Reading-Thinking Activity does much the same thing with texts that are read instead of listened to. It is described on pages 306–307. The strategy of Reciprocal Teaching (Palincsar and Brown, 1984), which we describe on pages 312–314, includes many of the same steps. So does the strategy of Questioning the Author (Beck et al., 1997), described on pages 309–312.

With beginning readers, many teachers work these comprehension-building steps naturally into their reading session. In the following section, we present a comprehensive framework for conducting explorations of books: Shared Reading. This strategy is intended to serve a range of purposes, not only developing students' comprehension, but also expanding their language, adding to their knowledge of print concepts, boosting their recognition of words, and—as important as all these—increasing their general enjoyment of books and literacy.

Shared Reading

Shared Reading (Holdaway, 1979) is a flexible means of working through a text with a student or students, calling the student's attention to the important features of texts, and inviting children's engagement and response. The technique is adaptable because it is based on the needs of the student and on the possibilities presented by the text.

Scaffolding and Shared Reading

The teacher's strategies during a Shared Reading session are summed up by the term *scaffolding* (Collins et al., 1986). That is, the teacher offers the students just as much help as they need, with the goal that they should function as independently as possible as soon as possible. The teacher withdraws support as soon as it is no longer necessary.

Modeling (Roehler and Duffy, 1991)

Here, the teacher behaves like a skilled reader who describes his or her own thinking and perceptual processes as she practices them. The teacher voices his or her own questions and lays out his or her own plans for inquiry. The teacher says what he or she wonders about and, as naturally as possible, draws out the students' own questions and suppositions: "You know, this title *Nobody's Mother Is in Second Grade,* makes me think some child's mother is going to come to school, and the child will be embarrassed about it. Think that's what will happen?"

Challenging

Here, the teacher gently challenges the students to practice specific comprehension strategies, especially ones that he or she has modeled: "I just told you my prediction of what will happen in this story, based on the title. What does the title make *you* think will happen?"

Praise

Here, the teacher congratulates the student for practicing a specific skill. The praise is highly specific: "Good for you! You got to the end of the sentence, realized that the word you read earlier didn't make sense, and went back and corrected yourself once you knew what the whole sentence was. That's a great strategy!"

Preparing for Shared Reading

The teacher prepares for a Shared Reading session by considering the needs of the student or students who will be participating and the kinds of challenges that the text presents. The teacher needs to make several decisions about the children's needs and the text's possibilities as he or she plans the session.

The teacher should think specifically about ways in which the text will challenge the students, and also help the students grow, in each of the following areas:

1. **Print Orientation.** Do these students need to be reminded that the print "talks," not the picture? Do they need to see the directional layout of print?
2. **Word Recognition.** What word patterns are presented that the children may be working on?
3. **Vocabulary.** What terms will the children need to know in advance, and what terms are they likely to learn from reading the text?
4. **Background Knowledge.** What knowledge will the children need in advance, and what are they likely to learn?
5. **Literary Genre.** Do the children have experience reading text of this type? What can be done to help them follow it successfully?
6. **Comprehension Strategies.** Which of the following comprehension strategies are the students already able to use? Which ones should be

demonstrated and practiced in this lesson? *Summoning up background knowledge, setting purposes for reading and asking questions of the text, making predictions, making inferences, monitoring comprehension, visualizing, finding main ideas, summarizing.*

Conducting a Shared Reading Lesson

Shared Reading is best done with a big book (a two to three foot high version of a children's trade book), with multiple copies of regular-sized versions. It can be done with a whole class or with a smaller group. The teacher should make sure the students are seated comfortably where they can see the book the teacher is holding.

A Shared Reading Lesson has a beginning, middle, and end. Teachers have different names for these three phases. Some call them *into, through,* and *beyond.* Others call them *introducing the book, reading and responding to the book,* and *extending the book.* Because we use similar phases with students in higher grades, too, we will use the same three terms for these phases at all levels: *exploration, inquiry,* and *reflection.*

Exploration is the phase in which the students first approach the text, find out what it is about, consider what they know about that, ask questions, and set purposes for reading.

Investigation is the phase in which students thoughtfully listen to or read the text, with their purposes and questions in mind, inquiring and seeking answers to their questions and satisfy our purposes, and also raising new questions as the text suggests them and pursuing new purposes for their listening and reading.

Reflection is the phase in which students do something with the new information they have gained: respond to it, question it, debate it, apply it, adjust their knowledge of the world in light of it—and decide where their inquiry should take them now.

In the Exploration Stage   In this phase, the teacher attempts to arouse the students' interest in the text and get them ready to read meaningfully. The teacher works the following steps into this phase.

1. The teacher encourages the students to inspect what is to be listened to or read, look at the cover, consider the title, peruse a few pictures inside the book, and perhaps listen to or read a few lines. Their purpose is to determine what *topic* the book is about and also what *form or genre of writing* it is (story, informational book, poem, etc.). For younger children, rather than to speak of genre, the teacher can point out who the *author* is, and recall other books by that author that the students have enjoyed. Then the teacher can gently direct their expectations by venturing a question such as, "Do you think George is going to do something goofy, as he did in the other *George and Martha* books?"

2. The students should be reminded of other books of the genre that they already know, being as specific as they are able to. If it is a biography, they should think of other biographies they have read and what kinds of things they found out. If it is a work of fiction, they might want to decide whether the book appears to be fantasy, realistic, or folk literature, because answers to this questions shapes the expectations they should have for what might happen in the book.

3. If it is an informational book or a work of realistic fiction, the teacher should ask questions that lead the students to reflect on what they already know about that topic. They should be aware of areas they don't know about or are unsure about that might be informed by this book. Then they should *formulate questions* about the topic that they hope to have answered by the text.

4. If it is a work of fiction, students should be asked to *make predictions* about what is likely to happen in the book, given the title, the illustrations, and the notes on the jacket.

5. The teacher should look through the book ahead of time to identify up to four words that the students might not be familiar with. These can be introduced into a discussion of what the book is about and defined in the course of that discussion.

In the Inquiry Phase   After the teacher has introduced the text, aroused students' interest and curiosity about it, and led them to set purposes for their reading, the teacher is ready to lead them into the text. We call this the *inquiry phase* of reading. The teacher can take different approaches here, depending on the students' needs. The teacher might focus on *print orientation,* on *word recognition,* on *language expansion,* or on *comprehension.* The teacher will always focus on *enjoyment:* keeping the exercise moving ahead at a good pace and showing enthusiasm all the while.

To Stress Print Orientation   If the teacher wishes to stress print orientation and word recognition, a big book should be used. The teacher reads a page of the book, reading very expressively (see the section entitled "Ten Pointers for Reading Aloud" Box 6.1, for read-aloud suggestions). Using a pointer or a finger, the teacher points to each word as it is read, makes the return sweep to the left, and drops down to the next line. If some of the students need extra help with print orientation, the teacher says aloud what he or she is doing: "Look. I'm going to begin reading up here in this corner. I'm going to read each word across, and then go down to the next word. See?" The teacher is careful not to belabor the talking *about* the print; it is important that the reading go along quickly so that students not lose the meaning.

To Stress Word Recognition   The teacher is reading a page of text aloud. He or she comes to a key word in the text and covers the word with his or her hand:

> Ahmed walked along, and walked along, until he came to a _____ *(this word is covered and the teacher skips it)* in the road.
> "Which way do I go?" he said.

Then the teacher asks the students what the word is. After they make several guess, the teacher uncovers the first letter: f: _____ and again asks students what they think the word is now. If need be, the teacher keeps uncovering letters until they correctly guess the word "fork."

To Stress Comprehension   To develop comprehension, the teacher can model questions and comments and offer probes that encourage the students to listen or read to find out. As the teacher or the students read the text, the students are reminded to keep their questions and purposes in mind and to be alert to what they are learning (and not learning). The teacher also encourages the students to visualize what they are reading and to be alert to new directions and new questions that arise from the text.

Working almost conversationally, giving cues to the students, and taking cues from them, the teacher works the following steps into the students' activity in this phase:

1. Having begun the lesson by asking the students to venture predictions and raise questions, the teacher encourages the students to read with their predictions and questions in mind.

2. The teacher stops the reading periodically (usually four or five times per session) and asks the students whether their questions have been answered and whether their predictions were correct. The teacher also encourages the students to be alert for other details they have noticed that lead to new predictions and new questions.

3. The teacher reminds students of places where inferences should be made and helps them to make those inferences.

4. The teacher encourages the students to visualize settings or actions that have been described. The children might do this through spontaneous drama, even by reading aloud expressively: "Janet, say those words to George the way you hear Martha really saying them. Bill, show us what George is going to look like while Martha says those things to him."

5. The teacher makes sure the students are aware when they are understanding what the text is meaning: "Jeannie, can you say what the author just said, but put it in your own words?"

In the Reflection Phase   After the students have read the book or have otherwise reached a stopping point, the teacher takes steps to get them to talk about the work and to respond to it in other ways. These steps include the following:

1. The teacher might ask for a retelling of the work. The purpose of the retelling is to invite the students to summarize the work.

2. The teacher might ask the students to reflect back on the questions and predictions they posed at the outset and how the material they found in the text answered the questions and fulfilled the predictions. If some questions were not answered, the students can discuss where they can now turn for answers. If the predictions strayed significantly from what happened in the text, they can discuss what led them astray or what surprises occurred in the text.

3. The teacher might ask the students to say what was the most important idea the author told us in this work. The purpose of this is to lead students to think about main ideas.

4. The teacher will certainly ask the students for their personal responses to the work, especially if it is a work of fiction or poetry. The teacher uses open-ended questions such as "What is in your mind about this book (or chapter, or passage or reading) right now?" or "What are you feeling right now when you think of this book? Why? What makes you feel that way?" or "What does this book make you think of?" or "What was your favorite part? Why?"

5. The teacher might follow the students' personal responses to the work with two or three interpretive questions. Interpretive questions are open-ended: They invite different answers, yet they are still close to the text. After reading *Where the Wild Things Are,* for instance, the teacher could ask, "Why do you think the supper was still hot?"

6. To help students visualize the work, the teacher might ask students to draw or act out their favorite part or the most important or exciting part.

EARLY INTERVENTION PROGRAMS

Some research shows that nine out of ten children who are not reading at the end of first grade still lag far behind their classmates four years later (Juell, 1989). Special help might push them ahead by inches, but their classmates are sprinting ahead by miles.

Recently, a chorus of critics have pointed out shortcomings in our ways of helping slower readers and are proposing bold new solutions. The chief criticisms of remedial programs are the following:

1. ***They Don't Work Well Enough.*** While they might move poor readers ahead, they do not close the gap between poor readers and the rest of the class. Typically, remedial reading instruction has yielded about seven months' gain in a nine-month school year (Allington and McGill-Frantzen, 1987).

2. ***They Make Children Miss Other Subjects.*** Remedial instruction has usually required that children be taken out of their other school subjects to get special reading skill instruction. Missing the information in these regular classes contributes to children's academic problems and even holds back their reading growth.

3. ***They Are Not Intensive Enough.*** Even teaching six children at a time, the smallest size of most remedial classes, can prevent a teacher from carrying out a careful diagnosis and giving each child fully responsive teaching and adequate amounts of real reading practice.

Reading Recovery

Perhaps the most promising solution proposed to date is early and intense literacy intervention. Reading Recovery™ (Clay, 1975), the most widely used program of this kind, targets the bottom 20 percent of the children in first grade and offers them one-on-one tutoring by an experienced and specially trained teacher. The tutoring lasts half an hour a day, five days a week, and continues until the children reach the median level of reading ability in their classes—usually in fifteen to eighteen weeks. It is the hope of Reading Recovery advocates that the children will be able to advance with their classmates after the training is complete and will not need further remediation.

Reading Recovery instruction begins with a comprehensive assessment of a child's emergent literacy, followed by a period of informal teaching, called "roaming the known," intended to further explore the child's concepts about literacy. After the preliminary assessment period, instruction begins in earnest—though continuous assessment is built into every day's activities. Each day's lesson usually contains seven elements:

1. ***Rereading of Two or More Familiar Books.*** Reading Recovery tries to keep the child immersed to the greatest extent possible in real reading and writing tasks. Reading books on the child's level is done every day. (More on this later.)

2. *Independent Reading of the Preceding Lesson's New Book While the Teacher Takes a Running Record.* A running record is a diagnostic procedure developed by Clay (1985). A child reads aloud and the teacher makes detailed notes of the accuracy and fluency of the reading. (Strategies for making a running record are presented in Chapter 2.)

3. *Letter Identification Using Plastic Letters on a Magnetic Board* (only if necessary). Many educators, including Fernald and Bradley and Bryant, have commented on the value of multisensory techniques in beginning literacy instruction. Plastic magnetic letters offer a concrete medium in which a child can call the letters by name as he or she arranges them to spell out words or to copy other words written out by the teacher.

4. *Writing a Story That the Child Has Composed, Including Hearing Sounds in Unfamiliar Printed Words via "Sound Boxes."* Sound boxes are a phonological awareness training technique developed by Elkonin (1973). Writing with invented spelling, as we saw in Chapter 2, has been shown to help children develop word and sound awareness, and awareness of phoneme-to-grapheme correspondences—in other words, to lay the foundation for learning to recognize words and to spell them. If a child cannot yet segment a word into its phonemes, the child's invented spelling will be very limited. Hence, the "sound box" may be used to develop phonemic segmentation ability.

5. *Reassembling a Cut-up Story.* A technique is included to help a child develop a concept of word and to practice word-to-word matching. A story that the child has dictated is cut into sentence strips; then these sentences are cut apart into words. The words are reassembled—first by matching them to another intact version and later by reading the words themselves.

6. *Introducing a New Book.* The teacher introduces a new book in each lesson, and the child will practice reading it several times on the day it is introduced and on subsequent days. Though the Reading Recovery program does not mandate any particular set of books, lists of books graduated by difficulty level are circulated among teachers who are trained to use the program. One of the aims of the running record is to make sure that the child is reading with between 90 percent and 94 percent accuracy in word recognition. (Easier material won't teach the child new words; harder material will frustrate the child.)

7. *Practicing the New Book.* Practicing might be done by means of echo-reading (teacher reads a line, child follows) or choral reading (they read simultaneously). The teacher aims to get the child to read the text over and over again (Iverson and Tunmer, 1993, after Clay, 1975).

Let us note that these lessons (1) base instruction on careful assessment and teach children what they need to know; (2) give practice that develops letter recognition, the concept of word, phonemic segmentation, and other concepts about print; (3) offer the child extensive daily practice reading real text on exactly the proper level for that child; (4) include writing as well as reading in a literacy lesson.

Questions about Early Intervention Programs

From its debut in the United States in the 1980s, Reading Recovery raised the hope that children who might otherwise fail to learn to read could be permanently "inoculated" against reading failure, by intensive one-on-one tutoring in the first grade by specially trained teachers. The program is costly, but perhaps not more so than the traditional alternative, once we add up the costs—financial and motivational—of keeping struggling readers in special reading classes year after year. Besides, the traditional alternatives have not worked well.

A lengthy review of research by Shanahan and Barr (1995) has tempered some of our rosier hopes for Reading Recovery. The hope that children could be remediated once and for all in first grade has not been borne out. Shanahan and Barr found that children's future success after leaving Reading Recovery depended on the regular classroom instruction they received. If children are given little reading support at home, and—most especially—if they are not exposed to reading materials that continue to offer appropriate challenges at ascending levels of difficulty, it should not surprising that some of their gains should be washed out. This is not an argument against Reading Recovery as much as an argument for constructive changes in regular classroom instruction.

Another question to be asked is whether the content of the Reading Recovery lesson might be improved upon. Most worthy of note, Reading Recovery lessons do not systematically teach phoneme-to-grapheme correspondences; rather, they leave it to the child to infer these correspondences indirectly. There is a raft of research, recently summarized in the National Research Council's *Preventing Reading Difficulties in Young Children* (Snow et al., 1998), that supports teaching children explicitly how the alphabetic writing system works.

Iverson and Tunmer (1993) compared the performance of 32 children who received Reading Recovery teaching plus these explicit procedures to teach phoneme-to-grapheme correspondences to another group of 32 who received standard Reading Recovery teaching and to still another group of 32 who received small group instruction in a Chapter I classroom. (Note that the group who received explicit phoneme-to-grapheme correspondences was taught according to the "making and breaking words" procedure described earlier in this chapter.)

The results? Children who received small group instruction in the Chapter I classroom gained very little in comparison to the two groups that used one-on-one teaching. Both of the Reading Recovery groups were successful in moving the children up to the median reading ability range of their first-grade classes and to sustain these gains at least through the end of the year. The group with the explicit phoneme-to-grapheme instruction, however, reached the desired level of reading performance in two-thirds the time it took the regular Reading Recovery groups (in forty-two lessons, on the average, instead of fifty-seven).

Given the expense of committing a teacher's time to providing one-to-one tutoring for a struggling child, speeding up the process will allow more children to be served; so the advantages of providing explicit instruction in phoneme-to-grapheme correspondences should be taken seriously.

Still another question is whether it is necessary to go to the expense of having a carefully trained teacher working one-on-one with the children. As for the importance of training, a research study by the core Reading Research advocates in the United States (Pinnell et al., 1994) found that reducing the training of Reading Recovery teachers markedly reduced their effectiveness. But efforts to construct a high-impact instructional program, according to current literacy principles, for small groups of Chapter I students (Hiebert et al., 1992) have shown impressive results that are comparable to those of Reading Recovery.

Early Intervention Programs Using Tutors

Finally, in an attempt to spread the benefits of tutoring to a larger audience than can be reached by professional teachers, several programs using volunteer tutors have come into being.

One of the best validated is Darrell Morris's **Howard Street Tutoring Program** (Morris, 1992), which began in a store front facility for inner city Chicago children in the early 1980s. Morris' program is aimed at second- and third-graders, who are taught by volunteering college students and retired people, under the supervision of an experienced teacher. The teacher assesses each child upon entry to the program and prepares daily lesson plans and packets of materials to be used by the tutors, who work with the children twice a week for about forty minutes. The lesson format is similar to that of Reading Recovery, except that the word study component explicitly and systematically teaches phoneme-to-grapheme correspondences.

Another successful program is Connie Juel and Marcia Invernizzi's **Book Buddies Program.** This program has involved college athletes in a tutorial program that has a lesson format very similar to that of Morris (Invernizzi et al., 1997).

Volunteer programs that recruit and field college students as literacy tutors recently got a boost from the federal government through the America Reads Program.

SUMMARY

In this chapter, after situating the concept of emergent and beginning literacy among many other kinds of understanding of early reading, we presented methods to structure your observation of children's *emergent literacy,* a term that applies to preliminary reading and writing, as well as their *beginning literacy.* The areas of literacy competence stressed in the chapter were *storybook reading, print orientation concepts, letter recognition, the concept of word, phonemic segmentation, sight-word recognition, oral language, comprehension,* and *the sense of story structures.*

After a discussion of the importance of each aspect of literacy, we described at least one assessment procedure.

Storybook reading turns out to be a rich indicator of children's emerging concepts about literacy. The assessment of children's storybook reading can be done by having a child pretend read a favorite storybook and categorize the results according to Elizabeth Sulzby's scheme.

A child's ability to make the *speech-to-print match* in a memorized written sequence can be assessed by using the dictated experience story or some other easily memorized material. The *voice-pointing procedure* is used with either type of material to determine whether children can match spoken and written words in a familiar portion of text and whether a supported rereading activity helps them to recognize new words in print.

A *phonemic segmentation task using invented spelling* was described for the purpose of investigating children's ability to divide words up into their smallest sound units, a necessary part of word knowledge related to the application of phonics.

Print orientation concepts can be assessed by using the *Concepts About Print Test* or by adapting this procedure in minor ways, such as varying the questions asked and the text used. The *Concepts About Print Test* represents a real reading experience with prereaders. It helps a teacher to learn what a child knows about book orientation; directionality of print and pages; concepts of letters, words, spaces, and punctuation marks; and the communicative nature of print and pictures.

Oral language development can be measured by several means. A test by Marie Clay et al., *The Record of Oral Language,* a device dedicated to the assessment of children's oral language fluency, was described in this chapter. We would suggest that teachers who are not adept at assessing children's language ability orient themselves to the task by using such a device. Once they know what they are looking for, they may be able to assess language ability informally while they are teaching: We suggested ways that the *Dictated Experience Story* can be used for this purpose.

A student's *comprehension* can be assessed in several ways. The Informal Reading Inventory, featured in Chapter 3, is one elaborate way of doing so.

A child's *sense of story structures* can be inferred in at least two ways. One method is the *directed listening-thinking activity,* in which children listen to a portion of a story and are asked to predict what might happen next. The predictions and comments can reveal whether a child has certain expectations about the structure of stories. Another method is to have children *retell stories* they have heard read aloud. Retellings can be analyzed to see whether critical elements of stories were included in their proper order.

The *acquisition of sight words* can be assessed informally by using a *sight-word inventory* made up of words frequently occurring in beginning reading materials. Words are presented in isolation, but the presentation is untimed. A similar inventory can be used to examine the *recognition of letters,* uppercase and lowercase.

The chapter also shared several means of helping children's literacy to emerge.

Big books, brought into popularity by New Zealander Don Holdaway, were suggested as an excellent aid for teaching print orientation concepts, since they enable children to read along with the teacher in a favorite story and notice features of the print as they do so.

Little books, short personalized texts to be taken home by children, are another useful sort of early reading materials.

Techniques that were advanced for making children aware of the correspondences between letters and sounds were the *word sort strategy* and the strategy of *making and breaking words.*

Techniques for developing reading comprehension are the Directed Reading-Thinking Activity, the Know/Want-to-Know/Learn procedure, Reciprocal Teaching, and Questioning the Author. All will be described in detailed in Chapter 9. In the present chapter, we described a variation of Shared Reading, enhanced with special emphasis on developing comprehension. The chapter closed with a section of early intervention programs, including Reading Recovery.

REFERENCES

Allard, Harry. *Miss Nelson Is Missing!* Illustrated by James Marshall. Boston: Houghton Mifflin, 1977.

Allen, R. Van. *Language Experiences in Communication.* Boston: Houghton Mifflin, 1976.

Allington, Richard, and Anne McGill-Franzen. *A Study of the Whole-School Day Experience of Chapter I and Mainstreamed LD Students.* Final Report of Grant #G008630480, Office of Special Education Programs. Washington, DC: U.S. Department of Education, 1987.

Bear, Donald, Marcia Invernizzi, Shane Templeton, and Francine Johnson. *Words Their Way.* Upper Saddle River, NJ: Merrill, 1996.

Beck, I., et al., *Questioning the Author.* Newark, DE: International Reading Association, 1997.

Berko, Jean. "The Child's Learning of English Morphology." *Word* 14 (1958): 150–177.

Brown, Anne, and Jeanne Day. "Macrorules for Summarizing Text: The Development of Expertise. *Journal of Verbal Learning and Verbal Behavior,* 22 (1983): 1–14.

Bruner, Jerome. *Child's Talk: Learning to Use Language.* New York: W.W. Norton, 1985.

Chall, Jeanne. *Learning to Read: The Great Debate.* New York: McGraw-Hill, 1967

Chomsky, Noam. *Language and Mind.* New York: Harcourt, Brace, Jovanovich, 1968.

Clarke, Linda. "Invented Versus Traditional Spelling in First Graders' Writings: Effects on Learning to Spell and Read." *Research in the Teaching of English,* 22, 3 (Oct, 1988), 281–309.

Clay, Marie. *What Did I Write?* Portsmouth, NH: Heinemann Educational Books, 1975.

Clay, Marie. *The Early Detection of Reading Difficulties, with Recovery Procedures,* 3d. ed. Portsmouth, NH: Heinemann Educational Books, 1986.

Clay, Marie, Malcolm Gill, Ted Glynn, Tony McNaughton, and Keith Salmon. *The Record of Oral Language and Biks and Gutches.* Portsmouth, NH: Heinemann Educational Books, 1982.

Collins, A., J.S. Brown, and S. Newman. *Cognitive Apprenticeship: Teaching the Craft of Reading, Writing, and Mathematics.* Report No. 6459. Cambridge, MA: BNN Laboratories, 1986.

Cunningham, Patricia. *Phonics They Use: Words for Reading and Writing,* 2nd Edition. New York: HarperCollins, 1995.

Dewey, John. *How We Think.* New York: MacMillan, 1910.

Ehri, Linnea. "Research on Reading and Spelling." Paper presented at the George Graham Memorial Lectures. University of Virginia, Charlottesville, April 1989.

Ehri, Linnea. "Development of the Ability to Read Words." In *Handbook of Reading Research,* Vol. 2, ed. R. Barr, M. Kamil, P. Mosenthal, and P.D. Pearson. New York: Longman, 1991.

Elkonin, Daniel. "Reading in the USSR." In *Comparative Reading,* ed. John Downing. New York: Macmillan, 1973.

Gardner, Howard. *The Unschooled Mind.* Garden City, NY: Basic Books.

Gessell, Arnold, and Frances Ilg. *Child Development: An Introduction to Human Growth.* New York: Harper and Brothers, 1949.

Goodman, Kenneth S. "Reading: A Psycholinguistic Guessing Game." In Harry Singer and Robert Ruddell (Eds.) *Theoretical Models and Processes of Reading,* 2nd Edition. Newark, DE: International Reading Association, 1976.

Goodman, Yetta. "Test Review: Concepts About Print Test." *The Reading Teacher* 34 (1981): 445–448.

Graves, Michael, Connie Juel, and Bonnie Graves. *Teaching Reading in the 21st Century.* Needham Heights, MA: Allyn & Bacon, 1998.

Griffith, Priscilla L., and Mary W. Olson. "Phonemic Awareness Helps Beginning Readers Break the Code." *The Reading Teacher* 45, no. 7 (March 1992): 516–523.

Harste, Jerome, Virginia Woodward, and Carolyn Burke. *Language Stories and Literacy Lessons.* Portsmouth, NH: Heinemann Educational Books, 1984.

Hiebert, Elfrieda. "Reading and Writing of First Grade Students in a Restructed Chapter 1 Program." *American Education Research Journal.* 29,3 (fall, 1992), 545-572.

Holdaway, Don. *Foundations of Literacy.* Portsmouth, NH: Heinemann Educational Books, 1979.

Invernizzi, Marcia, and Connie Juel. "A Community Volunteer Tutoring Program That Works." *The Reading Teacher, 50,* 4, (Dec–Jan, 1997), 304–311.

Iverson, S., and William Tunmer. "Phonological Processing Skills and the Reading Recovery Program." *Journal of Educational Psychology* 85 (1): 112–126. 1993.

Juel, Connie. "Learning to Read and Write: A Longitudinal Study of 54 Children from First Through Fourth Grades." *Journal of Educational Psychology, 80,* 4 (Dec, 1988), 437–447.

Lesgold, A., L. Resnick, and K. Hammond. "Learning to Read: A Longitudinal Study of Word Skill Development in Two Curricula." In *Reading Research: Advances in Theory and Practice,* Vol. 4, ed. G. MacKinnon and T. Waller. London: Academic Press, 1985.

Loban, Walter. *The Language of Elementary School Children.* Urbana, IL: National Council of Teachers of English, 1963.

Mann, Virginia, Paula Tobin, and Rebecca Wilson. "Measuring Phonological Awareness Through Invented Spelling." In *Children's Reading and the Development of Phonological Awareness,* ed. Keith Stanovich. Detroit: Wayne State University Press, 1988.

Marsh, G. Friedman, M. V. Welch, and P. Desberg. "A Cognitive Developmental Theory of Reading Acquisition." In *Reading Research: Advances in Theory and Practice,* Vol. 3, ed. G. McKinnon and T. Waller. New York: Academic Press, 1981.

McCormick, Christine, and Jana Mason. "Fostering Reading for Head Start Children with Little Books." In *Risk Makers, Risk Takers, Risk Breakers,* ed. JoBeth Allen and Jana Mason. Portsmouth, NH: Heinemann Educational Books, 1989.

McCracken, Robert, and Marlene McCracken. *Reading Is Only the Tiger's Tail.* Winnepeg: Peguis, 1987.

McGill-Franzen, Anne. "Early Literacy: What Does 'Developmentally Appropriate' Mean?" *The Reading Teacher, 46,* 1, (September, 1992), 56–58.

Morais, Jose. "Segmental Analysis of Speech and Its Relation to Reading Ability." *Annals of Dyslexia, 37,* 126–141, 1987.

Morris, Darrell. "Concept of Word and Phoneme Awareness in the Beginning Reader." *Research in the Teaching of English* 17 (1981): 359–373.

Morris, Darrell. "'Word Sort:' A Categorization Strategy for Improving Word Recognition Ability." *Reading Psychology, 3,* 3 (Jul–Sep, 1982), 247–259.

Morris, Darrell. *Case Studies in Beginning Reading: The Howard Street Tutoring Manual.* Boone, NC: Fieldstream Publications, 1990.

Morris, Darrell. "The Relationship Between Children's Concept of Word in Text and Phonemic Awareness in Learning to Read: A Longitudinal Study." *Research in the Teaching of English* 27, no. 2, (1993): 133–154.

Morris, Darrell. "The Relationship Between Children's Concept of Word in Text and Phoneme Awareness in Learning to Read: A Longitudinal Study." *Research in the Teaching of English, 27,* 2 (May 1993), 133–154.

Nagy, William, and Richard Anderson. "How Many Words Are There in Printed School English?" *Reading Research Quarterly, 19,* 3(1984): 304–330.

Palincsar, Ann Marie, and Ann Brown. "Reciprocal Teaching of Comprehension-Fostering and Comprehension-Monitoring Activities." *Cognition and Instruction, 1,* 2(1986), 117–175.

Pearson, P. David, and Dale Johnson. *Teaching Reading Comprehension.* New York: Holt Rinehart, and Winston, 1978.

Pearson, P.D., L.R. Roehler, J.A. Dole, and G.G. Duffy. "Developing Expertise in Reading Comprehension." In *What Research Has to Say About Reading Instruction,* 2d ed. Ed. S.J. Samuels and A. E. Farstrup. Newark, DE: International Reading Association, 1992.

Pinnell, Gay Su. "Comparing Instructional Models for the Literacy Education of High Risk First Graders." *Reading Research Quarterly, 29,* 1, (Jan–Mar, 1994), 8–39.

Pressley, M., C.J. Johnson, S. Symons, J.A. McGoldrick, and J.A. Kurita. "Strategies That Improve Children's Memory and Comprehension of Text." *Elementary School Journal, 90,* (1989): 3–32.

Raphael, T. "Question Answering Strategies for Children." *The Reading Teacher, 36* (1982): 186–190.

Read, Charles. *Children's Categorization of Speech Sounds in English.* Urbanna, IL: National Council of Teachers of English, 1975.

Roehler, L.R., and G.G. Duffy. "Teachers' Instructional Actions." In *Handbook of Reading Research,* Vol. 2, ed. Rebecca Barr, Michael Kamil, Peter Mosenthal, and P. David Pearson. New York: Longman, 1991.

Shanahan, Timothy, and Rebecca Barr. "Reading Recovery: An Independent Evaluation of the Effects of an Early Instructional Intervention for At-Risk Learners." *Reading Research Quarterly, 30,* 4 (Oct.–Dec, 1995), 958–996.

Sim-Sim, Ines. "News From Portugal." *The Reading Teacher, 47,* 5, (Feb. 1994), 424–427.

Sim-Sim, Ines. "Reading Around the World: News from Portugal." *The Reading Teacher,* 1994.

Slobin, Dan, and Charles Welsh. "Elicited Imitation as a Research Tool in Developmental Psycholinguistics." In *Language Training in Early Childhood Education,* ed. Celia Lavatelli. Urbana, IL: University of Illinois Press, 1971.

Smith, Frank, 1971. *Understanding Reading: A Psycholinguistic Analysis of Reading and Learning to Read.* New York: Holt, Rinehart, Winston, 1971.

Snow, Catherine, Susan Burns, and Peg Griffin, Eds., *Preventing Reading Difficulties in Young Children.* Washington, DC: National Academy Press, 1998.

Stauffer, Russell. *The Language Experience Approach to the Teaching of Reading, 2nd Edition.* New York: Harper and Row, 1975.

Stauffer, Russell. *The Language Experience Approach to the Teaching of Reading,* 2d ed. New York: Harper and Row, 1980.

Stern, Daniel. *The First Relationship.* Cambridge, MA: Harvard, 1982.

Sulzby, Elizabeth. "Children's Emergent Reading of Favorite Storybooks: A Developmental Study." *Reading Research Quarterly* 20 (1985): 458–481.

Temple, Charles, and Jean Gillet. "Developing Word Knowledge: A Cognitive View." *Reading World,* 18, 2 (Dec. 1978): 132–140.

Tough, Joan. *Focus on Meaning: Talking to Children to Some Purpose.* London: Unwin, 1973.

Trachtenburg, Phyllis. "Using Children's Literature to Enhance Phonics Instruction." *The Reading Teacher. 43,* 9 (May 1990): 653–654.

Treiman, Rebecca. *Beginning to Spell: A Study of First Grade Children.* New York: Oxford, 1993.

Trelease, Jim. *The New Read-Aloud Handbook.* New York: Penguin, 1989.

Vardell, Sylvia. "Looking for Literature: Lessons From Zimbabwe." *The Reading Teacher, 48,* 7 (Apr. 1995): 628–631.

Vellutino, Frank. "Alternative Conceptualizations of Dyslexia: Evidence in Support of a Verbal Deficit Hypothesis." *Harvard Educational Review; 47;* 3 (1977): 334–354.

Vellutino, Frank. *Dyslexia: Theory and Research.* Cambridge, MA: MIT Press, 1979.

Wagstaff, Janiel M. "Building Practical Knowledge of Letter-Sound Correspondences: A Beginner's Word Wall and Beyond." *The Reading Teacher, 51,* 4 (December 1997/January 1998) 298–304.

Walsh, Daniel, Gary Price, and Mark Gillingham. "The Critical but Transitory Importance of Letter Naming." *Reading Research Quarterly* 23 (1988): 108–122.

Yopp, Hallie Kay. "The Validity and Reliability of Phonemic Awareness Tests." *Reading Research Quarterly* 23 (1988): 159–177.

Assessing and Teaching Developing Readers

INTRODUCTION

In the previous chapter, we took a close look at the literacy development, assessment, and instruction of emergent and beginning readers. That was the first in a series of four chapters in which we look closely at the literacy issues of students at different points of development. This chapter is the second in this series on literacy at different points in development. Here, we look at developing readers, those children who are reading more and more text and more rapidly learning sight words. In the stage-bound parlance of Chapter 1, we would say that these children should be passing into and through the stages of building fluency and reading to learn and for pleasure. Normally, such readers are found from late second grade through fifth grade, after which we they could be entering a phase of mature reading. However, when children experience difficulty, this period of developing reading may begin later and last longer.

We begin this chapter with a case study of one such child who is lagging behind his classmates as he struggles to emerge from beginning reading and begin building his fluency. We proceed to describe the strategies of teaching that are available to help him and students like him.

Case Study

Let's consider the case of Jerry, a 9-year-old third-grader. Jerry is a quiet boy who takes little interest in school and avoids contact with adults when possible. Jerry does just enough schoolwork to get by, and what he does is poorly done. Without overtly refusing to work, he is adept at stalling and other strategies to avoid reading and writing tasks.

Jerry was retained in second grade, resulting in his being a year older than many of his classmates. He has always been an unsuccessful reader, and he received remedial reading instruction from the beginning of his second year through the present time, the spring of his third-grade year. In spite of this help, his reading progress has been slow. With the end of third grade approaching, Jerry has been given a fairly complete reading assessment. The findings of these assessments are shown as strengths and needs in Figure 7.1.

From Jerry's scores on the reading tasks and our notes, we can see that although Jerry is indeed becoming a problem reader, he also has a number of strengths.

It is important to search for and list the things that the student can do and enjoys doing, no matter how numerous the needs might be. Without rigorous attention to strengths and interests, we risk omitting the things that the child does successfully, and we risk becoming discouraged about attempting to help her or him.

We proceed now to creating goals for instruction. What are Jerry's most critical needs for reading improvement? We select the factors that we believe will help him to improve his reading most dramatically, as well as those strengths that we must not overlook in teaching, and we create a list of goals, in order of importance for this particular student. From these, our activities will be developed.

Jerry _____, age 9, third grade

Functional reading levels:

Independent: primer

Instructional: second

Frustration: third

Listening: fourth, possibly fifth

Strengths:

Comprehension solid at his instructional level

Working comfortably in low-vocabulary, high-interest material of second-grade readability

Enjoys being read to

Works cooperatively when he understands what the goal or outcome will be

Listening comprehension at least two grades above instructional level (that is, shows potential for improvement)

Has *some* sight vocabulary (although very small)

Can use decoding, and context to some extent, to figure out words

Has mastered most consonant and blend sounds

Tries to make sense of what he reads

Is interested in sports, cars, motorcycles, and outdoor life

Needs:

Small sight vocabulary, particularly beyond primer

Overusing phonics and underusing context in word recognition

Miscues usually resulted in meaning change

In phonics, has trouble with variant vowel sounds especially in medial position, and most polysyllabic words

Reading rate slow and halting due to small sight vocabulary

Very unsure of his ability to understand; says "I don't know" quickly

Hesitant to risk a guess or prediction

Avoids reading whenever he can and does no self-initiated reading

Gives appearance of passivity and boredom, his response to failure and frustration

FIGURE 7.1   Jerry's Strengths and Needs Chart

GOALS FOR JERRY'S INSTRUCTION

1. Develop a larger sight vocabulary.
2. Develop more effective word analysis skills, especially the judicious use of context.
3. Improve his reading fluency and rate.
4. Encourage his active comprehension, making predictions, and risking a guess.
5. Increase time he spends reading.
6. Develop his listening comprehension and story sense.
7. Encourage him to develop greater self-esteem and more positive attitudes toward reading.

Now we have clarified what Jerry can currently do, what he needs, and where we must place the most emphasis in our planning.

We are ready to select and devise activities that will fit our listed priorities and to develop some general plans for Jerry's instructional time.

Following are generic types of activities to fit different purposes. In the sections that follow, these activities are discussed and described in detail. We will select from them as we develop a lesson plan for Jerry and others whose reading is like his.

TO DEVELOP SIGHT VOCABULARY

Dictated stories
Predictable books
Repeated reading
Echo-reading and choral-reading
Shared reading
Sight word bank (or notebook)

TO DEVELOP FLUENCY

Repeated reading
Choral-reading with a group
Practice reading in order to read to others

TO DEVELOP WORD ATTACK SKILLS

Word sorting and categorizing
Word families and letter substitution
Confirmation exercises (in context)
Cloze and maze procedures

TO DEVELOP READING COMPREHENSION

Using predicting (directed reading-thinking activities)
Developing awareness of prior information: prereading, predicting, previewing, webbing
Developing awareness of story and text structures

Using story maps
Retelling
Reciprocal teaching and questioning

To Develop Listening Comprehension:

Being read to
Interpreting stories and text listened to through drama, art, and movement
Retelling stories and text listened to
Summarizing and paraphrasing material listened to
Storytelling

Developing Sight Vocabulary

Individual words become *sight words* (recognized immediately without analysis) when they are seen repeatedly in meaningful context. Many youngsters acquire some sight words before school entry, and without direct teaching or drill, by looking at the same favorite storybooks many times over. First they learn what words are on the page as they hear the same story read to them again and again. Soon they can recite the words along with the reader; soon after that, they can recite independently, role-playing reading as they turn the pages.

If at this point the reader casually points to the words as they are read, the child begins to associate the word spoken with its printed counterpart. This speech-to-print matching is an important foundation for learning to recognize words in print.

It is essential for readers to have a large sight vocabulary so that they can move through print quickly and efficiently. As we have already seen, youngsters like Jerry who have only a small store of sight words are forced to read very slowly with frequent stops to figure out words, stops that interrupt their comprehension and interfere with their getting meaning. Many youngsters read poorly for this reason. Increasing their sight vocabularies is mandatory for their reading improvement. This can be accomplished by a number of means.

Dictated Stories and Language Experience

Dictated stories are a part of the language experience approach to beginning reading (Allen, 1976; Hall, 1981; Nessel & Jones, 1981; Stauffer, 1980). The method of using dictated stories to teach reading has been used for many years. In fact, a variation of it was apparently used by John Amos Comenius in the 1600s! The method works as follows. An individual or a small group dictates an account to someone who writes down the account verbatim. The account is reread chorally until the students can recite it accurately and point to the individual words while reciting. Then parts, or the entire account, are read individually, and words that can be immediately recognized first in context, then in isolation, are identified. These new sight words go into the students' word banks, collections of sight words on cards or in a notebook.

It was long held that the value of dictated stories lay in the preservation of children's natural language, which might differ considerably from "book language." This is important, but a greater usefulness of dictated words for developing sight vocabulary lies in the repeated rereading of the material. Students might reread dictated stories more willingly than other material because the stories concern experiences the students have had themselves. Rereading the stories chorally and independently, regardless of the topic or syntax used, reinforces the recognition of the words in other contexts.

As the students' sight vocabularies grow, and their word banks come to contain about 100 or more words, this is a sign that the student will have an adequate sight vocabulary to read other kinds of texts. Now the dictated stories are usually phased out, and other material is introduced. Dictation works best as an initial means of establishing and fostering sight vocabulary and also as a confidence-building transition into reading.

When dictated stories are mentioned, some teachers of older poor readers associate the practice with very young children. They might immediately presume that older poor readers will be put off by what they assume is a juvenile practice. Although language experience is common in primary classrooms, it need not be reserved for little children. In fact, with many older and adult poor readers, what they dictate might be about the only print they can read successfully.

With young children, you need a concrete stimulus, or experience, to talk about: an object, picture, storybook, or immediate event. With older students, past or future experiences, hopes, fears, reminiscences, content area subjects, and abstract concepts can serve as topics. Older students can usually move through the steps more quickly than younger ones and can usually skip the voice-pointing step entirely. Older students often work best with this procedure individually or in pairs or threes rather than larger groups. A word notebook might replace the word bank card collection. And if the teacher presents the activity with a businesslike air and explains why it is being done, the experience need not feel like a juvenile one.

Figure 7.2 lists the steps in using dictated stories with younger and older students, in groups or individually.

Support Reading: Echo-Reading and Choral-Reading

Support reading means helping readers get through text that is too difficult for them to read independently. Although students should never have to read material at their frustration levels without support, sometimes it is necessary for them to get through some difficult material. This is most often the case with older poor readers who are expected to get information from a content area textbook that is beyond their instructional level. If appropriate material at their instructional level is not available, you can help them through difficult text using support reading methods.

In *echo-reading,* the teacher reads a sentence or two aloud, and the student immediately repeats what the teacher read while looking at and, if necessary,

WITH YOUNGER PUPILS:

1. Present a concrete stimulus—an object or event—to discuss.

2. Encourage describing and narrating so that the students will have plenty to say about it.

3. Tell students you will help them write the story using a chart tablet, transparency, or the board.

4. Ask for volunteers to contribute sentences for the story.

5. Print the account verbatim, allowing students to make changes or additions. Read aloud what you have written, including amended portions.

6. Read the completed account to the group.

7. Lead the group in choral recitation, pointing quickly to the words as you read. Repeat until the whole account can be recited fluently.

8. Ask for volunteers to read one or more sentences alone, pointing to the words as in step 7.

9. Ask for volunteers to point to and identify words they know. Keep a list of these for review.

10. Provide individual copies of the story for rereading and sight word identification.

11. Any words that a child can identify out of the story context can go into the child's word bank, to be used for sorting and other word study activities.

WITH OLDER PUPILS:

1. Work with groups of three or fewer.

2. Suggest, or allow students to suggest, a topic.

3. Lead discussion of the topic, encouraging as rich language use as possible.

4. Take the dictation as above, making minor word changes or additions as necessary to keep the story fluent. Cursive writing may be used instead of printing. Use a regular size sheet of paper if you wish.

5. Lead the choral rereading as above. Students might prefer to do more individual than group reading.

6. Provide an individual copy for each student, typed if possible, for practice rereading and word identification. Encourage rereading to a partner or someone else.

7. As individuals read to you and identify newly acquired sight words, have them enter the words in a sight word notebook. Older students might prefer a notebook to a traditional word bank.

FIGURE 7.2   Steps in Using Dictated Stories

pointing to the words. Only one or two sentences, or even one long phrase, are read at a time to allow students to use short-term memory as they "echo." Older students might use specially prepared tapes, with pauses for repetition, to practice echo reading independently. Echo-reading is an intensive support measure that is best used with short selections and material that is quite difficult or unfamiliar. Sometimes, it might be sufficient to echo read only the beginning of a longer passage to get students started. One important characteristic of echo reading is that it allows the teacher to model fluent reading and the students to practice it.

Choral-reading means reading aloud in unison. It is somewhat harder to choral-read than to echo-read, so this procedure is best for material that is easier or for text that has been silently previewed or echo-read first. Choral-reading, with the teacher's voice leading and providing the model, is an excellent way of practicing oral reading without the anxiety of a solo performance. Complicated or unfamiliar text should be read aloud to the students first and may be echo-read initially as well. Again, tapes can be used effectively for independent practice.

Choral-reading is a superb way to enjoy poetry. Poetry deserves to be read aloud; many poems that are read silently are only pale shadows of what they are when rendered aloud. Add a little movement, a sound effect or two, and a bit of variety with voices (high/low, loud/soft, fast/slow), and you have more than a poetry reading—you have a performing art! Choral-reading of poetry and prose is a low-anxiety experience; children's individual mispronunciations or lapses disappear into the sound of the collective voices, while everyone gets to experience fluent reading. It encourages the rereading of text, which contributes to fluency and sight word acquisition, while students barely recognize that they have read the same text many times over. Choral-reading has been shown to particularly help children who are nonfluent English speakers (McCauley & McCauley, 1992). Box 7.1 shows procedures for choral reading of poetry or other predictable text.

DEVELOPING READING FLUENCY

Poor word recognition and slow, word-by-word reading reduce comprehension. According to Allington (1983), lack of fluency is commonly noted as a characteristic of poor reading and can be taught but is often overlooked in corrective teaching. Allington proposed several hypotheses explaining why some children fail to become fluent readers:

- Some children are not exposed to fluent adult reading models or to prereading experience reciting memorized books.
- Good readers are more likely to be encouraged to read with expression, while poor readers get more instruction on individual words and word parts.
- Fast learners are given more opportunities for reading and hence more practice actually reading.

BOX 7.1

CHORAL-READING POETRY
OR PREDICTABLE BOOKS

1. Introduce the material by briefly discussing the topic with students.
2. Read the material aloud expressively.
3. Read the material a second time while children follow along in a large copy of the material (chart tablet sheet, transparency, or Big Book).
4. Choral-read the material several times until it is very familiar.
5. Begin adding pauses, sound effects, movement, tonal variety, or other expressive aspects to the reading.
6. Practice often so that all children feel very comfortable with it.
7. Ask children to suggest ways in which they can share their choral-readings with others, and follow up on their ideas.

Source: Joyce K. McCauley and Daniel S. McCauley. "Using Choral Reading to Promote Language Learning for ESL Students." *The Reading Teacher* 45, no. 7 (March 1992): 526–533.

- Successful readers more often read text that is easy for them, while poorer readers more often are faced with frustration-level material.
- Successful readers do more silent reading, which provides practice and experience.
- Children's ideas differ about what good reading is, with poorer readers often viewing reading not as meaning getting but as an accuracy competition. (p. 559)

Since reading fluency is an aspect of good reading that many students need to develop, methods that help students to develop this skill are both useful and necessary. With greater fluency, readers can concentrate on comprehending what they read, develop greater self-confidence, and enjoy reading more.

Rereading

Rereading means reading the same material more than once. Rereading helps students to gain fluency, bolsters students' self-confidence as readers, helps students to recognize familiar words at sight, and helps students use phrasing to support the meaning of what they read. It need not mean drudgery for students, however. There are a number of ways in which we can integrate rereading into our teaching. Some are as follows:

1. Have students read material silently before oral reading or discussion. If you will use predictive questions in your discussion, have them read silently up to a stopping point.
2. Encourage oral rereading for real purposes: to prove a point in a discussion, to role-play a dialogue, or to savor an effective descriptive passage, among other purposes.

3. Encourage the rereading of familiar or completed stories as seat-work or independent work or during free reading of sustained silent reading periods.
4. Use *buddy reading:* Select or have students choose reading partners or buddies, then reread completed stories or books aloud to their partners. (Buddy reading is discussed further below.)
5. Encourage children to take home familiar books to reread at home to family members. Since rereading is usually more fluent than the initial reading, children can show off their fluent reading at home this way.
6. Encourage rereading of favorite stories by revisiting old favorites when you read aloud to the class.
7. Have students listen to taped material, either professionally recorded or done by you or other volunteers. After listening and silently following along, have students imitate the reader as they listen, then eventually read the material alone. Tape-record their readings for self-critique.
8. Act out favorite stories using the technique of Reader's Theater, in which scripts are always read instead of memorized and recited.
9. Use choral-reading frequently and perform for others.

Repeated Readings for Fluency

Repeated reading refers to a systematic practice of using timed oral rereadings to develop reading fluency. Described by Samuels (1979), the method involves helping the student select an instructional level passage and a reading rate goal, timing the first unrehearsed oral reading of the passage and successive readings after practice, and keeping a simple chart of the student's rate after successive timings. When the student is able to read the passage at or beyond the goal rate, a new passage of equal (but not greater) difficulty is begun.

This method of repeated reading is not intended to directly aid comprehension, but rather to help students acquire sight words and practice reading fluently and confidently. As they practice rereading their passages for timing, their reading rate for that passage climbs dramatically; keeping a chart that shows these increases is highly motivating, especially for older poor readers.

Of course, we are not surprised that their rates climb as they practice reading the same passage. What is surprising, and what is the real benefit of this practice, is that their reading rates also increase on each successive unrehearsed oral reading. The reason that this happens is that all that rereading has helped them to acquire more sight words and has helped them learn to read aloud fluently and confidently.

Figure 7.3 shows the steps in using the timed repeated reading method, and Figure 7.4 shows a partially completed chart.

Of course it matters a great deal *what* students have to read. Expecting students to read frequently, copiously, and repeatedly in material that is at their level of competence assumes that plenty of lively and interesting reading material will be available at many different levels of difficulty. Fortunately, this is true. That is the topic of the next section.

1. Choose, or help each student to choose, a fairly comfortable, interesting selection to practice reading. It should be too long to memorize: 100 or so words for younger children, 200 or more words for older ones. Trade books and previously read basal stories are good.

2. Make up a duplicated chart for each pupil (see Figure 7.4). Omit the accuracy axis if you want to simplify the task.

3. Time each reader's first, unrehearsed oral reading of the passage. Mark the chart for Timed Reading 1.

4. Instruct the readers to practice the passage aloud as many times as possible for the next day or two. Let them practice in pairs, independently, and at home.

5. Time the reading again and mark the chart for Timed Reading 2, and show the students how to mark their own charts.

6. Continue timing at intervals of several days. As the rate increases for the first passage, help each child to set a new rate goal.

7. When the reader reaches the goal set, begin a new passage of equal (not greater) difficulty. Successive portions of a long story are perfect. Repeat steps 3 through 6.

FIGURE 7.3   Steps in Using Repeated Reading

Predictable Books, "Easy Readers," and Other Easy Reading Fare

If we acknowledge that "children learn to read by reading" (as reading guru Frank Smith put it), then children need material that they can and will read. Such material must be available at all reading levels, and it should appeal to a range of interests. Some of it should appeal to more mature interests even though its difficulty level is low.

It used to be that there were relatively few such books available. Primer-level basals were written in straight narrative style, and for that reason, dictated accounts and simple poems were often used in their place. Today, however, as the field of children's trade books has exploded to meet the demands of families and classrooms, more attention is being paid to the needs of developing readers. There are many wonderful predictable books for young readers, many of them available in big book format for group instruction. Some publishers, such as The Wright Group (19201 120th Ave NE, Bothell, WA 98011-9512) and the Rigby Publishing Company (P.O. Box 797, Crystal Lake, IL 60039-0797) have built their product lines around the use of predictable books in both big book and individual book formats. Many of the large commercial publishing houses, too, have special lines of books for young developing readers. In addition, a number of smaller education-oriented publishers publish collections of books that were written especially to appeal for students in the elementary grades and beyond

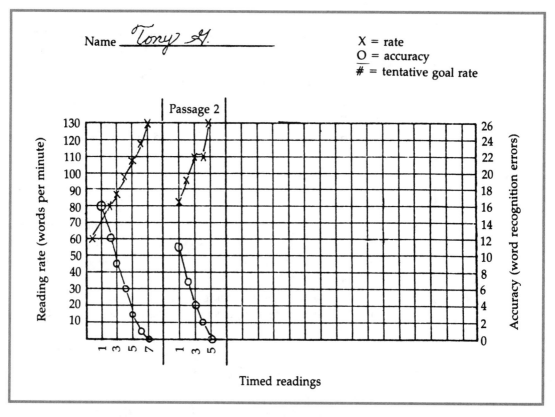

FIGURE 7.4   Sample Repeated Reading Chart

who need special motivation and easier fare. Three varieties of such books that will be discussed here are *predictable books, easy readers,* and *high-interest/low-reading level books.*

Predictable Books

Predictable books have a rhyming or repetitious element that make them easy to read, even for students who recognize few words at sight. The pattern of repeated words or phrases or the rhyme scheme helps readers remember and predict what words are coming next.

Some predictable books repeat the same sentences or phrases over and over. Eric Carle's *Have You Seen My Cat?* (New York: Franklin Watts, 1973) is an example of such a pattern. On alternate pages, the sentences "Have you seen my cat?" and "This is not my cat!" repeat, as a small boy asks a variety of people from many cultures and finds a lion, a panther, and a cheetah, among other cats. On the last page, which reads "This is my cat!," he finds his own cat with a litter of newborn kittens. The inside back cover shows all the varieties of cats, labeled. Even the least-experienced prereader can recite this book and point to the words after only a few pages. Repetition makes it predictable. Bill Martin, Jr.'s *Brown Bear, Brown Bear, What Do You See?* (New York: Henry Holt, 1983) is another example, familiar to many teachers. Each left-hand page identifies a color and animal and asks, "What do you see?" On the right-hand page the animal answers, "I see a _____ looking at me," and identifies the next color and animal: a yellow duck, a blue horse, a green frog, and so forth. Again, the last page lists all the animals cumulatively with small copies of the larger illustrations. Like many others, these books are available in big book, standard trade book, and miniature versions. Eric Carle's *The Very Hungry Caterpillar* (New York: Philomel Books, 1969), *The Grouchy Ladybug* (New York: Harper & Row, 1977), and *The Very Busy Spider* (New York: Philomel Books, 1984) are other examples.

Some predictable books rely on rhyme rather than repetition. Nancy Shaw's *Sheep in a Jeep* (Boston: Houghton-Mifflin, 1986) is an example. Although it has few words, the hilarious antics of the sheep that go for an ill-fated joyride make it appropriate for a wide range of ages. It sounds like this: "Uh-oh! The jeep won't go. Sheep leap to push the jeep. Sheep shove, sheep grunt. Sheep don't think to look up front." It is a great source of rhyming words, those that share the same spelling pattern (sheep–jeep) as well as those that don't (grunt–front), and colorful sound words (splash! thud!). The rhyming adventures of the sheep continue in *Sheep on a Ship* (1989) and *Sheep in a Shop* (1991).

Predictable books also serve as jumping-off places for students to create their own original books. Changing the topic and illustrations, while retaining the original pattern, can result in wonderful original versions that children enjoy reading as much as, or more than, the original version. For example, after mastering *Brown Bear, Brown Bear, What Do You See?*, a group of first-graders created *The Vegetable Book*: "Green pepper, green pepper, what do you see? I see a red tomato looking at me" and so forth. With the basic pattern written on chart paper and blanks for the color words and nouns, the group chose the vegetable theme and volunteered the word pairs to fill the blanks: brown potato, orange carrot, purple eggplant, for example. Each couplet was then printed on a separate sheet, and pairs of students were assigned to illustrate each page. The resulting Big Book was stapled together and reread numerous times. Meanwhile, the text was typed on individual pages with space for illustration, duplicated and stapled into individual copies. Each student then illustrated his or her own copy to keep. (During this time, the class brought in samples of the various vegetables for exploring and tasting.) Another group followed the same procedure with *Have You Seen My Cat?*, creating their original *Have You Seen My Dog?* and illustrating it with different breeds and colors of dogs. (This effort involved looking at numerous books about dogs to learn about different breeds.) These books remained very popular all year for independent reading.

Both commercial and student-written predictable books are extremely useful for independent reading and as springboards for creative writing. They help students to acquire and reinforce sight words while providing successful reading practice for even the least fluent reader. Here are some predictable books that you might use:

Abisch, Roy. *Around the House That Jack Built*. New York: Parents Magazine Press, 1972.

Barry, Katherine. *A Bug to Hug*. New York: Young Scott, 1964.

Becker, John. *Seven Little Rabbits*. New York: Walker & Co., 1973.

Bodecker, N.M. *It's Raining, Said John Twaining.* New York: Atheneum, 1973.

Bodecker, N.M. *Let's Marry, Said the Cherry and Other Nonsense Poems.* New York: Atheneum, 1974.

Brown, Margaret Wise. *The Important Book.* New York: Harper & Row, 1949.

Burningham, John. *Mr. Gumpy's Outing.* New York: Holt, Rinehart & Winston, 1970.

Carle, Eric. *Have You Seen My Cat?* New York: Franklin Watts, 1973.

Carle, Eric. *The Very Hungry Caterpillar.* New York: Philomel, 1969.

Carle, Eric. *The Grouchy Ladybug.* New York: Harper & Row, 1977.

Carle, Eric. *The Very Busy Spider.* New York: Philomel, 1984.

Charlip, Remy. *Fortunately.* New York: Parents Magazine Press, 1964.

Cohen, Carol. *Wake up, Groundhog!* New York: Crown, 1975.

De Regniers, Beatrice. *May I Bring a Friend?* New York: Atheneum, 1964.

Domanska, Janina. *If All the Seas Were One Sea.* New York: Macmillan, 1971.

Domanska, Janina. *Busy Monday Morning.* New York: Greenwillow, 1985.

Einsel, Walter. *Did You Ever See?* New York: Scholastic, 1972.

Emberly, Ed. *Drummer Hoff.* Englewood Cliffs, NJ: Prentice-Hall, 1967.

Fox, Mem. *Hattie and the Fox.* New York: Bradbury Press, 1986.

Galdone, Paul. *The Teeny Tiny Woman.* New York: Clarion, 1984.

Ginsburg, Mirra. *The Chick and the Duckling.* New York: Macmillan, 1972.

Hoberman, Mary Ann. *A House Is a House for Me.* New York: Scholastic, 1978.

Johnston, Tony. *Five Little Foxes and the Snow.* New York: Putnam, 1977.

Joslin, Sesyle. *What Do You Say, Dear?* Reading, MA: Addison-Wesley, 1958.

Joslin, Sesyle. *What Do You Do, Dear?* Reading, MA: Addison-Wesley, 1961.

Kalan, Robert. *Jump, Frog, Jump.* New York: Scholastic, 1981.

Keats, Ezra Jack. *Over the Meadow.* New York: Four Winds, 1971.

Kesselman, Wendy. *There's a Train Going by My Window.* Garden City, NY: Doubleday, 1982.

Kherdian, David, and Nonny Hogrogian. *Right Now.* New York: Knopf, 1983.

Krauss, Ruth. *What a Fine Day.* New York: Parents Magazine Press, 1967.

Langstaff, John. *Soldier, Soldier, Won't You Marry Me?* Garden City, NY: Doubleday, 1972.

Martin, Bill, Jr. *Brown Bear, Brown Bear, What Do You See?* New York: Henry Holt, 1983.

Martin, Bill, Jr. *Chicka Chicka Boom Boom.* New York: Simon & Schuster, 1989.

Martin, Bill, Jr. *Polar Bear, Polar Bear, What Do You Hear?* New York: Henry Holt & Co., 1991.

Martin, Bill, Jr., and Peggy Brogan. *Bill Martin's Instant Readers.* New York: Holt, Rinehart & Winston, 1971.

Matthias, Catherine. *I Love Cats.* Chicago: Children's Press, 1983.

Mayer, Mercer. *What Do You Do With a Kangaroo?* New York: Scholastic, 1973.

McGinn, Maureen. *I Used to Be an Artichoke.* St. Louis: Concordia, 1973.

Mendoza, George. *The Scribbler*. New York: Holt, Rinehart & Winston, 1971.

Nolan, Dennis. *Big Pig*. Englewood Cliffs, NJ: Prentice-Hall, 1976.

Numeroff, Laura Joffe. *If You Give a Mouse a Cookie*. New York: Harper & Row, 1985.

Numeroff, Laura Joffe. *If You Give a Moose a Muffin*. New York: HarperCollins, 1991.

Pomerantz, Charlotte. *The Piggy in the Puddle*. New York: Macmillan, 1974.

Quackenbush, Robert. *She'll Be Comin' Round the Mountain*. Philadelphia: Lippincott, 1973.

Sendak, Maurice. *Chicken Soup with Rice*. New York: Scholastic, 1962.

Shaw, Nancy. *Sheep in a Jeep*. Boston: Houghton Mifflin, 1986.

Shaw, Nancy. *Sheep on a Ship*. Boston: Houghton Mifflin, 1989.

Shaw, Nancy. *Sheep in a Shop*. Boston: Houghton Mifflin, 1991.

Slobodkina, Esphyr. *Caps for Sale*. Reading, MA: Addison-Wesley, 1947.

Spier, Peter. *Bored—Nothing to Do!* Garden City, NY: Doubleday, 1978.

Supraner, Robyn. *Would You Rather Be a Tiger?* Boston: Houghton Mifflin, 1976.

Sutton, Eve. *My Cat Likes to Hide in Boxes*. New York: Parents Magazine Press, 1973.

Tolstoy, Alexei. *The Great Big Enormous Turnip*. New York: Watts, 1968.

Wood, Audrey. *The Napping House*. San Diego: Harcourt Brace Jovanovich, 1984.

Wood, Audrey. *King Bidgood's in the Bathtub*. San Diego: Harcourt Brace Jovanovich, 1986.

Zemach, Harve. *The Judge*. New York: Farrar, Straus, 1969.

Zolotow, Charlotte. *Someday*. New York: Harper & Row, 1965.

Zolotow, Charlotte. *Summer Is* . . . London/New York: Abelard-Schuman, 1967.

Easy Readers

Children's books have been available in America for more than two hundred years, but it was only in the past two decades that quality works that children could read themselves have become regularly available. Traditional picture books were written to be read to children by adults and only rarely by children (Temple et al., 1998), so there has long been a need for accessibly written works that appealed to children's desire for interesting fare. Now many of the major trade publishers put out lines of easy readers. The Putnam & Grosset Group publishes the All Aboard Reading series. Dial Press has the Easy-to-Read Series. The series from Random House is called Step Into Reading, and HarperCollins publishes I Can Read. In conjunction with Bank Street College, Bantam publishes the Bank Street Ready-to-Read Series. Although Macmillan has no particular name for its easy reader offerings, it has published more than a dozen easy readers about *Henry and Mudge* by Cynthia Rylant.

Easy readers have been produced by some of the best children's authors and illustrators we have. Cynthia Rylant has won Newbery and Caldecott Awards. Other award-winning children's authors such as Dr. Seuss, James Marshall, Tomie dePaola, Arnold Lobel, Lee Bennett Hopkins, and Joanna Cole have also written easy readers.

An excellent source of reviews of easy readers is the *Adventuring with Books* series, published approximately every four years by the National Council of Teachers of English and containing nearly 2,000 annotated listing of books by topic and by difficulty level for students in grades Pre-K through 6.

High-Interest/Low-Reading-Level Books and Magazines

Since the 1960s, several educational publishers have produced works specifically for reluctant readers. According to Ryder et al. (1989), who have reviewed these books for the International Reading Association, the early efforts were not of particularly high quality. The quality improved by the late 1970s but had not improved further by the late 1980s. The books' strengths are also their weaknesses, note Ryder et al. To be "relevant" to reluctant readers, the books often highlight the experiences of boys in the inner city who (if they come from minority groups) are African American or Hispanic. Other students might feel as distant from the characters in these books as they do from white youths in gated suburbs. To be more readable, the books limit their vocabulary and sentence length, sometimes at the expense of comprehension.

An annotated review of the series books for reluctant readers, as well as for magazines such as *Cricket, Cobblestone, Stone Soup,* National Geographic *World,* the *Senior Weekly Reader,* and Scholastic *Scope,* are found in Ryder et al. (1989).

DEVELOPING WORD ANALYSIS STRATEGIES

Immediate, accurate recognition of more than 90 percent of the words in running text is necessary for effective instructional-level reading. As students read more widely and sample various kinds of text, they will necessarily encounter words that they do not recognize on sight. The role of teaching word analysis is to help students to acquire efficient strategies for figuring out unrecognized words.

Teaching the "P" Word: Phonics

The "debate" over phonics versus other means of figuring out words that are not recognized at sight has gone on for many decades. "Some people," wrote Steven Stahl (1992), "treat [phonics] as a dirty word, others as the salvation of reading" (p. 618). It is hard to explain why a means of figuring out printed words engenders so much strong feeling. What do you think of when you think of "phonics"? Stacks of boring worksheets? Children mindlessly sounding out letters at the expense of the word's meaning? Children "barking at print"? Lists of isolated skills to be mastered in some hierarchy? The opposite of reading whole words? The simple solution to our children's reading problems, if only teachers would teach it properly? Phonics means these things to some people. If you think of people's beliefs about phonics as representing a continuum, then these positions occupy the opposite ends. Most teachers and parents' beliefs would lie somewhere toward the middle of both positions. Richard Allington (1991) wrote, "I am tired of oppositional polemics and politics, of us-versus-them groupings, of good-guys-and-bad-guys characterizations" (p. 373). In recent years, though, it has seemed harder and harder to occupy the middle ground.

Recently the publication of Marilyn Jager Adams' provocative book, *Beginning to Read: Thinking and Learning about Print* (Cambridge: MIT Press, 1990) prompted a renewal of the debate. In it, Adams reinforces the notion that skilled reading requires rapid and accurate decoding as well as recognition of whole words. At the same time, she criticizes the mindlessness of much of the materials and methods that are used to teach phonics and reiterates that phonics skills and knowledge are useful only in the context of real reading and writing for meaning. She writes, "Written text has both method and purpose. It is time for us to stop bickering about which is more important. To read, children must master both, and we must help them" (1990, p. 424). As a variety of position papers featured in *The Reading Teacher*, February 1991, reveals, Adams has been both praised and vilified for her work. Barbara Kapinus (1991) wrote, "Adams's book is required reading to be an informed participant in the dialogue" (p. 379). Yetta Goodman (1991) charged that the purpose of Adams's book was "political" (p. 378), and Jeanne Chaney (1991) wrote, "I feel that her overriding message for beginning reading instruction is disturbing" (p. 374) and "Adams's book seems conspiratorial" (p. 374).

Given the continuing nature of the emotional and certainly polemic debate about phonics, what is the average teacher or parent to think? Will students be harmed if we teach them phonics skills? Will they be harmed if we don't?

A growing and convincing body of literature shows that good readers are able to use decoding skills rapidly and accurately, independent of the use of context, to recognize unfamiliar words in text (e.g., Adams, 1990; Ehri, 1991; Snow and Burns, 1998; Stanovich, 1980, 1991). While there are hundreds of words that appear over and over in running text and should be recognizable on sight for fluent reading, Adams (1990) estimated that 95 percent of the different words that children must read occur fewer than 10 times in a million words, or fewer than 10 times in a year's worth of reading (cited in Cunningham, 1990, p. 124). For this reason, all readers need to be able to decode letter patterns rapidly and accurately. According to Stahl (1992), "The fact is that all students, regardless of the type of instruction they receive, learn about letter-sound correspondences as part of learning to read" (p. 619).

What, then, should we teach as phonics? In Stahl's (1992) words, "There is no requirement that phonics instruction use worksheets, that it involve having children bark at print, that it be taught as a set of discrete skills mastered in isolation, or that it preclude paying attention to the meaning of texts" (p. 618). Stahl described these nine components of effective phonics teaching.

Exemplary phonics instruction:

1. ***Builds on What Children Already Know.*** It builds on what reading is about, how print functions, what stories are and how they work, and what reading

is for. This knowledge is gained by being read to, by shared reading of predictable books (see Chapter 6), by experience with dictated stories, and by authentic reading and writing tasks before reading begins. These are components of both whole language and traditional instruction in preschool, kindergarten, and primary grades.

2. ***Builds on a Foundation of Phonemic Awareness.*** It builds on a child's ability to perceive and manipulate sounds in spoken words. Phonemic awareness includes being able to think of words that rhyme; perceiving that some words have the same or very similar sounds at the beginning, middle, and end; and being able to segment and blend sounds in spoken words. A further explanation of phonemic awareness follows in a subsequent discussion.

3. ***Is Clear and Direct.*** Good teachers explain exactly what they mean, while some phonics programs appear confusing and ambiguous. Some years ago, debate raged about whether a phoneme, or letter-sound, had any existence outside of the spoken word. Teachers and programs who were influenced by this argument hesitated to pronounce any sounds in isolation, for example never explaining that *b* produced the /b/ sound at the beginning of words such as *box, bear,* or *bed.* Of course, we want to avoid inaccurate pronunciations such as "buh-eh-duh" for *b-e-d,* but more harm is done when we beat around the bush and never directly show at least the common and predictable consonant sounds.

4. ***Is Integrated into a Total Reading Program.*** Phonics instruction should not dominate, but instead should complement, the reading instruction children receive. The majority of time should be spent in reading real texts, discussing them, acting them out, writing about them, and interpreting them. Phonics instruction should spring from the words that children need to read in real texts, not from a preset hierarchy of skills or a scope-and-sequence chart. Stahl suggests that a *maximum* of 25 percent of instructional time be spent on phonics. On many days, even this will be excessive. In addition, the phonics skills that are taught should be directly applicable in the text being read at that time. A criticism of many basal phonics strands is that the skill being presented has only limited application in the accompanying story. Trachtenburg (1990) suggests using high-quality children's literature that features a particular phonic pattern to illustrate and practice the pattern, for example using *The Cat in the Hat* and *Angus and the Cat* to illustrate the short-*a* pattern. A fuller description of children's literature/phonics connections follows in a subsequent section.

5. ***Focuses on Reading Words, Not Learning Rules.*** Effective readers use patterns and words they already know that are similar, rather than phonics rules, when they decode. Most teachers already know that rules have so many exceptions that they are rarely useful, yet many phonics programs continue to stress them as though they were "golden rules." If a child can't decode *rake*, it is more helpful to point out that it has the same pattern as *make* and *take* than to cite the "silent *e* makes the vowel long" rule. Many poor readers can recite phonics rules fluently but cannot apply them in reading.

6. ***May Include Onsets and Rimes.*** Onsets, or beginning sounds, and rimes, or the part of the word or syllable from the vowel onward, have long been taught under the more common name of "word families." Teaching children to compare words using onsets and rimes helps them to internalize patterns and use known words, such as

make and *take* in the previous example, to decode the unfamiliar *rake*. It is certainly more productive than having children sound out letters in isolation.

7. ***May Include Invented Spelling Practice.*** It has been widely recognized that when children are encouraged to invent spellings for unfamiliar words that they write, using the sounds in the words as they are pronounced, they practice decoding strategies within the context of real language use. Encouraging invented spelling has become a widely used and welcome aspect of primary literacy instruction.

8. ***May Include Categorization Practice Such as Word Sorting.*** The practice of word sorting is a series of exercises in which children group together words with common phonic features, such as beginning consonants, phonogram patterns, and other spelling dynamics. Word sorting encourages students to study the words they know and abstract features from them that they can then use to read and spell words that they do not know. Word sorting was reviewed extensively in Chapter 6 and is given book-length treatment in a book by Bear et al. (1996).

9. ***Focuses Attention on the Internal Structure of Words.*** Good phonics instruction helps children to see and use patterns in words. Whether they use individual letter sounds, similar words with the same rime, or invented spelling, children are encouraged to look closely at the patterns in words. We learn to read and spell not word by word, but pattern by pattern.

10. ***Develops Automaticity in Word Recognition.*** The purpose of all phonics instruction is not to be able to sound out words or bark at print, but to be able to quickly and accurately "unlock" familiar words so that the reader's attention may be reserved for understanding and enjoying what is read. Strict decoding emphasis programs of the past, such as DISTAR, encouraged children to learn to decode at the expense of comprehension; they failed because they created "word-callers" rather than effective readers. Effective phonics instruction today encourages automaticity (LaBerge and Samuels, 1974) in word recognition so that the mind may be freed or comprehension (Perfetti and Zhang, 1996). That is what it is all for.

Assessing Decoding Ability

Most often, children's decoding ability is assessed by asking them to decode nonsense words that are similar to real words, such as *dap, rike, faught,* and *blunch.* Children must use decoding strategies (not memory or context) to pronounce pseudo-words, and such tests have been shown in research to identify children with potential problems in word recognition (see, for instance, Torgesen et al., 1987).

Nonetheless, teachers are cautioned against using nonsense words in teaching, since we are trying to help children make sense of the act of reading and apply sense-making strategies when they encounter unfamiliar words. Cunningham (1990) points out that many children are confused by such a task and attempt to read nonsense words as real words, convinced that their teachers would never ask them to read something that makes no sense. Cunningham suggested an alternative to nonsense word decoding assessments called *the Names Test* (see Figs. 7.5 and 7.6), a list of first and last names of fictitious children.

THE NAMES TEST

Jay Conway	Wendy Swain
Tim Cornell	Glen Spencer
Chuck Hoke	Fred Sherwood
Yolanda Clark	Flo Thornton
Kimberly Blake	Dee Skidmore
Roberta Slade	Grace Brewster
Homer Preston	Ned Westmoreland
Gus Quincy	Ron Smitherman
Cindy Sampson	Troy Whitlock
Chester Wright	Vance Middleton
Ginger Yale	Zane Anderson
Patrick Tweed	Bernard Pendergraph
Stanley Shaw	

FIGURE 7.5 The Names Test

FIGURE 7.6 Procedures for Administering and Scoring the Names Test

Preparing the Instrument
1. Type or print legibly the 25 names on a sheet of paper or card stock. Make sure the print size is appropriate for the age or grade level of the students being tested.
2. For students who might perceive reading an entire list of names as being too formidable, type or print the names on index cards, so they can be read individually.
3. Prepare a protocol (scoring) sheet. Do this by typing the list of names in a column and following each name with a blank line to be used for recording a student's responses.

Administering the Names Test
1. Administer the Names Test individually. Select a quiet, distraction-free location.
2. Explain to the student that she or he is to pretend to be a teacher who must read a list of names of students in the class. Direct the student to read the names as if taking attendance.
3. Have the student read the entire list. Inform the student that you will not be able to help with difficult names, and encourage him or her to "make a guess if you are not sure." This way you will have sufficient responses for analysis.
4. Write a check on the protocol sheet for each name read correctly. Write phonetic spellings for names that are mispronounced.

Scoring and Interpreting the Names Test
1. Count a word correct if all syllables are pronounced correctly regardless of where the student places the accent. For example, either Yó/lan/da or Yo/lan´/da would be acceptable.
2. For words where the vowel pronunciation depends on which syllable the consonant is placed with, count them correct for either pronunciation. For example, either Ho/mer or Hom/er would be acceptable.
3. Count the number of names read correctly, and analyze those mispronounced, looking for patterns indicative of decoding strengths and weaknesses.

Using Context

In addition to rapid, accurate decoding, good readers use the context of an unfamiliar word to help figure it out. Most words have meaning in isolation, but some have no real meaning, only a function in sentences; who can define *the*, for example? Many other words, including some of the most frequently occurring words, have many meanings, and only sentence context helps us to choose the right one; for example, there are at least six different meanings for *run:* a rapid gait, a tear in a stocking, a jogger's exercise routine, a small creek, a sequence of events, and a computer operation. Sentences have more meaning than the sum of the meanings of their component words. For example, even if you know what *time, a, saves, stitch, in,* and *nine* mean, it is only when they are combined in a sentence, *A stitch in time saves nine,* that comprehension can occur. Sentences have meanings beyond the meanings of individual words; paragraphs and larger units of text have meanings beyond that of individual sentences. In language, the whole is indeed more than the sum of its parts.

Using these larger meanings to help make "educated guesses" about what an unfamiliar word might be involves using context as a word recognition strategy. It requires a reader to ask the mental question "What would make sense here?" Several strategies may be taught to help students use context effectively.

Cloze procedures were described in Chapter 3 as a means of identifying students' reading levels in relation to a particular text. They are also helpful teaching tools for helping students to use context. To complete a cloze passage, students must think along with the author, so to speak, using prior information, the meaning suggested by the entire passage, and grammatical and meaning clues provided by the words preceding and following the omitted words. Systematic practice with cloze procedures helps readers to become sensitive to "context clues" and use them when reading.

For teaching, it is not necessary to delete every fifth word as you do when making a cloze passage for assessment. It might be better to delete fewer words and leave more of the text intact. Particular types of words, such as pronouns or verbs, could be deleted to highlight their function. Allow students to insert their best guesses, then discuss their choices. Discussion should guide students to consider how several alternatives might make good sense in one instance, while only one possible choice would make sense in another instance, and how different choices can lead to subtle but important changes in meaning. Cloze passages should be accompanied by discussion; their effectiveness is reduced if they are used as worksheets to be completed individually. Older students or more fluent readers may use text they have not read before, then compare their efforts to the original text. Younger students or less fluent readers might be more comfortable, and more successful, with text that they have read or heard before, such as dictated stories, predictable books, and familiar rhymes.

Confirming from text involves covering part of the text as it is read, predicting what might come next, then uncovering the hidden portions and proceeding. Whole words, parts of words following an initial letter, word groups, or phrases may be covered, depending on what cues you want your students to use as they read the passage. Big books and stories that are put on transparencies or chart tablets work best for this activity.

If you are using a transparency, use a paper or tag board strip to cover part of the text, have students read up to the covered part (and even a bit beyond it, in some cases), and ask them to predict what might come next. If you have covered a whole word, you might now uncover the initial letter or letters and have them predict again. Then slide the strip back and continue reading. At the end of the sentence, have students tell what clues they used to help them guess. If you are using a big book or chart tablet, words can be covered with small notepapers with a sticky strip on the reverse, and phrases or lines with a tag board strip can be held in place with paper clips. Keep the activity moving so that students don't get bogged down, and don't cover so many words so that context is lost. It is better to do a little of this activity fairly often than to do it infrequently and drag it out too long.

Approaching Word Attack Strategically

Students read many words every day that they must come to either recognize immediately or figure out through some kind of analysis. One team of researchers put the number of different words students will encounter by ninth grade in their school reading at 88,500 (Nagy and Anderson, 1984). Since more and more of those words are encountered when students are reading independently, the average students must identify more than a dozen new words every day. Students need to become *strategic* in their word recognition, which means both that they must be disposed to solve the problem of unlocking words and that they must possess the strategies for doing so.

David Cooper (1993) arrived at a set of six strategies that can be taught to students explicitly. The number of the strategies can be reduced and their working simplified when they are used at lower grade levels.

1. When you come to a word you do not know, read to the end of the sentence or paragraph and decide whether the word is important to your understanding. If it is unimportant, read on.
2. If the word is important, reread the sentence or paragraph containing the word. Try context to infer the meaning.
3. If context doesn't help, look for base words, prefixes, or suffixes that you recognize.
4. Use what you know about phonics to try to pronounce the word. Is it a word you have heard?
5. If you still don't know the word, use the dictionary or ask someone for help.
6. Once you think you know the meaning, reread the text to be sure it makes sense. (p. 202)

Figure 7.7 shows a simplified version of these strategies for primary-grade students.

BE A WORD DETECTIVE

When I Come to a Word That Causes Me Trouble...

1. I should read on to the end of the sentence or paragraph.

2. Look for word parts I know.

3. Try to figure it out from the letter sounds.

4. Ask someone or look it up in the dictionary.

FIGURE 7.7   Primary-Grade Strategy Poster for Inferring Word Meanings

DEVELOPING READING COMPREHENSION

Throughout this book, we have noted that comprehension is an active process of making meaning. Good comprehenders summon up their prior knowledge about the topic of a reading, they ask questions about the topic before and during the reading, they make appropriate inferences when ideas are not explicitly stated, they find main ideas, they summarize, and they make mental images from the words in the text. Comprehension, in this view, requires an active reader, one who is confident and curious enough to bring his or her own ideas to the reading and to question the ideas in the text.

However, in a decade-long study of what happens when elementary-grade students read textbooks, Beck and McKeown (1994) did not find many such readers. Traditional teaching required students to read and later answer factual questions about what they had read—questions that are more often intended to prove that they had understood the reading than to draw out their thinking about the subject matter. Too many students approached comprehension passively, as if comprehension worked by passively ingesting ideas from the text.

Since, as Isabel Beck's work suggests, the teacher's approach influences what students do when they attempt to comprehend, it is critically important that the instruction teachers provide students guide them into cognitive activities that bear fruit. In this section, we will describe several strategies for instruction that have been tested by research and practice.

As we did in Chapter 6, we will divide our treatment of comprehension into three phases, relating to what should be done before, during, and after a reading. We call these the phases of *exploration, inquiry,* and *reflection,* respectively.

For the First Phase: Exploration

Exploration, it will be remembered, is the phase in which students inspect a text, remind themselves what they already know about it, raise questions or make predictions about what they will find out from reading it, and set purposes for their reading.

Developing Prior Knowledge

Prior knowledge is what we already know or have experienced, directly or vicariously, that we bring to the act of reading. When we can somehow relate what we read to our prior knowledge, we understand and remember more clearly. When we lack prior knowledge to relate to what we read, chances are that we will become confused, misunderstand, and forget what we read. In this situation, we might also become disinterested in what we are reading, calling it boring or dull. And if our need is great to remember it, as in preparation for a test, we might resort to inefficient strategies such memorizing. Helping students to develop, organize, and become aware of their prior knowledge is critical to improving their reading comprehension.

But two problems are associated with prior knowledge. One is that we might lack sufficient prior knowledge about a topic, not having heard or read of it before. A second problem is that much of our prior knowledge about a given topic might not be readily accessible; it has been buried, so to speak, under other information, and we can't summon it up and think about it readily. Because we can't bring it to mind immediately, we think we've forgotten it or never had it. Activities that develop prior knowledge center on helping students to establish some basis for new information and helping them to remember and organize prior knowledge that is not readily accessible.

Webbing

A simple way to help students begin to recall prior knowledge and form relationships is to use webbing, an exercise in which the teacher writes a topic or term on the board, students offer terms or phrases that might be related, and the teacher draws lines connecting associated terms with each other. In the following reading, terms and relationships are noted, and the web may be revised to reflect new information acquired. The webbing exercise serves to help students remember old information related to the reading and to form expectations about what they will be reading.

For example, let's say that Ms. Brown, a fourth-grade teacher, plans to have her students read a nonfiction basal selection about how museums are organized and the jobs museum workers perform. She suspects that some of the students have never visited a museum and that the topic is relatively unfamiliar to many of them. She begins, then, with a web to explore with them what they already know.

First she writes *museum* on the board and begins a *brainstorming whip,* in which every student in turn offers a word or phrase related in some way to *museum.* Because some students look apprehensive, she suggests some questions to help get them started:

What is a museum for?

What are the names of some museums?

What might be in them?

What work do people do in museums?

As each student responds, Ms. Brown writes the response on the board around the key word. Because this is brainstorming, all responses are accepted without comment or evaluation. She notices that the first few responses appear to remind the others of things they might have forgotten and that many appear excited as their turn nears. After everyone has responded once, volunteers might offer other suggestions until their information begins to wane. Then she reads over all the suggestions from the board.

The next step is to help students organize this seemingly random collection of terms into categories. One way Ms. Brown could do this is to use different colors of chalk to draw connecting lines, but because there are a lot of items on the board, this might not help to clarify. So she selects one term, writes it below the web, and says, "What other words go with this one?" Items are checked off and listed in categories, with students explaining why these items go together. These categories resulted:

Students then suggest names for these categories: things in museums, museum workers, jobs in museums, and names of museums. Ms. Brown then says, "We're going to read an article about how museums are organized and what kinds of work must be done. As you read, watch for mention of the names of famous museums, their collections, and museum workers' jobs. Let's see which of the things we mentioned are in the article."

After the reading is completed, Ms. Brown leads her students in reinspecting the web, adding to the appropriate categories items from the article that the students had not mentioned and marking those not appearing in the article to look up in another source.

A webbing activity like this is effective for several reasons. One is that it encourages all students to draw on whatever prior knowledge they have, no matter how extensive or limited, and apply it to the reading task. Another is that hearing others' ideas often triggers a forgotten bit of information in another's mind, so all benefit from sharing of information. A third is that seemingly unrelated information is directly organized so that relationships are sought and explored. A fourth is that prereading participation fosters curiosity and gives readers something to watch for as they read, and a purpose for reading. A fifth is that the exercise helps the teacher to realize what prior knowledge, if any, students have on the topic before they begin reading.

Previewing

Another way to help students organize their prior knowledge and develop expectations about what they are going to read is to let them quickly preview a reading selection and predict what kinds of information they might find in it.

When students preview a reading selection, they do not begin to read it; rather, they scan each page, looking at illustrations and text features such as boldface print and headings. The time that is allowed for this is very short so that they can get an overall general idea of the content, just enough to begin to predict about specifics. Depending on the length of the selection, two minutes or less are usually sufficient. Previewing is effective with both fiction and nonfiction, as we will see in these examples.

Mr. Talbott works with a group of fifth-graders reading at a third-grade instructional level. He has selected a basal story for them to read and discuss that deals with events surrounding the celebration of the Chinese New Year. Because this holiday and Chinese-American customs in general are unfamiliar to his students, he uses previewing to help them form a basis for their reading. He tells the group to find the first and last pages of the story and then to look at the title and the pictures but not to begin reading yet. He gives them 30 seconds to do so, telling the group when to begin and stop. Then he asks them to close their books and tell him what they saw in the pictures. He lists all the responses on the board:

Chinese people
a parade
fireworks
people in costumes
people wearing masks

some kind of big snake or dragon
people inside a dragon suit
some children looking scared
people eating
a building with a funny roof

Then he asks, "What do you think is going on in this story? What could be happening?" Again he lists responses:

party
celebration
parade
holiday

Then he introduces some terms from the story and encourages predictions about what they might mean and how they might be related to the story: festival, calendar, temple, parade, and feast. The students' predictions begin to form around the idea that a Chinese holiday celebration is occurring in which people prepare special foods, observe religious customs, wear ceremonial clothing, and participate in a street procession with costumes and fireworks. From this basis of information, Mr. Talbott guides his students to reexamine the illustrations and predict what might happen in the story—for example, who might the children be who are pictured several times? Why might they be frightened in this picture? What might happen at the end?

At this point, the students have developed a good basis of information and expectation and are ready to begin reading. Their previewing has helped them to develop a context for the story's events, introduced some of the story's key vocabulary, and helped them to set purposes for their reading.

Ms. Niles works with older poor readers from several grades. Seven of her students must read an earth science selection on glacier formation, but prereading discussion reveals that both prior information and interest in the topic are lacking. She uses previewing to help overcome both problems.

First, she asks the group to tell what they already know about glaciers. Other than that they are made of ice, her question is met with shrugs and blank looks. "All right," she says, "you have exactly two minutes to look over these pages and find out as much as you can, and we'll see who is able to gather the most information. Sally and Becky, you look at headings and boldface print. Maurice and John, you look at maps. Sam and Daniel, you look for topic sentences at the beginnings of each major section. Jessica, you look at photographs and their captions. All set? Begin!"

Ms. Niles has adapted the previewing task to fit the special informational demands of this selection and has given each student a specific task. She has also used a team approach and introduced an element of competition to arouse the students' interest in the task. After two minutes of silent study, she asks each student or pair to report on the specified area and begins listing terms, topics, and descriptions on the board under general headings. She compliments each responder on the amount of information gathered, without designating any "winner." After a quick review of the lists on the board, the students begin to read the selection, armed with an array of facts, terms, and concepts they had not possessed before, as well as with some confidence that they can read the chapter successfully.

Previewing is an effective means of helping students to acquire some prereading information about topics of which they know little beforehand and set some expectations about the text that they can compare to what the selection conveys. The previewing time should be kept short, and the discussion period should be conducted in an accepting, encouraging manner. Reading should begin when interest is aroused and some basis for reading has been established.

Developing Prediction

Closely related to the topic of prior knowledge is the process of prediction, in which students compare what they already know or remember to what they think they are going to read. Prediction requires that students relate their prior knowledge to the reading task at hand and form expectations that they will apply to the reading. Thus, prediction forms the connection between prior knowledge and the new information coming in.

For the Phase of Inquiry

Inquiry is the phase of reading and finding out.

DRTA: Active Reading of Fiction

The directed reading-thinking activity (DRTA) is a guided group discussion activity that focuses on the formation and testing of prereading predictions. In essence, it is a set of procedures for guiding prereading and postreading discussion. In a DRTA, children develop critical reading and thinking by predicting possible story events and outcomes, then reading to confirm or disprove their hypotheses. As described by Stauffer (1975), in a DRTA, the students form a set of purposes for reading, processing ideas, and testing answers by taking part in a predict-read-prove cycle. The teacher *activates thought* by asking, "What do you think?"; *agitates thought* by asking, "Why do you think so?"; and *requires evidence* by asking, "How can you prove it?" (Stauffer, 1975, p. 37). The DRTA format helps students to read more critically and with improved comprehension because it engages them in this process of fluent reading in a structured fashion, slowing down and making concrete the phases of the prediction process.

Students might be asked to form tentative hypotheses about a story from the title, cover art, or first illustration. They might be asked to look at other illustrations or to read the first sentence, paragraph, or page. They are asked to predict what might happen in the story and how it might end up and to justify their predictions on the basis of what they have seen, read, and already know or believe. At preselected points in the story, they are asked to stop reading, review predictions and change them if necessary, form new predictions about upcoming material, and continue reading. Predictions might be recorded on the board to aid in recalling them later. Predictions that are disproved by later story events or that students no longer think are likely may be erased or crossed out. Students are continually asked to justify their positions on the basis of what they have already read. They may reread orally to back up their points. The predict-read-prove cycle continues through the story; as students get closer to the end, their predictions become more convergent as more and more of the story is revealed. At the story's end, predictions and clues may be reviewed, or other kinds of follow-up questions may be asked.

K-W-L: Active Reading of Nonfiction

K-W-L stands for the three questions readers should ask themselves as they read a nonfiction selection: "What do I *KNOW*? What do I *WANT* to learn? What did I *LEARN* from this?" The first two questions are asked before reading; the third is asked after the reading. They correspond to the mental operations of accessing prior information, determining reading purposes, and recalling information (Ogle, 1986). The procedure has three steps.

1. **Step K:** Before reading, the teacher guides students in brainstorming what they already know about the topic of the reading. The teacher records this information on the board or on a transparency. After the brainstorming, students are asked to use their prior information to predict what general types or categories of information they might expect to encounter when they read the passage. For example, if the topic is Columbus's voyage to the New World and students have recalled prior information about three ships, cramped quarters, and inadequate food, the teacher might lead them to identify categories of information such as "how they got there," "what the ships were like," and "what they ate and drank on the voyage." Since students often find this step difficult, the teacher needs to model and demonstrate this step numerous times until students begin to be able to perceive categories themselves.

2. **Step W:** As students complete the first step, disagreements and uncertainties will arise. These form the basis of the "What do I want to learn?" step. The teacher's role here is to highlight disagreements and gaps in prior information, raising questions that will help students to focus on the new information they will encounter. Students should write down the specific questions they want to have answered, thus making a personal commitment to the information. Students might be given a K-W-L worksheet to use for notetaking, with the three questions as headings. An example of a completed worksheet is shown in Figure 7.8.

3. **Step L:** After completing the reading, whether they read the whole article or a portion of it, students should write down the information they recall from the passage. They should check their written questions to see whether they found answers to them; some questions might require further reading or checking other sources. The teacher guides a discussion of the questions generated and the answers students found, including areas of disagreement; students refer to the passage to resolve disputes.

Carr and Ogle (1987) developed K-W-L Plus, an enhanced K-W-L with two additional steps for secondary students. After the reading and the use of the

Topic: _Crocodiles_

K	W	L
What We Know	What We Want to Find Out	What We Learned

K — What We Know

eats people
eats meat
reptile
lays eggs
about 6 feet long
leaves its babies
solitary
vicious
has about 6 babies

W — What We Want to Find Out

do they eat people?
What do they eat?
How do they get their food?
How big are they?
How does it have its babies?
How many babies at one time?

L — What We Learned

Do eat people
Also eat bugs, fish, ducks, birds, antelope
Actively hunt with others
Herds fish with tail
Shares its food
Live in groups
6–15 feet long
most common 6–8 feet
female digs a nest
use same nest year after year
guards the nest
helps babies dig out
helps babies break shell
father crocodile helps
can help break eggs
protects babies for 12 weeks

Categories of Information:

Diet
Size

Getting Food
Reproduction
Family Life

FIGURE 7.8 K-W-L Worksheet

three steps, students engage in *concept mapping* and *summarizing*. A *concept map* is a graphic organizer that allows students to group pieces of information gleaned from the text, helping students to see associations and relationships among various pieces of information. This process is considered important because many students, particularly poor readers, acquire information from text only as isolated facts, failing to organize them into any coherent units of meaning.

Practice in organizing information into main ideas or topics and supporting details improves overall comprehension. An example of a concept map is shown in Figure 7.9. The concept map is then used as the organizer for a written summary, which requires students to reflect on information gleaned and express it in their own words in a logical and readable form. Practice in *summarizing* helps students to organize and include all important information from a text, not just that information they found most memorable or interesting.

Questioning the Author: Close Reading for Comprehension

Students also viewed the text as infallible, even when the text did not state ideas clearly or when it asked for prior knowledge that the students were not likely to have. Summing up their findings, McKeown et al. (1996) concluded that "text-books . . . are not serving students well [and] students often react to inadequate text presentations by developing a view of themselves as inadequate readers" (p. 97).

Beck et al. (1997) saw breakdowns at each point in the process of comprehension: The students often did not have sufficient prior knowledge, did not make necessary inferences, did not come away with important ideas.

Beck et al. (1997) developed a comprehensive teaching strategy that would, first, reorient the students' thinking about texts and, second, lead them into using the kinds of thinking processes needed to understand the texts. They call their strategy *questioning the author*, or QtA (Beck et al., 1997).

Preparing for a QtA Lesson   The teacher prepares for a QtA lesson by deciding on a portion of text that can support intense questioning for a reasonable period of time, perhaps twenty to thirty minutes. Then the teacher follows three steps:

1. Reading through the text in advance and identifying the major understandings that the students should engage in this text;
2. Planning stopping points in the text that occur often enough to give adequate attention to the important ideas and inferences in the passage.
3. Planning the *queries* (probing questions) to be asked at each stopping point (These are tentative plans only. The teacher will take his or her cue for the actual queries from the students' own comments and questions.)

Conducting a QtA Lesson   The lesson proceeds in two stages:

1. ***Prepare the Students' Attitudes.*** The teacher begins the lesson by discussing the idea of authorship and explaining that texts are written by human beings who are not perfect people and their texts are not perfect works. Things might be unclear. Ideas might have been left out. Things might be hinted at but not stated. It is the readers' job to *question the author*. It might help to remind the students of what happens in a writing workshop (Calkins, 1986; Graves, 1982; Temple et al., 1992). When we listen to a classmate sharing her writing in a writing workshop, we know that sometimes she will mention something without telling us enough about it or even describe some things inaccurately. In a writing workshop, we question the

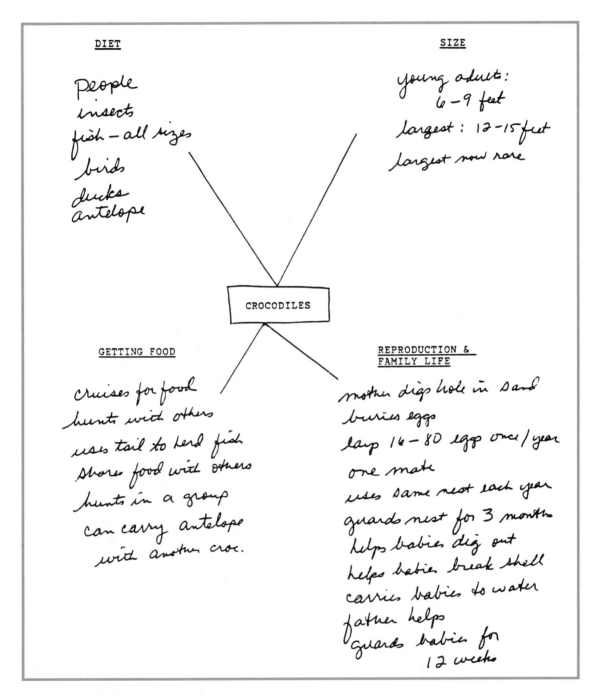

DIET

People
insects
fish – all sizes
birds
ducks
antelope

SIZE

young adult:
    6 – 9 feet
largest : 12 – 15 feet
largest now rare

CROCODILES

GETTING FOOD

cruises for food
hunts with others
uses tail to herd fish
shares food with others
hunts in a group
can carry antelope
    with another croc.

REPRODUCTION &
FAMILY LIFE

mother digs hole in sand
buries eggs
lays 16 – 80 eggs once/year
one mate
uses same nest each year
guards nest for 3 months
helps babies dig out
helps babies break shell
carries babies to water
father helps
guards babies for
    12 weeks

FIGURE 7.9   K-W-L Plus Concept Map

SAMPLE QUERIES FOR QUESTIONING THE AUTHOR

BOX 7.2

INITIATING QUERIES

What is the author trying to say here?
What is the author's message?
What is the author talking about?

FOLLOW-UP QUERIES

So what does the author mean right here?
Did the author explain that clearly?
Does that make sense with what the author told us before?
How does that connect with what the author has told us here?
But does the author tell us why?
Why do you think the author tells us that now?

NARRATIVE QUERIES

How do you think things look for the character now?
How does the author let you know that something has changed?
How has the author settled that?
Given what the author has already told us about this character, what do you think he [the character] is up to?

Source: From Beck et al., 1997. Used by permission.

author so that we can understand the writing better and also to help the author make the writing clearer. In a QtA session, students also question the author—but since the author isn't present in the classroom, the class will have to answer for the author.

2. ***Raise Queries about the Text.*** Next, the teacher has the students read a small portion of the text. When they stop, the teacher poses a query about what they have read. The kinds of queries the teacher might use are shown in Box 7.2.

The Role of the Teacher in QtA   The earlier research by Beck, McKeown, and their colleagues suggested that the kinds of tasks teachers set and the kinds of questions they ask have a strong influence on how students approach the cognitive activity of comprehension. This influence can lead students in productive directions, or it can lead them toward passive and inefficient practices.

In QtA, the teacher is knowledgeable about what comprehension is and how it should be approached. The teacher understands that comprehension requires activity on the part of the students, so he or she conducts discussions that require students to think and construct meaning. The teacher understands the difference between important ideas and details, so, in the words of McKeown and Beck (1996),

> he asks questions that focus . . . on meaning rather than on locating text information; for example, asking, "What did Tony mean when he said that to his brother?" rather than simply "What did Tony say to his brother?" (p. 114)

An Example of a QtA Discussion Here a class is discussing a single sentence from *Ben and Me* (Lawson, 1939). The sentence, which is narrated by a fictitious mouse named Amos, reads, "This question of the nature of lightning so preyed upon his mind that he was finally driven to an act of deceit that caused the first and only rift in our long friendship."

TEACHER: What's the author trying to say about Ben and Amos?

TEMIKA: That their friendship was breaking up.

TEACHER: Their friendship was breaking up? OK, let's hang on to that. What do you think, April?

APRIL: I agree with the part that their friendship did break up, but, um, I think that they got back together because when you were reading um, further, it said that he was enjoying the mouse.

ALVIS: I think that um, Amos is just, Amos is just lying because in the story it said if they weren't good friends, why would um, um, Ben build a um, kite for, build a kite for him so he could have fun?

TEACHER: OK, so Alvis is telling us that, why would Ben go to all that trouble and build that beautiful kite if they weren't friends? A lot of people agreed that their friendship is broken up. Alvis doesn't think their friendship is broken up. Can somebody help me out? What's the author want us to figure out here? (McKeown & Beck, 1996, p. 110)

Reciprocal Teaching

Reciprocal teaching (Brown et al., 1984) is a method for demonstrating and developing reading comprehension in a group setting. The teacher models a systematic way of approaching a passage by using a sequence of comprehension processes: summarizing, questioning, clarifying, and predicting. After the teacher models these processes in four steps, students take turns following the same steps and leading the others in discussing the passage read. This procedure is useful with any kind of text; it is particularly useful with nonfiction, which often contains a great many facts and pieces of new information. Here are the steps in using reciprocal teaching:

1. The teacher divides the passage to be read into fairly short sections; depending on the total length of the selection, one or two paragraphs at a time might be sufficient. For long selections such as whole chapters, long chapter sections, and longer stories, several pages might be better.

Or the teacher might wish to start the procedure with short sections, then make them longer as the reading progresses.

2. The teacher asks everyone to read the passage silently. To avoid having some students waiting for slower readers, the teacher should assign the reading before the activity begins. In this case, all students should quickly reexamine and review the passage before the discussion begins.

3. After the reading is completed, the teacher models the comprehension process by following these four steps:

    a. *Summarize* the section in one or a few sentences.

    b. *Ask* the group one or two good questions, avoiding picky details.

    c. Identify a difficult part of the passage and *clarify* it by explaining, giving examples, drawing analogies, or making other clarifying statements.

    d. *Predict* what the next section might be about or what might be learned from it.

4. The teacher should repeat steps 1 through 3 until the pattern is familiar to all students. Afterward, he or she can take turns leading the discussion steps previously mentioned: teacher-student-teacher-student or teacher-student-student. The teacher modeling and continued teacher involvement is critical to the students' success with the procedure.

Here is an example of how a teacher might use reciprocal teaching with a nonfiction passage: Ms. Brown has chosen an article about penguins from a nature magazine to supplement a science lesson with her fifth-graders. The article is three pages long, with lavish illustrations, so she divides the reading into passages of several paragraphs each. First, she distributes copies of the article with the stopping points marked on them. (If she were using a textbook, she would have each student locate the stopping point and mark it with a strip of paper across the page.) She directs students to read the first three paragraphs, which contain general information about penguins' habitat, habits, and diet. Then she models the use of the comprehension steps in this way:

First, I'll summarize this passage. In these paragraphs, we read that penguins are large birds that are unusual because they do not fly, but they are excellent swimmers. Their wings are specially shaped like flippers to help them swim very fast and over long distances. They live in icy frozen areas of the world where there is little or no plant life. They live on a diet of fish.

I would ask these questions about these paragraphs:

In what ways do we know penguins are different from other birds? (Students answer that they do not fly, they swim very skillfully, they live in icy places where there are no plants.)

- In what ways do you think penguins are like other birds? (Students answer that they have wings, other kinds of birds also eat fish, they lay eggs.)
- In what ways might their environment affect how they survive? (Students discuss the lack of plant life for making nests, the dangers of cold.)

I thought that the paragraph telling about their environment was a little difficult. The passage used some difficult words like *barren, antarctic,* and *ice floes* which might need discussion. Let's write these on the board and discuss what each one means." (Discussion follows about the meaning of these terms; one student gets a dictionary, and they refer to it.)

In the paragraphs to follow, I predict that we will find out more about how penguins adapt to extreme cold temperatures and find out how they raise their young in this environment.

Ms. Brown then directs students to read to the end of the next section, and she again models these four steps. After the class reads the third section, she calls on a volunteer to follow the same steps: summarize, ask a couple of good questions, clarify a part or term, and predict what might be upcoming. When the article is finished, students briefly discuss the main points of the article and evaluate how well they answered questions and followed the steps in the comprehension process.

Reciprocal teaching helps students learn how effective readers approach challenging texts and helps them to develop systematic ways of dealing with the information in them. After a number of repetitions, students might begin to internalize the comprehension steps and apply them independently to other text material.

Reciprocal Question-Answer Relationships

Successful readers use a variety of strategies to maximize their comprehension of text: They monitor their own comprehension, they self-question, they mentally summarize, and they seek relationships among ideas and facts presented in what they read. Unsuccessful readers often do not do these things; they tend to focus more on pronouncing the words and answering the teacher's questions, but they have few strategies for predicting what questions might be asked or for finding answers. Helfeldt and Henk (1990) propose an instructional strategy that helps at-risk readers use self-questioning to improve their comprehension. They call it reciprocal question-answer relationships (Re-QAR). The procedure consists of four general steps: explaining what the students will do, reciprocal questioning (wherein students and teacher take turns asking each other questions about a passage that was just read and answering each other's questions), categorizing questions and their answers according to where the information is found ("in the book" or "in my head"), and finally combining steps 2 and 3 by combining reciprocal questioning and categorizing the answers. In this step, students ask the teacher a question about the material, and the teacher answers it and categorizes the answer as "in the book" or "in my head"; then roles are reversed, with the teacher asking and the student or students answering and categorizing.

Helfeldt and Henk point out that ReQAR requires a high degree of student participation and that a lesson may span several days or longer. It would seem wise to break up both passages and steps into easily managed segments, at least until readers have had considerable practice with the procedure.

For the Phase of Reflection

Reflection is the phase of looking back on the meaning, questioning it, interpreting it, applying, or reexamining one's ideas about the topic in light of it.

Story Mapping

A good way to have students reflect on a story they have read is to have them construct a story map. A story map is a graphic representation of the parts of a story that shows how the story parts are related. Story maps "provide a practical means of helping children organize story content into coherent wholes" (Davis & McPherson, 1989, p. 232). "Story mapping," wrote Boyle and Peregoy (1990), " . . . helps children use story grammar for comprehension and composing" (p. 198). Story maps can be used to help readers perceive and understand plot structure and a variety of text structures such as literal and implied information, cause and effect, sequential ordering, and comparison and contrast (see Box 7.3). They

---

BOX 7.3 — STORY MAPS

Most texts that we call stories contain characteristic elements, called story structures, that occur in a particular sequence and serve to relate the story's characters and events in a logical order. These structures include the following:

1. *Setting:* a direct or implied statement that places the story in a physical, historical, or temporal context and introduces the protagonist.
2. *Initiating event:* an action, idea, or situation setting the story's plot in motion.
3. *Internal response:* the protagonist's response to the initiating event, including the setting of some goal and decision to pursue some course of action.
4. *Attempt**: an effort to achieve the goal.
5. *Outcome**: a direct result of the attempt.
6. *Consequence**: a result of the attempts to reach the goal and their outcomes. This may be an action, a change of behavior, or a state of affairs.

Some stories may have an optional final element:

7. *Reaction:* the protagonist's response to the consequence of the story's events, which may take the form of a change in opinion or belief, a statement of what has been learned, or a "moral."

Studies by Stein (1978) and others have shown that readers' understanding and recall of stories is influenced by their degree of experience reading or listening to stories and by the presence and order of story structures in what they read. Those who have heard or read a variety of stories in the past develop a set of expectations about how new stories will unfold. When what they read is organized logically and well structured, readers appear to compare what they expect to what they read, and they mentally reorganize and remember depending on those comparisons. When they have few expectations or when stories do not conform to their expectations, their understanding and memory of what they read decline.

*Sets of attempts, outcomes, and consequences make up episodes. A story may have many episodes or only one.

are similar to other graphic organizers such as structured overviews, story diagrams, and webs.

Figure 7.10 shows a sample story map for the Aesop's fable "The Crow and the Water Jug." This story map emphasizes the essential story structures described in the previous section: setting, initiating event or "problem," internal response or "goal," attempts and outcomes, and consequence or "resolution." Figure 7.11 shows another kind of story map, devised by Boyle and Peregoy (1990). In this model, the essential story grammar is boiled down to SOMEONE . . . WANTS . . . BUT . . . SO. Under each of these headings, the teacher or students list the character or characters and their problems, the goals, and means of achieving them. Other story maps might compare the advantages and disadvantages of some story action, the causes and effects of certain story events, or aspects of the various characters in a story.

To construct a story map, first think about the kinds of information or story structures you want to emphasize in your lesson. Make some notes about how this information might be arrayed. For example, comparison and contrast may be illustrated by listing items in two vertical columns; sequential order of story events might lend itself to a linear or timeline arrangement; details of characterization might be illustrated by a web-style arrangement of circles connected to a central circle with short lines; or the comparison of two stories or characters might be shown by two intersecting circles, sometimes called a *Venn diagram.* Examine your story map to make sure it emphasizes the logical flow of information. Don't make it too technical or detailed; emphasize just one pattern of organization at a time.

To teach with a story map, it is best to start with a straightforward, literal map of story events. Introduce it after the story has been read to help students recall and reconstruct what happened. When students are somewhat familiar with the story map and its use as a postreading activity, you might begin using story maps as a prereading organizer. Students might be given some minimal information and asked to predict story events or might be shown a partially completed story map and asked to predict what else might occur. Such prereading prediction has a positive effect on later recall and comprehension, just as it does with directed reading-thinking activities, K-W-L, and other related prediction strategies. After reading a portion of the story, the story map can be modified, and students can continue reading and changing the map until the story is completed. Story maps may also be used as a postreading activity, with students reconstructing a map individually or in cooperative learning groups; they may also complete partially completed maps, which Davis and McPherson (1989) call "macro cloze story maps."

Retelling

We know that retelling stories helps children to understand and remember stories and develop a sense of story. Retelling requires readers or listeners to organize information and make inferences about it based on text information and their own prior information by constructing a personal rendition of the text. Thus, retelling

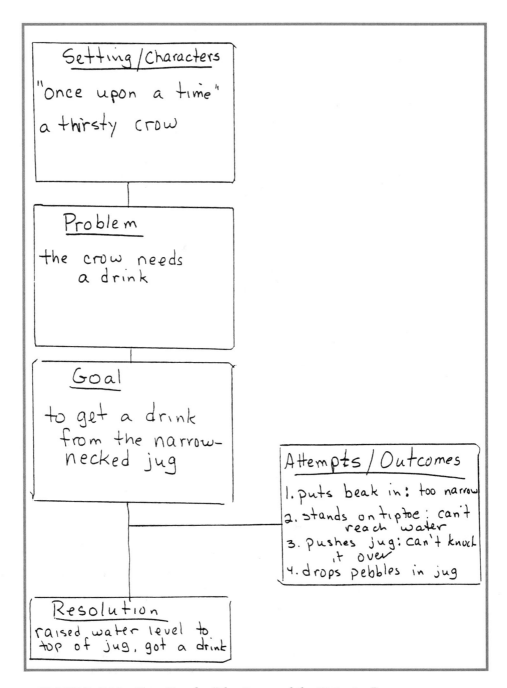

FIGURE 7.10   Story Map for "The Crow and the Water Jug"

focuses children's attention on relevant text information, sequences, and causes and effects. It requires that they organize that information into a coherent structure for retelling to another. Studies have shown that young children's story sense

SOMEONE	WANTS	BUT	SO
Little Red Hen	help to plant tend cut thresh grind bake The wheat	the other animals won't help her	she does it herself

FIGURE 7.11 **Story Map for "The Little Red Hen"**

and story comprehension are significantly improved by practice in retelling stories they have heard (Morrow, 1984, 1985, 1986; Pellegrini and Galda, 1982). Similarly, retelling has been shown to improve reading comprehension (Gambrell et al., 1985; Rose et al., 1984). You can use retelling strategies in your classroom to help all readers to improve their story comprehension.

According to Koskinen et al. (1988), in its simplest form, a retelling activity involves two students working together during direct instruction time or independent work time; one reads or listens to a portion of a text or a whole story and then teams up with a partner to retell the story. Since the listener's role is an important one and good listening is active, rather than passive, the listener is asked to provide helpful questions or comments to the teller and may be asked to complete a retelling reaction sheet.

Before students begin this activity, you need to model it so that students will have a clear understanding of what they are to do and why they are doing it. First, explain simply and clearly why retelling is a useful activity. Depending on the age of your students, you might say something like, "Retelling a story you have read or listened to helps you remember stories and helps you check to see if you understand what you have read or heard. It also helps you to learn to be a good storyteller. I will show you what to do to practice retelling stories and how to be a helpful listening partner. Then you will have time to practice retelling with a partner."

Model retelling by announcing to students what you are going to do: "I'm going to read a short passage from this story. Then I'm going to retell it to you without looking at the story. I'm going to try to include all the important ideas and information. As I read it, listen for the important ideas."

Next, read aloud a fairly short passage from a story or nonfiction text or a short, complete story. Afterward, retell the story or passage in a few sentences, including the most important information, sequences, and the like. Then ask students for feedback on the retelling by asking them whether you included all the important ideas, accepting their contributions or suggestions. Immediately after the modeling, students can read a short passage from a basal reader, textbook, or other material that they all have. Guide them in group retelling by having volunteers retell to the group, using question prompts that are appropriate for the type of text with which they are dealing (see Figure 7.12).

When children seem to have the idea of retelling, which might be after more than one model and group practice, create opportunities for students to practice retelling to a partner. In this practice, one student silently reads a passage or text for retelling, then retells it to a partner. Both students need not have read the same material; if the partner has not read the story and has trouble understanding it from the retelling, this is a good indication to the student that more practice retelling is needed. This is an excellent opportunity for students to read and share trade books they are reading in class, and it provides another important way for you to work trade books into your reading instruction. Students might practice reading and retelling during independent work time or free reading time. They should do this regularly, several times a week.

FIGURE 7.12   Prompts for Encouraging Retelling

Narrative text

Who are the main characters?

When did the story take place?

Where did the story take place?

What important events happened in the story?

How did the story end?

Expository text

What is the topic of the selection?

What are the important ideas in the selection?

Source: From Patricia S. Koskinen, Linda B. Gambrell, Barbara A. Kapinus, and Betty S. Heathington. "Retelling: A Strategy for Enhancing Students' Reading Comprehension." *The Reading Teacher* 41, no. 9 (May 1988). Reprinted with permission of Patricia Koskinen and the International Reading Association.

Name _____ Date _____

I listened to _____

I chose one thing my partner did well. _____

He or she told about the characters. _____

He or she told about the setting. _____

He or she told about events in the story. _____

His or her story had a beginning. _____

His or her story had an ending. _____

I told my partner one thing that was good about his or her story.

_____

Source: Adapted from Patricia S. Koskinen, Linda B. Gambrell, Barbara A. Kapinus, and Betty S. Heathington. "Retelling: A Strategy for Enhancing Students' Reading Comprehension." *The Reading Teacher* 41, no. 9 (May 1988). Reprinted with permission of Patricia Koskinen and the International Reading Association.

FIGURE 7.13 **Example of a Retelling Reaction Sheet**

Retelling is more effective for both students involved if the listener has an active role. Good listening is active and responsive, not passive. The student who is the listening partner should have something to do besides just listen. With guided practice, the listening partner can learn how to ask helpful questions by using the prompts referred to in Figure 7.12 or by suggesting other important information that the teller omitted, if any. Students can also complete a retelling reaction guide, such as the one in Figure 7.13. This procedure focuses on positive responses rather than criticism, which is very important. Providing this task for listeners helps them to set a purpose for listening and helps keep them focused on the task. Giving students systematic, structured opportunities to talk about what they have read helps develop comprehension and oral expression skills and provides teachers yet another way to incorporate fiction and nonfiction trade books in their regular instruction program.

More strategies to be used in the *reflection phase* of comprehension instruction will be found in Chapter 8.

DEVELOPING LISTENING COMPREHENSION

Listening comprehension is related to reading ability in that students who are not yet fluent, mature readers can usually listen to and comprehend text that is read to them that they cannot yet read for themselves. The most common example of this is with emergent and beginning readers, who can listen to and understand a wide variety of materials but might not yet be able to read anything for themselves.

As students' reading abilities develop and their instructional levels go up, the gap between the instructional reading level and listening level might begin to close, and by the time they have become fluent, mature reader, there might be no difference between what they can listen to and what they can read successfully. For much of the time before a student has reached this zenith in reading development, however, there will be a gap between these two levels.

Experience is an important factor in listening comprehension. Even if all other things are equal, a student who has been read to and whose school and home environments are rich in oral language (regardless of dialect or language origins) has an advantage over the student who has not had this experience. In the same way, students who can read fairly effectively have a greater store of information, concepts, and vocabulary than illiterate students or very poor readers, and the first group's listening comprehension levels are likely to be higher.

A student's listening comprehension level is important because it shows us how closely his or her ability to understand written text approaches the demands of the student's grade level and gives us an indication of how much potential for reading improvement the student has at this point in time. We must remember that unlike IQ or other intelligence measures, the listening level is not fixed; as the student's reading ability improves and he or she reads more, the listening level also rises. Thus, progress today paves the way for more progress tomorrow.

The Interaction of Listening and Reading Comprehension

There are several typical patterns in listening comprehension and reading. One is that a student might have a below-grade-level listening level and an instructional reading level that matches it. Take, for example, Sam, a fourth-grader whose listening and instructional reading levels are both at second grade. This means that Sam is currently reading about as well as he is able to and that he lacks the verbal concepts and vocabulary to understand third- or fourth-grade text either by reading or by listening. Attempting to raise Sam's reading level without also developing his listening comprehension will likely result only in frustration, for he will be asked to do what is beyond his present capability. In Sam's case, listening comprehension must be fostered so that his reading ability can grow.

Another common pattern is exemplified by Elaine, also a fourth-grader. Elaine's instructional reading level is also second grade, but her listening comprehension level is fourth grade and even includes some fifth-grade text when the topic is something she knows about. Elaine is a poor reader in fourth grade, but she already has verbal concepts and vocabulary appropriate to other fourth-graders and text typical of that grade. Elaine needs to develop her reading ability so that it more closely approaches her present listening level, which indicates that she has the present potential to improve her reading significantly.

Other patterns that occur less often are equally important. One is exemplified by Sarah, a fifth-grader. Sarah's instructional level is only about third grade, but her listening level is at seventh. Sarah is a poor reader in fifth grade, but she has the verbal capacity to understand much more difficult text. In Sarah's case, this capacity far outstrips present performance, and she can benefit from intensive remediation. Her problems might lie in motivation, inappropriate instruction, or other factors that must be overcome. But she has the measured potential for at least grade-level reading achievement.

Consider, in contrast, the case of James, a ninth-grader in a remedial program. James is functionally nearly illiterate, with only a second-grade instructional level. His listening level is fourth grade. James might be classifiable as a slow learner; he is certainly verbally impoverished, and his illiteracy has kept his listening comprehension from developing. Still, because there is a gap between the two levels, he can improve his reading somewhat. And if he does, his listening comprehension is likely to increase also, which in turn will make possible further reading progress if James is motivated toward such improvement. In his case, both reading remediation and listening comprehension development are needed.

Strategies for Developing Listening Comprehension

The key to developing students' listening comprehension lies in immersion in a rich language environment and stimulation of their language. First and foremost, such students must be read to, regardless of their age. Reading to James in ninth grade is every bit as important to his literacy as reading to a primary grader, for it is by listening that all readers develop their first concepts about stories, a sense of how written language differs from talk, and a store of information to bring to reading. Students whose listening comprehension levels are below grade level should be read to daily from a wide variety of kinds of materials. Good literature that is appropriate for their age and written at a level they can understand should be a mainstay and should include nonfiction and poetry as well as fiction. Older students should also be read to from newspapers and magazines, since we want to encourage them to use these sources as well as books. Tapes can be used, but they are not as effective as live readers because tapes cannot monitor listeners' interest, stop to answer questions, or reread a part for emphasis. Taped readings should never be used as a substitute for live reading but are useful for additional practice.

A directed listening-thinking activity (DLTA) is a good alternative to straight reading aloud. A DLTA is similar to the DRTA discussed previously in this chapter, wherein students make predictions about upcoming story events or, in the case of nonfiction, assert what they already know about a topic before reading and compare their predictions and assertions to what the text says. The only difference between a DRTA and a DLTA is that in the latter, the material is read aloud to students. DLTAs are an effective means of monitoring listening comprehension and fostering interest in listening.

Immersion in a rich language environment also means that students should be actively engaged in oral discussions and conversations. They must be guided to do more than just answer questions, the most common form of classroom talk. They should also describe, summarize, persuade and argue, using as specific, vivid, and precise vocabulary as possible. Many of the typical composition activities that are suggested in reading and English books, such as making up stories, recounting real events and reminiscences, describing objects, persuading others to some action or belief, arguing for or against some course of action, and composing directions, are just as useful for oral language and listening development. Speaking and listening cannot be separated; they will develop together. Students with underdeveloped listening comprehension need daily experience with both.

Oral reading by students for other students can be useful, too, but must be used with care. All oral reading should be rehearsed and prepared by the reader beforehand. No one is served by listening to someone stumble through text. Material for oral reading should be read silently several times, then read aloud for practice before the final reading. Also, oral reading should be done for some purpose, not as an end in itself. Some material deserves to be read aloud, and enjoyment of it is enhanced by being effectively read: poetry, vivid descriptions, and good dialogue are examples. The purpose of oral reading should be to share and enhance such material, not just to practice reading aloud.

Again, we return to the point of teacher modeling. The teacher sets the tone and provides the model by which students judge what is useful and important. Without dominating activities, we must show students by our modeling what we want them to be able to do. We should prepare what we read aloud to the class so that our reading will be fluent and expressive. We should share portions of material we find appealing or especially effective with them and work to make our descriptions and summaries colorful and precise. We should exhibit interest in and curiosity about words and expressions and share with students interesting and unusual language in what we read. We should respond to students' efforts to use language more effectively with sincere interest, attention, and positive reinforcement. We should listen more to what they say than to how they say it, and we should respond first to their message.

The more direct experience with language students have, the more their language use will expand. The more it grows, the more their listening comprehension will improve. The more listening comprehension develops, the more they will be able to bring to reading, and thus their reading will improve. The roots of reading ability are buried deep in oral language, and we cannot overlook this foundation if we wish to help our students read better.

TIME SPENT READING

So far in this chapter, we have concentrated on methods and issues that are related to reading instruction: helping students to develop sight recognition of words, use word analysis strategies fluently and effectively, organize and apply prior knowledge to new information acquired from reading, and use a variety of reading processes and skills to become more fluent and comprehend better. It might be thought that effective reading lies in instruction, and indeed, good instruction is an absolute requirement in helping children grow as readers. In spite of all the instructional techniques we apply, however, there is another factor that is critical: To become a good reader, a child must spend a lot of time reading.

This point seems self-evident. But how much time do children actually spend reading? A number of research studies have been conducted in attempts to determine this, and the results of these studies are disturbing.

Walberg and Tsai (1984) studied the out-of-school reading behavior of 2,890 American 13-year-olds. They found that the median child in their sample read 7.2 minutes per day and that the median child reported reading on about one day out of five. Forty-four percent of the subjects in the study reported spending no time reading for enjoyment, while only 5 percent reported spending three hours or more. Not surprisingly, these researchers found that frequency and amount of reading were related to reading achievement.

The relationship between reading achievement and out-of-school reading time was also documented by Barr and Dreeben (1983) and Rosenshine and Stevens (1984). Anderson et al. (1988) studied the out-of-school reading time of 155 American fifth-graders. Average time spent reading books, magazines, and newspapers was fourteen minutes per day. Variance between groups of children was extreme; those who spent the most time reading read nearly five times as much as those near the mean and more than 200 times as much as those who spent the least time reading. Again, time spent reading and reading achievement were positively related.

From the results of their own and others' research, Anderson et al. (1988) concluded

> that the typical child in the middle grades reads less than 25 minutes a day out of school. The amount appears to be considerably less than this in the United States, maybe as little as 8–12 minutes per day when all types of reading material are included, and maybe as little as 4–5 minutes a day when only books are counted. The amount of reading is almost certainly much lower than many have supposed." (p. 299)

On the topic of book reading from the same research, Wilson et al. (1986) wrote, "The likely significance of our data on book reading, then, is that 50 percent of American fifth graders read from books for 4.6 minutes per day, or less. About 10 percent of the children we surveyed never read from a book the entire interval of our survey (8 weeks and 26 weeks)" (p. 77).

These findings and conclusions should shock us. They reveal, in these authors' words, "a bleak picture" of most children's voluntary reading habits (Wilson et al., 1986, p. 76). We already know that in spite of our instruction, children generally do not do very much reading of connected text in school; of the hours they spend in school, only a few minutes a day are usually spent actually reading text. Much of the reading time is spent instead listening to the teacher and others, waiting, filling in blanks, or reading single sentences on worksheets and other exercises. According to Allington and McGill-Franzen (1987) and Gaskins (1988), in a major study of poor readers' time on task in reading, poor readers spent "an alarming amount of time in unproductive ways" (Gaskins, 1988, p. 751). These researchers noted that it was "not uncommon" for teachers to allow five or ten minutes of reading group time to elapse before instruction began, to allow students to gather for reading group slowly, to prolong delays with disciplinary and managerial tasks, and to assign many pages of workbook or skills sheets during independent work time, reducing the amount of time poor readers could spend reading connected text. They also noted many instances of groups beginning reading with no introduction or anticipation activity, engaging in tedious oral round-robin reading with all but one student waiting their turns, early finishers waiting idly for others to finish, and over-lengthy "discussions" of story parts dominated by short-answer questions, so that students spent more time answering questions than reading.

Reading must be practiced for a student to become proficient at it, and far too many of our children do not read enough to develop their real potential. This begins to sound like the makings of an epidemic—and it is. The National Adult Literacy Survey (Kirsch et al., 1993) studied the reading and writing abilities of 26,000 adults and projected that 21 percent of the adults in the United States— more than 40 million people over the age of 16—had only rudimentary reading and writing skills: enough to pick out key facts in a brief newspaper article but not enough to draft a letter explaining what was wrong with a credit card bill. Fifty-seven million more people, or 27 percent of the population, could not handle long material that required more than low level inferences. Together, these two groups make up half of the adult U.S. population. Many factors contribute to this problem, of course, but the failure of so many students to develop a robust habit of reading must be a major one.

Now for some good news. If the amount of reading students do is so small, it should not be too hard to increase it significantly.

If teachers and librarians can persuade all parents of the importance of reading with their children, or of making sure that their children have books and space and twenty minutes a day in which to read them, we will have doubled the average child's time spent reading, according to the numbers from the Anderson, Wilson, and Fielding (1988) study.

In school, if we have children drop everything and read for an extra twenty minutes every school day, that, also will double their average reading time. But we can do more. Classes that read books and also engage in peer discussions and teacher-student conferences about the books have better attitudes toward reading and produce greater gains in reading achievement than do those that practice only sustained silent reading practices, according to one study (Manning and Manning, 1984). These results suggest that students should not just drop everything and read, but also share their thoughts about what they read.

Some teachers worry that devoting more time to reading and book talks will deprive children of time to learn the skills they need, but those teachers who have done so almost always find that their fears were not justified. Children seem to learn as much or more by reading as by being taught reading. Empirical data to back this up come from Collins (1980), who reported that in studies of matched classrooms in second through sixth grades, those students who did sustained silent reading in books moved faster through their basal programs than those who did not and showed no decline in spelling or English skills, even though as much as half an hour a day was given over to silent free reading.

Books can and should be used in all subject areas in every grade. It is particularly important, however, that students read real books as part of their ongoing reading or language arts instruction so that they may learn the habits of sustained attention and other real book-reading abilities and may develop lifelong reading habits, tastes, and attitudes.

SUMMARY

Corrective teaching is directed toward supporting a student's strengths while teaching and practicing skills and strategies the student needs. From diagnostic data, strengths and needs are identified and priorities are established. Instructional time is planned to fulfill priorities and provide instructional balance.

Readers develop *sight vocabulary* when they see the same words repeatedly in meaningful contexts. *Dictated stories* feature rereading until students achieve fluency and can identify individual words in and out of context. *Support reading* helps students to get through difficult text and reinforces word recognition. Support reading includes *echo-reading* and *choral-reading*. *Predictable books* are useful because the same words appear repeatedly and help to build readers' confidence.

Fluency contributes to comprehension and is developed when students *reread* material.

Word analysis strategies are needed when students do not recognize a word at sight. Although debate still rages over the role of phonics instruction in learning to read, a growing body of evidence suggests that good readers are able to use decoding strategies automatically and accurately during reading, thus freeing the mind for comprehension. It also suggests that all students learn letter-sound relationships as part of learning to read. Exemplary phonics instruction builds on what students already know about letters, sounds, and words, emphasizes phonemic awareness, is clear and direct, is integrated into a total reading program, focuses on reading words rather than learning rules, includes the use of onsets and rimes, focuses on the internal structure of words and develops automaticity in word recognition. *Phonemic awareness* is the ability to manipulate speech sounds in words; it contributes to the ability to rhyme and use phonics. Phonics instruction may be integrated with literature by using trade books that feature particular phonic patterns. Decoding ability may be assessed by using the *Names Test*. *Using context* is also an important word analysis strategy. *Cloze procedures* and *confirming* help students to develop facility with context. *Word sorting* helps students to apply phonic regularities by categorizing words sharing a similar word feature.

We divided our treatment of reading comprehension into three phases: *exploration, inquiry*, and *reflection*. In the *exploration phases*, we presented teaching strategies focusing on readers' use of *prior knowledge, prediction, webbing*, and *previewing*. For the *inquiry phase*, we presented the strategies of the *directed reading-thinking activities, K-W-L* and *K-W-L Plus*, and also *Reciprocal Teaching, Reciprocal Question-Answer Relationships*, and *Questioning the Author*. *Story mapping* and *retelling* were presented as activities for the *reflection phase*. (Many more strategies for this phase will be found in Chapter 8.)

Listening comprehension supports and promotes reading comprehension. The *listening level* provides an estimate of the reader's present potential for reading improvement. Means of developing students' listening comprehension include *reading to students, directed listening-thinking activities,* and *teacher modeling.*

Recent studies show that most students do little, if any, reading outside of school. Yet they also show a significant relationship between *time spent reading* and reading achievement. All students, especially poor readers, must increase their time spent reading; ways of doing so are discussed in this chapter.

REFERENCES

Adams, Marilyn Jager. *Beginning to Read: Thinking and Learning about Print.* Cambridge: MIT Press, 1990.

Allen, Roach Van. *Language Experiences in Communication.* Boston: Houghton Mifflin, 1976.

Allington, Richard L. "Fluency: The Neglected Reading Goal." *The Reading Teacher* 36, no. 6 (February 1983): 556–561.

Allington, Richard L. "Beginning to Read: A Critique by Literacy Professionals and a Response by Marilyn Jager Adams." *The Reading Teacher* 44, no. 6 (February 1991): 373.

Allington, Richard, and Anne McGill-Franzen. *A Study of the Whole-School Day Experience of Chapter I and Mainstreamed LD Students.* Final Report of Grant #G008630480, Office of Special Education Programs, Washington, DC: U.S. Department of Education, 1987.

Anderson, Richard C., Paul T. Wilson, and Linda G. Fielding. "Growth in Reading and How Children Spend Their Time Outside of School." *Reading Research Quarterly* 23, no. 3 (Summer 1988): 285–303.

Barr, Rebecca, and Robert Dreeben. *How Schools Work.* Chicago: The University of Chicago Press, 1983.

Bear, Donald, Marcia Invernizzi, Shane Templeton, and Francine Johnson. *Words Their Way.* Upper Saddle River, NJ: Merrill, 1996.

Beck, Isabel, Maragaret McKeown, and Linda Kucan. *Questioning the Author: An Approach for Enhancing Student Engagement with Text.* Newark, DE: International Reading Association, 1997.

Boyle, Owen, and Suzanne E. Peregoy. "Literacy Scaffolds: Strategies for First and Second Language Readers and Writers." *The Reading Teacher* 44, no. 3 (November 1990): 194–200.

Brown, Ann L., Annemarie Sullivan Palincsar, and Bonnie B. Armbruster. "Instructing Comprehension-Fostering Activities in Interactive Learning Situations. "In *Learning and Comprehension of Text,* ed. Heinz Mandl, Nancy L. Stein, and Tom Trabasso. Hillsdale, NJ: Lawrence Erlbaum, 1984.

Calkins, Lucy. *The Art of Teaching Writing.* Portsmouth, NH: Heinemann, 1986.

Carr, Eileen, and Donna M. Ogle. "K-W-L Plus: A Strategy for Comprehension and Summarization." *Journal of Reading* 30, no. 7 (April 1987): 626–631.

Chaney, Jeanne H. "Beginning to Read: A Critique by Literacy Professionals and a Response by Marilyn Jager Adams." *The Reading Teacher* 44, no. 6 (February 1991): 374.

Collins, Cathy. "Sustained Silent Reading Periods: Effect on Teachers' Behaviors and Students' Achievements." *Elementary School Journal* 81, no. 2 (Nov. 1980): 108–114.

Cooper, J. David. *Literacy: Helping Children Construct Meaning.* Boston: Houghton Mifflin, 1993.

Cunningham, Pat. "The Names Test: A Quick Assessment of Decoding Ability." *The Reading Teacher* 44, no. 2 (October 1990): 124–129.

Davis, Zephaniah T., and Michael D. McPherson. "Story Map Instruction: A Road Map for Reading Comprehension." *The Reading Teacher* 43, no. 3 (December 1989): 232–240.

Ehri, Linnea C. "Development of the Ability to Read Words." In *Handbook of Reading Research,* Vol. 2, ed. Rebecca Barr, Michael L. Kamil, Peter B. Mosenthal and P. David Pearson. White Plains, NY: Longman Publishers, 1991, pp. 383–417.

Gambrell, Linda B., Patricia S. Koskinen, and Barbara A. Kapinus. "A Comparison of Retelling and Questioning as Reading Comprehension Strategies." Paper presented at the National Reading Conference, San Diego, CA, December 1985.

Gaskins, Robert W. "The Missing Ingredients: Time on Task, Direct Instruction, and Writing." *The Reading Teacher* 41, no. 8 (April 1988): 750–755.

Goodman, Yetta M. "Beginning to Read: A Critique by Literacy Professionals and a Response by Marilyn Jager Adams." *The Reading Teacher* 44, no. 6 (February 1991): 378.

Graves, Donald. *Writing: Teachers and Children at Work.* Portsmouth, NH: Heinemann, 1982.

Hall, Mary Anne. *Teaching Reading as a Language Experience,* 3d ed. Columbus, OH: Charles C. Merrill, 1981.

Helfeldt, John P., and William A. Henk. "Reciprocal Question-Answer Relationships: An Instructional Technique for at-Risk Readers." *Journal of Reading* 33, no. 7 (April 1990): 509–514.

Kapinus, Barbara A. "Beginning to Read: A Critique by Literacy Professionals and a Response by Marilyn Jager Adams." *The Reading Teacher* 44, no. 6 (February 1991): 379.

Kirsch, Irwin S., Ann Jungeblut, Lynn Jenkins, and Andrew Kolstad, *Adult Literacy in America: A first look at the findings of the National Adult Literacy Survey.* Washington: National Center for Education Statistics, 1993.

Koskinen, Patricia S., Linda B. Gambrell, Barbara A. Kapinus, and Betty S. Heathington, "Retelling: A Strategy for Enhancing Students' Reading Comprehension." *The Reading Teacher* 41, no. 9 (May 1988): 892–896.

LaBerge, D., and S. Samuels. "Toward a Theory of Automatic Information Processing in Reading." *Cognitive Psychology* 6, (1974): 293–232.

Manning, Gary L., and Maryann Manning. "What Models of Recreational Reading Make a Difference?" *Reading World* 23, no. 4 (May 1984): 375–380.

McCauley, Joyce K., and Daniel S. McCauley. "Using Choral Reading to Promote Language Learning for ESL Students." *The Reading Teacher* 45, no. 7 (March 1992): 526–533.

McKeown, Margaret, Isabel Beck, and Cheryl Sandora, "Questioning the Author: An Approach to Developing Meaningful Classroom Discourse." In *The First R: Every Child's Right to Read,* ed. Michael Graves, Paul Van Den Broek, and Barbara Taylor. New York: Teachers College Press, 1996.

Morrow, Lesley M. "Effects of Story Retelling on Young Children's Comprehension and Sense of Story Structure." In *Changing Perspectives on Research in Reading/Language Processing and Instruction,* Thirty-third Yearbook of the National Reading Conference, ed. Jerome A. Niles and Larry A. Harris. Rochester, NY: National Reading Conference, 1984, pp. 95–100.

Morrow, Lesley M. "Retelling Stories: A Strategy for Improving Young Children's Comprehension, Concept of Story Structure, and Oral Language Complexity." *Elementary School Journal* 75 (1985): 647–661.

Morrow, Lesley M. "Effects of Story Retelling on Children's Dictation of Original Stories." *Journal of Reading Behavior* 18 (Spring 1986): 135–152.

Nessel, Denise D., and Margaret B. Jones. *The Language-Experience Approach to Reading.* New York: Teachers College Press, 1981.

Ogle, Donna M. "K-W-L: A Teaching Model That Develops Active Reading of Expository Text." *The Reading Teacher* 38, no. 6 (February 1986): 564–570.

Pellegrini, Anthony D., and Lee Galda. "The Effects of Thematic-Fantasy Play Training on the Development of Children's Story Comprehension." *American Educational Research Journal* 19 (Fall 1982): 443–454.

Perfetti, Charles, and Sulan Zhang, "What It Means to Learn to Read." In *The First R: Every Child's Right to Read,* ed. Michael Graves, Paul Van den Broek, and Barbara Taylor. New York: Teachers College Press, 1996.

Rose, Michael C., Bert P. Cundick, and Kenneth L. Higbee. "Verbal Rehearsal and Visual Imagery: Mnemonic Aids for Learning Disabled Children." *Journal of Learning Disabilities* 16 (1984): 353–354.

Rosenshine, Barak, and Robert Stevens. "Classroom Instruction in Reading." In *Handbook of Reading Research,* ed. P. David Pearson. New York: Longman Publishers, 1984.

Ryder, Randall, Bonnie Graves, and Michael Graves, *Easy Reading: Book Series and Periodicals for Less Able Readers.* Newark, DE: International Reading Association, 1989.

Samuels, S. Jay. "The Method of Repeated Reading." *The Reading Teacher* 32, no. 4 (January 1979): 403–408.

Snow, Catherine, and Susan Burns, eds. *Preventing Reading Difficulty in Young Children.* Washington, DC: National Academy Press, 1998.

Stahl, Steven A. "Saying the "p" Word: Nine Guidelines for Exemplary Phonics Instruction." *The Reading Teacher* 45, no. 8 (April 1992): 618–625.

Stanovich, Keith E. "Toward an Interactive-Compensatory Model of Individual Differences in the Development of Reading Fluency." *Reading Research Quarterly* 16, no. 1 (Fall 1980): 3–71.

Stanovich, Keith E. "Word Recognition: Changing Perspectives." In *Handbook of Reading Research, Vol. 2,* ed. Rebecca Barr, Michael L. Kamil, Peter B. Mosenthal, and P. David Pearson. White Plains, NY: Longman Publishers, 1991, pp. 418–452.

Stauffer, Russell G. *Directing the Reading-Thinking Process.* New York: Harper & Row, 1975.

Stauffer, Russell G. *The Language Experience Approach to the Teaching of Reading,* rev. ed. New York: Harper & Row, 1980.

Stein, Nancy. *How Children Understand Stories.* Urbana, IL: University of Illinois Center for the Study of Reading, Technical Report No. 69, March 1978 (ERIC: ED: 153–205).

Temple, Charles, Ruthan Nathan, Frances Temple, and Nancy Burris. *The Beginnings of Writing,* 3d ed. Needham Heights, MA: Allyn and Bacon, 1992.

Temple, Charles, Miriam Martinez, Junko Yokota, and Alice Naylor. *Children's Books in Children's Hands: An Introduction to Their Literature.* Needham Heights, MA: Allyn and Bacon, 1998.

Torgesen, J., C. Rashotte, J. Greenstein, G. Houck, and P. Portes, "Academic Difficulties of Learning Disabled Children Who Perform Poorly on Memory Span Tests." In H.L. Swanson (Ed.), *Memory and Learning Disabilities* 27 (1987): 276–286.

Trachtenburg, Phyllis. "Using Children's Literature to Enhance Phonics Instruction." *The Reading Teacher* 43, no. 9 (May 1990): 648–654.

Walberg, Herbert J., and Shiow-ling Tsai. "Reading Achievement and Diminishing Returns to Time." *Journal of Educational Psychology* 76, no. 3 (June 1984): 442–451.

Wilson, Paul T., Richard C. Anderson, and Linda G. Fielding. "Children's Book-Reading Habits: A New Criterion for Literacy." *Book Research Quarterly* 2, no. 3 (Fall 1986): 72–84.

CHAPTER **8**

Adolescent Students with Reading Problems

This chapter addresses the needs of adolescent students with reading problems. Adolescent students, whether or not they are experiencing reading problems, differ from younger students in several ways. Their differences are marked by:

- changes in peer groups,
- separation from family,
- the search for one's individual identity, and
- changes in cognitive processes.

By the time children reach adolescence, their teachers and peers expect them to be able to read and write independently. If adolescents lack the ability to read at grade level, they risk following behind their literate peers academically. This often leads to other problems with social relationships and can ultimately result in severe behavior problems and finally school dropouts.

For these adolescents, the tasks of the reading teacher often go well beyond instruction in comprehension, vocabulary, word attack, writing, and other skills associated with literacy. The first step is often simply rebuilding their trust in the educational system.

This chapter addresses ways of meeting the needs of adolescent students who have reading problems. First, we present the principles and theories that guide our decision making about assessment and instructional procedures. We then present three case studies that illustrate ways to deal with adolescent students who have reading, writing, and motivational problems.

GUIDING PRINCIPLES AND THEORIES

Our approach is based on five principles:

1. establishing trust,
2. providing literate role models,
3. reducing the feelings of learned helplessness or passive failure,
4. legitimizing personal knowledge, and experiences.
5. developing a learning environment.

Establishing Trust

The keystone for success with adolescent students with reading problems is the establishment of trust between the student and teacher. Without trust, students do not view the teacher, or anyone in authority, as a credible source of information. Erikson (1963) proposed that as early as infancy, individuals begin to develop trust or mistrust in others. This early trust is based on having general survival needs met.

The family is perhaps the earliest influence—positive or negative—on trust. The trust that is established during infancy can be enhanced or diminished as people grow and have experiences outside the family. Their initial experiences with schooling also can enhance or diminish trust.

Many adolescent students with reading problems have a basic mistrust of authority, whether from family or school experiences. Without this trust, the outlook for subsequent positive social and academic development is poor (Erikson, 1963). However, trust can be established between adolescents with reading problems and their teachers. With this trust, teachers have a solid base upon which to address the problems of literacy for adolescents. Trust will foster risk-taking in the adolescents' writing and reading efforts.

Providing Literate Role Models

One reason children fail to develop the ability or motivation to read by the time they reach adolescence is the lack of literate role models in their lives. When we think back over our own academic histories, we often find that there were very few occasions on which we observed teachers reading silently. If adolescents have no literate role models in their homes and have had few opportunities to observe teachers or peers reading silently, there is little reason to expect that reading will be a normal part of their lives.

To address the lack of role models for literacy, the classroom environment must be one in which reading and writing are pursued for pleasure as much as for formal school tasks. Children and adolescents model behavior they observe in trusted adults and peers (Bandura, 1986). This modeling extends beyond fashion and social behavior to the areas of reading and literacy in general.

Reducing the Feeling of Learned Helplessness or Passive Failure

Adolescents who meet with repeated failure due to the lack of literacy skills often resist the most well-intentioned attempts at assessment or instruction. At the extreme, this results in learned helplessness. Learned helplessness is a sense that no matter what one does, nothing will help. We see this in adolescents with reading problems when they honestly believe that no amount of effort will bring about escape from a cycle of failure. They see all their attempts at success as leading to failure. Harter (1992) proposed that children and adolescents who feel as though they have little or no control over their successes or failures in school often attempt to evade tasks that might result in failure. These young people tend to make excuses for their failures based on either an external or an internal source of failure or success. Some students will blame the test or the teacher for failure. This kind of helplessness provides some protection against an additional example of personal inadequacy and reflects the view that forces outside the students control their fates. Other students will sit quietly and whisper, "I knew I was going to fail, I'm just too dumb." This kind of helplessness represents a sense that internal forces are limiting the students' performances. Perhaps the most depressing combination of the reasoning behind success and failure in school is for students to attribute failure to the lack of ability (internal inadequacy) and success to the fact that the test was "so easy anyone could pass it" or "I was just lucky" (external control).

Johnston and Winograd (1985) used the phrase *passive failure* to describe the way in which students who have feelings of learned helplessness view the reading process. They suggest that readers who exhibit passive failure are not aware of the relationship between effort and success, attribute success in reading tasks to luck or simplicity of task, attribute failure to the lack of ability, and generally fail to persist in difficult tasks. Adolescents who are experiencing passive failure are not moved by simple cheerleader-type statements such as "You can do it, all you have to do is try." They have heard that statement, they have tried, and they have failed.

One way in which learned helplessness and passive failure can be overcome is through modeling. Over time, modeling by a trusted and respected individual can be a strong motivation. If adolescents observe a trusted individual (e.g., a peer, a volunteer, or a teacher) modeling literate behavior and successfully reading a book or tackling a difficult writing assignment, they are more likely to attempt tasks involving literacy. When these attempts are used as building blocks instead of measuring sticks, the adolescents begin to overcome passive failure and learned helplessness. Some of the building blocks include

- being able to read a printed version of a short dictated story,
- coming to class,
- opening a book or magazine,
- asking for help reading a personal letter,
- listening to a story that is read to the class and asking questions, and
- attempting to write.

Some of these might appear insignificant. However, the goal is to recapture the adolescent as a learner and overcome passive failure.

Legitimizing Personal Knowledge and Experiences

Classrooms today are much more culturally diverse than those of a decade ago. This trend will increase in the future as more students come to school with greater cultural and social differences. These differences also are seen between students and their teachers. This diversity can lead to the selection of inappropriate materials, inappropriate topics, and the misinterpretation of word meanings.

Adolescents with reading problems reflect this broad diversity of cultural and personal experiences and knowledge. Reading and writing instruction are particularly suited to the use of students' cultural and personal experiences to enhance instruction. A teacher can create opportunities for students to use their personal knowledge and experiences through self-selection of topics for writing, reading, and class discussion, thus legitimizing personal knowledge and experiences.

In summary, adolescents with reading problems learn best in an instructional environment in which:

- a trusting relationship exists between the teacher and students,
- literacy is modeled,
- learned helplessness and experience of passive failure are replaced by a willingness to try and opportunities for success, and
- personal knowledge and experiences are valued and used.

These guiding principles lead us to an environment in which a variety of print material is available. It is structured to allow teachers and other literate participants to model reading and writing. When possible, students select their own writing topics, reading materials, and classroom tasks. Within these tasks, there are ample opportunities for legitimate successes in which efforts are related to outcomes. Finally, the students and teacher develop a trusting relationship through a freedom to express feelings, ideas, and opinions in a nonevaluative atmosphere.

Developing a Learning Environment

Although not without controversy, the whole-language philosophy is becoming more widely accepted as a means for empowering children and adolescents as learners (Altwerger et al, 1987; Weaver, 1990). Our selection of the whole-language philosophy is based on the guiding principles and theories that we have described. One point to be made is that whole language is, for many, a philosophy that guides the creation of a learning environment, selection of instructional and assessment strategies, and materials. Whole language is not a specified set of strategies, exercises, or materials used in teaching.

Within the whole-language philosophy, reading and writing are considered social as well as personal events. They are social in the relationship between the reader and the author of a text, the reader/writer and other members of a class, and the reader/writer and those who might be affected by the text. Reading and writing are also social events because when children observe others in their family or classroom reading or writing, they are more likely to read or write.

Classrooms that follow this philosophy provide many opportunities for sustained silent reading, reading aloud, free and guided writing, and class discussion. Davidson and Koppenhaver (1988) suggest that programs that have been successful in fostering literacy among adolescents

1. spend a high proportion of time on reading and writing,
2. teach skills in context,
3. stress silent reading,
4. teach strategies for reading comprehension,
5. build on background information and experience,
6. integrate speaking and listening with reading and writing,
7. focus on writing,
8. use modeling as a teaching technique,
9. use involvement or experience-based curriculum approaches that foster conceptual development,

10. facilitate discussions rather than lead them,
11. give students access to a wide variety of materials, and
12. use varied groupings and value collaborative learning (pp. 184–189).

These characteristics are often observed in whole-language classrooms. The methods by which each characteristic is realized and the specific strategies that are taught should be based on students' needs, interests, and abilities. Teachers typically can seize the teachable moment and create instructional lessons that are based on legitimate tasks such as preparing for drivers' license examinations, writing birthday cards for friends, or completing job applications.

Discussions of topics that are currently on the minds of adolescents also provide the basis for many literacy lessons in these classrooms. For example, child abuse, drug addiction, and teen pregnancy can be key topics for many readings, class discussions, and written and dictated compositions. In this way, the whole-language classroom provides an opportunity not only for fostering literacy, but also for addressing pressing social issues in the lives of adolescents. Within such a classroom, a variety of approaches can be implemented to address the complex needs of adolescent students with reading problems.

CLASSIFYING THE ADOLESCENT STUDENT WITH READING PROBLEMS

The earlier a child's problems are identified and appropriately addressed, the more likely it is that the child will succeed in school. Unfortunately, many reading problems are not diagnosed until high school. For example, if a child happens to be a younger sibling of a notorious troublemaker, any acting out by the child might be interpreted as a family trait instead of a symptom of academic difficulties. The child might be socially promoted through the elementary and middle school grades only to become frustrated at not being able to read high school material.

These adolescents with reading problems often fall into one of the following three classifications: nonreader, disenchanted reader, or remedial reader. A nonreader is one who lacks even the most rudimentary skills and strategies associated with reading. A nonreader has little in the way of sight vocabulary, often lacks even the most basic word-attack skills, and cannot read and understand written text. This student might be able to comprehend when a teacher or peer reads aloud and might be truly motivated to learn.

The primary problem associated with a disenchanted reader is lack of motivation or unwillingness to attempt the literacy tasks. This student often has had negative experiences associated with the social or behavioral elements of schooling or has experienced severe family or personal problems resulting in extreme emotional distress. In many ways, a disenchanted reader is the most difficult to understand, assess, and affect positively. This reader is often resistant to assessment procedures and foils even the best-intentioned attempts to motivate. A remedial reader might be able to recognize some sight words and might possess some limited word attack skills. In the majority of cases, however, a remedial reader experiences great difficulty in reading and comprehending grade-level texts. This student might be able to recognize enough words to perform at a minimal level on multiple-choice tests but probably will experience great difficulty in tasks that call for higher-level thought processes such as comparisons, finding the main ideas, and forming inferences.

As you will find in our case studies, patience and creativity are necessary to successfully address the needs of adolescents with reading problems. The three case studies that we will present provide insights into the assessment and instructional procedures that address the needs of adolescent nonreaders, disenchanted readers, and remedial readers.

Peter: A Nonreader

Peter is a 19-year-old nonreader who attends a secondary school that used to focus on vocational education but now functions as an academic alternative dropout prevention center. This section includes impressions about Peter that are based on his ninth-grade reading teacher's observations and discussions with his other teachers. Much of this information was informal but was useful for meeting his academic needs and creating an environment in which he could learn to read and write.

Peter was referred to the reading teacher for help in social studies and science. At that time, he was 16 years old and had been enrolled at the school since he was 13.

The teachers reported that Peter was a very sincere and caring individual. He openly expressed love for his family; however, his family did not always value school as an essential activity in Peter's life. Because of his admiration for his family members, Peter strove for their approval and acknowledgment. Hence, Peter often seemed less than enthusiastic about school. He had a handful of friends and developed strong attachments with his girlfriends; however, he never allowed them to uncover his "secret" of illiteracy.

Peter met with continued failure throughout his years in school. He had developed an uncanny ability to "escape" from the risk of failing, and he developed tricks for distracting a teacher's attention from the real academic problems. Such behaviors are common to many adolescents with reading problems.

Peter used several techniques to effectively avoid reading and writing. One very effective one was using his charm and his gift of gab. Peter's favorite topics were himself, his cars, his jobs, his girlfriends, and his family. Some conversations helped to develop the rapport that was needed to work effectively with him, but some discussion time was used to escape academic pursuits. Invisibility was another method Peter used to escape school. Often, he would sit quietly in a corner or the back of the room. When the teacher finally discovered him, he would smile coyly at the teacher as if to say "so you caught me . . . it's too late now!" Another technique that he mastered was misbehavior—confronting teachers or disrupting class. Disruptive behavior could be caused by having his secret illiteracy exposed, by being teased by a classmate, or by having family problems.

The most self-destructive method that Peter used to avoid failure was simply not coming to school. The reading teacher noted that he had dropped out of school during the second semester each year for the last four years to work with his father. We have presented this sketch of Peter to acquaint you with a fairly typical adolescent nonreader. The next picture of Peter is based on informal and formal assessments.

Assessment of Peter's Reading Skills and Levels

The reading teacher spent the first two sessions getting to know Peter and previewing his content area textbooks. He was required to read high school level texts, and his teachers reported that Peter experienced great difficulty. Peter blamed his academic problems on his teachers. This external orientation is typical of students who feel powerless and lack the confidence even to attempt academic work (Harter, 1992; Johnston & Winograd, 1985). When the reading teacher first began to tutor Peter using a high school textbook, he refused to read orally or silently and began moving around the room. The refusal and avoidance were indications that Peter felt defeated and required nurturing if he was to progress. After much prodding, he attempted to perform the oral reading task, but he was unable to read the passage. The reading teacher then offered to read selections of the text to him and ask him the end of chapter questions orally. This accomplished two goals: Peter was exposed to the content area material, and the reading teacher was able to assess his listening comprehension. With exchanges like these, Peter began to trust the reading teacher.

Peter and the reading teacher discussed his dilemma, and Peter agreed to take several reading tests so that a plan could be developed to improve his literacy skills. Testing began with a Word Recognition Inventory (see Chapter 3). He was able to pronounce 50 percent of the primer words on the automatic presentation. When given time to decode the unknown words on the primer list, he decoded three additional words, raising his score on the primer level word list to 65 percent. The test indicated that Peter had very few sight words and that his ability to use phonetic decoding was extremely limited. Asked whether he could read, Peter responded, "No" and looked down at the table. When asked whether he was ever placed in any special reading classes, he could not remember.

Next, Peter was asked to read the primer passage of an informal reading inventory (see Chapter 3). His oral reading was laborious. When he did not know a word, he would say the beginning consonant sound, then make a guess at the rest of the word, or he would not attempt to pronounce the unknown word at all. He required more than five minutes to get through the thirty-two-word paragraph. He yawned, fidgeted in his seat, got up, and said he really didn't want to go on. Because of his extreme frustration, the reading teacher read the passage to him. He was able to answer 80 percent of the comprehension questions correctly. Peter refused to attempt to read another primer level passage silently. He would, however, listen to the passages read to him. His listening comprehension level was assessed to be at least at the seventh-grade level. This was consistent with the initial assessment using content area texts. Peter's listening comprehension score demonstrated Peter's potential to become literate.

The reading teacher had discovered one of the many children who reach high school without being able to read. To obtain more information about Peter's academic past, the reading teacher referred to his cumulative record file. The decision to use the academic history found in the cumulative record as a final source, instead of an initial source, of information was a conscious decision. By first learning about Peter as a person, then assessing his reading in an informal manner, the reading teacher could make initial judgments that were less likely to be influenced by some expectation of failure or problem behaviors.

Peter's School Records and Academic History

The first entry in his cumulative record file was Peter's elementary cumulative record form. (Various types of information are contained in cumulative records, and this information differs from state to state.) Within this record, the teacher found early school pictures of him, a yearly evaluation of personal characteristics, a list of schools attended, psychological assessments, and teachers' anecdotal records and comments. The teachers' comments about Peter included such information as "Peter has spent two years in kindergarten. He is a nice child but sometimes he can act ugly." The reading teacher discovered that Peter repeated first grade and had attended six schools by the time he entered second grade. In second grade, Peter was referred for psychological testing. At the time of testing, he had been in school four years, and was 8 years, 11 months old.

Peter was referred for testing because he was working below grade level and was unable to cope with the learning process in the classroom. He was said to be disruptive in class, made inappropriate remarks, and talked to himself. He reportedly walked around the room at his own discretion and did not function as a group member. One early entry indicated that he could not retain information and could not sequence. A family interview revealed that Peter's mother and father divorced when he was 5 years old and that his mother had remarried and divorced again at the time of the interview. Peter's father lived out of town. His mother attributed Peter's behavior problems to the divorce and the adjustments after biannual paternal visits.

Peter took two intelligence tests. The scores on these tests indicated that he was functioning in the borderline range (see Chapter 9). These scores predict the likelihood of Peter's having difficulty becoming literate but did not qualify him for special-education services. He was reevaluated at age 10 years, 5 months while in third grade. These results were generally similar to the ones reported earlier. Again, he did not qualify for any special services, but recommendations were made to explore the possibility of vocational training. Peter repeated third grade, and his behavior was reported as very disruptive.

The third-grade teacher worked individually with Peter as much as possible, and a fifth-grade student came into the classroom to tutor him. He also attended a Chapter I reading program for remedial reading instruction. During this year, Peter was also tested by a reading specialist, who concluded that Peter had an "extremely severe reading disability." Using a standardized reading test, Peter's instructional reading level was found to be early first grade. The reading specialist stated that Peter had good listening comprehension and knew almost all his beginning consonant sounds. He did not, however, apply this knowledge to decoding unknown words. The reading specialist recommended several strategies to Peter's teacher, which included reading aloud to him, echo-reading and choral-reading, and language experience activities. In addition, a behavior technician was placed in the classroom to conduct a behavior modification program for Peter. This technician also provided him with individual academic tutoring. With this individualized intervention, Peter's behavior problems were significantly decreased.

Little more information was found in Peter's cumulative folder. He went on to fourth grade and, at the end of that year, was administratively promoted to the alternative secondary school that could provide him with vocational training and basic academics. He was 13 years old. His report cards show that he had failed his academic courses but passed his vocational training.

To summarize, this portrait of Peter was based on initial impressions by a reading teacher, informal assessments, and a review of his cumulative school record. These data showed that Peter was a student who became "invisible" in a group, got frustrated easily, and knew that he did not have adequate reading and writing skills. He moved frequently as a young child and had experienced family problems. He continued to perform poorly on tests of reading, but his listening comprehension scores and IQ scores indicated that he had the potential to become literate. Peter's behavior showed a significant improvement when a behavioral technician worked individually with him. On the basis of the initial contact with the reading teacher, Peter's test scores, and his positive experiences with the behavioral technician, individual tutoring by his ninth-grade reading teacher was continued.

Development of an Instructional Plan

The reading teacher's sessions with Peter included tutoring in content areas, reading to him, writing, language experience activities, word study activities, repeated readings, and sustained silent reading. The reading teacher met with Peter one period each day for individual tutoring. She read the required high school text to him, and he dictated the answers to the end-of-chapter questions. They discussed the text using a modified directed listening-thinking activity (DLTA). A description of the DLTA appears on pages 322–323. It is important to point out that often, particular strategies must be modified for individual students' needs. In this case, a nonfiction text was used. The reading teacher would read the section heading to Peter and ask, "What do you think the author might write about next?" or "What would the author want you to know?" This modification can be used with virtually any content area text.

Content Area DLTA

The procedure for a DLTA with content area material is basically the same as that for a directed reading-thinking activity (DRTA), explained on pages 306–307, except that the material is read aloud to the student. Stauffer (1975) developed the DRTA technique to assess young children's sense of story and prior knowledge and to provide a means to monitor and increase listening comprehension. Using the DLTA procedure with content area text provides remedial or nonreaders access to the information in a text that is too difficult for them to read. The DLTA provides a model for good reading and study skill practices and provides much-needed comprehension support for the older students. It can be done individually or with a small group.

The first step in the procedure is to preview the section or chapter to be read. Together, the teacher and the student look at the title, headings, subheadings, illustrations, and end-of-section questions. They discuss possible topics to be covered in the text and make predictions about the content. During this time, the teacher might probe to activate any information the student already knows about the topic. After predictions are made, the teacher reads the text to the student. The teacher selects stopping points within the text and directs the student to confirm, discuss, question, and make further predictions about the text.

The amount of text that is covered between stops for predicting is determined by several variables. They include listener attention, the amount of the student's prior knowledge about the topic, and the difficulty of the text being read. In addition to the amount of text that is included between stops, the teacher should set the length of the entire session so that the student does not become bored with the task and so that the amount of information is not overwhelming. When the teacher previews the text, points of closure should be noted so that sessions can end at a logical point. Time should be allocated for a discussion and review of each session. This review might address the end-of-chapter questions or specific assignments that might be required. The content area DLTA is a strategy that can be used by teachers, teachers' aides, or classroom volunteers. A summary of this procedure is presented in Figure 8.1.

In Peter's case, the DLTA was successful. His content area teachers required that the end-of-chapter questions be answered and gave examinations based on those questions. Peter successfully passed oral examinations on the chapters that were included in the DLTA.

One of Peter's goals was to learn to read and write well enough to function in society (i.e., read road signs and newspapers, apply for jobs, read directions, and write lists or notes). To do this, the reading teacher adapted the language experience approach to Peter's needs (Allen, 1965; Hall, 1981; Stauffer 1980).

FIGURE 8.1 Directed Listening-Thinking Activity

1. Preview the section. Read and examine titles, heading, subheadings, illustrations and end of section questions.

2. Discuss possible topics to be covered, making predictions about content.

3. Probe for prior knowledge about the topic.

4. Read text aloud to designated stopping points.

5. Confirm, discuss, question and make further predictions.

6. Read text aloud to next stopping point.

7. Repeat procedure.

Language Experience Approach with Adolescents

The reading teacher found dictation to be a way for Peter to express himself. By being given Peter an outlet for his knowledge, Peter became more confident in himself as a knowledgeable individual. He selected topics that were simple retellings of experiences he had had on the job or at home with cars or friends. To motivate him to dictate, the reading teacher assumed the role of secretary and would write whatever Peter wanted her to write. An important characteristic of this dictation is the verbatim transcription of the student's words. Once transcribed, the reading teacher echo-read (see Chapter 6) the dictation with Peter. He then read the dictation to the reading teacher. With increased fluency and confidence, Peter began editing his own work as he read. During daily silent reading time, Peter would self-select his dictations to reread. Periodically, these dictations were reread orally by Peter or were used as text for additional echo-reading. Peter was also asked to point to the words as he pronounced them (voice-pointing) to help him pay attention to the words.

One of the most important dictations consisted of a day-by-day description of his brick masonry class (Figure 8.2). Peter was motivated by the class and wanted to complete it so that he could get a job. This required a passing score on written tests. By reading and rereading his dictations about the class content, he was able not only to learn important vocabulary words, but also to orally rehearse procedures that are necessary in brick masonry. Peter passed his written examinations and finally began to recognize the connection between spoken words and written words. In addition, the study skill of rehearsal was made meaningful to him.

As Peter became more confident, he would dictate longer passages. His dictations were directly transcribed by the reading teacher using a computer program that recorded, printed, and analyzed texts for new vocabulary and word frequency. The reading teacher found dictation to be a way for Peter to express himself and to build confidence in himself as a knowledgeable individual. Figure

FIGURE 8.2 Peter's Dictated Text

Thursday, Sept. 13, 1990

My class is brick mason at George Stone from 11:00 to 2:00 and we are working on a house. My work is laying bricks, making mud, and a little bit of measuring, a little bit of math. Mud is sand, mortar mix, and water. It is used with a trowel. It makes the bricks hold up. We started to work as soon as I got there. I like getting an education doing something I can fall back on.

Friday, Sept. 14, 1990

I learned what the face of a brick was. It is the front side of the brick. The front will be coated with a white powder so you know what side is the back side. The face side is out. Laying a brick straight up and down means laying them like soldiers when it is the last topping of the house.

1. Work with groups of three or fewer.

2. Suggest, or allow students to suggest, a topic.

3. Lead discussion of the topic, encouraging as rich language use as possible.

4. Take dictation, making minor word changes or additions as necessary to keep the story fluent. Cursive writing may be used instead of printing. Use a regular size sheet of paper if you wish.

5. Lead the choral and/or echo rereadings of dictations. Students might prefer to do more individual than group reading.

6. Provide an individual copy for each student, typed if possible, for practice rereading and word identification. Encourage rereading to a partner or someone else.

7. Provide each student with several typed copies of the dictation. Have the student cut the story apart and paste it back together. Depending on the student's ability, use one copy as a guide. An alternative to this is to ask the student to cut it apart and create a "new" story.

8. Make a word bank or word list of words that the students know. Words that the students identify out of story context can go in their word bank/list. Older students often prefer to keep their words in a notebook. Students can read their list of words, do word sorts with their words, and get a running total of the number of words they know.

9. Have students circle all words they know or identify words of like classifications (e.g., underline all number words).

10. Students may choose dictations for sustained silent reading text.

FIGURE 8.3   Language Experience Approach (LEA) with Adolescents

8.3 provides guidelines for using the language experience approach with adolescent emergent readers.

Repeated Readings

For Peter, repeated readings helped to develop sight vocabulary, reading fluency, and confidence. In his case, the repeated readings of his own dictations helped him to acquire much needed job-specific sight words. As described in Chapter 6, repeated readings of text from content area or repeated readings from short stories are appropriate for any reader who is struggling with sight words. Elementary textbooks might be a good source of reading material for students like Peter. With these materials, photocopies or retypings can be used to avoid revealing the low levels of the books. A teacher might choose to write original text adapting material from content area or vocational texts.

Another method that is used to increase sight words and oral reading fluency is taped readings. Students listen to tapes and follow the text with their fingers and eyes. The tapes are available commercially or can be recorded by the teacher or a volunteer.

With students like Peter, the temptation is to abandon these support activities too soon. Even though progress is observed, making up years of failure in school requires time. These support activities must be conducted frequently until nonreaders can begin independent reading.

Word Sorts

Once Peter acquired some sight words, additional activities using word sorting were conducted, providing him with concrete ways of learning about words. In addition to sorting words on the basis of phonetic features, word sorting can provide practice in recognizing similar suffixes, grammatical categories (e.g., nouns or verbs), and meaning categories (e.g., animals or colors).

The open sort was particularly motivating for Peter. This type of sort and word sorting in general are discussed in Chapter 6. During open sorts, Peter was quick to discover ways to classify words. He often used words from his dictations about brick masonry as a source of words for sorting. Peter could sort his vocational vocabulary into such categories as types of brick or words associated with the process of laying brick. As Peter became more confident in his abilities with word sorting, he would often identify categories for sorting and attempt to fool the teacher by asking her to guess the category. This allowed Peter to assert some control over the task and to maintain his interest in the activity.

Journal Writing

Journal writing was used with Peter to provide another experience with print and to provide the teacher with an assessment tool. From Peter's writing samples, the teacher could note progress in the use of sight words, gain insights into his knowledge about letter-sound relationships, and assess his awareness of print and text structure. Peter knew that words had boundaries and that each word had a meaning. His writings were similar to those of other beginning readers/writers in that he wrote only words that he thought he could spell correctly and usually wrote from his own point of view. One writing reflected his feeling for his father.

I love to work with my dad and I love my dad.

To encourage risk-taking with print, invented spellings were encouraged when Peter was unsure of a word.

Any teacher can encourage learners by unconditionally accepting their first drafts and by making specific positive comments about the writing. For instance, Peter wrote:

I have a girl friend naum lori she a good girl but she is moving to texs this sumr but that is life but it gos on.

The teacher comment could be "Peter, I'm sorry your girlfriend is moving to Texas. I'm sure you will miss her. I like the way you expressed your feelings." In this way, the teacher reinforces the content of Peter's writing without critiquing his spelling.

Another method that was used to encourage Peter to write was simply to discuss experiences in his life. The reading teacher would retell Peter's story, emphasizing the story's importance, content, and relevance. Then Peter was told in a calm and pleasant voice to write down what he had said. If necessary, the reading teacher reminded him of information to be included in the writing. These discussions also gave the reading teacher an inventory of topics that interested Peter. The topics were noted on a topics list in his journal.

One of the motivational strategies that were used to encourage Peter to write was the parallel writing that took place between him and the reading teacher. Each day when Peter wrote, the reading teacher also wrote in a journal. During the writing time, Peter would observe the reading teacher having similar difficulties choosing a topic, deciding what to write, and figuring out how to spell difficult words. This served as a model for what all writers do and helped Peter to feel that he wasn't the only one who experienced difficulty in writing. At the end of each writing time, the reading teacher and Peter would share their respective writings and request clarifications when needed. They responded to some part of the writing with a positive comment. This sharing led to the development of trust and respect between Peter and the reading teacher. Peter's written interaction with the reading teacher built his confidence in himself as a writer. With this confidence came a willingness to edit for content and produce longer and more descriptive passages.

Summary of Peter

Peter was an adolescent who had progressed through eleven years of school without learning to read. His progress in a whole-language environment was slow but steady. The use of individual tutoring was indicated, given Peter's academic history and his unwillingness to share his secret of illiteracy with others. By reading aloud to Peter and asking questions about the content, the reading teacher was able to assess Peter's listening comprehension and present content area information to him. The fact that the content area interested Peter provided motivation to learn. His dictations were used to establish more sight vocabulary and provide a successful reading experience once Peter could read them to the teacher. By writing and reading with Peter, the reading teacher provided a role model for literacy. By addressing the problems of lack of trust, absence of role models, learned helplessness, and the need for validation of one's personal experiences, the reading teacher was able to move Peter along the path toward literacy.

Jayne: A Disenchanted Learner

Jayne was referred to a high school reading class during the first month of the school year. She was a 15-year-old ninth-grader who was not progressing in her classes. When given a standardized reading test, Jayne scored in the average range. Taken as a single indicator, this score would not place her in a reading class, but given her lack of achievement in other classes, she was enrolled. Attempts to communicate with Jayne were largely unsuccessful. She seemed to rebel every time conversations were initiated.

Jayne's entire demeanor appeared closed to adult intervention. She wore black jeans, T-shirts, denim jackets, and a black baseball hat every day. Jayne was overweight and seldom smiled. Unlike Peter, Jayne's history was largely unknown. She was an example of the many students whom reading teachers see because they have become disenchanted with school and refuse to read and write. As in Peter's case, Jayne's refusal to read or write in her classes could be interpreted in several ways. Jayne's reading test scores indicated that she was capable of reading her content area texts, but for some reason, she chose not to read them. Students like Jayne are often more difficult to deal with than is a student who wants to read but hasn't learned—she could read but would not! Jayne's case study differs from Peter's in another way. Peter's difficulties were addressed in an individualized tutorial arrangement. Jayne's needs were addressed in a large-group, whole-class environment.

The reading class that Jayne entered was part of the regular curriculum at an alternative secondary school and was based on whole-language philosophy. The class met each day for fifty minutes. Twenty to twenty-five students were enrolled in the class. Most were ninth- or tenth-grade students who scored at or below the 25th percentile on a standardized reading test. Others in the class were middle-school-aged expectant or teen mothers or students who had been recommended by teachers because of poor academic performance. Because of an open entry and exit policy at the school, new students enrolled each day and others withdrew.

Upon entry into the reading class, each student received a Unit Management Sheet (Figure 8.4), which outlined the requirements of the course. The students were required to complete all the activity sheets listed. (Sample activity sheets are shown in Figures 8.5 and 8.6.) Additional requirements included participation in whole-class discussion, strategy instruction, and cooperative learning activities. Each student was also required to read a certain number of books, to write each day, and to publish at least one composition. Records of completion of these activities were recorded on the Teacher

Student Name _____ Grade_____

Birthdate _____ Enrollment Date _____ Ending Date _____

Newspaper

Study Unit

Activity Sheet   Grade   Date

1. 5 W's and H   _____   _____
2. Main Idea   _____   _____
3. Classified Fact/Opinion   _____   _____
4. Word Groups   _____   _____
5. Following Directions   _____   _____
6. Classified Search   _____   _____
7. Other _____   _____   _____

Newspaper final grade   _____

Map

Reading Unit

Activity Sheet   Grade   Date

1. Where do you live?   _____   _____
2. Where in the World is Carmen Sandiego? or   _____   _____
    Where in the USA is Carmen Sandiego?
    (you must solve three mysteries)
3. Plan a trip: (Panhandle Trip or Miami Trip)   _____   _____
4. Using compass directions   _____   _____
5. Compass Points   _____   _____
6. Reading chart, graphs, diagrams & schedules   _____   _____
7. Other to be determined   _____   _____

Map Unit Final Grade   _____

Reference

Reference Materials Unit

Activity Sheet   Grade   Date

1. Timeline—"Famous Person"   _____   _____
2. Timeline—My Life—Past, Present & Future   _____   _____
3. The Yellow Pages   _____   _____
4. Using the dictionary   _____   _____
5. Field trip to UWF Library or   _____   _____
    Field trip to Pensacola Public Library
    Write a description of the field trip in
    black journal (prewriting concept map must be used)
6. Other activity   _____   _____

Reference Final Grade   _____

FIGURE 8.4 Student Unit Management Sheet Reading

Source: Samuel R. Mathews, Josephine P. Young, and Nancy D. Giles. *Reading and Writing: Providing Tools for Brighter Futures.* Pensacola, FL: The Educational Research and Development Center, University of West Florida, 1992.

Name _____   Date _____

SEARCH THE CLASSIFIED PAGES

1. How many pages are in the classified section? _____
2. There are many different categories in the classified section. Categories help you locate particular items you may wish to buy. For example if you wanted to buy a German Shepherd, you would look under the category "Pets." List five categories from the classified section in the newspaper.

   _____

   _____

   _____

3. Here are some items you wish to sell. In which category should each item be advertised?

   ITEM   **CATEGORY**

   a 1967 Mustang   _____

   refrigerator   _____

   used children's clothes   _____

   computer   _____

   lawn mower   _____

4. Suppose you were given $500.00 to move out to your own apartment. You have an old chair and some dishes your Mother was kind enough to loan you until you were able to buy them yourself. Your task today is to locate an apartment in the classified ads and furnish it. The $500.00 is for the furniture. Your family will pay the rent, but they will not pay over $200.00 a month. You may not rent a furnished apartment. List what you would need. Look for the items in the classifieds or advertisements and write down the price you would pay for the item and the phone number of the place of purchase. You may, however, move out with two friends each of whom have the same amount of money.

   use the back of this paper

FIGURE 8.5   Activity Sheet: Search the Classified Pages

Record of Student Progress Sheet (Figure 8.7). Requirements were modified to meet individual needs.

The Unit Management Sheet was part of each student's work folder and provided a personal guide through the completion of the course. This system allowed the students to be accountable for the management of their own learning. Students

> Where do you live?
>
> 1. Write directions to get to your school from your house. Include the name of the streets you must travel, the direction (north, south, east, or west) you must go on each street and the approximate number of miles on each street. Refer to the city map for this information.
>
> 2. Draw a map to your house using city maps for reference and graph paper.

FIGURE 8.6 Activity Sheet: Where Do You Live?

Source: Samuel R. Mathews, Josephine P. Young, and Nancy D. Giles. *Reading and Writing: Providing Tools for Brighter Futures.* Pensacola, FL: The Educational Research and Development Center, University of West Florida, 1992.

FIGURE 8.7 Teacher Record of Student Progress Reading I & II and Middle School Reading

Student Name _____ Course _____

Newspaper Study Unit	Grade _____	Date Completed _____
Map Reading Unit	Grade _____	Date Completed _____
Reference Materials Unit	Grade _____	Date Completed _____
Publish a Writing Selection	Grade _____	Date Completed _____
Reading Response Journal	Grade _____	Date Completed _____
Writing Workshop	Grade _____	Date Completed _____
Class and Group Activities	Grade _____	Date Completed _____
Sustained Silent Reading	Grade _____	Date Completed _____

RECORD OF BOOKS READ

	Title	Type of Book	Date Completed	Book Conference/Project
1.	_____	_____	_____	_____
2.	_____	_____	_____	_____
3.	_____	_____	_____	_____
4.	_____	_____	_____	_____
5.	_____	_____	_____	_____
6.	_____	_____	_____	_____
7.	_____	_____	_____	_____
8.	_____	_____	_____	_____
9.	_____	_____	_____	_____
10.	_____	_____	_____	_____
11.	_____	_____	_____	_____
12.	_____	_____	_____	_____

Type of Books:
A type book = less than 100 pages; B type book (Standard Book) = 100–150 pp.;
C type book = over 150 pages
- For 1/2 Reading credit a minimum of 3 B type books, 6 A type books, or 2 C type books must be read and the student must demonstrate comprehension of the book in the form of a book conference and/or book project.
- For 1 Reading credit a minimum of 5 B type books, 12 A type books, or 3 C type books must be read and the student must demonstrate comprehension of the book in the form of a book conference and/or book project.

made choices among class activities and were free to work at their own pace. These activities addressed literacy skills that are necessary to function in society. Skills such as using classified ads, reference materials, and maps were included.

Sustained Silent Reading

Jayne's reading class began each day with ten to twenty minutes of sustained silent reading. Although the class had a variety of reading materials available, students also were allowed to bring books or materials from their homes. The classroom materials included copies of the daily newspaper, paperback books, high-interest/low-vocabulary adult readers, magazines, children's books, and picture books.

In Jayne's case, the freedom to be able to read what she chose during sustained silent reading increased her participation in the class. She began by reading the newspaper each day. On some days, she looked at picture books; on others, she read short stories. Jayne's interest in the 1960s culture and heavy-metal music led her to a biography of the late Jim Morrison. This book was very long and probably would not have been selected by the remedial readers in the class. Jayne demonstrated through written and oral discussions (book conferences) that she could read the book with a high level of understanding. For example, she discovered and explained to the teacher interesting parallels between Morrison's life and Ozzy Osbourne's life. At one point, Jayne wrote a letter to Ozzy Osbourne warning him of the dangers of following Morrison's lead in drug and alcohol abuse.

Book Conferences

Book conferences are excellent means for students and teachers to share their feelings, opinions, and knowledge acquired through their readings (Atwell, 1987). Through guided discussions, a teacher can lead readers to a better understanding of what they have read, relate text to personal experiences, and give readers ideas about books or articles to read in the future. These conferences can be simple retellings or discussions generated by specific questions. Questions such as those in Figure 8.8 provide an informal way to evaluate students' general understanding of the selection. When students like Jayne are encouraged to openly express and discuss their feelings and opinions, mutual trust and respect develop.

Reading Response Journals

After sustained silent reading, Jayne's class participated in some form of writing. Several days each week, the class, including the teacher and any classroom volunteers, wrote in a reading response journal (RRJ) about the materials that they had read and their reactions to them. This writing allowed the students to report on what they had read and provided the teacher with a record of the students' participation and understanding of their chosen texts. Students in Jayne's class were told to write brief summaries of what they had read and their personal feelings and reactions to the text. (Other prompts are listed in Figure 8.9.)

1. Why did you choose this selection to read?

2. Who are the main characters in the story? Which one is most like you? Explain.

3. Tell me about the book in three or four sentences.

4. What was your favorite part? Explain why you selected this part.

5. Would you recommend this book to anyone else? Why or why not?

6. What do you think the author had to know to write this selection?

7. What do you think the author was trying to tell the reader in this selection? Explain why you believe this.

8. Do you think the main character handles situations the way you would? Give an example from the book.

9. Were there any words you didn't understand? What did you do when you came to these words?

10. Did your book have illustrations? What did you like about them? What part did they play in your understanding of the selection? Explain.

11. What information did you gain from reading the selection?

12. Do you think this story could really happen? Why or why not?

FIGURE 8.8 Book Conference Questions

After writing their entries, class members exchanged journals and responded to each other in writing. This exchange fostered the notion of writing as a form of communication and began building a trusting relationship among class members. Students were encouraged to respond to others' entries in positive ways. To do this, the teacher modeled examples of positive responses. The students then monitored each others' responses and explained to new students about RRJ etiquette. Students were taught to respond to what a writer had said, not to how it was said. The students were held responsible for exchanging journals and getting written feedback. Part of their reading grade was based on the participation in the writing and exchanging of the RRJ.

Jayne participated in the RRJ. She quickly learned to use the RRJ as a form of interpersonal communication about what she read and how she felt. An example of this communication follows:

> TEACHER: In your RRJs, write a brief summary about what you read. Then write your feelings, reactions, or thoughts about the way what you read relates to your life. After you finish, exchange with someone at your table and write them back. Sign your name after your response and pass the journal back to its owner. Remember, your journal entries are not graded for spelling, grammar, or structure.

Condensed from Nancie Atwell's (1990) Coming to Know: Writing to Learn in the Intermediate Grades.

• What did the author have to know about to write this story?

• Finish this sentence: I love the way the author . . .

• Tell about your favorite character in the book you're reading. What kind of person is your character, and why is he or she your favorite?

• How did you get to know the main character in your story? (Through what he or she said or did? Through description? How?)

• Tell what the setting was like in the book.

• Have you ever been to a place like the one described in the book?

• Is the setting of your story more or less important than the characters? Why do you think this is so?

• Tell the main things that happened in the story.

• Were you able to guess what was going to happen at the end? How?

• Write another way your story might have ended.

• Do you think the title of what you read is appropriate? Explain. Give details to support your answer.

• What kind of person do you think would like the book you're reading?

• Would you recommend your book to another? Why or why not?

• Write a letter to someone who says he or she doesn't like to read, convincing him/her to read your book.

• How does this book or story make you feel?

FIGURE 8.9 Other Prompts for Reading Response Journals

Jayne wrote:

I read a little bit of the jim morrison biography, it was really cool. It was talking about ALL these romors going round about him being dead and he wasn't.

I really like this book because it tells more about his life than anything eles. And in more detail its a really good thing to read even if you don't like the doors because it tells about his poetry too, and its almost like Fiction sometimes in the book.

The adult volunteer (Nancy) responded:

I used to listen to the Doors. I liked their music when I was in high school. He was a good looking guy. I remember that some of the other members of his group thought he was crazy. What do you think?
Nancy

No he had a rough childhood and he was drunk or drugged all the time.

I didn't know he had a rough childhood. Do you think that is the reason for him doing drugs? Nancy

On another day, Jayne wrote and a student responded:

I read about Jim Morrison in this old circus weakly 1978. It was real interesting

Sounds real intresting to bad I wasn't the one reading it.

Angie

In addition to providing Jayne with an opportunity to communicate with others about what she had read, the RRJ also provided her a place to express negative feelings about reading and writing.

I did not read to day.

The adult volunteer responded:

It seems today was one of those days. No one felt like reading very much. I don't want to nag either, but you need to just read something and quickly jot down the main idea of it. Bring one of your books. I know you're busy at home, but you have some spare time in here to read. Lisa

To summarize, RRJs serve many purposes. They provide the teacher with diagnostic information about the students' reading comprehension: the depth of their understanding and interpretation of the reading; their written communication abilities; and glimpses into their personal experiences, background, and beliefs. These written and dated entries also helped the teacher to determine a grade for Sustained Silent Reading by providing written documentation of student participation.

For the students, writing in RRJs helped them to discover that writing was a valid form of interpersonal communication and that what they wrote was important to others. RRJs also provided students with a record of what they had read. The exchanges among students fostered class cohesion and built mutual trust and respect for each other as learners.

Journal Writing and Process Writing

In addition to the writing in RRJs, the students in this secondary reading class wrote original works in composition books with sewn bindings. These books are excellent for writing journals because the bindings discourage students from tearing out unwanted drafts. This process helps the student to become aware of the concept of drafting. Writing journals were used for free writing, structured prewriting exercises, and other process writing steps. In this journal, entries remained confidential unless writers wished to share their work.

Free Writing

Free writing allows students the opportunity to express their thoughts, feelings, and ideas in a nonthreatening context. It is purely for self-expressions or a first draft in a process approach to writing. Allowing students to choose topics to write about encourages disenchanted learners to write about topics in which they possess knowledge and have an interest. Free writing also helps students to begin to feel comfortable as writers. Some points to remember about free writing:

- Writing is typically not graded.
- Students choose the topics.
- Teacher comments are on content only!
- If students do not wish to share their writings, they should not have to do so.
- Teachers must respect students' wishes for confidentiality.
- Verbal discussion of topics during free writing time is OK.

Free writing is not an activity that is readily picked up by students who customarily have been given topics to write about. Encouragement and verbal probing of interests, talents, experiences, and knowledge usually help to motivate them to write.

Jayne's journal writing allowed her to vent her frustrations and opinions without being concerned about others' reactions. Our first insight into Jayne's views about school are reflected in her first journal entry:

Monday

Today, for me, was a very bad day, but it was just like any other school day so I'm use to it all. The thing that makes it so bad is having to wake up befor noon. It really makes me feel kinda sick, literally sick.

Jayne was not happy to be at school, and she was willing to share those feelings with others.

Jayne used writing to express her opinions and feelings on a regular basis. Although her feelings were generally negative, she did express herself well and usually grounded her feelings with some rationale. For example, one day Jayne stomped into the classroom and asked for her journal. Jayne looked very angry, so the teacher gave her the journal immediately.

> I am sick of hearing all the people who are looking out for my best interest, and doing things that THEY think are good for me.
>
> I'm also sick of the goverment letting people, who don't know who I am or what I'm about, make decisions for my life.

Other opinions that she expressed were about world events. The day after the Persian Gulf War began, the class wrote about their feelings about the war. On this occasion, the teacher asked for students to volunteer to read their entries to the class. Jayne and many others shared their writings. Many other students' writings were equally strong, since many had relatives in the military and used this activity to express their personal concerns. The students responded passionately to each other's writing.

This activity represented a turning point in writing for many students who had once been afraid to share their written works with anyone. They felt comfortable enough with their writing and with each other to share. A student suggested a special-edition newspaper of their works about the war. To publish their writings, the students wrote and revised several drafts of their pieces, conferred together to clarify and extend their writings, edited their own and each other's work, and published their final products. This writing process is described in the next section.

The Writing Process

Although for the purpose of the special-edition newspaper, only one revision was made, the students developed an insight into the process that all writers must go through to publish. The edited writings were typed by using a desktop publishing computer program. The next day, students edited for typographical errors and misspellings. By the afternoon, the Special War Edition of the newspaper was distributed to the student body.

The newspaper experience affected Jayne in an interesting way. She chose to interview several students about their feelings and wrote a second article for the paper based on these interviews. This activity stirred something in Jayne. It gave her a cause that she could relate to her interest in the 1960s. After this publication, Jayne was anxious to write and to publish again. She joined the newspaper staff and quickly completed her reading class. For Jayne, the experience with the newspaper served to move her closer to the school in general and the acts of reading and writing in particular.

Any writing opportunity, whether a special-edition newspaper or a daily journal entry, gives students like Jayne an option for engaging in the process approach to writing (Figure 8.10). The writing process begins with the prewriting activity, which includes the selection of a topic either by individual students or by the class at large. (The process is also effective with a teacher-selected topic, although the selection of a topic must be made with the population of students in mind.) As part of the prewriting activity, students brainstorm for ideas to include in their writing. When this step is completed, students write first drafts without concern for mechanics or spellings. During this second step of the process, the primary concern is to put pen to paper or fingers to keyboard and produce prose. The third phase of process writing is sharing. In this phase, students share their works by reading aloud to their peers, a volunteer, or a teacher. The listener points out areas of strength and asks questions that which will help to clarify or expand the writing. The fourth step is the initial rewriting or second draft. In this draft, additional information is included as needed, and changes are made for clarification. As changes are made, the writer might enlist others' feedback for clarity and completeness. The fifth step is the editing phase, in which mechanics and spelling are stressed. Students might use spellchecker programs with word processors, dictionaries, or other sources for help. Once the students have completed the editing step, they begin the final step, publishing. In this step, they might choose to share their writing with others in the form of newspaper articles, entries in a class book, or letters and cards. The key to the success of the writing process approach is constant interactions between writer and reader/listener about the text. This ongoing conferencing is crucial and will promote cooperative learning. Figure 8.11 presents guidelines for these conferences.

FIGURE 8.10   Six Steps to Writing: A Process Approach

1. Prewriting: Writers generate or select a topic and brainstorm ideas for the text;

2. Drafting: Writers complete first draft without concern for mechanics or spelling;

3. Sharing: Writers read their draft aloud to another who responds with questions for clarification or expansion;

4. Revision: Writers reread their draft and revise based on the questions and areas in need of change;

5. Editing: Writers edit for mechanics and spelling;

6. Publishing: Writers complete the final draft of their work and if desired, distribute their work to others. (Statement about publishing student works and citation.)

Note: Throughout the process, conferencing between writers and readers/listeners is critical to the quality of the finished products.

(These steps were adapted from the works of Graves, 1985; Calkins, 1986; & Atwell, 1990.)

A. Guidelines for reader/listener comments:

  1. Respect the writer's integrity as a person;

  2. Be tactful!

  3. Give encouragement;

  4. Find something positive about the writing and express it to the writer;

  5. Emphasize meaning as the most important element of writing.

B. Sample comments to make to the writer after hearing/reading the writing:

  1. I understand you to be saying _____.

  2. I understand your main point to be _____ .

  3. What I like about this piece is _____.

  4. I would like to know more about _____ .

C. Questions to help writers read their works critically:

  1. Do you like what you have written? What part do you like best?

  2. Does it say what you want it to say?

  3. Did you include everything you wanted to say?

  4. Does it make sense to you?

  5. Is each new idea presented in logical order?

D. Questions and ideas for editing the final draft:

  1. What words do you think are not spelled correctly?

  2. Underline the words you think are not spelled correctly and look each one up in the dictionary.

  3. Read each sentence aloud.

  4. Does each sentence express a complete thought?

  5. Does each paragraph contain one central idea?

  6. Are capital letters and punctuation used correctly?

FIGURE 8.11   Guidelines for Conferencing During the Writing Process

Concept Mapping: A Prewriting and Postreading Strategy

Although Jayne had become motivated to express her feelings in writing and was beginning to participate more actively in class activities, she still needed to acquire strategies for organizing her thoughts and for analyzing others' thoughts. One such strategy that was used as a prewriting activity in the classroom was concept mapping. The steps for constructing a concept map are described in Figure 8.12.

This strategy has been shown to be useful for improving not only the organization of written material but also reading and listening comprehension (Heimlich & Pittelman, 1986; Novak, 1984). Jayne was not willing to use someone else's ideas. The use of a concept map as a strategy was somewhat of a compromise because the strategy was general, but the resulting structure was based on her own ideas of how a certain set of facts might be organized. So she used this strategy and participated in class activities when concept maps were constructed.

Again, Jayne used the concept map to express her personal feelings when the topic of running away from home was suggested. Her concept map (Figure 8.13) indicates that she was able to organize her ideas in a logical and hierarchical form.

The concept map that Jayne created is an example of an organizational scheme that is helpful during the prewriting step in the writing process. This same scheme is useful in attempting to organize ideas acquired from reading text (Novak, 1984). As a prewriting activity, concept maps represent a means of organizing concepts into topics and the topics into supporting facts.

The map provides a visual guide to follow while writing. Each topic can become a paragraph, and each supporting detail can become a sentence. Categorization of the supporting details occurs early in the mapping process, and the relationships among the details, topics, and concept can be identified. The use of the mapping procedure also stimulates the students to recall and organize their prior knowledge about some topic. In Jayne's class, the generation of concept maps was conducted as a class, small-group, and individual activity.

As a postreading activity, mapping allowed students in Jayne's class to formalize their organization of information acquired from reading text. (The directions for constructing a postreading concept map are given in Figure 8.14.) This activity also pro-

FIGURE 8.12 **Constructing a Concept Map as a Prewriting Activity**

1. *Identify a topic:* Independently, in small groups, or as a class, students select a topic with guidance from the teacher.

2. *Brainstorm:* Students generate ideas related to the topic. A student, volunteer, or teacher may act as class scribe.

3. *Categorize:* Students identify ideas which go together in some meaningful way and group them under category names (e.g., collie, doberman, and boxer can be categorized as dogs.)

4. *Graph:* Begin with the topic. Draw lines radiating from the topic to each category name and from each category name to appropriate members or ideas. When possible, words representing the relationships among ideas, category names, and topic should be written on the connecting lines.

5. *Discuss:* Describe how the concept map might be put into sentences, paragraphs, and larger text units.

6. *Writing:* Students begin writing their first drafts from the concept maps.

Note: At each point in the process, additional ideas and revisions in the map can occur.

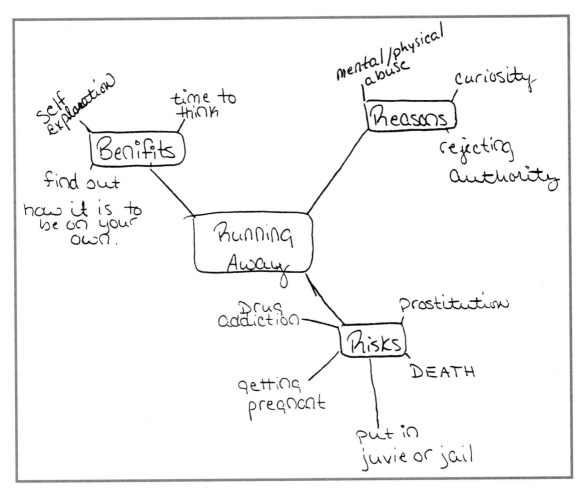

FIGURE 8.13 Concept Map: Running Away

vided the teacher with an assessment of the students' comprehension. It can be accomplished with the text present as a means for helping students to extract the text organization or from memory to provide a view of students' own organization of the text information. One exercise in which Jayne used the concept map as a postreading activity was in a text about trees. Her postreading concept map is shown in Figure 8.15.

FIGURE 8.14 Steps in Constructing a Concept Map as a Postreading Activity

1. Use the title or statement of theme as the topic of the map.

2. Brainstorm about the text.

3. Group the results of brainstorming into categories.

4. Graph, using category names and items from brainstorming.

A disenchanted learner poses one of the more difficult problems to a teacher. In our discussion of Jayne, we described her refusal to complete assigned tasks, which led her content area teachers to question her ability to read. The first task was to disentangle the problem of motivation from any strategic or ability difficulties. The way in which the teacher attacked this problem with Jayne was to provide access to a variety of reading materials, including those brought by the student. This encouraged free selection of topics and materials. By observing Jayne's selections and assessing her comprehension through oral discussion or entries in the reading response journal, her teacher identified interests and her competence in reading. This identification is especially important because a disenchanted learner often views formal tests as meaningless and performs accordingly, regardless of ability.

Writing was a key component of Jayne's school day. The strategy that was selected for helping Jayne to organize her thoughts was concept mapping. Using this strategy, Jayne was able to organize her thoughts using our organizational scheme. In the reading class, Jayne was allowed some control over instructional choices. Once her initial work was published, she was willing to revise her drafts to achieve cohesion and improve her mechanics. This empowered her to become an independent learner, and Jayne became an integral and contributing member of her class.

FIGURE 8.15 Concept Map: Trees

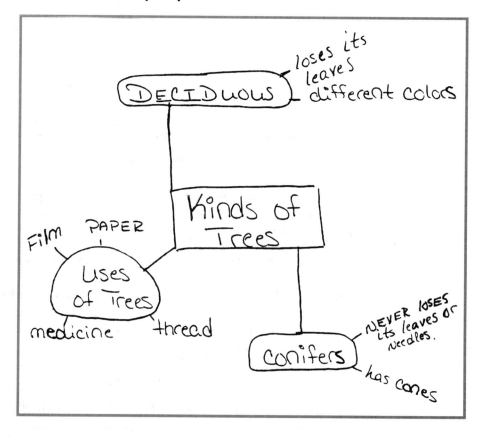

Sherita: A Remedial Reader

This case study follows Sherita, a remedial reader, through two years of reading courses. We will discuss remedial reading and writing strategies and informal assessment measures that are used in the reading classroom. Sherita attended the same alternative secondary school as Jayne but was enrolled primarily for the teen parenting program. She was in the same class as Jayne during her first year in the reading program. When Sherita enrolled in reading, she was 13 years old and in the eighth grade. Her baby was 4 months old. Unlike other teen moms in the class, Sherita's attendance was relatively good. She was present 150 days out of 180 school days.

Because Sherita was a teen mother, she had not only the normal social pressures of being a teen, but also the responsibilities of motherhood. In Sherita's situation, her strong drive to succeed and make something of herself became evident immediately when she participated in the class activities. During the first week of school, Sherita completed an interest inventory in which she expressed her desire to become a better reader and writer and stated her goals of becoming a lawyer and buying a house. The Personal Preference Inventory (Figure 8.16) gave the teacher a quick first look at Sherita's interest and writing ability.

Sherita was not formally tested at the beginning of the year, since screening was unnecessary for placement into middle school reading. Teacher observations of her reading and writing were used to assess her literacy skills and level of motivation. The teacher observed Sherita during the class time and quickly recorded these observations on paper. Those notes helped the teacher to understand Sherita and recognize her strengths and weaknesses as a student.

The reading teacher noted that Sherita had a difficult time settling down during daily sustained silent reading. She observed Sherita talking to her friends before she began to read and sometimes during the reading time. Some days, Sherita selected the newspaper to read, but on other days, she read short, high-interest books written on an elementary reading level. She also selected pamphlets and books about babies, child abuse, and parenting. She was observed on numerous occasions subvocalizing, or reading aloud to herself. Sherita made sweeping motions with her head as she read. The teacher interpreted these observations as signs that Sherita had little experience reading silently, had a variety of interests, and had limited attention to the task of reading.

Sherita's comprehension was assessed by examining her written entries in the Reading Response Journal. She would briefly write about the passage but needed encouragement to include details. For instance, after reading the newspaper she wrote in her Reading Response Journal:

> I read about mothers and fathers who are getting tired of their kids Because the childern are trying to take Over I can see what they are trying to Say, I think that the childern should give their mother and father a little respect

Name_____

Name you prefer to be called_____

Birthdate ___12-26-76___ Age ___14___ Race ___B___ Sex ___F___

1. List your favorite in each area below.

Movie _New Jack City_____

Music _rap_____

Sport _football_____

Hobby _Sewing_____

Magazines _ysb_____

Books _Horror_____

Subject in school _Math_____

Activity out of school _rideing bike_____

2. List 3 goals you have for yourself in the next 5 years? _To finish_

School to become a lawyer and

buy a house

_____

3. What are your goals for this school year? _To finish_

FIGURE 8.16   Personal Preference Inventory

School and make something of my
self.

4. What happened to get you to Beggs? I had a baby

5. How do you think Beggs can help you? To make some
thing out of my self

6. What must you do to attain your goals? Stay in School

7. How do you think a reading class can help you in school and in your life?
I will know how to read
and write.

FIGURE 8.16 (continued)

Sherita, I agree that children should respect their parents. What did the article say was getting the parents tired of their children? I didn't read the article, please give me some more information.

She was able to give the teacher more details upon request after rereading. It should be noted that the entry written by Sherita presented a general summary and stated her opinion. The teacher did not know initially whether Sherita failed to include details about the article because she (1) chose not to include details, (2) didn't know that she should include details in her entry, (3) didn't read the entire article, or (4) did not comprehend the article well enough to retell the details. Only after the teacher probed and orally discussed this article and other reading passages did she begin to understand Sherita's comprehension skills.

Other entries in her RRJ indicated that Sherita could express her feelings and opinions in writing. Sherita used her writing journal as another vehicle for expressing her feelings. Her first journal entry follows:

The worst day I had was when I was in the hosiptil and they would not let me go home And I wanted to go home. They would not let me go home because I had caught a fever and I would not eat and my baby had caught a fever and she was in the intevsive care nursery and they had put a IV in her head and I wanted them to take it out her head.

From this entry in Sherita's journal, the teacher discovered important information about Sherita's interests, life experiences, and writing skills. The teacher noticed that the entire paragraph consisted of one very long sentence. Most of her spellings were standard, and her invented spellings were easily deciphered. Since Sherita began writing without hesitation at the onset of writing time, the teacher interpreted that Sherita had no trouble selecting a topic. The teacher also noticed that Sherita wrote quickly but did not reread her writing upon completion.

The observations of Sherita's first weeks of school led the teacher to conclude that Sherita was a teen mom who was a very social adolescent with a variety of interests. She especially liked to read and write on topics pertaining to babies. While reading, Sherita exhibited behaviors that are attributed to inexperienced readers such as subvocalization and head sweeps. The teacher also noted that Sherita had a limited attention span for silent reading and writing. She read and wrote quickly but seldom included details in the RRJ entries or reread her other written work. She expressed her feelings easily and did not fear writing. In her writing samples, Sherita did not use standard sentence structure or include details to back up her opinions and conclusions. The following literacy activities served motivational, instructional, and assessment functions for Sherita's remedial instruction within a large-group setting. Individual modifications were made when necessary to accommodate her needs.

K-W-L: A Comprehension Strategy

One strategy that was found to help Sherita pay attention to what she read and obtain a better understanding of text was K-W-L (Ogle, 1986). As discussed in Chapter 7, this strategy activates prior knowledge by brainstorming about the topic, relates new information to old, organizes information, and sets a purpose for reading. K-W-L were especially effective for Sherita because of the social interactions they facilitated. In addition, by using what Sherita already knew about a topic, the K-W-Ls validated her own experiences and personal knowledge. She began to recognize that she did know important information. The term *K-W-L* identifies its three principles: recalling what is known about the topic, determining what the students want to know and what they have subsequently learned. The K-W-L is presented in Figure 8.17.

K-W-Ls can be a class, small-group, or individual activity. Students will be able to facilitate small-group and individual K-W-Ls after the teacher has modeled and explained the K-W-L process to the class a number of times. The teacher should select passages for K-W-Ls so that they represent a variety of topics. K-W-Ls are helpful for understanding content area text such as social studies and science.

The first step in the K-W-L strategy is to orally brainstorm about the topic. This step might take the longest but is particularly important for both student and teacher. Teachers have an opportunity to discover what the class knows collectively and which students are willing to take risks by adding to the oral discussion. Students learn classroom conduct for oral discussions and have a chance to activate and validate their own knowledge.

The teacher's responsibility is to conduct the orchestra of students and record their input so that they can see what is being discussed. The teacher must encourage all students to participate in the discussion, try to focus the discussion on the selected topic, and cue the students for additional information. Therefore, it is particularly important for the teacher to have read the selected passage carefully before presenting it to the class. An example of questions a teacher may use to initiate a discussion follows:

TEACHER: Today we will do a K-W-L activity about child abuse. Someone tell the class what a K-W-L is (probe if necessary).

- The title of the pamphlet is _____.
- It was published by _____.
- What do you know about child abuse?

K-W-L Comprehension Strategy Procedure

K-	Know-	What I already know—brainstorming ideas
W-	Want-	What I want to know—predicting
L-	Learn-	What have I learned—summarizing

Step 1   Read the title and look at the pictures.

Step 2   List some information known about the topic. Put this in the K column.

Step 3   List questions about the topic. Put these in the W column.

Step 4   Read the passage.

Step 5   Confirm or correct what was known.

Step 6   Write down all the information learned and the answers to questions. Put this in the L column.

Step 7   Organize the information into categories. (optional)

Step 8   Map the information. (optional)

Step 9   Write a summary using the map. (optional)

Step 10 If questions are unanswered, conduct additional research.

FIGURE 8.17   A Comprehension Strategy

Sources: Eileen Carr and Donna M. Ogle. "K-W-L Plus: A Strategy for Comprehension and Summarization." *Journal of Reading* 30, no. 7 (April 1987): 626–631. Donna M. Ogle. "K-W-L: A Teaching Model That Develops Active Reading of Expository Text." *The Reading Teacher* 38, no. 6 (February 1986): 564–570. Samuel R. Mathews, Josephine P. Young, and Nancy D. Giles. *Reading and Writing: Providing Tools for Brighter Futures.* Pensacola, FL: The Educational Research and Development Center, University of West Florida, 1992.

■ What do you do if you suspect child abuse?
■ What is child abuse?
■ What do you think you will find in this pamphlet?

After the discussion period, the teacher might request that the students copy notes from the board. Next, the teacher might ask the students to develop some questions about what they want to know about the topic. The class might come up with questions as a group or might decide to individually write questions down on paper. (A word of caution: Some adolescents in secondary reading classes might not want to know anything about the topic. Teachers must remember to begin the W step with careful wording.) The modeling of question statements will help students to phrase the questions. For instance, when the teacher asked the class, "What do you think you will find out about child abuse in this pamphlet?," Sherita wrote, "why people beat there children." Figure 8.18 shows Sherita's completed K-W-L on child abuse. The teacher could orally model Sherita's statement into a standard question. "Yes, Sherita, a good question is Why do people beat their children?"

At the conclusion of the W step, the reading material is distributed, and the students are asked to read silently. Teachers might choose to read the pas-

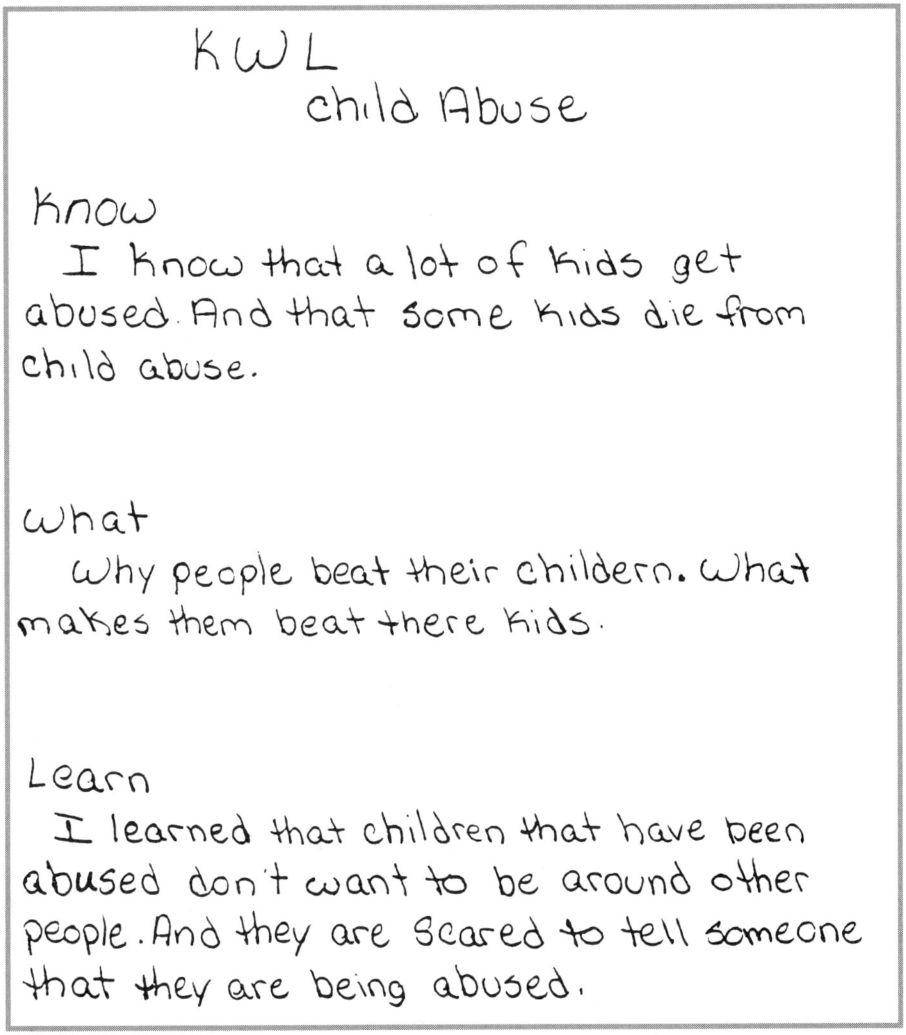

KWL
child Abuse

Know
I know that a lot of kids get abused. And that some kids die from child abuse.

What
Why people beat their childern. What makes them beat there kids.

Learn
I learned that children that have been abused don't want to be around other people. And they are scared to tell someone that they are being abused.

FIGURE 8.18 K-W-L about Child Abuse

sage to the class instead or have the class read it orally. After reading, students are asked to write down under the L—What we learned heading, new information, answers to their questions, and/or confirmations of their prior knowledge.

The K-W-L lends itself to a variety of follow-up activities. A natural follow-up is an oral discussion. Such a discussion can stimulate the students by confirming or validating their own knowledge, exchanging new information, and discussing unanswered questions and topics for research. Other times, the teacher might wish for the students to develop concept maps using the information acquired or to write a summary of the passage.

Teachers can adapt the K-W-L procedure as an interviewing exercise (Figure 8. 19) by asking students to select a partner and write what they think they know, what they want to learn, and, after an interview, what they learned about their partner.

KNOW
In the space below write everything you know about the person next to you.

WANT
Write three questions that you will ask this person to help you get to know them better.

1.

2.

3.

LEARNED
Ask the person the questions and then write everything you learned about him/her in the space below.

FIGURE 8.19   Getting to Know You: A K-W-L Interview

Sherita's ability to participate and read for specific purposes improved with time and repeated K-W-Ls. She became a facilitator for whole-class and small-group K-W-Ls. She would be the first to explain the purpose and procedure to new students. When asked by the teacher about how the K-W-L strategy helped her, Sherita replied, "K-W-Ls show you what you know, and what you have learned. They help you learn stuff you didn't know."

Reading to Adolescent Students

Reading to students like Sherita serves many purposes. One purpose is to expose them to a variety of literature. Another purpose is to build the attitude that reading can provide entertainment. It is also a way to discover different cultures, places, and people; is a stimulus for discussion; and is a means of acquiring knowledge about text structure and vocabulary. Reading aloud to adolescents also provides a vehicle for modeling comprehension, word study strategies, and the art of reading to children.

For the reading-aloud activity, the teacher selects a text to read to the class. It might be a poem, a newspaper article, a short story, a chapter or section of a novel or textbook, or a children's book. Since secondary teachers feel the pressure to fulfill course requirements within time constraints, the teacher might select material that could meet a requirement. These readings do not have to be long, and reading aloud does not have to take place each day. The readings might appear to be purely for enjoyment but may serve other purposes at the same time. For example, the teacher might read the children's book *Mufaro's Beautiful Daughters, An African Folk Tale,* by J. Steptoe (1987), to the class. The class will be able to discuss the story structure of folk tales, possibly relating it to other familiar tales. They also may find out about African tradition, different cultures, times and people. This particular book lends itself to a discussion of personality traits. Students could discuss orally or in writing the answer to the question "Which daughter do you most like and why?"

An extension activity that was used with *Mufaro's Beautiful Daughters* was a discussion of African word origins and general word-attack skills. For example, the text provides a pronunciation guide for names such as Mufaro (Moo-FAR-oh). As other unfamiliar names and terms were encountered, word attack skills could be continually practiced and reinforced. In addition to word-attack skills, vocabulary activities were incorporated. The name Mufaro means "happy man" in the Shona language of Africa. Students could first predict what the name meant and then confirm the actual meaning based on context clues from the text.

Reading aloud to students can fit into most course curricula. When studying biographies, an English teacher might choose to read the book, *Flight* (Burleigh, 1991), a children's book about Charles Lindbergh. A history teacher could choose *Flight* to enrich the study of the story of aviation, an art teacher might choose it to discuss book illustrations, and a reading teacher might choose the book to model the K-W-L strategy.

Reading children's books like *Flight* and *Mufaro's Beautiful Daughters* in secondary classrooms exposes teen parents and other adolescents to children's literature that their children might also enjoy. Once adolescents like Sherita began to build confidence in themselves as readers, they can practice their newfound strategies by reading aloud to younger children. This activity was especially helpful for Sherita, who had difficulty reading grade-level texts but who needed practice reading. By reading children's books to young children at a neighboring elementary school, she read texts at her independent reading level while at the same time she entertained and instructed younger children. For teen parents like Sherita, this activity provides guided practice and motivation for reading to their own children.

Summary of Sherita

Sherita was unlike Peter in that she did have the basic building blocks of literacy. She simply lacked more sophisticated strategies of comprehension and the guided practice in reading that brings about fluency in silent reading and deeper comprehension. While Jayne required a great deal of effort to gain the motivation to read and write, Sherita stated that her personal goals included becoming a better reader and writer. Capitalizing on her motivation and interests, the teacher was able to provide practice in sustained silent reading by supplying materials on child care, child abuse, and relevant children's literature. Higher-level strategies were demonstrated and practiced in whole-class setting through K-W-Ls and concept maps. To model fluency in reading, the teacher read aloud to Sherita's class. This also provided an opportunity to model comprehension strategies through think-aloud dialogues and prediction questions.

As Sherita became more confident in her own reading abilities, she volunteered to become a reader for a nearby elementary school. Her task was to read children's books aloud to kindergartners. This accomplished three goals. First, her participation made her a legitimate helper for others who were learning to read. Second, by reading aloud to others, her own reading fluency improved. Third, practice in reading to other young children gave her the confidence to read to her own child. This type of activity in itself might contribute to a second generation of readers.

SUMMARY

In this chapter, we have addressed many of the needs of adolescent students with reading problems. We presented three different classifications of these students:

nonreaders, disenchanted readers, and remedial readers. Adolescents with reading problems have many overlapping characteristics that can pose problems for the teacher. In the case studies, we described three adolescents who, for a myriad of reasons, performed poorly on literacy tasks: Peter, who lacked many of the very basic elements of literacy; Jayne, who had become disenchanted with the system and refused to try; and Sherita, who had the competing priorities of teen motherhood and was lacking sufficient literacy skills to perform at grade level.

Our proposed solutions to the problems centered on five guiding principles:

1. establish trust with the students,
2. provide literate role models,
3. reduce the feelings of learned helplessness and passive failure,
4. legitimize the students' personal knowledge and experiences, and
5. developing a learning environment.

Since adolescents seek to establish their own identities, our approaches had to provide unique and varied opportunities and nonthreatening assessment strategies. One way to achieve this goal was to provide reading materials that reflected a wide variety of interests. These materials included newspapers, magazines, and content area books.

Another way in which students exercised choice was in topic selection for writings or dictations. By selecting their own topics and using the writing process, the students acquired a strategy for generating and organizing their thoughts and for writing and revising drafts.

Adolescents were encouraged to write summaries and reactions about what they read using Reading Response Journals. The teacher's responses were nonevaluative and often were requests for clarification or more details. These responses served several purposes. First, by demonstrating respect for their feelings, a trusting relationship began to develop between the teacher and students. The second purpose that was served was a demonstration of the importance of supporting one's opinion or generalizations with detailed information. The Reading Response Journal served a third purpose: The students' written discussions of what they read provided the teacher with a comprehension measure of what they had read.

Through the use of K-W-Ls, students realized that they did possess knowledge about a number of topics. This realization increased their confidence and many times helped to overcome learned helplessness. Another strategy that allowed students to use their own ideas was concept mapping. Students were able to brainstorm about a topic and then apply their own ideas to the topic's organization. These strategies served to validate the students' own knowledge and to motivate class participation.

One of the key concerns in attempting to reach adolescent students with reading problems is providing access to literate role models. This access can be accomplished through classroom volunteers, literate peers, and, most important, the teacher. During sustained silent reading, everyone should read. When writing in the Reading Response Journals, the entire class, including the teacher, should participate. Class activities such as K-W-L and concept mapping provide opportunities for the teacher and peers to model and think aloud strategies for brainstorming and organizing ideas.

In working with adolescents, it is important to remember that they do enjoy having someone read aloud to them. Whether to an individual with a DLTA exercise or to a small group or the entire class, reading aloud provides an excellent opportunity for practicing class discussion, prediction, and comprehension strategies through thinking aloud. In addition, reading aloud can be beneficial for teen parents. Whether being read to or reading aloud themselves, they are gaining experiences that can support their efforts to foster literacy in their own children.

Each of the activities provided ongoing, informal assessments of students' prior knowledge and their use of reading and writing strategies. When the teacher discovered a student's strength, that strength was used as a building block for instruction. As areas of weakness were identified, whether skill-based or more strategic, instruction was tailored to meet their needs.

Adolescent students with reading problems come to the classroom with a broad spectrum of concerns. These concerns include the normal teen issues such as dating, peer acceptance, and establishing their independence from their families. In addition, adolescents with reading problems face the social stigma of illiteracy and the reality of falling behind same-aged peers in school. By providing an environment in which trust can be developed, literacy can be modeled, and choices can be made within the curriculum, the teacher can help adolescent students to return to the status of confident and independent learners.

REFERENCES

Allen, Roach Van. *Attitudes and the Art of Teaching Reading.* Washington, DC: National Education Association, 1965.

Altwerger, Bess, Carole Edelsky, and Barbara M. Flores. "Whole Language: What's New?" *The Reading Teacher* 41, no. 2 (November 1987): 144–154.

Atwell, Nancie. *In the Middle: Writing, Reading, and Learning with Adolescents.* Portsmouth, NH: Boynton/Cook, 1987.

Bandura, Albert. *Social Foundations of Thought and Action: A Social Cognitive Theory.* Englewood Cliffs, NJ: Prentice Hall, 1986.

Calkins, Lucy McCormick. *The Art of Teaching Writing.* Portsmouth, NH: Heinemann Educational Books, 1986.

Davidson, Judith, and David Koppenhaver. *Adolescent Literacy: What Works and Why.* New York: Garland, 1988.

Erikson, Erik H. *Childhood and Society,* 2d ed. New York: Norton, 1963.

Graves, Donald H. *Writing: Teachers and Children at Work.* Portsmouth, NH: Heinemann Educational Books, 1983.

Hall, MaryAnne. *Teaching Reading as a Language Experience.* Columbus: Merrill, 1981.

Harter, Susan. "The Relationship Between Perceived Competence, Affect, and Motivational Orientation Within the Classroom: Process and Patterns of Change." In *Achievement and Motivation: A Social-Developmental Perspective,* ed. Ann K. Boggiano and Thane S. Pittman. New York: Cambridge University Press, 1992.

Heimlich, Joan, and Susan Pittelman. *Semantic Mapping: Classroom Applications.* Newark, DE: International Reading Association, 1986.

Johnston, Peter H., and Peter N. Winograd. "Passive Failure in Reading." *Journal of Reading Behavior* 17, no. 4, (1985): 279–301.

Novak, Joseph. *Learning to Learn.* New York: Cambridge University Press, 1984.

Stauffer, Russell. *Directing the Reading-Thinking Process.* New York: Harper and Row, 1975.

Stauffer, Russell. *The Language Experience Approach to the Teaching of Reading.* New York: Harper & Row, 1980.

Weaver, Constance. *Understanding Whole Language.* Portsmouth, NH: Heinemann Educational Books, 1990.

CHAPTER **9**

Mature Readers
and Writers

FROM LEARNING-TO-READ TO READING-TO-LEARN

By third grade—certainly by fourth—the demands that are placed on students' reading ability change dramatically. In previous years, they had been given short, pleasant texts to read, and plenty of support and instruction to develop their reading skills and processes. By the later elementary grades, however, students must read longer passages, often from informational texts, and they must learn from them.

One part of the challenge is to read actively, to "mine information" from text. Another part of the challenge is to follow the patterns of text successfully to learn. Still another part is to develop the vocabulary with which to understand text. We deal with all three aspects of older students' literacy in this chapter.

A MODEL OF INSTRUCTION TO GUIDE READING-TO-LEARN

It will help both the teacher and the students approach the learning process if we organize our instruction and the students' study into three phases: *anticipation, investigation,* and *reflection.*[1] This three-part approach derives from a constructivist view of learning, which we might paraphrase this way:

> We learn by using the knowledge structures that we already have to interpret new phenomena that we encounter. As a result of interpreting new phenomena, we incorporate new insights into our existing knowledge structures. As we incorporate new insights into our existing knowledge structures, those knowledge structures change to become more sophisticated and capable of making finer distinctions about a wider array of phenomena in the future.

If we accept the constructivist view of knowledge in the above paragraph, it follows that we should think of learning episodes in the following three phases:

---

[1] Vaughn and Estes (1986) use the terms *anticipation, information search,* and *reflection* for what we mean here. Steele, Meredith, and Temple (1997) use *evocation, realization of meaning,* and *reflection* to correspond to these terms.

1. *Anticipation.* We often begin a lesson with strategies to get students curious about the topic—to get them to activate their prior knowledge. We might ask students what they know about the topic and what questions they have about it. We hope that by awakening their curiosity, their thoughts, and their questions, we will prepare the students (or they will prepare themselves) to enter the next stage, *investigation,* with alert and active minds.

2. *Investigation.* Once their curiosity is tweaked, their questions have been raised, and their purposes are set, students now use a variety of strategies to explore the topic—or, in psychological terms, to assimilate the new information to their old knowledge structures.

3. *Reflection.* In the reflection phase, students look back over what they have studied, consider what they knew about the topic at the outset and what they know now, consider the implications of what they have found out, and reassess their assumptions about the topic in light of what they have just learned. Again, in psychological terms, students are now asked to go back and reassess or update their knowledge structures (ideas, beliefs, and attitudes) to accommodate their old ways of thinking to the new insights they have gained.

We have a host of different methods to choose from the advance students' learning at each one of these phases. In the next several sections, we will outline teaching strategies that help students organize their thinking at each phase of the learning process.

STRATEGIES FOR THE ANTICIPATION PHASE

Activities in this phase of a lesson are meant to summon up the students' prior knowledge about a topic, arouse their curiosity, and lead them to set purposes for their further studies.

Advance Organizers

The educational psychologist David Ausubel (1970, 1978) developed the idea of the *advance organizer,* with the thought that beginning a lesson with a brief explanation of a topic to give students "the lie of the land" could help them make better sense of the information that was coming. So, for example, before having students read a passage about Marco Polo, the teacher talks briefly about the geography of Europe and Asia and the state of transportation in the late Middle Ages. The talk would give some context for the students' understanding of the passage on Marco Polo. (The passage on Marco Polo is included in the appendix to this chapter.)

Group Brainstorming

The teacher sets out a topic and asks the class to *brainstorm,* that is, to think of everything that comes to mind about a topic in a fixed period of time—say, five minutes. The teacher lists these ideas on the board. The teacher might help the students to arrange their ideas into categories to elicit better coverage of the topic. In the case of Marco Polo (see the text in the appendix to this chapter), for example, the categories might be "Who?" (Who was Marco Polo? Who else is involved in his story?), "What?" (What did he do?), "Where?" (Where did he do it?), "When?" (When did the major events happen?), "Why?" (Why did he do what he did?), and "So what?" (What was important about his accomplishments? Why is he remembered?).

Then the teacher has the students read a text (or listen to a lecture or watch a video) and see which of their ideas were borne out by the material they encountered.

Paired Brainstorming

This activity is similar to the one above, except that pairs of students list on a sheet of paper the facts and ideas that they know or think they know about a topic. They may also set questions to be answered in a reading. Teachers set a time limit set for this activity—usually five minutes or less. Again, it might help if the teacher has them arrange their ideas into categories.

Terms in Advance

In advance of a lesson, the teacher might choose four or five key terms from a text and write them on the board. Pairs of students are given five minutes to brainstorm how those terms might be related, how they *will* be related—in a historical chronology, in the explanation of a scientific process, or in a work of fiction—in the text they are about to read. Once the pairs have agreed on a set of relationships among the terms, the teacher asks them to consider the text carefully to see how those same terms played out in the text.

Scrambled Sequences

As a whole-group activity, the teacher might write five or six individual events from a sequence of events or from a cause-and-effect chain, each on its own piece of paper. They are scrambled and placed on the chalk tray of the board (or else individual students are asked to hold them up). Members of the class are asked to consider the proper ordering. One at a time, students are invited to come forward and place one item in what they think is its proper place. Once the class has more or less agreed on an ordering, the teacher asks them to scrutinize the text carefully as they read it to see whether the text had the same ordering as the one that the students came up with (Reutzel, 1985).

Free Writing

We can invite students to write down in five minutes, without stopping, everything that comes to mind when they think about a topic about which they are about to read (Elbow, 1989). When the five minutes are up (and it's advisable to call time after five minutes and give the students one more minute to finish up, as good ideas often come out under pressure), we might ask the students to read their paper aloud to a partner.

At this point, many options are available. We can invite pairs to share ideas with the whole group, as in the group brainstorming, or we might ask the students to underline the ideas in their paper that they are least sure about and pay close attention to the reading to learn whether it sheds light on their areas of uncertainty.

Semantic Mapping

Semantic mapping is a versatile technique that helps to summon up students' prior knowledge (Steele & Steele, 1991) in the *anticipation* phase of a lesson.

We begin by writing a word or phrase for the topic in a circle in the center of the chalkboard or piece of chart paper: "Marco Polo," for example. We might demonstrate how we would come up with a satellite idea: "What he did," for example. We write those words up to the right of "Marco Polo," draw a circle around them, and connect them with a line to "Marco Polo." Then we invite students to say all that they think they know about what he did. As each idea is listed, we write it up, draw a circle around it, and connect that circle to "What he did." If a student says "He was an explorer," the word "Explorer" goes in the circle; then, as more details come in about *where* Marco Polo explored, and so on, these are written up as satellites to the word "Explorer" (see the example in Figure 9.1).

After the students have filled out the cluster of ideas as far as they can, we ask them to think about where we need more information. We write big question marks next to the parts we are unsure of. We ask the students to pay close attention as they read the text: to confirm the things we correctly knew, to correct the ideas we were wrong about, to fill in knowledge we had questions about, and to tell us interesting things we hadn't thought of.

Know/Want to Know/Learn (K-W-L)

Called the K-W-L strategy for "What do we KNOW?" "What do we WANT TO KNOW?" "What did we LEARN?" (Carr and Ogle, 1987; Ogle, 1986), this procedure can be used within a single class period to guide a reading (or guide the attention of students who are watching a film or listening to a lecture), or it may be used to guide an inquiry that stretches over several days.

We divide the chalkboard (or a large piece of newsprint) into three broad columns marked, "KNOW," "WANT TO KNOW," and "LEARN." We also ask the students to produce their own version of the K-W-L chart in their notebooks.

Next we state the topic and ask students what they already know about it. We discuss this until a set of essential facts emerge, which the students are reasonably sure about. These we record in the "KNOW" column on the large chart (and invite the students to do the same in the notebooks in which they might be writing at their desks).

Once the students have offered, several ideas we ask them to help us think of categories into which the ideas can be grouped. For example, if we were doing a KWL about Marco Polo, we might group the facts under categories such as the "Who?," "What?," "When?," "Why?," and "So What?" that we saw earlier in this chapter. Then we might ask the students to find out whether they could offer any more ideas that could go within each category.

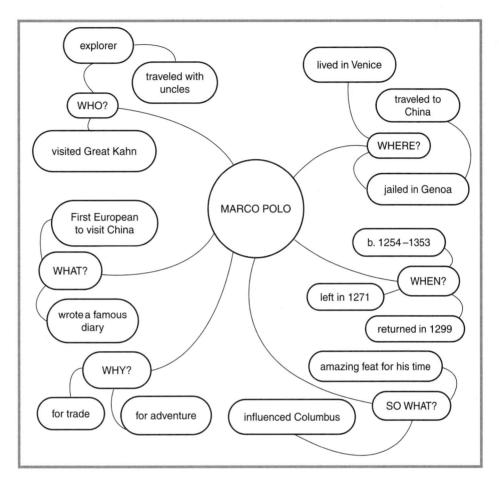

FIGURE 9.1 A Cluster on "Marco Polo"

As students think about the prior knowledge they have about a topic, areas of uncertainty will emerge, too. These can be entered into the "WANT TO KNOW" column. We ask students to think of other things they are curious about with respect to the topic, and record these, too, both on the chart, and in their individual notebooks. Again, if we invite students to think of questions within each category, more questions are likely to emerge.

Now, if the students are to read a text, we review the questions they raised and assign the reading. (Note, however, that if it is a broader inquiry we are undertaking, we must first discuss where they will find the information: From the library? If so, what books or periodicals? How will they find them? Or from informed sources? If so, how will we find them? How do we approach them? How do we interview them, and record and report what they have to say?)

The next parts of the activity take us beyond the anticipation phase. After the reading is complete, we turn to the third column, "WHAT DID WE LEARN?" We ask the students to record the main points they learned on their charts—lining up the answers with the questions they raised originally and writing the other information (the knowledge they had not anticipated) lower on the column. Now the students share with the whole group what they entered in the "LEARNED" column of their own charts, and this is entered into the large chart that is displayed before the whole class. The students compare how much they knew already with what they found out and compare the answers they found with the questions they raised. They decide what to do about the remaining unanswered questions, which might lead them into another cycle of KNOW/WANT TO KNOW/LEARN.

Think/Pair/Share

Think/Pair/Share (Slavin, 1996) is an engaging strategy that can be used at any point in a lesson in which we want students to think about issues. To use a Think/Pair/Share in the exploratory phase of a lesson, the teacher thinks of a discussion question that bears on the topic and that can be talked about briefly. The question might take the form of asking students to list what they know about a topic, recount a personal experience that has bearing on a topic, or reflect on a philosophical issue that has bearing on a topic.

During a period of four or five minutes, the teacher puts that question to the class and asks each student to prepare an answer. Then the student shares that answer with a partner and listens carefully to the partner's answer. Then the two of them may next prepare a joint answer. The teacher calls on three or four pairs to give a 30-second summary of their discussions.

The Anticipation Guide

An anticipation guide (Vacca & Vacca, 1989) is another activity that activates students' prior knowledge and stimulates predictions about the text. An anticipation guide is a set of statements about the text that students respond to and discuss before the reading of the text. The teacher's role is to create the anticipation guide, accept a broad range of student responses, and facilitate discussion before reading. After reading the text, the teacher should lead students to contrast their own predictions with the author's stated meaning. Vacca and Vacca (1989, p. 145) provide guidelines for constructing and using anticipation guides:

1. Analyze the material to be read. Determine the major ideas—implicit and explicit—with which students will interact.
2. Write those ideas in short, clear, declarative statements. These statements should in some way reflect the world that the students live in or know about. Therefore, avoid abstractions whenever possible.
3. Put these statements into a format that will elicit anticipation and prediction making.
4. Discuss readers' predictions and anticipations before reading the text selection.
5. Assign the text selection. Have students evaluate the statements in light of the author's intent and purpose.
6. Contrast readers' predictions with author's intended meaning.

A sample anticipation guide appears in Figure 9.2.

Directions: Before you read the article on mummies, mark those statements that you think are true *T* and those statements that you think are not true *NT*. Then discuss your responses with class members. After you read, mark the statements again using the information that you learned.

Before   **After**

1. _____   Egyptians believed everyone had a *ba* and a *ka*.   _____

2. _____   Bodies that were not preserved were said to be mummified.   _____

3. _____   People believed that Pharaohs became gods when they died.   _____

4. _____   To make mummies, embalmers took out the inner organs.   _____

5. _____   The embalmers did not take the brain out through the nose with hooks   _____

6. _____   Shabits are magical figures that were tucked into the mummy's wrappings. _____

7. _____   Everyone who died in ancient Egypt became mummies.   _____

F I G U R E 9.2 Anticipation Guide: Mummies in Egypt

STRATEGIES FOR THE INVESTIGATION PHASE

Once students have summoned up their prior knowledge, examined what they were sure of and not so sure of, raised questions, and set purposes for learning, they are ready for the next phase, the investigation phase. Several strategies are available to students in this phase, too.

The I.N.S.E.R.T. Model

I.N.S.E.R.T. (Vaughn and Estes, 1986) stands for "Instructional Note-taking System for Enhanced Reading and Thinking." The device is used in two parts. Only the first is relevant to the investigation phase of a lesson. Here, students are given a system for marking the text as they pursue different kinds of information in it:

✓ A check marks a statement that *confirms* an idea they already knew.

− A minus sign (−) marks a passage that contradicts something they thought they knew.

+ A plus sign (+) marks a passage of interesting information that they had not anticipated.

? A question mark (?) goes next to a passage that they would like to know more about.

As they read the assigned text, they place the appropriate mark in the margin next to relevant passages.

Since the categories of information that students will be marking in the text relate back to what they knew or thought they knew about the topic of the text, the I.N.S.E.R.T. system works best when preceded by an *anticipation activity* that asks students to summon up their prior knowledge about the topic. Brainstorming or paired brainstorming work well for this purpose.

ReQuest Procedure

When students need support in reading text for information, one way to structure a reading so that they give each other that support is to use the *ReQuest Procedure* (Manzo, 1970, 1991). In this procedure, two students read through a text, stop after each paragraph, and take turns asking each other questions about it. For example, after reading the first paragraph (silently) in the text about Marco Polo, the teacher asks David several good questions about that paragraph. She asks him questions about main ideas. She asks about nuances. She asks what importance some item in this paragraph might come to have later in the text. (She is trying not only to get David to think about the text, but also to model for David the kinds of questions he might ask when it comes to be his turn.) David has to answer those questions as well as he can. After David has finished answering the teacher's questions, it is his turn to ask her questions about the same paragraph, and the teacher has to answer them. When David and the teacher have both brought to light the important information in that paragraph, they read the next one. After that paragraph is read, David now gets the first turn at asking the teacher all the good questions he can think of about that paragraph. When he is finished, the teacher gets to ask him questions. When both are finished, they read the next paragraph, and so on.

After the teacher has introduced the activity by being a questioning partner, the teacher sets up pairs of students to ask questions of each other.

Reciprocal Teaching

An activity that is a significant step beyond the ReQuest procedure is the activity of *reciprocal teaching.* Developed by Brown, Palincsar, and Armbruster (1984), reciprocal teaching is a procedure for teaching comprehension skills systematically. The authors note that while word recognition skills are already taught in a carefully sequenced and managed fashion, comprehension instruction in many classrooms seems designed mainly to practice skills that have not really been taught (Brown et al., 1984; Pearson, 1985). Reciprocal teaching was developed to take students through the steps of reading with comprehension so that, after repeated practice, the students come to use, on their own, reading strategies that pay off in high rates of comprehension.

To carry out reciprocal teaching, the teacher meets with a group of five to fifteen students, each of whom has a copy of the same content area reading material. The teacher begins by modeling four tasks that are related to a segment of the material:

1. Summarize the segment in a sentence.
2. Ask the students one or two good questions about the segment.
3. Clarify the difficult parts.
4. Predict what the next segment will be about.

The students' responsibilities are to judge whether or not the summary is accurate, to decide whether or not the questions tap what is important about the passage and to answer them, and to help clarify the difficult parts.

After modeling the group leader's role five or six times, the teacher asks a student to be the teacher. Figure 9.3 and 9.4 are guidelines that provide support for students as they act out the role of teacher.

The student then carries out the same steps the teacher did, while the teacher

1. conducts the activity as often as his or her turn comes up;
2. joins the others in judging the accuracy of the summaries and the importance of the questions;
3. supports the student playing the role of teacher with frequent but appropriate praise;
4. keeps the students on task; and
5. challenges the "teacher" to perform slightly above her or his immediately past level of performance (give a more comprehensive summary, ask a main idea question following several factual ones, make a more logical prediction of what will follow).

Finally, at the end of each half hour's reciprocal teaching, the teacher gives the students a passage they have not read before and asks them to make a summary of it or answer a few substantial questions about it (Pearson, 1985).

After performing the outward activity of reciprocal teaching over several weeks, students internalize the strategies of summarizing, questioning, and predicting and use them when reading independently. Palincsar, Brown, and their colleagues have evidence of dramatic gains after reciprocal teaching with junior high school students who were fair in word recognition but poor in comprehension of content-area material (Brown et al., 1984).

FIGURE 9.3   Reciprocal Teaching

Source: Nettie Linton. "Reciprocal Teaching: An Update." Inservice Presentation. The School District of Escambria County, Pensacola, FL, 1989.

1. Question
FORMING GOOD MAIN IDEA QUESTIONS (WHAT IS IMPORTANT IN THE TEXT?)

2. Summarize
IDENTIFY THE MAIN IDEA.

3. Clarify
WHAT IS CONFUSING IN THE TEXT?

4. Predict
WHAT WILL BE DISCUSSED NEXT?

Student Name _____

Title of Selection _____

Paragraph 1

A. Predict: (*I believe this paragraph will be mainly about*) _____
_____

B. Read _____

C. Was prediction correct? (Yes or No)_____ Give reason: _____
_____

D. Question: _____
_____

E. Clarify: _____
_____

F. Summarize: (*This paragraph was mainly about*) _____
_____

Paragraph 2

A. Predict: (*I believe this paragraph will be mainly about*) _____
_____

B. Read _____

C. Was prediction correct? (Yes or No)_____ Give reason: _____
_____

D. Question: _____
_____

E. Clarify: _____
_____

F. Summarize: (*This paragraph was mainly about*) _____
_____

Replicate worksheet to match number of paragraphs in passage.

FIGURE 9.4 Reciprocal Teaching Guide for Students

Source: Nettie Linton. "Reciprocal Teaching: An Update." Inservice Presentation. The School District of Escambia County, Pensacola, FL, 1989.

Study Guides

Study guides help to guide students' processes of inquiry even when the teacher is not present, as when student are reading an assigned reading independently. The sample study guide in Figure 9.5 is intended to direct the students' attention to certain ideas that are woven through a text on the topic of corn. The students

1. In what wasy have humans adapted corn to our own uses?

2. How long have humans been manipulating corn plants for their own purposes?

3. Some people claim that it is unnatural, and therefore wrong, for people to "tinker" with nature. Using what you know about corn, construct an argument that agrees or disagrees with that position.

FIGURE 9.5   Study Guide for "Corn: What Good Is It?"

are expected to think about the questions as they read the whole piece and write down their answers either as they read or after they read. Later, their answers to the questions can frame a whole-class or small group discussion about the topic of the text.

For the purposes of promoting critical thinking, study guides work best when they

1. help students to follow intricate patterns of thought or subtle ideas that they probably would not have reached on their own but *do not* serve as a substitute for a careful reading of the text,
2. invite critical or higher order thinking at every step, and
3. are used as a springboard to discussion or writing, and not as an end in themselves.

Figure 9.5 shows an example of a *three-level study guide.* Students are given this guide to consider *before* reading a lengthy passage about corn, to guide their investigation.

Answers to the first two questions are woven through many parts of the assigned text. The third question asks readers to engage in higher-order thinking about the insights they were guided to assemble in the first two questions.

The questions that are asked on a three-level study guide such as the one above ask questions of this form (Vaughn and Estes, 1986):

1. "What did the author say?"
2. "What did the author mean?"
3. "What can we do with the meaning?"

In preparing a study guide, the teacher often proceeds in reverse order. That is, we decide what the most important use of the meaning in the reading is, and we formulate a question or questions about it. Then we decide which concepts or insights a student would have to have reached to get the main benefit from the article. Then we decide what facts the students would have to have noticed to derive those concepts or insights. Then we present the questions the right way around.

Study guides may take other forms, too. *Pattern guides* are specially constructed to call students' attention to the ways different genres of text organize information. An example of a chronological pattern guide is given in Figure 9.6. Other pattern guides will be considered later in this chapter when we discuss patterns of text organization.

A. Fill in the blanks with an event or events that happened in Burton in each time period:

Before A.D. 800	After A.D. 870	Tenth Century	Eleventh Century	Seventeenth Century
_____	_____	_____	_____	_____
_____	_____	_____	_____	_____
_____	_____	_____	_____	_____

B. Fill in the blanks with a brief description of what the town of Burton might have looked like in each period.

Before A.D. 800	After A.D. 870	Tenth Century	Eleventh Century	Seventeenth Century
_____	_____	_____	_____	_____
_____	_____	_____	_____	_____
_____	_____	_____	_____	_____

FIGURE 9.6 A Chronological Pattern Guide for "Burton"

Dual-Entry Diaries

Dual-entry diaries (Berthoff, 1981) are ways for readers to closely link material in the text to their own curiosity and their own experiences. They are especially useful when students are reading longer assignments, out of class.

To make a dual-entry diary, the students should draw a vertical line down the middle of a blank sheet of paper. One the left-hand side, they should note a part of the text that struck them strongly. Perhaps it reminded them of something from their own experience. Perhaps it puzzled them. Or perhaps they disagreed with it. On the right-hand side of the page, they should write a comment about it: What was it about the quote that made them write it down? What did it make them think of? What question did they have about it? As they read the text, they should pause and make entries in their dual-entry diaries. Some teachers assign a minimum number of dual-entry diary entries: so many entries for every ten pages read, for example.

As we shall see, reviewing the students' entries to their dual-entry diaries later in class can structure a whole-class discussion.

A Lesson in Cooperative Learning: Jigsaw II

Jigsaw II is a popular cooperative learning technique developed by Robert Slavin et al. (1992).

The teacher should go through the text in advance and prepare four different *expert sheets*, which are sets of questions that relate to the most important points in the reading passage that will be assigned. (One suggestion for an expert sheet would be a study guide, such as the one discussed above.)

The lesson should proceed as follows:

1. **Set the Stage.** Explain that the class will be doing a cooperative learning activity called Jigsaw II. Announce the topic of the lesson, and explain that everyone will be responsible for learning all parts of the text, but each person will become an expert on one part of the text and will teach others about it.

2. **Assign Students to Home Groups.** Assign students to home groups of four or five members.

3. **Read the Text.** Distribute copies of the text to all students. Also, distribute to each student in a home group a different *expert sheet*. (If there are more than four people in a home group, distribute copies of more expert sheets, so that not more than two people have the same expert sheet.)

   The expert sheet has questions to guide that person's reading of the text. The expert sheets differ, because later, each person will be responsible for helping the others in the home group to learn about the aspects of the reading covered by his or her expert sheet.

   Allow an adequate amount of time for everyone to read the passage. Everyone should read the whole text but should pay special attention to the material that answers the questions on his or her expert sheet. If people finish early, they should take notes on portions of the text that pertain to the questions on their expert sheet.

4. **Study the Text in Expert Groups.** Set up four tables or clusters of chairs to seat four *expert groups*. If there should be more than six students in any one expert group, divide that group into two groups. Appoint a discussion leader for each expert group. Spend a few minutes going over the rules of participation:

   a. Everybody participates. Nobody dominates.
   b. The group agrees on what the question means, or what the task is, before answering.
   c. When you are not clear about something that is said, restate it in your own words.
   d. Everybody sticks to the task at hand.

   Explain that the expert groups will have twenty minutes to discuss their questions and answers to them. They should already have located answers to the questions in the text, and they should take notes on answers their group offers to the questions. Also, they should decide how they are going to teach their material to their how groups. The teacher should circulate among the expert groups to help them stay on task.

5. **"Experts" Teach the Text to Home Groups.** When the study period is up, have the students leave the study groups and return to their home

groups. Now each student should take about five minutes to present to the home group what she or he learned in the expert group. The "expert's" task is not just to report, however, but to ask and entertain questions from the group, to make sure everyone learned his or her piece of the text.

6. **Evaluate the Process.** Ask each person to write about what he or she contributed to the discussion and what could make the activity go better.

Strategies for the Reflection Phase

Many of the strategies that are followed during the anticipation and investigation phases are designed to culminate during the reflection phase. Here are several that do.

Paired Brainstorming/Paired Summarizing

The same pairs that brainstormed what they knew as preparation for reading a text can now go back and review what they thought and compare it with what they found out. Just as they wrote out a list of points that they thought they knew, they may now write out a list of important points that they gained from the reading.

Terms in Advance, Revisited

Students who were given key terms in advance of a reading and asked how they might relate can be asked to construct a description of how those terms do relate, now that they have read the text. It might help if they create a *cluster* of those terms (see below).

Scrambled Sequences, Revisited

Some students were given items, terms, or events before the reading and asked to predict the proper order in which they should be arranged (following cause-and-effect chains or chronology). They can be asked to arrange those terms properly, now that they have read the text. Pairs of students should prepare to explain to the class why they arranged the terms as they did.

Semantic Mapping, Revisited

In the semantic mapping exercise that was conducted before reading, students arranged terms in "satellite formation" around the main topic. Ideas were introduced about which they were unclear; and some ideas, missing altogether, were represented by question marks.

Now that they have read the text, pairs of students (or, alternatively, the whole class) can construct clusters that properly denote the relationships between the key terms or concepts in the reading. The teacher might structure this exercise by giving the students a list of terms that they should include in their clusters. When they are finished, pairs of students should be called on to display and explain the arrangement of their clusters.

K-W-L, Revisited

If the *K-W-L* framework is used, before the reading, students will have made columns containing the information they already knew about the topic and questions they had about it. The information and questions will have been arranged into categories. Now, following the reading in the reflection phase, on the chalkboard for the whole group, the teacher add a larger last column for "What We LEARNED" from the reading. Students should be asked to contribute ideas to this column. It helps if they are quizzed about what they learned within the categories that were set up; then they can be asked about other information, even other whole categories of information, that also arose from the reading. As an alternative to the whole-group lesson, pairs of students can construct and fill in a K-W-L chart.

The I.N.S.E.R.T. Chart, Revisited

After they have completed the reading, students who have marked their text using the I.N.S.E.R.T system now create a chart in which they list in the columns three or four items of each category of information: information that they marked with a check mark because they were sure about it, information that they marked with a minus sign because it was contradicted, information that they marked with a plus sign because it was important but not anticipated, and information that they marked with a questions mark because it was unclear or because they want to know more about it (see the sample chart in Figure 9.7).

Study Guides, Revisited

If a study guide has been constructed well, it will have begun by asking students to gather insights from several parts of the text. These will be worth reviewing, because students are likely to have gathered different information. It will also have asked students to form an opinion or construct an argument, about which there are likely to be different points of view. These also are worth revisiting, since they are likely to yield lively discussion.

Dual-Entry Diaries, Revisited

After students have done the reading, dual-entry diary entries can help in the reflection phase, as the teacher moves through the text, asking students to share the comments they made on each page. The teacher should have prepared comments, too, to call attention to parts of the text that he or she wants to be sure to have discussed.

✔	−	✚	?
Marco Polo traveled from Italy to China.	He did not go alone.	The emperor made him a governor.	How did he talk to the Chinese?
He went in the 1300s.	The Chinese were nice to him—I thought he had trouble.	He had a family when he returned home.	Why didn't he keep exploring?

FIGURE 9.7 Example of an I.N.S.E.R.T. Chart

Think/Pair/Share, Revisited

As we saw above, the think/pair/share activity is a quickly performed cooperative learning activity that invites students to reflect on a text and have the help of a colleague in giving shape to their ideas. It may be done several times during the course of a reading or lecture and works well as a brief exercise in reflection. The teacher prepares a question in advance, usually of an open-ended nature, and asks individuals to write out a brief answer to it. Then students pair up and share answers with each other, trying to arrive at a joint answer that incorporates both people's ideas. Finally, the teacher calls as many pairs as time permits and has them give a thirty-second summary of their discussions.

Ten-Minute Essays and Other Free Writes

Following a reading or a class discussion, students can be helped to collect their thoughts if they are asked to write a ten-minute essay, using the free write technique. To set up a ten-minute essay, the teacher asks students to write without stopping on the topic of the reading and discussion.

Some writing teachers insist that the act of writing itself can open up wells of creativity in the mind that are unlike the more deliberate sort of thinking that we do when we plan what we are going to write (Elbow, 1989). Thus, in producing a free write, students write continuously without stopping If they can't think of anything to write, they write "I can't think of anything to write." The point is to keep the writing coming out without going back over it, examining it, or being critical of it.

Many teachers occasionally follow free writes with the invitation to go back through the free write, choose the most promising ideas, and craft a new essay, using these insights as the core of the paper—and eliminating all of the other chaff that usually comes out in a free write.

The Five-Minute Essay

The five-minute essay is used at the end of class to help students to get closure on their thoughts about the topic of study and to give teachers a better connection to the intellectual happenings of the class. The five-minute essay asks students to do two things: Write one thing you learned about the topic, and write one question you still have about the topic.

The teacher collects these essays as soon as they are written and might use them to plan the next day's lesson.

The Concept Chart

Another way to elicit and organize students' thinking about a topic they have read about is to use a *concept chart.* The concept chart is especially useful when three or more items or issues are being compared. The chart is set up by assigning the *rows* (the items arrayed horizontally) to the items being compared and the *columns* (the items arrayed vertically) to a particular feature according to which they are being compared.

For example, a concept chart might compare several vocations, as the example in Figure 9.8 does.

FIGURE 9.8 Concept Chart

	Preparation Required	Job Stability	Salary Level	Job Satisfaction
Physician	Extensive: University, plus medical school, plus internship	High	High	Moderately high
Artist	Moderately extensive: Training, plus long practice to reach proficiency	Low	Uncertain: Expect long periods of hunger!	Highest
Factory worker	Less extensive.	Moderate: Jobs can change, or move away.	Moderate	Can be low

Concept charts can be used as an exercise during a whole-class discussion, or teams of students, or even individual students, can use a concept chart to organize their thinking and discussion.

Three-Part Diaries

Students need to interact with the material, and interact with the teacher regarding the material, if their inquiry is to be powered by personal curiosity yet also have the benefits of a wise guide. For that reason, teachers use the *three-part diary.*

The diary is used throughout a whole course, and it is useful for shaping and recording a student's inquiry from day to day, as an aid to study, as a means of linking the student's learning in the course to his or her life outside of class, and as a means to frame longer written compositions. The three sections of the diary have different functions. The first section is used for the student to write his or her responses to the readings and discussions. A dual-entry diary format (see the discussion earlier in the chapter) is often used for this section; the student divides each page down the middle with a vertical line and writes notations on one side and comments on the other.

The second section is left for the student's own thoughts and associations about the topic. The student is encouraged to record thoughts that occur to him or her, notes from informal readings and other conversations—in short, any information and insights that further the student's understanding and appreciation of the topic of study. The material in this section will be used to inspire the writing of formal papers later on, but it will take some work by the teacher to make this happen. The teacher keeps his or her own three-part diary and, from time to time, reads to the class from the notes entered in this middle section. "Thinking aloud," the teacher demonstrates how he or she finds recurring patterns of interest or ideas strong enough to inspire further inquiry. The teacher then encourages students to do the same with this section of their diaries, meeting individually with students when there is time and encouraging students to interview each other about their entries in this section. The goal, again, is to find the thread of an inquiry, a recurring pattern of curiosity, an insight that is trying to be born.

The third part of the diary is reserved for letters to the teacher. Every month, at least, students are asked to write the teacher a letter, in which they comment on the class and their work in it, raise questions they have had, express hopes for their learning, and describe their own experience of learning in that course: What were their thoughts in the beginning? What goals do they have for themselves? How have they experienced growth in learning? What impediments are they facing? What would help?

The teacher collects the diaries (on a staggered schedule) every month and responds in writing to each students' letters.

Discussion Strategies

The difference between a rich and dynamic discussion and one that degenerates into the teacher doing all the talking with the students sitting in sullen silence is often elusive. Generally, those discussions are best where the students' curiosity sets the direction. The teacher has a critical facilitative role, though. J.T. Dillon (1986) has identified four "moves" or strategies that the teacher uses to keep a discussion going and keep it student-centered.

1. ***Statements.*** Statements are a way of expressing your own response or understanding or need for clarification of what has been said. They are less directive than questions, though, and thus they often invite a freer response in return. You might say, "So as I understand it, you're saying _____" or "That reminds me of something _____ said earlier . . ." or "wait a minute, though. You're saying _____, but Dan just said _____" or "I'm confused about _____."

2. ***Questions.*** Students will discuss their own questions more enthusiastically than the teacher's. So cultivate ways to ask students to venture questions about the text. Here are some useful prompts: "So what should we be asking about this text?" "What's been left out of our discussion so far?" "What's not clear about what has been presented in this text?" "What does anyone feel called on to agree with in this text?" ". . . to *disagree* with?"

3. ***Signals.*** Because the teacher's comments can often carry inordinate weight, it is often best to keep the discussion going with gestures and signals, rather than with comments. A quizzical expression can invite clarification. Two hands held out as if weighing two items can invite students to choose between agreeing with one statement and another. A look of friendly concern can encourage a student who is struggling to give words to an idea.

4. ***Silence.*** When a question is on the floor, allow time for it to be answered. A wait time of three, four, or five seconds serves as a powerful motivator for someone to fill the void. If the teacher doesn't fill it, someone else will.

The Discussion Web

An active discussion can cover a lot of ground, and it's not unusual for students to remember only the last things said or the ideas that were put forth most forcefully. Graphic organizers might help with this problem. Graphic organizers, written aids to capture and display the results of students' thinking, are useful at all stages of a discussion. They can help to frame a question, record and keep preliminary thoughts available for review, and communicate the group's findings to others.

One particularly useful graphic organizer, the discussion web, was adapted by Donna Alvermann from the work of James Duthie (1986). The discussion web is used to organize a five-step lesson, arranged around any text or topic that invites controversy (the taking of two different points of view):

1. The teacher prepares the students to read the selection by setting up the appropriate exploratory activity, that is, by giving them whatever background knowledge, vocabulary, or predictive questions they are likely to need.

2. After the students have read the selection and perhaps have had an opportunity to share their personal responses to it to a partner or in a small

group, the teacher assigns the students to pairs and asks each pair to prepare a discussion web like the one shown in Figure 9.9. The teacher should point out that the students will be asked to take sides on a question that is specific to the text. After reading the first half of Phyllis Reynolds Naylor's *Shiloh,* for instance, students might be asked, "Was Marty right to keep the dog Shiloh, even though it wasn't his?"

The discussion web has two columns, marked "Yes" and "No," and the pairs are asked to think of as many good reasons pro and con as they can—reasons why Marty was justified in keeping the dog and reasons why he was not. The students should try to list an equal number of reasons in each column.

3. After a few minutes, each pair is asked to join another pair and pool their reasons, pro and con. After they have considered all of the reasons, the foursomes are asked to reach a consensus agreement on an answer. They should write that answer at the bottom of the web, in the space marked "Conclusion," and also write the best supporting arguments. The teacher should remind them that individuals may dissent from the consensus, but they should try to keep an open mind.

4. When each foursome has arrived at a consensus, the teacher gives each of them three minutes to share their conclusion with the class and to discuss which of their reasons best supports their finding.

5. The teacher concludes the activity by asking students to write their own answers to the question, taking into account the other arguments they have heard. Post these answers on a bulletin board so that students can read what others have written.

The discussion web may stand on its own. It may also be used as a springboard for writing (have the students write a short essay in which they take and defend a side of the argument) or as the warm-up to a debate (have the class divide between those who are pro and con, with "undecideds" in the middle). In both these cases, it is preferable to stop the discussion web activity before step 3, that is, leave it to the individuals to reach their conclusions either in writing or by means of the debate.

Academic Controversy

Academic controversy (Kagan, 1992) is another cooperative learning activity that follows a pattern similar to that of the discussion web (see above). But unlike the discussion web, students are responsible for finding reasons to support only one side of an argument at a time. This is easier for some students, in our experience, than listing arguments for both sides during the same step. Also, the procedure includes an explicit invitation for students to step out of their roles and argue what they really believe—an opportunity that most students enjoy. The activity proceeds as follows:

1. The teacher assigns a reading, preferably one that raises an issues that invites diverse responses.

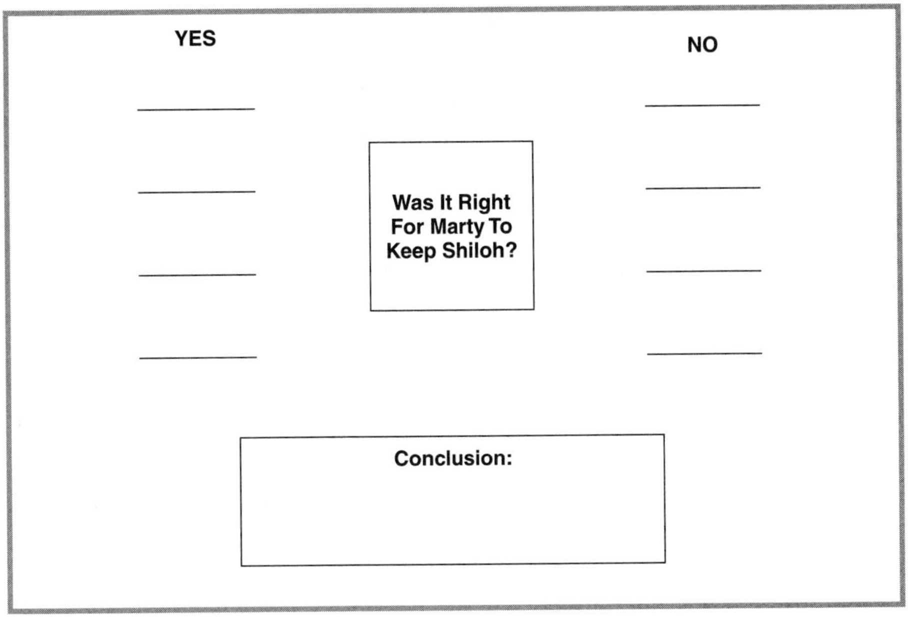

YES | NO

———————   ———————

Was It Right
For Marty To
Keep Shiloh?

———————   ———————

———————   ———————

———————   ———————

Conclusion:

FIGURE 9.9   Discussion Web for Shiloh

2. The teacher prepares at least one issue for discussion, stated in a form that is likely to elicit at least two justifiable positions from students (for example, "Was Jack justified in stealing from the giant?").
3. Students are assigned to groups of four.
4. Within the groups, pairs of students are assigned a position on the issue that they must defend.
5. The pairs list reasons that support their position.
6. The pairs temporarily split up and form new pairs with classmates who are defending the same positions. They share the reasons each of the original pairs listed in support of the position.
7. Students return to their original partners and set out a position statement followed by supporting reasons: "We want to argue for _____ because of X, Y, and Z."
8. Each pair presents its argument to the other pair within their group while the latter pair listens and takes notes.
9. The two pairs then debate.
10. Optionally, the pairs within each group may now be told to switch positions and repeat steps 4 though 8.
11. Finally, the students stop defending any point of view and construct the position on which they can find consensus, supported by the best reasons that came to light in the previous discussion.

Trade a Problem

Trade a Problem (Kagan, 1992) is a cooperative learning activity that has the advantage of inviting the students to find the important issues in a text, to investigate those issues, and to learn about them. The activity works as follows:

1. The teacher assigns a reading. (Appropriate exploratory activities should be used.)
2. After the reading, students are assigned to random pairs.
3. The pairs identify the four or five most important points in the reading.
4. These pairs join other pairs to form foursomes. They discuss the main points they found and clarify uncertainties and disagreements.
5. Each pair now writes a set of questions to answer or problems to solve for the other pair.
6. The pairs link up again. They take turns questioning each other: Each pair putting one of its questions to the other pair, who then offers an answer.
7. After the questions are all answered, the four students reflect on what they have learned from the exercise.

UNDERSTANDING PATTERNS OF TEXT ORGANIZATION

The way in which information is organized in text makes a difference in the way we understand and use the information. Good readers recognize and correctly respond to different arrangements of text; poor ones often do not (Marshall and Glock, 1978–1979). Consider how some typical patterns of text structure affect readers' responses to the text.

Taxonomy

What pattern of organization do you perceive in this passage?

The Guitar

The guitar is one of the most popular stringed instruments. Because it has a fret-board and strings stretched across a soundbox that are played by plucking, the guitar is considered a member of the lute family.

For centuries, the guitar had a rather small wooden body with soft strings fashioned of animal gut. In the present century, however, several distinct classes of guitars have emerged. The traditional version has lived on as the "classical" guitar, but there are now steel-string guitars and electric guitars as well.

The steel-string guitar has a long, narrow neck and an enlarged body. It makes a louder, more piercing sound than the classical guitar. The electric guitar, an offshoot of the steel-string guitar, has its sounds amplified and its tones modified by electronic devices. It can make sounds loud enough to deafen a rock musician. It can also make a variety of tones, many of which do not sound guitar-like at all.

This piece of text is organized by classifying, by listing and defining the different instruments collected together under the label "guitar," and by showing their relation-

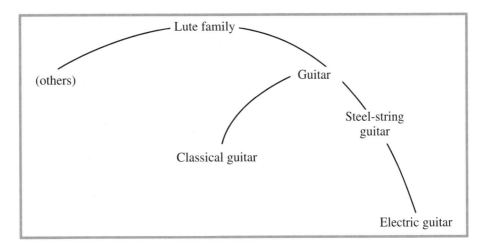

FIGURE 9.10   A Taxonomic Outline

ships to one another. Classifying is a fundamental act of the intellect, and text such as that in the passage is usually the result. This passage can also be outlined by means of a tree diagram, as in Figure 9.10. Classification charts like this are called *taxonomies*.

If readers are to understand this passage, they must perceive the taxonomic structure. If you asked them to recall what the passage said, you would expect them to remember the kinds of guitars that were discussed, what makes them different from one another, and how they are related within the "family." Taxonomic text structures are frequently encountered in science materials, especially in biology.

The key to creating a tree diagram for a taxonomic outline is identifying the author's most inclusive or most general category. In the *guitar* passage, the clue to the most general category is the statement "the guitar is considered a member of the lute family." This implies that the lute family would include other instruments that have "fretboard and strings." So *guitar* is a smaller class of instruments than *lute*. The remainder of the taxonomic outline follows the same logic. Classical and steel-string are two types of guitars, and electric guitar is one type of steel-string.

The ability to classify topics in a hierarchical structure is critical. Class discussion, using the guide to concept mapping found earlier in this chapter, provides an opportunity to model the development of a taxonomic outline. This time is also a good one to develop the idea of supporting details. For example, the steel-string guitar can be described in more detail by using the terms *long, narrow neck,* and *enlarged body*. The taxonomic outline can be expanded to include these details.

Chronology

What pattern of organization do you perceive in this passage?

Burton

The town of Burton, in the Midlands of England, has a history that is typical of trading villages of the region. Nothing of the town existed before the ninth century A.D.

Before 870 A.D.	After 870 A.D.	Tenth Century	Eleventh Century	Seventeenth Century
No town; thick woods	Northumbrian fortress built	Pastures cleared; manor houses built	Roads; market center	Town sacked by Cromwell; town abandoned

FIGURE 9.11 A Chronological Outline

The hill overlooking the Avon River where the town now sits was covered with an impenetrable wood.

In about A.D. 870, Northumbrian knights cleared the hillside and erected a rude fortress as an outpost against the South Saxons lurking across the Avon, which then served as the southern frontier of Northumbria. By the time peace was effected some thirty years later, a stone castle had been built, surrounded by about thirty dwellings. Some crops had been grown nearby.

With the peace and political stability of the tenth century, Burton grew in earnest. Pastures were cleared for five miles during the first half of the century, and fine manor houses were erected from the wood and the profits of sheep raising. Trails that criss-crossed the settlement grew to well-traveled roads, and by the middle of the eleventh century, Burton served as the chief market center for the surrounding thirty- or forty-mile area. The town grew comparatively wealthy.

But prosperity came to an end when Cromwell and his Roundheads burned the town in the seventeenth century. They marched the residents of Burton off into captivity, and few ever returned.

This account is arranged according to a sequence of events. Its most prominent organizational feature is *chronological*. To comprehend the passage successfully, readers have to picture the unfolding of events across the perspective of time. If you asked them to recall this passage, you would expect them to remember the events that were described, the time they occurred, and the order in which they occurred. Chronologically organized text can be reduced to a timeline, as shown in Figure 9.11. Chronological structures are frequently encountered in historical texts. Since both stories for children and chronological texts are organized by the sequence of events in time, the transition into this type of text might be less troublesome than other structures.

A strategy that aids students' comprehension of historical texts such as "Burton" is the construction of a timeline. To acquaint students with the concept of a timeline, one teacher asked them to develop timelines of their own lives—autobiographical time lines. This strategy communicates the concept of a sequence of events from an informed perspective—the students' own lives. Figure 9.12 shows a personal timeline activity.

Cause and Effect

The passage about the town of Burton also used cause and effect for organization. How would you outline the following passage, in which this pattern is more pronounced?

1. Look at sample time lines in class.
2. Think about your life since you have been born.
   A. What has happened in the world, in your family, at school, and within your peer group to affect your life?
   B. Think about your future—what wil you do this summer? What will you do when you finish high school? What must you do to accomplish these goals? (You may go to the library to use reference materials if needed.)
3. In your journal make notes of these events, one per line. (Include dates or your age when possible.)
   • Read over them, add or delete any events.
   • Number them in the order in which they took place and will take place.
   • Wait a day—talk to your parents and friends about your life.
4. Look over your notes, making adjustments.
5. Construct a first draft of your time line.
6. Conference with a volunteer or teacher. Edit. Redraw on white paper. Illustrate if desired.

FIGURE 9.12

Black Robes in the Desert

Scientists sometimes question the wisdom of "folk wisdom." The case of the Tuaregs' robes is a case in point. These nomadic people live in the area of the southern Sahara desert, the hottest terrain on earth. For centuries they have worn the same head-to-toe black wool robes. Since black absorbs more heat from the sun than any other color, scientists wonder why they've kept them through the years. Some people speculated that they had only black sheep as a source of wool, but an inspection of their herds dispelled that notion. Others speculated that black might have been chosen for its protection against the nightly desert cold, but scientific tests showed that black robes held heat no better than white ones.

Finally, through a series of experiments it was discovered that the black robes are actually cooler than white ones. The explanation is that the sun heats the upper part of the robe, which causes air to rise up through the loose-fitting robe and out through the open neck. In this way, a constant draft is maintained through the robes. This draft evaporates perspiration, which cools the wearer.

To understand this passage, readers must operate on at least two levels: They must recognize the larger cause-and-effect question "Why do the Tuaregs wear black robes in the desert?" and recognize its answer "Because their black robes keep them cool." They must also recognize the more specific set of cause-and-effect relationships that explain the seemingly contradictory statement that black is cooler in the desert.

A cause-and-effect flowchart is shown in Figure 9.13. This chart links the causes and effects and shows how one leads to another.

Cause-and-effect writing is found in many content subjects, including health, social studies, the sciences, and home economics. Other graphic organizers for cause-and-effect structures are depicted in Figure 9.14.

Written Directions

Some written materials give instructions for carrying out a procedure or performing some action. Simpler materials of this sort communicate a series of tasks that must be performed in some order:

FIGURE 9.13 Cause-and-Effect Flowchart

Source: Wisconsin Department of Public Instruction. *Strategic Learning in the Content Area.* Madison, WI, 1989.

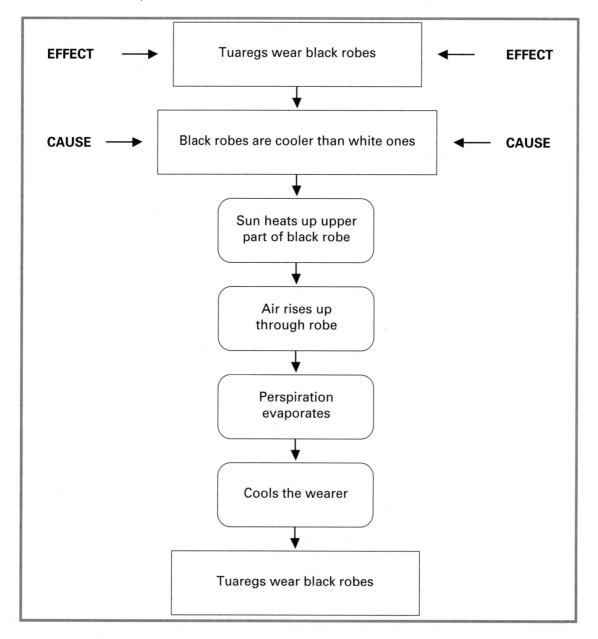

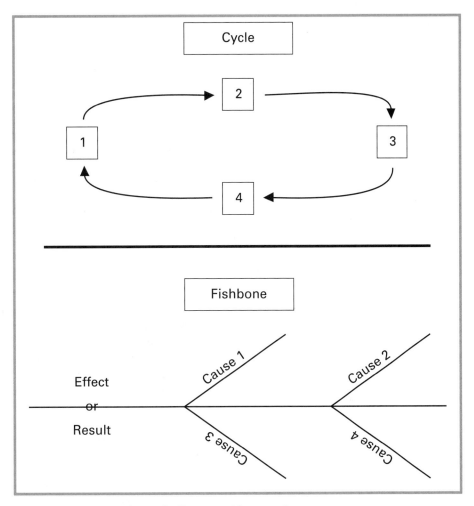

FIGURE 9.14 Cause-and-Effect Graphic Organizers

Source: Wisconsin Department of Public Instruction. *Strategic Learning in the Content Area.* Madison, WI, 1989.

Making Microwave Popcorn

Remove the plastic outer wrap from the package. Unfold the bag of popcorn, and place it in the center of the microwave oven with the directions facing *up*. Set your microwave to *full* (100 percent) power. Set the timer for 5 minutes, and listen carefully as the popcorn pops. When popping slows to 2 to 3 seconds between pops, stop. Note how long the popping took this time, and next time set the timer for the same length of time. Remove the bag from the microwave and open it carefully at the top, avoiding the hot steam that will escape.

To understand this passage adequately, readers must attend to the steps described and to the order in which they are given. Readers can demonstrate their understanding by arranging a set of picture cards in the right order, putting the sentences from the passage in correct order, writing the steps in order, acting out making popcorn, or actually making popcorn in a microwave oven.

What to Do in Case of Fire

In the event of a fire in this building, students must immediately and quietly stand beside their desks. The teacher should press his or her hand against the classroom door. If the door feels hot to the touch, the door must *not* be opened. Instead, the teacher is to lower the rope ladder stored in each classroom from the window ledge. The children will then climb down the rope ladder one at a time. As they reach the ground, they are to proceed at a walk to the west end of the playground, where they will line up and remain silent.

If the door is not hot to the touch, the teacher may open it and inspect the hall for flames or smoke. If the fire is at the north end of the building, the class will exit by the south stairway. Conversely, if the fire is at the south end of the building, the north stairway will be used. Each class will proceed at a walk to the west end of the playground to line up and remain silent. Each teacher will ascertain whether all the pupils are present at that time.

This passage cannot be understood by carrying out one sequence of tasks, because no *one* sequence is appropriate for all situations. Readers must recognize not only the tasks and their sequence, but also the situations in which each alternative sequence should be followed. They should be able to roleplay the correct procedure for each situation or answer questions such as "What should you do if the fire alarm rings and the teacher tells you the door feels hot?"

The relationship of the ideas in the fire drill passage can be outlined in a flowchart as in Figure 9.15. Material that takes the form of written directions is seen most frequently in math, science, home economics, and vocational education.

The writing-reading connection can also be used effectively to increase comprehension of written directions. Activities such as creating a piñata, making valentines for classmates, or making a model log cabin can serve as stimuli for creating a set of written directions. The process of creating a product, recording the steps for that process, and then exchanging these written directions with others provides students with the means to develop a schema for written instructions.

Comparison and Contrast

To understand what something *is,* it is often helpful to know what it is not. Comparison and contrast go beyond simple description by describing two or more things simultaneously and pointing out their likeness and differences.

Will the Real Cowboy Please Stand Up?

So many people pretend to be cowboys these days that it is getting harder to tell the real cowboys from the dudes. Dudes and cowboys both wear Western hats; wide, tooled leather belts; and ornate buckles, jeans, and boots. The jeans of both

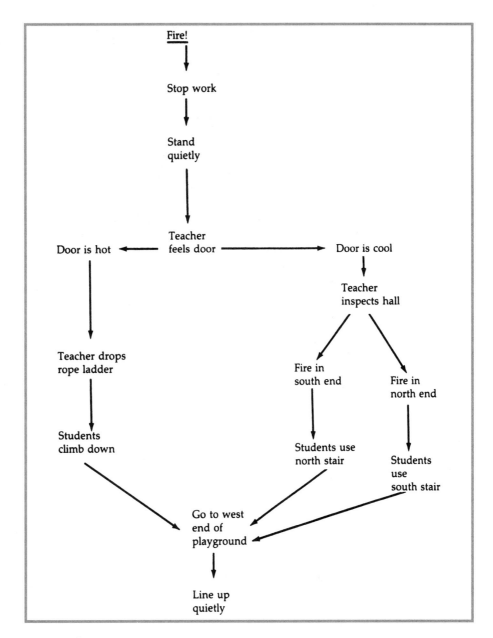

FIGURE 9.15   A Flowchart of Written Directions Containing Contingency Sequences

Source: Wisconsin Department of Public Instruction. *Strategic Learning in the Content Area.* Madison, WI, 1989.

dudes and cowboys may be worn or faded, in contrast to their boots. Both dudes and cowboys are likely to wear shiny, expensive-looking boots, but the real cowboy's belt is usually sweat-stained around the top edge, and he often tucks his jeans into the tops of his boots. The brim of the cowboy's hat is sometimes tipped at a rakish angle, but so is the experienced dude's. Neither is particularly bow-legged anymore, although this used to be one way to distinguish between the two. Nowadays, both dudes and cowboys are apt to drive pickups or jeeps instead of riding horses.

The surest way to tell a real cowboy from a dude is to look at his eyes. The cowboy's eyes are clear and steady, and he holds your gaze. The dude's eyes flicker this way and that, as if to see what impression he is making on others.

When a description is formulated for one of the things being compared but not the other, we must mentally supply its opposite to the things not described. For instance, if one man's belt is sweat-stained, the other's belt must not be so.

The ultimate test of a reader's comprehension of this passage would be to distinguish between a cowboy and a dude. To demonstrate comprehension, the reader might produce graphic organizers like the ones in Figure 9.16. Comparison-contrast structures are found in many content subjects, especially social studies and science.

Explanation or Exposition

Much text material in schools is used to describe or explain. Since its organization varies widely, it does not lend itself to a cut-and-dried description. The material might be entirely verbal, as in the following example, or it might include numbers and formulas, charts, graphs, and pictures.

The Deadly Cobra

The cobra is one of the most deadly snakes in the world. Many wildlife experts consider it *the* deadliest animal. Its venom, its mobility, and its behavior are legendary.

The cobra's venom is more powerful even than that of the rattlesnake. Its fangs do not inject the venom as do the fangs of other poisonous snakes; instead, they are used to pierce deep wounds in the victim's flesh, and the cobra releases venom from sacs in its mouth into these punctures. The deadly venom is carried by the bloodstream and attacks the victim's central nervous system. One African variety spits its venom at its victim's eyes; it can spit up to eight feet with almost pinpoint accuracy, and the highly corrosive venom blinds the victim unless it is immediately washed away.

The cobra's mobility is chilling. In spite of its size, it can move with great speed almost soundlessly. It creeps up on its intended victim undetected and can move on or above the ground with equal efficiency. It glides silently along the branches of trees or building rafters as well as along the ground. Its mottled skin provides a good camouflage, since it blends almost perfectly with dead leaves, tree bark, grasses, and dusty earth.

The cobra might be the only snake that seeks out humans. Most snakes and other animals avoid contact with humans at all costs and attack them only when escape is blocked or in defense of their young, but cobras seem to have no such avoidance instinct. Instead, they have been known to seek out and follow humans before attacking them without provocation. Their actions are those of a predator hunting, and the prey is human.

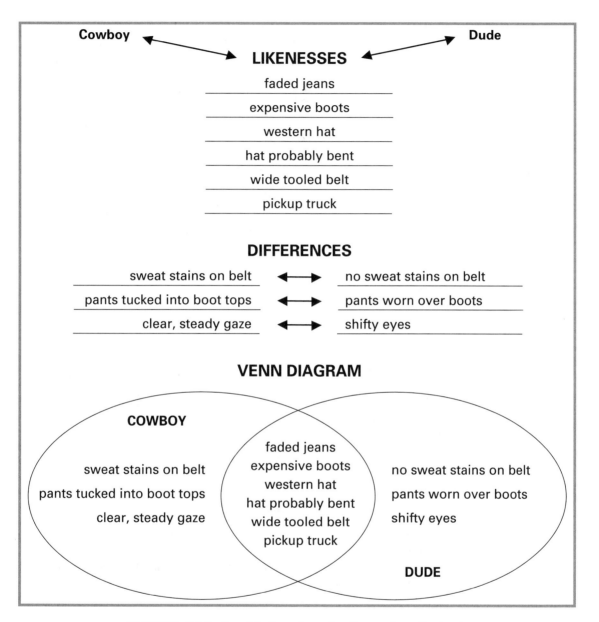

FIGURE 9.16   Graphic Organizers for Comparison-Contrast

Source: Wisconsin Department of Public Instruction. *Strategic Learning in the Content Area.* Madison, WI, 1989.

Comprehending expository material usually entails recognizing main ideas and supporting details. Expository material is often captured nicely by the traditional outline format because it explicitly shows the relation among ideas of

---

The Deadly Cobra

I. Venom
   A. More deadly than rattlesnake
   B. Puncture wounds made by fangs
   C. Released from sacs in mouth
   D. Attacks central nervous system

II. Mobility
   A. Has great speed in spite of size
   B. Moves silently
   C. Moves on or above ground easily
   D. Is camouflaged by coloration

III. Behavior
   A. Does not avoid human contact
   B. Seeks out, follows humans
   C. Attacks without provocation

FIGURE 9.17 Expository Outline

different levels of importance. Figure 9.17 shows an outline of this expository piece. Figure 9.18 shows another way to graphically represent expository text using a concept map.

Expository writing is encountered in virtually every subject in the curriculum. Whenever information has to be explained, expository prose is the choice.

Textbooks from elementary school through college employ a wide variety of patterns for organizing information. The mental activity that is involved in comprehending a passage written in one pattern may be somewhat different from that required to comprehend a passage written a different way (Estes and Shibilski, 1980).

These texts often include a variety of structures such as taxonomic, chronological, cause-and-effect, or comparison-contrast. The task in comprehending expository text is to identify how the various topics are related to each other. To accomplish this, it is helpful to understand each structural unit, one at a time. In the cobra text, there are examples of several structures. Figure 9.19 shows a guided practice exercise aimed at helping students identify these text structures.

VOCABULARY

Vocabulary is an important and troublesome issue in content area reading and writing. By the time they reach third grade, students must be able to read and understand many words that they usually do not use in speech (Chall, 1979). When they are successful at gleaning new words, we rightly conclude that reading has made a major contribution to their education. For those who do not suc-

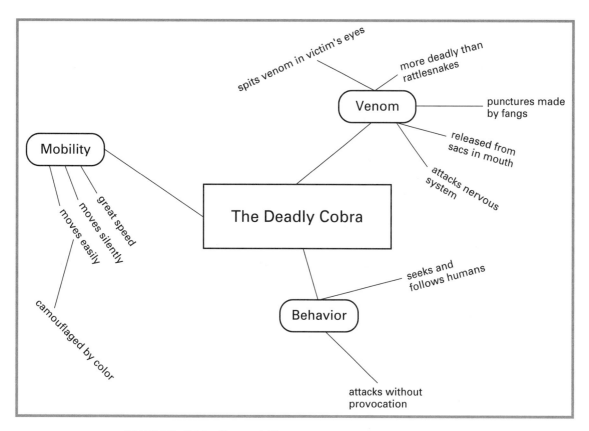

FIGURE 9.18   Concept Map

ceed, however, vocabulary constitutes a widespread problem in the middle and upper grades, especially in the content subjects.

We will deal with two main aspects of vocabulary: background concepts to which vocabulary words can be related and strategies to derive approximate word meanings from surrounding context.

Vocabulary and Background Concepts

If you're one of those who had to look up and write out endless lists of definitions in school, *vocabulary* might have have pretty boring associations for you. *Vocabulary* may mean using a word you didn't know where a familiar one would do.

To some extent, that criticism is justified: English does have "50 cent words" (these usually come down to us from the Anglo-Saxon) and "$64 words" (these almost always come from Latin or Greek) for the same thing: We can describe the same person as *stingy* or *parsimonious*. But in most cases, it turns out that each word in the language says something a little different about the world.

Directions: Write the signal(s) and the text structure used: taxonomic, comparison-contrast, cause-and-effect, chronology. Write a one- or two-sentence summary of each paragraph given. The teacher can use the following questions to provide guidance to the students:

"What is this paragraph telling me? Tell the main idea. Is it describing or telling something? If so, tell what. Is it comparing one thing to another? Tell what they are and how they differ or are similar. Is it explaining something? Tell why it happened and/or what happened. Is it telling about a sequence of events?"

1. One African variety spits its venom at its victim's eyes; it can spit up to eight feet with almost pinpoint accuracy, and the highly corrosive venom blinds the victim unless it is immediately washed away.

Signal	*and*
Text structure	*taxonomic*
Summary	*The cobra spits venom*

2. The cobra's venom is more powerful even than that of the rattlesnake. Its fangs do not inject the venom, as do the fangs of other poisonous snakes; instead, they are used to pierce deep wounds in the victim's flesh, and the cobra releases venom from sacs in its mouth into these punctures.

Signal	*more, even, than, instead*
Text structure	*comparison-contrast*
Summary	*Cobra venom is more powerful and is injected differently than other poisonous snakes*

3. Most snakes and other animals avoid contact with humans at all costs and attack them only when escape is blocked or in defense of their young, but cobras seem to have no such avoidance instinct. Instead they have been known to seek out and follow humans before attacking them without provocation. Their actions are those of a predator hunting, and the prey is human.

Signal	*but, instead*
Text structure	*comparison-contrast*
Summary	*Most snakes avoid human contact but cobras do not*

4. Its mottled skin provides a good camouflage, since it blends almost perfectly with dead leaves, tree bark, grasses, and dusty earth.

Signal	*since*
Text structure	*cause-and-effect*
Summary	*The cobra is camouflaged because its mottled skin blends with its environment*

FIGURE 9.19 Guided Practice: Expository Text

Source: Adapted from Jocelyn Perkins. "Integrating in the Content Areas." Paper presented at the International Reading Association Conference, Atlanta, GA, May 1990.

There is an interesting relationship between words and things. It may seem to us that we need words to express our ideas; that is, we have ideas first and then we use the words we know to express them. But it also works the other way around. We may never have the idea to start with unless we have the word that names it. That is because, as a friend of ours puts it, each word we have is like a flashlight that lights up a different part of our lives. We notice and remember experiences that we have names for. This has been demonstrated experimentally (Brown, 1958). The richer our vocabularies become, the richer and more varied our experiences will be. Having a rich vocabulary lets us know more about the world. There is a good reason why students need rich vocabularies: They enable students to experience their lives in more interesting detail.

With respect to vocabulary development, William Nagy offers us an amazing calculation (Nagy and Anderson, 1984): He figures that to understand the language of ninth-grade textbooks, a student needs a vocabulary of 88,500 words. There are estimates that the typical child comes to first grade with a vocabulary of about 6,000 words. To learn the remaining 82,500 words, students must average *a thousand words a month* for the rest of their school years. It is clear that we can't begin to *teach* students all the vocabulary they need to know; we must try instead to teach them habits of attentiveness to words that will help them to learn words on their own. The following strategies are intended to teach students those habits of attentiveness to words.

Semantic Webs

Traditionally, vocabulary instruction made students aware of *synonyms,* words that have similar meanings. Semantic webs allow us to show students relations among larger numbers of words. The relationships point out not just similarities, but also hierarchical relationships, that is, which word is more general and which is more specific.

To construct a semantic web, the teacher writes a word for a large category in the center of the board. Then the students help the teacher come up with subtopics for that category and then more specific words within each subtopic. In the end, a semantic web of words about feelings might come to look like the example in Figure 9.20.

FIGURE 9.20   A Semantic Web

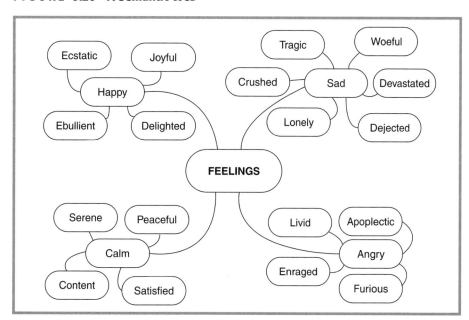

Concept Maps

Concept maps are similar to semantic webs. In semantic webs, the relationships are always those of similarity and variety (for example, "Kinds of FEELING WORDS include ANGRY; words for ANGRY include LIVID, APOPLECTIC"). In concept maps, however, we can specify any kind of relationship we want to be-tween the terms. In constructing a concept map about TREES, for example, we might set out relationships such as "kinds of," "attributes," and "growth cycle," as shown in Figure 9.21. Concept maps aid in vocabulary study at the same time that they reinforce disciplinary concepts.

FIGURE 9.21 Vocabulary Concept Map

Source: Samuel R. Mathews, Josephine P. Young, and Nancy D. Giles. *Student Literacy Volunteers: Providing Tools for Brighter Futures.* Pensacola, FL: The Educational Research and Development Center, The University of West Florida, 1992.

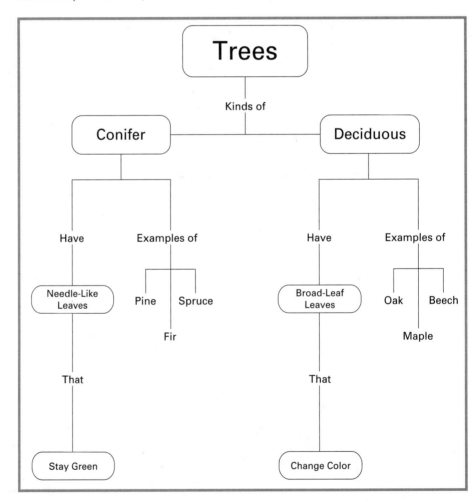

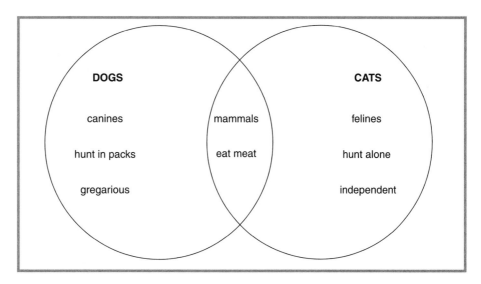

FIGURE 9.22   Venn Diagram

Venn Diagrams

A useful graphic organizer that demonstrates similarities and differences between items is the Venn diagram. To construct a Venn diagram, we put two terms side by side and draw circles around the terms so that they partially overlap each other. In the spaces inside the circle that surround each term and *do not* overlap, we write descriptors that apply only to each term, not to both. In the space where the two circles overlap, we write descriptors that are common to both. Figure 9.22 shows an example.

Etymologies and Word Webs

With half a million words, English has the largest vocabulary of any all the languages of the world. Many of the words are related in families, however, so it is possible for an educated person, equipped with knowledge of a few score word families, to have at least a sense of a good proportion of the English vocabulary.

In the concept mapping exercise, for example, we came across the word *conifer.* That word will be unfamiliar to many students. Yet it contains two parts that should be familiar to them, and by reflecting on those parts, the students might be able to approximate the meaning of *conifer.*

Coni- is related to *conical,* which means "like a cone." So the stem has the meaning of "cone." *-Fer* shows up in *ferry* (something that bears or carries cars and people) and *transfer* (to carry across), so the stem has the meaning of "bear" or "carry." Therefore, a *conifer* is a tree that bears cones.

Students might know that *biology* is the study of (this is roughly what *-logy* means) of life (this is the meaning of *bio-*). Then what is a *biography?* What is *symbiosis?* These words, too, have something to do with "life": A biography is a record of someone's life; symbiosis is a state of living together, depending on each other.

To look at words related to *-logy*, we have *psychology*, the study of the mind, and *theology*, the study of God.

But wait: Each of the words related to the parts of *biology* is made up of other parts that occur in still other words. "Biography" contains the stem *graphy-*, which also appears in "telegraph." And "telegraph" contains the stem *tele-*, which shows up in *telephone* and *telescope*. These two words contain stems (*-scope* and *-phone*) that show up in still more words (*microscope, stethoscope, symphony, phonics,* etc.).

One lively way of tracing the families of words is to construct a *word web*. A word web graphically shows the family relationships between words that share the same stems.

To demonstrate how a word web is constructed, let's take the word *biology*. The teacher writes the word in the middle of the chalkboard. Then the teachers asks students to think of any words that contain either of the parts of biology. One student thinks of "biography," which shares the stem *bio-*. The teacher writes "biography" on the board, draws circles around the stem *bio-* in both words, and connects both occurrences of the stem with a line.

Another student thinks of "psychology," which shares the stem *-logy*. The teacher writes that word on the board, draws circles around the stem *-logy* in both words, and connects the two with a line. Now other students think of other words with *bio-* and *-logy,* and the teacher treats them the same way. But another student things of "psychopath," because it shares a stem with "psychology." So the teacher writes "psychopath" on the board, then draws circles around the stem *psycho-* in both words and connects both occurrences of that stem with a line. The activity proceeds with students thinking of more and more words related to other words on the board. (See Figure 9.23).

Periodically, the teacher stops to ask the students what a particular stem might mean. The students should try first to infer the meaning from the words that share the stem, then check themselves with a dictionary that contains etymologies. The teacher might write the original meaning beside each stem.

Once students have done this activity as a whole class, they might make word webs in small groups or even in competing teams.

Vocabulary and Surrounding Context

Earlier in this chapter, we mentioned William Nagy's astounding estimate that students must learn 88,500 words to cope with the texts they are reading by ninth grade. It is clear from this estimate that students must learn most of those words on their own, without explicit instruction. Teaching can help, however. One way is by sensitizing students to the ways in which words convey meanings, using the strategies we have seen so far in this section. Another way is by making students aware of strategies that they can use to infer the meanings of words from their surrounding context.

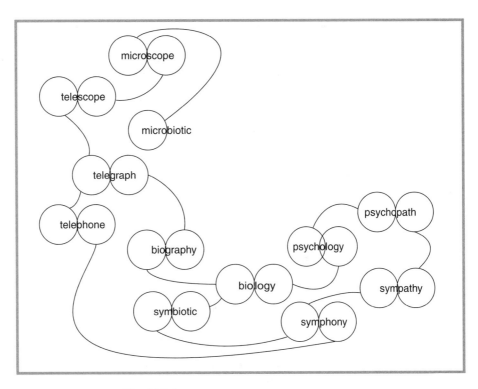

FIGURE 9.23   A Word Web

Several years ago, Dan Hittleman (1978) suggested that writers generally use five types of signals to shed light on the meanings of words:

1. **Definition.** They may use sentence forms like "X is (or "is called") Y." These sentences communicate an explicit definition of the word.

   An iconoclast is a person who deliberately breaks other people's traditions. A person who deliberately breaks traditions is called an iconoclast.

2. **Example.** When examples are given of an idea explained by an unknown word, we might be able to figure out the word if we recognize the example. Sentences that are so constructed often use words or phrases like *for example, such as, like,* and *especially.*

   Venomous snakes, such as the rattlesnake, the copperhead, or the coral snake, are to be avoided.

3. **Modifiers.** Even when a word is not known, the modifiers that are used to describe it might give an indication of what it is. Modifiers may be relative clauses as well as adjectives or adverbs.

   The minaret that the Moslems built stood tall, slender, and graceful above the other buildings in the town.

4. **Restatement.** Sentences sometimes state the unknown idea a second time using other, more familiar words. One such device is an appositive, a group of words following the word defined and set off by commas or dashes. Restatement is also done by using key words or phrases like *or, that is,* and *in other words.*

Chauvinism, an aggressive loyalty to one's own group at the expense of others, originally applied to national patriotism only.

They fired the attendant because of her indolence; in other words, she was lazy.

5. **Inference.** Following are several grammatical patterns that writers use to signal the meaning of unknown words:
   a. *Parallel sentence structure.* When series are used either in the same sentence or in groups of sentences, we can often get an idea of the nature of an unknown word by recognizing a known word in the series.

Each office contained some type of medical specialist. In one was a family practitioner; in another, an obstetrician; in another, a radiologist; and in another, a hematologist.

   b. *Repetition of Key Words.* Sometimes, if an unknown word is of sufficient importance in a passage, the author will repeat it enough times in enough different contexts for its meaning to be figured out.

It is sometimes said that only primitive people have taboos. This is not necessarily so. Even advanced cultures like ours have them. In America, for example, it is taboo to speak directly about death, or about a grown person's age, weight, or income.

   c. *Familiar Connectives.* Some familiar connectives, especially subordinating or coordinating conjunctions, show us the relationship between ideas and thus allow us to associate an unknown idea with a known one.

John was very excited about the award, but Judith seemed indifferent.

The devices for identifying meanings in context can be taught. If they are clearly introduced, well practiced, and returned to often, they can become a valuable addition to a readers's strategies for dealing with difficult material.

SUMMARY

In this chapter, we presented strategies for enhancing older readers' literacy skills. We began by setting out a teaching and learning model in three phases: anticipation, investigation, and reflection. Then we shared teaching and learning strategies appropriate to each phases. Because a major challenge to students' literacy by the middle of the elementary grades is to learn from text, and because they encounter texts with information arranged in many different structures, we devoted a section of this chapter to understanding and teaching text structures. Then came a presentation on learning vocabulary, which is another challenge that older students face.

REFERENCES

Alvermann, Donna. "The Discussion Web: A Graphic Organizer for Learning Across the Curriculum. *The Reading Teacher* 45, 2 (Oct. 1991): 92–99.

Ausubel, David P. *The Use of Ideational Organizers in Science Teaching.* Occasional Paper 3. Columbus, Ohio: ERIC Information Analysis Center for Science Education, Mar. 1970.

Ausubel, David P. "In Defense of Advance Organizers: A Reply to the Critics." *Review of Educational Research* 48, no. 2 (Spring 1978): 251–257.

Beck, Isabel, and Margaret McKeown. "Outcomes of History Instruction: Paste-Up Accounts." In *Cognitive and Instructional Processes in History and the Social Sciences,* J. F. Voss and M. Carretero eds. Hillsdale, NJ: Erlbaum, 1994.

Berthoff, Ann. *The Making of Meaning: Metaphors, Models, and Maxims for Writing Teachers.* Portsmouth, NH: Boynton/Cook, 1981.

Brown, Ann L., Annemarie Sullivan Palincsar, and Bonnie Armbruster. "Instructing Comprehension-Fostering Activities in Interactive Learning Situations." In *Learning and Comprehension of Text,* ed. Heinz Mandl. Hillsdale, NJ: Lawrence Erlbaum Associates, 1984.

Brown, Roger. *Words and Things.* Garden City, NY: Basic Books, 1958.

Burleigh, Robert. *Flight: The Journey of Charles Lindberg.* New York: Philomel, 1991.

Carr, Eileen, and Ogle, Donna. "A Strategy for Comprehension and Summarization." *Journal of Reading* 30, no. 7 (April 1987): 626–631.

Chall, Jeanne. "The Great Debate: Ten Years Later, with a Modest Proposal for Reading Stages." In *Theory and Practice of Early Reading, Vol. 1,* ed. Lauren Resnick and Phyllis Weaver. Hillsdale, NJ: Lawrence Erlbaum Associates, 1979.

Deighton, Lee. *Vocabulary Development in the Classroom.* New York: Teachers College Press, Columbia University, 1959.

Dillon, J. T. "The Remedial Status of Student Questioning." *Journal of Curriculum Studies* 20, 3 (Fall 1986): 197–210.

Duffy, Gerald G., Laura R. Roehler, and Beth Ann Herrmann. "Modeling Mental Processes Helps Poor Readers Become Strategic Readers." *The Reading Teacher* 41, no. 8 (April 1988): 762–767.

Estes, Thomas H., "Teaching Effective Study Reading." *Reading Improvement* 8, no. 1 (Spring 1971): 11–12, 20.

Elbow, Peter. "Toward a Phenomenology of Freewriting." *Journal of Basic Writing* 8, no. 2 (Fall 1989): 42–71.

Estes, Thomas H., "Teaching Effective Study Reading." *Reading Improvement* 8, no. 1 (Spring 1971); 11–12, 20.

Estes, Thomas H., and Wayne Shibilski. "Comprehension: Of What the Reader Sees of What the Author Says." In *Perspectives on Reading Research and Instruction,* ed. Michael L. Kamil and Alden J. Moe. Washington, DC: National Reading Conference, 1980.

Hittleman, Daniel R. *Developmental Reading: A Psycholinguistic Perspective.* Chicago: Rand McNally, 1978.

Kagan, Seymour. *Cooperative Learning.* San Juan Capistrano, CA: Kagan Cooperative Learning, 1992.

Lawson, Robert. *Ben & Me: A New And Astonishing Life of Benjamin Franklin as Written By His Good Mouse, Amos.* Boston: Little, Brown, 1939.

Manzo, Anthony V. "Reading and Questioning: The ReQuest Procedure." *Reading Improvement* 7, no. 3 (Winter 1970): 80–83.

Manzo, Anthony V. "Training Teachers to Use Content Area Reading Strategies: Description and Appraisal of Four Options." *Reading Research and Instruction* 30, no. 4 (Summer 1991): 67–74.

Marshall, Nancy, and Marvin Glock. "Comprehension of Connected Discourse: A Study into the Relationships Between the Structure of Text and Information Recalled." *Reading Research Quarterly* 14, no. 1 (1978–1979): 10–56.

McKeown, Margaret, Isabel Beck, and Cheryl Sandora. "Questioning the Author." In *The First R: Every Child's Right to Read,* eds. Michael Graves, Paul Van den Broek, and Barbara Taylor. New York: Teachers College Press, 1996.

Nagy, William, and Richard Anderson. "How Many Words Are There in Printed School English?" *Reading Research Quarterly, 19,* (1984): 304–330.

Ogle, Donna M. "A Teaching Model That Develops Active Reading of Expository Text." *Reading Teacher* 39, no. 6 (February 1986): 564–570.

Pearson, P. David. "Changing the Face of Reading Comprehension Instruction." *The Reading Teacher* 38, no. 8 (April 1985): 724–738.

Reutzel, D. Ray. "Story Maps Improve Comprehension." *Reading Teacher* 38, no. 4 (January 1985): 400–404.

Slavin, Robert E. "Cooperative Learning in Middle and Secondary Schools." *Clearing House* 69, no. 4 (March–April 1996): 200–204.

Slavin, Robert, et al. "Putting Research to Work: Cooperative Learning." *Instructor* 102, no. 2 (September 1992): 46–47.

Steele, Jeannie L., and Patty Steele. "The Thinking-Writing Connection: Using Clustering to Help Students Write Persuasively." *Reading Horizons* 32, no. 1 (Oct. 1991): 41–51.

Steele, Jeannie, Kurt Meredith, and Charles Temple. *A Framework for Critical Thinking Across the Curriculum.* Washington, DC: The Reading & Writing for Critical Thinking Project, 1997.

Steptoe, John. *Mufaro's Beautiful Daughters: An African Tale.* New York: Lathrop, Lee, and Shepard, 1987.

Vacca, Richard, and Joanne Vacca. *Content Area Reading,* 3rd ed. Glenview, IL: Scott, Foresman, 1989.

Vaughn, Joseph, and Thomas Estes. *Reading and Reasoning Beyond the Primary Grades.* Needham Heights, MA: Allyn and Bacon, 1986.

Wisconsin Department of Public Instruction. *Strategic Learning in the Content Area.* Madison, WI, 1989.

APPENDIX: MARCO POLO, ADVENTURER

In 1298 a Venetian adventurer named Marco Polo wrote a fascinating book about his travels in the Far East. Men read his accounts of Oriental riches and became eager to find sea routes to China, Japan, and the East Indies. Even Columbus, nearly 200 years later, often consulted his copy of *The Book of Ser Marco Polo.*

In Marco's day the book was translated and copied by hand in several languages. After printing was introduced in the 1440s, the book was circulated even more widely. Many people thought that the book was a fable or a gross exaggeration. A few learned men believed that Marco wrote truly, however, and they spread Marco's stories of faraway places and unknown peoples. Today geographers agree that Marco's book is amazingly accurate.

Marco Polo was born in the city-republic of Venice in 1254. His father and uncles were merchants who traveled to distant lands to trade. In 1269 Marco's father, Nicolo, and his uncle Maffeo returned to Venice after being away many years. On a trading expedition they had traveled overland as far as Cathay (China). Kublai Khan, the great Mongol emperor of China, asked them to return with teachers and missionaries for his people. So they set out again in 1271, and this time they took Marco.

From Venice the Polos sailed to Acre, in Palestine. There two monks, missionaries to China, joined them. Fearing the hard journey ahead, however, the monks soon turned back. The Polos crossed the deserts of Persia (Iran) and Afghanistan. They mounted the heights of the Pamirs, the "roof of the World," descending to the trading cities of Kashgar (Shufu) and Yarkand (Soche). They crossed the dry stretches of The Gobi. Early in 1275 they arrived at Kublai Khan's court at Cambaluc (Peking). At that time Marco was 21 years old.

At the Court of the Great Khan

Marco quickly became a favorite of Kublai Khan. For three years he governed busy Yangchow, a city of more than 250,000 people. He was sent on missions to far places in the empire: to Indochina, Tibet, Yunnan, and Burma. From these lands Marco brought back stories of the people and their lives.

The Polos became wealthy in Cathay. But they began to fear that jealous men in the court would destroy them when the khan died. They asked to return to Venice. Kublai Khan refused. Then came an envoy from the khan of Persia. He asked Kublai Khan for a young Mongol princess for a bride. The Polos said that the princess' journey should be guarded by men of experience and rank. They added that the mission would enable them to make the long-desired visit to Venice. The khan reluctantly agreed.

Since there was danger from robbers and enemies of the khan along the overland trade routes, a great fleet of ships was built for a journey by sea. In 1292 the fleet sailed, bearing the Polos, the princess, and 600 noblemen of Cathay. They traveled southward along Indochina and the Malay Peninsula to Sumatra. Here the voyage was delayed many months.

The ships then turned westward and visited Ceylon and India. They touched the East African coast. The voyage was hazardous, and of the 600 noblemen only 18 lived to reach Persia. The Polos and the princess were safe. When the Polos landed in Venice, they had been gone 24 years. The precious stones they brought from Cathay amazed all Venice.

Later Marco served as gentleman-captain of a ship. It was captured by forces of the rival trading city of Genoa, and he was thrown into a Genoese prison. There he wrote his book with help from another prisoner. Marco was released by the Genoese in 1299. He returned to Venice and engaged in trade. His name appears in the court records of his time in many lawsuits over property and money. He married and had three daughters. He died about 1323.

Source: Compton's Encyclopedia. Used by permission.

CHAPTER 10

Strategies for Teaching Reading and Writing to English Learners

This chapter addresses the special needs and challenges of the significant number of children in our schools with apparent problems in reading and writing whom we characterize as *English learners,* those whose mother tongue or home language is not English. Their difficulties are most often not so much with reading and writing as with reading and writing in their second language: English. These children have been variously referred to as *bilingual, migrant, immigrant, language minority, ESL, limited English-proficient,* and *non-English speaking students,* among many other terms. We tend to focus on the weaknesses of these students, rather than the many strengths they bring to reading and writing. As Miramontes (1990) points out, identifying, using, and valuing "the things students *can* do can help teachers purposefully engage students in bringing those abilities to bear on meaningful academic tasks."

THE CONTEXT OF TEACHING ENGLISH LEARNERS TO READ AND WRITE

English Learners: Who Are They?

When we think of English learners, we tend to think of Latino children; indeed, they make up the largest population of English learners. For that reason, most examples and references in the chapter will relate to this group. But there are many other significant populations of English learners, and how their needs are met in our schools depends not only on how many there are, but also on how concentrated they are. Clusters of children who have a mother tongue in common present special challenges, but also unique opportunities.

According to a recently published census of English learners (Henderson et al., 1993), about 6 percent of the more than 42 million public and nonpublic school students in the United States and its territories were classified as limited English proficient, almost 2 1/2 million children at that time. Annual growth has continued at almost 10 percent per year. According to Fleishman and Hopstock (1993), two-thirds were in grades K–6, and the mother tongue of 75 percent of them was Spanish. About 5 percent of them spoke Vietnamese, with about 2 percent each speaking Hmong, Cantonese, Cambodian, Korean, or Native American languages.

English learners are not a monolithic population. Some are very proficient in speaking and understanding their mother tongue, and some are literate in that language. Some became literate in their home countries and others in programs of bilingual education here in the United States. As a result of living in refugee camps, some upper elementary and adolescent children have arrived in this country with little or no school experience at all. Some English learners are migrant children from rural areas without educational opportunities, and others were working and contributing to the family income. And some English learners have limited proficiency even in their mother tongue, just as some native English speakers are limited in their English proficiency. As we consider the situation of these many categories of English learners, then, we must think in terms of many solutions.

What Do We Know about the Context of Learning and of Learning in a Second Language?

Several major principles guide our understanding of providing the best context for learning and for learning in a second language. Cummins (1986, 1989) contrasts two levels of language proficiency that underline the need for high-level proficiency in the second language before academic instruction is provided in the second language. Basic interpersonal communications skills are those that permit English learners to carry on a simple conversation in the new second language, and they appear to be proficient. But a higher level of proficiency, cognitive-academic language proficiency, is required for the student to learn to read in the second language or, for example, to learn the distributive principle of multiplication in mathematics. Cummins maintains that there is a threshold of language proficiency in the mother tongue that must be reached in order for the student to attain academic proficiency in the mother tongue and a second language.

Cummins's (1986, 1989) related linguistic interdependence principle indicates that what students learn in two languages is interdependent. It forms a common underlying proficiency (CUP) (Cummins, 1981) that provides the basis for positive transfer of skills. Children have knowledge and skills that they have learned in the mother tongue, and they can use them in the second language. They do not have to learn this knowledge and these skills again. In fact, it is axiomatic that children learn to read only once. They can transfer reading and writing skills to their new second language, just as we do as adults when we study a foreign language. Cummins indicates that CUP explains why children who have attended school in their country (and language) of origin tend to demonstrate higher achievement in English later than children who lack that experience.

Lambert (1975) contrasts additive and subtractive bilingual education programs. In the former, children add a new language and culture, with mother tongue and its accompanying culture, along with a positive self-image. In a subtractive program, English and its accompanying culture are substituted, often leading to low self-esteem, leaving school, low academic achievement, and other negative consequences.

These principles lead us to a counterintuitive but inescapable conclusion that success in English language proficiency is closely related to students' learning of reading, writing, and academic concepts in the mother tongue (Collier, 1989; J. Crawford, 1989; Cummins, 1989; Hudelson, 1987; Krashen, 1985; Krashen and Biber, 1988; Ramírez, 1991).

The Legal Status of Programs to Serve English Learners

Perhaps the most sweeping policy change to affect the education of English learners in recent years was the 1974 *Lau* v. *Nichols* decision of the U.S. Supreme Court, which ruled that equal education did not result from providing exactly the same education to all children (J. Crawford, 1989). It required that school districts take affirmative steps to overcome the educational barriers experienced by students who did not speak English. Soon after, Title VII of the Elementary and Secondary Education Act was amended to make limited English-proficient students eligible for federal funds and to permit their enrollment in bilingual education programs. More recently, the 1998 Unz English Initiative in California prohibits most bilingual education in that state, mandating instead a one-year period of immersion instruction in English as a second language, the efficacy of which is largely unsubstantiated in the literature.

Bilingual Education: One Solution

Although the *Lau* v. *Nichols* decision did not mandate bilingual education as a remedy, school districts soon found that it was one of the few ways to ensure that English learners had equal access to education, that is, education in their mother tongue while they learned English. Most programs have taken the transitional form, in which children learn to read and write and also study the other subjects of the academic curriculum, mathematics, social science, science in the mother tongue. Simultaneously, the children study English as a second language, a process that typically takes two to five years or more. Through a transition process called positive transfer of skills, children can then do in English what they learned to do in the mother tongue. Even learning to read in English as a second language is a relatively smooth and effortless process—we learn to read only once. When children do not have the opportunity to learn academic subjects in the mother tongue, they fall behind in those subjects during the period of time they are learning English.

Children in transitional bilingual programs usually continue their academic studies only in English after the onset of transition to English, although they typically receive continuing support in the mother tongue, as needed. More infrequently, children are placed in maintenance bilingual education programs and continue to receive instruction in the mother tongue even after transition, the goal being to be a bilingual, biliterate, and bicultural individual at the end. Because of the lack of instructional materials in the mother tongue and often a lack of trained bilingual teachers in many languages, non-Spanish-language bilingual education programs are less common and usually limited in scope.

Language Policy Decisions about the Language of Instruction: The Transition Process

A fundamental precept of literacy for children from language minority populations is that they will learn to read and write more rapidly and more effectively in their mother tongue than in a second language that they learn later. One of the first important and authoritative positions taken on this issue was that of a UNESCO conference (UNESCO, 1953), which concluded that children learn better to read in a new second language if they first learn to read in the mother tongue. This work was corroborated by many investigators in subsequent years.

Saville and Troike (1971) concluded that once a child has learned to read, transferring that ability to another language is not a difficult matter. In an important study, Modiano (1968) found that Mayan children in Mexico who were learning to read learned more rapidly in their mother tongue of Quiché than others who learned to read in their second language of Spanish. Later, they read better in Spanish than those who first learned to read in Spanish. Through succeeding years, the preponderance of evidence indicates that children learn to read most effectively in their second language by first learning to read in their primary language (Cummins, 1986, 1989; Krashen and Biber, 1988; UNESCO, 1953).

English-as-a-second-language instruction is the keystone of programs to meet the academic needs of English learners. It is especially important where only small numbers of children speak the same mother tongue or where a lack of trained personnel and appropriate instructional materials prevents the implementation of programs of bilingual education. It is also the major element of those full bilingual education programs in which we use the mother tongue for academic instruction while children develop sufficient proficiency in the second language to benefit from academic instruction in that language.

The foundation for communicative approaches to second language acquisition is based on concepts, theories, and hypotheses that have converged around the interaction of constructivist notions about making meaning. Vygotsky (1978) defined the zone of proximal development as "the distance between the actual developmental level as determined by independent problem solving and the level of potential development as determined through problem solving under adult guidance in collaboration with more capable peers." This key concept emphasizes the social dimension of learning that results from the support of mothers, teachers, older siblings, and other caregivers. The collective wisdom of the cooperative learning group has an obvious role here, as well. The convergence between communicative approaches to second language acquisition and literacy is particularly prominent in the constructivist paradigm.

Language policy is a factor of great importance in literacy for children. Clearly, children will learn to read and write most quickly and most effectively in the mother tongue. Many factors must be taken into consideration, however, before that decision is made (A. N. Crawford, 1995). For example, if children speak a minority language for which there is a well-developed written form, if skilled bilingual teachers are available, and if there are instructional materials in that language, then we can provide instruction in that mother tongue. If this is not the case, then we should consider using the language experience approach described in Chapter 6 and later in this chapter.

If children speak a minority language for which there is not a well-developed written form, such as Hmong, then we must teach the children to speak and understand English and then to read and write in English, probably using the language experience approach. If bilingual teachers are not available, then even the presence of instructional materials will not be sufficient to permit mother tongue instruction. A literate speaker of the minority language might be trained as a paraprofessional to work under the supervision of a fully trained teacher who is not proficient in the mother tongue of the children.

Finally, some families will insist that their children learn to read and write only in English, although they do not speak or understand that language. Some might even believe that using the minority language for literacy is a tool to maintain speakers of that minority language in an inferior social position. In this case, teachers need to demonstrate respect for the mother tongue, and they need to assure the children and their families that they will also have the opportunity to learn to speak, read, and write English. In addition, they need to reinforce the idea that children learn to read and write only once and that learning to read and write in another language that they learn later is a relatively simple transfer process. Finally, they need to reinforce the idea that reading is *comprehension*, not pronouncing or "reading" sounds. Nonetheless, some families will still insist on English only.

SECOND LANGUAGE ACQUISITION

Whether or not children learn to read and write in their mother tongue, they must learn to speak and understand English. It is difficult to even address literacy for English learners without considering the close links that must exist between the teaching of reading and writing and the teaching of English as a second language. Because of the nature of the most effective approaches to teaching both, those that are constructivist or whole-part-whole, we know that they complement each other very effectively. In addition, literacy in English is so closely related to learning to speak and understand English that they must be considered together.

At this point, we should also examine the dichotomy between constructivist and reductionist models of instruction. A constructivist view of instruction focuses on the construction of meaning, using what the child already knows and combining it with new ideas to be integrated. It is learner-based, an important factor in working with the students from diverse backgrounds who are often at risk in any case. The factor of background knowledge is well recognized as being a key to success in reading and writing, especially in reading comprehension. English learners have no lack of background knowledge, but there is often a discontinuity between the background knowledge they have and that assumed by the texts from which they will learn to read and read to learn. Within the constructivist view, language acquisition is embedded in function. Skills are taught in a meaningful context, not in a systematic, artificial, and fragmented way. Reductionist or skills-based models conversely focus on the disassembly or fragmentation of curricular elements so that isolated skills and concepts can be mastered within a linear paradigm.

Until recent years, most students have studied a second language, whether English or a foreign language, using such grammar-based approaches as the grammar translation and audiolingual methods. These are reductionist or skills-based approaches that move learners from part to whole. We recall the grammar translation approach from foreign language courses that we took in secondary school and university in the 1950s and even later (Chastain, 1975). We learned vocabulary in terms of English from lists in which teachers paired words in the foreign language with their English counterparts. We also studied the grammar of the new language. English was always the window through which we viewed, and contrasted, our new second language. Few of us became functional in speaking and understanding our new second language. At best, we succeeded in written tests of grammar, translated with difficulty, and read with halting comprehension.

The audiolingual approach is rooted in structural linguistics and behavioral psychology, resulting in a methodology based on a grammatical sequence, with mimicry and the memorization of pattern drills, but without the heavy grammatical analysis of the grammar translation approach (Chastain, 1975). This approach is characterized by the unconscious mastery of sequenced grammatical forms, learning as the result of teaching patterned oral drills, and an emphasis on correct oral production of grammatical forms in response to oral stimuli (Finocchiaro, 1974).

The results of recent research have changed our conceptions of how a second language is acquired and how this acquisition is best promoted in the elementary and secondary classroom. There has been a major paradigm shift away from these grammar-based approaches to language learning and toward those we call *communicative*, which are also consistent with meaning-based or constructivist approaches to literacy (A. N. Crawford, 1994).

Underlying Principles of Communicative-Based Approaches

Krashen's Hypotheses

Krashen (1982) has offered several important hypotheses that underlie current practice in most communicative approaches to second language acquisition. Among Krashen's most important contributions is his input hypothesis. He concludes that growth in language occurs when learners receive comprehensible input, or input that contains structure at a slightly higher level than what they already understand. The input hypothesis corresponds to Vygotsky's zone of proximal development. The context of the input provides clues to maintain the integrity of the message. According to the input hypothesis, a grammatical sequence is not needed. The structures are provided and practiced as a natural part of the comprehensible input that the child receives, much as it occurs with infants acquiring their mother tongue. Krashen (1981) relates the input hypothesis to the silent period, the interval before speech in either the mother tongue or second language in which the child listens to and develops an understanding of the language before beginning to produce language.

In his acquisition learning hypothesis, Krashen illustrates the difference between the infant's subconscious acquisition of the mother tongue and the secondary school French student's conscious learning of a second language. We *acquire* language subconsciously, with a *feel* for correctness. *Learning* a language, on the other hand, is a conscious process that involves knowing grammatical rules. Of course, the infant is almost always successful in acquiring communicative competence, while the secondary school foreign language learner is usually not (A. N. Crawford, 1994).

According to Krashen's natural order hypothesis, grammatical structures are acquired in a predictable sequence, certain elements usually being acquired before others. He has concluded that the orders for first and second language acquisition are similar but not identical. It is important to note, however, that Krashen does not conclude that sequencing the teaching of language according to this natural order is either necessary or desirable.

Krashen's related monitor hypothesis describes how the child's conscious monitor or editor functions to make corrections as language is produced in speaking or writing. Several conditions are necessary for the application of the monitor: (1) time to apply it, a situation that is not present in most ordinary oral discourse, especially in classroom settings; (2) a focus on the form or correctness of what is said, rather than on the content of the message; and (3) knowledge of the grammatical rule to be applied. These conditions serve to illustrate why so few children or adults learn to understand and speak a foreign language in a grammar translation or audiolingual secondary school or university foreign language course.

In his affective filter hypothesis, Krashen concludes that several affective variables are associated with success in second language acquisition. These include high motivation, self-confidence and a positive self-image, and, most important, low anxiety in the learning environment.

Other Basic Principles

Results from recent research have led to other major changes in educators' conceptions of how a second language is acquired and how this acquisition is best facilitated in the elementary and secondary classroom, one of which is the obvious similarity between primary and second language acquisition. Both include the formation of an incomplete and incorrect interlanguage by both primary and second language learners (Selinker et al., 1975), with most children moving through similar stages of development in this incomplete language.

The role of correction is also similar in both primary and second language acquisition. Approximation is a related process in which children imitate language in all of its dimensions, oral and written, and test hypotheses about it. The process of approximation underlies oral and written language in that children are acquiring new skills and understandings within the context of authentic wholes. Children exhibit behaviors in which they approximate the language behavior of their models, growing closer and closer to their levels of proficiency. In his view of successive approximation, Holdaway (1979) describes the process as one in which Vygotsky's adults and more capable peers use the output from children's responses to construct, adjust, and finally eliminate the scaffolding that facilitates progress in learning. According to Terrell (1982) and Krashen and Terrell (1983), we should therefore view correction as a negative reinforcer that will, at best, raise the affective filter and the level of anxiety in a language classroom, whether with children or adults. When there is no interference with comprehension, we should recognize that the correction of errors has no more place in the second language acquisition program than it does when infants acquire their mother tongue. Caregivers might expand incorrect or incomplete forms, such as *Kitty gots four feets*, and say *Yes, Kitty has four feet*. There is little evidence, however, that this expansion has any positive effect. Errors can be viewed as signs of immaturity, not incorrectness; they will disappear naturally as a part of approximation in the development process of language acquisition.

These similarities between primary and second language acquisition are not consistent with either the grammar translation or audiolingual approachs. Children learning their first language do not rely on grammatical rules or on systematic acquisition of vocabulary. With its emphasis on early production instead of a silent period, on correct production instead of an acceptable, though immature and incomplete, interlanguage, and on grammatical sequence instead of function and communicative competence, the audiolingual approach bears little resemblance to the way in which primary or second languages are successfully acquired.

Finally, age is an important factor in second language acquisition. Collier (1987) examined the relationship between the age of language minority children and their acquisition of a second language. She found that children who entered the second language acquisition program at ages 8 to 11 were the fastest achievers. The lowest achievers entered the program at ages 5 to 7; and they were one to three years behind children from 8 to 11 years of age. Children from 12 to 15 years of age had the most difficulty acquiring the second language. She projected that they would need six to eight years of instruction to reach age-level norms in academic achievement. When Collier (1989) later analyzed other research on age and academic achievement in the second language, she found that children who had academic instruction in the mother tongue generally required four to seven years to reach national norms on standardized tests in reading, social studies, and science and as little as two years in mathematics and language arts, including spelling, punctuation, and grammar. She also found that children from ages 8 to 12 who brought at least two years of schooling from their home country in their mother tongue needed five to seven years to reach the same levels of achievement in second language reading, social studies, and science and two years in mathematics and language arts. Young children with no schooling in the mother tongue from either the home country or the new host country needed seven to ten years of instruction in reading, social studies, and science. Adolescent children with no second language instruction and no opportunity for continued academic work in the mother tongue were projected, in the main, to drop out of school before reaching national norms, both those with a good academic background and those with interrupted schooling.

Basic Instructional Strategies for Second Language Acquisition

The implications of Krashen's hypotheses and of related similarities between first and second language acquisition are that approaches to second language acquisition should provide comprehensible input, focus on relevant and interesting topics instead of grammatical sequences, and provide for a silent period without forcing early production. There are approaches to second language acquisition that meet these criteria. They are categorized as communicative approaches; the ones that are most appropriate for elementary and secondary classrooms include the total physical response method and the natural approach.

The Total Physical Response Method

Asher's (1982) total physical response (TPR) method is an important communicative approach in the initial stages of second language acquisition. The TPR method provides for comprehensible input, a silent period, and a focus on relevant content, rather than on grammatical form. The focus of TPR is on physical responses to verbal commands, such as "Stand up" and "Put your book on the desk." Because little emphasis is given to production, the level of anxiety is low.

Lessons can be given to small groups or to an entire class. In the beginning, the teacher models one-word commands. This is done first with a few children, then with the entire group, then with a few children again, and finally with individual children. The teacher says, for example, "Sit," and then models by sitting down. Later, the teacher issues the command without modeling. As the children's levels of language increase, the teacher begins to use two- and three-word commands, such as "Stand up" and "Bring the book." The children demonstrate their understanding by physically carrying out the commands. The order of commands is varied so that the children cannot anticipate which is next. Old commands are combined with new ones to provide for review. Whenever the children do not appear to comprehend, the teacher returns to modeling. After a silent period of approximately ten hours of listening to commands and physically responding to them, a child then typically reverses roles with the teacher and begins to give those same commands to other children. It is important for the teacher to maintain a playful mood during classroom activities.

The total physical response approach can be extended to higher levels of proficiency by using the technique of nesting commands. The teacher might say the following:

Jamal, take the book to Svetlana, or close the door.

Noriko, if Jamal took the book to Svetlana, raise your hand.

If he closed the door, stand up.

A high level of understanding is necessary to carry out such commands, but no oral production is needed. Parents of young children will recognize that their infants can understand and carry out such commands long before they begin to speak themselves.

The Natural Approach

Terrell's (1977) original concept of the natural approach provided for three major characteristics: (a) classroom activities were focused on acquisition, that is, communication with a content focus leading to an unconscious absorption of language with a feel for correctness but not an explicit knowledge of grammar; (b) oral errors were not directly corrected; and (c) learners could respond in the target language, their mother tongue, or a mixture of the two.

Krashen and Terrell (1983) later added four principles that underlie the natural approach to language acquisition. The first is that comprehension precedes production, which leads to several teacher behaviors: The teacher always uses the target language, focuses on a topic of interest to the children, and helps the children to maintain comprehension. The second principle is that production emerges in stages ranging from nonverbal responses to complex discourse. Children can begin to speak when they are ready, and speech errors are not corrected unless they interfere with communication. The third principle is that the curriculum consists of communicative goals. Topics of interest make up the syllabus, not a grammatical sequence. Finally, activities must lead to low anxiety, a lowering of children's affective filter, which the teacher accomplishes by establishing and maintaining a good rapport.

Terrell's (1981) natural approach is based on three stages of language development: (1) preproduction (comprehension), (2) early production, and (3) emergence of speech.

The Preproduction Stage   Topical, interesting, and relevant comprehensible input is provided by the teacher in the first stage, which closely parallels Asher's (1982) TPR approach. The teacher speaks slowly, using gestures to maintain comprehension. Children may respond with physical behaviors, shaking or nodding their heads, pointing at pictures or objects, and saying "Yes" or "No." It is important that input is dynamic, lively, fun, and comprehensible. A. N. Crawford (1994) provides an example in which the teacher uses a pet turtle and says:

> *This is a turtle. It is four years old. Is it green? Who wants to hold it?* [Hand to child.] *Who has the turtle? Does Tran have the turtle? Yes, he does. Does Rosa have the turtle? No, she doesn't.*

This basic input can be repeated with other objects in the classroom, such as large-format illustrations and posters (A. N. Crawford, 1994). Crawford suggests that each child in the group be given a different illustration, and the teacher provides input:

> *Who has a picture of an airplane? Yes, Olaf, you do. Is the boat large? Olaf, give your picture to Zipour. Who has a picture of a boat? Yes, Nicole has a picture of a boat.*

These examples include three primary preproduction techniques: using TPR, using TPR accompanied by naming objects, and using pictures. The required responses include movement, pointing, nodding or shaking the head, and using the names of other children in the group. We should remember that nodding the head for an affirmative response and shaking it for a negative one are not appropriate in all cultures; it is the converse in Albania, for example. Children might also have to acquire these nonverbal behaviors. Since the emphasis at this stage is on listening comprehension, verbal responses in the mother tongue are also acceptable. This can be a problem if the teacher is unable to understand the children's mother tongue, but they usually find a way to help the teacher understand.

Classroom props allow for relevant expansion of this and subsequent stages of the natural approach (A. N. Crawford, 1994). Any manipulative or concrete object is helpful, including flannel boards and puppets. Large, colorful illustrations, such as those in travel posters and big books, are also very helpful. Sources of free color illustrations include calendars, outdated or otherwise, large posters available from textbook and trade book publishers, and colorful illustrations in the annual reports of many large corporations, usually available on request through announcements in major business magazines.

The Early Production Stage   In the stage of early production, the child begins to produce one-word utterances, lists, and finally two-word answers, such as "little dog" and "in house." Some of the latter, such as "me like" and "no want," are grammatically incorrect or incomplete. According to A. N. Crawford (1986), we should view these errors as immature, not incorrect. In the presence of good models, these errors will disappear in time, just as they do among infants developing their mother tongue.

Several types of questions can be used to elicit the one- and two-word responses within the reach of children as they transition into the early production stage:

Question Type	Question
Yes/no	*Are you hungry?*
	Do you like ice cream?
Here/there	*Where is the picture of the dog?*
Either/or	*Is this a pen or a key?*
One-word	*How many apples are there?*
Two-word	*What animals are in the picture?*

As in the preproduction stage, these strategies should be integrated into activities that permit a variety of responses, ranging from physical responses from those who are not ready for production, to brief oral responses from those who are. As the children begin production, conversations should increasingly require one-word responses. Within the same conversation, the teacher can address questions calling for longer responses to those children who are ready.

> *Kjell, show us your picture. What is in Kjell's picture?* [A sandwich.] *Yes, it is a sandwich. What is on the sandwich?* [Catsup.] *Is there apple on the hamburger?* [No. Laughter.] *What else is on the sandwich?* [Meat, mayonnaise.] *How does it taste?* [Good.] *What do you like with a sandwich?* [Chips. Soda.] *I like milk with mine.*

The Emergence of Speech Stage   During the emergence of speech stage, children begin to produce structures that are longer, more complex, more rich in vocabulary, and more correct. This production proceeds from three-word phrases to sentences, dialogue, extended discourse, and narrative. At this stage, Terrell recommends such activities as preference ranking, games, group discussions, skits, art and music, radio, TV, filmstrips, pictures, readings, and filling out forms. An example of a chart that incorporates preference ranking is provided by A. N. Crawford (1994) below:

Favorite Pizzas						
Name	**Cheese**	**Sausage**	**Pepperoni**	**Tomato**	**Anchovy**	**Mushroom**
Margarita		X		X		X
Sofik		X				
Abdul						
Nguyen	X		X	X		
Petra		X		X		X

Does Sofik like pizza? [*Yes.*] *What kind of meat does Sofik like?* [*Sausage.*] *How many like tomato on their pizza?* [*Three, Margarita, Nguyen, and Petra.*] *How does Abdul like pizza?* [*He doesn't like it.*] *Which children like the same kind of pizza?* [*Margarita and Petra.*] *Is there a topping that no one likes? What is it?* [*Anchovy.*] *How do we know?* [*Nobody wants anchovy.*]

Not only is the chart a valuable source of comprehensible input, but the process of gathering the data for the chart is, as well. In addition, children begin to read each other's names and the words for popular foods.

The Curriculum of a Communicative Program

According to A. N. Crawford (1994), teachers who would advocate teaching the first person present indicative tense to a 7-year-old English-speaking child in a primary school classroom would be incredulous at the suggestion that a parent teach the same concept to a 3-year-old at home. Of course, both children can use the tense correctly, neither as the result of instruction. This leads us to conclude, as do Krashen, Terrell, and others, that the content of second language acquisition programs should be based primarily on content, not on gramatical sequence.

Under the assumption that needed language structures will emerge and be acquired naturally within the context of topical lessons, a communicative second language curriculum is usually organized around a set of topics to ensure the introduction of new vocabulary and concepts of interest and utility to the children. Grammatical sequences also appear as a subcategory of some communicative curricula.

Terrell (1981) suggested that the initial content should be limited to following commands for classroom management, names of articles in the classroom, colors and description words for articles in the classroom, words for people and family relationships, descriptions of children, clothing, school areas, school activities, names of objects in the school that are not in the classroom, and foods, especially those eaten at school. Later, in the acquisition process, topics of interest to children would include the children's families, their homes and neighborhoods, their favorite activities, and pleasant experiences they have had. They also enjoy discussing their preferences about food, colors, television programs and films, and other aspects of their lives.

We begin to see the close link between literacy and the acquisition of second language when, as a part of the natural approach, Terrell (1981) recommended that key words be written on the chalkboard in the second language for older children who are literate in their mother tongue. This corresponds to the key word to reading approach (Veatch, 1996; Veatch et al., 1979) described later in the chapter. In the early production stage of Terrell's natural approach, children may express themselves quite appropriately in one- or two-word utterances as they begin to acquire a second language. A. N. Crawford (1994) indicates that it is altogether proper that they also begin to read key vocabulary that they have expressed for their teacher to write for them. They might later produce lists of related ideas, such as foods to eat at a carnival or fair, words that describe a favorite friend, or things to do after school. These topics and this output reflect the oral language common in the early production phase of Terrell's natural approach to language acquisition.

Assessing English Language Proficiency

There are many commercial instruments for assessing English language proficiency. Most examine pronunciation, knowledge of syntax, vocabulary knowledge, and other discrete skills. To teach English learners to read in English, teachers need to know how well they comprehend English.

The use of the informal reading inventory (IRI) as a test of listening comprehension, often termed *capacity level,* is not as common as its use to determine instructional, frustration, and independent levels (see Chapter 3), but teachers can use it very effectively for this purpose. A. N. Crawford (1982) suggested that the informal reading inventory, a set of graded reading passages ranging through the levels of primacy school, shows promise as a measure of second language proficiency when used as a test of listening comprehension or reading capacity. The teacher can use the IRI to determine readiness for reading instruction in given materials by reading a selected passage aloud to the child. Crawford reported that children who read in the mother tongue and respond correctly to 75% of comprehension-level questions about the material usually have sufficient second language proficiency to begin learning to read at the highest level at which they are successful in meeting that criterion. For children who are learning to read in their mother tongue in a bilingual program, this is often at or near the grade level at which they are reading in that mother tongue.

TEACHING ENGLISH LEARNERS TO READ AND WRITE IN ENGLISH

Let us now examine some approaches and strategies to reading and writing that promote second language acquisition within a constructivist perspective. Only a few years ago, it was commonly held that second language learners should not begin learning to read and write in the second language until they had reached an intermediate level of fluency. We now recognize that the processes of reading and writing in the second language can begin early in the acquisition process, especially for those children who have developed literacy skills in the mother tongue. In addition, literacy can play a major role in support of the acquisition of the second language. Krashen and Terrell (1983) describe reading in the second language as an important source of comprehensible input.

Early Literacy Experiences

According to A. N. Crawford (1993), most English learners have had some emergent literacy experiences at home and in the community. They recognize food and soft drink labels, they know brands of automobiles, and many have watched a parent read, refer to a calendar, respond to a letter, or write a check. In many homes, parents and grandparents tell stories and read to their children. Except in the most rural and isolated areas, most children also have abundant print in their environment. In this way, many children have begun to understand the underlying concept of print representing spoken ideas, often even for a second language that they are only beginning to understand.

A classroom environment that is rich in print is an important step toward providing meaningful material to read (A. N. Crawford, 1994). Children don't need to know letter names or sound-symbol correspondences to begin recognizing and discussing their own names, labels, and other forms of print to which they are exposed. Surrounding them with sources of print in the classroom will serve to extend their experiences with authentic text. When reading instruction is provided in the mother tongue, teachers will often label their classrooms in that mother tongue until the children are ready for labels in English, a relatively short time. Teachers should avoid labeling simultaneously in both languages so that children are not in the position of learning English in terms of the mother tongue. Children should learn English terms through direct experience with their classroom environment, not through translation from the mother tongue.

Most bilingual teachers who teach reading in the mother tongue recognize that children's motivation to begin reading and writing in a second language early is strong. Although we have already noted that it is most beneficial for children to learn to read and write first in the mother tongue, when possible, teachers can begin an early introduction to literacy in a second language to take advantage of that motivation. The key vocabulary and language experience approaches should be used with caution, however, to ensure that the second language acquisition program does not evolve into just a second language literacy program presented before the child is ready. Being able to read and write in the mother tongue is always the most desirable base from which to establish literacy in the second language later because of the positive transfer of literacy skills to that second language.

If children have an extremely limited background in the language of initial instruction, especially if it must be in English as a second language, then the key vocabulary approach (Veatch, 1996; Veatch et al., 1979) might serve well as a bridge to literacy from the mother tongue that children use to communicate orally. Emerging from Sylvia Ashton-Warner's key word or key vocabulary strategy, this approach is a major source of written language for providing authentic, meaningful, and early literacy experiences.

During an individual meeting with the teacher, each child in the key vocabulary approach selects a word of personal importance, which the teacher writes on a card. After the child traces the word with a finger, the teacher records it in a key word book or a sheet of paper and also records a sentence or phrase that is dictated by the child about the word. The child then reads the dictation back to the teacher and illustrates it. Finally, the child copies the word and the sentence.

Adapting the Language Experience Approach for English Learners

Moving from the dictation of key vocabulary to predictable language patterns in the language experience approach (LEA) is a natural step, and one that quickly leads to more traditional LEA strategies (Heald-Taylor, 1989). A dictation about story theme preferences might result in each of several children dictating an idea conforming to this predictable pattern (A. N. Crawford, 1994):

I like stories about animals.
I like stories about airplanes.
I like stories about children in other countries.

And so on.

Using the language experience approach in the second language is an excellent way to initiate children into print that is interesting and relevant to them (Dixon and Nessel, 1983; Moustafa and Penrose, 1985; Nessel and Jones, 1981). According to A. N. Crawford (1993), LEA also provides a means through which children can experience literature, and the new culture that it represents, in their second language that is above their ability to read and comprehend. After a teacher tells or reads a story aloud, English learners can then retell it for the teacher to record, though usually in a less complex version than the original. Peck (1989) found that listening to read-aloud stories in this way helps children to develop a sense of story structure, which should be reflected in the dictated version, and enhances their abilities to predict in this and other stories. The dictated text allows children to think, talk, read, and write about the piece of literature and to be exposed to its valuable cultural content. At the same time, they are actively interacting with it at a level of comprehension and of second language proficiency that is appropriate for their stage of development. They will be able to activate background knowledge from this experience that will transfer positively into the second language when they later read the literature for themselves in their new second language. This background knowledge also underlies their comprehension of what they read.

Beginning an LEA activity with a piece of literature or a story will often result in a better structured dictation than the random list of sentences that often results from LEA dictations stimulated by an illustration, a manipulative, or other prompts (A. N. Crawford, 1993). Heller (1988) describes a process for eliciting dictations that incorporates aspects of story grammar and supports the composing process. She recommends adding several components to traditional LEA procedures, including the activation of background knowledge through discussion before the dictation, the setting of a purpose and identification of a target audience for the dictation, the discussion of a model LEA dictation, the modeling of metacognitive strategies by teachers who describe their thoughts about creating an interesting story, and asking the children to make notes about the story they will dictate. They can then discuss, edit, and rewrite the dictated story in much the same way that the writing process would be applied in independent writing.

The language experience approach (A. N. Crawford et al., 1995) for teaching reading and writing is an approach in which a small group of children or an individual child and a teacher talk about an idea or topic, such as a favorite story or another topic of interest. Children tell their own ideas to the teacher, who writes them down sentence by sentence to use as reading material. The children read the text many times with help from the teacher. After many exposures to the text, children begin to recognize words that are used over and over in the dictated material, and soon they are able to read other materials as well. Children also begin learning to write early in this approach.

The LEA is particularly useful for teachers who work with older English learners who are preliterate, an increasingly common phenomenon. Migrant children or the children of refugees might never have been in school, even when they are 10 or 12 years of age, or older. The LEA is also useful where books and other instructional materials might not be available to teachers at all in the children's mother tongue.

The LEA to reading works well because it is based on the children's oral language; children understand what they are reading because the ideas and language are their own. It is more interesting because they read about real ideas, not artificial syllables, leading English learners to quick and early success in reading with this approach. One way to reinforce for English learners this concept that we read for meaning, not for pronunciation, is to have them read aloud from LEA charts in different voices. Ask one child to read the chart in an angry voice, another in a happy voice, and another in a questioning voice.

As children dictate text for the teacher to record, some will use incorrect syntactical structures and inappropriate vocabulary. There is some controversy about whether or not teachers should record exactly what the children dictate. Children will most easily learn to read the type of oral language they use. When teachers correct the language of children as they dictate, it often signifies to the children that the teacher lacks respect for them. It is best to write exactly what the children say, especially at the beginning. But words that are not pronounced correctly should be spelled correctly.

The language experience approach is best captured in an old Chinese proverb, which can be paraphrased as follows:

- What I can think about, I can say.
- What I can say can be written by me or someone else.
- I can read what I can write.
- I can read what other people write for me to read. They can also read what I write.

Multiple readings of the text are helpful to English learners (Crawford et al., 1995). Children can practice reading the text as an oral cloze procedure, based on a copy of the text with some words left out and with empty spaces where words are missing. Tell the children that some words are missing and ask whether they can predict what should be in the space. Reading the text with the children, the teacher pauses briefly when encountering a missing word, writing in the missing words as they children identify them. The teacher might write the missing words at the bottom of the page before starting this activity.

There are many practice activities that can be done with LEA text. Practice with sentences is more meaningful than practice with separate words. The sentence meaning can help children to remember the words more easily than practicing the words in isolation.

Children may accumulate new words they learn, these collections serving as their personal word files. After they have fifteen or twenty words, they can do classification activities with their word files. Finding words that start with the same letter and sound is a way some children learn to associate letters and sounds, allowing them to learn best about letters and sounds from words they already know. They can look for words that are names of people, places, animals, colors, foods, and clothing.

If children are collecting the words they can read, they can try to build sentences with them. The teacher may need to demonstrate before asking them to try it. The teacher should read their sentences to them if they cannot read them independently. Children can also try to reconstruct the same sentences that they have used in their dictated texts.

One nonthreatening way to elicit text that reflects more mature syntax and vocabulary is an adaptation called the collaborative chart story. When children are dictating and beginning to read with confidence later in the process, the teacher can ask children to negotiate their suggested text with the group. The teacher can invite questions from other children about a suggested sentence, for example, by asking how they feel about the way it is stated and how effectively the vocabulary provided expresses what the group wants to say. When children who have dictated sentences with grammatical errors hear suggestions from other children about how it might be said in another way, they invariably agree to the change. The children do not view this collaboration as correction, but rather as reflecting the contributions they all make together in communicating with the audience that will read their text later. It is probably better to accept exactly what is dictated at the beginning of the LEA process so that children can see the direct links among what they say, what the teacher writes down, and what the group reads back later.

Text-Based Strategies

English learners will indicate their readiness to move from the language experience approach to reading by expressing their interest in what they will call *"real books."* A valuable form of written text for second language learners early in the reading process is the big book, particularly big books with predictable or repetitive language patterns (A. N. Crawford, 1993).

Teachers read to children, who then read with them and finally back to them, although this *reading* might consist of telling about the story while looking at the illustrations (Trachtenburg and Ferruggia, 1989). Using big books provides an opportunity for the teacher to model so that children can clearly see what they will later do in their own independent reading. In addition, children begin to notice correspondences between letters in familiar texts and the sounds they represent (Holdaway, 1979). If parallel versions of a text are available and have been used in the mother tongue, then children will not only bring that background knowledge to bear in the English version, but also grow in English proficiency as a result of this early literacy experience.

According to Lynch (1986), the shared reading process begins with consideration of the book language that may already been acquired by children whose parents or other family members read to them. For those who lack this experience, shared reading takes on increasing importance. English learners will sometimes come from homes where printed material is scarce or where parents' own literacy skills may be limited. We cannot make assumptions about the conceptual knowledge of print that any English learner brings to the classroom (A. N. Crawford, 1993).

By looking at the cover and at illustrations inside a book together, children begin to understand that they can make predictions based on what they already know, their background knowledge, and what they think the author is trying to say to them. As the teacher begins to read the story to them, they will notice and discuss connections between their predictions and the story line.

With beginning readers, their first reading may take the form of group echo-reading with a teacher or lead reader, usually following a read-aloud by the teacher (Peetoom, 1986). As the lead reader reads very expressively, the time gap between that person and the group of children will diminish. When an individual or a part of the group stumbles, the lead reader should take charge and read until the group is together again. This activity lowers anxiety about oral reading because children's approximations, a very natural aspect of early reading, are not noticeable and comprehension is maintained. Most important, everyone is reading.

Peetoom (1986) describes timed and repeated readings in which children read aloud passages of about 150 words from carefully selected literature. With practice, children read them more accurately and in less time. Dowhower (1987) has reported that such repeated and rehearsed readings can result in gains in the reading rate, accuracy, and comprehension of 7-year-old children, with some evidence of transfer to unpracticed passages, as well. As a part of her study, children read along with an audiotape until they read easily, or they practiced reading a passage until they could read at a preestablished set rate. This can be an especially useful independent activity for dyads of children working together. Again, they will be reading instead of completing written drill and practice activities on skill development. Samuels (1979) associated repeated readings with the development of automaticity, the stage at which children read and recognize words unconsciously, permitting their full attention to focus instead on meaning. Automaticity in reading seems to parallel the process of oral production without employing the monitor in language acquisition. It also has much in common with Terrell's (1986) concept of *binding*, in which a linguistic form evokes meaning without any delay.

A. N. Crawford (1993) suggests that a bilingual teacher present a piece of literature from English in a read-aloud or storytelling format but in the mother tongue. The children will interact with it by dictating and reading a retelling in their mother tongue, but they will be exposed to the cultural content and background knowledge that it contains. When they are later able to read it in their new second language, they will have background knowledge from the earlier experience that will transfer positively into English.

Many teachers are concerned about how children can begin to read a big book or a predictable book before they have learned to read, that is, to decode or call the words. Smith (1988) describes the process as one of demonstration in which the teacher or parent reads the big book to the child, who in turn *reads* it back to the teacher or parent. As children gain confidence through this early successful experience with reading and through a process of approximation, they begin to read with increasing accuracy and faithfulness to the actual text. Predictable text is a characteristic of some children's literature that makes it especially well suited for the shared reading process. Predictable patterns are often repetitive, with small changes often signalled by accompanying illustrations.

Sometimes, these patterns are cumulative, in that early repeated elements are added to new elements so that children must remember them in sequence.

When children read to the teacher as a group, a process that Peetoom (1986) calls echo-reading, there is an even greater sense of success because individual errors are not noted. Children can either correct themselves or go right on, with a correspondingly low level of anxiety about reading. This process is very much parallel with the need for a low level of anxiety in the acquisition of a second language and with the role of correction in that process (A. N. Crawford, 1994).

Children soon begin to identify which parts of the text tell about corresponding parts of the story, and they also begin to recognize certain words of interest to them. These words are not necessarily easy words from an adult's point of view. In terms of the frequency of their appearance in primary texts or in the number of syllables they contain, they are instead easy from a child's point of view because of their interest and utility. Such words as *elephant* and *yellow* are more likely to be remembered and read correctly on second or third reading than more difficult words, such as *come* and *as*.

Lynch (1986) points out that repetition of familiar stories leads to increased success, not to boredom on the part of the children. Their abilities to predict will grow, and they will increase the kind and variety of cues they use to predict, moving from illustrations and background knowledge of a story to familiar words and other visual cues. The later use of graphophonic cues, the phonics and structural analysis skills that are of so much concern to some educational decision makers, emerges then as a result of this process, not as its cause (Smith, 1988).

Vocabulary Development

We have already considered Krashen's assertion that second language acquisition and literacy contribute mutually to each other's development, with reading providing much comprehensible input. Reading is also a major factor in the vocabulary development of English learners.

In keeping with a meaning-based approach to teaching English learners, Harmon (1998) provides an excellent contextualized strategy for vocabulary development that reflects the philosophy of the natural approach to second language acquisition. She describes how a teacher uses a new term and then elaborates and extends its meaning immediately:

> "Let's start *recounting* the events of the story. *We will tell about the beginning, middle, and end.*"
>
> "This is an *excerpt—one tiny piece.*"

In another strategy described by Nagy et al. (1993), Spanish-speaking students can use cognates they recognize from Spanish and English to support their reading comprehension in English. Words such as *general* are the same in spelling and meaning in both languages, and many other cognates are the same in meaning and similar in spelling, such as an example provided by Nagy et al.: *transform* in English and *transformar* in Spanish. But looking beyond their study, children must also be taught to be wary of false cognates, such as *actual*, which means *nowadays* in Spanish, and *dime*, which means *give me* in Spanish.

Adapting Phonics and Decoding Strategies for English Learners

A constructivist view of learning tells us that children unify what they already know about the world with new information that they gain through authentic experiences. Even in the largely synthetic process of learning about the isolated letters and sounds of a language, we will find that English learners have background knowledge about the sound system of their mother tongue, phonemic awareness, and usually some knowledge about the symbols that represent those sounds, as well. Phonics, then, is the process of unifying that knowledge of sounds and letters in an authentic experience that permits children to generate new knowledge, that is, how to pronounce the sound of a letter or combination of letters in an unknown word. When this is accomplished within the context of what children already know, then instruction in phonics is not inconsistent with the constructivist paradigm.

We have already recognized that English learners bring to the classroom phonemic awareness of sounds in the mother tongue. They should then learn phonics in the mother tongue out of the context of words they already recognize on sight, probably learned from the print environment and from language experience charts and big books. Children who learn phonics in the mother tongue generally have a much easier time learning phonics in English than do children who must learn phonics first in English. Some languages, such as Spanish and Korean, are very regular in their phoneme-grapheme relationships; and not only is phonics more simple to learn, but children have more confidence in them than do children learning to read in a language in which phoneme-grapheme relationships are not regular, such as English.

The real dilemma for English learners is when they must learn phonics in English first. Although they might have learned to speak and understand English, they still lack the phonemic awareness skills in English of a native speaker. For example, a native Spanish-speaking child will speak the forty-three sounds of English using the twenty-five sounds of Spanish. There are only five vowel sounds in Spanish but fifteen in English. This accounts for the difficulty that Spanish-speaking children have in pronouncing short vowels in English, especially the schwa; they have similar difficulty in "reading" (correctly pronouncing) these sounds in a phonetic approach to reading. Although there are variations in the differences between other languages and English, similar difficulties arise for children who speak most other languages. For those who learn phonics in their mother tongue, the process of learning English phonics is much easier because they have already figured out how the process works. It transfers from the mother tongue, even if many of the sounds do not.

The language experience approach and shared reading are holistic strategies for teaching reading. In these strategies, we do not begin with phonics. But learning about letters and sounds (phonics) is a part of learning to read in all methods, including these. In a constructivist approach to teaching about letters and sounds, children should learn about reading first. They should dictate many LEA charts and read them, learning to read some 100–200 words on sight. They should have many shared book reading experiences, and then they are ready to learn about letters and sounds using words they already know.

Writing and Spelling

A major principle of the constructivist view of literacy is the interdependence of listening, speaking, reading, and writing. Hudelson (1984) observed that second language learners address the four language processes as a totality, not as separate entities. According to Fitzgerald (1993), writing begins when children can draw, and there is no need to wait for reading. We can certainly extend these ideas to English learners, who should be encouraged to write in the second language early, especially if they have writing skills in their mother tongue. The errors that they make should be viewed in the same way that we view errors in oral production, as a part of the natural processes of approximation and acquisition (A. N. Crawford, 1994).

Ferreiro (1991) described the process of writing as one of making meaning through construction and reconstruction. Samway (1993) reinforced this idea in her study of how a sample of non-native-English-speaking primary school children from 7 to 11 years of age evaluated their own writing and that of others. Although these high-risk children were experiencing difficulties in school, they tended to focus on meaning in their evaluative comments. Most of their comments were categorized as *crafting*, how well a story had been developed, or *understanding*, making sense of the text.

For English learners, we have already seen that writing flows out of a variety of language acquisition activities, including the key vocabulary and language experience approaches to reading and the postreading strategy of written retellings. The structuring of their writing or their selection of vocabulary might be further supported through the use of semantic maps and cumulative semantic maps.

In a six-month observational study of six upper primary school Southeast Asian children in the United States, Urzúa (1987) found that feedback between children in the writing process caused them to develop a sense of audience. Their peers asked them questions and made suggestions about their writing. The children also developed a sense of voice, preferring to select their own writing topics. Finally, she observed that they developed a sense of power in language as they learned to add to their writings, to discuss vocabulary with each other, and to take risks as they manipulated language.

Spelling is another area in which instructional strategies must be adapted for English learners. Consistent with the communicative approach principle of minimizing error correction and with the developmental nature of second language acquisition and literacy, teachers of English learners, like teachers of English speakers, should accept the invented spellings of their children as a very natural aspect of their developmental growth in writing. There are differences, however, in how English learners will progress through some of Gentry's stages of invented spelling (see Chapter 2).

In the semiphonetic stage, English learners begin to approximate an alphabetic orthography and to conceptualize the alphabetic principle. They begin to demonstrate the relationship between sound and letter, and they sometimes use letter names as words. They begin to understand the left-to-right convention of most Western languages, and they may begin to segment words. Differences in the nature of invented spelling between languages will appear. The use of consonants tends to predominate over the use of vowels when children write in English as a mother tongue, for example, but vowels predominate over consonants when children write in Spanish as a mother tongue (Ferreiro and Rodríguez, 1994).

In the correct stage, children have learned most basic rules of the orthographic system. They are aware of such word structures as prefixes, suffixes, contractions, compound words, and homonyms, and they continue to learn some less common spelling patterns and rules. It is at this stage that they begin to recognize when a word *looks* correct, a phenomenon that corresponds to the natural approach characteristic in which second language learners begin to recognize when something *sounds* right or *feels* right. They are able to spell a large number of words automatically.

English learners who are literate in another language will tend to move much more rapidly through Gentry's stages in their new second language of English than in their primary language. Nathenson-Mejia (1989) found that in their English writing, Spanish-speaking children in the beginning stages of English spelling made extensive use of their Spanish pronunciation in their invented spellings in English. Edelsky (1982) made the same observation in a more generic sense. She took the positive point of view that children are applying some mother tongue writing skills to the second language, rather than the negative point of view that it reflects interference from the first language on the second.

SCAFFOLDING STRATEGIES FOR IMPROVING READING COMPREHENSION

In recent years, reading instruction has moved away from the controlled environment of the traditional basal reader toward authentic children's literature, often in anthologies, including fiction and nonfiction trade books. According to A. N. Crawford (1997), children are exposed to oral and written ideas that demand higher levels of background knowledge, vocabulary, and language proficiency. In their work with English learners, teachers face great challenges in providing for the equitable access of all children to authentic literature in English while helping them make progress in reading and writing.

Whether or not English learners read literature in the primary or the second language, we can organize a set of scaffolding strategies to support their reading comprehension into three categories: prereading strategies, guided or directed reading strategies, and postreading strategies. Scaffolding is the temporary support that teachers provide when children are engaged in a task within Vygotsky's zone of proximal development. Bruner (1978) has described scaffolding as a temporary launching platform designed to support and encourage children's language development to higher levels of complexity. Pearson (1985) later elaborated the temporary nature of scaffolding in describing it as the gradual release of responsibility. Good teachers intuitively use such scaffolding strategies as higher-order questioning, prompts, illustrations and other visual resources, demonstrations, dramatization, gestures, comprehension monitoring, graphic organizers, and rephrasing (A. N. Crawford, 1994). These strategies help children maintain their participation in learning activities.

According to A. N. Crawford (1994), the difference between these recommended scaffolding strategies and those ordinarily used for English learners is substantial. Some English learners have tended to have been placed in perpetual compensatory or remedial programs, in which we expect them to learn to read and write by acquiring isolated skills through interaction with incomplete fragments of language. These children rarely move successfully into the mainstream curriculum, more frequently leaving these programs only when they complete their schooling, all too often as dropouts. The recommended strategies resemble most closely the enrichment or additional activities that teachers of English learners sometimes never have time for because they are busy teaching the isolated skills that the children seem to lack. We need to develop those skills directly and, within the context of language, in an authentic mode.

The recommended strategies that follow are those that will provide the underlying support or scaffolding needed for reading comprehension. It is the isolated skills that teachers should set aside. We should view skill development as an outcome of learning to read, not as its cause (Samuels, 1971; Smith, 1985). When a child's needs suggest that a directed skill lesson is needed, teachers should seek out an appropriate one in the teacher's editions and workbooks of traditional reading and language arts programs.

Prereading Strategies

There is increasing recognition of the importance of bringing background knowledge to bear on making sense of new information (Smith, 1988). The activation of this background knowledge, and often its development, constitute a vitally important prereading activity for the English learner. The background knowledge that we have acquired about the world forms the structure through which we assess new information and incorporate it. We use this knowledge to make and verify predictions about the new information to which we are exposed. According to Krashen (1991), background knowledge also makes second language input more comprehensible and therefore facilitates second language acquisition. In addition, we can consider vocabulary itself as an important aspect of background knowledge to be activated or installed.

Background Knowledge

All children have acquired background knowledge, but there is often a discontinuity between the background knowledge a child has, what Moll and González (1994) refer to as "funds of knowledge," and the assumptions that teachers, authors, and textbook publishers make about that knowledge. A. N. Crawford (1994) indicates that this discontinuity must be assumed to be deeper when the child comes from a language or culture different from that of those for whom the materials are designed or intended, usually middle-class native English speakers. A story about a birthday leads a Mexican child to activate background knowledge about a piñata, while most children in the United States activate background knowledge about a party, a cake with candles, and gifts. Children from Senegal and Morocco don't think about birthdays at all because birthdays are not celebrated in their cultures. If children lack a schema or background knowledge for a birthday tradition that is presented in a literature selection representing a culture they do not know, then background knowledge must be activated or developed as a prereading activity. Instead of a deficit in knowledge, then, we must view the funds of knowledge that all children bring to the processes of reading and writing as an asset, a resource. Our task is to tap that knowledge.

Many prereading activities were introduced in earlier chapters. We will elaborate some of them here and add a few more that are of particular value to English learners.

Group Discussion

The activation or development of background knowledge in children without previous exposure can often be accomplished through a sharing of the group's knowledge. Although no individual child might know a great deal about a topic, several children in a group will each have some knowledge (María, 1989).

Semantic Mapping

A useful strategy for providing structure to the development of background knowledge is semantic mapping (Heimlich and Pittelman, 1986). Knowledge is activated from long-term memory, shared with other children, and discussed in terms of needed vocabulary. It is then recorded in a graphic format that promotes organizing schemata so that relationships become more clear. The resulting semantic map might also serve as an advance organizer that will promote reading comprehension when the children later read the selection.

The teacher writes a word on a chart, chalkboard, or transparency and asks children to tell what they know about that concept. Although most children won't know much, a few will know something. The process of discussing and systematically recording their background knowledge on a semantic map permits them to share what they know while the teacher organizes it into logical categories. Semantic maps are widely used to develop vocabulary in the same way. In fact, a major difference between authentic literature and basal reader stories or so-called decodable text is the variety of vocabulary that the skilled author uses, selecting the precise word needed to best express an idea.

According to A. N. Crawford (1993), semantic mapping is not a strategy to use every day. The nature of the literature selection, the desirability of formally structuring the background knowledge into a semantic map, and the existing background knowledge of the children should all be factors in deciding when and if the gains from devoting a considerable amount of instructional time to the activity are warranted.

The cumulative semantic map acts as a graphic thesaurus (A. N. Crawford, 1994). Ordinarily, a semantic map for activating background knowledge or vocabulary is developed and completed during one or two related lessons and is not referred to subsequently. However, teachers often find that they are dealing with some concepts on repeated occasions. It can be useful to return to a semantic map on such a topic, to add to it, and to consider new additions in contrast with earlier ones.

We can see in Figure 10.1, for example, a cumulative semantic map as it might appear after two months of school (A. N. Crawford, 1994). A teacher might introduce the new word *furious* from a piece of literature and ask children where it should be added to an existing cumulative semantic map for words about feelings and emotions. At that point, the children can discuss how angry *furious* is in comparison to *miffed, enraged,* and *upset,* which had been added to the semantic map on earlier occasions. When written on removable self-stick notes, the various words can be arranged and rearranged in ascending order of increasing anger as children negotiate their meaning with each other. Moustafa (1996) suggests placing words on cards with cellophane tape across the top. Using the same tape over and over, the teacher can then stick these to a large wall chart made of plastic shower curtain material. Moustafa's strategy can be adapted to the cumulative semantic map, facilitating the moving of words from one place to another on the chart or in making room for a new word to be added. Many weeks later, the map has been elaborated, as

FIGURE 10.1 A Cumulative Semantic Map

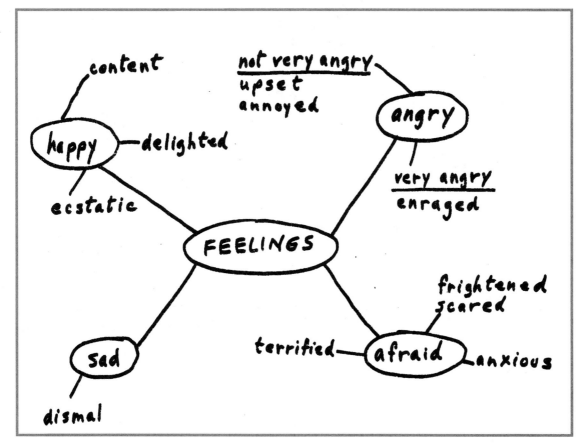

seen in Figure 10.2, and, of course, this process continues through the school year.

In a later writing assignment, English learners might again refer to the cumulative semantic map on the wall when they want to select just the right word to convey the degree of anger they have in mind (A. N. Crawford, 1994). Discussing the choice of word with the teacher or with other children will be particularly helpful. When children are ready to add yet another synonym for *angry* a week or a month later, they will have the opportunity to review other words or expressions for the same feeling within a context of known or somewhat familiar vocabulary. We can view a well-developed cumulative semantic map as a graphic thesaurus. Other suitable topics for cumulative semantic maps might include *seeing* (stare, peek, glare, etc.), *motion* (crawl, creep, dawdle, dash, poke along, lope, etc.), and *touching* (poke, tap, jab, stroke, etc.). Only the topics come from the teacher; the source of vocabulary is the literature the children are reading.

FIGURE 10.2 An Elaborated Cumulative Semantic Map

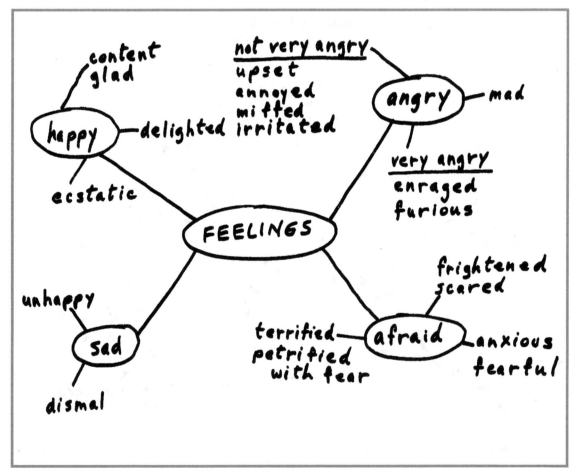

Advance Organizer

The advance organizer (see Chapter 9) is another useful tool for activating background knowledge. It is perhaps most common to find advance organizers provided in content area textbooks, such as history, geography, and the sciences, but they can also be a useful addition to literature readings, whether prepared by authors and publishers or by teachers. Some stories or literature selections provide a brief summary, often on a book jacket or on the back of a soft-cover book. Occasionally, this includes a question or comment that is designed to entice the reader into reading the selection. Teachers can use these to interest their children in stories, to activate background knowledge, and to help them make predictions about the story. Even an adult will rarely purchase a book without examining the advance organizer or publisher's summary on the back cover, not to mention the illustration on the front cover.

Vocabulary Development

When children read, their lack of vocabulary knowledge is often an obstacle to comprehension. Because they might have insufficient academically related background knowledge and vocabulary development in the mother tongue that would accompany it, this can be an even greater problem for children who must read in their second language, We can consider vocabulary as an aspect of background knowledge in prereading, but we will treat it separately here to examine several concepts that relate more specifically to vocabulary.

Let us consider two different aspects of the question of vocabulary development. One is the richness of language that surrounds children. It is well recognized that children become familiar with the meanings of words when those meanings are highly contextualized, not when they are studied in isolation as new vocabulary words. It follows, then, that a richer language environment should result in increased exposure to contextualized vocabulary and therefore to understanding of their meanings (A. N. Crawford, 1994b).

We often postpone or even eliminate instruction for at-risk children, however, in the very areas of the curriculum in which new vocabulary words will be offered in the most highly contextualized ways—in science, social studies, art, music, health, and other areas of the curriculum. This is even more common for children who are learning in their second language. According to A. N. Crawford (1993), we must ensure that these areas of the curriculum are provided for all children, including English learners, and that they are presented so that contextualized exposure to a rich vocabulary is promoted.

Another aspect of vocabulary is the issue of direct instruction. Although many vocabulary words will be acquired incidentally, some literature or content selections will contain a few vocabulary words that must be clearly grasped if the text is to be understood. There will be other words not known to the children that need not be addressed through direct instruction because they are not critical to understanding the selection or because they can be quickly analyzed through the context in which they appear.

Many of the strategies that are recommended for the activation or development of background knowledge constitute direct approaches to vocabulary instruction. Semantic mapping is one of these strategies, but its application should be limited to those key and conceptually difficult vocabulary terms that are more in the realm of background knowledge. Otherwise, there will be little time left for reading after prereading activities are completed.

English learners often benefit from read-aloud activities by the teacher, followed by discussion. A read-aloud is simply the process of having a teacher read a literature selection, or a part of one, aloud to the children before they read it themselves. Vocabulary will have been presented in context, and someone in the group will likely have some knowledge of most words. Other words might be analyzed by reviewing the illustrations in a story or an appropriate illustration, manipulative, or visual aid provided by the teacher. Because illustrations provide important visual information, paging through a selection and discussing them before reading provide an opportunity for presenting new vocabulary and also for making predictions about the text. A partial or complete read-aloud of a literature selection as a prereading activity may be called for in a particularly challenging piece.

Guided Reading Strategies

According to Smith (1985), we learn to read by reading. This fundamental and obvious idea should underlie our thinking as we consider how children's time is spent during reading instruction. Rather than having children study about reading by mastering skills, we must instead maximize the amount of reading that they do. Some obviously counterproductive strategies are pencil-and-paper exercises. Another is the still common practice of round-robin oral reading, in which each child takes a turn reading aloud to the group or class. This usually consists of having a child laboriously reading aloud a passage that she or he has never before read, even silently, while the rest of the children in the group pretend to listen or read along. The child who is reading focuses on pronunciation, not on understanding what is being read, and the other children are alternatively bored or preparing to read when their turn comes. This practice is especially deceiving with children who read in Spanish, for example. They can read orally with confidence in English, albeit with a Spanish accent and no comprehension. They are, in fact, pronouncing, and not reading.

Our own experiences in learning another language remind us of the importance of reading for comprehension, as opposed to word calling. Most of us had the experience of being asked to read aloud in a secondary school or university foreign language class. We read with great intensity, attempting to correctly soften the intervocalic d of Spanish or accurately pronounce the difficult initial r of French. When we finished, the teacher asked us to tell about the content of what we read in our own words. Of course, we had little idea, because we had been focusing on pronunciation. We must remember that communication and comprehension are the focus of reading and writing, just as they are in a communicative approach to oral language development. There are many guided reading strategies that will help us to ensure that children focus on comprehension instead of only on correct pronunciation.

As we noted above, when English learners begin to read themselves, they may benefit from having their teacher read to them from the selection first. Occasionally, the teacher might find that presenting the entire selection as a read-aloud is helpful. When a parallel version of a text is available in the children's mother tongue, the teacher might read it aloud before the children read later in the second language. Children in school are not bored or disturbed by several exposures to the same literature selection, any more than a 3-year-old objects to hearing the same story before bed every night. The familiarity of a story that is an old friend becomes a real comfort. Familiarity with the background knowledge and structure of a story permits a child to read with good comprehension and with fewer time-consuming visual cues, especially for children's early literacy experiences in the second language. The teacher's read-aloud also provides the teacher with the opportunity to model predicting, thinking about context, and other strategies by talking through some of the metacognitive processes that are used during the teacher's oral reading.

Elementary school children should read silently on an extensive basis. It is through more rapid silent reading that children can read for the most practice and be exposed to the most background knowledge and contextualized vocabulary. It is more difficult for teachers to provide extra support to second language learners, however, because their need for it might be less obvious during the largely independent activity of reading silently. The need should be based on children's abilities to interact with the teacher and each other about what they have been reading, that is, their comprehension of what they have been reading.

One strategy for providing this support during the silent reading of literature selections is to direct or structure children's reading with questions. Some would decry this as an annoying and unnecessary strategy that is destined to destroy any enjoyment of the selection by the child. That might indeed be the case for some children. The reality is, however, that many English learners struggle to read, and their many failure experiences can result in a lack of motivation and interest in reading. Their teachers often have difficulty reading themselves during silent sustained reading because of their need to supervise closely the reading of their sometimes reluctant students.

According to A. N. Crawford (1993), guiding children's reading with questions, a variation on directed reading-thinking activity, provides valuable support in maintaining comprehension. The teacher should precede the children's reading of a page or passage of a piece of literature by asking a higher-order question, that is, an open-ended question whose answer requires the child to use background knowledge and combine it with information that is in the selection to be read. An example of such a question is "Please read page 71 to find out why the main character is worried." Students will read page 71 to find the answer to the question; it focuses them on comprehension, not on production and accurate oral reading. This questioning strategy brings key story concepts to their attention as they read and, perhaps more important, provides moral support, interest, and motivation from someone who cares about them, the teacher. Children who cannot or will not read a lengthy selection alone might do so a page or two at a time within the security of a supportive teacher-directed group. Their reading can be structured by questions that elicit predictions, with timely resolution of those predictions through discussion and any needed mediation. Finally, these questions should be formulated to require higher-order thinking on the part of the children, demonstrating the teacher's high expectations for them. Peetoom (1986) suggests chunking stories by having children read them in manageable and comprehensible sections. Questions can be used very effectively and naturally to accomplish this chunking.

Although there is considerable debate about the value of teaching reading comprehension skills through direct instruction, there are sufficient other reasons to guide silent reading with questions. A teacher will take no longer to formulate and ask a higher-order comprehension question than a low-level recall question before asking children to read to find the answer. It is often said that teachers have low expectations for at-risk children and English learners. Guided silent reading provides an opportunity for children to make inferences and predictions, identify cause-and-effect relationships, and apply other higher-order critical thinking skills when their comprehension is supported (A. N. Crawford, 1993).

Postreading Strategies

After children read, there are other opportunities to provide scaffolding. We have already considered the retelling of stories that are told or read to children as a means of producing text through LEA for them to read themselves. Retelling is also an excellent postreading activity for English learners. An oral retelling provides children with the opportunity to negotiate with each other about the meaning of the selection. It is often through this process that children can incorporate new information gained through reading into existing background knowledge. Koskinen, Gambrell, Kapinus, and Heathington (1988) found that the verbal rehearsal that occurs in the retelling process also serves to improve the reading comprehension of less proficient readers. Some children may elect to retell in their mother tongue what they read or heard in their second language. Brown and Cambourne (1990) observe that retelling also promotes multiple readings of text as a part of the negotiation process.

Retelling also provides a means for integrating writing into the program. Either through a cooperative learning process or through individual or paired writing, children can prepare a written retelling (Strickland and Feeley, 1985). As a result of their earlier discussion, of the knowledge they gained through reading, and of such prereading activities as semantic mapping and the examination of story grammar, children are better prepared to write a well-structured retelling. Like the modeling that teachers provide during reading, teachers should also model retelling with an actual example.

The most obvious postreading activity should not be overlooked: more reading. If we are successful in providing high-quality literature that children will choose to read and also in supporting their comprehension, then we should expect gains in all areas of the language arts. Krashen (1985, 1993) has concluded that reading is more powerful than direct instruction in developing vocabulary, grammar, spelling, and reading comprehension, especially for English learners. He advocates extensive free voluntary reading with messages that are understood in low-anxiety situations. Finally, he believes that good writing is promoted more by extensive reading than by writing.

SOME ISSUES IN ASSESSING THE READING AND WRITING OF ENGLISH LEARNERS

Instruments and Procedures

Most assessment strategies used with English speakers will function well in other languages and also with English learners in English. There are, however, some adaptations indicated. For example, one element of evaluating oral reading accuracy in the informal reading inventory (see Chapter 3) is the mispronunciation, each occurrence of which is counted as an oral reading error or miscue. When a mispronunciation error can be attributed to a conflict point with the mother tongue and when it does not interfere with comprehension, a short *i* pronounced as a long *e*, for example, then an error would not be counted.

In a personal communication with the author, Kenneth Johnson (1977) provided a test sentence to illustrate this principle for the African-American child whose mother tongue is southern regional dialect or Black dialect. The sentence often elicits a mispronunciation that has the potential to interfere with comprehension. The child is asked to read the following aloud:

> *As I passed the sign,*
> *I read it.*

In conformance with Southern Regional dialect, the African-American child sometimes pronounces *passed* as *pass*, dropping the *-ed* suffix that is also a past tense marker. If the child comprehends the marker, that is, if he or she understands that *passed* is in the past tense, even though pronounced as in the present tense, then the child will pronounce *read* in the past tense. If not, he or she will pronounce the identically spelled word in the present tense. According to Johnson, the child will invariably correctly pronounce *read* in the past tense. In a study of teachers who administered IRIs to Spanish-speaking children, Lamberg et al. (1978) concluded that, to avoid such problems, teachers need special training to use them with English learners.

Grouping for Instruction

Using assessment data to group English learners for reading instruction is always a challenge. When most or all children speak another language in common, such as Spanish, and when the teacher is bilingual, then a mother tongue reading program and a strong ESL program are in order. As children become ready to transition to English language reading instruction, the grouping structure becomes more complex, often resulting in instruction in two languages at several levels within each language. It is tempting to move children who speak English to another classroom at that point, but this practice leads to a phenomenon called *fossilization,* a danger that Selinker, Swain, and Dumas (1975) point out as the isolation of English learners from native speakers, leading to a stopping-in-place of language development caused by a lack of comprehensible input from expert speakers of the new second language.

One school district developed a model that effectively alleviates this problem at the elementary level (Krashen and Biber, 1988). English learners are organized for mother tongue instruction in reading and the language arts during the morning, along with a natural approach program of acquiring English. In the afternoon, English learners are mainstreamed with English-speaking children in art, music, and physical education. As English learners gain proficiency, they begin to receive sheltered instruction in that second language in the more concrete areas of the curriculum, such as mathematics and science. Social studies in English are introduced later.

Sheltered instruction is a context-embedded intermediate ESL methodology in which content in provided to English learners in English, but with special support through strategies such as those developed by the Los Angeles Unified School District (1985). They recommend that teachers simplify input by speaking slowly and enunciating clearly, using a controlled vocabulary within simple language structures. When possible, they should use cognates and avoid the extensive use of idiomatic expressions. They suggest that teachers make frequent use of nonverbal language, including gestures, facial expressions, and dramatization. They also recommend the use of manipulatives and concrete materials, such as props, graphs, visuals, overhead transparencies, bulletin boards, maps, and realia. Comprehension should be maintained through extensive use of gestures, dramatization, illustrations, and manipulatives. Teachers should check frequently for understanding by asking for confirmation of comprehension; by asking students to clarify, repeat, and expand; and by using a variety of questioning formats. Schifini (1985) additionally recommends a focus on student-centered activities, especially at the secondary level, at which lecturing and textbook use predominate.

Selection of Literature and Other Instructional Materials

The principles of selecting literature for English learners do not differ greatly from those for English-speaking students. Authentic children's literature in languages other than English is increasingly available, especially in Spanish. The interests, culture, and background knowledge of the students must, of course, be considered. Children are anxious to see themselves in the literature they read, whether in English or the mother tongue.

Most major publishers now provide anthologies of literature for children that are parallel in English and Spanish. The best ones are not translations from English to Spanish, but rather those that are parallel and similar in thematic content, with many stories overlapping in both languages. At least some of these stories have been translated from Spanish to English for exposing English-speaking children to literature from another culture.

The use of these programs provides many advantages. Children can begin learning to read in the mother tongue, moving into English two to three years later when they have learned enough English to reach the level of cognitive-academic language proficiency. When they later read many of the same selections in English, they have the advantage of prior experience with concepts and story grammars, providing a strong support to their comprehension as they move into their new second language.

SUMMARY

In this chapter, we have addressed the special needs and challenges of the significant number of children in our schools with apparent problems in reading and writing that we characterize as English learners, those whose mother tongue or home language is not English. The difficulties they have are more often with second language issues than with reading and writing. We have presented interrelated strategies for teaching English as a second language and literacy, strategies that are based in meaning, rather than isolated skills development.

English learners must first learn to speak and understand English, and communicative approaches, such as total physical response (TPR) and the natural approach, provide very effective strategies to meet this need. They parallel the development of the mother tongue, in which children are almost universally successful.

Evidence suggests that when English learners can learn to read and write in their mother tongue, it will benefit their long-range acquisition of English and their abilities to read and write in English. Strategies for teaching reading and writing to English learners should be based on meaning, with the key vocabulary and language experience approaches serving well at the level of emergent literacy. As English learners move into English text, they will need extra support for comprehension. Their program should include prereading, guided reading, and postreading activities that provide scaffolding for comprehension in their new language.

REFERENCES

Asher, J. J. "The Total Physical Response Approach." In *Innovative Approaches to Language Teaching*, ed. R. W. Blair. Rowley, MA: Newbury House, 1982, pp. 54–66.

Au, K. H. "Social Constructivism and the School Literacy Learning of Students of Diverse Backgrounds." *Journal of Literacy Research* 30 (1998): 297–319.

Brown, H., and B. Cambourne. *Read and Retell: A Strategy for the Whole-Language/Natural Learning Classroom*. Portsmouth, NH: Heinemann, 1990.

Bruner, J. "The Role of Dialogue in Language Acquisition." In *The Child's Conception of Language*, ed. A. Sinclair, R. J. Jarvella, & W. M. Levelt. New York: Springer-Verlag, 1978, pp. 241–256.

Chan, J., and B. Chips. "Helping LEP Students Survive in the Content-Area Classroom." *Thrust* (1989): 49–51.

Chastain, K. *Developing Second-Language Skills: From Theory to Practice*. Chicago: Rand McNally College Publishing Company, 1975.

Collier, V. P. "Age and Rate of Acquisition of Second Language for Academic Purposes." *TESOL Quarterly* 21 (1987): 617–641.

Collier, V. P. "How Long? A Synthesis of Research on Academic Achievement in a Second Language." *TESOL Quarterly* 23 (1989): 509–539.

Crawford, A. N. "From Spanish Reading to English Reading: The Transition Process." In *Claremont Reading Conference Yearbook*, ed. M. P. Douglass. Claremont, CA: Claremont Reading Conference, 1982, pp. 159–165.

Crawford, A. N. "Literature, Integrated Language Arts, and the Language Minority Child: A Focus on Meaning." In *Whole Language and the Bilingual Learner*, ed. A. Carrasquillo and C. Hedley. Norwood, NJ: Ablex, 1993, pp. 61–75.

Crawford, A. N. "Communicative Approaches to ESL: A Bridge to Reading Comprehension. In *Claremont Reading Conference Yearbook,* ed. M. P. Douglass. Claremont, CA: Claremont Reading Conference, 1986, pp. 292–305.

Crawford, A. N. "Communicative Approaches to Second Language Acquisition: From Oral Language Development into the Core Curriculum and L_2 Literacy." In *Schooling and Language Minority Students: A Theoretical Framework,* 2nd ed., ed. C. F. Leyba. Los Angeles: Evaluation, Dissemination and Assessment Center, California State University, Los Angeles, 1994a, pp. 79–131.

Crawford, A. N. "Estrategias para Promover la Comprensión Lectora en Estudiantes de Alto Riesgo." *Lectura y Vida* 15, no. 1 (1994b): 21–27.

Crawford, A. N. "Language Policy, Second Language Learning, and Literacy." In *A Practical Guidebook for Adult Literacy Programmes in Developing Nations,* ed. A. N. Crawford. Paris: UNESCO, 1995, pp. 9–16.

Crawford, A. N. "Estrategias para Promover la Comprensión Lectora." In *Hacia un Futuro sin Fronteras,* ed. M. Lavadenz and C. Velasco. Santa Barbara, CA: University of California Linguistic Minority Research Institute, 1997, pp. 77–85.

Crawford, A. N., R. V. Allen, and M. Hall. "The Language Experience Approach." In *A Practical Guidebook for Adult Literacy Programmes in Developing Nations,* ed. A. N. Crawford. Paris: UNESCO, 1995, pp. 17–46.

Crawford, J. *Bilingual Education: History, Politics, Theory and Practice.* Trenton, NJ: Crane, 1989.

Cummins, J. "The Cross-Lingual Dimensions of Language Proficiency: Implications for Bilingual Education and the Optimal Age Issue." *TESOL Quarterly* 14 (1980): 175–187.

Cummins, J. "The Role of Primary Language Development in Promoting Educational Success for Language Minority Students." In *Schooling and Language Minority Students: A Theoretical Framework,* ed. California State Department of Education. Los Angeles: Evaluation, Dissemination and Assessment Center, California State University, Los Angeles, 1981, pp. 3–49.

Cummins, J. "Empowering Minority Students: A Framework for Intervention." *Harvard Educational Review* 56 (1986): 18–36.

Cummins, J. *Empowering Minority Students.* Sacramento: California Association for Bilingual Education, 1989.

Cummins, J. "Primary Language Instruction and the Education of Language Minority Students." In *Schooling and Language Minority Students: A Theoretical Framework,* 2nd ed., C. F. Leyba. Los Angeles: Evaluation, Dissemination and Assessment Center, California State University, Los Angeles, 1994, pp. 3–46.

Dixon, C. N., and D. Nessel. *Language Experience Approach to Reading and Writing: LEA for ESL.* Hayward, CA: Alemany Press, 1983.

Dowhower, S. L. "Effects of Repeated Reading on Second-Grade Transitional Readers' Fluency and Comprehension." *Reading Research Quarterly* 22 (1987): 389–406.

Edelsky, Carole. "Writing in a Bilingual Program: The Relation of L_1 and L_2 Texts." *TESOL Quarterly* 16 (1982): 211–228.

Ervin-Tripp, S. M. "Is Second Language Learning Like the First?" *TESOL Quarterly* 8 (1974): 111–127.

Ferreiro, E. "La construcción de la Escritura en el Niño." *Lectura y Vida* 12 (1991): 5–14.

Ferreiro, E., and B. Rodríguez. "Las Condiciones de Alfabetización en Medio Rural." México: CINVESTAV, 1994.

Finocchiaro, M. *English as a Second Language: From Theory to Practice.* New York: Regents, 1974.

Fitzgerald, J. "Literacy and Students Who Are Learning English as a Second Language." *The Reading Teacher* 46 (1993): 638–647.

Fleischman, H. L., and P. J. Hopstock. *Descriptive Study of Services to Limited English Proficient Students*. Arlington, VA: Development Associates, Inc., 1993.

Harmon, J. M. "Vocabulary Teaching and Learning in a Seventh-Grade Literature-Based Classroom." *Journal of Adolescent & Adult Literacy* 41 (1998): 518–529.

Heald-Taylor, G. *Whole Language Strategies for ESL Students*. San Diego: Dormac, 1986.

Heimlich, J. E., and S. D. Pittelman. *Semantic Mapping: Classroom Applications*. Newark, DE: International Reading Association, 1986.

Heller, M. F. Comprehending and Composing Through Language Experience." *The Reading Teacher* 42 (1988): 130–135.

Henderson, A., et al. *Summary of the Bilingual Education State Educational Agency Program Survey of States' Limited English Proficient Persons and Available Education Services 1991–92*. Arlington, VA: Development Associates, Inc., 1993.

Holdaway, D. *The Foundations of Literacy*. Sydney: Ashton Scholastic, 1979.

Hudelson, S. "Kan Yu Ret an Rayt en Ingles: Children Become Literate in English as a Second Language." *TESOL Quarterly* 18 (1984): 221–238.

Hudelson, S. "The Role of Native Language Literacy in the Education of Language Minority Children." *Language Arts* 64 (1987): 827–840.

Johnson, K. R. (1977). Personal communication,.

Jiménez, R. T. "The Strategic Reading Abilities and Potential of Five Low-Literacy Latina/o Readers in Middle School." *Reading Research Quarterly* 32 (1997): 224–243.

Jiménez, R. T., and A. Gámez. "Literature-Based Cognitive Strategy Instruction for Middle School Latina/o Students." *Journal of Adolescent & Adult Literacy* 40 (1996): 84–91.

Koskinen, P. S., L. B. Gambrell, B. A. Kapinus, and B. S Heathington. "Retelling: A Strategy for Enhancing Students' Reading Comprehension." *The Reading Teacher* 41 (1988): 892–896.

Krashen, S. D. "Bilingual Education and Second Language Acquisition Theory." In *Schooling and Language Minority Students: A Theoretical Framework,* ed. California State Department of Education. Sacramento, CA: Office of Bilingual Bicultural Education, California State Department of Education, 1981, pp. 51–79.

Krashen, S. D. *Principles and Practice in Second Language Acquisition*. New York: Pergamon Press, 1982b.

Krashen, S. "Theory Versus Practice in Language Training." In *Innovative Approaches to Language Teaching*, ed. R. W. Blair. Rowley, MA: Newbury House, 1982a, pp. 15–30.

Krashen, S. D. *Inquiries and Insights: Second Language Teaching, Immersion & Bilingual Education, Literacy*. Hayward, CA: Alemany Press, 1985.

Krashen, S. D. *Bilingual Education: A Focus on Current Research*. Washington, DC: National Clearinghouse for Bilingual Education, 1991.

Krashen, S. *The Power of Reading*. Englewood, CO: Libraries Unlimited, Inc., 1993.

Krashen, S., and D. Biber. *On Course: Bilingual Education's Success in California*. Sacramento: California Association for Bilingual Education, 1988.

Krashen, S. D., and T. D. Terrell. *The Natural Approach: Language Acquisition in the Classroom*. New York: Pergamon/Alemany, 1983.

Lamberg, W. J., L. Rodríguez, and D. A. Tomas. "Training in Identifying Oral Reading Departures from Text Which Can Be Explained as Spanish-English Phonological Differences." *The Bilingual Review/La Revista Bilingüe* 5 (1978): 65–75.

Lambert, W. E. "Culture and Language as Factors in Learning and Education." In *Education of Immigrant Students, ed.* A. Wolfgang. Toronto: O.I.S.E., 1975.

Lynch, P. *Using Big Books and Predictable Books*. New York: Scholastic, 1986.

Los Angeles Unified School District. *Strategies for Sheltered English Instruction*. Los Angeles: Los Angeles Unified School District, 1985.

María, K. "Developing Disadvantaged Children's Background Knowledge Interactively." *The Reading Teacher* 42 (1989): 296–300.

McQuillan, J., and L. Tse. "What's the Story? Using the Narrative Approach in Beginning Language Classrooms." *TESOL Journal* 7 (1998): 18–23.

Miramontes, O. B. "A Comparative Study of English Oral Reading Skills in Differently Schooled Groups of Hispanic Students." *Journal of Reading Behavior* 22 (1990): 373–394.

Modiano, N. "Bilingual Education for Children of Linguistic Minorities." *American Indígena* 28 (1968): 405–414.

Moll, L. C., and N. González. "Critical Issues: Lessons from Research with Language-Minority Children." *Journal of Reading Behavior* 26 (1994): 439–456.

Moustafa, M. "Children's Productive Phonological Recoding." *Reading Research Quarterly* 30, no. 3 (1995): 464–476.

Moustafa, M., and J. Penrose. "Comprehensible Input PLUS the Language Experience Approach: Reading Instruction for Limited English Speaking Students." *The Reading Teacher* 38, (1985): 640–647.

Nagy, W. E., G. E. García, A. Y. Durgunoğlu, and B. Hancin-Bhatt. "Spanish-English Bilingual Students' Use of Cognates in English Reading." *Journal of Reading Behavior* 25 (1993): 241–259.

Nathenson-Mejia, S. "Writing in a Second Language: Negotiating Meaning Through Invented Spelling." *Language Arts* 66 (1989): 516–526.

Nessel, D. D., and M. B. Jones. *The Language-Experience Approach to Reading*. New York: Teachers College Columbia University, 1981.

Peck, J. "Using Storytelling to Promote Language and Literacy Development." *The Reading Teacher* 43 (1989): 138–141.

Peetoom, A. *Shared Reading: Safe Risks with Whole Books*. Richmond Hill, Ontario, Canada: Scholastic, 1986.

Ramírez, J. D. (1991). *Final Report: Longitudinal Study of Structured English Immersion Strategy, Early-Exit and Late-Exit Bilingual Education Programs*. NTIS 300–87–0156. Washington, DC: U.S. Department of Education.

Samuels, S. J. "Letter-Name Versus Letter-Sound Knowledge in Learning to Read." *The Reading Teacher* 24 (1971): 604–608.

Samuels, S. J. "The Method of Repeated Readings." *The Reading Teacher* 32 (1979): 403–408.

Samway, K. D. "This Is Hard, Isn't It?": Children Evaluating Writing. *TESOL Quarterly* 27 (1993): 233–257.

Saville, M. R., and R. C. Troike. *A Handbook of Bilingual Education*. Washington, DC: Teachers of English to Speakers of Other Languages, 1971.

Schifini, A. *Sheltered English: Content Area Instruction for Limited English Proficient Students*. Los Angeles: Los Angeles County Office of Education, 1985.

Selinker, L., M. Swain, and G. Dumas. "The Interlanguage Hypothesis Extended to Children." *Language Learning* 25 (1975): 139–152.

Smith, F. *Reading Without Nonsense*. New York: Teachers College Press, 1985.

Smith, F. *Understanding Reading*. Hillsdale, NJ: Erlbaum, 1988.

Strickland, D. S., and J. T. Feeley. Using children's concept of story to improve reading and writing. In *Reading, Thinking and Concept Development*, ed. T. L. Harris & E. J. Cooper. New York: College Entrance Examination Board, 1985, pp. 163–173.

Terrell, T. D. "A Natural Approach to Second Language Acquisition and Learning." *Modern Language Journal* 6 (1977): 325–337.

Terrell, T. D. "The Natural Approach in Bilingual Education." In *School and Language Minority Students: A Theoretical Framework,* ed. California State Department of Education. Los Angeles: Evaluation, Dissemination and Assessment Center, California State University, Los Angeles, 1981, pp. 117–146.

Terrell, T. D. "The Natural Approach to Language Teaching: An Update." *Modern Language Journal* 66 (1982): 121–132.

Terrell, T. D. "Acquisition in the Natural Approach: The Binding/Access Framework." *Modern Language Journal* 70 (1986): 213–227.

Trachtenburg, P., and A. Ferruggia. "Big Books from Little Voices: Reaching High Risk Beginning Readers." *The Reading Teacher* 42 (1989): 284–289.

UNESCO. *The Use of Vernacular Languages in Education*. Paris: UNESCO, 1953.

Urzúa, C. "You Stopped Too Soon: Second Language Children Composing and Revising." *TESOL Quarterly* 21 (1987): 279–304.

Veatch, J. "From the Vantage of Retirement." *The Reading Teacher* 49 (1996): 510–516.

Veatch, J., F. Sawicki, G. Elliott, E. Flake, and J. Blakey. *Key Words to Reading: The Language Experience Approach Begins*. Columbus, OH: Merrill, 1979.

Vygotsky, L. S. *Mind in Society*. Cambridge, MA: Harvard University Press, 1978.

Assessing Factors Related to Reading Problems

In this chapter, we discuss intellectual, physical, language, and learning factors that can be secondary or contributing causes of reading problems. Although these factors are often considered peripheral to reading, they can affect the entire enterprise of learning.

Most classroom teachers are more or less accustomed to assessing reading within their classrooms. Assessing intelligence, vision and hearing, emotional and personality development, and special learning problems, however, is usually done outside the regular classroom; the school nurse might provide vision and hearing screening, the school psychologist might administer intelligence tests, the counselor might do personality and interest assessments, the speech-language pathologist might administer speech and language tests, and so forth.

Teachers might or might not be familiar with the assessment devices used and the results they yield. These results are often used to determine whether students qualify for special programs and to guide in providing interventions for students who are experiencing difficulty. In the sections that follow, we will discuss legislation related to students with special educational needs, the referral process, generic ways in which special learning problems are assessed, and how these issues are related to reading.

PHILOSOPHICAL AND LEGAL ISSUES RELATED TO SPECIAL-NEEDS STUDENTS

In the past, children with special intellectual, physical, or emotional needs were largely excluded from the regular curriculum. Changes in educational policy for special-needs students are the result of growing public awareness and legislative action (Patton et al., 1991). Public schools are required by law to provide "appropriate educational experiences" for all students, including those with emotional, physical, intellectual, and/or cognitive processing problems. The key issue is what is "appropriate" in each case.

Legislation Affecting Special-Needs Students

Legislative action to ensure that students with handicapping conditions receive appropriate educational experiences began with Public Law 94-142, the Individuals with Disabilities Education Act (IDEA), enacted in 1975. It was amended in important ways in 1986 and 1990 and was reauthorized by Congress in 1997.

PL 94-142 mandated a number of far-reaching changes in the education of students with special needs. Following is a list of the law's major provisions and amendments, the immediate implications of each provision for the classroom teacher, and a summary of the basic rights of handicapped students under the law.

Provision: Free public education will be provided for all handicapped persons between the ages of 3 and 21 years of age.

Implications: Schools must serve the needs of students who are both older and younger than those served in the past. The traditional concept of "school-age children" between ages 5 and 18 has been drastically modified. Since the law provides for grants that create financial incentives for schools to identify handicapped preschoolers and provide special services for them, kindergarten and primary-grade teachers are involved in early identification programs.

At the other end of the age scale, teachers in all grades are affected by the inclusion of handicapped older students into regular classes. This is particularly important in high schools, where pupils up to the age of 21 may be included in regular classes. Teachers must be aware of the special needs and interests of handicapped older students and young adults who are placed in classes with younger pupils.

In 1986, PL 94-142 was amended by PL 99-457, which extended the requirements of the original law to children ages 3 to 5 even in states that do not provide free public education to children under age 5. In addition, Part H of PL 99-457 established a federal grant program to provide funds to states to develop and implement statewide, comprehensive, coordinated, and multidisciplinary interagency programs of early identification and intervention for handicapped infants and preschoolers from birth to age 2. This is not a requirement, but the program provides incentives to states to develop such programs.

Public Law 101-476 amended PL 94-142 in 1990. It added the requirement for transitional services for students 16 years of age and older with disabilities. These services promote the transition from school to the workplace. Services include postsecondary education, vocational training, rehabilitation services, and referrals for social services.

Provision: Handicapped students will be placed in the least restrictive environment whenever and wherever possible. This often means mainstreaming handicapped children into the regular classroom and curriculum.

Implications: The inclusion of handicapped students in regular classrooms for part or all of the school day affects nearly every teacher. All teachers must clearly understand how students' handicapping conditions affect their learning, how materials and activities must be adapted appropriately, how students' performance is to be evaluated, and how to deal positively with these students' social and interpersonal problems. In addition, regular classroom teachers have to be routinely involved in the assessment of these students' special needs.

Provision: Each handicapped student will be provided with an individualized educational program, called an IEP, which spells out present abilities, short- and long-term goals, and the means by which goals will be achieved. Each student's IEP will be developed jointly by teachers, parents, and the student where possible.

Implications: All teachers who work with disabled students have direct responsibility for the planning, implementation, and evaluation of instructional programs. Teachers must expand their understanding of handicapping conditions, management techniques, teaching strategies, and materials to develop and use IEPs. In developing and updating IEPs, teachers have to join forces with the parents of handicapped students for greater parental involvement and teacher accountability. In many cases, the students can be included in the development of their IEPs, to the extent that they are able to participate.

Provision: *All tests and evaluative instruments used will be prepared and administered in order to eliminate racial and cultural discrimination.*

Implications: Tests and assessment devices have to be closely scrutinized to eliminate discriminatory aspects. Results of a single test or measure cannot be used to classify students. In addition, tests must be modified when necessary so that students with disabilities can respond to them in ways that are best for them—for example, in Braille or in sign language. Tests must be administered in the student's native language or in sign language or cued speech for hearing-impaired students. These modifications entail widespread changes both in test construction and in the ways tests are administered and interpreted.

This provision has also been interpreted to mean that schools must provide a multidisciplinary team as an integral part of the identification process.

The provisions of the Individuals with Disabilities Education Act also establish certain basic rights for handicapped students:

1. *the right to due process*, which protects the individual from erroneous classification, capricious labeling, and denial of equal education;
2. *the right of protection against discriminatory testing* in diagnosis, which ensures against possible bias in intelligence tests (and other tests) used with ethnic and minority children;
3. *the right to placement in the least restrictive educational environment*, which protects the individual from possible detrimental effects of segregated education for the handicapped;
4. *the right to have individual program plans*, which ensure accountability by those who are responsible for the education of the handicapped.

The law also stipulates that a child receiving special education services must be given a review at least once every three years. The purpose of this review is to determine whether the child is still eligible for special services. The review must include a complete reassessment of learning aptitude, speech and hearing, school achievement, adaptive behavior, and the like.

The Individuals with Disabilities Education Act mandates that students with special educational needs be given opportunities to achieve their full potential. However, the ways in which states and local school districts interpret the law and its provisions sometimes raise issues that must be decided by the courts. For example, as we will see in the section on identifying special needs, the law provides for a variety of experts to "reason together" to determine a student's handicapping condition(s) and remediation. But parents, who are considered partners with educators in the schooling of their children, may interpret their child's needs differently. In most cases, parents and educators who are in disagreement reach compromises, sometimes with the assistance of an appeal process; sometimes, however, legal action is necessary. Parents have, in some cases, won the right to require that school divisions pay for private schooling if the parents can convince the court that an "adequate" education is not possible within the local schools.

Inclusion and the Regular Education Initiative

The concept of *inclusion* (sometimes referred to as *mainstreaming*), or integrating handicapped students into regular education classes, has long been a source of controversy. PL 94-142 does not require all children with disabilities to be placed in regular classrooms with support services. Nor does it suggest that regular-education teachers should be expected to teach all handicapped students without guidance and assistance from special educators. It does, however, call for the education of students with special needs to be conducted in the *least restrictive environment* in which the students have probable chances for success (Lewis and Doorlag, 1991).

Better ways of meeting the needs of exceptional learners are being explored today, including helping regular-education teachers to use teaching practices that have been found to be effective with exceptional children, using special educators as teacher consultants rather than direct providers of instruction, establishing teams that ensure that only students who truly need special services are so identified, structuring classrooms to promote cooperative learning between students of all ability levels, and using materials and methods to help create more positive student attitudes toward handicapped and exceptional peers.

These procedures have all been advocated by those supporting the *regular education initiative* (REI), the goal of which is to make regular educators more responsible for the education of handicapped children. Although not without controversy, REI has gained support across the nation in recent years.

To implement REI, extensive inservice and modified preservice training for regular educators is needed. Some states now require preservice special education teachers to be certified both in special education and in regular education. Greater communication, trust, and cooperation between special and regular educators have been called for as critical to implementing REI and restructuring an educational system that better serves the needs of all students in regular, special, remedial, and compensatory programs (Patton et al., 1991).

Another approach that has gained popularity in recent years is to provide special services to identified students on a "push-in" basis, rather than as a "pull-out" program. In a pull-out, identified students leave their regular classroom for group and/or individual instruction by a special-education teacher. This has the advantage of allowing these students privacy and reducing distractions during their instruction, but it has the disadvantages of isolating special students, disrupting their daily schedule, and inhibiting regular- and special-education teachers' efforts to work together.

When services are provided on a push-in basis, the special educator works with identified students within the regular classroom. Special-needs students do not miss regular classroom events while they receive the extra support and attention they need. In addition, special educators and classroom teachers can work closely together, sharing their areas of expertise and supporting each other's efforts. However, push-in programs require teachers who might have very different skills and expectations to work closely together in the same workspace. Administrative support and encouragement are usually needed to make this cooperative effort successful.

Since regular-education teachers will continue to have greater responsibility for teaching children who are identified as having special needs, informal diagnostic methods like those described in this book take on even greater importance and usefulness.

Identifying Special-Needs Students

Individual school divisions differ in minor ways in the procedures they follow regarding referral and classification, but a sequence of events such as this is typical:

- A request is made to have a student considered for screening or diagnostic testing. Either teachers or parents can make such a request. Since each school must have a standing committee to handle identification procedures, this committee receives such requests.
- Parental permission for testing is sought by the principal, the special-education supervisor, or the head of the screening committee. If parents or legal guardians refuse to give permission, no further action can be taken. The student's progress can be monitored and further requests can be made, but without parental permission, no examination can take place.
- After permission is granted, the committee usually meets to discuss the child's progress and difficulties, determine what measures have already been taken to help the child, and decide what further assessment might be called for. If further assessment is recommended, arrangements are made for these assessments to be done. The committee must be multidisciplinary and typically includes a special-education representative, a school psychologist, the school principal or principal's designee, one or more classroom teachers, and one or more parents. Other committee members might be a reading specialist, a speech-language pathologist, a visiting teacher or home-school liaison, or other specialists.
- After assessments are completed, the team reconvenes to discuss the results and make recommendations. The student's parent(s) or guardian(s) and classroom teacher are included in this meeting. Parents might bring their own advocate to help them to understand the results and recommendations if they so choose. Teachers who work with the student are invited to share any informal assessment data they have, as well as any other information or observations about the child's performance, behavior, and so forth that might assist the committee.
- After all available information has been collected, the committee makes a joint recommendation about the student's eligibility for special services,

what types of services can be offered, and the most appropriate placement for the student. Parental consent is again needed, this time for services to be provided and placement to be made. If parents do not give their permission, an impartial mediator reviews the case and makes a determination that is binding on all parties.

■ After eligibility has been determined and parental permission has been received, an IEP must be developed for each student. Included are the student's present achievement or performance levels, short-term and long-term goals, beginning and estimated ending dates for special services, evaluation procedures and criteria that will be used to determine whether goals have been met, detailed descriptions of services to be provided, accomodations that the student will be permitted (such as being allowed to take tests orally or have an interpreter present), and estimates of the student's involvement in regular education classes. Once again, parental agreement is required before an IEP can be implemented. If agreement cannot be reached with parents on aspects of the IEP, a hearing is held to ensure the family's right to due process. No special services can be provided until parental permission is given in writing.

■ Finally, the student is placed in the least restrictive educational environment, and IEP implementation begins. Every educator or agency that is involved with the student's educational plan is required to make "good faith efforts" to help the student to achieve the goals set forth in the IEP. Parents can request program review and revision if they believe that such good faith efforts have not been made, but if in spite of such efforts, the student does not achieve the goals of the IEP, no individual is to be held accountable. IEPs are reviewed and revised yearly to ensure that goals and procedures are appropriate. In addition, all special-education students must be reassessed triennially to determine what changes have taken place and whether services are still required.

Assessment of Special Educational Needs

The Individuals with Disabilities Education Act requires that assessment for special services must include educational, psychological, medical, and sociological components. This ensures that the assessment a student receives is as comprehensive as possible. The use of a combination of standardized and informal assessments is common and in some states is required.

As you read in Chapter 5, formal assessment devices are usually standardized, normative tests. Administration, scoring, and interpretation procedures are clearly set forth. Formal tests yield many different types of scores and are given for many different purposes, but most are given to provide information about a student's standing in relation to other students.

As you may remember from Chapters 2 and 3, informal procedures are usually less structured than, or are structured differently from, standardized tests. Devices such as informal reading inventories and spelling inventories, and classwork such as math worksheets fit this category. There is an element of subjectivity in their scoring, if they are scored, and in their interpretation. However, while they lack the kind of normative scores that standardized tests yield, informal assessments yield results that are directly related to instruction. They often show what a student can and cannot do more directly and precisely than formal tests. Thus, both kinds of assessment provide useful information about students' abilities and achievement.

Screening assessments are mandated and reviewed by the school's identification or child study team, of which the regular classroom teacher and/or reading teacher are often a part. A team approach to assessment acts as a safeguard against potential assessment biases. As you might recall, the Individuals with Disabilities Education Act contains two provisions to safeguard against test abuses:

- Testing must be conducted in the language of the student, measures used must be nondiscriminatory and validated for the purpose for which they are used, and no single test score may be used as the sole basis for determining special education placement.
- In determining mental or cognitive disability , concurrent deficits in both intelligence test performance and adaptive behavior must be detected.

Assessment instruments have different purposes and assess different aspects of performance and potential. They fall into these general categories:

1. ***Learning Aptitude Tests***. Learning aptitude refers to the student's capacity for altering behavior when presented with new information or experiences. These often include intelligence tests, which measure scholastic aptitude, not general aptitude or intelligence, and also indirectly assess achievement in areas such as vocabulary and math computation. Intelligence tests are the primary means used to assess learning aptitude. Learning aptitude is also sometimes referred to as cognitive ability, learning potential, cognitive factors, and similar terms. Some school achievement batteries contain sections that assess learning aptitude, comparing it to present achievement levels.

2. ***Achievement Tests.*** These are the primary means used to assess students' present levels of scholastic performance. These tests assess what has been learned, not what the child is capable of learning. Achievement test batteries include subtests dealing with reading, spelling, mathematics, written language, and the like. Tests that assess achievement in single areas only, such as separate reading, spelling, mathematics, and writing achievement tests, may be used instead of a battery.

3. ***Adaptive Behavior Tests.*** Adaptive behavior refers to how effectively an individual meets standards of personal independence and social responsibility that are normally expected of her or his age and cultural group. These measures are used when mental or cognitive disability is suspected.

4. ***Tests of Specific Learning Abilities.*** These test various single learning processes such as auditory discrimination, short-term memory, visual perception, motor abilities, and the like. Some tests assess only one process; others are batteries

with subtests assessing different processes. Most intelligence tests also include measures of many of these abilities, such as short-term memory, visual perception, and visual-motor coordination.

5. ***Classroom Behavior and Adjustment Tests.*** These include evaluation scales and rating scales for behavior, self-concept scales, and interest inventories. These are most often used in the identification of emotionally disturbed students or those with behavior disorders, either as the primary or a secondary problem.

INTELLECTUAL FACTORS

When diagnosing a reading problem, one of the most frequently used instruments is an intelligence test. Why?

Broad trends in the research literature show what seem to be contradictory findings:

1. that good readers tend to perform better on IQ tests than poor readers and

2. that reading problems are not limited to lower-IQ students but are found across the whole range of intellectual abilities.

There has long been some general agreement that intelligence and reading achievement are fairly well correlated, particularly in the upper grades. What this factor means is that better performance on reading tests and intelligence tests tends to occur together; students generally do well on both or poorly on both. It does *not* imply causation; we cannot infer from positive correlations that one factor causes the other, only that they coincide.

It might be that above-average intelligence encourages above-average reading achievement. It might be equally true that good reading helps students to do better on intelligence tests. Or it might be that *both* reading tests and IQ tests call upon the same kinds of abilities and knowledge. But poor readers can come from all ability levels.

What *do* IQ tests tell us? That depends very much on which test is used. Not all measure the same skills, and to evaluate results, we have to know something about their characteristics.

Tests of Intelligence and Learning Aptitude

Intelligence tests are essentially measures of verbal abilities and skills in dealing with abstract symbols. However, they are not intended to measure innate intelligence or potential, but rather to sample behavior already learned in an attempt to predict future learning. The premise of these measures is that present performance is a predictor of future performance (McLaughlin and Lewis, 1990). They are appropriately viewed as predictors of academic success; misinterpretation of their purpose and results leads to misunderstanding and inaccurate judgments about children. The issue of intelligence tests and cultural bias is discussed in a subsequent section.

Group Intelligence Tests

Some tests that yield an IQ or some kind of "ability quotient" are group tests. Group tests usually require students to read and mark answers; they consequently penalize poor readers, who generally score poorly on such measures. Thus, they tend to underestimate poor readers' potential. Group intelligence tests or tests of learning aptitude are useful only as general screening devices, and results generalized only to large numbers of students, not individuals.

Individual Intelligence Tests

An individually administered test that does not require a student to read or write will give a better estimate of real academic potential than a group test.

The **Wechsler Intelligence Scale for Children-III (WISC-III)** (1991) is the individual test that is most often used to assess intellectual performance of children between the ages of 6 ½ and 16. It is one of several related tests that span all age levels. **The Wechsler Preschool and Primary Scale of Intelligence-Revised (WPPSI-R)** (1989) is appropriate for children between 4 years and 6 ½ years of age. The **Wechsler Adult Intelligence Scale-Revised (WAIS-R)** (1981) is used for individuals between 16 and 74 years of age. These tests may be administered only by someone who is specially trained and certified to do so. Modified instructions for administering the WISC-III to deaf children are available (Sattler, 1992).

The WISC-III assesses intellectual functioning by sampling performance on many different types of activities. The test attempts to assess verbal and nonverbal aspects of intelligence separately with thirteen subtests: ten required and three optional or supplemental. The thirteen subtests are organized into two scales, those involving language operations directly in one, the Verbal Scale, and those involving the nonverbal or indirectly verbal operations in the other, the Performance Scale. Each scale yields a separate scale IQ, which can be compared to determine whether both aspects of a child's intelligence seem to be equally well developed, and the scale IQs can be converted into a Full Scale IQ.

Raw scores from each subtest are converted to *scaled scores*, standard scores ranging from 1 to 19 with a mean of 10 and a standard deviation of 3. Transforming raw scores into standard units makes it possible to compare results of different subtests.

The Full Scale IQ represents a subject's overall intellectual functioning as measured by performance on the 10 subtests. The Verbal, Performance, and Full Scale IQs all have a mean of 100 and a standard deviation of 15. The test uses the following classification scheme for IQ scores:

130 and above	Very superior
120–129	Superior
110–119	High average
90–109	Average
80–89	Low average
70–79	Borderline
69 and below	Mentally deficient

It is important to avoid overinterpreting IQ scores by keeping in mind that they represent a sample of behavior taken at one point in time and by considering IQ scores only in relation to the *range* in which they occur, rather than as single, fixed scores. The average standard error of measurement for the Full Scale IQ score is 3.2 IQ points. A Full Scale IQ could therefore be expected to vary by plus or minus three or four points because of probable random effects. It is more accurate to speak of a student's IQ score as "within the high average range," for example, than to say that the student "has an IQ of 117."

Clinicians often look for differences between Verbal and Performance IQs and patterns of scores on individual subtests to recommend further psychological and academic testing (Sattler, 1992).

The **Kaufman Assessment Battery for Children (K-ABC)** (1983) is another widely used individual measure, appropriate for children between 2 ½ and 12 ½ years of age. The K-ABC battery contains mental processing and achievement subtests. A Mental Processing Composite, an index of intellectual functioning, is derived from the mental processing subtests. Two other global scores are derived from groups of subtests: Sequential Processing and Simultaneous Processing. Global scores have a mean of 100 and a standard deviation of 15.

A nonverbal scale is available that allows the examiner to conduct several of the subtests in mime with only motor response required. The scale is useful with hearing impaired, emotionally disturbed, speech or language impaired, and non-English-speaking students.

The manual gives remedial suggestions for improving students' sequential and simultaneous processing abilities, but these have not been well validated. Also, norms are available only for children up to age 12.6.

The **Stanford-Binet Intelligence Scale** (1986) has recently been radically changed from its old format. Earlier versions of the Stanford-Binet were developed on the premise that as a child grows older, he or she develops knowledge and skills in a fairly steady, sequential way, resulting in a measurable "mental age." For example, if a 7-year-old could correctly respond to items that are typically correctly answered by 9-year-olds, the student's mental age would be 9 years and some months. IQ scores were converted from mental ages.

However, the concept of mental age has been convincingly attacked over the years; the development of the Wechsler Scales was a successful attempt to measure intelligence on the basis of a scale other than age. The 1986 version of the Stanford-Binet is not an age scale. Items are arranged in ascending order of difficulty into fifteen subsets, which attempt to assess abilities other than strictly verbal ones.

Scaled subtest scores can be combined into several global scores in Verbal Reasoning, Abstract-Visual Reasoning, Quantitative Reasoning, and Short-Term Memory, with an overall score similar to a global IQ score. These changes make the new Stanford-Binet more like the Wechsler Scales.

The **Kaufman Brief Intelligence Test (K-BIT)** (1990) is a brief assessment of verbal and nonverbal intelligence of children and adults from the ages of 4 to 90. It was developed to be used as a screening device, not as a substitute for more comprehensive individual IQ tests.

The K-BIT has two subtests: Vocabulary and Matrices. Designed to measure verbal and school-related skills, the Vocabulary subtest assesses a person's word knowledge and verbal concept formation. The Matrices subtests measure the ability to solve problems and other nonverbal skills.

The K-BIT yields age-based standard scores having the same mean and standard deviation as the Wechsler and Kaufman scales. Scores are generated for each subtest and for an overall K-BIT IQ Composite or IQ standard score (Kaufman & Kaufman, 1990).

These individual intelligence tests assess both verbal and nonverbal intellectual abilities. Academic skills such as reading and writing are deemphasized. Although these tests yield results that can be used to predict academic success, no single test, used exclusively, can predict or evaluate a child's academic achievement. Many factors can influence test results. One of these factors is the role of experience.

The Role of Experience

When we consider the concept of intelligence in terms of a student's personality, background, interests, and other related aspects as well as in terms of subtest behaviors and IQ points, we must take into account the role experience plays in intellectual development. It is difficult to overestimate the importance of experience, both real and vicarious, in shaping intelligence and IQ test performance.

What kind of experience are we talking about? Essentially, we learn about ourselves and our world in two ways: *directly*, by having real, concrete experience with objects and events, and *vicariously*, by observing and remembering the experiences of others.

Real experiences in the formative years contribute to what most of us think of as an enriched environment. Enrichment means having plentiful opportunities to manipulate things; experiment with causes, effects, and consequences; talk and be talked to; and be encouraged to extend cognitive horizons and try new things.

These characteristics of an intellectually enriching environment know no economic, ethnic, social, or linguistic boundaries. They flourish where adults respect and nurture children's attempts to become competent and where those adults give conscious thought to providing opportunities for children to become independent and capable.

Direct, concrete *experience with things and events* is one critical aspect; *experience with language* is another. Verbal intelligence flourishes in the home, and later the school, where children are talked to by adults, where adults really listen to their responses and encourage conversation, where events and behaviors are explained and verbal reasoning is demonstrated, and where adults model language use by expanding and elaborating on what children say.

In environments in which children are rarely addressed except in commands, in which their spontaneous utterances are rarely listened to or responded to, where their requests for explanations are routinely answered by "Because I said so, that's why!" and explanations are rarely given, verbal intelligence is stunted. These children enter the world of language poorly adapted to participate in it fully. Their learning opportunities are restricted by language, rather than expanded by it. Whatever their socioeconomic status, they are disadvantaged in school readiness.

The other important aspect of experience is *vicarious experience*. Fortunately for all of us, we can learn from observing others as well as by experiencing things ourselves. Learning from the experiences of others saves us from having to experience everything personally, and we can derive nearly as much from those experiences as from our own.

Perhaps the greatest benefit of literacy is that through reading, we can vicariously experience events, emotions, and ideas that are completely outside our own environment. We can travel to places we will never go to, including places that exist only in the mind; visit the past and the future with as much ease as the present; meet the most famous people of history and share their innermost thoughts; and experience joy, rage, grief, amazement, and every other human emotion by reading. All this makes good reading a lifelong joy and avocation.

Reading and books, however, are more than a source of pleasure. They remain, in spite of the inroads of TV, videos, and cyberspace, the largest source of information for many people. Schools still use books and other forms of print as the major vehicles for transmitting information.

This learning, whether vicarious or direct, occurs within a cultural context. The knowledge that is passed from one generation to another differs among different cultures. The issue of cultural bias in assessment is of major concern in assessing factors associated with reading.

Issues of Bias in Assessment

Since the 1970s, the disproportionate number of minority and/or economically disadvantaged children who are placed in special-education classes has led to controversy regarding the use of traditional intelligence and learning aptitude tests with these children. Attempts to address this inequity by creating alternative assessment devices have lacked sufficient psychometric rigor (Sattler, 1992) or lack the research and developmental efforts to be useful in school settings (Laughon, 1990).

Helms (1992) has presented arguments for examining racial and ethnic differences in performance of intellectual abilities from a cultural perspective. She suggests that when selecting and interpreting assessment instruments, the examiner consider cultural differences in a subject's knowledge and tradition.

PHYSICAL FACTORS

Many physical conditions and processes can be related to reading problems. The factors that are most commonly considered are visual and auditory. Each of these areas has been extensively studied in relation to reading difficulties, but the research data and the various conditions and processes themselves are complex and sometimes confusing. In this section, we will consider vision and hearing.

Vision and Visual Problems

Reading is a visual act for sighted people, because we cannot read in the dark. It is, of course, much more than just a visual act because more goes on behind the reader's eyes than in front of them, but some visual competence is needed to activate the cognitive processes involved in reading. To make sense of print, the reader must be able to gain information from print through vision. For this reason, poor readers are often subjected to vision screening in diagnosis.

Teachers are often the first line of defense against vision problems. They are usually in an ideal position to spot potential problems and refer children for appropriate screening because they, more than parents, observe children in close contact with reading and writing materials. Also, children with vision problems often don't realize that others see differently, and they don't call adults' attention to their difficulty. Therefore, it is important for teachers to understand vision problems and their symptoms. Figure 11.1 summarizes the nature and symptoms of some common visual difficulties.

Astigmatism, hyperopia, and myopia are by far the most common problems. *Astigmatism* (blurring of part of the image) can occur in conjunction with either

FIGURE 11.1   Vision Problems

Technical Name	Common Name	Condition	Symptoms
Myopia	Nearsightedness	Clear vision at near point; blurring of distant images	Squinting at the board; holding print close to face; inattention to board work
Hyperopia	Farsightedness	Clear vision at far point; blurring of close objects	Holding print well away from face; disinterest in close work; eye fatigue during reading
Astigmatism		Distortion and/or blurring of part (or all) of visual field, far and near	Eye fatigue; headache; squinting; tilting or turning head; nausea during reading
Amblyopia	Lazy eye	Suppression of vision in one eye; dimming of vision without structural cause	Tilting or turning head to read; eye fatigue on one side; headache
Strabismus	Crossed eyes	Difficulty converging and focusing both eyes on the same object	Squinting; closing or covering one eye to focus; eyes misaligned
Phoria or fusion problems; binocular coordination		Imbalance of ocular muscles; difficulty converging and focusing both eyes equally	Squinting; closing or covering one eye
Aniseikonia		Differences in size or shape of image in each eye	Blurring; squinting; difficulty focusing or fusing image; closing one eye

nearsightedness or farsightedness, but both conditions are corrected simultaneously with lenses. *Hyperopia* (farsightedness), blurring of the image at the near point, makes reading and writing uncomfortable and tiring and has long been associated with reading problems (Grisham and Simons, 1986). After more and more close work in the first few years of school, this "developmental farsightedness" disappears for most children, and many become mildly myopic as they learn to read.

Myopia (nearsightedness), better acuity (keenness) of vision up close than at a distance, does not interfere with reading. There is some evidence that myopia may be largely developmental and environmentally produced by the demands of close work with print during the school years (Javal, 1990). Although nearsightedness does not contribute directly to reading problems, it can give children difficulty in doing board work and can be a cause of inattention during such activities.

These vision problems can be so minor that they have few if any symptoms, and even the reader might be unaware of any problem, or they can be so severe that normal classroom activities are extremely difficult. Usually, the teacher is in a position to detect fairly minor problems that, if treated promptly, are easy to correct. All of the aforementioned vision problems are correctable, most with glasses or contact lenses, some with a combination of corrective lenses and muscle exercises.

Although vision problems might be very different, they often have identical symptoms. Teachers can do little more than guess about the precise nature of the problem in many cases, but they should be alert to the continuing presence of these symptoms, which are listed in Figure 11.2.

These symptoms are sometimes demonstrated by poor readers whose vision is unimpaired. When any of these signs are displayed frequently, are not com-

FIGURE 11.2 Symptoms of Possible Vision Problems

Appearance	Chronic redness or swelling of eyes or eyelids
	Matter encrusted in or around eyes
	Sores near or on eyelids
	Excessive watering or tearing of eyes
	Eyes appear misaligned
Complaints	Headache in or near eyes
	Burning, itching, or watering eyes
	Nausea or dizziness during visual tasks
	Blurring or "jumping" of print during reading or other visual tasks
Behavior	Excessive blinking during reading or visual tasks
	Squinting, closing or covering one eye
	Tilting or turning head to read or write
	Straining forward to see board
	Holding book or head abnormally far or near

mon to the rest of the class, and are evidenced even when performing easy tasks, they signal a need for a parent conference and referral to an eye specialist. Referrals should be made through the principal, school nurse, supervisor, or other designated personnel.

Hearing and Auditory Problems

The relationship between auditory problems and reading difficulties has long been established. Hearing and language are as intimately related as language and reading. As teachers observe the oral and written language of their students, they can become aware of possible hearing problems.

When children learn to read, they use their whole experience with oral language. We know that oral language development and learning to read are closely related and that the ability to process and understand *written* language depends in large part on being able to process and understand *oral* language. Hearing problems can interfere with, delay, or even prevent the development of oral language fluency, and it is in this respect that hearing problems can affect reading.

Another factor is the heavy reliance on oral activities and phonics instruction. Across the entire spectrum of approaches, some features of every beginning reading program are standard: learning letter names and sounds, use of simple phonic analysis strategies to decode words, and frequent oral reading. These activities put a premium on clarity of hearing, and the youngster with auditory problems is at a distinct disadvantage.

Thus, hearing problems that occur any time in the first eight to ten years of life can affect a child's reading by interfering with language development in the preschool years or with the largely oral reading instruction of the primary grades.

Testing of auditory *acuity* (keenness) involves assessment of the ability to hear speech sounds, music, and noises. In reading, it is the speech sounds that are critical.

Speech sounds are measured in terms of pitch and volume. *Pitch* refers to the frequency of a sound; *speech* sounds are high-tone or low-tone depending on their pitch. Pitch is measured in *hertz,* or cycles per second. High-frequency, or high-tone, sounds have a higher number of cycles per second than low tones. Speech sounds of the normal human voice range from 128 to 4,000 cycles per second; consonant sounds are higher in pitch than vowel sounds.

Volume, or loudness, is measured in units called *decibels.* Normal conversation is usually between 20 and 60 decibels.

Hearing losses can affect the perception of pitch or volume or both. If the child can hear some sound frequencies but not others, this can be devastating in learning to read because it means that the child can hear some speech sounds accurately but not others. Hearing loss involving the high-frequency sounds is more common than loss of low-frequency sounds. Children with high-frequency hearing loss can accurately hear vowel sounds and maybe some consonant sounds, but not all of them.

Those with high-tone losses may hear spoken words in a garbled, indistinct fashion, depending on how many consonant sounds are affected. If only vowels can be heard, words are almost totally meaningless because consonant sounds are what make spoken words intelligible. (Read a line of print aloud to someone, pronouncing only the vowel sounds. Repeat the line pronouncing only the consonant sounds. Which version could the listener more easily understand?)

Hearing losses are not always as severe as the previous example. Often, only a few consonant and blend sounds are affected, but phonics instruction is made very difficult by this loss, and the student may be very poor at word analysis and word recognition. Also, the words that are most often taught in beginning reading frequently vary only in their consonant sounds, as in the word families and rhyming word patterns (*cat-hat-pat-mat-sat*). Learning these words can be very difficult for a child with high-tone hearing loss.

Some hearing problems are caused by volume impairment at most or all frequencies. These cases can be helped by hearing aids, which amplify sound at all levels. Since volume loss affects the perception of all types of sounds, it is probably the most obvious and the easiest to spot in the classroom. Loss of only certain sounds is more difficult to spot because the student will hear many sounds normally and problems may be blamed on inattention or carelessness.

Symptoms of both types of hearing loss are similar. The main difference is that a child with volume loss will have trouble consistently, whereas a child with selective frequency losses will hear many sounds normally. Common symptoms of hearing losses are shown in Figure 11.3. Screening should be conducted if a student exhibits one or more of these symptoms.

At first glance, some of these signs are similar to those of children with vision problems. Behaviors such as inattention, strained posture, scowling, or squinting can be common to children with hearing or vision problems or to children who have no physical problems but are simply frustrated in reading.

Another very important factor in the diagnosis of hearing problems is the *duration* of the problem. While volume losses are usually of a more or less chronic nature, many selective frequency losses are temporary. It is very common for children to experience temporary loss of some sounds during and after a heavy cold or upper respiratory infection. These hearing losses can last from a few days to a few months, and while they exist, they can interfere with normal classroom activities.

FIGURE 11.3 Symptoms of Possible Hearing Problems

Complaints	Ringing, buzzing or pain in ears
	Ears feel blocked or "stuffy"
Behavior	Frequent requests to have statements repeated
	Confusion of simple oral directions
	Turning or tilting head toward source of sounds
	Cupping ear toward source of sound
	Straining forward during listening
	Unusually loud or monotonous voice
	Frequent pulling or rubbing of ears
	Chronic inattention during listening activities

Children with colds or other upper respiratory infections and respiratory allergies are subject to middle-ear impairment called *conductive hearing losses.* Two types of conductive problems are particularly common in school-age children. One condition is *otitis media,* a collection of fluid in the middle ear. Fluid in the middle ear distends the eardrum outward, inhibiting its ability to vibrate freely and thus reducing the signal transmitted inward.

A second common conductive loss occurs when air pressure on either side of the eardrum is unequal. From the middle ear, a tunnel, the *eustachian tube,* runs to the back of the throat at the level of the nose. This tube's function is to equalize pressure on both sides of the eardrum. When heavy upper respiratory congestion is present, the eustachian tube can collapse or become blocked. As a result, the eardrum cannot properly conduct sound. Implantation of plastic tubes in the eustachian tube now corrects the problem.

Children who do not receive the necessary medical treatment for chronic infections may suffer these temporary hearing losses. Those with chronic colds and those returning to school after a particularly severe upper respiratory infection should have auditory screening at regular intervals, with particular attention paid to perception of the high-tone sounds.

Although middle-ear disorders are more common in children, inner-ear disorders called *sensorineural losses* can also cause hearing impairment. Within the inner ear, the *cochlea,* a bony structure that looks like a coiled shell, contains the sensory organs of hearing and the components of the body's balance system.

Here the sound waves that have been transmitted by vibration to the inner ear are transformed into mechanical, electrical, and chemical signals and transmitted to the brain (Berg, 1986). The cochlea and its delicate transmission functions can be damaged by excessive noise, certain drugs, and exposure to infections such as mumps and rubella. Although early immunization programs have minimized the number of cases of these once-common childhood illnesses, alarming numbers of preschoolers are still not properly immunized before school entry.

The most reliable auditory screening method examines volume in decibels and different frequencies in cycles per second. An instrument called a *pure tone audiometer* is used to produce pure tones generally ranging from 125 to 8,000 cycles per second in pitch and from about 10 to 110 decibels in volume.

An audiometer can be used for screening groups of students, but the most accurate screening is done individually. The subject is seated so that the audiometer controls are not visible. Headphones are worn so that each ear can be tested separately, and a buzzer or other signaling device is used as a means of responding to the test. The examiner, an audiologist, uses the audiometer to produce each tone at a full range of volume from soft to loud, and the subject signals when the tone is first audible and also indicates its duration. The examiner can occasionally check to see that the subject is not just signaling randomly by using an interrupter switch to cut off the signal momentarily.

If the student fails the initial part of the screening, indicating inadequate perception of any of the pure tones, a *pure tone threshold test* is given. In this procedure, sounds are presented at several different frequencies, and the intensity of the sound is varied to determine the exact decibel level at which the student can detect the sound, called the *threshold level.* Another auditory screening measure is *speech audiometry.* The audiometer is used to determine threshold levels for speech sounds. Speech audiometry is useful in detecting high-frequency hearing losses, which cause affected students to have difficulty perceiving some high-frequency consonant sounds in speech.

A topic that is related to auditory acuity is *auditory discrimination,* the ability to distinguish between highly similar sounds and to detect whether two (or more) sounds are alike or different. Being able to detect subtle differences in speech sounds helps students to master phonics; those with poor auditory discrimination might have persistent trouble with phonic analysis and may also have speech impairments.

Auditory discrimination can be assessed formally or informally. The student is required to distinguish between pairs of words or syllables that differ minimally (*rat-rap, ome-ote*). Teachers frequently make up and give such exercises themselves. Formal auditory discrimination tests are also common, and some standardized readiness tests include such a subtest.

In beginning reading, it is common to combine phonics instruction with auditory discrimination practice. Beginning readers or prereaders who at first seem to have difficulty with auditory discrimination often need only to learn what to listen for and how to respond. In other words, they have no auditory disability but have to learn what the task is.

Auditory discrimination skill seems to improve sharply as children progress through the primary grades, a finding that implies that it develops at least partly in response to instruction and experience with the task. It might well be a learned skill as much as an innate perceptual ability.

LANGUAGE DIFFICULTIES AND DISORDERS

Print is a form of language, and to be a reader, one must be a language user. Serious language disorders can inhibit children's development as readers and writers. Those that occur in the early years, when language is being acquired, have the most serious effects on later literacy.

Language Acquisition and Difficulties in Infancy and Early Childhood

As we discussed in Chapter 6, children begin to use language, first to understand speech and then to produce it, in the first two years of life. Most children show that they can understand simple speech before they can produce any intelligible words and begin using one-, two-, and three-word utterances before the age of 3. First words are most often names of things (*ball, doggy, mama*) and social expressions (*bye-bye, no-no*) (Nelson, 1973). Words referring to animals and sounds, childhood games, and food and drink names occur very frequently among toddlers' first 50 words (Tomasello & Mervis, 1994).

Between $1\frac{1}{2}$ and 2 years of age, babies begin putting words together. Using just two words, they can express an amazing number of ideas, relationships, and needs; comment about objects and events; announce their own or others' actions; and even confess their own transgressions. Two-word, or *telegraphic*, utterances such as "Allgone milk," "Doggie bye-bye," "Baby poopie," "Coat on," and "No nap!" convey a wealth of information with an economy of expression; indeed, as Trawick-Smith (1997) put it, "Babies speak as though they were paying for every word!" (p. 202).

Longer utterances quickly follow, gaining in complexity. Young children seem to intuit and apply simple rules of their native language to determine the order of words in their two-word and longer utterances; rarely do they make word order errors such as "On coat" instead of "Coat on." When they are unsure of word order, toddlers often produce the utterance with a rising, or questioning, inflection, as if to say, "Is this right?" At 24 months, Jenny produced the following sentences, as well as many others:

"Two doggies, Mama."

"Read it Moon Book one time."

"Any trains coming?"

"Can't reach it."

"Jenny boo-boo hurts."

"Gramma boo-boo ona leg. Gramma fall down ona sidewalk."

"Toast coming, Daddy. Get it toast out now."

"Daddy change it diaper."

"Go see Shadow, okay?"

"Becky play Pla-Dough."

"Go Helen see Bill now."

Although children acquire their language at somewhat different times and rates, most children have begun to babble expressively by the end of the first year, speak individual words by about $1\frac{1}{2}$, and combine words by $2\frac{1}{2}$. When these language features are absent, parents and caregivers often suspect a problem that could be interfering with normal language acquisition.

Hearing impairment is one condition that can delay language. In the early months of life, hearing-impaired babies cry and coo just as hearing babies do, and many people never suspect their hearing loss. But by about 6 months, vocalization begins to decrease drastically, and these babies do not progress to the complex babbling and production of speech sounds of hearing babies. Hearing impairment severely disrupts the development of oral speech.

However, it appears that hearing-impaired babies do not stop developing their communicative abilities at this point, as was traditionally believed. Deaf babies often begin to use gestures to communicate at about the same time that hearing babies begin to use single words; at about the time hearing babies begin to produce two-word utterances, deaf babies often begin to combine two gestures to express more elaborate ideas. Deaf babies who are exposed to sign language have been observed to babble, or playfully repeat the same gesture, in sign (Petitto & Marentette, 1991).

Down Syndrome is another clearly identified source of language delay. Like the hearing impaired, Down syndrome babies show significant disruption of language development in the second six months of life. They are slower to begin to babble and produce speech sounds, begin to use words much later than others, and show difficulty with general communication; that is, they pay less attention and respond less when parents and caregivers talk to them, make fewer requests, and initiate conversation less often. Thus, a concurrent problem of Down syndrome is interference with socialization caused by difficulties in language interactions.

General language delay (Ratner, 1989) is a term used to describe significant language delays that have *no apparent cause*. Even when no obvious cognitive, perceptual, or emotional deficits occur, some children aquire language much more slowly than the average child, have limited vocabularies or begin using words much later than others, or appear to have trouble understanding others' spoken language. Their language is usually typical of much younger normal children; for example, a 4-year-old with general language delay might be producing only one- and two-word sentences.

The term *delay* might imply that these children will later catch up to their average peers, but this is not usually the case. Usually, their language development occurs in the same stagewise progression as that of their peers, but at a continually slower rate. Because learning to read requires language facility and complex cognitive activity, language-delayed young children are likely to have academic problems, particularly related to literacy acquisition, and are often identified as learning disabled or having other special educational needs (Ratner, 1989; Tallal, 1987).

Language Development and Difficulties in Preschool and Primary Grades

For most children, language acquisition and development proceed rapidly in the years between the ages of 2 and 6. In the early childhood years, children learn to recognize and use the most common sentence forms, including statements, questions, commands, and exclamations. They acquire a working vocabulary of 5,000 to 8,000 words and can understand several thousand more words that they hear adults use but don't use themselves (Reich, 1986).

In the preschool years, children's language develops along four equally important fronts:

- Their speech becomes clearer, articulation improves, and fluency develops. These areas of speech production are referred to as *phonology*.
- Their vocabularies grow as they acquire many new words and expressions, while they learn to understand even more words than they produce; thus, both *expressive* and *receptive* language grows. The system of word meanings is referred to as *semantics*.
- As they learn more words, their sentences become both longer and more complex. They begin to use imbedded clauses, past and future tenses, plural forms, and the common sentence forms that adults use most often. These aspects of language are referred to as *syntactic*.
- They develop greater skill in using language socially: to get things done, to get their needs met, and to direct the behavior of others in socially acceptable ways. The social uses of language are referred to as *pragmatics*.

Atypical phonology is fairly common in the preschool years, and most problems of pronunciation can be addressed with speech intervention. Many English phonemes, or phoneme clusters such as *skw* or *sl*, are not typically mastered until 7 to 9 years of age. Children who make irregular or inconsistent sound substitutions (such as pronoucing *rabbit* as "babbit" one time, "dabbit" another time), who are highly disfluent after most children have developed fluency, or who generally cannot be understood, are at risk for significant language delays, and need identification and intervention.

Bilingual children often use the phonemes of their first, or more dominant, language when speaking their other language. A child who is bilingual in German and English, for example, might pronounce the English word *will* as "vill" or *valley* as "falley." These are language differences, not difficulties; they are caused by the great challenge of trying to learn and coordinate two different phonological systems.

Atypical semantic development is seen in children who suffer general language delay, as well as in Down syndrome children and others with serious cognitive deficits. These children often understand and produce words at a level similar to that of normal children who are much younger.

Some children show a somewhat different difficulty; they appear to have difficulty retrieving words and may use a variety of compensatory strategies to "fill in the blanks" in their communication. Children with word retrieval difficulties might stutter or pause for long periods as they try to recall the name of an object or a particular describing word, they might use very general terms such as "that," "things," or "stuff" instead of labels for common objects, or they may describe objects by their function rather than by their names, as in "what you put your cereal in" for *bowl*.

Speech-language pathologists often use tests of receptive and expressive vocabulary to determine whether a child has a language retrieval disability or a general linguistic delay. Two commonly used diagnostic tests for children up to the age of seven are the **Receptive One Word Picture Vocabulary Test** (1985) and the **Expressive One Word Picture Vocabulary Test-Revised** (1990). In the former, the child points to the correct picture that goes with a word pronounced by the examiner; the child does not need to speak. In the latter test, the child names pictures of objects that the examiner shows. For subjects from age 7 through adulthood, the **Peabody Picture Vocabulary Test-Revised** (1981) is often used. This test of receptive vocabulary also requires subjects to point to the correct picture, and does not require speech.

Atypical syntactic development is evidenced when children do not construct sentences in age-appropriate ways. In this case, children might not acquire, or acquire much more slowly, the basic sentence forms, questions, negatives, and word parts such -ed, -s, and -ing that average children use by about the age of 5. Children with atypical syntax usually also use shorter utterances and fewer words overall than their peers. Their utterances tend to be grammatically confusing, and others often have trouble understanding what they mean.

Atypical syntax can be caused by intellectual deficits or mental retardation, deafness, and general language delays. A subtest of the **Clinical Evaluation of Language Function** (1980) called "Producing Model Sentences" might be used as a diagnostic tool. This assessment requires children to repeat sentences of increasing grammatical complexity. Special, long-term language intervention is required for these children.

Finally, children with quite profound disabilities often have ***atypical pragmatics development.*** The ability to use language socially, to get along with others, influence others and get one's needs met typically develops in the preschool years, as children learn how to use words, tone of voice, and body language to affect others' behavior. Most children quickly learn how to use language to get other children to give them a toy, share materials with them, or allow them to join in play.

But children with disabilities such as cognitive deficits or mental retardation, emotional disturbance, autism, and deafness might have great difficulty learning how to use language effectively in social ways. Intervention for these children involves teaching them to speak so that the listener understands, take turns talking, show interest in others' talk, use appropriate position and body language, ask and answer questions, and so forth. When these children's social use of language becomes more effective, they are often better able to form relationships, become active members of a group, and experience enhanced feelings of self-worth.

Language Development and Difficulties in Later Childhood

Between the ages of about 5 and 12, children continue to develop as language users, primarily broadening their vocabularies and polishing their language use. They acquire the few sentence forms that are less common, including passive forms such as "A passing grade was earned by only three students," and produce longer, more grammatically complex sentences with imbedded clauses. Their spoken vocabularies grow from around 5,000 to 20,000 or more words. By about age 12, most children's language equals that of most adults.

The greatest part of language development, then, occurs in the early childhood years and around the age of school entry. The middle and later childhood years are periods when language does not change substantially but becomes broader, richer and more precise. The pragmatic system develops fully, and by middle childhood, most children have a variety of types of language that they use in different social settings and for different purposes. The language of school, for example, might be somewhat more formal and more precise than the language of the playground or basketball court, and most children speak differently to a grandparent or a teacher than they do to their best friends. Children learn more effective turn-taking, and in general use language in a variety of ways to influence others.

Language intervention for older children often takes the form of direct teaching of language pragmatics, vocabulary development, and effective use of statements, questions, and other sentence forms. Children with disabilities or language delays can progress in language development when given appropriate special instruction.

The Special Challenges of Bilingualism

Bilingualism is not a language problem, but a condition that can present special challenges to the young child. Bilingual babies progress from single-word *holophrases* to two-word utterances at about the same time as monolingual babies, but may have more difficulty than monolingual babies in putting words together because of differences in word ordering between the two languages.

For example, verbs appear at the ends of sentences in some languages, in the middle in others; adjectives follow nouns in some languages, precede them in others. As an example, an English speaker would say, "the white cat," whereas a Spanish speaker would say, "el gato blanco." Many bilingual babies seem to select the ordering system of one language and use it nearly exclusively; others appear to use the ordering system of the language that is being spoken at the moment, as an adult would.

Bilingual children face special challenges in semantic development, as they must learn two separate vocabularies. Young children often use words from both languages in their speech ("Here, gato," for example). By about age 5, bilingual children usually begin to sort this out and use each language exclusively, depending on the language context.

SPECIAL LEARNING PROBLEMS

Learning disabilities and *dyslexia* are terms that are used for special learning problems. The issues involved in defining the terms, identifying students with these problems, and discovering methods of remediation have aroused considerable controversy for the past several decades. Disagreement over these issues still abounds, but educators appear to be moving toward a greater understanding of them. In this section, we will attempt to clarify some of these issues.

Learning Disabilities

A learning disability is a severe problem in learning that qualifies a child for special education services. In 1977, the federal government adopted the following definition of specific learning disability, based on a 1969 definition proposed by the National Advisory Committee on Handicapped Children. This definition reappeared in the 1990 version of the Individuals with Disabilities Education Act (IDEA), Public Law 101–476, and its 1997 reauthorization:

> A *specific learning disability* is a disorder in one or more of the basic psychological processes involved in understanding or in using language, spoken or written, which may manifest itself in an imperfect ability to listen, think, speak, read, write, spell, or to do mathematical calculations. The term includes such conditions as perceptual handicaps, brain injury, minimal brain dysfunction, dyslexia, and developmental aphasia. The term does not include . . . learning problems which are primarily the result of visual, hearing, or motor handicaps, or mental retardation, or emotional disturbance, or of environmental, cultural, or economic disadvantage. (*Federal Register*, December 29, 1977, p. 65083)

In 1990, the National Joint Committee on Learning Disabilities adopted the following definition of learning disabilities:

> *Learning disabilities* is a general term that refers to a heterogeneous group of disorders manifested by significant difficulties in the acquisition and use of listening,

speaking, reading, writing, reasoning, or mathematical abilities. These disorders are intrinsic to the individual, presumed to be due to central nervous system dysfunction, and may occur across the life span. Problems in self-regulatory behaviors, social perception, and social interaction may exist with learning disabilities but do not by themselves constitute a learning disability. Although learning disabilities may occur concomitantly with other handicapping conditions (for example, sensory impairment, mental retardation, serious emotional disturbance) or with extrinsic influences (such as cultural differences, insufficient or inappropriate instruction), they are not the result of those conditions or influences.

These and other similar definitions of learning disability share these characteristics:

- learning disabilities are seen as being caused by central nervous system dysfunction;
- they presume some degree of information-processing difficulty that interferes with academic or learning tasks;
- learning-disabled children are seen to show marked discrepancy between their potential and actual achievement; and
- other causes for the difficulty are ruled out.

Students who are identified as learning disabled constitute a very diverse group, similar only in their unrealized academic potential. Although not all children who are identified as learning disabled have reading problems, poor reading ability is often associated with learning disabled students (Helveston, 1987; Merrell, 1990; Stanovich, 1988).

Many students who are identified as learning disabled have basic sight recognition and decoding problems. As we described in Chapter 8 in our discussion of Peter, the adolescent nonreader, poor sight recognition of words and inefficient or inaccurate decoding skills lead to poor comprehension, avoidance of reading and writing, deficits in the amount of reading these students do, and deficits in general knowledge usually acquired by reading.

Thus, learning-disabled poor readers tend to share many of the same problems as other poor readers. These students tend to have problems reading right from the start, especially with word recognition strategies taught in primary grades. It has been suggested that learning-disabled students experience a lag in the development of phonological sensitivity, the awareness and perception of speech sounds in words (Ackerman et al., 1986).

Because these students might not intuit how letters represent speech sounds in words by wide exposure to print, as more able learners do, they may need more systematic exposure to letter-sound patterns in words and more practice with decoding than their peers. Many of the remedial techniques that we have discussed for helping poor readers to develop sight recognition and word analysis skills are effective with students who are identified as learning disabled.

Although remedial instruction for these students often focuses on the teaching and practice of reading skills, it should be emphasized that learning disabled poor readers need the same emphasis on meaningful reading of connected text that other poor readers need. Practicing reading skills without using them in the context of real reading is not effective instruction for any student.

In the long run, LD teachers work with many youngsters who are poor readers, and both regular classroom teachers and reading specialists will find that some of their poor readers might have been identified as learning disabled. Whether or not they have been so identified, poor readers *all* need help in consolidating skills that they have mastered, acquiring strategies that they do not yet have, and closing the gap between their potential as readers and their present performance.

We must all keep firmly in mind that being classified as learning disabled does not mean that a child has a particular set of problems or symptoms that set him or her clearly apart from other poor readers. Nor does it indicate that a particular method of instruction or set of materials is appropriate. Children who are so classified differ from each other just as much as others do, and no particular method or means has been shown to be more effective than others in remediation.

All poor readers, learning disabled or not, require instruction that is tailored to their individual strengths, needs, ages, interests, and prior experiences. All poor readers need to be given appropriate materials at their instructional levels; provided instruction that achieves a balance in word identification, comprehension, listening, speaking, and writing; and taught at a pace that is appropriately challenging without frustration.

Dyslexia

Dyslexia is a medical term for a profound inability to read or to learn to read. Dyslexia is a condition that everyone seems to agree exists but about which there is little agreement otherwise. No single set of symptoms, means of diagnosis or identification, or method of remediation has been identified.

One of the first definitions was proposed by Samuel Orton (1937), who described dyslexic children as being delayed in reading compared to their peers, suffering from frequent letter and word reversals, and often being able to read only by holding the print up to a mirror. This led to widespread belief that dyslexia was primarily a neurological disorder involving visual perception and memory.

Today, many theories exist to explain the apparent anomaly of otherwise bright, verbal, motivated people who experience profound difficulty learning to read even when provided with an abundance of special instruction. Most of these theories propose that dyslexia is the product of some central nervous system dysfunction centering in the perceptual and language processing capabilities of the brain.

Likewise, no single set of symptoms exists that would clearly define dyslexic children and distinguish their characteristics from those who have other learning disabilities. In general, however, many people who have been labeled as dyslexic share many or most of these characteristics:

- measured intelligence at least in the average range but often significantly above average;

- profound difficulty with phonemic awareness, phonemic segmentation, and decoding operations;
- frequent reversals of letters and words in both reading and writing;
- poor spelling, particularly in attempting to use phonetic strategies to spell unfamiliar words;
- both reading and writing far below their intellectual potential;
- continued reading and writing failure in spite of personal motivation and appropriate special instruction.

According to Vellutino (1979), dyslexia is "commonly used in reference to severe reading disorder in children who are apparently normal in other respects" (p. 321). Vellutino and Denckla (1991) describe dyslexic children as having difficulty establishing a link between the visual and linguistic components of the printed word, thus hindering their efforts at learning to read. They further suggest that these learners are not apparently experiencing other cognitive processing problems such as attention, problem solving, and sequencing.

In spite of these ambiguities, the term is used frequently and widely, particularly in the media. However, it is difficult to know whether people discussing the condition mean the same thing. Reporters discussing illiteracy and what they call "the crisis in education" might refer to "illiterates" and "dyslexics" as though the terms were synonymous; educators and parents sometimes refer to *dyslexics* when they mean *poor readers* or even *students reading below grade level*. Physicians and other medical personnel might use *dyslexic* to describe *learning-disabled patients who read poorly*. Perhaps no other term in education has come to mean so many things to so many people.

Efforts to determine which instructional methods are most effective in remediating dyslexia are similarly confusing. The individuals who have been referred to as dyslexic are, like everyone else, more different from each other than alike. Most methods that have been proposed have been successful with at least some people who are thought to be dyslexic. But none are reliably effective with everyone.

Most often, remediation centers around efforts to help the person who has been labeled dyslexic compensate for his or her difficulties by using audiotaped books and texts, as are useful to the visually impaired student, teaching them to use special study skills and procedures that help them to organize and learn material aurally, and teaching them to depend on spelling aids like digital dictionaries and spell-checking and grammar-checking computer programs.

Some general approaches that have been somewhat successful for those students thought to be dyslexic are:

- emphasizing whole-word or sight word recognition and the use of context as a word recognition strategy, rather than overemphasizing phonic decoding;
- developing listening comprehension and general background knowledge by listening rather than relying on reading to convey information;
- using oral aids such as taped texts and lectures, voice-activated microrecorders, and oral note-taking;

- teaching students how to break down writing assignments into manageable steps using the steps in the writing process;
- emphasizing specific thinking skills such as comparison-contrast and cause-and-effect using oral discourse so that dyslexic students can comprehend what they see and hear and not have to read everything;
- teaching students to compose written work orally first, such as dictating onto audiotape, then write while listening to the tape (some students need to have their oral compositions typed for them); and,
- teaching students how to break academic tasks into their component parts, adapt such tasks to their special academic needs, and tackle one part of a task at a time.

SUMMARY

This chapter dealt with special factors associated with reading. Among these factors are those that qualify learners for special-education services under *the Individuals with Disabilities Education Act (IDEA)* and related legislation.

Within this legislation are provisions that mandate serving these learners with appropriate educational programs that use the least restrictive environment. The identification of these learners and subsequent placement in special education programs must be conducted with assessment instruments and methods that protect against discrimination, erroneous classification, and undue labeling.

One alternative to placement of students who qualify for special education is the *Regular Education Initiative (REI)*. This initiative provides for the special-education student to remain within his or her regular classroom under the regular-education teacher who receives support from special education specialists.

Identification of the special-needs student typically is initiated by the classroom teacher. Before additional assessment and screening can occur, permission must be obtained from the parents or legal guardians of the child. Once permission has been granted, *assessment* and *screening* can take place. This assessment typically includes one or more of the following areas: intellectual, physical, special learning, or affective factors.

Initial assessment of *intellectual factors* typically includes the use of an initial screening instrument such as the Kaufman Brief Intelligence Test (K-BIT). If these initial screening instruments indicate a potential problem, additional testing is conducted by using a more comprehensive assessment of intellectual factors such as the Weschler Intelligence Scale for Children, III (WISC III). These tests typically provide scores for subtests, Verbal, Performance, and Full Scale IQ scores. In selecting assessment instruments, care should be taken to select instruments that do not penalize a child with cultural differences.

Vision and *hearing problems* are also associated with reading difficulties. Again, a classroom teacher is often the first to notice potential problems during daily classroom activities. As with intellectual factors, the referral for additional screening begins with parental or guardian permission. Screening in the areas of vision and hearing is typically conducted by professionals or paraprofessionals in the allied-health fields.

Language disabilities most often occur in late infancy and the preschool years, when normally oral language appears and develops fully. Most children are fluent language users, with extensive *receptive and expressive vocabularies* and well-developed grammatical capabilities, by the age of 5 or 6. In the early years, *hearing impairment or deafness, Down syndrome,* and *general language delay* can impair or inhibit language acquisition. In the later preschool and school years, difficulty with speech sound production (*atypical phonology*), acquisition of vocabulary and word meanings (*atypical semantics*), acquisition of grammatical forms and rules (*atypical syntax*), and use of language for social purposes (*atypical pragmatics*) can inhibit language learning and impact literacy.

Special learning problems include *learning disabilities* and *dyslexia.* Although universally accepted and detailed definitions of these terms have yet to be identified, professionals do agree that they include a wide range of problems related to the acquisition, comprehension, and production of written language. Children who manifest these problems typically possess average or above-average intelligence but exhibit serious, longstanding learning difficulties.

Reading is a complex process that is affected by a student's level of intellectual functioning, experiences, motivation, and physical and emotional well-being. By assessing the impact of these special factors on a student's literacy, appropriate changes in instructional strategies, referrals, and placements are more likely to be made.

REFERENCES

Ackerman, Peggy T., Jean M. Anhalt, and Roscoe A. Dykman. "Inferential Word-Decoding Weakness in Reading Disabled Children." *Learning Disability Quarterly* 9, no. 4 (Fall 1986): 315–324.

Berg, F. S. "Characteristics of the Target Population." In *Educational Audiology for the Hard of Hearing Child,* ed. F. S. Berg, J. C. Blair, S. H. Viehweg, and A. Wilson-Vlotman. Orlando, FL: Greene & Stratton, 1986.

Grisham, J. David and Herbert Simons. "Refractive Error and the Reading Process: A Literature Analysis." *Journal of the American Optometric Association* 51, no 4 (Jan. 1986): 44–55.

Helms, Janet E. "Why Is There No Study of Cultural Equivalence in Standardized Cognitive Ability Testing?" *American Psychologist* 47, no. 9 (1992): 1083–1101.

Helveston, Eugene M. "Volume III Module I: Management of Dyslexia and Related Learning Disabilities." *Journal of Learning Disabilities* 20, no. 7 (August–September 1987): 415–421.

Javal, E. "Essay on the Psychology of Reading." *Opthalmic and Physiological Optics,* 10, no. 41 (October 1990):381–384.

Kaufman, Alan S., and Nadeen L. Kaufman. *Kaufman Brief Intelligence Test Manual.* Circle Pines, MN: American Guidance Services, 1990.

Laughon, Pamela. "The Dynamic Assessment of Intelligence: A Review of Three Approaches." *School Psychology Review* 19, no. 4 (1990): 459–470.

Lewis, Rena B., and Donald H. Doorlag. *Teaching Special Students in the Mainstream,* 3d ed. New York: Macmillan, 1991.

McLaughlin, James A., and Rena B. Lewis. *Assessing Special Students,* 3d ed. Columbus: Merrill, 1990.

Merrell, Kenneth. "Differentiating Low Achievement Students and Students with Learning Disabilities: An Examination of Performances on the Woodcock-Johnson Psycho-Educational Battery." *Journal of Special Education* 24, no. 31 (Fall 1990): 296–305.

Nelson, Katharine. *Structure and Strategy in Learning to Talk.* Chicago: University of Chicago Press, 1973.

Orton, Samuel. *Reading, Writing, and Speech Problems in Children.* New York: Norton, 1937.

Patton, James, James Kauffman, J. M. Blackburn, and Gweneth Brown. *Exceptional Children in Focus,* 5th ed. New York: Macmillan Publishing Company, 1991.

Petitto, L. A., & Marentette, P. F. "Babbling in the Manual Mode: Evidence for the Ontogeny of Language." *Science* 251 (1991): 1493–1496.

Ratner, N. B. "Atypical Language Development." In *The Development of Language*, ed. J. B. Gleason. Columbus: Merrill, 1989.

Reich, Philip A. *Language Development.* Upper Saddle River, NJ: Prentice-Hall. 1986.

Sattler, Jerome M. *Assessment of Children,* 3d ed. San Diego, CA: Jerome M. Sattler, 1992.

Stanovich, Keith E. "Explaining the Difference Between the Dyslexic and the Garden-Variety Poor Reader: The Phonological-Core-Variable-Difference Model." *Journal of Learning Disabilities* 21, no. 10 (Dec. 1988): 590–604, 612.

Tallal, P. "Developmental Language Disorders." In *Learning Disabilities: A Report to the U.S. Congress.* Washington, DC: Interagency Committee on Learning Disabilities, 1987.

Tomasello, M., and C.N. Mervis. "Commentary: The Instrument is Great, but Measuring Comprehension Is Still a Problem." In *Monographs of the Society for Research in Child Development* 59, no. 242 (1994).

Trawick-Smith, Jeffery. *Early Childhood Development: A Multicultural Perspective.* Upper Saddle River, NJ: Merrill, 1997.

Vellutino, Frank R. *Dyslexia: Theory and Research.* Cambridge, MA: MIT Press, 1979.

Vellutino, Frank R., and Martha B. Denckla. "Cognitive and Neuropsychological Foundations of Word Identification in Poor and Normally Developing Readers." In *Handbook of Reading Research, Vol. 2,* ed. Rebecca Barr, Michael L. Kamil, Peter Mosenthal, and P. David Pearson. White Plains, NY: Longman Publishers, 1991.

Index